Christian
Personal
Ethics

Other Books by
Dr. Carl F. H. Henry

REMAKING THE MODERN MIND
THE UNEASY CONSCIENCE OF MODERN FUNDAMENTALISM
NOTES ON THE DOCTRINE OF GOD
THE PROTESTANT DILEMMA
FIFTY YEARS OF PROTESTANT THEOLOGY
THE DRIFT OF WESTERN THOUGHT
STRONG'S THEOLOGY AND PERSONAL IDEALISM
GIVING A REASON FOR OUR HOPE
GLIMPSES OF A SACRED LAND
CONTEMPORARY EVANGELICAL THOUGHT (Ed.)
REVELATION AND THE BIBLE (Ed.)
BASIC CHRISTIAN DOCTRINES (Ed.)
CHRISTIAN FAITH AND MODERN THEOLOGY (Ed.)
JESUS OF NAZARETH: SAVIOUR AND LORD (Ed.)
THE BIBLICAL EXPOSITOR (Consulting Ed.)
BAKER'S DICTIONARY OF THEOLOGY (Consulting Ed.)

CHRISTIAN PERSONAL ETHICS

BY

CARL F. H. HENRY, TH. D., PH. D.

EDITOR, CHRISTIANTY TODAY

Baker Book House
Grand Rapids, Michigan

Paperback edition issued 1977 by
Baker Book House
with permission of copyright owner
ISBN: 0-8010-4165-1
Library of Congress Catalog
Card Number: 57-6671

First printing, April 1977
Second printing, August 1979

PHOTOLITHOPRINTED BY CUSHING - MALLOY, INC.
ANN ARBOR, MICHIGAN, UNITED STATES OF AMERICA
1979

TO MY STUDENTS
in ETHICS and CHRISTIAN ETHICS

CONTENTS

SECTION II: CHRISTIANITY AND THE MORAL REVELATION: THE REDEMPTION OF THE MORAL LIFE

INTRODUCTION

At one time Ethics might have been considered a dull hobby of a duller academician. This is not true today. Ethics is the incisive and universal requisite for survival.

Since Christianity's first attack upon the pagan morality of the Western world, no generation has faced such decisive moral issues as today's. The crises in ethics will determine both the continuance of present-day civilization and the destiny of individuals within our culture. The forums of national and international debate cannot escape far-reaching moral decision; culturally and literally, life and death hang in the balance.

Flares of distress signals emblazon the whole field of human behavior. Christianity's millennium-long barricade against a resurging paganism is weakening before the onslaughts of iniquity. Powerful forces aim to alter, to discredit, even to replace it. As a result, the strength of Christian loyalties bulwarks modern man's conduct less and less; moral earnestness almost everywhere halts indecisively at the Christian-pagan crossroads. In our decade, as many habitués of Sodom have detoured into the "civilized" as into the "uncivilized" half of the world.

The severance of ethics from fixed values and standards, ardently promoted by John Dewey and the naturalists, has brought moral chaos. Theological sanctions discarded, the modern man covets only social, and sometimes only individual, approval of his behavior. The sense of ethical imperative is evaporating from one range of life after another. The obligation to durable principles is no longer insisted upon. The soul of the twentieth-century man no longer feeds on objective and eternal norms, but is content with ethical leftovers.

One fact is certain: simultaneous with this relativity of moral imperatives, human life has lost its worth. The soul-nausea and dread of modern man has reached depths unknown even to the ancient Greek skeptic. The sense of cosmic lostness and of personal insignificance frames modern man's window on life.

On a mass scale, the value of human existence is almost totally discounted. The nadir of man's worth finds its supreme illustrations not in the deeds of earlier centuries, but in those of our own: barbarism in Nazi concentration camps; brutal state compulsion under Soviet totalitarianism; slave labor camps; suspension of human rights upon the whim of political machines; scientific devotion to weapons efficient for wholesale death-dealing; mass atomic destruction of whole civilian populations (Nagasaki and Hiroshima) by world powers promoting the cause of human dignity. The power which awes modern man is his capacity to destroy a million lives a minute, to eradicate the vestiges of civilization almost overnight, to shake the very globe on which he exists. In our day the "might makes right" credo of Thrasymachus and Machiavelli and Nietzsche has become a politico-social option beyond the worst dreams of the tyrants who shaped it.

The dissolved and lost value of human life is a fact not only in the aggregate, but in the individual composition of society. The evaporation of ethical restraints has emptied life of meaning and of a sense of destiny. The fibres of morality have disintegrated in society, in fact, because they first deteriorated in the family. Basic to the chaos in social ethics stands the decline of personal moral conviction and its accompanying sense of futility. Individual life seems cut-rate, even give-away, with the loss of fixed standards and of an enduring goal. Personal existence in the 1950s means the malnourished soul, the diseased moral life, and dissipated sense of worth.

For the first time since the Christian era, relative, subjective ethics looms as the approved cultural philosophy. Abetted by deliberate moral revolt, indifference to conscience has been followed by a wave of iniquity as seedtime begets harvest. The shocked conscience is today a minority phenomenon; indeed, it is lampooned and caricatured. Decency is placed on the defensive; dogged determination to "do the right thing" is flouted as a trait less enviable than prudish. Our generation not only flaunts its iniquities before men; it actually approves those who delight in them.

In such a moral vacuum no more crucial question exists than this: is the recovery of life worth and meaning related to a revival of "Christian ethics"? Does the current upheaval in society and in personal life mean Western man's release from theological myths to a whoring after false modern gods? Is the Christian option antiquated? Must we tabulate Christian ethics with the "also ran's"; have we been scratched from the race of life?

Interestingly enough, in some quarters the cry for recognition of a moral universe is being voiced anew. "It has been evident for a long time," Ernest F. Scott writes, "that there was something wrong with the old order, and that world as we knew it has now fallen in utter ruin. The task is laid on us of re-building society on a new basis, and all thinking men are agreed that this must be found in the moral principles which are set forth most clearly and authoritatively in the New Testament."[1] The quotation gains special significance as a witness to a rising interest in religion along with a rising barbarism. A return to religion made in pagan dimensions provides only a false security. Records are worse than ever in the spheres of crime, sex, divorce, narcotics and alcoholism.

[1]Ernest F. Scott, *Man and Society in the New Testament* (New York: Scribner, 1946), p. vii.

Christianity's insistence upon absolute values insults the spirit of our age. The futility of seeking any permanent definition of the good infects the modern temper. Scientific relativism is the god of the sophisticated modern. Even some ethics textbooks aim deliberately to vindicate the absence of fixed and final moral norms. In fact, the teaching of morality has become unfashionable. And why not, if principles of universal validity are untenable? Taught that the boundary line between right and wrong is not a rigid one, high school and college students are expected to make the transition into military service where absolute relativism becomes relative absolutism: totalitarianism is always wrong and democracy worth the eternal sacrifice.

As long as the illusion of automatic progress served as a modern mirage, the ethical inertia of evolutionary ethics remained hidden from view. Lost confidence in this shallow doctrine has now reinstated the moral question to central urgency. Either we shall witness the dissolving of all our duties into mere conventions, or we shall mature afresh to the conviction that Hebrew-Christian ethical realities alone can lift the Western world from the mires of paganism. The principles of love, purity of life, the worth and dignity of the soul, the fundamentally spiritual character of social service, will be defined in these pages in the climate of biblical theology and ethics. No slim sub-Christian thread can today provide a sturdy rope by which the storm-tossed moral life can any longer be anchored; the pagan refabrications have rotted away. Apart from a new hold on biblical realities, there seems little moral hope. We may soon find ourselves past the ability to break with evil, if we ignore biblical Christianity's known way of severance.

Through its flight from moral accounting, the present generation has invited an almost certain bankruptcy. Hardly a home in America today is unshadowed by the ethical hesitancies and ambiguities of these tense times. The writer knows this tragic cleavage in moral outlook from personal experience as representative rather than exceptive of those who live in the twentieth century. He has stood on both sides of the pagan-Christian tension in this Christian-pagan world. He cannot keep silence. To shirk sustained thinking about ethical priorities is neither good humanity nor good Christianity.

In childhood, Episcopal Sunday school emphasized the moral ideals of Jesus Christ in the Gospels.

Home life and the classroom, however, were conspicuously unrelated to ecclesiastical claims. The incarnation and the resurrection were Sunday doctrines; they nowhere intruded into the family or into history or science during the week.

The years of vocational effort at first enlarged, and then in a fundamental way transcended, this disparity. Years spent in newspaper reporting and editing multiplied the conviction that the American mind is confused to frustration on the question of moral standards. Then, utterly strange though it seems still, came the writer's dynamic conversion to Christ. With it came the reinforcement of an absolute ethic.

The more earnest academic contest with the moral problem still lay ahead. At Wheaton College, J. S. Mackenzie's text, *A Manual of Ethics,* dominated the course in ethics. It grappled competently with the vast history of secular ethics, but merely skirted the ethics of revelation. Its 450 pages allotted a one-page discussion to Christian ethics, only to assimilate it to Stoicism; Jesus Christ counted for two index references, one of which catalogued him with Buddha and Socrates, while another, if memory does not fail me, made him out a Kantian. Admittedly the professor's lectures somewhat supplemented the text. But a comprehensive revealed ethic, full-orbed as Christian theology, was hardly delineated, nor even identified.

Seminary studies added little in the way of a consistently integrated Christian life view. In fact, the seminary offered divinity students, at the theological college level, a curious choice between enrollment in the course in ethics or in economics. For many moderns, no doubt, these are, indeed, alternate options.

During graduate studies, Indiana University's philosophy department presented a modern rarity. Comprising it was a Thomist, a post-Kantian, and a high Calvinist its chairman. The latter, Professor W. Harry Jellema, taught secular ethics, a course in which he unhesitatingly acknowledged Christian ethics as the source of weighty answers to some of the unresolved problems of speculative morality. Likewise he portrayed Christianity, despite its divine and revelatory nature, as an ethics of cognitive and philosophical implications, as well. In my own handling of the sweep of speculative ethics, I retain a frequent debt-at-a-distance to Professor Jellema.

Doctoral studies at Boston University swung the pendulum in the opposite direction. Ethics was one of the stipulated fields for qualifying examinations. Both the approved reading list and the lectures by Professor Edgar S. Brightman moved solidly in the idealistic tradition. There was a semi-concealed, albeit gentlemanly, distaste for an ethic or religion of special revelation. The long tradition of biblical ethics, and equally the dialectical and existential theology and ethics of the Continent, were almost wholly ignored in deference to an autonomous morality in the post-Kantian mood.

Along the way came strategic opportunities for teaching Christian ethics and theology. Earliest days in the ethics classroom reflected, I fear, a rather inadequate articulation of Hebrew-Christian morality. Doubtless, there yet remains much to learn. The years have shaped two convictions: the impotence and sterility of speculative ethics derive largely from its self-enforced segregation from the ethics of revelation; Christian ethics becomes impoverished when unrelated to the problems of secular morality to which the man of the world seeks an answer.

This volume is, I trust, an enlargement of these theses, especially in the sphere of personal ethics.

For the timely appearance of this work I owe particular appreciation to those whose designated contributions have provided research assistance to gather source materials, confirm references, and check the final manuscript for publication. They include: Mrs. Dorothy M. Bisbee, Lawrence C. Lamb, Carl V. Lawrence, Dan Schirman, and several others whose insistence on anonymity I must honor. Chaplain Warner A. Hutchinson (U.S.N.) provided editorial assistance. And I would be remiss not to acknowledge the competent aid of my wife, Helga Bender Henry, always a very present help in time of literary trouble. To Professor Gordon H. Clark, head of the philosophy department at Butler University, I am especially indebted for penetrating criticisms and suggestions.

CARL F. H. HENRY

Washington, D.C.

Section I

Speculative Philosophy and the Moral Quest

1

NATURALISTIC ETHICS AND THE ANIMALIZATION OF THE MORAL LIFE

THE QUESTION of right and wrong elbows itself into prominence wherever human beings exist. No one is able wholly to evade it. The moral inquisition persistently confronts the spirit of man, if not as an existential anxiety, at least as a distressing theoretical consideration, or as a practical nuisance. Even the lives of social primitives, and not alone of cultured intelligentsia, are made tense by this conflict of good and evil. To the more reflective, a systematic analysis and evaluation of the nature of the moral claim is unavoidable. The restless and expansive spirit investigates the whole of reality. But especially in the moral realm, the quest for coherent scrutiny of the ethical imperative, and for the consistent reconciliation of apparent conflicts, is inescapable.

Whatever man's relationship to the other animals, the fact is that brute life is not harassed by this controversy over ethics. The history of mankind is relatively recent, but almost the whole of it — the Bible would delete the qualifying "almost" — is incontrovertibly vexed by a life-and-death debate over right and wrong, over truth and error. The power to form a scale of moral judgments by which to weigh himself and the race in the balances of good and evil, is a unique differentium of human kind. Even those who brand the distinction illusory or damaging admit man's persistence in discriminating right from wrong.

Since moral and rational distinctions are non-existent for the lower animal world, the beasts do not bother to "explain away," nor do they seek to "buttress" the moral claim. If an unleashed canine wandered into an unguarded meat shop, and after devouring a hindquarter of choice beef returned a second time to continue the foraging, we would hardly ask a jury to determine premeditation of crime, nor would we sentence the culprit to six months on biscuits for grand larceny. Instead, we would charge the dog's master with violating the leash law, and we would expect the penalty to include at least some restitution for the shopkeeper's loss. Dogs obviously are guilty neither of crime nor of immorality. True, some domestic animals may be conditioned to shame, through associating certain forms of behavior with the displeasure of their masters, as Freudians never weary of pointing out. This shame differs, however, from guilt accompanying conscious violation of a moral code. For man, not brute, unendingly accounts and seeks to account for the sorrows and shadows of guilt.

Each man's judgment of the nature of the moral claim is at one and the same time an evaluation of himself and of the universe of reality in which he lives. The cribbing collegian; the workman on an injudicious vacation fling; the prostitute on solicitous saunter; the gangster thrusting his gun at a bank cashier — each is working out an implicit world-life view. The values which men give priority, and equally those they repudiate, imply a definite, however inarticulate, concept of God, of man, and of the moral order. No competent thinker presumes to issue pronouncements-in-a-vacuum about the ultimate nature of the good and the bad. The philosopher shapes conviction into systematic statement, showing the implications of a given view of reality for a certain expression of conduct. While the man-in-the-street does not do this, his life attitudes are conditioned nonetheless and in the same manner by certain controlling assumptions. To judge the moral order spurious, or, conversely, valid, is at the same time to pass a verdict upon the whole of reality and, unavoidably, to define the nature of man himself.

Historically, secular philosophy has propounded two antagonistic interpretations of ethics: Naturalism and Idealism.[1] Into these competitive philosophies almost all speculative ethics may be classified. Their differences center in two different views of conscience and reason, and in the consequent elaboration of competing statements concerning the nature and station of man in the space-time world. The outcome of this dispute over man's moral and mental nature determines the significance and worth of human life.

Idealism, emphasizing the priority of mind and values, and emphasizing the reality of the spiritual world, without doubt was until modern times the generally accepted and preferred philosophy. Naturalism, in contrast, exerted an influence devoid of cultural significance. During the past century, however, Naturalism has grown in popularity and strength. Today the naturalistic view of life places idealistic and supernaturalistic systems on the defensive. A prestige and vigor which to the great moralists of earlier generations would have appeared incredible and fantastic, has accrued to Naturalism. It has become the chosen creed not only of many distinguished intellectuals, but also of a large segment of the average populace. It has reared its head as a political and cultural force both nationally and internationally. The

[1]A division of the history of ethics, or of philosophy, into Naturalism and Idealism, may seem to be unfortunate since, while Naturalism is a type of metaphysics, Idealism is today usually thought of as a type of epistemology. The terms, therefore, do not seem to be mutually exclusive; whereas epistemologically Berkeley was an idealistic supernaturalist, Hume was an idealistic naturalist. If Idealism is taken only in the sense that the mind contributes something to reality, there can be a naturalistic Idealism. But the terms are used here to designate contrastive metaphysical views: the one asserts the contingency of the mental and spiritual, and the other its absoluteness and ultimacy. Hume, indeed, made ideas ultimate and not contingent or derivative, but he denied the priority and existence of any eternal spiritual reality.

Russia that once battled Nazism in Germany paradoxically enough has realigned the entire world by its plumb line of atheistic Materialism.

Naturalistic ethics offers a great diversity of explanations and systems of morality. Adherents of this view disagree as to the precise determinant of right and wrong (the pleasure of the moment, the pleasure of a lifetime, the pleasure of the multitudes, the preference of the strongest, and the like). All of them, however, share assumptions which clearly define distinctions between right and wrong as relative and subject to revision rather than as fixed and eternal. The controlling tenets of naturalistic ethics are: (1) that nature is the ultimate reality; (2) that man is essentially an animal; (3) that truth and right are intrinsically time-bound and changing. The various forms of naturalistic ethics differ only in the ingenuity, consistency and profundity with which these basic assumptions are used to explain the phenomena of the moral life.

Every moment yields to the claims of the space-time universe. Nature is real! Heat or cold, tranquility or storm, flood, fire, hurricane, earthquake: each enforces acceptance and adjustment. Man is an animal, classified by all philosophic traditions as in creaturely subjection to space-time laws. His very survival is a struggle, attested by the necessities and satisfactions of relieving hunger and thirst three times a day, seven days a week, four weeks a month, twelve months a year. A time-bound creature, man is born into a changing, tormenting world that snatches him up at last into death. Obviously, distinctions in truth and morality are likewise both time-bound and localized, demonstrated by conflicting cultural codes and practices. Local tradition and culture undeniably influence the innumerable views of right and wrong. ("When in Rome, do as the Romans do.")

Naturalism does not stop here, however. Nature is not only real, it is also *ultimate*. Man is only animal and *all* distinctions of morality and truth are changing and relative. That is its irreducible doctrine.

I. ELEMENTAL NATURALISM

The difference between naive or elemental Naturalism, and systematic Naturalism, rests chiefly in the naked assumption by the one and the consistent, thorough elaboration by the other of the premises underlying naturalistic morality. Naive Naturalism lives by a naturalistic credo without endeavoring to apply its implications consistently to all behavior, and without elaborating a world-life view to interpret the data of experience.

The business man who decides that while honesty is the best policy as a commercial rule, yet now and then considers it is permissible to strike it rich by clever duplicity; the college freshman who accepts grading as necessary for ability grouping but does not hesitate to cheat occasionally, especially on finals; the statesman who deliberately violates a treaty or agreement in pursuing a reputation for integrity in order to gain strategic advantages — these agents may not have systematized Naturalism as an unyielding world-life view, but they nonetheless repudiate the ultimacy of values. For such persons, moral distinctions may retain a periodic usefulness in the transitions and routines of life, but the climaxes of life yield to experience or to subjective preference. In the most crucial and important decisions, the ethical imperative serves as a means to something extra-moral. The novice, while unconcerned about systematizing his conduct so that it expresses an inner unity of conviction, may often swerve indecisively between one act and its opposite, unsure when to depart from prevailing custom and social expectancy. In this respect doubtless he differs conspicuously from the moral agent who devotes himself loyally and unbendingly to the naturalistic creed, and who for their temporary service tolerates what appear to be exceptions to this pattern of operation. It is characteristic of the naive ethical agent that, when pressed about specific attitudes and deeds, he can offer no elaborate and systematic vindication of them. For him, it is enough to say that this is the way he prefers things, or to appeal to the fact that he does not stand alone in these preferences, or that they reveal a more or less traditional answer, or that, at any rate, there is no more reason for an alternative course than for this one.

No one — not even the skilled moral philosopher — lives his life in absolute conformity to the system of values implicit in his motives and conduct. The frailties of mankind are such that conduct does not flow from thought and will with geometric necessity. In contrast to other earthly creatures, however, man is of such a nature that it is impossible for him to live completely devoid of schematization and pattern. A certain bent of will and conviction appears, requiring at least an elemental justification of conduct even where no all-embracing world-and-life view is elaborated. Elemental Naturalism fluctuates between no sustained and convincing justification of its moral attitudes, and a weak, half-hearted defense of them.

A. ANCIENT: SOPHISM

The sense world impinges relentlessly upon conscious human experience. To this fact the ancient Sophists added the concept of sense experience as being conclusive for all knowledge. This was the framework in which Greek Sophism taught nature as the ultimate reality of which all else is a differentiation. Man is limited, the Sophists contended, to a knowledge of his own sensations. This limitation of knowledge to the flux of sense produced the emphases of Protagoras (b. 490 B.C.) that the existence of the gods is uncertain (*i.e.,* we must not affirm the reality of the supernatural) and that all truth (including the principles of morality) is relative. But the ancient Sophists felt compelled to account for universal belief in the supernatural; and their explanations are not unlike some accounts usually considered modern. Bio and Euhemerus contended that belief in gods originated with the veneration of distinguished men (a view not without anticipations of Herbert Spencer's theory that it arises in ancestor worship). Critias, head of the thirty oligarchical despots, on the other hand, maintained that existence of the gods was first published abroad by wise statesmen eager to secure the willing obedience of the citizenry to public legislation (a view with some kinship to the humanist notion that the god-idea has functional rather than ontological validity). Gorgias (c. 427 B.C.) pursued the Sophist dogma beyond relativism and agnosticism to the nihilistic and pessimistic conclusions that nothing exists; if it did, he said, it would be unknowable; if knowable, this knowledge would be incommunicable to others, since the *same* idea could not be common to two *different* individuals.

Alongside the denial of the supernatural ranged the denial of man's immortality and uniqueness. Critias considered blood as the seat and the substratum of the soul.[2] While this may seem crude and unaesthetic, it is nonetheless akin to later theories that the psychic is dependent upon man's physical nature. The Presocratics were generally physiological in their view of sensation and thought. Man does not differ from the animals in kind; like them, he bows to time. The human predicament, basically, is simply that of making an advantageous adjustment to nature.

Identification of reality with the flux of immediate sense experience involved a thorough relativism in knowledge and morals for Sophism. The dictum of Protagoras — "all truth is relative" — clearly mirrors its inner spirit. The Sophist denied even the very existence of law and gave room only to custom or convention. Whatever passes for morality represents to the Sophist only a convention, a social claim invented by groups for their own interests. The denial of any abiding reality beyond that of sensation led directly to a critical skepticism regarding ethics. Sophism abandoned the speculative search for a *summum bonum*. It disallowed any one rule of life; from the eddy of sensations it filtered out no single universal purpose for man.

Such a view represents simple Naturalism in its most spontaneous and unsophisticated form. That the whole of existence is a differentiation of time-space process; that man is a creature of time only; that right and wrong are artificial and subjective distinctions: these tenets Sophism shared with all naturalistic movements. It attempts no elaboration of these convictions into a rationale of action; in fact, it abandons the effort to superimpose permanently valid ideas upon the sense process. Since everything is in change, truth and morality are mobile distinctions; even man has no permanent significance. Many cultivated Greeks favored sophistic views, ranking ethical distinctions as simply the prejudices of the mobs.

[2]Cf. Aristotle, *De Anima*, i, 2.

B. ANCIENT: CYRENAICISM

It was Cyrenaicism which sought to distill from Sophism's flux of sensation a reliable, continuing principle for life conduct. Named for its founder, Aristippus (b. 435 B.C.) of Cyrene, a Greek colony in North Africa, this movement hoped to combine the Sophist's insistence upon sensation-of-the-moment as our only object of knowledge, with the conviction of a permanent sensory value, *viz.*, the subjective pleasure of the moment. This rule of human conduct was to Aristippus the performance of whatever yields the maximal momentary pleasure. This moment-by-moment devotion to subjective pleasure becomes the purpose of life.

Aristippus' argument is simple enough. Since we know only the sensation of the moment,[3] pleasure as a past or future experience is non-existent. Present pleasures differ only in intensity or degree. They cannot be said to differ in kind because no knowledge is given to sensation of the causes nor of the ultimate consequences of pleasure. Physical or bodily pleasures are preferable to all others because they are more intense, more simple. No pleasure is bad, for pleasure is "the good," but weaker sensations are less desirable than intense pleasures. We are to wrest the maximum pleasure from nature (the sense manifold) before each fleeting moment passes, aware that even while we calculate values the present eludes us. Only the present is ours; the future may never be. We can no more anticipate prospective pleasures than we can live in retrospect. The moving present alone is ours in which to live. We are children of time, not of eternity. Therefore we seek joys within the compass of the momentary present. A life of pleasure, heedless and unthinking, undisturbed by reason, is the ideal of the pagan Cyrenaic spirit. "Eat, drink and be merry, for tomorrow we die" becomes the Cyrenaic credo.

The simple Cyrenaic formula had to weaken, however. The attempt to correlate sense flux with the maximum pleasure of the moment was thwarted by the disruptive fact that some pleasures entail disproportionate pain. Long before the modern Seltzer age the confirmed glutton faced the reality of enforced abstinence; long before the Kinsey report, people recognized physical exhaustion and mental sluggishness as the price of intemperate sex indulgence. The "good life" (most pleasure-filled) is the life of "gentle wind" rather than its contrary extremes of "sea calm" (indifference) or of "tempest" (trouble). The truly happy man exercises a sort of prudence. Says Aristippus: "He who enjoys without being carried away, is master of his pleasures." The man of pleasure governs his pleasures, rather than being governed by them. Wise men, says Aristippus, live in such a way that, if all existing laws were abrogated, their manner of life would experience no change. Thus the promised novelty of the pleasure-of-the-moment morality was retrieved.

[3]Cf. *Diogenes Laertius,* ii, 92, 93.

Actually this control of pleasure is incompatible with the principle that the intensest pleasure of the moment is the highest good. To limit the intensity of momentary pleasure (in the name of the avoidance of excessive pain) by an awareness of the pleasure-pain relationships in experience is to admit an alien element, a principle of discrimination, not derived from immediate sensation. This is an appeal beyond immediate sense experience to a principle of prudence. It forsakes what one experiences immediately for reflection upon more-than-immediate experience.

Cyrenaicism comes to frustration over inability to realize its original purpose. While it professes to find a rule of life predicated wholly upon adjustment to the momentary sense flux, it is driven to acknowledge a decisive relevance to the rational and moral life of realities outside this immediate experience, all the while refusing to conform its approach to the rule of this acknowledgment. Cyrenaicism is therefore a species of simple or naive ethics, and affords no scientific or systematic discussion of the moral life. It hesitated half-way between the Sophist abandonment of ethical to unrelieved relativism, and a principle of action to which moral behavior could be oriented. To avoid pain, therefore, the Cyrenaic consequently fluctuated uncertainly between the maximal pleasure of the moment and its own grudging compromise.

Several important factors can be detected. One is the unconcern of nature for that superlative momentary pleasure in which Cyrenaicism professed to find the supreme good. The attempt to force nature into the service of everyman's pleasure-of-the-moment succeeds only in extracting from Cyrenaicism a confession of the futility of such an effort. Nature as a manifold of sensations does not minister to this rule, but often grinds away with bland indifference to it, and even in stark contradiction of it. If there is any scheme by which the world of space-time events and the life of man are to be coordinated, it is not one which constantly furthers the utmost sense pleasure of each individual. Actually, the sensationalistic position that knowledge is individual, and hence that scientific inquiry into nature is useless speculation, made no room for the Cyrenaic appeal beyond immediate sensations. In deference to the inner conviction of some implicit rule of life the sensationalistic theory of knowledge was compromised by an appeal beyond momentary experience. Another element worthy of notice is the Cyrenaic curtailment of maximal pleasure not for the sake of a higher kind of pleasure, but for the sake of future physical pleasures of greater intensity. Thus the theory works against itself. It admits that maximal present pleasure will undercut the possibility of maximal future pleasure, but can offer no guarantee that the anticipated future pleasure, when it becomes present, will be exempt from this same curtailment.

A third difficulty was inevitable. Man lacked any guarantee not only of the future's fuller intensity of pleasure for the sake of which a lesser intensity was now tolerated, but also of a future's experience of promised pleasure to compensate for renounced pleasure. Here not empirical skepticism about nature in the modern sense, but rather the brevity and uncertainty of life, and the certainty of death, posed the problem. Why postpone the pleasures of today for those of a tomorrow which may never come?

The unresolved contradictions in Cyrenaicism required a fundamental change of perspective. Two schools arose. One sought a higher justification of pleasure as the supreme good of life, and bore the name Epicureanism. The other moved downward to the pessimism already latent in the Sophism against which Aristippus of Cyrene revolted, and was called Cynicism. Both Epicureanism and Cynicism modified the Cyrenaic interpretation of Naturalism to prevent maximal pleasure of the moment being the rule of life. Neither, however, repudiated the underlying dogma of the unreality and nonexistence of the supernatural.

C. ANCIENT: CYNICISM

The downward course to nihilism began in Cynicism, a reactionary movement.

The title Cynic derived from *kuon,* dog, which teachers of the movement adopted as a sign of their return to the simplicity of animal existence. "Return to nature" was their motto. But the epithet was applied to them also by antagonists because of the coarseness and immodesty which characterized the Cynics. Antisthenes (444-399 B.C.), founder of Cynicism, was called the "downright" dog; his most notable follower Diogenes (412-323 B.C.), the "royal" dog.

In common with the Sophists and Cyrenaics, the Cynics abandoned philosophical systems and contemplated merely a way of life. Theoretical solutions were regarded as impossible, so that Cynicism involved rational skepticism; the major interest of personal knowledge was in its practical usefulness. Science and culture held only a pragmatic value. According to Cynic epistemology, based on the empiricism of Gorgias, Antisthenes' early teacher, only particular things are real; nominalism is championed. Diogenes told Plato that he could "see a table and a cup, but . . . no 'tableness' and 'cupness.'"[4] This involved the impossibility of any judgments but those of identity (man is man; good is good). The impossibility of error, that is, the equal truth of all propositions, was defended.[5]

Socrates, with whom Antisthenes later studied (Plato implies he was too aged to learn [*Soph.* 251]) stressed the renunciation of the lower life as a means to a higher: "To have no wants at all is, to my mind, an attribute of godhead; to have as few wants as possible, the nearest approach to godhead" (*Xenoph. Mem.* i, 6). The Cynics fixed upon

[4]Diogenes Laertius, vi, 55.
[5]R. M. Wenley, "Cynics," in *Encyclopedia of Religion and Ethics,* James Hastings, ed. (New York: Scribner, 1924-27), IV, 381a.

the negative ascetic element as an end in itself and championed renunciation. They acknowledged nothing holy, withdrew from society, flouted contemporary norms and human ties. Civil and social relations were regarded as impositions. Society is an accident, said Cynicism; man should be sufficient unto himself. Law and civil institutions are tyrannical interferences with the simple life, often compelling men to act against their unitary nature. Self-sufficiency, as an inherent possession of every man, was to be guarded at all costs; complete sacrifice for its realization was the essence of virtue. Self-sufficiency must be set free from social convention. The usual values of life, health, position, wealth, like poverty, shame, sickness and death, were to be treated with total indifference. Hippias taught that social laws and institutions are arbitrary and harmful, enslaving true human nature which is individual and specific; the good life consists in renouncing them. The innate prerogative of simple manhood alone provides escape from social ills. Self-control meant not the ethicizing, but the cessation, of human relations. The professed ideal of Cynics was to be homeless beggars, cityless wanderers.

Cynicism contained a concealed theoretical element of which its spokesmen were unaware, but which provided its later point of contact with Stoicism.[6] While man was not related individually to an unchanging rational and moral order, he was bound by an inner rational principle operating as a pragmatic universal of the will. The essential unity of mankind was assumed to be evident not in the realm of theory but in that of overt conduct. Cynicism itself, however, was tantamount to "a confession of failure" — a denial of the moral problem. By 275 B.C. Cynicism reaped its ripe harvest of "antinomianism and quixotry."

Its significant elements were caught up in Stoicism, which eliminated the Cynic contempt for science and liberal culture. Its resultant deletion from human life of all individual desire and preference was not hard to foresee. It lurked in the spirit of Prodicus, who declared that death is a desirable escape from the evils of life. Only a step behind lagged the "death-counselling" Hegesias. Proclaiming human life devoid of positive happiness, he located its only good in the avoidance of trouble, and declared life to be intrinsically valueless.

These ancient expressions of simple, unelaborated Materialism issued a confession which led rather swiftly to their displacement as satisfactory and convincing accounts of the moral situation. By espousing the dogma that what cannot be sensed is nonexistent, Sophism,

[6]Stilpo prepared the way for Stoicism, by blending Cynic morality with an interest in metaphysics. The central emphases of Cynicism were later absorbed by Stoicism, but in a radically different manner, a pantheistic frame. "Return to nature" would imply in that view no reversion to animality, no reduction of human needs to a bestial level, but required the basic discrimination of the reasoning man from the unreasoning brute as well as from inert matter, and his spiritual relationship which lifted him from individual isolation to conscious unity with all minds.

Cyrenaicism and Cynicism reduce human life to moral anarchy, and foredoom every attempt to rescue it in the name of principle. A strictly sensate view empties life of all worth and meaning. The Sophists spell out this teaching to a relativistic conclusion, the Cynics to a nihilistic conclusion, and the Cyrenaics to the deduction that sense experience alone does not support the maximal momentary pleasure of the individual, but rather frustrates it.

D. MODERN REFLECTIONS

Hebrew-Christian ethics, grounded in the principle of special revelation, and the prestige of theistic and idealistic ethics in modern times, allowed scant development for that of Naturalism even in its elemental and unsystematic forms, until the nineteenth century. The ancient Hebrew writer in the early chapters of Ecclesiastes, delineating the frustration of those who grasp only after the delights of sense and time, provided evidence that the careless and unthinking abandon to momentary pleasures is a universal temptation. The same abandon as an escape from moral reflection may be sensed in Omar Khayyam. Through an appeal both to a naturalistic philosophy of science and to one of evolutionary origins, naturalistic ethics gained prestige and thus gained systematic formulation.

Nevertheless, it was in the form of elemental Naturalism that the theory found popularity first among many university students and then among the masses. The prejudice against high moral decision found a rationalization of its ethical revolt in the temper of the times. Rather than wrestle earnestly and systematically with the questions of world and life view, and rise above the inadequacies and inaccuracies of ordinary thought, Naturalism rationalized ethical revolt by upholding current prejudice against high moral decision. In the nineteenth century, revivals of the Cyrenaic ideal are found in Byron, Heine and Oscar Wilde.

II. SYSTEMATIC NATURALISM

Systematic Naturalism deliberately supersedes its elemental anticipations to stress a needed life principle which exposes the inner relationships of the super-sensory natural world. Nature is more than momentary sensation; it is organization, network, configuration, pattern. The structure of nature undergirds the life of human decision in reliable ways. Naturalism explicates a metaphysics with scientific thoroughness, and by attaching itself to a world view, articulates this connection between the natural and supernatural and exhibits the program of human action implied therein.

A. HEDONISTIC NATURALISM

One of the earliest expositions of systematic Naturalism attempts to vindicate pleasure, or Hedonism, as a universal rule of life. In two ways this attempt goes beyond elemental Naturalism: first, by venturing a cosmic orientation for morality, and secondly, by repudiating moral relativism and pessimism, in order systematically to conform conduct to the rule of pleasure already anticipated by Cyrenaicism in a cruder way.

1. ANCIENT: EPICUREANISM

Epicurean ethics refuses to accept both the Sophist disavowal of any permanent life value and the Cynic turn to nihilism. It regards both these systems as too simple and superficial an index to the moral situation. Epicureanism instead proposes the return to a positive rule of life, as alone meeting the complexities of human nature. It criticizes the Cyrenaic formula as too naive a reading of nature and man, and ventures to schematize the world of reality and life by a more convincing chart of the ethical problem.

The manner in which Epicureanism modifies the Cyrenaic morality is twofold. First, it articulates a comprehensive world-life view alongside its morality, to give the life of human decision a cosmic justification. It thus becomes the first materialistic view of life entitled to the designation of scientific or systematic Naturalism. Second, it replaces discredited Cyrenaicism — the motif of short-term immediately-exhausted physical pleasures — by another view of life — that of long-term, productive mental pleasures.

While the Epicurean scheme substitutes long-term pleasures for short-term pleasures as the rule of life, its fundamental similarity to the Cyrenaic view, of which it is a development, is nevertheless easily discerned. Not only are both views expositions of the naturalistic credo, but both seek in pleasure, and in the pleasure of the individual, the rule of life which the space-time process is thought to justify. They are variant expressions of egoistic hedonism. Both movements share the assumption that a universal and permanent rule of life, that of the individual's pleasure, may be wrested from the life context. The only essential difference is that whereas Cyrenaicism stressed momentary pleasures, and those of a physical nature, Epicureanism stressed the pleasures of a lifetime, to be found in long-term mental application.

The only prospect of sketching a rule of life lay in a precise, detailed statement of the larger world movement in which man exists. To reveal the associations in the sense realms from which man seeks pleasure would provide a tangible basis of adjustment, for world view and life view would then imply each other. Epicurus was confident that the naturalistic framework supplied a foundation for principled human living, if only it were fully projected. In *De Rerum Natura,* a didactic poem "On the Nature of Things," Lucretius, a pupil of Epicurus, states the classic exposition of Epicureanism.

Epicurus (341-270 B.C.) found his materialistic metaphysics ready-made in the philosophy of Leucippus and of his brilliant student, Democritus. According to Democritus, all reality is a system of atoms, or indivisible particles of matter of all sizes and shapes, in motion.

Consistent with this materialistic dictum, Democritus explained all spiritual entities — the soul and the gods included — as complex manifestations of these mobile atoms, differing from other collocations of atoms only in structure. Qualitative differences are nothing but differences of structure. Mental atoms are smoother and rounder, hence more functional, he contended. But the soul eventually bows to time. The gods, he said, have longevity, but not eternity.[7]

The elaboration of the materialistic credo is here carried through with rigorous precision: some events are uncaused, all others have natural causes. The intervention of gods is unnecessary to explain phenomena; animals and men are products of the earth; the soul is material; the quantitative arrangement of atoms, not any qualitative distinction in kind, is the key to the whole of existence; pleasure is the smooth movement of atoms, pain is their collision with each other. Thus the "good life" is explained purely in terms of physics; pleasure and pain are not conscious states occurring on the occasion of certain physical processes but, like consciousness itself, are reduced to the process. The highest good is pleasure, which by an avoidance of extremes observes the limits fixed by nature.

This all-embracing atomistic physics, with its emphasis on the deterministic flow of events, brought support to the thesis that the world of nature is not simply the flux of momentary sense impressions, but is a system of dependable relationships. The recognition of some such persevering connection between existing things and events had driven Aristippus to the acknowledgment that man's reason must prefer some pleasures above others in order to moderate their physical intensity. Democritus, however, transcends a merely sensationalistic Materialism. Thereafter it becomes necessary to connect the rule of life more securely with the inner system of nature which man apprehends through super-sensory experience. Behind the fleeting sense realities is the real world of nature: invisible, imperceptible atoms, endowed with motion in a necessary system of law. Nature is not what is sensed, but rather is this system of atoms, constantly in motion, qualitatively alike, and forming temporary combinations according to necessary law.

If the rule of life, or "the good," is to be equated with pleasure, this equation must now involve a choice between pleasures, not merely in respect of their intensity, but in the repudiation of momentary, immediately exhausted physical pleasure for productive pleasure. Law obtains in nature; the way to derive pleasure is to obey that law. The happy life accepts the limits fixed by nature, and avoids extremes; it observes the systematic restraints, and is not overly-given to the pleasures of eating, drinking, sex, or anything else. Hence there is little

[7]Lucretius, *De Rerum Natura* (ii, 646) asserts the gods are everlasting, *Diogenes Laertius* (x, 123), immortal. Cf. Cyril Bailey, *Greek Atomists and Epicurus* (Oxford: University Press, 1928), pp. 441-467.

crass hedonism in Epicureanism. The "good" is pleasure; every pleasure is good. But we are driven by the system of nature to the more fruitful, long-range mental pleasures. A merely quantitative approach is inadequate; the measure of pleasure is not in direct proportion to the duration of existence. Not every species of pleasure is desirable, nor is every species of pain to be avoided. The worst pains are psychical, not physical; man suffers from the memory of the past and from the anticipation of the future. The correct praxis is to weigh the foreseen pleasures and pains, to anticipate the likelihood of preponderance. Hence Epicurus introduces a new definition of pleasure, *i.e.,* absence of pain, not sensory stimulation. We must seek pleasure in accordance with the laws of nature. The system of nature, Epicurus contends, will delight the man who devotes himself to long-term, productive mental pleasures.

If the Democritian system of nature, or atomistic physics, by which Epicurus supplemented the modified Cyrenaicism of Aristippus, allowed a confident basis of behavior by the new rule of life, its inviolable determinism nevertheless posed great problems.

If what happens must happen, what room does the mathematical necessity of Democritus leave for duty and an ought? If the world exists only with reference to necessities, whatever happens, must happen. Then free decision is excluded, and no action can be better than another. To retain significance for choice or freedom, Epicurus and Lucretius depart from the doctrine of necessity, and introduce into nature the feature of chance or unpredictability. For Democritus, chance was nothing but a law of necessity of which we are ignorant, but for Epicurus it constituted the possibility of free choice. Not all events follow the laws of motion necessarily; there are some exceptions. Not only have the atoms at one point in history deviated without cause from their line of fall, but the power of choice in man is explained as a causeless function of the will. Alongside the validity of causal law, whose universal operation is denied, exists uncaused occurrence, or chance, particularly human freedom. Epicurus asserts that the future is not wholly ours, nor wholly not ours, and that therefore we can organize our lives to a considerable degree. Men are not completely subject to nature but can choose.

This reduction of freedom to the problem of chance is no real solution of the moral problem, nor does it shed light upon the subject of free choice. The admission of unaccountable deviations in the regularity of nature does not constitute the actuality of free will. Whatever man's actions, he ventures them all as a creature bounded either by necessity or chance. Non-necessity in Epicurus' moral philosophy reduces simply to capriciousness, or action without a view to an intelligible criterion. This falls far short of granting man the possibility of organizing his behavior in conformity to rational principle, and of allowing him freedom to bind life to a moral ought. The reality of freedom is never constituted simply by man's exemption from absolute law, nor by the brute possibility of chance deviation from necessity. Doubtless the admission of chance introduces the element of unpredictability. But the freedom of the will and moral accountability require more than chance deviation in a spontaneous, uncaused direction. Rather, they have in view man's capacity to act voluntarily in accord with certain principles.

Even if the Epicurean view had made room for such action in view of principles, the system itself was too narrow to allow for the concept of duty. The materialistic world of reality does not exist with reference to good and bad; it allows no qualitative distinctions between pleasures. Only where the good is connected with the holy, with the eternal and unchanging, in contrast with the transitory and perishing, does a genuine distinction between kinds of pleasure arise, as over against a measurement only of degrees of pleasure. True as it is that Epicureanism stresses long-term mental pleasures, the reason for seeking these is that they promise man a pattern for outsmarting nature. Man is to choose the long-range pleasures not because God approves them, nor because they are intrinsically better, and lead to future rewards, but because they shrewdly turn the necessity of nature to his own advantage. He is to repress momentary lusts, and to deny himself short-term, swiftly exhausted pleasures of the flesh, not because they are supernaturally condemned, inherently wrong or below the true dignity of human nature, nor because the pleasures of a higher spiritual world are better, but because nature as a system frustrates the attempt to live by the Cyrenaic formula. Because nature does not sustain the intensest bodily enjoyments, but rather the enduring mental delights, prudent selection of pleasures is necessary. In such a sketching of the *summum bonum* there exists neither duty nor an *ought,* simply the *is,* the necessary movement of atoms, to which man inevitably conforms. While Epicurus transcends sensationalistic Materialism, he nonetheless enthrones Naturalism as a philosophy, and in approving the prevailing "scientific view," accommodates ethics to its deliverances. Such a complaint may seem, for the moment, circular, since Epicurus would admit the accusations. Nonetheless, the concept of duty is evaporated and the essence of morality dissolved by such a view. For where the good enjoys no prior and determinative role in the construction of reality, its significance is inevitably destroyed.

Man's rational ability to discern the invisible system of nature, and to govern life by fixed necessities which are not disclosed to sense experience, reflects in Epicureanism (a recognition of the complexities of human rationality as over against the world of lower animals). Man is a complex animal who swiftly understands nature as operative in more than the present: reality contains continuity and necessity as well. The materialistic stance of the system provides no explanation for this intricate rationalism, other than to refer it to a peculiar organization of atoms. Cyrenaicism failed, as we have observed, because even an efficient sentient life implies the operation and guidance of thought. The life which is not rationally ordered is soon wrecked on the shoals of appetite and passion, because a merely sentient good cannot satisfy a creature which is not merely sentient but rational. The Epicurean emphasis on mental pleasures suggests even more conspicuously a distinction between man and the beasts in this regard. The true good of a reflective being cannot be unreflective. Man's construction of the ideal life requires a strategic reference to reason. In this sense, his rationality seems to lift him above complex animality and operates rather as a non-animal element. A decisive rational component is thus admitted into human experience for which Naturalism is unable to make room; man is explained as a product of nature, and yet his distinctive characteristic is to transcend and anticipate nature. This rational side holds a priority among the facets of human nature which demand satisfaction, and yet the naturalistic credo is precluded from providing a home for man's reason except as an emergence which is neither essential to nor definitive of ultimate reality. Once it is conceded that the real world is not sensed, but thought, the larger problem which remains to be worked out is whether the ultimate world may not then be a world of thought and reason, rather than of unthinking matter.

The Epicurean brief for long-term as against short-term pleasures intensifies the moral tension already found in Cyrenaicism, due to the circumstance that man is regarded only as a perishing creature of time. The fact of man's mortality and his indefinite tenure of life works against the appeal for long-term pleasures. The invitation to repress short-term, immediately-exhausted fleshly pleasures for long-term, productive mental pleasures, meets an almost insurmountable obstacle in the possibility that death may intervene to cheat the Epicurean of remote pleasures, so that he will be deprived of both short-term and long-term gratifications. Yet the Epicurean knows that the life of Cyrenaic patterns does not yield consistent and abiding pleasure. In the name of pleasure, therefore, he must advocate repression and self-denial, and even the possibility of the pain and disillusionment of death. The consequence of this dilemma is pessimism, a development of Epicureanism which is not accidental, but which flows from its unresolved contradictions. When man is informed that life may outwit futility only by the pursuit of long-term pleasures, while he is continually aware that death may come tomorrow, and that time for physical gratifications is short, even if they carry the possibility of disproportionate pain, the paralysis of the moral life is close at hand. The more expansive the "long view" of pleasures, the greater threat does nature pose that their distant realization will be interrupted.

The Epicurean emphasis on absence of pain, its gesture in the direction of human freedom, and its extension of the significance of the rational aspect of human experience, serve to create enlarged expectations of a mutuality and correspondence between man's own interests and welfare and the space-time universe which bounds him. Yet the hard fact is that, in the materialistic account, nature is a system which whirls through its paces with total indifference to man's pleasures, whether short-term or long-term. The problem of pain and suffering is one for which every comprehensive philosophy must venture to account, but for naturalistic systems of ethics which allow a significant scope to individual happiness, it is the Achilles' heel. The universe and man, sketched in materialistic terms, do not blend the thesis that pleasure is the assured rule of life, neither long-term mental nor short-shrift bodily pleasures. Egoistic hedonism does not supply the text by which the mystery of nature can be disentangled. Epicureanism, which sets out affirmatively with the dictum "seek long-term pleasure" reduces to the negative counsel "avoid pain." Not the anticipation of positive pleasures, but the avoidance of the distresses of life, becomes its keynote.

Pain, however, is unavoidable for human beings in this present world; in a naturalistic universe, in which all entities bow to time, the certainty of death, and the possibility of the shortness of life, are constant reminders that the last word belongs to the system of nature, not to man. Epicurus, indeed, sought to remove the terror of death, by pointing out that when the atoms which constitute the body dissolve, consciousness ceases. By this artifice, he aims to deny that death is pain. But he did not deal with the real problem. The man who transcends the sense flux, whose complex rationality enables him to discern the underlying system of events, who has a certain freedom over against these necessities, is cast aside finally as but one of the trivialities in the process which grants him no permanent significance. No persuasive speculative argument that death is not pain can convince man that death is long-term pleasure. The Epicurean sets out to vindicate mental pleasures, only to see them grudgingly cut off at last by death. He has a perturbing fear, in the crises of life, that nature which at last discloses its indifference to him, actually maintains that indifference in all the experiences of life.

So it happens that Epicureanism comes finally and characteristically to say: take things as they are. The good life consists in *ataraxia,* in the undisturbed state. The Greek word *tarasso* means to be tossed like the sea; *ataraxia* is its contradictory. Nature being as it is, there is no justification for exulting over good fortune, since the corresponding possibility of bad fortune exists on the same scale. The Epicurean steels himself against abounding pain, by withholding himself from abounding pleasure. To insure exemption from negative excitements, he deprives life of its positive excitements. What took its rise as a long-term pleasure philosophy thus settles at last into *ataraxia* as the rule of life, now far removed from pleasure. The positive notion of pleasure yields to the negative. The purest "pleasure" becomes the absence of desire for pleasure in any form, short-term or long-term, physical or mental.

Thus Epicureanism joins Cyrenaicism in a joint confession. Cyrenaicism had said, avoid the life of tempest, enthrone the life of sea calm, but ended only in shipwreck on the shoals of indifference. Epicureanism sought anchor in the deep currents of mental pleasure, but it too was driven by the winds of nature to a pleasureless haven. It is impossible for the individual to prize personal pleasure when nature is viewed as an impersonal, non-providential system of events. Even if there were more to nature than system and necessity, and room were made for chance variations, the outcome would be *ataraxia,* not simply as the end but as the whole of life. To reconcile pleasure and ethics in these dimensions is impossible. If nature were more complex than the naturalistic reduction, the situation might indeed be remarkably different. In the mold of Naturalism, however, no alternative to the repudiation of personal pleasure as an element in the rule of human life lay at hand. In ancient Naturalism's search for pleasure in life, both the elemental and systematic forms turned melancholy and pessimistic. The pursuit of pleasure reduces to the avoidance of pain, first short-term and then long-term, and death is cherished as the supreme prospect that human life will be placed beyond the consciousness of pain in any form.

2. *MODERN: UTILITARIANISM*

Utilitarianism is the revival in modern times of the pleasure principle which ancient Cyrenaic and Epicurean ethics projected unsuccessfully as the rule of life. Champion of Utilitarianism Jeremy Bentham (1748-1842) ". . . evaluated Epicurus as the only one among the ancients who had the merit of having known the true source of morality."[8] But the modern development imposes on hedonism three dramatic and far-reaching modifications. It repudiates egoism and champions altruism; it is almost incorrigibly optimistic, resisting any mood of pessimism and melancholy; it is highly rationalistic and technically complex, thereby increasing the tension between the animality and rationality of man.

The supreme rule of life for Utilitarianism is neither the short-term nor the long-term pleasure of any individual as such, but rather the greatest happiness of the greatest number of people. If the Cyrenaic formula is the pleasure of the moment, and the Epicurean the pleasure of a life, the Utilitarian is the maximal earthly pleasure of all lives. It is altruistic with a vengeance, proposing a scheme of action which secures for all men the greatest preponderance of pleasure over pain.

Why hedonism now appears in an altruistic rather than in an egoistic form, is not difficult to answer. Christianity had intervened as a determinative cultural influence separating the history of the ancient

[8]Jeremy Bentham, *An Introduction to the Principles of Morals and Legislation,* (Oxford: Clarendon Press, 1892), ch. 2.

from the modern world. Even hedonism as an ethical philosophy could not escape the unique pervading influence of Christianity with its concern for human welfare. Not pleasure as an isolated objective, but rather concrete righteousness, comprises Christianity's proper rule of life. The special happiness necessary to man as a creature, it contends, is a concomitant of dedication to "the kingdom of God and his righteousness" (Mt. 6:33). Naturalism, however, admits no orientation of life to an eternal world, nor does it permit the good and the true a determinative role in the world process. Hence it gives primacy to what supernaturalistic metaphysics regards as the secondary circumstances of a moral life. Yet the inevitable impact of Christian ways of thinking and living upon Utilitarianism marked a new era in moral philosophy. No longer could pleasure or happiness — synonymous terms for the Utilitarians — be limited to excessive regard for self to exclusion of others' welfare in the social whole.

Not only is Utilitarianism avowedly altruistic; it is also characteristically optimistic, rising above the melancholy and pessimistic pall which hung heavily above the ancient hedonisms. The reason for this change of mood is two-fold: first, the modern philosophy of science, and second, a post-Christian appraisal of nature and history.

The nineteenth century increasingly regarded nature both in its structure and detailed behavior as a system of unrelieved uniformity and necessity. This conception of the world process as an unrelieved uniformity which grinds away unconcerned over man and his interests, could only have multiplied the hopelessness of the ancient world. But to the modern man came science. He learned how to master and to control this vast cosmic machine, how to snatch away its inner secrets for personal advantage. Thus science offered the possible elimination of whatever is contrary to human comfort and pleasure. Over against the ancient ethics of hedonism, overwhelmed always by the stark impression of nature's aloofness to man's pleasure, Utilitarianism shared a growing confidence in science to outwit nature and to channel its forces for the greatest pleasure of the greatest number.

Alongside this faith in science, the Utilitarian movement was conditioned by religious considerations as well. A faith in God involving broad implications for history and nature tends to supplant the idea of an indifferent cosmos with a silent assumption of nature not only harmoniously directed to man's interests, but actually promotive of man's welfare. This religious motif is not traditional Hebrew-Christian supernaturalism, although it is conditioned thereby. The Christian concept of creation had long displaced the old Greek view of matter as essentially evil and antagonistic to the spiritual world; instead, Christianity enforced the conviction of nature's subservience to thought. The modern optimism over nature, even as an inviolable sphere of mechanical uniformity (as Democritus had insisted centuries before), in Utilitarianism is correlated with vague ideas of God. The new theological notions are not spun into a closely-knit metaphysics, specifying a distinctive view of nature and history, and of man and his duty. They reveal, in fact, considerable variance both in theology and in departure from biblical supernaturalism. Notwithstanding, they concur in the conviction of nature's concern for man and his needs. While the prevailing scientific-mechanistic view of man and the world replaces traditional theology in forging the moral situation, the traditional viewpoint is permitted the mollifying contribution of nature's friendliness to man. This contribution, however, is then correlated with peculiar religious and moral presuppositions; in theology, the biblical doctrine of special providence and revelation is subtracted; in ethics, hedonistic interpretations of the moral life are added. While the historic view of God is not basic for fashioning Utilitarian moral views, it somewhat conditions the whole movement, nevertheless. The inherited God-concept does not disappear instantly. Rather it retreats step by step to become but a phantom of the Jehovah of biblical theology. God is merely the original source of the laws of nature, and therefore the guarantor of its kindly disposition toward man despite nature's inexorabilities. While the idea of God is greatly reduced from that of its first Christian dimensions, it nevertheless infuses a measure of spiritual piety and confidence into the whole. God gets only cool recognition; the only warmth he contributes to human life is to kindle the curious assurance of a benign nature, despite the acceptance of scientific materialism.

Among the Utilitarians were a few who held supernaturalistic views without permitting them to dictate a theistic ethics. John Locke, for example, although a theist and a believer in an unchanging Divine rule of right and wrong, denied innate principles of morality, and assimilated evangelical morality to inductive and empirical considerations. William Paley anticipated some of Bentham's system, and while he cannot be regarded as a Utilitarian, he is one of the last who compounds features of that position with the Christian framework. For him, the salient points of moral philosophy included not only the greatest pleasure of the greatest number, but also the doctrine of Consequences, the Will of God, and the Future Life. By conceiving virtue as a "doing good to mankind in obedience to the will of God for the sake of everlasting happiness," he regarded the Christian sanction of charity and brotherliness as the mainspring of ethics. When the sensationalistic epistemology was no longer crossed and swayed by inherited religious considerations, its implications for the moral life became unreservedly delineated. Notions of right and wrong are then founded not on an eternal reason and on the created nature of things, but proceed rather from sense associations alone. Hume is the real progenitor of the movement in ethics which is identified so prominently with the names of Jeremy Bentham and John Stuart Mill. Hume writes on morals with an entire disregard for supernaturalistic considerations; his orientation, instead, to sensationalism has won him the designation of the Scotch Epicurus. Bentham, popularly regarded as the founder of the Utilitarian school, discarded all theological sanctions and applied these earlier principles in actual practice.

The Utilitarian movement does not break with Christianity officially, although Christian determinations are not decisive for its ethics. What survives conspicuously, by way of addition to the ancient Greek view, is an unconscious debt to Hebrew-Christian metaphysics in the new attitude toward nature.

A third feature of Utilitarianism is its increasing emphasis on man as a distinctively rational animal, by which the tension already observed in Epicurean ethics is pushed to troublesome intensity. Indeed, it is said that this element of the morality of Utility is more significant even than its espousals of altruism and optimism as adjuncts of an hedonistic approach. For it is over the significance of the rational side of human nature that the Utilitarian movement at last falls into dispute, and an irreparable breach arises which inundates the movement with insurmountable difficulties.

The enlarged scope assigned to reason in the analysis of the ethical situation is related to the modern scientific confidence that man can chart the behavior of nature in detail. Universal intelligence is thus called upon to assert itself with new precision. Bentham proposed a "felicific calculus" for the individual measurement of the probable pleasures attending alternate possibilities of moral action. His aim was to make morals as accurate as physics by measuring the quantity of pleasures scientifically. In Bentham's mathematics of ethics the following criteria measured the rightness or wrongness (pleasure-productivity) of a possible act: intensity, duration, certainty or uncertainty, propinquity or remoteness, fecundity, purity, and extent, or the number of persons affected by the act. Bentham's formula called for an exacting application of reason in the measurement of pleasure. For Aristippus, durability had played no part in determining the goodness of a pleasure, since it was an unknown factor; only immediacy and intensity were considerations. Bentham retains the emphasis that the basis of morality is the feeling of pleasure, but the method of discriminating right from wrong becomes "as rational as mathematics."[9]

It was John Stuart Mill (1806-1873) who lifted the significance of human reason to a yet higher dimension. Virtue consists in acting according to reason, for man is a reasonable being. To Mill, this meant more than a rational method for measuring the value of pleasure or pain. It meant, indeed, the necessity of distinguishing between pleasures qualitatively and not merely quantitatively. Human nature is too complex to rest in animal satisfactions. The complex, loftier elements of

[9]Gordon H. Clark and T. V. Smith, *Readings in Ethics* (New York: F. S. Crofts, 1935), p. 288.

man's nature require more in the ethical situation than merely prudential calculations.

Mill becomes the great heretic of the Utilitarian school by his insistence that pleasure is not the only good, and that pleasures differ in kind as well as in amount and intensity. The Utilitarian school, like the Epicureans before them, had found "the superiority of mental over bodily pleasures chiefly in the greater permanency, safety, uncostliness, etc., of the former — that is, in their circumstantial advantages rather than in their intrinsic nature." Mill's essay on "What Utilitarianism Is"[10] had championed this qualitative distinction as over the merely quantitative.

Unfortunately for Mill, no external induction can prove distinctions of quality. Nevertheless, Mill retained an empirical approach to ethics.

Such a formula marks a significant departure from a consistent ethics of hedonism. It insists upon an essential distinction between man and the animals, even as it insists upon a qualitative distinction between pleasures. It does not indeed securely buttress these convictions in terms of a carefully-forged metaphysics, by which the inner connection of world view and life view is convincingly set forth. There is doubtless a connection, however tenuous, between Mill's belief in supernaturalism, even if attached to the theory of a finite god, and the special distinction which he confers upon man. It is remarkable, nonetheless, that Mill could regard his version of Utilitarianism as the essence of Christianity, declaring that "in the golden rule of Jesus of Nazareth we read the complete spirit of the ethics of utility. To do as one would be done by, and to love one's neighbor as one's self, constitute the ideal perfection of utilitarian morality."[11] Between the golden rule and Utilitarianism there is doubtless this similarity, that both express a concern for human welfare, but the differences are far profounder, and Mill is oblivious to them. The world did not need to wait for Utilitarianism to assert that benevolence is good, that whatever imperiled the public good was not virtuous, that true morality tends to the welfare of the social whole; the revealed morality of the Bible had affirmed all of this. The bare doctrine of Utility will not be found there, of course. Yet Mill modifies the conclusions of Utilitarianism without altering its determinative presuppositions. More is needed to sublimate the devotion to pleasure to devotion to virtue than inferences from fleeting sensations and a world of change. Disparaging the disjunction of pleasure from right-

[10]John Stuart Mill, *Utilitarianism,* ch. 2. Mill presses for a distinction between kinds of pleasure, and their discrimination on the basis of quality and not quantity alone. While he insists that such a distinction is "quite compatible with the principle of utility," he nowhere shows how a genuine distinction of quality can be made between pleasures on the basis of inductive experience alone. His real argument is that the complexity of human nature is such that merely animal satisfactions are for man an insufferable fate. "It is better to be a human being dissatisfied than a pig satisfied," he urges. Reprinted with a study of *The English Utilitarians* by John Plamenatz (Oxford, Blackwell, 1949).

[11]*Ibid.,* p. 24.

eousness in the search for wellbeing or happiness, the Scriptures speak of those who are "lovers of pleasure more than lovers of God" (II Tim. 3:4).[12]

Emphasis on the peculiar significance of the rational and spiritual life of man militates against Utilitarian disregard of motive, and of innate moral principles, as well as against its regard of only empirical considerations as the guide to moral action. If morality is reasonable, and if man as rational can find his proper place in the world only in the service of reason, may this not be — indeed, must this not be — a rational universe? Curiously, Hume had protested that traditional moral philosophy had erected "schemes of virtue and happiness, without regarding human nature, upon which every moral conclusion must depend."[13] But it was precisely such neglect of an adequate analysis of human nature which provided the basis of Utilitarianism. Similarly, Utilitarianism's connection of morality with an ultimate mind and will had been the very strength of the inherited theories of virtue. John Stuart Blackie notes that "the ancients, while acknowledging Utility as a principle, kept Reason in the foreground, while the moderns push Utility into the van, and use Reason only as an instrument to make that point alone prominent."[14] Similarly he observes that "to deny God in the macrocosm necessarily leads to the denial of Mind in the microcosm,"[15] an observation which suggests the corollary, that to take reason seriously in the moral situation eventually raises the issue of its ontological significance.

If Mill from an inductive study of pleasure-claims failed to show how it is possible objectively to distinguish some as different in quality from others, it remained for Henry Sidgwick (1838-1900) to carry and raise the Utilitarian position to another perspective. Sidgwick contends that man is gifted with self-evident moral intuitions. He insists that particular and general happiness are correlated in a universal harmony. He regards immortality as the greatest guarantee of happiness for the individual who seeks the happiness of the greatest number. The vista which he opens by insisting upon the innate disposition of human nature to morality, and its connection with the eternal order, separates him by only the slimmest of threads from an elemental Idealism. Yet he halts short of a Divine disposition of all things, refusing to postulate an objective moral order.[16] It is difficult to speak conclusively, but the fact of Sidgwick's acceptance of evolutionary theory, alongside his

[12]Doubtless the term "pleasure" does not here fully coincide with the term in the ethics of Bentham and Mill. But what they said about pleasure cannot be separated from the principles they imply, and these determine the content of pleasure by a reference other than the love of God.

[13]Cf. John Hill Burton, *Life and Correspondence of David Hume* (Edinburgh: W. Tait, 1846), I, 35.

[14]John Stuart Blackie, *Four Phases of Morals* (Edinburgh: Edmonston and Douglas, 1874), p. 308.

[15]*Ibid.*, p. 319.

[16]Henry Sidgwick, *The Methods of Ethics* (7th ed., New York: Macmillan, 1922), pp. 506-509.

flimsy theism, may account for his hesitancy at this point. He is the first moralist to assign an important role to evolutionary considerations: "I do not doubt that the whole fabric of human thought—including the conceptions which present themselves as most simple and elementary—has been developed, through a gradual process of psychical change, out of some lower life in which thought, properly speaking, had no place."[17] He abandons Mill's distinction of kinds of pleasure, arguing that a consistent application of the empirical quantitative principle excludes qualitative distinctions.

Even the Utilitarian espousal of altruism is not, however, as impressive as at first it seems. It is not, in fact, a clear-cut contradiction of egoism at all. Deep down, the pleasure of all men is to be sought because this brings the self long-term pleasure. Hence a kind of Utilitarianism arises which is really Epicurean. Does not Utilitarianism reduce to an intricate form of egoism? How are we to determine what moral content is productive of the greatest pleasure of the greatest number? How are we to arrive at a confident definition of that in which human happiness everywhere and always consists? How, within the limited empirical situation, is this ideal enthusiasm for the greatest possible happiness of all creatures implied in the direct stimulus of pleasure? "Epicureanism to win a hearing [in the last century] is constrained to profess a standard which shall not fall beneath that laid down in the Sermon on the Mount or in the 13th chapter of 1st Corinthians; and to do this with nothing but the individual selfish love of pleasure to start with . . . one is forced to explain how the original, individual, and personal love of pleasure [as Bentham admits] . . . manages from mere external considerations . . . to take the shape of benevolence."[18] Benevolent instincts in man do not blend easily with the thesis that he is only an animal upon whose consciousness nature alone makes impressions. How is the thesis, this act *is* the means of the greatest pleasure of the greatest number, convertible into the thesis that therefore this act *ought* to be performed by me?

If pleasure is the only motivation for conduct, what if the pleasure of the greatest number should not coincide with the pleasure of a given individual moral agent? If the pleasure of the individual and of the majority are to be convincingly exhibited as consistently harmonious, something more is required than Bentham's mere assumption of it, and his dependence primarily upon legal enforcement of the social good. If there are no sanctions above the legislator, what is to prevent him, in turn, from seeking his own pleasure through the pain of the masses, rather than general welfare?

Churchmen distrustful of traditional theology, and ready to find the essence of Christianity in nothing beyond an ethical concern for the social whole, supported Utilitarianism. Sidgwick halted short of the

[17]*Ibid.*, p. 32.
[18]Blackie, *op. cit.*, p. 331.

emphasis that God harmonizes individual and group welfare through intuitions which prescribe the greatest happiness of the individual and of the social whole. Prudence, he contends, is the intuition which prescribes the individual's *greatest* happiness, in contrast with approximations of it; benevolence, another intuition, prescribes a regard for happiness of others; the intuition of justice, or equity, dictates equal regard for both. Even this departure from empirical ethics failed to guarantee an individual's always finding his own greatest happiness in promoting that of others. Consequently, Sidgwick appeals to the doctrine of immortality for a solution.

In an effort, therefore, to prevent altruism from capitulating to selfishness, Sidgwick borrows an attenuated and secularized version of the Hebrew-Christian doctrines of creation, preservation and an after-life. But the metaphysics and ethics of revelation are not allowed in any decisive sense to determine his position. Even the case for immortality wins its way primarily because of Sidgwick's interest in psychical investigations. (He became first president of The Society for Psychical Research.) While he therefore bases altruism on intuitive morality, and disregards all consequences except those immediately derived from the principle of Utility, thereby seeking to elevate the greatest happiness of the greatest number to an unconditionally prescribed rule of duty, yet in the last analysis he invokes intuition as a justification of Utilitarianism, but not because Utilitarianism flows — as indeed it does not — from a revealed metaphysics and theology. "If . . . we may assume the existence of such a Being, as God, by the *Consensus* of theologians, is conceived to be, it seems that Utilitarians may legitimately infer the existence of Divine sanction to the code of social duty as constructed on a Utilitarian basis."[19] But the idea of God is detached from any effective connection with altruistic hedonism, except to assume Divine approbation, if there be a divinity. Sidgwick, no less than Mill, thinks he finds in Utilitarianism the ethics of Jesus, and cites the Golden Rule as a special application of the self-evident and innate principle of justice, *viz.*, that whatever action one judges to be right for himself, he implicitly judges to be right for all similar persons in similar circumstances. The real conflict between selfishness and unselfishness is not, in fact, resolved this simply, however. For while altruism is formally established as an *ought,* its content is still indeterminate, and the problem of supplying its content, of defining approved acts, remains to be solved. The intuition of justice may guard the theory from relativism, but the calculation of the ideal content of morality must always be faulty while it is suspended upon subjective empirical determinations.

If the altruistic temper of Utilitarianism appears superficial, even more can this be said of its spirit of optimism. Ancient hedonism had been driven finally to conceive the purpose of life as flight from pain,

[19]Sidgwick, *op. cit.,* p. 506.

rather than realization of positive enjoyments. The ethics of Utility stressed the greatest pleasure for the greatest number as its confident expectation. Faith in science to control nature for man's ends, plus a romantic view of nature attaching to scantily-defined views of God, provided the avenues to this modern confidence. It now remains to show that neither of these assumptions justifies such optimism, and that the recent reassertions of pessimism are more consistent with the naturalistic frame of reference.

Consider first the phantom-god of the Utilitarians. In some few cases the outlines of Christian theology are dimly perceptible, as with Locke. In others, the finite god of pre-Christian metaphysics may be detected, as with Mill. In yet others, little more is asserted than the bare reality of some supernatural Being. This notion of God is correlated with warm expectations from nature, and sometimes reduces to little more than this. Doubtless this cheerful attitude toward nature is a reflex of the Hebrew-Christian creation doctrine that man stands as the apex of the original forms of life and that the world of nature and the lower creatures are called into being with a view to him as their vice-regent. But a naturalistic view of things is, in fact, not entitled to the admission of a genuine supernatural principle; it can capitalize neither on the existence of God, nor on a doctrine of creation and providence. Beyond all doubt, naturalistic schematizations of reality do not exclude all conceptions of deity. Most of the Greek naturalists dignified some aspect of the space-time world as divine. Epicurus spoke of atom-constituted gods existing in the stellar spaces between the worlds. But the Epicurean gods, like all naturalistic gods, are dependent upon the universe, and not the universe upon them. The first-principle of Naturalism is that nature is the ultimate real. It is therefore wholly unclear why, in a naturalistic view, the assertion of deity in any form should involve a fundamental change in the concept of nature. If God, and not nature, is the ultimate and controlling principle of reality, the first-principle of Naturalism is deserted, and its replacement should then be allowed to dictate the moral situation and its own moral claim. In that event hedonistic Naturalism, in any form, would be excluded; instead, a difference in kind between pleasures would be vindicated; man's peculiar dignity would be found in an orientation to the eternal spiritual world; and the rule of life would be supernaturally defined and sanctioned. The silent assumption of a naturalistic world which in modern hedonism suddenly loses its indifference to man, and harmonizes both individual and general interests, either involves the invocation of a deity to which Naturalism is not entitled, or it involves the uncritical inheritance of the medieval confidence in providence,[20] unjustifiably divorced from an acceptance of

[20]It is one of the curiosities, and ironies, of the Utilitarian movement that in view of its altruism, and the correlation of ethics with a vague doctrine of "the Fatherhood of God" — used loosely as a synonym for the friendliness of nature to man's interests — it came to regard itself as expressive of Christian ethics.

the God of Hebrew-Christian revelation. In the last century, the awkwardness of this dilemma has been evaded, as will be noted later, because of the rise of evolutionary views. According to the developmental theory, nature is evolving in increasingly complex patterns, whose intrinsic harmony is demonstrated by the production and support of man. Thus the doctrine that nature is personality-producing and personality-sustaining, and not hostile to man, gains a wholly secular basis.

Before this more recent and post-Utilitarian tenet is evaluated, one ought to consider Utilitarianism's confidence in scientific control of nature as an optimistic foundation for hedonistic Naturalism. The rise of scientific techniques encouraged the belief in man's control and use of nature, and in the approaching day when nature and man may coexist in a millennial atmosphere. Thus the pessimistic view of nature yielded to meliorism, and at last to optimism. Science stands between man and nature, gifted with a methodology that guarantees technological discoveries, and that turns the inexorable necessities of nature to support human pleasure.

To read the benefits of science in this way, however, was to exceed the bounds of actuality. The ground of pessimism in the ancient views lay not alone in nature's unstable support of pleasure in day to day experience, but especially in the brevity of life and in the certainty of death. The changes which science has been able to contribute at this level, important as they are, do not in any significant way mitigate the essential problem. Beyond all doubt, modern science has combatted human diseases with great skill, has reduced an entire range of erstwhile fatal illnesses to the category of minor nuisances. But does this development essentially modify the older complaint?[21] Science has extended the life expectancy of man not only in lands laden with poverty and disease, but in lands of plenty and health. The average length of life from ancient to modern times seems to disclose a progressive increase, although nothing yet compares with the curious longevity of the patriarchs of early biblical history. But the most striking average gains have been made in modern times, and one researcher comments that "the average length of life has undoubtedly increased more in the past century than in all prior centuries together, since the dawn of civilization." Approximate estimates based on fragmentary

[21]A Scottish medical officer, curiously, has recently expressed doubt, after long experience with old people in his district, that the prolongation of life is necessarily "progress." In his annual report, R. B. Clayton asserts that "many authorities believe that it is not really kind to prolong the lives of so many to a stage of 'sans teeth, sans eyes, sans taste, sans everything.' The physician exhibiting penicillin or M and B will not allow . . . pneumonia to give . . . quietus, but saves the patient, often for a matter of mere months, to endure a lingering, painful end. . . . A brilliant operation which prolongs life for a month or two, or maybe a year — part of which is spent in recovering from the operation, part in learning the use of artificial apertures and the remainder in a slow death — is not 'progress' to the individual."

data suggest that the life span of prehistoric man was 18 years; that in ancient Rome, 22 years; in the Middle Ages, 35 years; a century ago in England and Wales, 40.9 years; in the United States in 1900, 49.2 years, compared with 65.8 years in 1945.[22] The latter 16-year lengthening of the life span in less than a half century "is undoubtedly without parallel in the whole range of human existence, and may never again be equaled."[23] Contemporary scientists look anticipatively to the development of new weapons to fight disease and to extend life in the atomic era, and are not without the fond hope of achieving an expectancy of 100 years for man in our times. One scientist has already ventured the prediction that one out of ten Americans eventually may live to be a centenarian. Yet all magic formulas for longevity are bounded by the same distressing limits which plagued the ancient naturalistic mind. They leave the individual's life-span indeterminate, and they exclude death for no one. The role of these facts in modern experience is seen in the growing tendency to regard death as an unmentionable.[24] In no case has science conquered the inevitability of death. The modern man has only found more fascinating diversions from sober contemplation of this fact. Moreover, the optimistic reading of science ignored almost entirely an aspect of the inventive enterprise which, in our generation, has been painfully obvious, the fact that science has placed at the disposal of man techniques for human destruction which are powerful enough to undo in a single day all the positive achievements of centuries. It is the very methodology which brought to modern man his capacity for turning nature to the service of human pleasure which has equipped him with a demonic power for human destruction. Furthermore, even if science should be channeled constructively, and should succeed in the significant extension of human life, which appears an unlikely anticipation, no merely quantitative approach to a hedonistic ethics is adequate to cope with its inner difficulty. No multiplication of flat pleasures can satisfy man; as Mill emphasized, the pleasures for which man is fashioned are intrinsically different. Mill does not spell this out, to emphasize that immortality and spiritual pleasures, and theism and the peculiar dignity of man, are essential elements of a genuine distinction of kinds, or qualitative differences, in pleasure. Alongside the problem of adding years to life stands the problem of adding life to years. Modern hedonistic optimism over science does not really sense the fact so obvious to pre-Christian hedonism, namely, that the fact of inevitable human death is a standing reminder of the indifference of nature, and mute evidence that the universe cannot really be coordinated with a pleasure ethics.

[22]*Statistical Bulletin* of the Metropolitan Life Insurance Co., Vol. 28, No. 10 (Oct., 1947), p. 1.

[23]*Ibid.*, p. 3.

[24]The British anthropologist Geoffrey Gorer (reported in *Time* magazine, Nov. 7, 1955) gives the reason: without the traditional belief in a future life "natural death and physical decomposition have become too horrible to contemplate."

3. MODERN: EVOLUTIONARY ETHICS

From what has been said, it is apparent that neither the phantom gods of Naturalism nor the fact of science can adequately justify the optimistic view of nature. During the past century, however, naturalistic ethics has found added support in the philosophy of evolution for its confidence in nature's disposition toward human concerns. Utilitarians supporting the evolutionary philosophy hoped to make ethics "scientific." Moreover, by finding in the concept of development a wholly natural account of the emergence of complex rationality in man, they evaded the tension between reason and sensation arising from that larger significance which Utilitarianism assigned to reason, albeit incompatibly with the earlier naturalistic theories.

The evolutionary view of nature and history implied, to the proponents of hedonism, an age of boundless pleasure in which advantage to both the individual and to society would blend absolutely. "From the laws of life it must be concluded that unceasing social discipline will so mould human nature that eventually sympathetic pleasures will be spontaneously pursued to the fullest extent advantageous to each and all. The scope for altruistic activities will not exceed the desire for altruistic satisfactions."[25]

The determination to combine evolution and optimism, like the earlier correlations of a phantom god with optimism, and of science with optimism, should prepare us for a remarkable fact about the whole hedonistic movement in its modern beginnings. It did not actually derive its basis for optimism from its own foundations, but rather injected optimism into them. What really tempered modern hedonism, both in its altruistic disposition and in its incorrigible optimism, was a view of history which was inherited from medieval Christian thought and secularized. There was no forging of a rival view wholly dictated by the naturalistic reconstruction. The inherited thesis of history's final goal being a kingdom of millennial bliss hedonism reduced easily to the maximal pleasure of the greatest number. In the biblical setting, the kingdom of righteousness is inaugurated by Divine cataclysm; in secular reconstructions, it becomes an achievement of human effort in cooperation with nature. With this assumption, the acceptance of nature as evolving could mean only one thing, progress. In fact, the developmental theory becomes the guarantor of progress; its denial seems to involve static and pessimistic views of reality. In this inheritance of medieval optimism about the end-state of history, evolutionary Naturalism ignored the basic concept, namely, the reality of a supernatural creator and governor of the universe. Minus the doctrine of Divine providence, both the suppositions of unlimited progress and of nature increasingly disposed to man's advantage were without a convincing basis. More than that, evolution divorced from such providence with equal readiness feeds pessimism. In the pre-Christian

[25]Herbert Spencer, *The Data of Ethics* (New York: American Publishers Corporation, n. d.), p. 289.

world, in fact, pessimism was associated, inevitably, with the concept of nature as the only reality. At any rate, nothing definable as scientific knowledge supplies any criterion for establishing an absolute future.

Apart from the discussion of evolution as an adequate account of origins, another question arises. Does, as some enthusiasts believe, the harmony which evolution postulates between nature and man provide within an empirical framework any sure basis for unlimited progress in pleasure? Herbert Spencer, for example, wrote that "The inference that as advancement has hitherto been the rule, it will be the rule henceforth, may be called a plausible speculation. But when it is shown that this advancement is due to the working of a universal law; and that in virtue of that law it must continue until the state we call perfection is reached, then the belief in that state is removed out of the region of probability into that of certainty."[26] This assumption of a universal and absolutely uniform law, which the evolutionary hedonists correlated with the theory of development, is no longer dominant either in physics or in biology, but has yielded place to the acknowledgment of discontinuities in nature. The laws of nature now are regarded more as "statistical averages" which justify only probability, rather than absolute conclusion, about the future. But the attempt to read even the probability of future progress, and the melioristic notion that nature and history will minister more largely to human pleasure than at present, can both be challenged. Bertrand Russell emphasizes the fact that the evolutionary principle supplies no basis whatever for optimism over man and his future destiny.[27] If the evolutionary movement is such that its shifting front instantly exhibits forms of enlarging complexity, then, just as the amoeba, which at one point in the space-time process occupied the strategic and significantly central role, yet in time was retired to oblivion, so also the future apex of the evolutionary process may outrank *homo sapiens* and relegate him to a peripheral position in the ongoing developmental movement.

The difficulty of correlating a nature friendly to man was already acknowledged by some pre-evolutionary Utilitarians. Mill's reference to the "imperfect state" of the world, which he expands into an oration on the injustices of nature, leads to an almost pessimistic remark that "the conscious ability to do without happiness gives the best prospect of realizing such happiness as is attainable."[28] Only Mill's confidence in a world improving because of science and implementing the smooth operation of virtue cancels out the force of his admission. He asserts: "All the grand sources . . . of human suffering are in a great degree, many of them almost entirely, conquerable by human care and effort."[29] From the first, however, the concept of an intrinsic harmony between

[26]Spencer, *Social Statics* (New York: Appleton, 1883), p. 78.
[27]Bertrand Russell, "Current Tendencies," in *Selected Papers of Bertrand Russell* (New York: Modern Library, n.d.), pp. 324ff.
[28]Mill, *op. cit.*, p. 23.
[29]*Ibid.*, p. 22.

nature and man was challenged by supporters of the evolutionary view, although their interpretations were overwhelmed by the apostles of optimism. It was T. H. Huxley who insisted that a fundamental antagonism exists between the cosmic process and the ethical life. He therefore regarded the hedonistic attempt absolutely to equate virtue and happiness as impossible as squaring a circle in geometry.[30]

The recognition, by evolutionary naturalists, that the romantic view of nature is based in medieval theology rather than in data available to a naturalistic evaluation, curries a distrust of hedonism as the rule of life. If moral distinctions evolve out of natural processes, they are a necessary unfolding, and the process, not morality, is the ultimate and decisive thing. The really perpetual element in nature is its drive, its power. Thus, in the growing awareness that all forms of hedonism presume too sentimental an interpretation of nature, there arises as a cosmic device for human pleasure, an equal recognition that what nature really implies is not a pleasure-ethics but a power-ethics. Whatever evolves, evolves by sheer process. What is the necessary expression of natural law is "better" only in the sense that it is a manifestation of the most powerful. The deepest drive of nature is not pleasure, but rather the use of power in overcoming all obstacles. As evolutionary ethics turns from pleasure to power as the rule of life, it makes a point of contact with another interpretation of naturalistic premises, one which is spiritedly antihedonistic, and which likewise has ancient precedents.

B. POLITICAL NATURALISM

Naturalistic ethics may orient man to the world of nature, rather than nature to human life, and thus produce a hard-hitting power-ethics. In such a scheme the essential thrust of the universe is not man's pleasure, contrary to sentimental theories which combine the ultimacy of nature with the happiness of the individual. The indifference of nature to personal desires evidences quite convincingly that the universe offers neither benevolences nor condolences to man. Nature is power, and whoever succeeds in taking up this power in himself, stands as an incarnation of the greatest force in existence, and holds the fulcrum of history. Power determines the course of reality. Might makes right.

All the ethical norms of life are but convention; if one wishes to avoid relativism in morals, he must go to nature itself. What is rooted in nature is power, not moral law; whatever prevails is right.

1. ANCIENT: THRASYMACHUS

Perhaps everyone at some time or other has entertained the thought: "If I could get away with it, I'd do it." The taxpayer would cheat with liberty, he may think, if he were a director of internal revenue. The pickpocket could go for lucrative game if the police would arrange

[30]T. H. Huxley, *Evolution and Ethics* (New York: Appleton, 1896).

their vacations the same month. The adulterer could extend his indulgences if he could guarantee privacy and confidence. The lack of control over consequences is a restraining force upon conduct.

But this is not political Naturalism, or Naturalism with a polity, or settled administration of the thesis that might is right. It is only a very naive mood. It lacks a consistent exposition of the thesis, and a comprehensive application and defense of it. The connection between the nature of reality and the course of conduct is not set forth, even in the barest form. Callicles, an aristocrat of Plato's day, had said: "Nature herself, I believe, declares that it is right for the superior man to get an advantage over the inferior, and the more capable man over the less capable." In the *Republic,* Thrasymachus proposes the thesis that power is the rule of life. "Justice is nothing else than the interest of the stronger." The dictator who imposes his "rights" by sheer force becomes the ideal example of the thesis that all forms of government exist only for their own interests, and that laws are fashioned for the sake of the superior force. "Everywhere there is but one principle of justice, which is the interest of the stronger." The most powerful legislate in their own interest, and this legislation becomes the good.

When Thrasymachus ventures a systematic and comprehensive defense of political Naturalism, Socrates and the *Republic* swiftly move into the discussion of the moral problem with full earnestness. Thrasymachus argues that those who honor moral norms are always disadvantaged, both in private contracts and in dealings with the state. But he does not stop there. He stresses that the advantage of a power-ethics is most obvious when it is not confined to segmented experiences of life, but applied as a comprehensive and unrestricted rule.

The words of Thrasymachus read like a prophecy of Hitler's march on Czechoslovakia, or of Russia's invasion of Poland, or Red China's plunder of Korea. "I am speaking," says Thrasymachus, ". . . of injustice on a large scale in which the advantage of the unjust is most apparent; and my meaning will be most clearly seen if we turn to that highest form of injustice in which the criminal is the happiest of men, and the sufferers or those who refuse to do injustice are the most miserable — that is to say tyranny, which by fraud and force takes away the property of others, not little by little but wholesale; comprehending in one, things sacred as well as profane, private and public; for which acts of wrong, if he were detected perpetrating any of them singly, he would be punished and incur great disgrace — they who do such wrong in particular cases are called robbers of temples, and man-stealers and burglars and swindlers and thieves. But when a man besides taking away the money of the citizens has made slaves of them, then, instead of these names of reproach, he is termed happy and blessed, not only by the citizens but by all who hear of his having achieved the consummation of injustice. For mankind censure injustice, fearing that they may be victims of it and not because they shrink from committing it. . . . Injustice, when on a sufficient scale, has more strength and freedom and mastery than justice; and . . . justice is the interest of the stronger, whereas injustice is a man's own profit and interest."

The state thus becomes an achievement of shrewd leaders who employ it as an instrument for selfish ends. According to Thrasymachus, rulers are like shepherds fattening their sheep for the kill. The cleverest man is the one who is able to impose his will upon all others. A democracy involving many leaders, obviously then, allows only mediocre achievement in such a scheme. Even an aristocracy, with a select few, halts short of the ideal tyranny, wherein one person prevails over all others.

Not sheer animal or physical strength alone determines the content of right. Political Naturalism increasingly stresses that nature is much more than what is usually designated "physical nature." All kinds of power which reduce others to a position of dependence and subservience — social power, economic power, political power — establish the right which prevails. Might alone makes right; any other reference for the good is sentimental and contrary to nature.

2. *MODERN: MACHIAVELLI*

The impact of Christian ethics upon the Western world subdued political Naturalism until 1500 A.D. Its reviving voice was that of Niccolo Machiavelli (1469-1527), in Italy, the land of the popes. His most influential work, *The Prince,* helped to mold the modern mind and, in consequence, modern history.

The Prince is directed to the rulers who sway states and dominions. Machiavelli's primary interest is not how rulers ought to rule, but in how they do rule — not in the ideal, but in the actual. His theme is plain: the ruler "who abandons what is done for what ought to be done, will rather learn to bring about his own ruin than his preservation." The epithet "Machiavellian" gains its meaning from the eighteenth chapter: "In What Way Princes Must Keep Faith." There he remarks that humanity because of its dual human and bestial nature, is tempted to wage war by law or power. "The prince must know how to use both natures, and that the one without the other is not durable." The successful ruler is a human lion and fox, keeping faith when it is for his interest, breaking faith when new conditions arise (*i.e.,* when it is against his interest). Since the art of war secures his rise to power, and preserves his position, it is the Prince's only needful study. Hence, even in peacetime by consolidating military and political power in himself the ruler prepares for inevitable war. He foments disorders in bordering nations, he bribes allies of rival states, he divides and conquers. Then he wages aggressive war, installs an unscrupulous tyrant over the conquered people, stamps out the previous rulers, and at last liquidates even the unscrupulous tyrant to gain the favor of his subjects. Machiavelli does not sketch this as an ideal pattern; he simply holds up Cesare Borgia, the acknowledged son of Pope Alexander VI, who forged a kingdom for himself by force and fraud, as "an example to be imitated by all who by fortune and with the arms of others have risen to power."

The ironic fact is that the political authoritarianism of the Roman Church, centered in the popes, contributed to the notion of an arbitrary human power from which there was no appeal. Naturalism made the transition from the dogma that the emperor is the pope's vicar, to the dogma that the citizen is the emperor's. Romanism held that the empire exists for the sake of the church; political Naturalism held that it exists for the sake of the ruler.

John K. Ryan remarks that, on Machiavelli's view, might not only makes right, but it constitutes duty.[31] Whatever strength can achieve by way of imposition, it axiomatically ought to achieve; if it cannot conquer, it ought not. Thus the Machiavellian keynote is not "my country, right or wrong" but rather, right is whatever strengthens the state, and wrong is whatever weakens it. If we do not here arrive at the thesis that might is right, at least the Machiavellian formula is clear that might can never do wrong, even if the ruler employs fraud, crime, or other arbitrary means in the reach for power. No legislation or moral code ought ever to frustrate the uninhibited assertion of power. "Moral principles" are determined with a view to the party which successfully imposes its arbitrary will upon others. The Prince, as the center of power, is above all restrictions of religion and ethics. Machiavelli regarded a national religion as a valuable patriotic aid to strong government, but he hated Christianity because it negated the strong military virtues of Rome. The moral qualities he prizes are patriotism, exaltation of the fatherland, honor, the general good. The state, however, is an end in itself; it owes allegiance to no law superior to its own interests, and those self interests are justifiably advanced by whatever means the state uses.

Like Thrasymachus, Machiavelli was a Mussolini before Mussolini, except that the opportunity to latch the state to political Naturalism was never afforded him. The defeat of Florence had ended his public life and led to imprisonment for his supposed part in a plot against the Medici. *The Prince* was written during the fifteen years of exile from the royal courts, and his longing to give the state forceful leadership was unfulfilled. But his nationalistic appeal has a ring which those familiar with modern dictators will readily detect: the masses are "without a head, without order, beaten, despoiled, lacerated, and overrun." Italy waits "to follow any standard if only there be someone to raise it"; indeed, she waits for "her liberator," through whose courageous leadership the "fatherland" will be raised up.

[31]John K. Ryan, in *The Great Books,* Harold C. Gardiner, ed. (New York: Devin-Adair, 1949), p. 56.

The full bloom of Machiavelli's thought waited four centuries for historical actualization in the sphere of *realpolitik. The Prince* was written in 1513; the outlines of the modern totalitarian state, it has often been noted, first emerged with international fury in 1913. Embodied in the dictator, with inventive science and industrial technocracy as allies in the expansion of power, totalitarianism repudiates human rights except by definition and tolerance of the state, suffers religion only to the extent that it strengthens the state, aims to liquidate individuals, groups, social classes and even races when this seems to further the state's interest. The features of Machiavelli give way, and in their stead appear the outlines of Mussolini, Hitler, Stalin and his Communist successors. Mussolini, interestingly enough, submitted a thesis on Machiavelli for the doctor's degree.

3. MODERN: THOMAS HOBBES

Before the rise of the totalitarian state, however, several intermediary voices are heard. The first of these is Thomas Hobbes (1588-1679). The fact that he is an Englishman lays the ghost of that subtle race prejudice which would identify political Naturalism with "the Italian spirit," "the Germanic spirit," "the Russian spirit." The power-ethic line is not peculiar to certain nationalities; it is characteristic of all exponents of Naturalism interpreted animalistically rather than sentimentally. Hobbes shares with Thrasymachus and Machiavelli the thesis that man and the state are aspects of nature alone and hence can be understood only naturalistically. He develops the "might makes right" thesis before Nietzsche and Hitler, before Marx, Lenin and Stalin, with the important qualification that in Hobbes' approach the people voluntarily transfer their rights to the king.

Already in ancient times the advocates of Naturalism argued that moral distinctions are unnatural, that the human race accepted them only to render social life predictable. In Plato's *Republic,* Glaucon distressingly reports the naturalistic theory that justice "is a mean or compromise, between the best of all, which is to do injustice and not be punished, and the worst of all, which is to suffer injustice without the power of retaliation; and justice, being at a middle point between the two, is tolerated not as a good, but as the lesser evil, and honored by reason of the inability of men to do injustice."[32] Thus moral rules are viewed as imposed by social sanctions; as having their origin in human reason and will; as resting on tacit consent. Hobbes' *Leviathan* (his designation for the state) ventures to account for the ruler and his power by a social contract theory of origins. Man's original "state of nature" is barbarian egoism, each individual seeking his own survival. The inclination after power to ensure survival, the drive for self-preservation, is deeper than the drive for pleasure, and, if uncontrolled, would issue in man's counter-destruction of man. Man, as a part of

[32]*Republic,* ii, 359.

nature, inherits this drive for survival. Since none would know when his goods may be stolen or his life assailed, and since men are fairly equal in strength and cunning, one would destroy the other. A shrewd animal, he organizes as a social unit to outwit the natural circumstances which peril his existence. He inaugurates a power-ethics of self-preservation. To achieve his egoistic ends (survival) he presumably becomes altruistic, designating an omnipotent ruler. To promote self-preservation, the people enter into a social contract conferring their personal rights upon a ruler who is empowered to legislate for all. Who the sovereign is matters little. The all-important consideration is that the ruler be all-powerful, since where there is no adequate power there is no law, and consequently no injustice. In the original condition of nature man has a right to do anything he pleases, to aggrandize to himself whatever he can take and hold. But the Leviathan's power becomes the *terminus ultimus* of the total forces of all citizens.

There can be no appeal from the decisions of the Leviathan, for if one person prevails to change his will, another may also, and the social state would soon return to its unpredictable and insecure condition. Since self-preservation is achieved through the sovereign state, that sovereignty must never be weakened. The worst kind of government is "better" than none. The *ought* is not derived from God, any more than is the state; both are artificial. The state rests originally upon the preference of the people, and the moral law is simply the will of the ruler. The *ought* is not eternal, but man-made, not by the *vox pop,* but by the dictator. Right and wrong are distinctions made by the sovereign. The state and all moral authority are rooted simply in man's shrewd recognition that this is the technique for achieving self-preservation. The fear of the sovereign alone keeps men from devouring one another.[33] The proclamations of the ruler are to be obeyed for no other reason than that what the ruler proclaims is, *ipso facto,* for the good of the ruled. Thus Hobbes blends political Naturalism with hedonistic egoism as a universal descriptive fact.

The king is above all laws, for he makes them. Once set up, the state is beyond criticism. This was the thesis of Hobbes before Hitler and Stalin. The supreme command is "to make and abrogate laws, to determine war and peace, to know and judge all controversies, either by himself, or by judges appointed by him; to elect all magistrates . . . ." The sovereign's formal law is the law of God and nature. Hence, in the sphere of religion as in every other, the sovereign has complete power. Probably no post-Christian naturalistic writer quotes the Bible as frequently as Hobbes, although it is always made to subserve naturalistic dogma. Hobbes does not mean by God what the

[33]That the state is to be feared is New Testament doctrine — but the justification of dutiful submission is its status as a minister of Divine justice, and hence as an instrument for the enhancement of the moral claims of the will of God in human life. The state exists, according to biblical ethics, to protect law-abiding citizens, and to restrain those who are not.

Hebrew-Christian movement means; instead, he follows the premise that nature is the exclusive reality, that man is wholly determined, and that all his actions are referrable to biological and psychological factors. The terms "good, evil and contemptible are always used with relation to the person that uses them, there being nothing simply and absolutely so."[34]

The thesis of Hobbes, like that of Thrasymachus and Machiavelli, lacked an actual application in practice whereby its historical consequences might be measured, except for the limited realizations of Charles I and Borgia. Today it is more obvious that power-politics, instead of ministering to human self-preservation, robs individual life of dignity and reduces it to a pawn of the state. Defenders of traditional morality have always pointed out that political Naturalism, while it set out as a theory of ethics, actually evaporated all ethics, for it inverts the ideas of injustice and justice. The internal criticism in Plato's *Republic* has enduring value, and modern statesmen who keep an anxious eye on totalitarian powers echo its ancient convictions in our far-removed century. There Socrates replies to Thrasymachus that injustice is inferior to justice in character and wisdom because: (1) the man who recognizes no principle or proportion is neither wise nor good; (2) the repudiation of all principle involves an incapacity to act cooperatively and consequently brings disruption; injustice is therefore not a source of strength, any more than of wisdom and of goodness; (3) the repudiation of justice involves the impossibility of happiness.

No theory, however, is ever challenged adequately by an exhibition of inner difficulties alone. The lack of a more convincing and compelling alternative retains a poor theory's hold upon the minds of men. The idealistic alternative, and the alternative of revelational theism, remain to be considered. It should be noted here that attempts to reply to Hobbes from the standpoint of naturalistic Utilitarianism proved unconvincing. The difficulty was not only in meeting Hobbes' insistence that man's perpetual and restless desire for power is not reducible to a quest for more intensive pleasure, but the fact that the Utilitarians proceeded from within the same naturalistic assumptions which undergirded Hobbes' own view, and which undercut in advance the confidence in changeless moral norms to which ruler and citizen alike are answerable.[35] Already in the *Republic* Socrates was impelled to contra-

[34]Hobbes, *Leviathan* (New York: Dutton, 1950), Pt. I, ch. 6.

[35]It was to the merit of John Locke (*Two Treatises of Civil Government*) that he stressed man's right to revolt against an unjust king. Locke appealed to an eternal law, a law that judges the king as well as the people, over against Hobbes' arbitrary law. Locke is the great philosopher of democracy — to whose political writings many modern students of political science have not fully matured — because he appealed (not simply to the will of the majority, as even Hobbes had done in his own way, but) to a moral law over and above nature. The Renaissance mood that the human good consists in the individual's complete freedom to pursue his own purposes is a superficial reply to the thesis that the good is the complete

dict political Naturalism not alone by an analysis of its inner weakness, but also by the explicit contradiction of the naturalistic world-life view as a unit. He asserts, against Thrasymachus: (1) proportion holds life and the universe together; (2) some element of unity, or tacitly recognized standard, is necessary for efficiency and success (even among thieves); (3) the function of the soul is to live, and its virtue is to live well, for it involves justice, or the harmonious recognition of all legitimate claims. The *Republic* is an enlargement of these premises into a carefully articulated metaphysics which supplies a context for the moral life.

The political naturalists have scant sympathy for any doctrine which espouses the essential goodness of human nature, and which implies that man acts from selfish and wicked motives only by neglect. The superficial view of human goodness unwittingly prepared the way for the naturalistic reaction, because advocates of the optimistic view of man often labeled it as Christian doctrine and thereby confused the biblical statement. In contrast to the whole tide of classic Graeco-Roman ethics, which deified man, Christianity proclaimed original sin and the need of supernatural redemption for the natural man. Political Naturalism emphasized that the individual cannot be trusted to comprehend and actualize the good of the community. Its profound error lies in proclaiming human baseness as evidence of man's essential animality, while actually the real tragedy of man stems from the egoism of his moral revolt against the Creator and the consequent perversion of the absolute ethical claim. The naturalistic despair over the attempted infusion of harmony into this chaos is more realistic than the naturalistic confidence that human egoism can be cultivated into love.[36] In resorting to an external sovereign will that maintains itself by fear and force, political Naturalism suggests a perversion of the necessity for reorienting human behavior to an external, omnipotent will. Christianity presents not an arbitrary tyrant, but the Living God as the ultimate source of all abiding moral distinctions.[37] Only a super-

---

subordination of the individual to the community or state or ruler. Locke's thesis is far more profound, for he stresses that the individual and the state alike exist under God, so that the state has duties not alone to the citizenry, but to the Deity as well.

[36]Rousseau, in the eighteenth century, combined the notion of social contract with the optimistic notion that man is by nature morally good. Insofar as this reflected the notion of the inherent goodness of primal man, it marked a surface agreement with Hebrew-Christian theology, over against the animalistic view. But the notion that man still has a guileless nature and natural instincts which would preserve him in purity, if he could divorce these from the artificialities of contemporary society, had its roots actually in an optimistic view of man which ignored the dimension of sin stressed by biblical thought.

[37]The doctrine of original sin, as dialectical theology restates it today, is hardly the biblical doctrine, but Reinhold Niebuhr points out forcefully that by Hebrew-Christian ethics "Egoism is not regarded as harmless because imbedded in a pre-established harmony (Adam Smith), nor as impotent because reason can transmute its anarchies into a higher harmony (utilitarianism), nor as the basic reality of human existence (Thomas Hobbes)." *An Interpretation of Christian Ethics* (New York: Harper, 1935), p. 39.

naturalistic view can affirm God as the chief end of human life, while a naturalistic view may depict man as a mere means subject to the ends of the state. Thus we are again brought face to face with the fact that the major decisions in ethics are already implicit in the metaphysical credos men confess.[38]

4. MODERN: FRIEDRICH NIETZSCHE

With the appearance of Friedrich Nietzsche (1844-1900) the philosophy of power-ethics gained an exponent who radically promulgated the mood of anti-reason, anti-morality, anti-Christ. The insistence that ultimate reality cannot be grasped from the standpoint of reason, but only by immediate contact with the powerful forces of man's environment, marks him as a predecessor of oncoming existential ethics. The call for a complete transvaluation of the inherited Hebrew-Christian values exposes political Naturalism's most daring attack on Western traditions, and thus prepares the way for Communism. The violent castigation of biblical religion as a "crime against life" intensifies the growing secular antagonism to Christian theology and ethics. Nietzsche complains that Christianity's assertion of the sinfulness of man makes him dependent upon the ministrations of the church; that Christianity's equality of man by virtue of creation precludes Superman and reduces everyone to the herd-level; that Christianity's insistence upon an absolute morality involves a slave-ethic. In his *Ecce Homo,* Nietzsche writes: "Christian morality is the most malignant form of all falsehood. . . . It is really poisonous, decadent, weakening. It produces nincompoops, not men."[39]

[38]Over against the notion of Hobbes, that society and the state find their origin in a primitive social contract, stands the Hebrew-Christian representation of the social and political order as existing within the will of God. The history of Israel takes its rise in a special covenant, not in a contract which is the "generation of that great Leviathan . . . that mortal god" but in the initiation of the holy Lord in his redemptive activity. Hobbes would transfer the absolute obedience which Israel reserved for Jehovah to the earthly sovereign, would rob it of its moral absoluteness, and relate it only to the concerns of egoism and self-preservation. Of equal importance, Hobbes makes the continuance of the social contract necessary for the survival of the sovereign no less than of the people, whereas the Hebrews, in contrast with the pagan conception of religious covenants in their day, acknowledged God's transcendence over the covenant. Cf. Paul Ramsey, *Basic Christian Ethics* (New York: Scribner, 1953), p. 376.

[39]"I am proceeding, as you see, in this essay," he writes, in *A Genealogy of Morals,* "from an hypothesis which, as far as such readers as I want are concerned, does not require to be proved; the hypothesis that 'sinfulness in man is not an actual fact, but rather merely the interpretation of a fact, of a physiological discomfort, — a discomfort seen through a moral religious perspective which is no longer binding upon us" (p. 166). In *Anti-Christ* he writes: "I condemn Christianity and confront it with the most terrible accusation that an accuser has ever had in his mouth. To my mind it is the greatest of all conceivable corruptions . . . it converted every value into its opposite, every truth into a lie, and every honest impulse into an ignominy of the soul. . . . I call Christianity the one great curse, the one enormous and innermost perversion, the one great instinct of revenge, for which no means are too venomous, too underhand, too underground and too petty, — I call it the one immortal blemish of mankind" (p. 230). (*A Genealogy of Morals,* New York, Macmillan, 1924; *Anti-Christ,* New York, Knopf, 1920).

Yet Nietzsche was in advance of his age, forging the implications of the naturalistic premise with greater consistency than his mediating contemporaries. He sees that thorough-going Naturalism requires the abandonment of the Christian life view, as well as its Christian metaphysics. He perceives, likewise, that Naturalism cannot justify hedonism's confidence in a universal pleasure ministering reality. He discounts as futile the attempt to organize experience in terms of reason. Nietzsche as the Anti-Christ[40] pits himself against the whole tradition of the western world. It is ironic that in 1910, from within the optimism of post-Hegelian absolutism, James Ward wrote: "I do not think the growing Nietzsche cult will last long or in the end do harm."[41] Nietzsche at first sought to deepen the connection between Utilitarianism and Positivism, and the prevailing scientific world-view but finally, however, convinced that the modern view requires a more radical approach to the ethical problem than an attenuation of Christian morality, took an anti-Utilitarian turn. As the moderns sketch reality, he asserts, the only basis for morality is individual, not universal. The majority exist for the sake of the individual, not vice versa. While then still ahead of the general Anglo-Saxon mood, Nietzsche's viewpoint was realized in German Nazism and Russian Communism during the present generation. Many leaders in the free world, in the United States and in Great Britain, while they reject Nietzsche's conclusions in the interest of alternatives which political Naturalism regards as

[40]Nietzsche endeavors to distinguish his attack upon Christianity from an attack upon the person of Jesus Christ. He views the Christian Church as a product of the work of Paul, and not of Jesus. Thus Nietzsche resists an identification of Christianity with Christ, a dogma for which liberal Protestantism afforded him support, except that Nietzsche turned it against Christian ethics as well as Christian theology. Paul is a power-seeking monster, the vengeful Jew imposing a slave morality upon the Roman empire as a means of gaining revenge on the master-race. Christian doctrine originated not with Christ but with Paul. "A God who died for our sins, salvation through faith, resurrection after death — all these things are the counterfeit coins of real-Christianity, for which that pernicious blockhead Paul must be held responsible" (*Will to Power,* I, 138). He even goes so far as to say that Christ would deny everything now regarded as his Gospel. Jesus "died too early; he himself would have disavowed his doctrine had he attained to my age" (*Thus Spake Zarathustra,* I, 16). He puts it this way: "there has only been one Christian and He died on the Cross" (*Anti-Christ,* p. 178). Yet it is difficult to get at Nietzsche's precise opinions of Christ. At times he sees Christ as the fulfillment of his own morality, and in that sense the model for superman, exceeding the accepted morality. More generally, Christ is viewed as a misguided man who wasted his words on the common herd. It rankles Nietzsche that Christ "stuffed so much into the heads of paltry people." Stronger dislike is shown when Christ is called "an interesting decadent" who is out of touch with reality, a person who is living in a vague dream world envisioning imaginary rewards for his followers. (*Will to Power,* New York, Macmillan, 1924; *Thus Spake Zarathustra,* New York, Macmillan, 1924).

[41]James Ward, *The Realm of Ends* (London: Cambridge University Press, 1911), p. 451.

highly insecure,[42] nevertheless share the basic assumptions which made Nietzsche possible. Perhaps the greatest strength of political Naturalism lies in the general romantic optimism which doggedly refuses to contemplate as a live possibility the reconstruction of society as naturalistic leaders envision it. The refusal of a nominally Christian culture to acknowledge its inability to forestall such a development is equally devastating. The generation which tore itself free from Christian religion has now produced a generation which is tearing itself free from Christian morality, and in so doing from any confidence in an objective ethic. At long last Nietzsche becomes relevant: "There is an old illusion. It is called good and evil." The question of the essential nature of good and evil sounds throughout the modern world with new urgency.

Nietzsche refuses to read the present in terms of the past, but only in anticipation of the future. Nature, therefore, is not the minister of pleasure but rather the harbinger of power. This conquest of obstacles is nature's essential reality and fundamental principle. All life and instinct are an expression of this inner thrust for power (physical, mental, moral, spiritual). The Superman emerges to demonstrate this surge of nature; all others (including the exponents of the Christian morality) are sentimentalists. The "he-man" incorporates in himself the will to dominate. The principle of self-assertion, with the consequent repudiation of sympathy, reaches its superlative manifestation in the Superman.

Through Nietzsche's speculations the utility of the state as a weapon of political power, and hence as an instrument of Superman, gains new importance in Western thought. A distinctive attitude toward the state parts political Naturalism from hedonistic Naturalism. Utilitarianism was not indifferent to the state, but it looked for a blending of egoistic and altruistic impulses which would involve ultimately the dispensability of the state, since the good lay in society rather than in the state. Political Naturalism shares in the denial of any absolute and transcendent basis of the state, but it views the state as a supreme weapon of aggression for the imposition of the will to power. Hence "the good," or the power-furthering, lies outside society as such in the directive state. This thesis modern totalitarianism inherits from Thrasymachus, Hobbes, Machiavelli and Nietzsche.

Behind Nietzsche's "will to power" stand two influences. One is Schopenhauer's doctrine of the primacy of the will, which Nietzsche frees from its pessimism and narrows to the will to power. The other

[42]The world of English thought made a household phrase of George Eliot's defense of "peremptory and absolute" duty, although God may be considered "inconceivable," and immortality "unbelievable." But it neglected Nietzsche's taunt: "They have got rid of the Christian God, and now think themselves obliged to cling firmer than ever to Christian morality; that is *English* consistency . . . with us it is different. When we give up Christian belief, we thereby deprive ourselves of the *right* to maintain a stand on Christian morality" (*The Twilight of the Idols. The Works of Friedrich Nietzsche* [trans. Thomas Common]. New York: Macmillan, 1927, III, 167f.).

emphasis assimilated by Nietzsche is the new concept of evolution. The concepts are not unrelated in Nietzsche's thinking, however. For he takes exception to the Darwinian premise that evolution is the result only of the instinct to survival. If life is an evolutionary struggle for existence accommodating the survival of the fittest, strength becomes the primary virtue, and weakness the worst of faults. The struggle for might according to Nietzsche is more primary than the struggle for existence. For him whatever heightens the feeling of power, and the desire for it, is good; whatever weakens it, is bad.

Nietzsche applies Darwin's thesis to the whole of reality — logic, religion, ethics, matter, society, philosophy. He detaches the theory from optimistic elements which Darwin included, *e.g.*, that chance variations in species invariably contribute to survival, and that each species continues to progress. Not only do some changes hinder survival, contends Nietzsche, but there are limits which no species may exceed, for species do not develop from lower to higher, but appear simultaneously and by chance. Most important, the human species is not developing, nor is it an advance upon other animals, nor is it as exempt from perishability as the less complex forms. Darwin's notion of the self-preservation of species is but the lingering ghost of medieval teleology, albeit a secularized version. The real ego is but an aggregate of competing urges.

Since no species is any more important than another, the only key to nature and life is the non-rational will to power. Nature is not miserly, but extravagant, even wasteful in the production of forms; it is indifferent to the survival of all and to the importance of any. (Nietzsche detaches the evolutionary theory from all teleology and appends it to a theory of eternal recurrence. Every possible combination will be actualized an infinite number of times in "the great game of chance" which constitutes the universe's existence. The pantheistic determinism of the Stoics reappears with its fire-reason, its divinity, its teleology, displaced by mere flux, chance and power. Nietzsche does not stop to reconcile this deterministic emphasis with his theory of the Superman, whose emergence we are to facilitate. Why is not the so-called decadent morality of the herd simply one of the combinations which nature necessarily actualizes?) Hence Nietzsche's reaction against the rationalistic Hegelian attempt to vindicate truth and morality by ascribing deity to every man culminates at last in a denial of worth to any man.

Uniqueness is shorn from all except Superman, the incarnation of power. Only the occasional appearance of a super-species, especially of a superman, breaks the monotony of this prodigal activity. This specimen's superiority lies in his superlative manifestation of the will to power. The Superman recognizes no norm superior to himself. He does not exist for the sake of the whole; the whole exists for him who is the incarnation of the will to power.

Behind this construction lies the tenuous notion that whatever is "higher" in the evolutionary scale is also "better," *i.e.*, ethically higher as well as physically more intricate. Apart from this assumption, Nietzsche's naturalistic context left no room for the idea that whatever is favorable to the developmental process, *e.g.*, the will to power, is ethically good. Neither in the case of the apex of evolution, nor in the case of what advances evolution, however, can an objective ethical criterion be introduced without reinstating the reality of cosmic, supra-human absolute values with the complete denial of which Nietzsche begins. A bare nature-principle hardly constitutes a principle of ethical valuation. Even Nietzsche, therefore, does not escape the tacit recognition of the transcendent ideal, of an "ought" or "better" by which life is to be measured.

The second fundamental postulate which permeates Nietzsche's view, alongside the will to power, is the contrast of "the master and slave morality." Whatever weakens and frustrates the will to power is bad. Nietzsche does not assert, what later pragmatism ventures to contend, that what is life-furthering is therefore true. The question of truth and falsehood to him is quite irrelevant. Be it true or false, whatever is serviceable to the will to power is desirable. Hence courage becomes the highest virtue, and intellect, energy, virility, self-assertion, self-reliance and self-determinism are prized as means to power.

By the same measure, humility, meekness, obedience, compassion and forgiveness are despised as evidences of weakness. The Hebrew-Christian morality decreases the feeling of power. Instead of ministering to natural strength, it shapes a disciplined existence which Nietzsche scorns as weak and ignoble. Nietzsche, therefore, calls for the restoration of the bold military virtues of the Greeks and Romans. The virtues of the masses represent a form of resentment and attempted recrimination against the leaders. "All noble morality takes its rise from a triumphant yea-saying to one's self" while, in contrast, "the slave-revolt in morality begins by *resentment* itself becoming creative and giving birth to values."[43] The master and the resentful masses thus become the symbols of two opposing types of human nature and morality, aristocratic and slave. The chief weapon by which the weak endeavor to enfeeble the strong is by an appeal to moral principle. The priests, the "shepherds of the herd," who themselves are numbered with the slaves, graphically symbolize this resentment. The Jews are especially despicable, since the curtailment of the power-virtues is chargeable particularly to their influence. "All that has ever been accomplished on earth against the 'noble,' the 'powerful,' the 'lords,' the 'mighty' is not worth speaking of, when compared with that which *the Jews* have done against them; the Jews, that priestly people, which finally succeeded in procuring satisfaction for itself from its enemies and conquerors only by a transvaluation of the values, *i.e.*, an act of

[43]Nietzsche, *A Genealogy of Morals*, p. 35.

the keenest, most spiritual vengeance."[44] In these Anti-Semitic lines, Nietzsche pays unwitting tribute to the remarkable cultural vitality of Hebrew revelational ethics. But it is especially for Jesus Christ, through whose life and death the biblical values have shaped the dominant moral tradition of the West, that Nietzsche reserves his bitterest outbursts: "This Jesus of Nazareth, as the personified gospel of love, this saviour bringing blessedness and victory unto the poor, the sick, the sinners — did he not represent seduction in its most awful and irresistible form — the seduction and by-way to those same Jewish values and new ideals? Has not Israel, even by the round-about-way of this 'redeemer,' this seeming adversary and destroyer of Israel, attained the last goal of its sublime vindictiveness?"[45] This Jewish "ethics of vindictiveness" found its supreme expression in the crucifixion of Jesus, "the tool of its vengeance . . . so that 'all the world,' namely all enemies of Israel, might quite unhesitantly bite at this bait. . . . The symbol of the cross — that awful paradox of a 'God on the cross' " then, is the most "seducing, intoxicating, narcotising, corrupting" influence, the epitome of all those virtues that characterize the lives of the slaves as inferiors, which, when accepted by the aristocratic man, reduce him to impotence, bound by slave moral ideals. Christianity is depicted as a system of revenge, a disguised means of obtaining power. The Golden Rule is a maxim of the herd, aimed at destroying the strong through an attempted enforcement of the "virtues which facilitate the happiness of the lowly, a standard of all values."[46] To this condemnation of the Christian ethic as a slave morality of love, Nietzsche adds the charge that it is ascetic and world-denying, contradicting man's natural instincts. Christianity is branded as the most triumphant announcement of man's absolute unworthiness.

Nietzsche calls, therefore, for a transvaluation of existing Christian values. Too long has the true "elite" suffered under the ignominy of slave morality: man must rouse himself and kill the poisonous snake of ignoble values:

" 'Thou shalt not rob!' 'Thou shalt not commit manslaughter!' Such words were once called holy; before them the folk bent their knees and heads and took off their shoes.

"But I ask you: Where in the world have there ever been better robbers and murderers than such holy words?

"Is there not in all life — robbing and manslaughter? And by calling such words holy, did they not *murder* truth itself?"[47]

"To redeem what is past in man and to transvalue every 'It was' until will saith: 'Thus I willed! Thus shall I will —.'

[44]*Ibid.*, p. 30.
[45]*Ibid.*, pp. 32f.
[46]Nietzsche, *The Will to Power*, I, 154f.
[47]Nietzsche, *Thus Spake Zarathustra*, p. 293.

"This I publicly called redemption, this alone I taught them to call redemption."[48]

And what is the new moral code in Nietzsche's thought? The Christian "thou shalt love thy neighbor as thyself; this is the fulfillment of the law" becomes a new virtue: "It is power, that new virtue; one dominating thought it is, and round it a cunning soul: a golden sun, and round it the serpent of knowledge."[49] A new nobility is needed; and what is noble? To be able to command. The new nobility will be based on real values, the signs of which Nietzsche propounds in *Beyond Good and Evil.* The morality of the new nobility marks a reversion to the morality of the paganism of Greece and Rome before the spread of Christianity. The Christian ideals are useful only to the mass of men, the herd.[50]

The doctrine of the Superman follows naturally from what has been considered. Some interpreters have suggested that the doctrine rises from Nietzsche's atheism, compensating for it with a creaturely object "worthy of his adoration."[51] Nietzsche writes: "Up! Up! ye higher men! It is only now that the mount of man's future giveth birth unto anything. God hath died. Now *we* wish beyond-man to live."[52] Superman thus takes the place of God; instead of looking beyond the stars, man will find a goal in mankind.

To bring in this "man of the future," a higher race of men is required as forerunner of the Superman. As a step toward this higher race, Nietzsche calls for drastic practical measures including the revision of marriage laws and elimination of the unfit. It is unclear whether Superman is one dominant individual or a race of new individuals incarnating a power-ethics. Superman will incarnate the dominant will, superior physical strength, great courage, pitilessness, and, being himself "beyond good and evil," will himself determine all values.

As with every false philosophy, the cornerstone of Nietzsche's outlook on life is partial and inadequate. Nietzsche's postulate of "will to power" does not cover the whole of reality as he supposes, but oversimplifies the complexity of the space-time world and man, to say nothing of the moral and spiritual realm. By reducing it to one single

[48]*Ibid.*, p. 288.

[49]*Ibid.*, p. 105.

[50]The moral temper to which Nietzsche was led pays its own unintended tribute to the unyielding revision which biblical ethics requires of the pagan conception of virtue: "One does well to put on one's gloves when reading the New Testament. The proximity of so much pitch almost defiles one. We should feel just as little inclined to hobnob with 'the first Christians' as with Polish Jews; not that we need explain our objections . . . they simply smell bad. In vain have I sought for a single sympathetic feature in the New Testament; there is not a trace of freedom, kindliness, openheartedness, and honesty to be found in it. . . . Every book becomes clean, after one has just read the New Testament" (*Anti-Christ*, pp. 193f.).

[51]R. Motson Thompson, *Nietzsche and Christian Ethics* (New York: Philosophical Library, 1951), p. 16.

[52]Nietzsche, *Thus Spake Zarathustra*, p. 419.

factor Nietzsche mistakenly thinks he has found the key to the whole. What Nietzsche has not validated is the tenuous naturalistic assumption on which his argument everywhere proceeds: "I am not much more than an animal which by means of blows and titbits hath been taught to dance."[53]

In fact, Nietzsche is placed in constant jeopardy, as are all speculative naturalists, whenever he seeks to persuade readers of the truth of his views, and of the falsity of their own. If the key to life is eternal recurrence, or the will to power, why the attempt to persuade? Furthermore, Nietzsche's insistence that his interpretation of reality is indubitably true, not only complicates his "only an animal" theme, but also elevates reason to a place of centrality which demands a revision of the naturalistic concept. What differentiates man from the lower animals becomes now not a fuller assimilation to the will to power, but a participation in changeless truth — a position overwhelmingly contrary to the denial of changeless moral truth. Ramsey effectively points out that "if the proponent of naturalism asserts that his theory is *true* and that he *knows* it to be true, then, no matter what the theory itself says about man . . . the man who as subject holds this theory and puts forward this claim to truth is himself manifestly a truth-apprehending animal, and this constitutes his distinction from all other animals (no matter what his theory says). If ever the *truth* of some form of naturalism were established, precisely then nothing could be more certain than that naturalism is false."[54]

It is precisely here that the concept of man as the bearer of the image of a rational-moral Creator-God is conspicuously more forceful and adequate than Nietzsche's will to power as a sufficient principle. It is impossible to explain even Nietzsche, let alone the "whole universe," by the simple axiom of will to power.

Nietzsche declares that Christian moral ideals have brought about a weak and dwarfed Europe, a morality of pity which is "the most sinister symptom of our modern European civilization."[55] But past history discloses that where the will to power and not Christianity (the will to holy love) has shaped the world's ideals, this worship of power has thrown nations into disorder and decay, and even today threatens to bankrupt civilization. Nietzsche's misunderstanding of the Christian virtues is nowhere so apparent as in his depiction of them as feminine. The strength of meekness, the force of love, the courage of forbearance, the energy of submission, and the greatness of humility, are lost to him. Actually the war-like virtues he enthrones are not the

[53]*Ibid.*, p. 15.
[54]Ramsey, *op. cit.*, p. 269.
[55]Thompson, *op. cit.*, p. 69.

true dignity of manliness at all, for in Nietzsche's formulation they veer close to animalism uncontrolled by a pure heart.[56]

Nietzsche's demand for the transvaluation of values sprang, of course, from his premise of the will to power as the criterion of all morality, and his consequent rejection of Christian morality. The phrase "transvaluation of values" in Nietzsche means not a change in the values themselves, but rather a change of valuations. The values Nietzsche prized — courage, energy, intellect, etc. — assuredly hold a place even in Christianity, but when they are defined so as to exclude such Christian virtues as pity, sympathy, love, and humility, the determining presence of the naturalistic bias is clear. Nietzsche's counter claim to biblical ethics is but the violent protest of the sinful, natural man, which Christian redemption contradicts with the requirement of spiritual and moral regeneration.[57]

5. MODERN: KARL MARX

With the influence of Karl Marx (1818-1883), a political Naturalism begins to emerge from its seclusion and becomes a national and international force. Marx and Friedrich Engels (1820-1895), with whom he co-authored *The Communist Manifesto* in 1848, had little to say directly about ethics in this tract and in their many other volumes. But the *Manifesto* — a mere 15,000 words — helped organize the simmering mood of socialism into a vast movement, and constituted a bridge between the discontented masses and the scattered intellectuals who shared such a vision. Behind the tense and bitter social conflict of

[56]The whole sweep of the Bible teaches that sin against our neighbor is "to sin against Life" (as Nietzsche would say) and against God. Love treats each man according to his worth. The question Christianity raises is not "How powerful is he?" but "Is he human?" If so, I must love him. The aristocrats of society, in the Christian view, are the spiritually and morally regenerate who salt the earth, infusing society with a dynamic, transforming level of life.

[57]Precisely Nietzsche's antagonism to the ethics of revelation blinds his eyes to the dramatic fact that the man of moral transformation is the "new man" of regeneration, the man renewed in the image of Christ, who is indeed the genuine and original moral archetype, the Superman who stands by his life, death and resurrection at the crossroads of human history. Nowhere does the Christian transvaluation of secular values come to more graphic propositional expression than in the Beatitudes, and nowhere is it more strikingly manifested in flesh and blood than in the life of Jesus. Not only do the teachings of Jesus and Nietzsche stand in stark contrast, but their lives, the lowly Nazarene on one side, and the renegade clergyman's son who lived in seclusion and died at last in an insane asylum on the other, and who by his own criterion "ought" to have been cast on the scrapheap of second-rate humanity. George F. Thomas comments that Christ's "interpretation of leadership and greatness in terms of service and suffering rather than of domination wrought a revolution in men's thinking which has been the basis of much that is best in Western political and social life. . . . It has brought about a genuine transvaluation of values in the Western world as a result of which the humility of the will to serve has supplanted the egoism of the will to power as the highest ideal of character." *Christian Ethics and Moral Philosophy* (New York: Scribner, 1955), pp. 72f. May not the Christian doctrine of man in sin and moral revolt far better explain Nietzsche, than Nietzsche and his speculative philosophy "explains" Christianity?

our times and the struggle over the future of civilzation one may discern the impact of this century-old pamphlet. In its pages, a world divided over basic tenets was roused to social revolution.

The *Manifesto* projected a new social order whose controlling assumptions are not found in religious or moral realities, but rather in emphases peculiar to the new social sciences. Its life-view implies a quite definite ethical theory, one which shares with Nietzsche both the repudiation of a supernatural moral order and a specific hostility for the Christian ethic.

Among the naturalists, Marx and Nietzsche stand as the influential nineteenth-century spokesmen for irrationalism. Marx was already allied with Engels in the formation of radical Communist groups, and had already edited a radical daily paper even before Nietzsche was born. Marx died when Nietzsche was thirty-nine. But both accepted that materialistic view of the universe to which science paid almost exclusive tribute in the second half of the nineteenth century. Both were atheistic and vigorously anti-Hegelian. Both were evolutionary, Marx more in the spirit of historical dialectic by way of inheritance from Hegel, while Nietzsche reflected more Darwinian influence.

Just as Ludwig Feuerbach (1804-1872) and Friedrich Strauss (1808-1874) deserted Idealism for Naturalism, professing to find only a humanistic basis for the religious and moral life, so Marx revolted against the philosophy he learned from Hegel. But in contrast with Soren Kierkegaard's resort to supernatural-irrational religion as a remedy, Marx projected the reform of society on the thesis that the ultimate malady of the race is economic. What the masses need is not Divine power, but economic power. And, since supernatural religion consoles men in their afflictions, rather than incites them to revolution, it is an opiate requiring elimination. Feuerbach had already viewed religion as a divisive force in a nation, and an obstacle to a democratic republic. Marx, with Engels, spawned the Communist interpretation of life based on dialectical Materialism. As Feuerbach retained Hegel's dialectical method but rejected his Idealism, so Marx merges the dialectic with economic determinism as the comprehensive key to reality.

Marx and Engels project a moral theory consciously and deliberately relativistic. Ethical and religious sentiments alike are regarded as mere reflexes of the economic situation. An absolute ethic is always the disguised front of class interest. Rights are simply class assertions, and which yields to the other is a matter of power alone. Thus the first dogma, of the cultural relativity of all moral values, is attached to a second dogma, namely, that all values reflect class interests, and these in turn attach to a third dogma, that value-claims are but the propaganda of self-seeking groups. This compounded dogmatism is then latched to the metaphysical schematization of materialistic economic determinism (absolute determinism being avoided by considering only the end and general procedure, but not the details of the process, as determined). Thus the standpoint of moral relativism is dogmatically transcended, in order dogmatically to relativize all dogmas of non-relativity. The dogma that only such action is "right" which yields the desired social changes is the eventual outcome.

The emphasis on universally obligatory moral imperatives is deplored as "bourgeois ethics."

This revolt against eternally fixed moral distinctions Marx inherited, curiously enough, from the direction which his teacher, Hegel, gave to the idealistic tradition. The Hegelian dialectic, depicting the Absolute in a process of logical evolution, excluded immutable principles upon which a permanent ethics could be predicated. The moral consciousness, involved historically in this process, lacked universal validity. Marx grasped the Hegelian concession that a community's ethical system reflects the interests of the dominant class, denuded the concept of its religious and idealistic remnants, and conformed it to the naturalistic view of nature and man. That view, in brief, is deterministic and economic. The economic factor replaces the Absolute as the impersonal (or super-personal) force which controls the destinies of life. The essence of man is the totality of his social relationships. He is formed by his environment, causally connected to the economic milieu, yet he also forms his environment and hence is more than its passive reflection. The basic conflict of human existence is economic. The *Manifesto* has no reference to "justice" or to "moral law." It pulsates to the theme that law rests upon society, and not society upon law.

Yet an idealism of sentiment, an ethos, runs through the program for social reform nonetheless. It has often been noted that no more vigorous condemnation of economic injustices can be found in Marxist writings than were pronounced centuries ago, by the Hebrew prophets and by the apostles, especially James, the brother of Jesus (cf. Jas. 5:1-6). Marx's picture of capitalism as essentially an exploitation of the worker was extreme and overstated. The working class lived a life, it was asserted, more miserable than that of draft animals. The bourgeois class deprives the proletariat of everything but its labor power, reimbursing their works just enough to accommodate their survival and yet to keep them in abject dependence. The worst side of capitalism — inadequate wages, poor working conditions, lavish luxury among the wealthy — was propagandized to support this picture. The state of the laboring class in the mid-century was lamentable by any estimate, and the social and political revolutions in France, Prussia, Italy, and elsewhere, arose in this provocative climate. The propaganda that a capitalistic system could not pay more than subsistence wages and succeed, because it is allegedly based on the principle of exploitation, waited for a century after the *Manifesto* for its most impressive answer, in the contrast of the living standards of the American worker and the Russian worker under two rival economic systems. But in the mid-eighteen hundreds the picture was different. Admittedly, in England, the evangelical awakening worked remarkable social reforms among the oppressed and under-privileged. But as a social strategy it moved rather slowly because it called for high spiritual decision on a personal basis. The Marxist thrust was not without real basis in socio-economic injustices requiring a vigorous Christian critique. But the effective initiative in economic criticism passed to the Communist leaders, who compromised whatever protests issued from Christian circles by even more radical demands, and by including the churches within the range of their criticisms. Indeed, there was reason to criticize the indifference of many religious movements to the misery of the lower classes. But the anti-religious spirit of political Naturalism in its Marxian form was yet to show its unveiled face.[58]

Lenin transformed Marxian theory into infallible dogma, as his essay "Materialism and Empiro-criticism" attests. Sharing Marx's view that religion deludes the worker with visions of imaginary satisfactions to compensate for their actual deprivation, he branded it the instrument of social passivity. His hostility was more aggressive and violent, calling for the extermination of religion except when its provisional toleration served the Marxist cause more effectively. Rather well-known today is his letter to Gordii in 1913: "The difference between seeking God and constructing or creating or inventing, etc., a God is no greater than between a yellow or a blue devil. . . . A million sins, bestialities, rapes and infections of a physical kind are more easily seen through by the crowd and therefore less dangerous than the refined spiritualized idea of God decked out in the most gorgeous costume. . . . From the social, from the personal standpoint, every theory of God is nothing but the adoring self-concern of the stupid *petite bourgeoisie,* of the destructive middle class spirit."[59] Stalin later implemented Lenin's anti-religious program until World War II, when it was relaxed within stringent limits.

The Marx-Engels strategy called for radical social change, not mere improvement or revision. The program included abolition of private property; of individual freedom to buy and sell service as well as goods; of the family in its traditional sense; of individual nations; and of the prevailing bourgeois culture centering in the free enterprise social system. In *Das Kapital* (Marx wrote it in London, although only the first of the three volumes appeared prior to his death), the platform is delineated fully. The abolition of private property and of state

[58]The Communist International, at its 1928 Congress, declared that the cultural revolution requires the systematic and unswerving combat of religion as "the opium of the people" — a Marxian phrase — and asserted that "The proletarian state, while granting liberty of worship and abolishing the privileged position of the formerly dominant religion, carries on anti-religious propaganda with all the means at its command and reconstructs the whole of its educational work on the basis of scientific materialism." *Handbook of Marxism,* Emile Burns, ed., (New York: Random House, 1935), pp. 1009f.

[59]Quoted in Robert Pierce Casey's *Religion in Russia* (New York: Harper, 1946), pp. 77f.

regulation of labor and wages is set within the mechanism of history as a necessary element in progressing to the ideal Communistic state. Not only does this outline of the future represent philosophical prophecy; it assertedly represents scientific prediction. History moves inevitably toward the triumph of the proletariat. Class struggle is the law of history, and bourgeois society is but a temporary and already obsolete phenomenon, in the transition from the enslaved masses of ancient times to the classless Communist order of the future.

This social strategy combined three elements which held a fascination for the discontented masses in the great cities of the West. One was the promise of swift and easy material gain, a prospect seldom burdensome to men predisposed to find the abundance of life in a larger share of this world's goods. At the same time, it appealed to the humanitarian instinct of man, precisely in the manner in which Utilitarianism had shaped the quasi-Christian ethical climate of the day, by affording him an opportunity to promote the general welfare, *i.e.*, the widest distribution of wealth. Thus the Utilitarian notion that the rule of life is the greatest good of the greatest number prepared the way for a theory that forced economic redistribution to achieve the maximal good of the working class, even at the forced sacrifice of the bourgeoisie, if necessary. More than this, a metaphysical buttressing was afforded this program of social action by asserting both the historical inevitability of the outcome, and its scientific basis in the economic determinism of nature and history. One further consideration, actualized by the later Communistic successors of Marx, lent further force: the comprehensive elaboration of the implications of Marxism in all areas of culture interpreting religion, ethics, philosophy, literature and art, as well as economics and politics, in conformity with the bias of dialectical Materialism. All that was necessary to enlist the hesitant and half-hearted, was some tangible, visible evidence of the theory's truth, *i.e.*, its pragmatic success as an aggressive revolutionary force to which the initiative of social change belongs.

The "scientific" character of Marxism is among its first claims to be disputed. To make the economic factor the exclusive index to the class struggle in history is an illicit oversimplification of the complexity of social actualities. Doubtless the history of mankind has been plagued by class struggles, and the economic element has been a conspicuous source of tension. But almost the whole tide of non-Marxist social ethics would dispute as unrealistic the notions that distinctions among men are an expression primarily of economic considerations. Nor would Marxism guarantee a future of peace and justice by a levelling of society through removal of distinctions among men. The fact is that the Communist revolution in Russia did not bring class distinctions to an end, but succeeded only in introducing new and more vicious lines of division. The multitudes owe absolute allegiance to the military leadership which, surrounded by a circle of propagandists in the service of the party-line, exercises absolute control in the name of the state.

If the anchoring of Communism in history bolstered the confidence of its first generation of advocates, inciting them to great risks, and even to sacrifices for the future, the assertion that the new order is an inevitable goal of history must eventually discourage such sacrifices. If the new order is linked with the mechanism of history, the temper of reform may for a season be sustained by ethical idealism, until a generation has passed in which the anticipated reforms have not been realized. Then the suspicion must grow that what belongs to the mechanism of history cannot be hurried, and that the hope for social progress no longer turns upon the initiative of the people as the active agents of achievement, but rather upon those impersonal laws asserted to govern the constitution of nature and man. Beyond this melancholy disappointment stands only one further step, pessimistic doubt that history, any more than life itself, has a goal — not to mention the goal of a Communist utopia for which man reached, only to fall into a new working-class misery. Thus the problem which overwhelmed naturalistic ethics in ancient times—the fact that nature has the last word—casts its dark shadow over dialectical Materialism also. Communism can modify[60] its insistence on inevitability here only by weakening the certainty which it claims for the outcome. Yet this insistence may place the historical climax of proletariat bliss out of reach for generations. And indeed, apart from a teleological view of nature, and a reintroduction of that very factor of providence which Communism excludes, is there any firm basis for thinking that nature and history, in any generation, future or present, have a special view to man and society? Is there not more likelihood that a superman — or at most a supreme soviet, or highest organ of state authority — may extract from nature and history defined in these terms a purely personal advantage?[61]

The Marxist concern for "human justice" is something radically and obviously distinct from the inherited Judeo-Christian concern. The latter sets out from the insistence that truth and the good are ontological realities, that God is logically and chronologically prior to nature and man, and constructive of the universe; the former sets out from the deliberate repudiation of these emphases. In the Communist program,

[60]Yet Communism modifies its notion of historical determinism every time it charges the bourgeoisie with injustice, and assumes its moral responsibility for acts which do not spring out of the inevitabilities of history.

[61]"The conflict over the 'right of property' wavers in vehement commotion. The Communists affirm that 'the earth belongs to him who tills it, and its products to those who bring them out!' I think it belongs to him who knows how to take it, or who does not let it be taken from him, does not let himself be deprived of it. If he appropriates it, then not only the earth, but the right to it too, belongs to him. This is egoistic right: i.e., it is the right for me, therefore it is right. . . . The tiger that assails me is in the right, and I who strike him down am also in the right. I defend against him not my right but myself." Max Stirner, *The Ego and His Own* (trans. from the German *Der Einzige und sein Eigenthun,* Modern Library Edition), p. 199.

whatever contributes most efficiently to the proletarian aim is justice. The moral ideal thus becomes a floating propaganda weapon to promote class war. In its conduct, the welfare of the group-ideal is prized above the welfare of individuals, for the individual is regarded as but a means to the social goal. Christianity assigns the individual man a unique dignity and worth on the basis of creation and redemption; Marxism refuses to elevate man beyond animality, and suspends all his rights upon the tolerance of the state. Thus Marxism is caught in a strange inconsistency. On one side, its great protest is against the exploitation and degradation of the individual man; on the other, its whole world view is shaped by tenets which exclude any genuine role for the dignity and worth of the human being.

The role of the state in Communist history is thus strikingly different from its role in Communist propaganda. The Marxist program set out as anti-state, for the state was identified as an instrument of oppression. The elimination of class distinctions would involve the dissolution of the state. But this opposition to the state has disappeared wherever Communism has grasped control of political machinery. Since the Bolsheviks seized the apparatus of the Russian state in 1917, political Naturalism in its Communist form has brought to the philosophy of political power-ethics an accumulation of military, scientific and industrial strength which would have seemed incredible to earlier generations. Government control is extended to all spheres of culture, which are regarded merely as branches of the state. Thus Leviathan appears as a twentieth-century colossus: the owner of all wealth, the employer of all labor, the controller of all science and education and religion and art. Communist policy involves, in the present generation, the most ruthless display of "might makes right" ethics that world history has ever beheld. Aggressive violence, bloody revolution, ruthlessness, deception and false witness are justified as means to the movement's ends. A spirit of mathematical treachery and mercilessness is the symbol of its expansion.

It was Lenin's phrase that "an oppressed class which does not learn to use arms, to acquire arms, only deserves to be treated like slaves."[62] Today enslaved multitudes behind an iron curtain, their very survival and rights suspended entirely upon the tolerance and whim of the Communist state, are gradually awakening to the fact that immoral earnestness can only lead to profounder bondage, and that freedom requires the reference of all human decisions to norms addressed to the state, rather than invented by the state. The earlier Marxists proclaimed: "We do not believe in eternal principles of morality and we will expose this deception." Modern victims are tempted to regard their predecessors as doubly deceived.

The practical consequences of the doctrine of political Naturalism are no self-sufficient criterion, for these have not yet been completely

[62]Lenin, *Selected Works* (London: Lawrence and Wishart, 1953), I, Pt. 2.

manifested, nor have they passed through final judgment. But the pain, misery and turmoil which political Naturalism has spawned in the twentieth-century world are written large for all to see. The choice was not between slave-morality and an elite-morality at all; rather, it was between two types of bondage, enslavement to Satan, or voluntary servitude to the Divine will. Political Naturalism deliberately repudiates the latter. The consequences are apparent enough: racial hatred, concentration camps, disregard of treaties, suppression of human rights, aggressive warfare, wanton destruction of life and property. In his *Ecce Homo* Nietzsche asserted: "I am not a man. I am dynamite." Adding a potentially terrible violence to the side of this philosophy, air and atomic power stand in stark contrast to that spiritual and moral power with which the small company of Christian apostles ventured forth to turn the world upside down. Nietzsche's doctrine of Superman contributed largely to the moral degeneration of modern Germany,[63] as Machiavelli's doctrine did in Italy. Ruthless dictators taught citizens to regard their nations as comprised of supermen, to which other races or peoples are inferior. Thus a high tide of hate was loosed in the erstwhile Christian West. The aftermath of Hitler and Mussolini, of Stalin and of the terrors of Soviet totalitarianism, was to plunge civilization into the valley of the shadow of death. The "might makes right" philosophy was the ideal of Nazism, which, by controlling the activities, thoughts, and ideals of the German nation, sought to "coordinate" its spirit and structure under its centralized direction.[64]

C. RELIGIOUS NATURALISM

Naturalistic ethics does not necessarily exclude religion, any more than it excludes gods of a sort. It may, in fact, even be strategically coordinated with religious faith as the crucial and determinative reference for the moral life. Sophist Naturalism was agnostic about the gods; Epicureanism tolerated them a remote and uninfluential existence which reappears as the climate of much of the ethics of Utility; political Naturalism conceives of religion and the gods as a device for patriotism and nationalism. Religious Naturalism regards the order of nature not simply as an inexorable necessary system, but

[63]On September 1, 1939, Hitler told the Reichstag: "I desire nothing other than to be the first soldier of the German reich. I have again put on that old coat which was the most sacred and the most dear to me of all. I will not take it off until the victory is ours or — I shall not live to see the end. There is one word that I have never learned: capitulation." *Encyclopaedia Britannica* (1952), II, 598f.

[64]The totalitarian motif was plainly set forth by Hitler: "National socialism must claim as a matter of principle the right to force upon the entire German nation its principles . . . and to educate it to its ideas and thoughts. The National-Socialist doctrine . . . is to be ruler of the German nation. It has the life of the people to destine and to regulate anew . . ." *Mein Kampf* (New York: Stackpole Sons, 1943), p. 559. What the political naturalist insists upon is not merely the right to rule men's practical activity, but their minds as well.

as a Divine necessity. The champions of an ethics of religious Naturalism are both ancient and modern.

The system of nature, as a necessary movement of events indifferent to the whims and preferences of the individual, constituted the Achilles' heel of every hedonistic ethics. Recognizing that nature — the ultimate reality — appears indifferent to our desires, how are we to retain significance for any rule of life?

The answer of religious Naturalism is unhesitating: the order of nature is a *Divine rational necessity*; worship it! The uncompromised entrustment of the whole of life to nature as a Divine necessity alone lends significance to human existence and conduct. The ethics of Stoicism in ancient times, and of Spinoza in the modern era, exemplifies this mood.

1. ANCIENT: STOICISM

The demarcation between Pantheism and Naturalism is small. Both views agree that no reality exists transcendent to the system of nature. But Pantheism regards this inner, invisible order as a rational Mind and Will, as a living Divine order, of which the visible phenomenal world is the outward manifestation. Naturalism, on the other hand, conceives the space-time process as essentially non-mental or non-spiritual. Stoic metaphysics has much more in common with theism than does its later Spinozistic counterpart; the former conceives nature as rational and teleological, the latter as mathematical and non-teleological order. But even the Stoic form of Pantheism must be sharply distinguished from those modern forms shaped and influenced indirectly by the Hebrew-Christian conception of God as personal. Stoic divinity is impersonal, fate is an impersonal power, and providence is impersonal. The Stoics denied any personal relation whatever between the soul and God, and hence deprecated prayer. Death for them involves the cessation of human personality; individual souls exist only until their absorption into the Divine reason. It is no mere accident that, shaped in the climate of post-medieval thought, the modern extension of Stoic ethics as seen in Spinoza, himself a Jew, should deliberately enforce this impersonalistic side. Even in Stoicism (300 B.C.), the teleological element appears as an inheritance from the Aristotelian metaphysics from which as a successor philosophy it is unable wholly to free itself, yet to which it allows no determinative force. Even the conception of nature as rational does not imply ultimate personality. The Stoics spoke, indeed, of the reason and wisdom of nature. Yet they were indebted to Heraclitus, identifying reason with fire, and retaining for reason a corporeal sense of rarefied matter against which the idealistic tradition of Socrates-Plato-Aristotle protested. Instead of defining reason in an unqualified incorporeal sense, Stoicism identifies it as the logical fire which animates the space-time world. Hence the line between Stoic Pantheism and hylozoism, the view that nature is alive, is a narrow one; Stoicism is essentially Naturalism imbued with a religious motif in search of significance in life.

Stoic metaphysics, basically, considers that nature is reason or law, a Divine fire, and therefore just, since everything conforms to law. The invisible necessity of things is fate; everything falls by Divine law into its appointed place. The Stoic conception of fate excludes chance and indeterminacy for absolute determinism. Yet the entire movement of things is regarded as providential. Zeno the Stoic asserts that, were we omniscient (absolute Reason), we would know that everything occurs according to Divine reason and hence for the best; therefore we should accept all the developments of life with equal readiness, rather than assert contrary preferences.

The Divine reason, or essence of reality, is manifested at various levels of purity. The universe is its debased expression, for matter is solidified reason, which reason itself is seeking to dissolve and consume. But the spark of pure reason survives in man. Man is to order his life by this Divine reason; he is to live "according to nature." This phrase, already discussed in connection with the Cynics, means that human life becomes significant only as man is absorbed into the universal reason. The Stoic world-view is calculated to supply the moral life with a scientific basis. Man, the seed of reason, finds completion only in the comprehensive Divine reason, for this intelligent fire constitutes the inner harmony of the whole of reality. Rather than begrudging the unconcern of nature with man's desires, and abdicating life to Cyrenaic indifference or to Epicurean *ataraxia,* man is called upon for a major ethical and spiritual decision, namely, to conversion. He is to commit his life enthusiastically to the necessities of nature, thus transforming nature's compulsion into freedom. The all-important consideration in ethics is whether the necessity of nature occurs despite us, and hence breeds resentment, or whether it occurs with our concurrence. Whether we are slaves or the masters of life depends upon whether we assert our own preferences, or whether we worship the system of nature. The Stoic rule of life is *apatheia* — an acquiescence to the unyielding firmness of the order of nature.

Stoicism asks for a sudden conversion, a total change of attitude. Feelings and personal emotions give a false valuation of things. Conduct must be elevated incessantly into reason-conformity; the individual must find the "mind of nature" and cultivate an impassive disposition. Apathy becomes the key word of Stoic ethics. It involves both a distaste for personal desires and a resting of the mind in the unmodifiable *must* of things, accepted as the *ought* of life.

The Stoic is thus called upon to set his life outlook against that of the human race in general, against the voice of the populace, which attaches the false valuation of emotional preference to its experience. And he is called upon equally to contradict his own inclinations, and to rise to the plane of universal reason. He becomes indifferent, both to himself as an individual, and to the race in this personal dimension. The Stoic philosophy universalizes conduct by stressing the importance of universal reason above that of individuals and nations, and by addressing humanity at this dimension only. The universal reason is man's only "fatherland"; every decision of life is to be looked at rationally, from "the standpoint of the universe." All social and national differences between men fall away as artificial. A humanitarian ethics arises for Roman and Greek and Hebrew, for emperor and slave alike.

Stoicism influenced a number of men outstanding in the history of moral thought. Both Greek and Roman responded to it. In its ranks were the emperor Marcus Aurelius and the slave Epictetus. But the Stoic morality never expressed itself as a cosmopolitan popular movement of the masses. It remained, for the most part, the luxury of intellectuals. Even at this level, its support was unstable and eventuated in a two-level morality, due to the difficulty of actualizing the ideal of apathy.

Elements of Christian ethics have often been compared with the Stoic view, and a dependence suggested.[65] The Christian doctrines of the fatherhood of God, and of the brotherhood of man, are doctrines which the Stoics popularized in the Roman empire. The Christian appeal for a sudden and decisive change of life is likened to the Stoic. The biblical emphasis on acquiescence in the will of God is compared with Stoic *apatheia.*

But the line between Stoic and Christian ethics is a sharp one, as decisive as that between Stoic and Christian metaphysics.[66] The Stoic doctrine negates the significance of individual personality. The "universal fatherhood" of God reduces to the thesis that the universe no more respects my neighbor's desires than my own. The worship of the system of nature means that I must renounce the thought that I, as an individual, am significant in the universe. The "universal brotherhood" of man means only that I must regard my blood brother in the same impersonal way that I do a stranger. This is far removed from the

[65]The early residence of the Apostle Paul, Tarsus, was the location of a Stoic center of learning, and in one of his addresses he quoted a Stoic poet (cf. Acts 17:28, "as certain even of *your own* poets have said"). In addition, however, not only Stoic terms (*antarkes,* content, Phil. 4:11, I Tim. 6:8; *eusebeia,* godliness, I Tim. 2:2, 4:7f., etc.), but Stoic ideas have been charged to him. But these Greek words were not the exclusive property of the Stoics. And the distinctive framework of the Pauline conceptions disputes Clement C. J. Webb's notion that Stoicism supplied the framework for Christian ethics.

[66]Albert Schweitzer remarks: "The ethic of the later Stoicism is so near akin to the universal charity of the Christian ethic, that by the tradition of later times Seneca is declared to be a Christian. . . . Yet the two movements cannot amalgamate. . . . Marcus Aurelius is responsible for the most terrible persecutions of Christians, and Christianity, on its side declares war to the death against the Porch. . . . It helps not at all that their ethical teaching is almost identical. Each appears as part of a philosophy which is irreconcilable with that of the other. All contradictions in the world may be concealed, but not that between two world-views . . ." *The Philosophy of Civilization* (New York: Macmillan, 1949), pp. 138ff.

Christian doctrine of particular Divine providence and of neighbor-love.[67] Lightfoot, in his work on St. Paul and Seneca, remarks that in Stoic phraseology " 'imitation of God' signifies nothing deeper than a due recognition of physical laws on the part of man, and a conformity thereto in his actions."[68] The Stoic doctrine of moral apathy, of stoicism in the experiences of life, eliminates passion and compassion alike. The very notion of sympathy for others in their misfortunes is excluded, just as congratulation of them in fortune is ruled out, not only by the dogma of the indifference of nature to the individual, but by the insistence upon *apatheia.* Pathos and passion are excluded, and the life of passive disaffection, of impersonal disinterestedness, of impassivity, replaces them. While compassion, as an expression of love for individual persons, holds a central role in Christian ethics, it is a contradiction of the Stoic attitude. The contrast with Stoicism is made painfully obvious by Epictetus' reference to the consolation of a father who has lost a son by death. It is permitted to the Stoic to groan with such a person, says Epictetus, provided one does not groan inwardly. Here an essential distinction between the Stoic and Christian conceptions of life, and of the significance of the individual, is painfully obvious. The Stoic doctrine of impersonal universal reason robs the whole dimension of human life of love.

Beneath this contrast, moreover, stands another equally important doctrine. An uncompromising acquiescence to the flow of events is contrary to the Christian view of life. It calls for protest against, and the repudiation of, elements which seem to belong to the *must* of things. Death, suffering, and disease are, from the Christian point of view, experiences which cannot be reconciled with an ideal universe, but belong rather to a world in sin. Christian acquiescence to them is never as to the ultimate and ideal, but as to penal evils, which the redemptive power of God invests nonetheless with a disciplinary significance. To accept death as final is contrary to Christian faith and ethics. Mourning for the dead and the consolation of the bereaved have New Ttestament as well as Old Testament precedent, whereas for the Stoic, death is a matter of indifference.

The moral philosophy of Stoicism arises as a solace and support for man's inability to find a home for his personal desires in the context of nature. The Stoic appeal to absolute reason does not solve this problem, but rather requires the heroic confession that man as a

[67]The writer once heard Prof. W. Harry Jellema express the contrast in this way: "Christian ethics affirms: think of everybody as meaning as much to God as you think you mean to Him. Stoicism: think of yourself as being as insignificant in the universe as other individuals appear to be to you."

[68]"What is the duty of a good man?" asks Seneca. "To resign himself to his destiny. It is a great consolation to share the fate of the universe. Whatever it be that decrees how we are to live, how we are to die, it binds even the gods by the same inexorable law; an irresistible current bears along terrestrial and celestial things" (*De Prov.,* 6). The Christian doctrine, on the contrary, may be found in Romans 12:1f.

personal moral agent is insignificant in the universe. The pursuit of virtue for virtue's sake within the Stoic cosmology cannot be productive of personal happiness or personal anything, for it involves the negation of personality. But because man is a personal agent, the Stoic conversion cannot effectively restrain the individual's overwhelming sense of the emptiness and worthlessness of existence, nor erase the soul's protest against this realization. The exclusion of all personal compensation or reward for the pursuit of virtue is destructive of enthusiasm for virtue, since its price is the cancellation of all self-interest. What begins as an affirmative worship of the order of nature concludes at last with the confession to which Cyrenaicism and Epicureanism were already led in a more elemental manner, that if the system of nature is the ultimate reality, I must stop thinking that I as an individual am significant in the universe. "Regret nothing, desire nothing . . . frame your will in harmony with your circumstances," says Epictetus in his *Manual*. Human existence reduces finally to resignation to the inevitable, whether man worships the inevitable or not.

Perhaps nowhere is this depressing conclusion delineated more aptly than by Albert Schweitzer:

> The vacillation which is characteristic of Stoicism comes . . . from the fact that the results it attains do not match its aspirations, but are much poorer than these. The spirit of antiquity tries to find an optimistic-ethical life-affirmation in nature-philosophy, and to find in it also the justification of those instincts for reliable activity which it has possessed since the days when it was entirely unsophisticated, but it cannot do so. Whenever it acknowledges what has happened, it sees clearly that thinking about the universe leads only to resignation, and that a life in harmony with the world means quiet surrender to being carried along in the flood of world-happenings, and, when the hour comes, sinking into it without a murmur. Stoicism talks, it is true, with deep earnestness of responsibility and duty, but since it cannot draw either from nature-philosophy or from ethics a well-established and living notion of activity, it lays out in these words nothing but beautiful corpses. . . . Nature-philosophy only provides the cosmic background for the resignation to which ethics have come. . . . An inconceivable impoverishment takes place in the representation of the moral. The notion of action cannot be worked out to completion.[69]

Whatever role Stoicism seeks to vindicate for man as a cause in nature productive of moral effects, is compromised by these larger determinations. When ethics is conceived only as acquiescence in the universe, it cannot be conceived as producing an effect on the universe. It then fails really to give an ethical character to the relation of the individual to the universe, and ends in what Schweitzer describes as a world and

[69]Schweitzer, *op. cit.*, p. 120.

life negation which reduces ethics to impotence. It arrives not "at real ethics, but only at an ethically-coloured resignation";[70] altruistic ethics is lost. Inward liberation from the world means the end of ethics working in and on the world.[71]

All naturalistic ethics, beginning as it does with nature as ultimate, arrives finally at resignation, a desire for inner liberation from the world and never at an ethical motive for the transformation of the world. In the ancient world of Naturalism, only Stoicism ventured a monistic, optimistic ethic. Its worship of the universe supports its world-affirming, optimistic-ethical world-life view. But Stoicism, too, ends in world-and-life negation. It cannot really find absolute meaning in the world, which it does not recognize as fallen, hence cannot really reach its goal of an "optimistic-ethical affirmation of life," but "arrives only at resignation, not at ethics."[72]

2. *MODERN: SPINOZISM*

The worship of nature's inner necessity as the essence of virtue, whereby its compulsion is turned to freedom, is far more complicated for Benedictus Spinoza (1632-1677). His problem gains an orientation from the modern world: how to retain religion and morality in view of the account of reality which science gives us.

Stoicism maintained a teleological view of the universe, asserting a sort of general providence, but Spinoza's view excludes all teleology in favor of a mathematical explanation. The universe is explained in terms of previous efficient causes only; all final causes, all ends, fall away.

If Spinoza's interaction with the moral problem is post-scientific, it is also post-medieval. His famous *Ethics* is not only replete with Hebrew-Christian vocabulary, but follows the pattern of classic works on systematic theology: theology, anthropology, soteriology. God is the *summum bonum*; in this assertion he maintains a formal connection with the revelational tradition. He shares its conviction that metaphysics determines ethics, that the way in which reality must be defined is decisive, in turn, for the conception of the moral life. God, for Spinoza, is the *causa sui*, the self-caused. Thus he sets himself against the later

[71]*Ibid.*, p. 301.

[72]*Ibid.*, p. 192. "From every point of view, vigorous ethical world-and-life affirmation is made difficult for the ancient world. That is why it falls more and more a prey to pessimistic conceptions of the universe, which draw its thoughts away from reality, and celebrate the liberation of the spiritual from its bondage to the material in a succession of cosmic dramas. Gnosticism, Oriental and Christian, Neo-Pythagoreanism, which arose as early as the first century B.C., the Neo-Platonism which originated with Plotinus (A.D. 204-269), and the great Mystery-religions, all come to meet the religious world-shunning disposition of the masses during the break-up of antiquity, and offer it that deliverance from the world of which it is in search. In this chaos of ideas Christianity emerges victorious because it is the most robust religion of redemption, because as a community it possesses the strongest organization, and because beneath its pessimistic world-view it has at its disposal living ethical ideas" (p. 140).

tendency to define the problem of ethics by a consideration merely of the sphere of psychology, or biology, or anthropology bounded by evolutionary process. For Spinoza, it is the fixed framework of reality which is decisive for ethics. God is the "self-caused . . . (or) that of which the essence involves existence."

The traditional vocabulary, however, is used in a new sense, and has a different context. Spinoza, a Jew, was in conscious revolt against the Hebrew tradition. Spinoza's *causa sui* is not the Jahweh of the Old Testament, not the Creator-Redeemer of Hebrew-Christian revelation, not the triune God of medieval theology and philosophy. The synagogue excommunicated Spinoza, and the Roman Catholic church placed his writings in the prohibitory index. While he retains the vocabulary of the inherited tradition, he presents a novel content to his philosophy.

The order of the universe, according to Spinoza, is its inmost reality. The mathematical system of the universe, on which science insists, is God. God is wholly immanent, is identical with the mathematical necessity of nature. Not teleology, but this mathematical structure, determines everything. The new emphasis on mathematical equations as the key to reality becomes decisive for metaphysics. The priority of logic, of which mathematics is an example, stands out even in Spinoza's work on *Ethics*. The work is conceived much like a book of geometry, beginning with a series of definitions, supplemented by a set of axioms, and then followed by propositions with their proofs. The first definition is of the self-caused. This is the mathematical system of nature.

In Spinoza's naturalistic world-view, God is the sum total of nature, not an ethical personality outside it. He expounds this position with sophisticated finesse and thoroughness, and seeks to win a place for ethics within it. Descartes, indeed, had already referred man's physical existence to the network of nature alone, although he did not propose a geometrical mechanism covering the whole of reality. Spinoza retains Descartes' view of nature, and he revises Descartes' view of God and man in his entire being to accord with mathematical determinism. *Ethics,* Spinoza's major work, is really nature-philosophy: man must lose himself spiritually in nature.

God, or the mathematical system of nature, does not overrule the movement of things for the sake either of a favored few, or for a favored creature-man. The *ought* is the *must* of nature. The "favored few" are those who adjust to nature. Happiness comes when man, who belongs naturally to the universe, "surrenders himself to it consciously and willingly."[73] God acts not with a view to final ends but from inner necessity. So does the man of ethics: he is no longer a ship tossed by an unstable sea, but lives constantly adjusted to the invariable necessity of nature, in submission to changeless laws. He avoids sympathy, since everything happens by an unchanging necessity in the Divine Nature. Hatred and contempt vanish as utterly futile.

[73]*Ibid.*, p. 191.

The life of resignation is the life of power, for it triumphs over circumstances, self, and others. Becoming one with God means acquiescence to the necessity of things.[74]

Spinoza begins with the fact that man's desires for riches, fame and sensual pleasure in the universe are disappointing. No rule of life can be predicated upon the desires of man, for they are foredoomed to frustration. He concludes that providential teleology therefore is excluded.[75] The only way to achieve the fulfillment of desire is to learn the mathematical structure of reality and to conform life to it, since ignorance of this structure is the cause of all disappointment. Man's salvation from frustrated desires is achieved by the intellectual love of God, acquiescence to the order of nature. The volitions and emotions are to be placed in the service of the reason, and the reason in the service of the unfailing mathematical regularity of nature.

Spinoza's key concept is *resignation* to the causal network of the universe, although Spinoza designates it the intellectual love of God. The spirited recognition that every detail of life is bracketed by inevitabilities imparts to life an enduring worth. Whether existence is significant or not turns upon whether it is conformed enthusiastically to life's fateful necessities. The knowledge of what is, and that what is must be — this is the only avenue of freedom from emotional conflict. The increase of scientific knowledge, or of the intelligible order, brings an active emotion of joy as we recognize that this order is divine and conform ourselves to it, *i.e.,* to God. The worship of God, or the universe, delivers the individual from resentments toward experience. If the system of nature were suspended upon individual preferences, the reliability of its behavior would be destroyed; man could no longer relate his life dependably to it. To allow experience to be wholly dominated by the necessary causal order of the universe is the only

[74]It is Schleiermacher who later paints Spinozism as Christian ethics. Religion is the sense of dependence: man must realize his essential oneness with the Infinite, the universe, experienced in feeling. The only added factor is derived from the evolutionary climate of his day, the notion that progress is immanent. Inherent in things is their own perfection as an automatic principle. The moral law is only the law of nature developing in man.

[75]Spinoza acknowledges that if adequate independent evidence could be adduced for a personal God, whose benevolent purpose is operative in the stream of events (as Hebrew-Christian theology asserts) the frustration of desire would then not overthrow the providential interpretation. But the only evidence Spinoza will admit is human experience interpreted by mathematical analysis; any appeal to special Divine revelation is excluded in advance. The biblical emphasis that man's desires are sinful, and unentitled to a favorable issue in every respect, is also ignored. Spinoza has broken with this conception of God. Hume, too, asserts that if we had *a priori* assurance that the universe is the creation of an infinitely wise, good and powerful God, then the presence of misery in the world would be insufficient evidence for overthrowing a benevolent interpretation of nature. But Hume asserted not only that we have no such *a priori* demonstration, but that only the empirical observation of all effects can yield us knowledge of their causes. Both thinkers *a priori* exclude the possibility of *a priori* knowledge of a teleological universe and of special Divine revelation.

way of moral growth, for such resignation weans us from personal desires and attaches us rationally to dependable causal connections.[76] The joy of unfrustrated desires and the confidence in the regularity of nature promote the love of God. Our desires and actions are religious insofar as they spring from the knowledge of God, or the scientific apprehension. Delight in the inflexible system of the universe increases as one realizes that dependable anticipations arise only in dependence upon this rigorous causal structure. Thus the attachment of the mind to the inimitable system of the universe issues at last in comprehending the whole of life *sub specie aeternitatis*. When our thoughts and deeds are controlled by scientific insight, God may be said to be thinking in us.

How far this is from Christian ethics should be clear. Spinoza's God does not love the world; the *causia sui* — which we are to love — is impersonal necessity. In place of "God works all things together for good to them that love Him, to them that are the called according to His purpose" (Romans 8:28), Spinoza would assure us, in effect, that "the system of nature grinds away dependably for all who intuit its necessity, and who conform their lives to its mathematical invariability."

In contrast with Stoicism, altruism for Spinoza does not belong to the essence of ethics. In the last analysis, despite the existence of universal laws, all ethical action aims at our own interests as spiritually supreme. Spinoza gives some scope to organized society, to man's civic responsibilities, yet there remains no room for genuine devotion to the community. The perfect society appears automatically in proportion as individuals adjust to the necessity of nature. No practical and purposive aims are to be realized in the world: ethics consists only in the relation of acquiescence to nature as a system of mathematical determinism.

The verdict of Stoicism and Spinozism is essentially the same: If the system of nature is the ultimate reality, the negation of the individual, the denial of personal significance, follows as much from the repudiation as from the assertion of hedonism or other personal preferences. Stoicism admitted a limited scope to providence, but never vindicated the presence of purpose in its scheme of cosmology. Spinozism eliminates this inconsistency, and is frankly anti-teleological. The Stoic does not merely drift to *apatheia,* but makes a religion of it. Spinozism does the same thing with *resignation,* without even a glimmer of providence in the sequence of events.

In contrast with the more reserved *ataraxia* of Epicureanism and the attitude of indifference of Cyrenaicism before it, the ethics of religious Naturalism arrives contentedly in the land of apathy and resignation, by attaching an even profounder significance to reason than any of these

[76]"Acquiescence in one's very own self can arise on the basis of Reason, and only that acquiescence which arises out of Reason is the highest which can be given" (*Ethics,* IV, 52). "Truly acquiescence in one's self is the highest thing we can hope for" (*Ethics,* IV, 52S). Quotation from edition published by Van Nostrand, New York, 1876.

earlier naturalistic views had done. Man can intuit the very reason of the universe, and only by conforming himself wholly to it can he be at home in nature. But this same affirmation of at-homeness makes man really an outcast in the world of reality. It not only requires him to repress the emotional and volitional sides of life, and to repudiate any significance of his personal existence, a position to which Cyrenaicism and Epicureanism were led in a more elemental way, but it requires a sustained and fixed attitude toward life which reduces man at last to merely an aspect of the impersonal necessity of nature. While Stoicism never solved the problem of freedom in metaphysical determinism, Spinoza makes the effort. He defines freedom (for everything less than God) as the ability to accomplish the same (essential) act under varying conditions. Freedom is absorption in God. Yet Spinoza dismisses the conception of human freedom, as well as of external teleology, as imaginative and erroneous.[77] There is no spontaneous power of decision and no choice, no ability to accomplish two purposes, but one condition allowing but one necessarily determined assertion or denial. Man is free to the extent that he himself has actualized the necessities of nature with conscious desire. But, as Harold H. Joachim points out, man's conscious desire is not to be traced to purposive causes, but in Spinoza's system must be referred to "an indefinite chain of causes which are not teleological in their *nexus*. Hence man's 'freedom' is illusory: for the basis of the so-called 'free' action, is itself necessarily determined *a tergo* by forces over which man has no control."[78]

But what then is the point of telling man that he "ought" to conform his life to a scheme of inexorable necessity which already permeates the whole? And if Spinoza writes his *Ethics,* is it not because he *must* do so, rather than because the unconformity of others to the *must* provokes him to? Is not Spinoza self-deceived about his own freedom, as well as about theirs? And is not even the recognition or non-recognition of "what is," and that "what is,.must be," and equally much the endeavor "to make the best of what is" also an essential element in "what is and must be"?[79] As every naturalistic view, Spinozism is unable to save significance for the moral agent. It reduces him to a fragment of impersonal reality. The only immortality Spinoza acknowledges is not that of an indestructible soul, but the imperishable mathematical necessity of the universe, in conformity to which man more and more is called upon to depersonalize his existence.

3. MODERN: HUMANISM

The empirical emphasis, which appeared alongside the mathematical in modern natural science, leads to a modification of the ethics of

[77] *Ethics,* Appendix i.

[78] Harold H. Joachim, *A Study of the Ethics of Spinoza* (Oxford: Clarendon Press, 1901), p. 229.

[79] *Ibid.,* p. 285, n. 3.

religious Naturalism in the form of Humanism. The mathematical key to nature, based on intuitive insight and deductive consistency, did not give the scientist access to the details of nature's behavior. But modern science had a passion to unveil the order of nature in its smallest minutiae, not primarily to lay bare the eternal system of nature, but with a view to control of the immediate future. Even Spinoza's exposition of nature contained a concealed agnosticism about the order of nature as an eternal and immutable system. Edwin A. Burtt points out that "if Nature is a necessary structure, operating with no reference to human good or ill, it follows that she is under no obligation to conform, in detail at any rate, to man's ideas about her, and hence may at any moment present him with perceptions which disappoint his most confident expectations."[80] This may be somewhat superficial, if intended as a reply to Spinoza, but it indicates nonetheless the humanist shift of interest from the eternal order of nature to its verifiable continuities. In the quest for scientific knowledge, therefore, demonstrative certainty yields priority to adequacy of information for future experience. Scientific knowledge becomes tentative; its function is not to systematize the future absolutely, but to anticipate it efficiently. Thus the scientific ideal of certainty is displaced by the ideal of tentative empirical knowledge, suspended upon experience, and subject to revision.

From this setting Humanism rises as an ethical philosophy. Nature is to be reverenced as the ultimate real. But our tentative knowledge of nature requires the moral life to be defined with modesty and openness. Tolerance for others' convictions is a virtue (not because God reserves for himself the right to judge the hearts of men, or because the New Testament implies the right of conscience) because, since we have no right to claim absolute truth, others may be right. The distinction between views is that of greater or lesser conformity to the data of experience, not between an eternally fixed right and wrong. Moral ideals are not certain, but tentative; no fixed rule of life may be asserted as universally valid for all men in all times and places.

Contemporary Humanism thus accepts the prevailing empirico-naturalistic view of the world, and abandons the teleological notion that goodness and perfection furnish determinative clues for the interpretation of nature. But, as an evolutionary view, it seeks to vindicate a place for social values in the experience of man. Whether the universe is hostile, unconcerned, or friendly to man depends upon what significance is given to the space-time universe's "cooperation" in man's emergence from the evolutionary process. While man is not to be regarded as the favored object of some prevenient personal agency, yet the universe functions conducively to his emergence and survival. And, on the human level, a psychologically peculiar organization of natural forces has emerged, facilitating a devotion to the social good. This

[80]Edwin A. Burtt, *Types of Religious Philosophy* (New York: Harper, 1939), p. 466.

social aspiration becomes the heart of religion itself. Humanism consists of devotion to the dependable supports of human welfare, to man's ideal needs and highest values as disclosed in experience. Just as evolutionary Naturalism has a pleasure-tradition, and a politico-power tradition, so it has a tradition which emphasizes social values. The indirect effect of Hebrew-Christian influences upon this latter emphasis is clear from the fact that Humanism of this variety is a reaction against Protestant Liberalism, which itself had appeared as a reduction of evangelical Christianity. The values which seem particularly commanding to Humanism, a movement described as "Naturalism which goes to church," are those promotive of individual and social well-being. Humanists oppose capitalism and incline toward socialistic theories of economics on the theory that the distribution of material goods multiplies the enrichment and enjoyment of life. Above totalitarianism they champion "democracy" in its Renaissance form of the absolute freedom of the individual from all objective constraints, and hence they are usually socialistic. Humanists have unlimited faith in education as a great socializing force, assuming that the knowledge of the truth assures its practice. Above material values available to human enjoyment, humanists stress artistic enjoyment and creativity, the joys of cooperation, friendship and love as examples of the aesthetic and the spiritual good.

Significantly, in view of its empirical method of scientific tentativity, Humanism in principle abandons devotion to the love and apprehension of objective and eternal truth, which the classic form of religious Naturalism prized as the central value. The importance of this limitation to relative values, and the corresponding repudiation of absolutes, has escaped even many humanists, who do not consistently apply the principle. Most humanist thought uncritically resists the relativity in morals actually implied in its suspension of validity upon future (rather than past) experience. This is seen, for example, in the repudiation as "radical" of those humanists who, in addition to advocating lenient views of divorce (as humanists generally do), encourage "free love" as well. It is seen even more conspicuously in the prevailing humanist devotion to science as the *only* and *enduring* guide to truth about reality, and to scientific truth, artistic creation, and love as permanent values. Obviously the permanent disvalue of "free love" and the permanent value of honesty in scientific research, and of artistic creation and love, can be asserted with justifiable confidence only from a context which designates some values eternal and unchanging. Only with great impropriety are such permanent values smuggled inside a frame of interpretation which affirms all judgments as tentative and subject to revision, and which professes to suspend the validity of such judgments upon future confirmation. That moral values are relative to man's changing social experience can be earnestly harmonized with inherited values as permanently retentive of their excellence only by a compromise of the dynamic and relative approach to reality.

The reaction to this basic compromise leads to a despair over the worthwhileness of human good. In the Anglo-Saxon world, this evaporation of "the humanism from Humanism" has seldom yet manifested itself; George Jean Nathan is perhaps exemplary of the exception, and Joseph Wood Krutch also. But as Humanism is devoided of its glimmer of interaction with Protestant Liberalism, and absorbed fully in a materialistic view of reality and life, this concern for individual and social welfare vanishes, as well as the optimistic thesis of their coincidence. In the Communist alternative, Humanism gives way to pragmatic Naturalism, whose consistent elaboration must suspend faith in all values, including faith in the scientific method and in man, on day-to-day justification. While the values of Humanism are still prized, they are regarded with greater tentativity. Consequently the prevailing humanistic values are called into question. Humanism yields to a power-ethic in which the end justifies the means. Science exists to enhance the power of the state. Honesty in research is no longer supremely prized. Love gives way to hate as a justifiable social attitude. But before this transition to power-naturalism is possible, religious Naturalism must devoid itself of the significance of God, and also of religion, in the formulation of a rule of life.

If Spinoza's view, despite its thorough-going religious Naturalism was colored by Christian terminology, a striking indebtedness also characterizes Humanism: it refuses to refer the god-idea to nature, even as an invisible system. Rather, Humanism identifies the god-idea with man's social ideals, thus carrying forward a religious ethic in the naturalistic tradition; or it refers the god-idea to an imaginary supernatural world, thereby bequeathing the moral life little more than a religious overtone.

The identification of the religious with the axio-sociological is found in A. Eustace Haydon, Edward Scribner Ames, John Dewey, Shailer Mathews and Gerald Birney Smith. Whereas the others speak of God as the highest social values personified,[81] Haydon discards the term God, preferring to speak only of religion, which he equates with enthusiasm for social values.

Mathews and Smith, however, insist that God or social value has a reality beyond that which emerges in human moral experience; it is rooted also in the cosmic process as an object of experience. Thus the idea of God gains an ontological reality, as an aspect of the larger space-time process within which man appears. Henry Nelson Wieman defines God as the sum total of those processes which make for righteousness. Values are grounded in the cosmic structure, as an aspect of

[81]The term God here has simply a functional or symbolic sense, and to that extent — apart from the assertion of specific values to which it is attached in modern Humanism — makes a return to the usage of Sophists like Antiphon and Critias.

the creative activity of the universe. They are not prior to the universe, and determinative of it as changeless spiritual realities, as in supernaturalistic Theism or Idealism, but are conceived dynamically as the moving front of the evolutionary process. Values are not something which emerges, but are the emerging process itself. Thus modern Humanism returns to an ancient form of religious Naturalism, by identifying God with the invisible system of nature, conceived as an evolutionary spiral.[82] This identification of God with a dynamic aspect of the universe is not the prevailing humanist notion, however.

A growing number of humanists assert that the god-idea has supernaturalistic overtones, from which it is awkwardly and unconvincingly detached. They refer the god-idea to an imaginary supernatural postulation anchored in individual psychological needs or explain it as a community necessity rising out of collective feelings. To these thinkers, the retention of the god-idea in connection with ethical considerations is confusing if not misleading. Haydon, as indicated previously, surrendered the term God but developed a religious ethic.

A large and growing company of humanists finds this exposition of a religious ethic without God to be superficial. If John Dewey regarded belief in a supernatural God as a stumbling-block to progress, so religion too, since it takes its rise in theistic conceptions, is regarded, in turn, as a barrier to ethical advance.[83] So reason the Communist thinkers, following the tradition of Marx, Lenin and Stalin. A religious ethic is the opiate of the people; ethics must be divorced from religious considerations no less than from supernaturalistic metaphysics. And here the declension of religious Naturalism becomes complete. Nature is an impersonal materialistic system of necessity; man is an animal whose insights are relative. There is nothing about nature to be worshipped; religious Naturalism, like the ethics of hedonism, is sentimental and romantic. The essential thrust of nature is power. Thus it is that communist Humanism repudiates religious Naturalism and finds in force or power both the rule of life, and the instrument of state policy.

III. RELATIVISTIC NATURALISM

It has already been pointed out that the assumption of relatively durable values — of "truth and value for this generation" — reflects an abandonment of the empirical suspension of all judgments upon present verification. To vindicate the value of love, honesty, and of under-

[82]Recent emergent evolutionary theories even attempt to reintroduce a certain limited teleology which they do not really accommodate (cf. Samuel Alexander's *Space, Time and Deity* [London: Macmillan, 1927]).

[83]It was Dewey, more than any other modern thinker, who indoctrinated the West in the dogma that the repudiation of supernatural and eternal realities is the precondition for scientific respectability and ethical progress. The cleavage between science and the religion and ethics of Christian theism gained an intellectual foundation in his Gifford Lectures, and was popularized through his influence on American educational philosophy.

standing the world, Humanism appeals to past experience in order to validate an expectancy about future experience. Thus it assumes a continuity in events which is not in fact determinable within experiential limits. When the humanist speaks of "truth" or "value for a generation," he usually identifies that generation neatly with the time-span of his own life, quite oblivious to the fact that another person's life-span may have begun or ended last night.

A. PRAGMATISM

Pragmatic Naturalism tends to enlarge the confession of the relativistic factor in all judgments of value, and divorces naturalistic ethics from those overtones of divinity and religion which characterize Stoicism, Spinozism, and Humanism. A wider range is allowed to subjective creative preference as a crucial factor in discrimination of value.

John Dewey devotes himself consciously to the "relation of science and values" as the true problem of philosophy: "How shall our most authentic and dependable cognitive beliefs be used to regulate our practical beliefs? How shall the latter serve to organize and integrate our intellectual beliefs?"[84] Dewey's answer is clear: morality is to be given a scientific basis, *i.e.*, it is to be brought within the scope of the experimental method. Scientific knowledge is to serve as the guide of conduct. Moral standards are to be discovered through the methodology of the natural sciences.[85]

Yet Dewey never clarifies for us the manner in which science can discriminate which values are genuine, although he implies repeatedly that some are not (*e.g.*, totalitarianism, murder, dishonesty). On the one hand, we are told that whatever works is right; the test of the validity of ideas is their workability. On the other hand, the assumption constantly reoccurs (inconsistently with the main thesis) that some consequences are at all costs to be avoided. It is this latter mood which barricades the theory of Dewey and the humanists most effectively against a power-ethic exposition of Naturalism. The Communist strategy employs murder, false-witness, theft of private property and adultery (the substitution of marriage based on party loyalty for marriage based on other considerations) with remarkable potency. All the necessary elements of moral discrimination within the experimental and pragmatic limits of Dewey's approach to reality are met by the Communist theory of values. Dewey avoids the moral anarchy latent in his theory only by the optimistic importation, into the crude experimental formula, of certain prevailing moral notions. Thus he undercuts his pragmatic credo that no values are worthy of absolute devotion, that no final end exists, and that ends are to be regarded merely as

[84] John Dewey, *The Quest for Certainty* (New York: Minton, Balch, 1929), p. 18.
[85] *Ibid.*, p. 273.

means (to other ends which are means — and so on, *ad infinitum*). Dewey never shows us, from within his methodology, how science can discriminate values which are genuine from those which are not, nor why, if some ends better promote the subjective preferences of others, I ought to assert subjective preferences to the contrary.

Dewey's revolt against the Christian approach to life goes far beyond those who sought to honor the ethical principles of Christianity in detachment from Christian metaphysics. Instead, he makes the repudiation of enduring moral principles a necessity to ethical progress, because, for Dewey, the fulcrum on which his philosophy revolves is that the individual's activity supplies his own norm and end.

In actuality, the pragmatic school has revived the fundamental presuppositions of the Sophists, in their bearing upon ethics and life as a whole. The distrust of permanent principles of morality, valid for all men in all times and places, has been popularized by the reduction of all thinking to experimentation. The existence of knowledge is disallowed, even to the denial of the Protagorean identification of sense perception with knowledge. Empirically-verified hypotheses are regarded as "the nearest approach to knowledge . . . available to man."[86] Yet modern Pragmatism hesitates to go with Protagoras' extreme relativism: "There are as many truths as individuals . . . the individual is the measure of the true and the false," although it concurs that "there are no universally valid truths or principles."

B. LOGICAL POSITIVISM

The naturalistic pragmatist shares with the logical positivist the notion that meaning is to be limited to the empirical content of experience. But the positivist contends that ethics is descriptive and not normative, descriptive of personal attitudes or feelings, and "normative" only as emotive. On the other hand, the pragmatist contends that ethical statements contain a descriptive content above emotive preference, becoming normative because of this informative content. Men employ moral norms, like the norms of thought, because of their workability, and not simply as emotive preferences, argues the pragmatist.

The positivist is unconvinced that, once the analysis of value requires the measurement of all claims by physical tests, any such descriptive content beyond emotive preferment can be vindicated. Supernaturalistic ethics has insisted on such norms, but as part and parcel of a super-scientific methodology. But when experience-claims are measured by physical correlates alone, what cannot be so measured is meaningless, and hence, the positivist argues, ethical propositions are assertions of personal preference. Hence, Positivism involves a revolt against any effort to find, describe, and vindicate values and methods which are to supply rational guidance to conduct, whether that effort is made by supernaturalistic or by naturalistic morality. The positivist rebels against

[86]Donald Butler, *Four Philosophies* (New York: Harper, 1951), p. 400.

eternal values imposed upon human nature fixed by creation, and also against changing values supposedly derived from an evolutionary universe to supply rules of conduct for changing human nature. He denies the very possibility of a fixed objective reality from which tentative rules of conduct may be gleaned as reasonable (*i.e.*, workable) hypotheses, to be imposed as duties. Not even workability can be justified as a criterion by which moral rules are to be discriminated.

Behind the recent analysis of values lies the sensationalistic dogma that valid explanation requires measuring all claims by physical tests. Unless experience-claims are measured by physical correlates, they are meaningless. This formula has been applied in several ways. One is that of Logical Positivism, which stresses the dictum that only that is valid which may be confirmed by sense experience. Another is that of Marxism, which appends moral relativism to Dialectical Materialism and deterministic economics. Still another, which must be evaluated later with those existentialist theories which repudiate any effort to grasp the meaning of life by reason, turns this emphasis on resolute subjective preference to confer absoluteness upon the meaninglessness of life.

Humanistic ethics, pragmatic Naturalism, and so-called scientific morality, have been hard pressed to elaborate a convincing defense against positivistic attacks. Their position is compromised by the fact that, whereas Humanism and Pragmatism assert that democratic ideals and the principles of love resolve the ethical tensions in human nature, Communism has given a strategic centrality to undemocratic ideals and principles of hate whose workability for Soviet purposes is difficult to dispute. The pragmatist tends to reply that these Communist ideals will be found to be wrong, *i.e.*, unworkable; they are self-destructive guides of conduct. But why is self-destruction an unworkable premise? And do not the Communist rules seem remarkably potent? May it be that the pragmatist has a secret absolute, or perhaps a series of them, which he cherishes along with his methodology? Moreover, in contending for workability as a methodology, he assumes a uniform view of man and nature which he cannot vindicate within his initial premises. Even his definition of the "tensions" in human nature which require relief gains a meaning which he cannot verify empirically. When he speaks of happiness as the condition of the resolution of these tensions he can point to nothing in sense experience by which the definition is validated. If workability is the only norm, and if no eternal and changeless norms can be predicated on the basis of supernaturalistic ethics, the highway from religious Pragmatism to Communism is a short one, and that to Logical Positivism not much greater.

The expansion of this subjective factor in ethics is carried through with determination by Logical Positivism. Underlying the positivist dogma is the insistence that all valid explanations must be framed in physically measurable terms. Only what can be validated by sense experience can be approved as true or false; all else is subjective emotion. The Golden Rule, according to Herbert Feigl, means: "Would that everybody behaved toward his fellowmen as he expects them to behave toward him. This sentence, having its accent in emotional appeal . . . is neither true nor false."[87]

The objections to Logical Positivism have not been wanting. The theory dogmatically assumes what renders its conclusions necessary, that is, that all reality is sensate. If verification of valid judgments is limited to sense validation alone, this can only be on the theory that physical realities alone exist. This is hardly a *proof,* however. Not even the basic dogma that "only that is valid which is confirmed by sense experience" is capable of sense verification; hence the theory transcends its own limits at the very outset, and cannot really make room for itself. Indubitably it is true that many value judgments are, in part if not in whole, emotive preferences. But the one such judgment which is wholly a matter of emotive preference, and is invalid, is the positivist distortion of the actualities of the ethical situation which represents moral principles as nothing but emotive preferences.

It has also been pointed out often that the positivist seeks to persuade others of the "truth" of his philosophy, and is not engaged merely in oratory. Therefore even he presupposes in practice the very realities he denies in theory.

The Marxist assertion of the cultural relativity of all moral values is appended to the further dogma that all values reflect economic class interests and are the propaganda of self-seeking groups. These theses, which represent the reintroduction of supportive absolutes to the dogma that all values are relative, are then attached to a whole schematization of metaphysics, in the form of materialistic economic determinism. Thus the standpoint of relativism is dogmatically transcended, in order dogmatically to relativize all dogmas of relativity.

The fundamental instability of every naturalistic scheme of ethics is thus laid bare. The mind and will of man cannot rest in sheer relativism, yet its search of the horizons of only space-time process accommodates no absolute guides of conduct, nor workable rules with an imperative sanction. Naturalistic ethics moves within this distressing tension, disillusioning itself in romantic pretensions or yielding to nihilistic exhaustion.

So, at least, it seemed before the rise of existential ethics. Rebellion against any objective comprehension of reality, against any rational rules for conduct, against any definition of man and his tensions in general or universal terms, is existentialism's keynote. It orients the whole discussion of values to the particular man and to his own inner experience. The disavowal of all standards of good or of right, and emphasis on personal decision as the only escape from moral anarchy,

[87]Cited by T. E. Hill in *Contemporary Ethical Theories* (New York: Macmillan, 1950).

is its distinctive characteristic. The logical positivist says that every man makes his moral world; the existentialist says, personal moral decision makes the man.

IV. IRRATIONAL NATURALISM

The nihilistic outcome has been avoided in our century by the rise of this ethics of desperation, *i.e.,* existential ethics. Its outlines come into view with the post-Hegelian revolt against reason, to which the naturalistic mood contributes largely. Existential ethics, which requires separate attention, aligns itself over against both naturalistic and idealistic ethics. And, reviewing the modern naturalistic temper, one may find evidences of a speculative ethics in the process of suicide. In previous ethics, the enlarging significance of reason creates the very possibility of a rule of value. But modern Naturalism progressively limits and doubts the role of reason. And it contributes at last to an ethical theory which abandons any objective rule of life, and yet seeks to maintain significance for values through anguished personal decision.

Because existential ethics revolts against both the naturalistic and idealistic traditions, it is best to consider it at a later point. But this anti-rational emphasis by which naturalistic ethics prepared the way for an existential alternative may be noted here with propriety. The revolt against reason becomes a characteristic — perhaps the most characteristic — feature of the modern naturalistic constructions of morality. Indeed, this same anti-rational tendency comes increasingly to the fore in modern idealistic traditions as well. The emergence of existential ethics as a definitive twentieth-century viewpoint suggests an observation about the whole of modern ethics.[88] Its crowning tendency, as seen from the alternative to which it leads, is the disparagement of the rational in relationship to the moral. Thus it may develop that Hume and Kant, Marx and Dewey, Nietzsche and Kierkegaard, William James and Karl Barth, are not as antithetical as many writers assume.[89]

Be that as it may, the growing disposition of modern naturalistic ethics has been the enlarging disqualification of reason in the evaluation of reality.

Hume, the Scotsman, argues that men know nothing but their sensations.

Marx, the German Jew, extends the secular, anti-religious revolt against reason. He anticipates Nietzsche in several respects. Both

[88]It suggests also that after pursuing rival courses, Idealism and Naturalism suddenly draw near to each other, appearing as divergent expressions of a single perspective. The search for an alternative to both, today, centers in the question whether the live option is Christian ethics or existential ethics.

[89]"For the understanding of both Kierkegaard and Nietzsche it is of importance to study them together and to interpret them mutually. What is common to both is . . . the return to the Existenz of men in this contemporary Western situation." Karl Jaspers, *Reason and Existenz,* trans. William Earle (New York: Noonday Press, 1955), p. 151.

accepted the mechanistic-materialistic view of the universe to which science paid almost exclusive tribute in the second half of the nineteenth century. Both were atheistic and anti-Hegelian. But Nietzsche stated his view with more deference to the Darwinian evolutionary premise. Marx merges the dialectic with naturalistic determinism as the comprehensive key to reality. This leads to a moral theory consciously and deliberately relativistic; ethical and religious sentiments alike are regarded as reflexes of the economic situation.[90] Rights are simply class assertions, and which defers to the other is suspended upon force alone. The assertion of an absolute ethic is simply the disguised front of class interest. Ethics is nothing more than the vigorous assertion of group will.

Nietzsche asserts that reality is not to be "understood" from the standpoint of reason; consciousness actually distorts existence, for nothing is really identical with anything else. Nature is to be used, not comprehended; life aims at utility, not truth. The ideas which survive in experience are those which subserve the desires by imposing useful correlations upon the chaotic sense world. The forms of thought are an *a priori* equipment of the individual, but they arose *a posteriori* in the species. Logic is but a convenient mode of organizing experience, not a device for comprehending it rationally. The irrationalistic mood is so fundamental in Nietzsche that he divests the evolutionary theory of teleological elements, instead attaching it to a theory of eternal recurrence. Ethics gets an essentially pragmatic turn, oriented to the immediate ends of the Superman. Be it true or false, whether an opinion is life-furthering is all that matters. Even a lie is justifiable if it is serviceable for the Superman's ends.

The disparagement of reason gains expression in French naturalistic ethics also. Comte is not only the proponent of the morality of Positivism, but he assigns the conceptual life a greatly restricted significance. The duty of rejecting all absolute notions of truth and ethics becomes the price of a scientific mind. The concepts of human reason not only arise from experience alone but, as Emile Durkheim proposed, are relative to particular civilizations.

In America, John Dewey narrowed the significance of reason further, in the interest of the pragmatic-instrumentalist view of knowledge. Dewey's great appeal is to experience; whatever science neglects is not worthy of a hearing. Science is disinterested in discovering the nature of reality. It aims, rather, to anticipate how reality changes. By exhibiting the relations in nature, it purposes to control its behavior. Thought is prospective and creative, not retrospective and ontological. The test of the validity of ideas is their consequences. And this prospective methodology of science is to discover, *i.e.,* to establish,

[90]Gordon H. Clark points to the Marx-Engels "technique of abusive language" and "the distortion of history" as further evidence of the abandonment of reason and logical consistency, as well as to the Marxist avoidance of "a coherent explanation of the hitherto prominent problems of philosophy."

the only "values" and "ends" in existence. The ends which work in experience are right, *i.e.,* work. Dewey is compelled, moreover, to abandon the quest for a unitary and objective rule of life, in view of his denial of final ends. No ethical belief is inherently true. Modern man is precluded from an objective verdict about the "moral order" by the merely instrumental significance of reason.[91] But if a principle works in given situations, it should be retained; if another works better, *i.e.,* more efficiently, this should be substituted.

An enlarging company of thinkers now contend that value-claims are simply subjective feeling-claims which cannot be supported by objective rational considerations. Among them are A. J. Ayer, Rudolf Carnap, Bertrand Russell and C. L. Stevenson. The skepticism which Immanuel Kant attached to metaphysics they extend to basic values. All assertions of moral value are regarded as nothing but the expression of individual desires, lacking in rational persuasiveness.

The correlation of values with the non-intellectual phase of experience has been furthered by the value-studies of Joseph Wood Krutch. He voices the acknowledgment of one wing of humanists that, when approached within the tolerated limits of empirical science, the appraisal of values destroys their very worth. To understand values, in the humanist sense, is to disintegrate their claim and usefulness. Krutch emphasizes that love and understanding cannot be considered valid ultimate ends. Dispassionate scientific analysis forfeits the *worth* of love, reducing it to the trivial. The sense of its worthwhileness rises from emotional rather than from rational considerations. "Realistic" humanists, who find this cleavage between knowledge and value unresolvable, have suggested that the disparity can be transcended only by the emergence of a new humanity. Such a suggestion is not far from a kingdom in which the new being comes into existence through moral decision. But it does not take the existential leap: "Ours is a lost cause and there is no place for us in the natural universe, but we are not, for all that, sorry to be human. We should rather die as men, than live as animals."[92]

Logical Positivism has carried through this non-rational orientation of ethics with great vigor. By this school, all ethical judgments are reduced to nothing but emotive preference. Moral evaluations are regarded as neither true nor false, but as assertions of emotional preferment.

[91]It was a remarkably different Dewey, whose insights were closer to truth, who in 1887 penned words which the subsequent development of his thought give an ironic relevance: "In spite of the vigor and ardor with which these ideas [of evolutionary morality] are urged, some of us, at least, remain unmoved. We believe that the cause of theology and morals is one, and that whatever banishes God from the heart of things, with that same edict excludes the ideal, the ethical, from the life of man. Whatever exiles theology makes ethics an expatriate." "Ethics and Physical Science," in *Andover Review,* VII (June, 1887), p. 576.

[92]Joseph Wood Krutch, *The Modern Temper* (New York: Harcourt, Brace, 1929), p. 249.

The connections between the foregoing tendencies and existential ethics are not difficult to discern. The appeal to empirico-pragmatic considerations in the construction of the moral life involves progressively the restriction of the significance of reason. Its ontological importance is denied. Its adequacy to life and experience is denied. The quest for an all-inclusive rule of life is repudiated. The world of reality and experience, in consequence, are bracketed more and more by the category of the irrational. And the absolute significance of the ethical is increasingly suspended upon passionate personal decision and upon a prospective and creative approach to reality.

The road through the mountainous and rugged terrain of naturalistic ethics has included many viewing points, some outlooks contrasting sharply with others, some appearing only as modifications of others. But each has led in turn to a common impression: that a world of reality engulfed wholly in process and change leads to no secure basis for ethical distinctions, least of all to the notion that reality conceived in these shriveled dimensions is disposed toward man's universal or individual happiness. At every juncture such a course discloses open highways which lead directly to the animalization of life. Man is a creature of this life only; he not only bows to nature, but nature's indifference gives him an uncertain tenure and a secret obsession for death. He finds no assurance that unthinking nature "predisposes" social and individual interests, nor that it "legitimizes" long-term mental over immediately-exhausted sense pleasures. Neither does it "respond" to man's adoration and worship, nor "resist" the dedication of its vast powers to corporate or individual destructive uses, to "work" in the service of radically hostile goals. Nature is what Theism and Idealism have always warned that it is — no independent source of moral distinctions and imperatives, but, when regarded only as space-time process, a very absent source of comfort in a time of moral trouble. The shrewd naturalist may profess to discern a permanent imperative (at least for his generation or lifetime, or for this time and place), but it is the idealist who can unhesitatingly insist that a genuine *ought* can be distinguished from the changing *is* only if some realities, moral and spiritual, abide forever. The naturalist contends that complex animality is able to render life worthwhile, even in the face of life's uncertainties and limitations, but the Hebrew-Christian moralist emphasizes the Bible's representation of prudence as among the greatest gifts the Creator-Redeemer God offers to man. Apart from the conviction, adequately grounded, that the moral claim is objective, and constitutive of an unchanging spiritual world to which man is accountable, the notion of right and wrong in Naturalism deteriorates constantly into a matter of personal preference.

Naturalism can neither explain human life, and its moral claim, nor ennoble it. It inculcates inevitably a complacency towards moral evil.

The more consistent its revolt against truth and morality, and against the supernatural spiritual world, the more it seeks not only to justify sin, but to hallow its manifestations, until at last it ventures a scheme of life predicated upon counter-morality. Some followers of Naturalism may revolt against objective morality and yet retain some of its elements for prudential reasons; others may discard the whole, yet halt short of Nietzsche's lust for power. Thoroughgoing Naturalism, however, uncontained by factors of sentiment and prudence, leads to sheer immoralism which rises from the disturbing recognition that, if space-time nature constitutes the whole of reality, the moral imperative is but an arbitrary and external imposition upon the changing movements of reality. The long sweep of naturalistic ethics has coalesced to encourage widespread unbelief in objective standards. For that reason vast multitudes have had only the feeblest standards to invoke, to resist or to challenge those aggressive forces of totalitarianism, which seek by sheer violence to enforce their arbitrary external claims. The much-publicized "strength and maturity" of disbelief in changeless moral distinctions at last exacts as its costly toll man's own weak inability, especially in a tired age which lacks faith in anything eternal, to defy the arbitrary imposition of an ethics sanctioned only by might.

2

IDEALISTIC ETHICS AND THE DEIFICATION OF THE MORAL LIFE

SOMEONE HAS REMARKED that in attempting to escape from moral issues we of necessity collide with them head on. The history of naturalistic ethics is a history of such collision. Naturalism depicts man as an animal trapped in the relativities of the space-time universe for whom it hopefully elaborates a rescuing and sustaining life principle. Idealism recognizes the impossibility of forging such a rule of life on a naturalistic basis. It therefore repudiates Naturalism, as a falsification of reality.

I. ELEMENTAL IDEALISM

Reality involves more than space-time. Man is more than complex animality. Truth and morality include more than convention.

Elemental Idealism emphasizes this "moreness." Suspicious of the naturalistic credo, and even disputatious of it, although not always judiciously so, its criticisms of naturalistic ethics are mostly internal, by the process of checking weaknesses and inconsistencies in the successive efforts of the naturalistic schools. Idealism, however, has little to offer in the way of a convincingly-formulated alternative. It replies by mood and feeling, rather than by the persuasive exposition of a coherent option. It asserts faith in a fringe of reality above nature, in man's superanimality, in distinctions of truth and morality which endure, but it presents no competent vindication.

In this form, Idealism may succeed — for a generation — in preventing a landslide to naturalistic theories of ethics, but it will win few converts from the opposing forces. Idealism could well anticipate a decline of enthusiasm for its own position in a future generation removed from a convincing grasp of the essential bases of the inherited tradition, and continually exposed to a vigorous case for its naturalistic alternative. The naturalistic view requires far less in the way of spiritual decision than its idealistic alternative. The lusts of life predispose man to favor a view which comforts him in the neglect of the noble and in the pursuit of egoistic and fleshly pursuits. Ethics requires, for the sustained realization of the noblest levels of life, the implementation not only of emotional and volitional, but of rational and religious drives as well. Elemental Idealism is content merely to "hold to the high view." It does not state that view with compelling force, frequently even misunderstands it and makes needless and harmful concessions to the opposition. Because of its failure to refute the opponent with the force of reason, the future of such Idealism is not promising. Its spirit becomes eclectic; it selects what it prefers from other views, and maintains its position without a serious devotion to consistency.

A. ANCIENT: POLEMARCHUS

Twice, in Plato's *Republic,* do the representatives of elemental Idealism intrude in character. The first instance is that of Polemarchus. He is the son of Cephalus, an enthusiastic defender of the idealistic view of life, but who, when pressed to vindicate it against pointed objections, begs leave to offer sacrifice to the gods, and bequeaths the debate to the oncoming generation. Polemarchus, who sets out to uphold his inherited view, soon compromises its essential turning-points; he knows the broad outlines only superficially. Under cross-examination, he attaches to the term "justice," in a series of philosophic retreats, a variety of senses, and settles at last for relativizing it according to the nature of the recipient of one's acts: justice is giving every person his due according to his friendship or enmity toward the actor or moral agent.[1] Thus the moral *ought,* even in the mouth of a spokesman for the "high view," becomes only a rule of expedience.

B. ANCIENT: GLAUCON

Elemental Idealism has abler representation than that of Polemarchus; it may stand rather with Glaucon and Adeimantus. *The Republic* graphically pictures their moral temper. They are, on their own confession, ranged with Idealism against Naturalism. They are able not only to repeat the arguments for Naturalism with precision, but to repeat the naturalistic objections to idealistic ethics so incisively that they seem to be speaking for ethical relativism. "They say," volunteers Glaucon, picking up the naturalistic temper, that the practice of justice arises simply by way of social necessity, that men practice it unwillingly, and that all the benefits of the just life accrue to those who merely appear to be just, without actual submission to its demands. About the only justification which they have heard for virtue in the traditional sense, even in the house of its friends, is that the gods approve it; that is, virtue is to be practiced for the sake of the rewards to which it leads (as an instrumental good only) and not because it is intrinsically good. Glaucon and Adeimantus challenge Socrates to show that virtue must be pursued for its own sake, and not simply as an instrumental good.

C. MODERN REFLECTIONS

An underlying characteristic of "grass-roots Idealism," in contrast to sturdier philosophical expositions, is the ready acceptance of the

[1]Cf. Plato, *The Republic,* i, 332.

"prevailing" view of man and of the universe, and the effort to append thereto an objective moral system, or to modify it only at the secondary level. The moral cannot be reduced to the natural; there is more to reality than nature. If this concept were outlined competently, it would involve a revision of the naturalistic view of nature and of man, rather than simply the attachment of a mysterious fringe to currently-accepted naturalistic explanations. Despite the pressure of the contrary view, most moderns, whose doubts have not been undergirded by a comprehensive naturalistic schematization of reality, as in Communist-indoctrinated circles, still incline to the view that moral distinctions basically are not man-made, and that man, despite his animality, has a peculiar awareness of moral realities to which he owes an allegiance. He has a special responsibility — strange in the animal world — to his fellow men. Sometimes the Golden Rule, which among the Utilitarians was attached to a naturalistic base, gains through this elemental Idealism the meaning only that we are obliged — in Polemarchus' ambiguous words — to accord to every man "his due." "The Good" is not reducible to relativism, nor to pleasure nor power, nor to a resignation to space-time determinism. It is to be found in something distinct from these, in something called justice, righteousness, goodness.

But the intelligible exposition of this position is not forthcoming from elemental Idealism. There is confidence that moral realities exist, but how they constitute moral order, what are their inner relationships, and their connection with natural laws of physics, biology, zoology, and anthropology, remain a mystery. No attempt is made to articulate the moral order with the same zeal with which the naturalists venture to define the natural order. No science of the moral world is placed alongside the science of the physical world. And where there is only a science of nature, and no science of morals, the elemental idealist is removed only by pious imagination from the naturalistic account of life and reality.[2] Consequently, the elemental idealist does not forge a pattern of life compellingly different from that of the naturalist who sets the fashions of behavior; he is not prepared to raise a well-formulated protest when his children are indoctrinated by a naturalistic philosophy of education (in modern times, John Dewey's). The political views he holds and the candidates he supports, and the basis on which he suspends moral action, draw no clearly discernible line which sets him in contrast to the naturalist who applies his own tradition with some hesitancy and inconsistency. The line between elemental Idealism and elemental Naturalism frequently blurs. And this blur can be eliminated only by elaborating a science of the moral order.

[2]Some naturalists (cf. Henry Nelson Wieman's *The Source of Human Good* [Chicago: University of Chicago Press, 1946]) more fervently attempt the definition of the moral situation than many who hold a firm but elemental conviction that moral distinctions are genuinely objective and unchanging.

II. SYSTEMATIC IDEALISM

To make the idealistic view practically significant it must be demonstrated as metaphysically significant. When, alongside knowledge of the natural order, there is a knowledge of the moral order equally articulate, idealistic ethics gains scientific standing.

A. RATIONAL IDEALISM: PLATO, ARISTOTLE, HEGEL

Although he may be simply Plato's mouthpiece, Socrates in *The Republic* carries the burden of argument in behalf of the idealistic interpretation of ethics. To show that the good life is not merely extrinsically good, but intrinsically good, is the volume's high objective. The good life is to be pursued not simply for the sake of the rewards to which it leads, but for its own sake.

The positive presentation of the idealistic view is preceded by an incisive criticism of naturalistic ethics. This critique holds permanent value not only because of its refutation of ancient views, but because of its anticipation of positions which Naturalism came to champion in strength in later eras — the natural origin of laws by social contract, the equasion of justice with political might, and so forth.

Socrates does not wrestle systematically with the naturalistic view until he finds in Thrasymachus an advocate who earnestly attempts its justification by relating it to a comprehensive naturalistic account of the world and of life. It is then that Socrates drives Thrasymachus gradually to the admission that the man who recognizes no principles is neither wise nor good, while the life of the wise and good man is held together by the principle of proportion or harmony; that the man who recognizes no principle is not strong but is foredoomed to disunity and dissolution; that the man who recognizes no principle is not happy, since the function of the soul is to live, and its virtue is to live well.

But Socrates is aware that a systematic presentation of idealistic ethics requires more than an exhibition of the inadequacies of its alternatives, and even an acknowledgment of these weaknesses by its partisans. Even more indispensable is the exhibition of the idealistic option in order to show its superiority as an explanation of the phenomena of the moral life. To do this, Socrates appeals not to immediate experience alone, but to the experience of the human race, to man as a socio-rational being, in the larger sweep of history, in order to find there the supportives of a science of the moral order. Reflective Idealism transcends common sense Idealism in the thoroughness with which it wrestles with the foundations of morality. It enforces the disbelief that all moral distinctions are relative by showing that a proper interpretation of reality excludes this possibility. The metaphysical order undergirds the moral order in a decisive manner, and the bearing of one on the other may be detected by critical analysis of man in his setting. This setting is not merely geographical, biological, and economic; it is rational and social, and as such, includes the climate of eternity.

The great turning points of the idealistic interpretation of morality set forth in *The Republic* have been pressed against the naturalistic interpretation of life ever since. The basic convictions represent not only the Socratic-Platonic-Aristotelian tradition, or the so-called classic Greek mind, but also the dominant tradition of modern philosophy — from Descartes and Leibnitz through Hegel and Lotze to Royce, Hocking and Flewelling.

The factors which Naturalism elevates to prime importance, the idealistic tradition brackets by larger considerations. Nature is real, but it is not the only reality, nor is it ultimate. Man is an animal, yes, he has a physical nature subject to space-time laws and to death, but that does not exhaust his personality; he is unique in the creature world. Much that passes for knowledge is opinion, subject to revision. Many requirements of behavior are nothing but convention, but the sphere of truth and goodness cannot be reduced to subjective and arbitrary distinctions.

More precisely, the idealistic elaboration of the ethical situation asserts the logical priority of an eternal, invisible supernatural realm, of an ultimate spiritual and mental reality over the natural space-time world. It affirms that man is superior to other creatures by virtue of a unique relationship to this supernatural world, which constitutes him distinctively a rational animal. As a bearer of Divine reason, he transcends the space-time world, and is destined for spiritual immortality beyond death. Idealism stresses that genuine distinctions of truth and morality are eternal and changeless; they are an aspect of reality objectively addressed to man as fixed norms which he cannot violate without impugnity.

Whatever distinctions part idealistic moralists in their separate expositions of this sober handling of ethical realities, they share this common framework. Their essential differences arise beyond this setting of initial conviction. The ethical views of *The Republic* or *Laws* of Plato are not in some important respects dissimilar from Aristotle's *Nichomachean Ethics,* and from Hegel's *Philosophy of Right,* and Hocking's *The Meaning of God in Human Experience*; the dissimilarities are not as fundamental as the basic agreements. According to Plato, rational analysis of man in his social and historical setting yields an insight into the changeless order of truth and morality. Critical reflection on man's ratio-moral situation in life yields demonstrative proof of this objective eternal order. Man as man stands in constant interaction with this invisible spiritual realm. He is peculiarly related to this supernatural sphere, and in and through this relationship transcends the mere limits of animal complexity, and gains a unique status in the creature world.

That human nature and its presuppositions are best analyzed by critical reflection upon the social whole, upon the larger Man, is a basic idealistic emphasis. The happiness of the individual, defined as the rationally pleasurable, is harmonious with the interests of society. An analogy exists between the just man and the just state. Hence Plato proposes to arrive at a definition of justice, or virtue, by an analysis of the state. What, he asks, are the essential conditions for its well-being?

Because man has an animal, or physical side, the biological and economic aspect of life must be conserved; the neglect of the natural basis of life spells disaster and death. In his analysis of the state, therefore, Plato first stresses the necessity of craftsmen, whose energies are devoted to ministering to the material needs of mankind. While theoretically each individual might be his own baker, carpenter, dress-maker and farmer, the interests of all are best served even on this level if society is tempered by individuals who specialize in the area of their peculiar vocational gifts. Some will minister to the aesthetic and cultural sides of life, for a society which lacks such emphasis might be fit for brutes, but would leave human nature unsatisfied.

Once a state elaborates the cultural and technical sides of life, however, it invites aggression by an enemy state. It becomes necessary, therefore, to maintain troops for purposes of defense. In keeping with the principle already established for craftsmen, Plato opposes a citizens' army and urges a professional standing army skilled in the devices of warfare.

But a social group with only craftsmen and soldiers, and lacking in executive leadership, is not worthy of designation as a state. The state has a soul as well as a body; it has a rational-spiritual, as well as a physical, reality. Even here Plato, though dead, speaks still to modern political science. Just as the natural basis of the state is sustained by its craftsmen, and protection is provided by its troops, so the state gains its guarantee of endurance from qualified rulers. The rule of the state is not to be entrusted to just any of its citizens; a skilled haberdasher fulfills his contribution best as a craftsman, a skilled general as a warrior. The direction of the state must fall to those who specialize in a disciplined insight into those invisible spiritual and moral principles that supply the timeless ideals of a just society. Thus Plato stipulates a rigid course of study for those who are to have a role in guiding the destinies of the states. They are to go, without compulsion, beyond the study of physics and the natural and biological sciences, and beyond mathematics, to acquire comprehension of the invisible metaphysical realities, including the ultimate principles of morality. They are to gain practical experience by public service in subordinate posts; from those who have reached the age of fifty, the most able, who have reached the vision of the good, will be asked to divide their time between further meditation and government service in a role of supreme counsel. Even among these rulers Plato distinguishes guardians, who are assigned legislative responsibility, from the larger class of auxiliaries, whose responsibility is executive. The ultimate ideal as ruler of the just state is the philosopher-king.

The perfect, or just, state is one which is rightly-ordered. There is concord in all its classes as to the ultimate seat of authority. The craftsmen provide, through their unity in diversity, the element of temperance; the warriors supply the state with courage; the rulers provide the state with wisdom in their deliberative role. Thus the perfect state reflects the cardinal virtues of wisdom, courage, and temperance. And where is justice? Justice is simply the proper concord of all these virtuous elements within the whole.

From the "social man" or the ideal state, Plato is able to read off the characteristics of the just individual. The analogy between the ideal state and the virtuous man is found in justice defined as right harmony or proportion. As the craftsmen are to the state, so the emotions are to the individual — diverse, yet tempering life favorably when consecrated to superior ends. As the warriors are to the state, so the volition is to the individual — supplying life with its spirit and drive. As the rulers are to the state, so reason is to the individual — the supreme authority which the will and feelings are to subserve. Justice is the proper harmony of reason, volition, and emotion in the individual life, and is achieved by the enthronement of reason as the soul's seat of authority.

This insistence, that the microcosm mirrors the macrocosm, that man on the spiritual side of his being is a part of the Absolute Reason and Ethical Will, and that the social whole therefore reflects ultimate moral and rational reality in large letters, is characteristic of all idealistic expositions of man and of the universe. Alongside the experience of the moment, and of the individual life in detachment from its social and cosmic setting, a larger dimension is brought into view, and man is exhibited as constantly confronted by the claims of the ultimate spiritual and moral world.

Beneath this idealistic construction stands an exorbitantly optimistic view of human nature. The essential continuity of human and Divine reason is affirmed. On the spiritual side of his being, man is pictured as a fragment of Divinity; the Absolute Reason and Good are simply a totality of human rational and ethical experience. That is why the ideal ruler in Platonic thought is the Philosopher King, rather than the Redeemer-Messiah of Hebrew-Christian revelation. The dogma that man is a fragment of Divinity means that his moral problem reduces to one of forgetfulness, of ignorance, of rational and moral norms always accessible to him on the basis of his intrinsic Divinity.

The fact that universal moral reflection has not articulated identical accounts of the ideal content of morality has cast doubt on the validity of the idealistic statement of the ethical situation. Even those who seek to vindicate the objectivity of the moral order are not without some measure of contradiction in their statements of its nature. Plato does not identify the Idea of the Good with the will of God, but regards it as a reality external to Deity. Hegel regards the Good as identical with the Absolute, yet as emerging only by a gradual evolutionary process in human history. Edgar S. Brightman depicts ethical values as autonomous, regarding only moral norms as theonomous, representing God as finite and contending with an "irrational given" in his own nature. In modern times, the thesis that moral imperatives may be more clearly distilled from the conduct of the social whole, rather than from the individual, has been under special attack, on the ground that group principle and behavior are often more evasive of their responsibilities than are individuals.[3]

The Hebrew-Christian view has its own way of accounting for this diversity. It protests that idealistic ethics conceals man's dependency as a creature, and obscures, therefore, his need of Divine general revelation for the knowledge of the Good. The knowledge of God and of his will may be stamped upon man by creation, but it is never accessible to him as a corollary of intrinsic divinity. Man's access to the moral and spiritual realm is not simply a matter of his rational initiative but, in view of his finitude, involves a dependency upon the reality of supernatural revelation.

This brings us to a second characteristic of idealistic ethics. It tends to equate the knowledge of the good with realized virtue, assuming its performance to follow automatically. The Socratic formula "knowledge is virtue" pointedly gives voice to this weakness. Plato regards virtues not as abstractions but as "powers"; a man of great virtue is for him a man who actualizes his ability to live in a certain manner.[4] The Aristotelian notion, that virtue is habit, reflects the same basic weakness. The good is already implied in the will; the problem of ethics is only to preserve the *mean*. The will is thought to be in the service of the good automatically,[5] except for the invasion of life by emotional factors

[3]This is the thrust of Reinhold Niebuhr's *Moral Man and Immoral Society* (New York: Scribner, 1932).

[4]In Latin, the word *virtus* gains the meaning "power."

[5]"One of the greatest of the ideas taught by Socrates, and immortalized by Plato, is that no one can ever do anything wrong on purpose, that evil doing is ignorance, and that the man who knows can never do wrong." Freeman and Appel, *The Great Ideas of Plato* (New York: Lantern Press, 1952), p. 85. To show the fallacy of this contention by demonstrating the contrary thesis, that men knowingly desire what is evil for them, is no light task, for this thesis is especially repugnant to man as sinner. But the biblical threat of final judgment stresses man's guilt in view of a deliberately spurned knowledge of the truth. There is greater comfort, of course, in a doctrine of ignorance which exempts one from accountability. But the Christian doctrine is not that man lacks all knowledge of God, nor of his personal revolt against the Divine will, nor of a consequent eligibility for future retribution. The distinguishing factor here is the biblical emphasis on man's inordinate will, by which reason is enslaved. The natural man is directed against the good will of God and does not strive after the good. Man as sinner not only wills inferior goods above the absolute, but he wills evil in the guise of good, through rationalization. He does not perform evil

which are tangential to the real core of man's being. But human history does not support this confidence. The universal plight of man is that, limited as his knowledge of the good may be, his actual performance is beggarly; he stands constantly condemned by light to which he shuts his mind. The Hebrew-Christian doctrine, that man is a sinner, that his will is in bondage to evil, that he is in revolt against the will of God, thus lays hold of idealistic ethics at a vulnerable point.

Enforced by this principle, Hebrew-Christian ethics also assailed the confident rationalism of classic Idealism by pointing out that sin has noetic consequences, enslaving the mind. It charged idealistic ethics not only with concealing the necessity of general revelation for man's creaturely acquaintance with the knowledge of God and of his will, but it leveled a further charge, namely, that the concealment of man's sinfulness also obscured his need of special Divine revelation for the normative definition of the content of morality. Moreover, this irrelevance of a redemptive framework severed the Platonic and Aristotelian ethic from those higher and fuller moral energies necessary for sustained ethical earnestness.

Hebrew-Christian ethics thus resisted both the naturalistic animalization and the idealistic divinization of moral experience. The strength of the idealistic theories, that the rule of life is to be discerned rationally by sustained meditation about the very presuppositions of experience and not by an attempt merely to organize sense experience into a universal principle of conduct, also supplied its great danger. It gave way to speculative rationalism, which denied any limits to human reason, either on the basis of creation or in the predicament of sin, and thus prepared the way for a reactionary type of ethical Idealism which would seriously compromise the role of theoretical or conceptual reason in the moral experience of man.

A third characteristic of idealistic ethics is that, while defending the objectivity of ethical distinctions, it does not convincingly transcend its anthropological starting-point. Despite the emphasis that all concerns of this life are to be viewed from the standpoint of eternity, the development of this supernatural perspective rises out of the untenable assumption of the essential divinity of the rational soul of man. Plato indeed rises above the standpoint of the later Kantian ethic in implicitly acknowledging that the moral law cannot be defended simply in terms of autonomy. Man requires contact with the intellectual-moral-spiritual world which exists outside, as well as within, the moral agent. Man possesses a latent capacity for recognizing the good, and the doctrine of recollection is invoked in order to link the inner with the

---

unknowingly. Man as sinner is capable of a generous self-deception, of pursuing evil in the false comfort that he is exempt from punishment, although he is never wholly ignorant of his compromised position before God. Against the Platonic view, the Pauline doctrine emphasizes that the unregenerate man does not perform what elements of good he knows, nor indeed can he. Neither does he will to do the good despite his knowledge that God punishes wickedness and approves goodness.

outer order. But the doctrine presupposes both the pre-existence of the soul and its essential Divinity. The collapse of this assumption necessarily capitulates Idealism into the welter of Naturalism. The sacrifice of this starting-point cuts man off from objective moral norms.

Hebrew-Christian ethics adduced two considerations which tended to lift ethical discussion above this anthropological point of view. They have supplied for multitudes an answer to the uneasy question which haunts idealistic ethics: how can we show that what man salutes as an objective *ought* is ultimately and actually so? How can we be sure that what we regard as the *ought* actually structures reality as one of its constitutive features? Lacking a convincing answer, idealistic ethics could not lift the individual with assurance above himself, nor enlist him effectively in the social task.

These two aforementioned considerations were the doctrine of creation, with its corollary implication of general Divine revelation, and the assertion of special redemptive revelation. The idealistic correlation of man and the Absolute may leave room for a doctrine of pantheistic emanation, but it does not accommodate a creation doctrine with its emphasis on the otherness of God. Without such a creation doctrine, idealistic ethics falls into frustration — as did naturalistic ethics before it — in the attempt to vindicate alongside the halting moral prejudices of man an objective and eternal order of the *moral ought*. The idealistic traditions tend to obscure the person and will of God, except as they come in their later expression under the influence of Hebrew-Christian emphases. Plato's writings attempt to vindicate the good as a reality independent of the will of God (cf. the *Euthyphro*); whether the gods love it or not is no central consideration. Thus absolute morality loses the attractive power which it gains through the conceptions of an ethical creation and an ethical redemption. Worse yet, Plato does not derive the content of morality from the Idea of the Good, but starting with the accepted virtues of the Greeks, and their social manifestation, he appears to allow popular psychology to dictate the content of the virtuous life. This complaint is even more forceful when turned against Aristotle, for his ethics is even more in accord with common opinion than Plato's. If the sense of *ought* in man becomes the exclusive and decisive criterion for the construction of the moral order, then two consequences follow. One is that if the moral order is identified with man's ethical sense, it can no longer be shown that the moral order exists independently of him as a reality by which his sense of *ought* is objectively measured. Can we be sure that the compunction of conscience is at the same time the compunction of reality as a whole? The doctrine of creation provides an answer which inverts the question, placing man on the defensive. The moral purposes of the supernatural Creator confront man as a responsible moral creature in the claims of conscience. Is man sure that, in his creaturely existence, he has not obscured nor transgressed those purposes?

The other consideration is that the specific content which individual conscience attaches to the ethical situation is brought under the effective criticism of the moral order by the doctrine of special redemptive revelation, proclaimed by the Hebrew-Christian movement. Conscience is quickened in relation to the eternal moral order, by bringing man as sinner under the criticism of absolute morality. The thesis that the True and the Good are the ultimate constitutive elements in the universe of being, and that the thrust of reality is providential and teleological, gains peculiar vividness from the appeal to the special redemptive acts of God, and from the miraculous works of Jesus Christ whereby he exhibited the laws of nature as instruments of Divine providence and as symbols of the influence of Divine grace.

The idealistic tendency to distill absolute moral principles from the nature of man in his present condition of sin and revolt, as if he were in fact a part of God, thus clashed with the Hebrew-Christian message, which proclaimed to the Graeco-Roman world that ethical standards are not to be based upon man, but upon the will of God who is man's judge. This tension recurred with the rise of modern philosophy, but its outlines were blurred by the capitulation of large segments of Christian thought, in the form of Protestant Liberalism, to the essential emphases of the Kantian and Hegelian statements of the moral situation. Beneath the contrastive idealistic and Christian expositions of morality, however, stood distinctive epistemological, anthropological, soteriological, and theological assumptions. For Plato, human reason is able to comprehend Divine reason because it is in principle an extension of the Divine; for Hebrew-Christian theism, man is a finite and dependent creature and, even as a bearer of the image of God, stands in constant dependence upon Divine revelation. For Plato, man delights in the good, so much so that education in the truth will assure the performance of virtue; for the revelational view, man is a fallen sinner inclined toward ethical disobedience and in need of Divine regeneration for the achievement of the good life. For Plato, sin is mere imperfection, or ignorance, and hence man's salvation lies in reason; for the biblical tradition, man is involved in moral disobedience, and exposed to Divine penalties, from which the only deliverance is to be found by recourse to redemptive atonement and forgiveness. For Plato, the reality of the supernatural is not clarified beyond ambiguity as to the nature of God, except for the identification of Cosmic Reason with justice; for the Judeo-Christian view, God is the sovereign, personal Creator, Redeemer and Judge of the race, the source and sanction of ultimate distinctions of truth and morality. A staggering difference is implied by these alternatives for the moral situation. But none is more important than the idealistic tendency to frame ethical realities by a moral order which has impersonalistic overtones. It is this vulnerable element which, in fact, gives to Idealism in its modern expressions a novel turn in the history of ethics.

B. POSTULATIONAL IDEALISM: KANT, PERSONALISM

While rationalistic Idealism is revived in modern times by Hegel and Lotze and their successors, ethical Idealism in its distinctively modern form gains its decisive features from Immanuel Kant (1724-1804). Kant shares the classic Greek determination to preserve the absolute character of the ethical idea. But the manner in which he does so gives rise to the tradition of postulational Idealism.

Against the rising tide of naturalistic speculation set in motion by Hume, Kant undertook the vast task of elaborating a critique of knowledge, analyzing its limits and presuppositions. Whereas Hume aimed to ground all experience — moral and every other — in nothing but sense impressions and memory images of these, and thus assigned a relative character to all judgments, Kant sought to vindicate the universal and necessary character of truth and morality.

The new scientific explanation of the world left as profound an impression upon post-medieval Idealism as upon post-medieval Naturalism. Plato and Aristotle represented the forms of Goodness, Truth and Beauty as constituting the whole of reality a teleological order, and on the ground of its essential divinity pictured the rationality of man as capable of conceptually knowing the ultimate and objective order of things. Kant begins, however, with a twofold debt to the prevailing modern scientific philosophy. He accepts the prevailing explanation of the space-time universe as a mechanically-determined order in which the objective existence of rational purposes and benevolent goals is an unimportant consideration for charting its behavior. In contrast with both utilitarian and optimistic evolutionary schools of thought of a later day, Kant held that morality is unrelated to nature, and that the phenomenal man is bound to the sense world; ethics attaches only to the world of reason, so that only as the man of moral decision does man have an ethical destiny. And, while Kant aims to overthrow the sensationalist theory of knowledge, he concedes to the empirical theories the important assumption that the content of knowledge is supplied by sense experience alone. The Newtonian concept of scientific method not only combined mathematical deduction with empirical verification, but also assigned the ultimate emphasis to sense verifiability. Kant allows the new science to give sensationalistic orientation to his knowledge theory.

In the *Critique of Pure Reason* Kant strikes hard against the attempted reduction of all knowledge experience to sense percepts. Such a theory would degenerate man from a rational and moral agent to a complex animal. For that reason Empiricism represented a more serious attack upon human dignity and uniqueness than the later Darwinian derivation of man's physical features from an animal ancestry. If man's rational and moral experience was essentially that of complex brutes, plus only a special perseverance in comparing and adding sensations, it would matter little how man's physical nature was explained, for he could not in any event aspire to any permanently valid knowledge, and all prospect of a durable culture would be threatened. Kant saw the latent implications of the Humean theory of knowledge and aimed to overthrow it.

Kant stresses that knowledge experience contains features which are not derivable from sensation, particularly synthetic judgments *a priori*. In the spheres of science and mathematics, truths are cast in a universal and necessary form which exceeds the limitations of experience. What is needed to explain the facts of epistemology is the recognition that reason supplies the form while sensation supplies the content of knowledge. Without the innate categories of reason and forms of perceiving, the flux of sensation would be an unintelligible conglomerate. Without sensations, the forms would be devoid of content and unproductive. Knowledge is a joint product of the rational innate forms and of the sense-contributed content; only through the innate categories does sensation become orderly and intelligible.

This theory of knowledge stands in sharp contrast to that of classic Graeco-Roman Idealism, and to that of medieval theism as well. The primary difference is Kant's surrender of all cognitive or theoretical knowledge of the metaphysical world, in view of his adoption of the empirical emphasis that sensation (and hence the phenomenal world) supplies the only content of knowledge. For Kant, the reality of the spiritual world, and its nature, is never a matter of knowledge, but is postulated for other than theoretical considerations. Man can have no knowledge, he asserts, of spiritual realities nor of objective purposes and ends; these are affirmations of faith in the absence of knowledge. Hence the framework of Kant's ethics is postulational Idealism. Plato and Aristotle, like Hegel in modern times, asserted that man's knowledge extends to the invisible spiritual and moral order, of whose reality and nature he can frame a demonstrative rational proof. Hebrew-Christian Theism asserted that evidence of the absolute character of the ethical idea confronts man in the fact of general Divine revelation, and that further conclusive and normative testimony concerning the content of morality is set forth in the special biblical revelation; therefore, what cannot be proved by rational demonstration is nonetheless accessible to human reason on the basis of Divine revelation. But according to Kant, the moral order can neither be rationally demonstrated nor divinely revealed, because of the limits of human reason. Its status is simply that of a necessary postulate, if men are to live and act as rational beings.

While man is shut off from any knowledge of the metaphysical world, he is not, on that account, according to Kant, to draw a skeptical and animalistic interpretation of life. For man is constituted not only by certain rational forms, but by a moral *a priori*. He is structured by an "I ought!" This is a *categorical imperative* — not merely a declarative ("I shall"), but an imperative; not an hypothetical ("if I will") but categorical. The voice of duty is absolute; it tolerates no "if's and but's." Only to the extent that man recognizes this "I ought" and conforms his life to it, acting out of a sense of duty, does he really exist in the dignity of humanity. He may disregard the "I ought," but he can never destroy it. If he disregards it, he lives as an animal; if he lives rationally, conforming his conduct to the moral ought, he acts by a universal moral criterion which confers dignity and worth upon life. To shrug off one's oughts is to shrug off humanity. The sense of duty does not oppress him, but rather constitutes him as man. *I am* to the extent that I recognize the "I ought" and conform life to it, not simply because "I doubt" or "I think" (Descartes), nor because I have a complex animal existence. The denial of the moral ought amounts to a denial of self-consciousness. The essential nature of the self involves an *ought*: "I ought" therefore "I am."

For Kant, nothing is good except the good will. Virtue which is performed by accident, or for the sake of rewards, or of advantageous consequences to which it leads (*e.g.*, pleasure, whether egoistic or altruistic) is not virtue at all. Only duty done for duty's sake, out of reverence for moral law alone, is duty.

How is this formal sense of duty to be translated into meaningful action? The categorical imperative implies the universality and impartiality of moral action; the ethical life is to reflect that universality and necessity which characterize all rational experience. We are to act toward others by a principle which at the same time we may will to serve as universal law. We are not to treat others merely as means, but always as ends. Kant regards this as the essence of the Golden Rule, even as Mill and the Utilitarians thought it could be equated with that viewpoint.[6]

What the Hebrew-Christian tradition identified as the revelation in conscience of the will of God for man as a creature fashioned in rational and moral responsibility, Kant regarded only as the interior demand of reason asserting universal law. This feeling of duty, according to Kant, confronts us *as if* it were a Divine command. The categorical imperative drives us to postulate God as the ultimate source of the moral nature; the sense of "I ought" requires (the sense of) "Thou shalt." Only thus can man be assured that the universe itself is a rational world which aims at duty, and that disinterested virtue is rewarded by ultimate happiness rather than frustrated. Faith therefore

[6]Doubtless Kant is influenced, in his doctrine of the good will, by the Christian idealism of his pietistic upbringing, with its emphasis on a virtuous will in opposition to externalism. He rightly protests, also, against all who think the performance of right acts out of a sense of duty is inferior, and represents a low conception of the moral life. Undoubtedly ethical conduct which springs from the sense of duty in a legalistic spirit, and apart from personal enthusiasm, is subethical; the Hebrew-Christian movement constantly contrasts the law as a mere outward and foreign compulsion with the ideal of the law written upon the heart. But Kant's ethics is nonetheless separated by a great gulf from the spirit of the Golden Rule, which excludes any abstraction of duty from the revealed will of God as its supreme source and sanction.

is given a determinative scope in the sphere of practical reason, in the necessary absence of all knowledge of the supersensible moral and spiritual world. While man has no conceptual knowledge of God, he is impelled therefore to postulate God as a regulative ideal. And, although no logical demonstration of freedom and of the immortality of the soul is possible, yet these are to be postulated by faith. The moral inequities of this life imply a future redress, without which the present moral life would lose significance. God and immortality and the objectivity of the moral order are thus postulated as faith-constructs after Kant's initial disavowal of all knowledge of them. The impossibility of metaphysical knowledge, he contends, renders such faith forever secure; if no man can adduce a logical demonstration of the objective spiritual order, neither can any man adduce a logical disproof thereof.

The most remarkable feature of Kant's theory of ethics is his assertion of the priority of the moral life, or of the practical reason, over metaphysical and theoretical considerations. The whole history of thought prior to his day had asserted the dependence of the ethical upon the metaphysical. Define the nature of reality as a whole, it asserted, and the rule of life becomes plain. Naturalism exhibited one cosmic setting for man, and alongside it, a corresponding rule of life; classic Idealism sought to vindicate an alternate metaphysics, and a corresponding interpretation of the moral life; biblical theism presented a distinctive view of God and of the world, professedly revelational, and alongside it a revelational ethics. As the German scholars expressed this interrelationship, *Weltanschauung* determines *Lebensauschauung* — world-view determines life-view. But Kant's metaphysical skepticism excludes a knowledge of the noumenal world. The moral *a priori* structures human nature, and demands a certain faith-view. Hence, for Kant, life-view determines world-view, ethics determines metaphysics — although we must be careful to regard the spiritual world as only regulative and not as literal.

Thus Kant is able to crown his optimistic moral view only by a denial of any theoretical grasp of the metaphysical world, and by refusing to make any claims about the space-time world except from the subjective standpoint of how it exists for man as its perceiver. Only by such a costly epistemological transaction could the moral demands and ideals of human nature be rendered "secure."

If there was much which was objectionable in the ethics of rational Idealism, those objections were compounded by Kant's alternative view. Both share the staggering assumption of man's direct moral continuity with the Divine, the one by affirming also his spiritual identity with the Divine, and the other by venturing to postulate God in the moral image of man's ethical nature. Both excluded any radical judgment or condemnation of human ideals from a Divine standpoint, and hence ruled out in advance the biblical doctrine of the sinfulness of man.[7] Imperfection there might be, through the yielding of life to sub-rational impulses, yet man as man, in his rational and ethical activity, was taken as the direct manifestation of the Divine mind and will. When human nature supplies the central locus of the tension between the *is* and the *ought,* the deification of the rational or intelligible self follows as a matter of course. The attempt to define the *ought* merely by an empirical analysis of the *is* involves always a highly optimistic view of man. Moreover, while the affirmation of an *ought* involves at the same time an assertion that the ought *is,* the existence of a genuine *ought* tends to be placed in doubt through the concealment of its differences from the *is* in the sphere of created and fallen human life.

Both traditions therefore — the Socratic and Kantian alike — set in motion a vast tide of moral reflection aiming to vindicate the absolute character of morality. The quest for a basic principle of morality, in this optimistic climate, frees itself from the necessity, and then from the propriety, of all external sanction and transcendent aims, until introspection supplies the totality of the moral demand apart from any philosophical or theological considerations. What begins as a venture to buttress the moral claim places it at last in great jeopardy, by seeking to define its nature apart from the rational vindication of any metaphysical order, and by centering increasing interest upon the personal decision of the moral agent as the ultimate foundation of the ethical situation.[8]

Besides this, the Kantian exposition is weakened by certain internal difficulties. One is the purely formal nature of Kantian ethics, and the consequent difficulty of applying it to the practical problems of the moral life. From the definition of virtue merely as the good will, even expanded into the categorical imperative of a universal principle of action, it is not possible to arrive at the material content of ethics.[9] Emil Brunner points out that even the pessimistic Buddhist ethic of renunciation appeals to universality as a decisive ethical principle.[10] Kant gives us in the categorical imperative only a formal principle

[7]Kant's doctrine of "radical evil," indeed, ascribes to every man a tendency to evil, and some of his idealistic contemporaries accused him of surrender to the theological tradition. But, in the outworking of his system, he evaporates the doctrine of radical evil in order to maintain the doctrine of autonomous reason, and by identifying the higher self with the intelligible man. Perhaps at no point did Kant approach so closely to the Christian theology as in grappling with the fact of radical evil. And at no point does his loyalty to the idealistic tradition appear more clearly than in his ultimate refusal to develop this into a doctrine of sin and the fall, and in his defense instead of an autonomous ethic.

[8]The doctrine that God is disclosed to faith in the tug of the categorical imperative, and that in affirmative ethical decision man saves significance for the moral life, thus prepares the way for the contemporary emphasis on the existential leap of faith.

[9]Gordon H. Clark, *A Christian View of Men and Things* (Grand Rapids: Eerdmans, 1952), p. 185.

[10]Emil Brunner, *The Divine Imperative* (Philadelphia: Westminster, 1947), p. 40.

which is obscure as to content, and thus leaves all the ethical issues of practical life in jeopardy.

The deficiency previously found in rationalistic ethics, of showing that ultimate reality corresponds to the moral consciousness of humanity, is even more serious in postulational ethics. To secure this correspondence, rationalistic ethics virtually identifies human rational and moral experience with the Divine nature. Kant is cut off from this possibility by his metaphysical agnosticism, and is compelled to introduce an alien consideration into his system to accomplish the same end. After divorcing moral responsibility from all reference to utility, and after equating virtue with duty for duty's sake, Kant finds it necessary to assure man that the good actually furthers the interest of all, and through faith considerations to connect man's well-being with ethical performance. There is force in Schweitzer's complaint that Kant actually puts "utilitarian ethics under the protectorate of the Categorical Imperative,"[11] as one is tempted to observe both in this connection and in the content which he attaches to the form of morality. But it is only by an abandonment of the regulative nature of these considerations that man can derive the confidence that the individual pursuit of virtue indubitably furthers the general welfare.

Only the Hebrew-Christian revelation of creation transcends this idealistic void between man's sense of absolute obligation and his assurance that it is validated by the structure of ultimate reality. The connection between the subjective conviction of obligation or duty, and the objective world of reality which supplies man's larger setting, cannot be convincingly maintained. Neither the rational idealistic view that the Divine is but the upper side of human experience taken as a totality, nor the postulational view of an "as if" moral order which invests the immanent sense of duty with the aura of Divine command, can accomplish this. If, on the other hand, the moral law within is based in a moral external law addressed to man on the basis of creation, the loss of the Divine in the human is precluded, and of the human in the Divine, as well.

A. E. Taylor rightly stresses that no purely immanentistic ethics can really take morality seriously, because apart from an assured relationship with a superhuman reality the motivation for the pursuit of the good weakens. He writes: "The whole problem is how a man who is absolutely under the domination of 'inclination' ever comes to exhibit pure 'reverence for duty,' uncontaminated by all 'inclination,' in even the least and most trivial act of life."[12] Since the initiative for remaking ethical personality cannot issue from the personality which needs to be remade, Taylor contends, all genuine morality presupposes a supernatural or Divine dynamic.

[11]Schweitzer, *The Philosophy of Civilization*, p. 184.

[12]A. E. Taylor, *The Faith of a Moralist* (London: Macmillan, 1951), p. 217.

A second deficiency of idealistic ethics, therefore, which reaches its most complete expression in the Kantian form, is its immanentistic basis. The intelligible world of moral ideas and ideals is for Kant a product of the practical reason. The categorical imperative thus has a this-worldly origin; moral values are the prescriptions of the autonomous reason. "Even the Holy One of the Gospel must first be compared with our ideal of perfection before he is recognized as such."[13] Not only is the necessity and possibility of a transcendent revelation of the moral law denied, but its exclusion is made the very starting-point of Kantian ethics. Only what is self-legislated can be regarded as duty. The point is not merely that obedience to a moral law without personal enthusiasm is subethical but that for Kant the conception of theonomous ethics is subethical. Kant's view is deliberately antithetical to the Hebrew-Christian view which bases ethics upon the general and special revelation of the will of God. In biblical ethics, man's knowledge of the will of God always presupposes a theistic setting, and rules out an autonomous ethic. Does not even Kant's categorical imperative lean upon a certain Christian atmosphere, which already dominates the sense in which his majestic imperative is to be understood? "Act so your principle of action may become the principle on which all others act" is intended by Kant to exclude egoistic ethics and political Naturalism. But why so? Why could not a Sophist apply the rule, with a resignation to universal relativism? Why not a Nietzsche—allowing to each the imposition of his will to the measure of his ability? The vanishing trail of a Christian doctrine of neighbor-love clings to Kant's categorical imperative and preserves his autonomous ethic from consistent self-expression.

It should create little surprise that Kant's correlation of autonomy and moral earnestness, instead of lending itself to the postulation of a phantom God as a regulative ideal, has been thought to require the deliberate exclusion of every last vestige of theism as a presupposition of the moral situation. This is the unyielding standpoint of Nicolai Hartmann, who contends that an ethical universe requires the rejection of a God who addresses morality to man, and hence rejection of any regard for the categorical imperative as if it were a Divine command.[14]

The hostility to commandment, as irreconcilable with the standpoint of virtue, reflects in actual fact both the Kantian antipathy for a transcendent basis of ethics and Kant's insistence that duty must be self-legislated. "No imperatives hold for the *Divine Will* or in general for a *holy* will; the 'Thou Shalt' is out of place here, because already 'I will' is necessarily of itself in harmony with the law."[15] Now it is well enough to insist that God would be less than God if the good confronted him outwardly, rather than expressed the demand of his

[13]Kant, *The Fundamental Principles of the Metaphysics of Ethics* (New York: Appleton-Century-Crofts, 1938), p. 24.
[14]Nicolai Hartmann, *Ethics* (Allen & Unwin, 1932).
[15]*Op. cit.*, p. 30.

own inner holy nature and will. Likewise it is well enough to insist that moral obedience which is humanly yielded to outward compulsion without inward assent has no genuine ethical significance. It is quite another matter, however, when contemporary moralists like Emil Brunner and Reinhold Niebuhr profess to speak from the standpoint of revelational ethics when they stress the incompatibility of commandment and love. For such a disjunction is essentially Kantian, and its proper atmosphere that of an autonomous ethic.

Kant's influence on recent moral theory has been great, reaching even into traditions which dissent from his position in important respects. His impact is reflected in W. R. Sorley's Gifford Lectures, in which "the argument begins with a discussion of values and ends with the idea of God,"[16] in harmony with Lotze's post-Kantian emphasis that "the true beginning of metaphysics lies in ethics." Sorley, however, seeks to bridge the Kantian and Hegelian traditions; instead of contenting himself with a merely postulated and regulative God, he voices the conviction that an intuitive leap may be made from values to God as their source and support. It is seen also in Edgar S. Brightman's Personalism, with its non-rational "Given"; in the unyielding Kantian rather than Hegelian thesis, that reality is broader than logic; in the assertion that while ethical norms are theonomous, moral values are autonomous.[17]

The focal problem of idealistic ethics has been to bring together the objective good and the inner moral sentiment. Plato accomplished this union by the artificial scheme of the pre-existence and essential divinity of the soul, with its consequent capacity for recollection. The collapse of these notions left Idealism without a new concept until Kant's day. His emphasis on the autonomy of conscience and of the moral law regarded man himself, albeit the universal man, as the sufficient source of clear and infallible moral principles. If Plato jeopardizes both the outer moral order and the inner moral sense, Kant surrenders the former and daringly intensifies the latter. Since God is a moral postulate, no external sanction for morality remains, while the categorical imperative, no longer regarded literally as the *imago Dei* on the basis of creation, is conceived as self-sufficient. But this maneuver ends at last with the robbery even of the inner vision of morality of its reserves. By its neglect of the transcendent basis of ethics, and by its neglect of the active distortion of the internal *imago* through sin, the Kantian view contributes indirectly to the loss of the imperative character, and to the substitution of the optional character, of the inner moral sentiment. Over against Naturalism, the idealistic tradition wrestles more earnestly with two essential elements of the moral problem: first, the conviction that ethical distinctions must not be imposed upon the human spirit entirely from without, as by an

[16]W. R. Sorley, *Moral Values and the Idea of God* (Cambridge: University Press, 1935), p. 1.

[17]Edgar S. Brightman, *Moral Laws* (Nashville: Abingdon Press, 1933).

alien and arbitrary dictator, else man would not be morally responsible by nature, and second, the conviction that unchanging and objective truth and goodness alone secure the moral life from relativism and change. Christian ethics recognizes the importance of these considerations, and it finds the prospect of moral solution in the fact of the *imago Dei.* What Idealism lacks in terms of an effective link between the inner moral imperative and the eternal moral order, Christian ethics professes to possess in the realities of the Divine image in man.

Kant's shadow may be detected on the background of modern existential and dialectical ethics, which we have yet to discuss. To the former he contributes a metaphysical climate of moral experience devoid of all objective teleology and rational synthesis; to the latter, the emphasis that the categories of thought stand to the spiritual world in a relationship of antinomy. But, in a broader sense, the larger tradition of idealistic ethics, by its bold claim to speak for the standpoint of ultimate and absolute Reason, while yet its deliverances are generously particularistic and cultural, contributed to a loss of confidence in the standpoint of "objective reason." Idealistic ethics especially has represented itself as the impartial reflection of universal reason upon the ethical predicament of the human race. But the longer the trail of idealistic systems, the longer becomes the list of divergences to confirm skepticism over any idealistic analysis of ethical judgments from an impartial, rational perspective which is wholly unconditioned. "The perspective of the moral philosopher," George F. Thomas reminds us, "is not that of universal reason reflecting impartially upon the *general* moral experience of mankind; it is that of his own reason conditioned by the *particular* moral experience of his time and place."[18]

C. IRRATIONAL REACTION

Not until the post-Hegelian reaction against absolute Idealism sets in, does the anti-intellectual spirit assert itself consciously in the interest of supplying a deliberate moral and spiritual perspective. The reaction to the ethics of rationalistic Idealism and postulational Idealism only gradually shapes itself into an ethics of irrationalism.

This drift to irrationalism was already mildly underway in the post-Kantian romanticism of Fichte and Schopenhauer. Even the restricted significance which Kant attached to reason came soon to be disowned, and his emphasis on reason's limitations enlarged. The revolt against reason acquires full momentum with the rise of an anti-Hegelian reaction. Hegel himself had prepared the way for doubt as to an absolute reason and morality by regarding the whole of reality as a

[18]Thomas, *Christian Ethics and Moral Philosophy,* p. 376. Thomas scores the important point that the idealist has no right to reproach the Christian moralist for according a special place to Hebrew prophets and Christian apostles, since he "accords a 'privileged position' to the particular moral experience of ancient Greeks or modern Europeans." There is a difference, however, in that the idealistic moralist does this unwittingly, the Christian moralist, intentionally.

process, and by his acknowledgment that "without the world there is no God." Instead of the emphasis that the world of reality is conceived rationally by the knowing subject, the notion prevails that the world is falsified by attempts to conform it to reason; reality answers, rather, to the category of the irrational.

That the real is the irrational gains a twofold exposition, one supernaturalistic and religious, the other naturalistic and anti-religious. The former is fathered by Soren Kierkegaard (1813-1855), who becomes the forerunner of existential ethics; the other, as we have already noted, by Marx (1818-1885) and Nietzsche (1844-1900).

With the rediscovery of Kierkegaard and Nietzsche, the ideological connection between these two neglected thinkers of the past generation has come to the fore. Indeed, since each boldly (but independently) repudiated reason, it was the overconfident rationalism of the nineteenth century which ignored them. Their significance does not lie in the fact of a mere hostility to reason, however, but, as Jaspers notes, "both questioned reason from the depths of *Existenz*"[19] and proposed a new orientation of the human spirit to reality. The attempt to drive to ultimates by the avenue of reason reveals only an illusory detour. Descartes' "I cogitate, therefore I am" is a deceptive lie; for Kierkegaard true being is the leap of faith; for Nietzsche, the will to power. Both brought to nothingness the attempt to relate man and reality through reason. Kierkegaard said, "Nobody today is a real believer," while Nietzsche said, "God is dead."[20] For Kierkegaard the contrarational world presents the great creative opportunity to the man of faith; for Nietzsche, to the superman.

Kierkegaard therefore shares in the modern revolt against reason, and proposes to consecrate this revolt to the services of religion. He opposes the socialistic emphasis with its depreciation of the individual, which socialism Hegel had furthered, and which Marx was to develop on a naturalistic base. Idealistic-rationalistic tradition had emphasized the reality of universal, abstract reason, with little interest in the particular. But for man as a knower, not essences but existences are important, particularly *my* existence. Reality cannot be grasped rationally, as the Platonic-Hegelian movement thought; it must be experienced in decision. The essence of human nature is not the intellectual and cognitive, but the passionate. The unique individuality of each person is actualized in spiritual-moral decision.

Even Denmark's prevailing church life in Kierkegaard's time obscured the significance of personal decision and was little more than Christianized Hegelianism blended with formalism. As his means of rescuing the absolute significance of the religio-ethical, Kierkegaard projects its inward appropriation in a context of subjectivity and paradox. The truth and the good are real only for the individual in the place of

[19] Jaspers, *Reason and Existenz*, p. 25.
[20] *Ibid.*, pp. 29f.

passionate decision; outside this intense subjectivity God does not exist. There is no knowledge of God in objectivity; the historical becomes religiously significant only through immediate subjective experience as the locus of the experience of God. Thus Kierkegaard thinks that the absolute nature of the ethico-religious can be preserved for the individual only by the repudiation of all attempts to vindicate God by rational demonstration or by appeal to Divine revelation addressed objectively, historically and propositionally to man through chosen prophets and apostles. The happenings of the past, the events external to subjective decision, are not only valueless as evidences for the reality of God and of his claim, but to appeal to them represents a rationalistic betrayal of the indispensable standpoint of passionate resolve. Extra-rational decision, not rational perception or illumination, supplies the meeting between man and God. The real world has the category of the irrational for its shroud; it stands over against the conceptual man as "wholly other." The objective existence of God has no significance for faith, any more than for reason; what matters supremely is that he exists *for me* in inward decision. Only in the existential leap of faith — and not by rational synthesis — is the tension between eternity and time resolved. And the truth experienced in passionate inwardness is never objective reality, or knowledge of an object; this must always remain a matter of intellectual uncertainty. The truth is true *for me*; whether it is true for another is his problem, but not mine.

Thus the irrationalist movements of idealistic and naturalistic ethics unite in repulsing every attempt to systematize the world of reality. Not only is metaphysical knowledge disowned, but the very ambition for it is repudiated as an attempted freezing of reality in dogmatic concepts, and, in addition, as a perversion of man's authentic situation in life. There is no promise of any theoretical resolution of ultimate problems. All man's concepts are denuded of a distinct objective content. The crucial center of individual life is *Existenz,* inwardness. In passionate decision man may reach momentarily beyond reason and touch the reality outside. The experiences of the self standing at this threshold of Transcendence are propositionally incommunicable. Except for signs or pointers, which are not to be regarded literally, man can make no affirmations about the objective world, which stands outside the limits of reason. The ultimate meaning of human existence is unspeakable.

In this desperate reversal the history of philosophy works a dreadful revenge upon the idealistic attempt to exhibit the present world of reality as essentially identical with the mind and purpose of God. The Greek polytheistic myths wrestled with Fate; classic Greek philosophy, with non-being and formless matter; ancient Naturalism, with "the void." Hebrew-Christian religion swept all these notions aside by its confident assertion of Absolute Providence, while yet it posited the dread reality of the fall and sin. But for the modern movement of philosophy, Reason alone (the capitalized speculative substitute for God) becomes the sufficient reference point for all reality. The price of the idealistic refusal to take the counter-rational seriously is the naturalistic refusal to take reason seriously. The attempt rationally to justify the moral chaos of human existence is now countered by the intentional assertion of a chaotic and counter-rational existence. The existential reaction is a refusal to take anything seriously, — anything, that is, but human decision.

3

EXISTENTIAL ETHICS AND THE INTENSIFICATION OF THE MORAL LIFE

We are now aware that two rival moral philosophies, Naturalism and Idealism, are seeking the mastery of Western thought. Each delineates its own comprehensive interpretation of life and morals. Each likewise contends for an exclusive explanation and integration of the components of human experience. In this twentieth century, however, a third perspective, repudiating all forms of systematic morality, has garnered a large and enthusiastic following. Because of its revolutionary orientation of the whole of life, the ethics of Existentialism demands close scrutiny.

Contrary to speculative philosophy's attempt to explain the world and life rationally, Existentialism repudiates as the inordinate "pride of reason" the effort to correlate the cumulative and aggregate experiences of life into a consistent whole.

Decision, rather, constitutes the warp and woof of life for existential ethics. The existentialist scorns every endeavor to define moral and spiritual claims by rational criteria. Such realities, he contends, are grasped solely by "practical-existential" decision. Traditional ethical studies, with their systematic schematizations, become therefore a speculative luxury. To the existentialist, they represent an evasion of life itself via abstraction. Systematic ethics appears to him as grotesquely irrelevant to the stark realities of daily problems and pressures.

Once Reason was King. In the movement of thought extending from Descartes through Hegel, the supremacy of Reason reached the whole of reality. More than this, reason provided the comprehensive and reliable human chart to the metaphysical and moral worlds. It supplied man an index to the self and to his universe. Hegelian philosophy, and that wing of Protestant thought which followed in its train, set no limits to the possibilities of human reflection. As a fragment of Divinity, man needed merely to work up to his own innate greatness.

Today, however, Reason is a refugee. The popular allegiance is to the "cult of unreason," even in some professing Christian circles. The optimistic trust in reason has been shattered by an anti-Hegelian reaction. The Hegelian philosophy tried to give man significance by making him a part of the Absolute Mind. But as Pantheism and the immanentistic systems collapsed, they left human reason as an isolated fragment of reality. Reason was now in exile.

Many other factors contributed to this deposition of reason. The more important ones are easily discovered. When David Hume denied the possibility of knowing the supernatural and equally of accounting for things and their causal relations with the categories of conceptual reason, he spawned agnosticism into the stream of Western thought. In doing so, he virtually undermined the then-accepted Christian morality, supported as this was by confidence in the rational certainty of God. This agnostic spirit soon moved beyond Hume's own circle of followers, inhibiting even those who regarded themselves as his antagonists. Immanuel Kant, while venturing a rebuttal of Hume's views, likewise denied any possibility of knowing the spiritual world conceptually. Abandoning the religious grounding of morality, he oriented the discussion of ethics to the practical reason and to immanent value-experience. Kant's categorical imperative and "transcendental ego," detached from metaphysical considerations as they were, fell prey to evolutionary thought. Reason itself was demoted to a late stage in the developmental process of man and society. Reality more and more was regarded as "broader than logic."

The preparation of the pre-existential world for its modern mood is not without other observable influences. Kant did more than to cut off the conceptual man from metaphysical realities. He justified metaphysical interests for their intensely practical significance, and encouraged a regard for the ethical sense "as if" it were divinely commanded. Both Nietzsche and Kierkegaard have made their contribution. Whatever their differences, each repudiates the attempt to grasp reality rationally, and each seeks instead to do so from the standpoint of *Existenz,* or of subjective immediacy. From the second decade of the twentieth century onward, the philosophic initiative even in the Anglo-Saxon world begins to transfer to movements which, in one way or another, emphasize that reason is not ontological. The life of virtue must now be justified, if at all, by other considerations than an appeal to eternally valid principles. Naturalism replaces Idealism as the predominant cultural viewpoint. Aggressively it attacks in principle any suggestion that reason objectively structures the real world. Humanism emerges as a hesitant accommodation of the anti-rational revolution, for some reflections of the rational approach to values linger still in the humanistic effort to seek the rational integration of life by devotion to the values of love, honesty, and understanding of the world. The humanistic rebellion against Hegelian supernaturalism and rationalism is not yet an outright revolt against reason. For while Humanism regards the whole of reality as sheer evolutionary process, and hence disqualifies all value-claims from any absolute status, yet inconsistently enough, it nonetheless acknowledges the permanent validity of the values just stipulated as the fount of meaningful human experience. But contemporary morality, by its insistence that reason, while not worthless, nevertheless supplies no final basis of conduct, nor trustworthy external guidelines, carries the revolt against reason much nearer its climax. Human reason is maligned either as objectively invalid or as unable to cope with life in its complex totality.

In earlier statements of ethics, the validity of the rational process has been silently assumed in the sphere of value experience, even when the larger metaphysical relevance of reason was discounted. But with the collapse of the idealistic movements and of the naturalistic attempt to accommodate ethical experience, the link between values and reason became severed. With Marx and Nietzsche to set the pace, the callous naturalistic wing, in contrast with the humanistic, dismissed values as being merely subjective preferences lacking in objective validity. Today the thesis that values are simply a reflection of class or of individual interests has influential support on both sides of the Atlantic. Logical Positivism decrees with cold heart that both morality and metaphysics must bow to the dictum that only the physically measurable is valid. It repudiates any attempt to discover values and methods that furnish rational guidance for behavior. Scholars such as Russell, Ayer, Carnap, and Stevenson distrust the writings of contemporary humanists and pragmatists, in which moral rules are rationally defended. Instead, they boldly reduce value to emotive preference. The pragmatic notion that "ethical truth" is whatever works in experience is modified to the notion that "ethical truth" is the vigorous assertion of the will. The logical positivists do not, however, impart to this thesis the Nietzschean turn, that "ethical truth" is whatever the most vigorous will asserts.

The dilemma of contemporary ethics is poignantly expressed by Joseph Wood Krutch. He speaks especially of love, but his comments may be extended to the other values of life also. What happens, he asks, when values are approached in a "scientific" manner? To analyze and appraise values by the prevailing naturalistic criteria is to paralyze their claim and their utility. To cold, rational analysis, values appear subjective and arbitrary. To dispassionate reflection, they are a personal whim. Such calm detachment and scientific objectivity only nullify their force. Hence the real key to value experience is passionate self-concern. Without this the dynamic of the ethical life evaporates. In order to retain their force in personal living, values require personal commitment. The moral life therefore gains its compulsion only in an "extra-scientific" assent to the genuineness of values. The problem of ultimate values thus becomes a focal point of debate. The importance of the question is indubitable, for the solution to the enigma of human worth, at the end, corresponds always with the answer to the question of values.

Precisely in this mood existential ethics offers a new orientation for life and reality. Bluntly hostile to any rational attempt to discern universal essences and eternal principles, the existential philosophy insists that to "understand" values and the moral question is but to misunderstand them. The demand for a scientific or theoretical formulation as a test of the rightness or wrongness of any ethical decision, obscures the essential nature of ethical living. The genuinely ethical life is one of existential decision, and not of rational synthesis.

Existentialism grants to reason a pragmatic significance in this world of physical events. But it cuts reason off from any ontic relation to universal essences and changeless absolutes, and, indeed, denies the very reality of such. Its emphasis falls not on reason at all, but rather on decision. It stresses man's ability to shape his own future, unnecessitated and undetermined by his environment. The man himself is *in the making* by his ethical commitments. Man is no mere character in a Platonic essay or Humean dialogue whose main function is now and then only to nod assent or monotonously to utter the phrase "I grant it." Rather, man is himself the minor premise, and perhaps the major premise, in the syllogism of life, upon whose declarations the very outcome of the syllogism depends. The important thing is to decide, not to speculate about deciding.

The moral life needs no clarification of the metaphysical hinterland before posing the question "What ought I to do?" Such inquiries as "What kind of universe is this?" or "What life-view is demanded by this world-view?" only divert the individual from the task of living passionately at the moment.

Not only is rational discrimination of moral claims irrelevant to the task of living, but the rational integration of life is an illicit goal. Existentialism scorns the attempt to formulate a world-and-life view. *Weltanschauung* and *Lebensanschauung* are futile attempts to comprehend the essence of things in a rational synthesis. Any claim to an objective understanding of existence is thrust aside as sheer pretense, even when (and, as we shall see, especially when) the authority of Hebrew-Christian revelation is invoked in its behalf. Thus the entire moral tradition of the West, except for occasional strands influenced by postulational ethics, is repudiated as speculative rationalism.

The existential moralist proposes, instead, a "practical" morality. He inquires: "What shall I do in this concrete predicament in view of its specific alternatives?" and not, "What is the nature of duty?" or "What is the nature of the self that it should be required to do anything at all?" The disintegrating and frustrating experiences of life serve constantly to alert us to the awareness that human life is intense subjective decision. The existentialist pleads for a life-or-death approach to ethics. The ethical man comes into being through moral commitments. In dynamic decision man creatively makes his own tomorrow in a context of existence which is neither bound by necessity nor hemmed in by reason. The problems of life are psychological, not logical. Hence ethical decision must be ventured on the existential-practical plane, rather than from the theoretical point of view.

This perspective supplies the rallying cry for an enlarging circle of contemporary moralists. A century ago Existentialism was a neglected frontier; today it is the prospering center of ethical debate. The community of existentialists includes scholars whose conclusions, and even premises, about the ethical life are radically diverse. They share in common the approach to reality in terms of *Existenz,* but thereafter the unanimity ends. This was already the situation a century ago, when both Nietzsche and Kierkegaard deliberately disowned a rational approach to reality and called for its grasp in terms of subjective immediacy. Kierkegaard sketched the ethical life in a vocabulary climate of supernatural revelation and Christian realities as well as of *Existenz.* Nietzsche regards the standpoint of subjective immediacy not only as anti-reason but as anti-Christ. In the mid-twentieth century, Existentialism is likewise exposited with equal passion by agnostics and atheists, as well as by theists. In fact, its influence is being registered in both dimensions in wide currents of popular life.

I. ELEMENTAL EXISTENTIALISM

The distrust of reason, as we have already noted, is a primary characteristic of contemporary life. An uneasy fear persists that the problems of humanity are beyond rational solution. Man appears helpless to resolve the meaningless drift of things and events. Tense anxiety is the modern man's constant companion.

Naive Existentialism is the flight of the human individual from what he considers life to be—cosmic absurdity and misery and hopelessness. He flees to sense pleasures. Caught in a universe which provides him with no principles for making choice, one which closes him up to empty subjectivity, he is free to do as he pleases to outwit the boredom of absurdity and the frustration of despair.

This wondering about human value is especially widespread in post-war France. She is clamped in the vise of European turmoil and ambition. She no longer is a major power. And this present generation has experienced her fall. Disillusion, discouragement, disenchantment, and *immobilisme* are France today. The young intellectuals, later known as the bearded *Existentiales,* adopted Jean-Paul Sartre's atheistic stress on the misery and absurdity of life to justify loose living. The university set, governed by naive Existentialism, renounced ethical claims and gave themselves to pleasure. The first impression which the existentialist revolt against reason makes among many persons is that of dissolving the moral imperative. But this is hardly the intention of most existential moralists today.

II. PHILOSOPHICAL EXISTENTIALISM

A. ATHEISTIC: SARTRE, HEIDEGGER

Atheistic Existentialism admittedly begins with subjectivity, and it never rises above the repudiation of fixed values and supernatural claims, yet it often defends moral earnestness. Its chief spokesmen, Martin Heidegger (1889-) and Jean Paul Sartre (1905-), disown the appeal to the supernatural for solution of the disorders of life. They are atheists. With Kant and Hegel, curiously, they derive all values from the immanent freedom of man and lodge the essence of duty in the willing subject. This position, however, Heidegger and Sartre adopt not as theists, but rather as anti-rational existentialists. Existentialism is always characterized by the fact that it adduces the priority of individual existence as the starting-point of significant decision, and rejects rational criteria as marginal to spiritual and moral considerations. As the French novelist Simone de Beauvoir points out, this willing subject is no longer an impersonal universal man; instead, for Existentialism, the concrete individual is the source of all values.[1]

Yet both Heidegger and Sartre condemn the life of raw hedonism as an unjustifiable implication of atheistic Existentialism. The tragic side of life serves as introduction for various possible ethical decisions. It is an element in the classic Greek tension between reason and sense, in the Hebrew-Christian tension touching the sinfulness of man, and in the Hegelian conflict between the finite and Absolute. Why may not the tragic factor lead also to ethics without God and without the supernatural? By passionate living in a world wherein he is a homeless vagrant enduring unrelieved nausea, man is free to sponsor his own values, and thus to create himself a moral individual.

As Heidegger sees it,[2] the individual is thrown, rudderless, into a world which he cannot comprehend rationally, but in which he must decide and act. No rational grounds, or objective criteria of goodness and rightness, can guide him in these choices. The individual's nature is forged by his choices and deeds; previous to them, he has no nature. He becomes what he decides and does. His environment bends to what he makes it through free choice. Duty is not an imperative which confronts man in advance; rather, the valuable becomes valuable in the choosing. Man's solitary ethical choice in the irrational environment of his existence actualizes his possibility of projecting hope into the universe of despair.

The ethically-affirmative existentialists in the atheistic camp regard the tragic dimension of man's experience as a silent acknowledgment that he is separated, not from God, but from his real self. His sense of the tragic is forced on him from the inside, not from the outside. It arises because, while other creatures merely undergo their experiences, man is conscious of his. For man to affirm his identity with the distraught self would be to acknowledge himself a failure, and to deny the ambiguity of the self. The alternate option is a dynamic

[1]Simone de Beauvoir, *The Ethics of Ambiguity,* trans. Bernard Frechtman (New York: Philosophical Library, 1948), p. 17.

[2]Heidegger's definitive work, *Zein und Seit* (6th ed., Tübingen: Neomarius Verlag, 1949) has not yet been translated into English. Sartre's *L'etre et le neant* (Paris: Gallimard, 1943) has been issued in translation (*Being and Nothingness*) by Philosophical Library, 1956.

"conversion" which, accepting this ambiguity, strives to actualize the transcendent self.

The very absence of absolute values means his freedom is unthwarted. Death is the only certainty in man's experience. Hence he must make his decisions and act under the shadow of death. Life must gain its whole meaning from the present act alone.

Man's decisions gain an absolute significance in that he is the god who shapes his own destiny. His will alone may lodge itself determinatively in the free historical movement.

To set forth a rational synthesis of man and the world of existence would be idolatrous. Such rational objectification springs from man's desire to transform his existence from becoming into being and to seek an external guarantee of his existence. But man would thereby cease to be man. The existential conversion begins with the candid recognition that no such exterior rational supports exist. One must avoid rising above the pessimism of life from wrong motivations. The rejection of impersonal rational objectivity is the first requirement of moral progress.

The atheistic approach nowhere convincingly answers the question *why* man should make himself a finite god or legislator of moral distinctions in a universe which is indifferent to morality and which holds forth only the final prospect of death to everyman. Heidegger states that to choose and act is to exist authentically; not to do so is but to eke out half-being. Unless the individual decides, he evades or denies his freedom and responsibility. But this is assertion, not argument. That an ethically-indifferent environment would supply man an opportunity for ethical creativity is obvious enough, but that this constitutes a moral imperative to do so is not at all evident. Why ought the individual not to be sensual? Why be passionate about anything? Why will his freedom?

The one intolerable "evil" which atheistic Existentialism acknowledges is human existence at half-mast. But this complaint, if intended seriously, would seem to require the rejection of the existential approach to life, rather than its acceptance, for a solution. For existence is not as free and undetermined as the existentialist would have us believe. In fact, he admits that death has the last word, as the only certainty in life. Man cannot then will his own existence. Why therefore should he imagine that he can will the reality of values — if he cannot even will his own reality? For the value of his existence is depreciated in advance. Why fancy that he is ethically creative, when personal extinction is the surest of his encounters with reality? And, since all is in change, are not man's ethical achievements also doomed? Are not all man's decisions bounded by the meaninglessness and indifference of the space-time process?

The existentialist is a victim of his own advance repudiation of a providential order of fixed moral purposes and rational ultimates. His argument is unconvincing that values and the correlative risk of total loss require that nothing be decided beforehand, and that whatever is so decided threatens man's liberty. If the moral agent himself creates the distinction between right and wrong, and subjectively supplies their content, the absolute significance even of existential decision will sooner or later disclose its nature as mere psychological deception. May not the risk of total loss exist only where values are "given," and where they persevere to judge and condemn the man who repudiates them?

Equally difficult is the existentialist notion that man is wholly without light in the darkness of his moral predicament. That man is to will his freedom is said to imply no concrete content for ethical action. No objective content is attached to the moral act. The existentialist formula is *that* man ought to choose; *what* he chooses would appear a matter of indifference. If this representation is accepted, it confronts the existentialist himself with insuperable problems. For each influential existentialist makes the transition to a platform of ethics which rivals his competitors. Those who argue, along with Sartre, that to intend freedom involves a program of revolutionary socialistic (but non-Marxian) action represent but one wing. Contend though they do that the individual should will not only his own freedom but the freedom of others, and that science, technics, art and philosophy involve legitimate ethical claims, they do not show how existential analysis actually yields these ethical conclusions. Nazis and anti-Nazis, theists and anti-theists, a Nietzsche and a Kierkegaard have latched their value-claims to the existentialist mast. An existential repudiation of the bald invocation of the "will to power," with its arbitrary imposition of one's own value preference on others, can be convincingly sustained only on the supposition that a universal principle exists which excludes subjectivism in ethics. Either the existentialist must tell us concretely what to choose, and thereby recognize special objects or principles of commitment, and thus retract his repudiation of rational criteria, or he must allow the empty form of decision to go the way of moral anarchy. Moral distinctions suspended only upon isolated existents or individuals acting out of their freedom cannot avoid a subjective end-result except by an appeal to that very universal and objective rational criterion which Existentialism disallows. If erotic wants and desires are subject to no external criteria, the sphere of moral choice is uncontrolled by any principle or *ought* delivering existential decision either from relativism or the whimsical imposition of one's personal preferences upon other selves, as well as upon the universe, by force of will. Strive though the existentialists may to avoid the subjectivistic outcome, they offer no convincing escape. In John Mothershead's words, "it is hard to see why an absolutely free resolve, undetermined by antecedent conditions and not guided by any objective values, should have one content rather than another."[3]

The existentialist, as we have emphasized, does not in fact free himself from rational propositions in his definition of the ethical predicament of man. The extent of his speculation in ethics extends beyond the content which he attempts to attach to ethical decision. It extends also to the presuppositions of such decision. That there is no reason for existence is already a well-formed speculative judgment, as is his notion that there is no objective reality beyond subjective existence.

We have already stressed that existential ethics is not marketed today only in atheistic brands. The existential approach does service for a variety of formulas which share the emphasis that the moral imperative is addressed directly to the individual. One of these is specially significant because it suggests a revival, in existential form, of the ethics Kant postulated in the face of metaphysical agnosticism. Divorcing ethics from religion, it nonetheless defends the universal validity of ethical action.

That human consciousness is by definition social, standing in perpetual "I-thou" relations, is a fundamental emphasis of existential ethics. In contrast to that impersonal knowledge of the world of objects which is conveyed by science and history, the knowledge of other selves in an existential dimension is a primary mode of experience. The personalism of Ferdinand Ebner and Martin Buber has popularized this emphasis that human selves are characterized by an original existential awareness of other selves.

The German moralist Eberhard Grisebach has infused the spirit of Kant's postulational ethics into this insistence of existential personalism. Kant's dictum, that a person ought never to be treated as a thing or as a mere means to an end, gains in Grisebach's writing an existential statement: The "I-thou" relation ought never be reduced to an "I-it" relation. The whole range of the unethical is traced to this prohibited distortion which deals with another knower, or personal center of consciousness, as though he or she were merely a part of the impersonal world.

Grisebach develops the ethical implications of person-knowledge in his work *Gegenwart* (Face to Face), a title which fixes attention upon the present moment as the decisive zone of reality.[4] To Grisebach, reality is what confronts us objectively, the not-ourselves.

It is impossible to regard this reality which stands over against us simply as the physical world. For one thing, modern idealistic philosophy has cast doubt upon the world's reality in total independency of the human knower. For another, modern physics dissolves its apparent

[3]John L. Mothershead, Jr., *Ethics: Modern Conceptions of the Principles of Right* (New York: Henry Holt, 1955), p. 309.

[4]Eberhard Grisebach, *Gegenwart: Eine Kritische Ethik* (Halle-Saale: Max Niemeyer Verlag, 1928).

solidity into electrical charges. Even the objectivity of so-called "invariable laws of nature" is placed in question by the contemporary reaction against absolute uniformity and by the acknowledged subjective element coloring the statistical averages of phenomenal events. Man can twist the "facts" of the impersonal world to suit his purposes.

But the irreducible reality which confronts us, refusing to be thrust aside or ignored, is the reality of other subjects. The real world is another person, who cannot be manipulated but rather stands over against us with a claim identical to that which we ourselves make. The implications of man's encounter with reality are therefore ethical.

From the circumstance that other selves constitute the real world, Grisebach elaborates a complete system of ethics. Its underlying thesis is the requirement of an equality of respect for human selves who confront us. All the relations of life are worked out within this pattern of the equal dignity and rights of human personality — those of husband and wife, brother and sister, parents and children, teacher and student, friends, fellow citizens, and those in the sphere of international relationships as well.

The striking element in Grisebach's system of morality is his professed derivation of ethical content by existential analysis of human experience, without any necessary reference to a Divine Other. Man plays an extempore role in a non-theistic universe. As if he were a God-prototype, he is free to fashion himself existentially. Yet the presuppositions of everyday living are worked out by Grisebach in the spirit of Kantian ethics, with its exclusion of conceptual knowledge of God and its virtual agnosticism. But in Grisebach's statement, the ethical claim is blended with the recent existential emphasis on reality as it is directly experienced in personal encounter — an encounter with other selves who are not to be commanded as mere means to our ends, but who possess the same inherent claim and make the same demand upon others that we do, to be treated personally as an end rather than impersonally as a means.

Grisebach's approach shares the weaknesses already observed in the Kantian ethic. The grandiose bias that an ideal moral content can be drawn immanently from man's moral experience, and the detachment of the ethical life from its true religious source and sanction, structure both presentations. Contemporary European existentialists who combine the defense of existential "I-thou" knowledge with a primary emphasis on Divine self-revelation seek to avoid these difficulties. They repudiate an autonomous ethic. They exhibit man as sinner confronted by a holy God with the dread alternative of repentance or wrath. The essence of moral duty, as they see it, is obedience to a transcendent Divine command.

B. THEISTIC: JASPERS

Before we turn to revelational Existentialism, however, some reference should be made to the ethics of Karl Jaspers (1883-). Jaspers' exposition of existential immediacy is philosophical in spirit, rather than strictly theological. The relation between the moral claim and God or the Unconditioned is a central emphasis of his writings. The ethics of decision is oriented, apparently, to supernatural metaphysical realities. But if one reads alertly, he soon discovers that no compromise of the existential standpoint is intended. Existential experience does not allow one to delineate realities transcendent to one's own experience. The Unconditioned is not the transcendent God of whom man has rational knowledge at all.[5]

Jaspers tells us that knowledge is possible only of the phenomenal world. This world is organized in experience by the knower's creative contribution to the knowing-process. The term "Knowledge" cannot be applied to what transcends this experience-realm or is external to it. These assumptions, which underlie Jaspers' moral philosophy as well, are clearly post-Kantian.

The moral and spiritual distinctions man makes must then be distinctions within his experience, not cognitive assertions about what is transcendent to his experience. For nothing transcendent to man's experience is eligible for consideration. Man is prohibited from rational affirmations about a reality distinguished from his experience and transcending it. Even such a term as the "Unconditional," within this approach, cannot mean anything superior to an "area of man's experience," despite the capitalization. The Unconditioned is, in consequence, wholly immanent in experience.

It will be recalled that Kant stressed that the essence of the moral life lies in a regard for the categorical imperative as a Divine command. A postulational, or *as if,* relationship was thus asserted between the phenomena of the moral life and the transcendent metaphysical world inaccessible to cognitive experience. For Jaspers, too, the unconditional imperative "comes to me as the command of my authentic self to my mere empirical existence."[6] The real man, in fact, is identical with his

[5]Jaspers' exclusion of rational knowledge of the metaphysical world is apparent: "The reality of God and the immediacy of our historical relation to God exclude any universally compelling knowledge of God." *Way to Wisdom* (New Haven: Yale University Press, 1951), p. 47. The same note is sounded by Gabriel Marcel's Gifford Lectures: "In the manner of the Kantian philosophy one speaks of what lies outside experience, what lies beyond the limits of experience. That, in the last analysis, can mean nothing, since the judging of something to be *outside* experience is itself empirical, that is to say, it is a judgment made *from within* experience." *The Mystery of Being,* I (*Reflection and Mystery*), p. 46. The second volume carries, of course, the same accent: "We are completely debarred from putting ourselves in the position of a judge who can pronounce exclusive judgments or even decide degrees of precedence." II (*Faith and Reality*), p. 172. (Both volumes published by Harvill Press, London, 1951.)

[6]Jaspers, *Way to Wisdom,* p. 55.

ethical decisions.[7] Man makes himself a partaker in the eternal by valid moral decisions.

One consequence of Jaspers' existential ethics should be crystal-clear. When the only object of knowledge is experience, one may set up an imposing psychology or anthropology, but he ought no longer to speak of theology. There is a vast difference between the biblical proverb "as a man thinketh in his heart, so is he" (Prov. 23:7) or the Pauline thesis that in the absence of charity "I am nothing" (I Cor. 13:2), and the post-Kantian view that the real self is identical with the moral self. The latter view, carried forward by ethical Existentialism, sacrifices objectivity as a correlate of the position that the real self is the moral self, and it assumes that man becomes moral only in passionate decision.

For Kant and ethical existentialists influenced by him, all talk of metaphysical reality objective to man's experience, and to which his experience must be related, is nonsense. Their presuppositions rule out any such theory of knowledge. When they discuss the "unconditioned" they speak of an area of experience, of uncompromising decision, but never of a reality which exists independently of experience or is transcendent to it. Their presupposition excludes a knowledge of supernatural moral principles which man possesses on the basis of Divine revelation. Jaspers finds "an element of helplessness in grasping at the support of reliable laws and authoritative commands."[8] The only unconditional imperative accommodated by such views is what the higher self legislates for the empirical self — not what a supernatural God imposes as his will upon human experience. The individual fulfills his authentic self by moral decision that constantly answers the summons of the higher moral claim within his experience. In this higher way of life the real self is born and perpetuated. The moral tension in the soul is located between the two phases of man's internal experience. One is valid because it claims the form of universality, and it claims allegiance from within as a categorical imperative. The human personality, and not transcendent Divine personality, is the authority.

The tradition of existential ethics associated with the name of Soren Kierkegaard, however, brings us to a distinctive orientation of the principle of subjective immediacy. The proponents of theological Existentialism substitute "Divine revelation" for immanent experience. "Divine revelation" is spiritual immediacy which is joined with subjective decision viewed as ethical response to the Divine summons to obedience. It is necessary therefore to examine its claims, especially in view of the growing insistence that Christian ethics gains its legitimate and proper formulation within this movement.

[7]*Ibid.*, p. 56.
[8]*Ibid.*, p. 73.

III. REVELATIONAL EXISTENTIALISM: KIERKEGAARD, BARTH, BRUNNER

Soren Kierkegaard first expounded existential morality as the primitive form of revealed Christian ethics. In the Danish churches of Kierkegaard's day, Hegelian Absolutism was almost universally mistaken for Christian doctrine. This form of religious rationalism involves many failures, but few as conspicuous as its failure to do justice to the significance of the individual. As Kierkegaard saw it, this misconception of the importance of the person could best be contradicted by asserting the priority of individual existence as the starting-point of significant decision. This Kierkegaard did in the name of Hebrew-Christian revelation. And thereby he set in motion a radical anti-rational individualism upon which a growing company of scholars have sought to erect a modern exposition of Christian ethics.

The practical and anti-speculative thrust of Existentialism drew swift attention from modern theologians and moralists in the Christian tradition, especially those already influenced by anti-metaphysical tendencies. Since Hebrew-Christian theology propounds an ethics of Divine revelation, the existential emphasis on the nothingness of the human being and on the insignificance of human thought could be viewed as the introduction to revealed ethics. This ethics of revelation is then centered in an encounter with God defined as the Transcendent or Wholly Other.

The fresh appeal of the existential approach should be clear. Traditional speculative ethics often devoted less attention to the need to *act* morally than to its rationalist disputations of what morality is. For the call to moral decision, it substituted a thick fog of words and tortuous argument. The path of speculative ethics is littered with systems that elaborate general life-views but blunt the need for decision and action in the life of the individual. But now man is commanded to act morally with his whole being in the midst of his moral tension. Existentialism makes contact with man as he is.

If revealed ethics disowns anything, it is the notion that Divine revelation aims merely to satisfy human curiosity about the nature of spiritual and moral realities. Personal response to the absolute Divine claim is no mere secondary consideration. God calls for decision. Over against the whole stream of speculative ethics, with its one-sided interest in "knowing the truth" of metaphysical and moral realities, the biblical emphasis is on *"doing* the truth." This phrase sounds awkward simply because our modes of thought have been so much shaped by the speculative tradition. The truth as something not simply to understand, but to *do* by moral activity, is a distinctive New Testament conception.[9]

The Hebrew-Christian revelation sets moral light before darkened man and calls him to obey. It stands in judgment against him if he

[9]Cf. John 3:21, "He that doeth the truth cometh to the light"; I John 1:6, "If we walk in darkness we do not the truth."

merely knows what the light is like, and then lives in indifference or rebellion to it. Biblical theology requires a yielded life and will, not just the proper words. Its byword is "submit," not "know intellectually."

Recent ethical study tends to link revelational ethics and the existential mood. This is because biblical theology rejects idle speculation as much as Existentialism does. The burning question in the present-day study of ethics is the real identity of Christian ethics. Revealed ethics assertedly moves on a different plane from speculative ethics and it admittedly requires urgent personal involvement. Is Christian ethics therefore wedded to the existential? or to the rational? Does revelational ethics spurn the idea of an intelligible world-life view? Does it dismiss casually all interest in metaphysics as a base for morality? And does it rest its case on the subjective leap whose only test for validity is the subjective assurance of the immediate Divine confrontation of the soul? Or does revelational ethics set the urgency of personal moral choice within the framework of a rational and divinely revealed world-life view?

The writer contends that it *is* possible for Christian ethics to maintain — and to do so in a profounder way — those sound elements that are found in existential ethics without being caught up in the tide of the anti-metaphysical and irrational thought that is so decisively a part of Existentialism today. The service of existential philosophy has been to set in bold relief the unsatisfactory course modern speculative ethics sought to follow.[10] The existential revolt also protests against an inadequate representation of Christian ethics. It stands in stark contrast to such a view of the fall and depravity of man as would imply he had no ability for significant moral decision. To recover the emphasis that truth is for the sake of obedience, and to underline that truth is not impersonal and impractical are invaluable gains indeed. To point out clearly that life is confronted moment by moment with decisions of vast and terrifying import to the person is most worthwhile. But to do these things it is not necessary to give up, as the existentialists do, reason as a means of knowing God and his moral order. A lasting devotion to morality cannot be rooted in a will-o'-the-wisp experience alone. There must be a spiritual meeting between the person and the Lord God, but the ethical will of God must also be grasped as a rationally consistent and coherent orientation to life. Only then will the claim from God for ethical living have its greatest hold on the person.

[10]It would be too much to say that speculative ethics is concerned only with ethical abstractions and not at all with practical directives for life. Such a criticism issues easily, but superficially, from modern theories which regard all interest in moral principles as abstractions from life and which arbitrarily define the ethical situation by existential immediacy. But the sense of individual moral urgency, of life-and-death earnestness about personal destiny, is not a conspicuous feature of speculative ethics. The history of moral philosophy is often tedious and pedantic, its discussions sometimes arid and academic and quite removed from real life. Evidence is close at hand for the existentialist dissatisfaction with the fruits of speculative ethics.

Moral earnestness will soon weaken unless the person pursuing the good life treats questions that lie outside the self-limited scope of existential concern. It is not necessary to insist upon the irrelevance and harm to moral living of rationally valid principles of conduct in order to keep passionate ethical concern. One reason so many existentially-oriented moralists are so passionately concerned about ridding ethics of rationality is that they have adopted an anti-rational, anti-metaphysical, and anti-Christian philosophy. And this is their one remaining apologetic strategem. Every system bears its fruit. The fruit of ignoring a rational basis for ethics will be an age of moral despair. There will be little hope of recovery from ethical despair in a climate of deliberate anti-intellectualism.[11]

The problem existential ethics presents is that of evaluating to what extent, if any, the form and content of ethics comes genuinely into purview by an analysis of existential experience. Kierkegaard did not himself combine the ethical element of decision with the faith-leap which he so much emphasized. Whether the contemporary "neo-orthodox" writers are in all respects "pure Kierkegaardian" or not, however, they share in the exclusion of conceptual knowledge of any reality transcendent to human life, and hence in the abandonment of rational knowledge of ethical realities. And the problem which remains is that of saving significance for the ethical imperative.

Recent dialectical theology disagrees over whether existential analysis can be correlated with revealed ethics.

Karl Barth professes to derive ethics from the sovereign transcendent command of God alone. The Word of God seeks man out and confronts him from above. No point-of-contact in man's moral life supplies continuity between God and man. The Wholly Other shapes his own point-of-contact *in* the confrontation. It is in the Spirit's address that man in the midst of his existential involvement deals with God.

But for other adherents of a revelational ethic, this seems too arbitrary. They question Barth's total separation of the Divine command from the spiritual nature of man who is created by God. Barth, they say, gives too little heed to the scope of the general Divine revelation that is still addressed to men and survives the fall.

[11]It is bad enough to lose moral hope temporarily. It is worse to lose moral hope permanently through a philosophy of despair, to which ethical Existentialism attaches itself. The door of transition opens in only one direction with the collapse of a moral hope which has already lost its lifeblood by being rooted in despair. That direction is Nihilism. "A philosophy of despair arises out of a disparagement of beliefs which were once trusted. Such a repudiation of beliefs which once were regarded as sound is the hardest type of disillusionment to endure because it injures an individual's sense of his reflective competence. . . . Just such injured pride . . . accounts for the emotional intensity with which disillusionment is itself defended in articulate systems of skepticism. . . . The tragic nature of much modern life . . . is that in rejecting what turned out to be a deceptive way of life, many have come to the resolute conclusion that there is no trustworthy way." Ben Kimpel, *Faith and Moral Authority* (New York: Philosophical Library, 1953), p. 91.

Emil Brunner seeks to vindicate a "twilight knowledge" of God's will in conscience. There is at least a formal survival of the image of God in man. But Brunner denies significant cognitive value to this image, for he seeks to derive its content from the saving encounter alone, and does not relate its formal aspect to rationality.

Reinhold Niebuhr assigns a somewhat fuller scope to general revelation, as does Paul Ramsey. Ramsey hesitates to sketch the content of Christian ethics independent of the best insights of speculative ethics. He places special value on idealistic ethics.

Thus the relationship of Christian ethics and speculative ethics is re-introduced by contemporary ethical controversy as a subject for serious and lively debate. The section devoted to the *imago Dei* must deal with this issue in considerable detail.

But the vulnerable point in recent theological ethics is already clear. The existentialists inherit from Kierkegaard the refusal to grasp the spiritual and moral world with the instrument of reason, and insist instead that individual existence supplies the only starting-point of significant decision. Man stands at the crossroads of time and eternity, unable to resolve their contradictions and claims rationally. As Paul L. Holmer remarks, in Kierkegaard's view "ethical and religious truth is not cognitive, but it is 'subjectivity.' "[12] The passionate and responsive leap of faith, detached from any indebtedness to reason, alone secures a synthesis in which the finite will of man stands recurrently confronted by the absolute claim of the infinite God. The post-Kierkegaardian movements insist that there can be no objective discrimination between ethical claims. Deliberately they do away with a rational basis for morality.

The surrender of all objective certainty regarding moral ultimates, or what is the same thing, the deliberate insistence on objective uncertainty in all matters involving ethical decision, is an emphasis indebted to the anti-metaphysical epistemology of Kant. Kierkegaard's contrast of religious and ethical propositions to propositions about the empirical world is related to Kant's confinement of conceptual knowledge to the phenomenal world. Kierkegaard's position constituted, as Holmer acknowledges, "a slashing attack upon the view that logic [is] ontological."[13] He opposed the application of logical categories to God and to the good. The Kantian cleavage between the rational man and the spiritual-moral man is thus perpetuated. Not only is man related to moral claims only by non-cognitive decision, but only man-in-decision is the real man. "The real subject is not the cognitive subject . . . the real subject is the ethically existing subject."[14]

This bias against the relevance of rational criteria to moral distinctions poses for Christian thought an ironic decision of passionate

[12]Paul L. Holmer, "Kierkegaard and Ethical Theory," in *Ethics,* LXIII, 3, (April, 1953), p. 165.

[13]*Ibid.*

[14]Kierkegaard, *Postscript* (Paris: Gallimard, 1941), p. 287.

inwardness that is profounder than any proposed even by Kierkegaard. Should the Christian irrationally limit ethical and religious commitment to a "leap of blind faith"? If so, would it not seem futile to seek agreement on competitive ethical issues? Would he not thereby exchange the coherence of the Christian view of God and man for subjective value preference? If the conflict between competing and contradictory moral judgments is to be resolved only by passionate inwardness, does not ethics cease to involve any longer an "I ought" according to principle, and become instead an "I give myself wholly to" according to one's feelings and desires?

Or should he consider the whole Christian revelation, ethics, and theology, as rationally binding? In this event, he must confront men with the reality of the good as the objectively revealed will of God. For if reality is an objectively structured moral order, then it is deception to maintain, as Kierkegaard does, that reality gains the moral dimension only from personal decision.

Neo-orthodox theology, as it has drawn up an ethical theory, has insisted that the Christian faith requires its own ethic, and then has tended to identify revelational ethics with the existential and to repudiate the theoretical. There are many reasons for this. Certain of them characterize the new theology. The starting-point is the ruling out of metaphysics as a valid subject for thought and knowledge. This gives rise to a dialectical valuation. The dialectical process involves affirming both thesis and anti-thesis about spiritual realities, and then it demands a personal faith-repose that cannot be resolved into rational synthesis. The Kantian approach to morality by the " 'as if'-leap" is given impetus by its connection with "special revelation." "Special revelation" here means that man is confronted with an absolute summons to ethical obedience by a personal Divine encounter.

Special revelation thus bears a definition which it did not carry in the tradition of Christian thought prior to Schleiermacher's day. Reason and revelation are broken apart. This means that "revealed" theology and ethics have nothing in common with any rational world-life view. Barth says that the *humanitas* is no reception-center for Divine revelation. Brunner sharply distinguishes revelation-truth from rational truths. Ethics becomes a mother of practical existential living — with no *raison d'etre* in metaphysics.[15] The possibility of either an ethical or

[15]This is more fundamental than Barth's repudiation since 1932 of Existentialism as an erroneous philosophical basis for the theology of the Word, since it presumed to find, to Barth's dislike, a point of contact for revelation in human experience. Barth's statement of an ethics of revelation in terms of dialectical non-existential theology, grounding the ethical exclusively in the vertical encounter in which the Holy Spirit creates in man his own point of contact for revelation, assuredly marks his theology as more radically transcendent even than that of Brunner. And it means that ethics for Barth comes into purview only insofar as it can be actualized within the rim of dogmatics. Since it is defined as the command of God, which is essentially the definition of revelation, ethics is an integral phase of dogmatics. The human existential predicament becomes theologically relevant for Barth only through vertical encounter by the Word, and the relation to the

theological *system* is ruled out by the infinite qualitative difference between God and man. Ethical thought based on revelation must be dialectical, or thought in contradiction. The good life allegedly has no fixed content, and cannot be charted in advance by guiding principles. It must gain its content afresh, moment-by-moment, in each changing situation, from a vertical Divine command. A pattern of life and conduct in advance of this recurring Divine-human confrontation is ruled out. Indeed, the content of ethics cannot be made into a system at all, for all principles of duty and virtue, all charting of moral values, is excluded. God communicates no truths, neither about his purposes nor about himself. He only commands obedience in particular situations which are to be met in faith as they arise.

It is necessary to show that the ethical perspectives of Kierkegaard, Barth, and Brunner are rooted fundamentally in a philosophical perspective rather than in any special Divine revelation. Two important elements cut neo-orthodoxy loose from the historic Christian view of biblical ethics. One is the rejection of propositional revelation, thus denying a rational base for theology and ethics. The other is making revelation to be an immediate encounter only. This by-passes an inspired and authoritative Scripture.

Dialectical theology may make an appeal to special revelation in order to give some transcendental basis to an inner ethical drive. But really this is begging the question. For it shares with post-Kantian Existentialism the repudiation of all objective moral guides as inadequate and irrelevant. Its disparagement of all "sacred" commandments and venerated ethical codes goes beyond the claim that ethics must be experienced internally, not merely accepted as external authorities. For a standard feature of the theology of crisis is its insistence that daily living is not to be guided by moral principles. "Principles" imply a rational content that can be objectively analyzed. It regards as idolatrous the attempt to conform the ethical life to a rationally coherent system of behavior. Human life lived in accord with ethical principles asserted blunts the tension of moral choice. Dialectical theology has no more use for objectively revealed ethics than it does for objectively revealed truths about God. And this renunciation of a revealed system of Christian morality follows from a fundamental bias of neo-orthodoxy. It is the old Kantian dogma that no meaningful propositions can be formed about the spiritual and moral world.

Existenz question of existential theology is for him therefore a purely formal one. For Brunner, by virtue of his emphasis on general revelation, the existential sphere already bears theological implications. But, at the moment, it is well to note that the theology of crisis as a movement breaks with the whole tradition of Christian ethics by its renunciation of a revealed theoretical life view. It does so in one way by saluting primarily the existential, and in another by saluting primarily the dialectical approach to reality.

The fact that recent theologies import into this context an emphasis on special revelation in no way modifies the essential difficulties which inhere in this repudiation of objective ethics. It may appear that by binding moral decision to the transcendent element of a Divine confrontation, one escapes from an ethical anarchism. It may be argued that this type of ethic is consistent with the uniqueness of the person. It insures moral earnestness by calling for ethical decision at a depth of intense inwardness. But a little reflection will indicate that an ethics of direct Divine confrontation alone cannot securely transcend subjectivity. An irrational view of Divine revelation can have no more effect in giving status to ethics than can an irrational metaphysics. The allegation that God confronts man does not alter the view at its essential point. It makes little difference in the end whether one calls the confronting element "God" — as do the neo-orthodox, or whether they call it the "transcendental ego" — as do Kant and Jaspers and Marcel and Sartre. Individual life is still too unique to allow morality to be stated in principles. Ethics still cannot be objectively stated in advance of the decision — nor indeed after it.

The hinterland of the biblical ethical appeal, however, is an objective revelation of the eternal spiritual realm which Jesus and the Old Testament prophets lay bare to man. This spiritual realm is transcendent to human life. Man must be related affirmatively to it if he would be a child of God. The Bible nowhere insists that knowledge-claims are to be confined to the phenomenal world. Rather, its message centers in the disclosure to mankind of a transcendent supernatural reality. Jesus, in the tradition of the Hebrew prophets, upholds unconditional imperatives which are transcendent to individual experience, objectively confronting man as divinely authoritative. He asserts principles which have not arisen *in* human experience but which are to be received as universally trustworthy and dependable guides for life. They reflect ethical realities external to human existence. That which he finds in human experience will be judged by God, and needs to be oriented anew *to* the transcendent moral world.

George F. Thomas rightly complains that the insistence on the absolute uniqueness of each moral situation, so that no approach in terms of presuppositions is possible, discloses a "nominalistic tendency to stress the particular at the expense of the universal aspects of moral situations," and that this neglect of the constant factor "leads . . . perilously close to the abyss of irrationalism."[16]

[16]George F. Thomas, *Christian Ethics and Moral Philosophy,* p. 386. The strange fact is that Thomas himself holds to the dogma that Divine revelation is not identical with words and commandments in their propositional form (*ibid.,* pp. 373f.), thinks that imaginative images stimulate the will more than concepts (p. 371), asserts that the interpretation of revelation is not divinely given but belongs to the individual (p. 374), holds that personal experience rather than biblical authority validates the biblical content of morality to us (p. 375), and regards reason as "simply a function of the human self" (p. 381).

To this we may add a further observation. It is one of the ironies of the history of ethics — and perhaps instructively so — that abstracted concentration on the present moment of decision, when divorced from enduring moral principles, has been associated hitherto with hedonistic ethics. It is dubious indeed that such an association can be avoided long, even by more pious exhibitions of moment-by-moment ethics, unless the connection of decision with an objective and principled morality is made.

The uniqueness of human existence is better safeguarded by the universal validity of moral law than by an insistence that there is no moral law. Granting differences do exist among men, still they are involved in moral situations which are *not* at every point unique. And the ethical significance of each man is kept by his involvement in an objective and all-embracing moral order. Men are responsible because of the Divine moral will. This will has universal application to all men. Ethics then can be intelligently defined and can be studied systematically. *Intellectual* evaluation and assent are indispensable elements in significant moral decision. Moral decision which is wrenched from man in the absence of rational criteria is deficient. Moral obligations can only be understood with some rational grasp of their essential nature. An unwillingness to relate moral action to universal principles will soon bring down such action to the level of whim and fancy. Human behavior will have the same moral direction that animal behavior does, *i.e.,* none.

Kant held that man can know nothing beyond his conceptual experience of the sense world. Knowledge of the transcendental is ruled out. This means that there can be no appeal to the will of God as the supreme moral authority for human life. The "voice of God" is an aspect of the individual's higher experience. It is not something that transcends and confronts that experience. The pre-Kantian interest in metaphysics is exchanged for an interest in moral psychology. And it is a psychology that has nothing in common with the biblical doctrine of the crucifixion of the old nature and the birth of a new man through a supernatural activity of the Holy Spirit. No doctrine of Divine revelation could possibly modify this structure *unless* it made possible knowledge of things beyond this physical world. Only by reaffirming rational knowledge of the metaphysical world can the "will of God" have meaning for ethics. Otherwise, such concepts as God, revelation, and all that they entail reduce to distinctions within human experience. They are not other than an aspect of human experience. The concepts do indeed exist within the experience of the person thinking about them, but it is an open question whether there is a real God or real revelation that corresponds to the concepts. At best one can only be wistfully agnostic.

Whatever else such a theory may involve for ethics, at the very least "it cuts at the very foundation of religious faith that there are principles, such as the Ten Commandments or the Beatitudes, which are trustworthy directives for all human life."[17] It rules out Scripture, Divine commandments, and the moral teaching of Jesus as an authoritative rule of life.

And it cannot but involve the renunciation of logically consistent moral behavior since such behavior is clearly dependent upon logically consistent principles of conduct. Ethics surrenders its high status as a science in dialectical theology. Ultimate judgments about the nature of the good are deprived of their inherent right to be tested and vindicated by rational coherence. If ethics involves no synthesis of propositions conveying moral truth, it is reduced to sheer decision, unable to construct a rational self-defense of its claims. Therefore, this view threatens to lead to moral disorder and relativism. What else is left when objective criteria for the evaluation of morality are set aside?

Moreover, if the good, as the existential viewpoints maintain, is legislated subjectively in a decision of faith, then the religious life cannot judge the worth of any of the competing patterns for living. None may any longer be prized and all are to be dismissed as unrelated to real life.

Unfortunately for the existentialists, they are themselves included in the tide of relativism. They cannot say, "You *ought* to be an existentialist; here are some principles to convince you that we have the true view of life."

Say what one will about the passionate sobriety which Existentialism claims to impart to the moral life, there need be no doubt about the dispossessions it also requires. For existential ethics involves the loss of those cherished principles of action and sacred commandments which revealed religion has sanctioned; the loss of ethics as a science and the consequent surrender of behavior to rational inconsistency; the denial to Christianity of the right to vindicate the superiority of its ethical claim by exhibiting its coherent claim, in contrast with the logical inadequacies and incongruities of its competitive systems of morality; and the reduction of ethical earnestness to the subjective enthusiasm of theological Existentialism, which aims to inject hope into the world's moral despair but is precluded from giving a reason for that hope.

The new moral theory, that principles are irrelevant for ethical life, springs, as Ben Kimpel stresses, out of "a confident dogmatism that no general principles can be known for the dependable direction of human life."[18] This position is shared today by the advocates of moral Existentialism and of moral relativism, who make common cause in the revolt against objective authority. There is not merely a distrust of the efficiency of reason regarding moral and spiritual inquiry, but there is a deliberate denial of the validity of the reasoning process in these areas. This rational skepticism is not a conclusion to which the con-

[17]Kimpel, *op. cit.*, p. 3. Cf. also Kimpel's *Moral Principles in the Bible* (New York: Philosophical Library, 1956).
[18]*Ibid.*, p. 2.

temporary mood is logically driven by its assessment of reality; rather, it is implicit in the anti-metaphysical theory of knowledge with which it dogmatically sets out, and within the arbitrary limits of which it seeks to rescue the moral life.

Christianity does assuredly share the existentialist concern for moral action which is relevant to all the immediate and momentary crises of life. But it does not on that account discredit the undeniable demand of human nature for the comprehensive rational integration of the whole of life's experiences. It protests against existential ethics because the latter sets out with an artificial universe which it has substituted for the world as it really is. Existence takes on vanity and absurdity because the existentialist cultivates an awareness of the movement of reality on a subhuman, and almost animal, plane of interaction. Lewis Mumford well remarks, "almost all meaning above the animal level of response comes through abstraction and symbolic reference; in fact, the symbolic medium . . . is the very one in which man, as man, lives and moves and has his being . . . without constant reference to essences, as represented by symbols, existence would become empty, meaningless, and absurd — which is, precisely, what it seems to the mere existentialist. But what the existentialist, in horror and despair, finds lacking in his world, is merely what is lacking in his philosophy."[19] The defaced universe and the distorted life to which this philosophy leads are evident when one contrasts it with the Christian representation of reality. Formally at least, the central tradition of Western thought is right in the emphasis that reality is to be teleologically evaluated. Life does have meaning and purpose. There is a master plan. Eliseo Vivas is right in detecting that existential pessimists "have not done justice — as the main tradition of European philosophy has — to the fact that existence is valuable, is never utterly devoid of value."[20] The fallen world, even when approached with biblical realism, is indeed an anguished world, but it is not a total loss. Life is not meaningless nothingness.

Existential ethics reconstructs reality in contours strange to the Hebrew-Christian's revelation of a providentially-ordered universe. In biblical revelation no area of life is wholly barred to the presence of God. An anguished existence totally devoid of intelligibility and design is utterly foreign to Christianity. Christ does not require man's leap into another realm to touch the true and the good. Moral rebellion and separation from the Living God, not living in a God-forsaken world, produce soul-nausea and dread. Actually, Existentialism is a revolt against human responsibility and against those imperatives which God imposes upon moral creatures. Insistence upon the universe as wholly free, and upon existence as rationally incomprehensible is

[19]Lewis Mumford, *The Conduct of Life* (New York: Harcourt, Brace, 1951), p. 53.

[20]Eliseo Vivas, *The Moral Life and the Ethical Life* (Chicago: University of Chicago Press, 1950), p. 340.

the course of human pride in its refusal to bow before the claim of God. The evasion of ultimate responsibility, which the existentialist so passionately imputes to others, is supremely manifested in his own repudiation of objective value and of all rational criteria of goodness. Life's tragedies, ambiguities, and monstrosities of evil demand attention, but as Mumford rightly insists, "it is possible to recognize the tragic struggle in the world without making a religion of it."[21] Anguish of spirit is not a necessary concomitant of human finiteness. Rather, it is the product of sin and can be alleviated in redemption.

Kierkegaard's verdict that only the Christian believer is free from life's conscience-plaguing disquietudes and disharmonies is right. But the peace which Kierkegaard promised his followers differs radically from the peace which alone can placate the hunger in the heart of man. The search for human happiness is at the same time a quest for wisdom. As Jesus made strikingly clear, the good man is also the wise man, and the wicked man, a fool.

To attach the aggressive defense of the moral to the modern revolt against reason is therefore a tragic error. Such strategy reflects one last desperate effort of civilization to rescue the ultimate significance of love from a universe where the ultimate significance of reason has been abandoned. May it not be a reflex of the prevailing culture pattern, in view of its surviving dispositions toward Christian thought, that Kierkegaard, rather than Nietzsche, furnishes the focal Anglo-Saxon interest in the revolt against reason? Were the swift modern decline one degree farther removed from Christian presuppositions, may not rather the German Heidegger or the French Sartre have captured the imagination of contemporary scholarship? Has not a past leadership in Germany already found Nietzsche intriguing, and does not the present Russian leadership couple the revolt against reason with a revolt against love? Love without ultimate reason eventually discloses an inner spirit as repulsive as reason without ultimate love. Biblical ethics holds no brief for rationalism. Hence it can only endorse Kierkegaard's indignation over the proclamation in ecclesiastical circles of Hegel's speculation as the essence of Hebrew-Christian revelation. But at the same time biblical ethics in its defense of the life of virtue and love does not regard irrationalism as any less formidable a foe than rationalism. The Hebrew-Christian perspective sounds stern warnings to the ethical explorations of our turbulent times: the revolt against the Logos is a revolt also against Agape, and the only genuine prototype of Agape is the Logos become flesh.

[21]Mumford, *op. cit.*, p. 157.

Section II

Christianity and the Moral Revelation: The Redemption of the Moral Life

4

THE IMAGE OF GOD CREATED AND SULLIED

THE RELATION between Hebrew-Christian ethics and speculative ethics in general is vigorously debated today. It is true that biblical ethics is part of a theological structure, with such categories as the will of God, sin, atonement, and sanctification. No exact parallel can be found to these categories in speculative ethics. Yet there is much in common between them. They are both earnestly concerned with duty and value, with motives and consequences, with the question whether moral distinctions are to be objectively or subjectively given.

Christian ethics insists upon the unitary character of truth and the universal validity of moral norms. It is not ultimately defended by a hopeful appeal to non-rational considerations that are valid only for those who accept them and that admit no test besides existential commitment. The unique Divine revelation in an authoritative Scripture, the centrality of Jesus Christ for moral solution and example, and the Church as it exhibits the ethical sensitivity of Christians down through history, all these contribute to the content of Christian ethics. But there is more — there is also an insistence upon universal criteria and standards in ethics.

There is tension and debate between revelational and speculative ethics. Part of the tension springs from an objection to the emphasis by Christian ethics on its unique derivation and from a rejection of the Christian imperative of universal compliance to its content. Tension also arises between the two systems because the Christian rejects the tendency of speculative ethics to dismiss biblical ethics as being only an interesting appendage of a particular system of thought — and nothing more. The Christian believes this cavalier treatment of revealed ethics jeopardizes the authority of the moral consciousness. Christian thought also judges speculative ethics for raising spurious alternatives that reflect man in the service of sin.

The warfare is carried on by each successive generation of moralists. Strategy and tactics vary with the times. The combatants deploy in changing positions on the battlefield. Sometimes one side seems to have conquered, then the other side finds resources for a counter-offensive. And the war continues. One side may wholly ignore the other as a specious venture to be avoided. Sometimes each will view the other simply as a reflection of its own concerns. At other times each will insist that the other supplement it. What shall we say about this conflict?

The first emphasis of Hebrew-Christian ethics must always be the absolute uniqueness of its revealed character. Every attempt to explain Christian ethics as being merely a more complex development of the insights of general ethics either conceals or minimizes the basis that it has in special revelation.[1] Only an uncritical and alien philosophical bias can blend with confidence the Hebrew-Christian ethic into the tradition of speculative morality.

What separates biblical from secular ethics is that the latter is conceived not in special revelation — but in sin. The continuity between secular and biblical ethics is broken by the natural man's rebellion against God. Even when secular ethics presents theological ethics as the highest achievement of ethical thought, as now and then it does out of a sense of lostness in the wilderness of speculative morality, it obscures this basic fact of man's sinfulness. It misrepresents him as capable of reasoning his way back to God. Every speculative ethics presents, in its own peculiar way, an inadequate and distorted reflection of the Divine ethical claim.

The connection between biblical ethics and all speculative systems is fluid. No meeting place of philosophical ethics and biblical ethics can be once for all diagrammed. There is a shuttle-service between the two, but even identical ethical propositions do not imply a precisely identical content. Sin and corruption in fallen human life frustrate the natural morality of man. Because of moral rebellion man suffers moral distortion. This distortion of moral content in man is so severe that the surviving content is no longer serviceable as the basis of a morality of special revelation. The ethics of Jesus Christ is no mere supplement or capstone for the ethics of Plato, Aristotle, Kant, Hegel, Royce, or Brightman. Any attempt to conceive of Christian ethics as a subspecies of speculative ethics does not account for two vital factors: special revelation and ethical revolt.

The distinctiveness of Christian ethics is sensed by the radical naturalistic thinkers more than by the idealistic thinkers. Idealistic moralists, in the Western world at least, tend to exhibit Christianity as the highest expression of the idealistic viewpoint. And they cut out its determinative features of revelation and redemption as the price of this "tribute." Nietzsche saw that idealistic views shrank from Naturalism because of a peculiar certainty and intensity of conviction about the supernatural that came to them from Hebrew-Christian tradition. Despite his own unabashed Naturalism and his distaste for both Idealism and Christianity, Nietzsche was aware that modern supernaturalism was the more persuasive because of its dependence

[1] Josiah Royce's effort to account for Christianity as "the most highly developed religion of loyalty" in *The Problem of Christianity* (New York: Macmillan, 1913) is but one of a long list which might be adduced.

upon specially revealed theology and ethics. The philosophical moralists are prone to ignore this essential difference between the revelation-motif and the speculative-motif because the admission of revelation makes the question of sin and redemption the central issue of ethics.

But the relationship of theological and philosophical ethics is not one of total contradiction. While insisting on its distinctive basis in revelation, Christian ethics does not view the whole of speculative ethics as unrelieved and systematized error. Formally, an idealistic ethic may assert much to which Christian ethics can voice no objection and to which it may even subscribe with enthusiasm. The logical priority of the supernatural, the uniqueness of man in the creature-world, the objectivity of the moral order are all presuppositions of Christian ethics. Nor must Christianity borrow these controlling points for the construction of its own approach. Only the stubborn non-Christian will insist on that artificial way of stating the matter. Rather, since human experience has a *general* Divine revelation as its background, man cannot forge his secular alternatives to the biblical way of life without imbibing something of the truth. Indeed, this witness to general revelation is found even in naturalistic ethics — at the very least because naturalists continue to speak of ethics. The speculative moral schools always borrow at a distance — some at quite different points and some more generously than others — elements which can be consistently retained only in the Christian view of morals.

If controlling ethical assumptions possess a content which Idealism assigns to them, then the agreement between speculative and revelational ethics is more formal than actual. Ideas about God, man, and the good never occur in a system of thought in a purely formal sense devoid of any material content. Every speculative philosophy has a *specific* view of God and man. For Plato, the logical priority of the supernatural means the primacy of the eternal Ideas (crowned by the Idea of the Good). The uniqueness of man means pre-existence and recollection of those eternal Ideas. The objective moral order is a sphere of values to which man is so closely related that he needs no revelation to have an understanding of the Good. So it is with every system of idealistic ethics: it sets forth a view of God, man, and the moral ought. This view is competitive with the Christian view. Christian ethics cannot be distilled from an attempted purification of speculative ethics. Man in idealistic ethics is always a creation of speculative philosophy, a man who on the psychic side of his being is Divine, whose spiritual core is a fragment of God. Such a race of men has never really existed. And no system of ethics based on such a mythical race can ever be elevated to Christian ethics. Between every system of idealistic ethics and the Christian system of ethics stands an impassable wall, a barricade which becomes more rigid when the basic assumptions of each are clearly defined.

To avoid unnecessary dilution of its intentions, Christianity speaks of man, not as a rational animal merely, but rather as a creature bearing the Creator's image. Such definition stands verbal guard against both the naturalistic animalization and the idealistic divinization of man. It emphasizes on the one hand man's finite, contingent existence, and his dependence upon God. Man is subject to change, limited in knowledge and strength, related to the world of nature by a bodily existence exposed to suffering and death. Christianity, on the other hand, however, stresses also man's capacity to transcend the natural world and his own self, and man's ability to act in responsible relation to the will of God in response to the Creator's claim. Man is a rational, moral, spiritual creature, pre-eminent among the animals as gifted with dominion over them; through his ability to conceive general ideas he is freed from absorption in sense particulars, and is fashioned for a life of values and ends in devotion to the will of the Divine Spirit. To comprehend the uniqueness of man in such dimensions is characteristically Hebrew-Christian, and involves a distinct alternative to the naturalistic and idealistic misconceptions of man's creaturehood.

Every proposal to arrive at the content of Christian ethics by a synthesis of speculative morality and revealed morality minimizes the extent to which secular ethics is forged from the standpoint of revolt, and is over-optimistic about the precise continuity between speculative systems and the Hebrew-Christian world and life view. George F. Thomas' recent study, *Christian Ethics and Moral Philosophy,* properly repudiates the existential surrender of rational criteria in the sphere of spiritual-moral realities, on one side. On the other, it discounts the Thomistic moral synthesis of pagan and Christian ethics as tending to conform the latter to the former, rather than "sufficiently modifying" the former.[2] Yet Thomas would allow the speculative systems of morality to contribute to the content of Christian ethics, provided that such insights be "transformed or converted" to accord with "Christian faith and love" as the exclusive norm of ethics. The relation here implied between speculative and revealed ethics is that revealed ethics is not the exclusive source of an approved morality. Revealed ethics supplies the norm (we shall not here dispute the slender statement of this norm: "Christian faith and love"), yet a synthesis of the content of secular systems with revealed ethics is allowable. Such an adjustment does not, in the writer's opinion, handle with sufficient realism the secular orientation of speculative systems to the standpoint of moral revolt.

And yet a point of continuity does exist between biblical and non-biblical ethical writers, if not in their respective systems. The Christian ethical ideal is not to be defined entirely apart from the ethical ideal of all humanity. If Truth is one, and if the Good is one, and if God is everywhere with a witness — and these are basic Christian assertions —

[2]George F. Thomas, *Christian Ethics and Moral Philosophy,* p. 392.

then such a connection must be insisted upon. Christianity stresses the unity of Truth, and the universal validity of the Good and Right, and the universality of rational norms, along with its emphasis on special revelation, because it sets special revelation against the background of general revelation.

The Christian emphasis is that revelation supplies philosophy with its only secure presuppositions and that a coherent philosophy is the handmaid rather than the jealous rival of theology. In that Christianity recognizes that the special moral revelation of the Bible authoritatively enlarges the general revelation in man's conscience, Christian ethics may be considered a species of philosophical ethics. This is provided the latter term is not arbitrarily restricted to speculative ethics and thus made to exclude an ethical content derived from supernatural disclosure. If philosophical ethics "always categorically rejects the basis of a transcendent revelation,"[3] it does not do so because the ethics of biblical revelation renounces universally valid norms of goodness and truth nor because Christian ethics does not deal with many of the same problems. But it rules out special revelation as a live option because man flees from the acknowledgment of his true condition before God. To admit the existence of a revealed ethics involves at the same time the admission of much about the nature of God, and of man, and of redemption, and of human destiny. Because Christian ethics appeals distinctively to a unique Divinity, to an authoritative literature, to a peerless moral example, it refuses to be grouped with those views that derive the nature and content of the good only by theoretical speculation or by existential decision. But the appeal to transcendent revelation does not involve a denial of the ultimate unity of Truth nor of rational consistency.

The tension between Christian and speculative ethics rises from the fact that the latter term usually designates those movements that erect a standard for the will through rational speculation, independent of any appeal to special revelation. Brunner points out that a "philosophical ethic is not necessarily . . . irreligious; but its distinguishing feature is the fact that it always categorically rejects the basis of transcendent revelation."[4] Seen in this light, Christian ethics must be set against speculative ethics. But this is due to the arbitrariness of philosophical definition and bias. Speculative ethics is in competition with Christian ethics because it conceals sin by repudiating the necessity for and reality of specially revealed ethics.

Civilization and culture are possible because of the Divine endowment of man-as-creature with a rational and moral nature. The image of God in man establishes man's capacity for fellowship with God. Christianity means nothing more by the uniqueness of man than his dignity derived from the Divine purpose in creation and redemption. Concern for

[3]Brunner, *The Divine Imperative*, p. 35.
[4]*Ibid.*

morality and truth is a native and original feature of the human spirit only in view of his particular origin. The only impression the Bible gives of man's condition on the basis of creation is that of moral uprightness. Man possessed an ability to discern the will of God concerning all the duties required of him. He had a disposition to perform those duties. And he was eager to translate that disposition into ready compliance and performance. The important truth that even the Gentiles have the work of the law written on their hearts has an Old Testament as well as New Testament basis. It rests on the view that man has been granted from the first a divinely inscribed ethic on the basis of creation. This constitutional endowment has been working universally in the interest of virtue and against vice from the very beginning of mankind. It has been calling forth the continual exercise of conscience. Ethical responsibility has characterized man throughout fallen history. Not only does the biblical record represent Adam as capable of moral choice from the start, but it views the first murderer as morally culpable. Christian ethics is based specifically on the specially-revealed Divine will as the source and ground of the moral law. But it does not thereby deny an original moral revelation to man at the beginning of the history of the race. The revelation on which Christian ethics rests is not totally alien to human nature. While addressed to man from without, it is not imposed by a brutal assault upon the intellect. It is a scandal to man, not from crucifying his reason, but by driving him to his knees as sinner. It demands from him the acknowledgment that his high-sounding objections do not come from sound morality nor sound logic, but are the rationalizations of a proud mind and rebellious will.

The separation which the fall of man and his disobedience in sin produce between man and God does not detach man from moral realities and responsibilities. He remains morally accountable in sin. He does not, even at his worst, degenerate to a state of animalism in which all ethical distinctions are lost. But man as sinner erects spurious alternatives to the Divine moral law which enable him in self-delusion to "justify himself" by works. Or he raises humanistic standards for himself while the genuine claim of the Divine is dismissed as myth. Man demonstrates his sinfulness by this thought and behavior. But he is not done with ethics nor with God.

It has already been argued that no system of pagan ethics possesses an effective point of contact with Christian ethics. It is the systematic developing of ethics by non-Christian presuppositions that diminishes this point of contact. The Christian life-view is a coherent and self-consistent revelation of moral realities, and it operates on its own distinctive assumptions and controlling ideas. The more self-consistent are its competitive moral theories, with their compromised starting-point in sin, the more their viewpoint departs from an acceptable ethical content. For non-Christian ethical theory seeks self-consistency by the extension of a framework which is already concessive, and thus compounds its errors.

The contact point with revealed ethics is to be found not in the systems of speculative morality, but in the ethically-accountable person who bears the image of God even if in a sullied manner. The denial of a point-of-connection between a system of Christian ethics and the particular systems of philosophical morality is not meant to suggest that no coherent ethical content is possessed by man on the basis of creation. The ethical knowledge man possesses through the image of God is rational. Christianity does not object to secular ethics' attempt to work out a rationally consistent pattern for living. Rather, it holds that secularism views the ethical situation in an artificial and false manner. After the fall the natural man still bears the image of God, even if in a distorted way. But his ethics is worked out by a mind that is finite and out of fellowship with God and in the service of a perverse will. This process is a commentary on the strategy of man's revolt against the general Divine revelation. No ethical system based on general revelation set forth by man as sinner has succeeded in developing an ethics which is essentially Christian. Rather, nothing but competitive views of life have come from non-revelational moralists.

The question is not whether Christian ethics can account for the actual moral situation in history, in contrast with an ideal climate of morality. For only Christianity can adequately account for the present world of moral behavior.

Man differs at one essential point from all other creatures. He alone bears the *imago Dei* — the image of God. Only he has, as part of his essential nature, the forms of reason and morality. Only he is given a distinctive content of knowledge. Because he is so made, he cannot escape ethical responsibility. R. L. Ottley highlights the crucial role that the *imago Dei* plays in the experience of every man. He says a "distinctive of the Old Testament is the view that man was created in the divine image, that by the law of his original constitution he was a personal, self-conscious and spiritual being, designed for communion with his Maker, and endowed with faculties enabling him to fulfill a spiritual destiny."[5] This intriguing phrase — the *imago Dei* — is not an archaic Latinism; it embraces the essential nature of man as he is on the basis of creation.

Hebrew-Christian thought views the *imago Dei* with primary emphasis on conscience. It holds to an unchanging moral standard on the basis of Divine creation and preservation. And it says that man possesses an ineradicable ethical content. But it does not limit man's knowledge to this aspect of experience. The moral *imago* does not stand alone. It is part of a more comprehensive Divine-human relationship that distinguishes man as unique in the creature world. The *imago*

[5]R. L. Ottley, *Aspects of the Old Testament,* Bampton Lectures (London: Longmans, Green, 1909), p. 59.

embraces at once the forms of rational as well as of moral experience and a knowledge of God as the Truth and as the Good. The *imago* cannot be broken up so that moral experience on the basis of creation takes place in a vacuum, unrelated to reason and distinct from an awareness of God. On the contrary, the feeling that God is, the forms of reason and morality, the innate possession of certain moral convictions are elements of one whole. All the factors condition each other. The moral *imago* is at once rational and religious. The rational *imago* is part of man's experience as a moral and religious being. And the reason for this is that the image man bears is the image *of God.* The consequence is that man is made with a religious reason and a religious ethical nature. That is why his revolt against truth and against the good is at one and the same time a revolt against God.

The biblical doctrine of the *imago Dei* includes man's rational capacity to rise above the mere impressions of sensation and to pursue an intelligent purpose in life. This capacity to distinguish true from false, right from wrong, and to defend rationally his moral choices and desires is essential in his responsibility for conduct. Man is fashioned for a moral destiny. He possesses the discerning and reasoning faculty as an indispensable tool for moral responsibility. The writer of Genesis emphasizes his superiority to the animal world in this regard. To unfallen Adam the Creator gave the privilege of naming the lower creatures in Eden. This task involved the ability to discriminate their essential nature, and clearly implied the ability to discriminate his own nature from theirs. Among them he could not find a help meet. When Eve was brought to him, he saw their relatedness in character. The total impression of the creation narrative is that Adam, while not gifted with omniscience and universal knowledge nor with a direct insight into obscure mysteries, clearly *was* gifted with the rational and moral qualities necessary for ethical judgment and behavior in conformity with eternal principles of right and wrong.

The primary question which ethics raises about the *imago Dei* concerns the moral *imago*. Obviously this involves abstraction. A discussion of the ethical image must consider the questions of the innate form of ethics and an innate content.

The form of ethics, given as a universal and necessary structure of human experience, accounts for the universal conviction that the distinction between right and wrong, good and bad, is a genuine one — and that it is not merely a matter of personal prejudice. The indisputable fact that in actual life the same action is often labelled "good" by one culture and "bad" by another does not discredit the truth that all men make a distinction between good and evil. Human experience is by definition ethical, in the sense at least that questioning the rightness and wrongness of thoughts and deeds is universal and inescapable.

Equally important is the question whether man possesses a moral content as part of the *imago*. Does man as a specially endowed creature possess only some vague and indefinite feelings of morality that are at best confused and indistinct? Are these moral distinctions merely reflexes of his make-up? Or does the *imago* include some content of moral principle? A knowledge to some degree of ethical realities? Does such a content come under the law of contradiction so that it binds the whole man, rational and moral, to its claims?

Indeed mankind does fill out the content of the good in various ways. In some respects there is overlapping, and in others sharp competition. But this need not rule out the possibility that a universal moral content does exist. Three things need to be shown to establish its reality.

The first is that human moral experience must be shown to be intelligible and significant because of a conviction of an objectively fixed moral order. This conviction may be tacitly or implicitly expressed. The universality of moral codes is a fact profounder than the fact that they disagree. Men not only know that the distinction between right and wrong is a genuine one, but they know that they are obligated to be virtuous. More than this, there is not *total* disagreement about ethical content. For there is culture among all men. And there must be some unanimity of ideals for culture to exist. Oswald Spengler's thesis that there is no culture, but only diverse cultures, their meaning wholly individual, is destructive of meaning. Even between competitive codes some point in common may be found. The fact is that even when considered universally, the moral scene does not reduce to animal relativism. The adage, "one man's food is another man's poison," is as true of universal ethics as of universal diet. Some men's food is some men's poison. But the human menu will disclose, for all its variations, some common denominator despite the differences of preparation.

The second is that this varied content of ethics can be explained readily by the principle of distortion. There is no need either to deny universal ethical content or to insist on ethical relativity. Sin produces this distortion of content. It is, in fact, a preferable explanation because the denial that man possesses innately any ethical criteria leads to moral relativism. It is impossible to arrive at an absolute distinction between what is right and wrong from observation of human experience alone. One cannot even hold that the distinction between good and bad is a permanent one. Moreover, the fact that man universally, in his compromises of ethical norms, retains the capacity for a feeling of guilt enforces this conviction that moral realities are outraged by his present violations of them.

The third factor is the biblical sanction for a universal ethical content. For a Christian any belief he holds must be rooted in biblical theology. It is clear from the Scriptures that conscience has transcendental significance because of man's created relationship to God. Man's superiority to the animal creation is due to his possession of a unique life in which the Logos is "the Light of men" (Jn. 1:4) who "lights every man" (1:9). Men have a knowledge of God by external nature (Rom.

1:20). Also, the law is "written on their hearts" (2:15). They know "the just judgment of God, that they which commit such things [cf. Paul's list of vices in the immediate context] are worthy of death" (1:32).

Despite all the subjective and environmental factors that enter into conscience, man is still brought before the moral judgment of God by his conscience. The fall and the consequent moral deformities of Gentile life have not destroyed all the moral elements of human nature. Some ethical factors are indestructibly written on the heart of even the most depraved. The Apostle Paul writes to the Romans that the Gentiles, who lack the Mosaic law, "show the work of the law written in their hearts, their conscience also bearing witness to it, and their thoughts accusing or excusing one another" (Rom. 2:14f.). The law is written on the heart of pagans who do not have special revelation. Man not only has this law on the basis of creation, but he also hears it. The conscience is a second "knowing," a "knowing alongside" of the moral instinct. By its assent it validates the implanted moral law. Reason accuses or excuses as conscience directs.

Calvin noted that it is in and through conscience that man "appears before the judgment seat of God." This transcendent judgment "is as it were appointed sentinel to man, which observes and examines all his secrets that nothing may remain buried in darkness."[6] The significance of conscience is not merely the formal distinction of right and wrong. It is in some sense an immediate — yet implanted — Divine revelation that has a definite conceptual content. The principles of moral law confront man in and through conscience.

Man is a creature responsibly bound to the will of God. His Maker delights in righteousness and abominates wickedness. Man's turning aside into sin disrupts his service of the Creator and places him in the service of idols. These are immediate implications of his moral nature.

Hence, the phenomenon of conscience possesses more than an immanental basis. Rather, it secures a transcendent basis for ethical experience in and through the fact that man has the moral image of God. Conscience in fallen man cannot be identified uncritically with the will of God. Nonetheless it is the point at which the content of the moral *imago* is brought to bear on the moral predicament. It links man at once to his responsibility before God and to the sense of impending judgment for sin. "For our conscience," writes Calvin, "does not permit us to sleep in perpetual insensibility, but is an internal witness and monitor of the duties we owe to God, shows us the difference between good and evil, and so accuses us when we deviate from our duty.[7] . . . The conscience cannot sustain the load of iniquity, without an immediate discovery of the Divine judgment."[8]

[6]Calvin, *Institutes*, III, xix, xiv.
[7]Calvin, *Institutes*, II, viii, i.
[8]*Ibid.*, II, viii, iii.

When it comes to a detailed exposition of the moral content of the *imago,* however, difficulty multiplies. The reason is threefold.

Man as sinner knows the *imago* only from the perspective of revolt. He is one who distorts it in the handling. And he cannot by his own initiative reconstruct from within moral rebellion what the *imago* is really like. The point is not that the objective clarity of the *imago* is gone. That it is *not* destroyed is presupposed from man's universal accountability for personal sin, and from the explicit teaching of the New Testament. But the *imago* is seen falsely by man in his subjective reception and exposition of it. If this negating process were merely a necessity of his nature, he would not be personally responsible for it. But he is responsible, for it grows out of an inherited disposition to which he consents, and which he enforces. Man from within his moral revolt so greatly mars the *imago* given him as a creature that he himself needs spiritual reconstruction through redemption.

An added difficulty is that special revelation does not define for us the precise content of the original *imago.* Scripture assuredly exhibits the moral claim in its fullness. It is certainly more comprehensive in content than is our knowledge solely from general revelation. For it speaks of man's predicament in sin, from which it proposes at last to rescue him entirely by the gradual fulfillment of the Divine program. Special revelation is historical and progressive: the incarnate Ideal and Redeemer, and the completed Scripture, are its peaks. It follows that the eternal and universal will of God is exposited in this long redemptive history with greater completeness than what fallen and pagan man can distill from the *imago* alone.

A further consideration is that from the earliest history of man the Divine image was not regarded as a self-sufficient moral guide to be considered apart from dependence upon the Creator. Even though the discerning and reasoning faculties of unfallen man were indispensable to him in the moral situation, God still addressed him in statutes and precepts in external revelation. Thus, even prior to the fall of man we find in the creation narrative evidence of a necessary dependence upon supernatural Divine revelation for adequate content of the will of God.

The Old Testament sets forth precepts which were externally addressed to man both before and after the fall. The New Testament imposes on the righteous man precepts known neither by general revelation nor through the Old Testament disclosure. Even if it be emphasized that New Testament moral requirements are implicit in the Old, not all are explicit. This should caution us against a too hasty insistence that the content of general moral revelation through the *imago* is broader than the moral content of special revelation. The epistemological predicament of man-as-sinner indeed suggests the opposite. The experience of redemption brings an enlarged and purified expression of the will of God. But redemptive ethics purposes more than to restore man to the spiritual relationship with God which was his to enjoy on the basis of the *imago Dei.* The revelation in Scripture enlarges the moral knowledge that natural man had before or after the fall.

But this fact should not be interpreted to give comfort to those who tend to find only a flimsy, vague, and indefinite content in the moral *imago*. The fall of man does indeed mean the loss of genuine piety. But it does not mean the loss of *all* knowledge of God and moral claims. Nor does it mean the loss of man's ethical accountability. The clear teaching of the epistle to the Romans is that the natural man is constantly confronted by general revelation and is morally responsible.

The continuity of special revelation with general revelation is everywhere a biblical assumption. The very commandments given to man-in-sin in a "thou shalt not" form suggest as their presupposition a "thou shalt" addressed to man on the basis of creation. Special revelation does not supersede the general revelation, but rather republishes the moral knowledge enjoyed by man in the state of integrity. Divine revelation is one. It represents a comprehensive unity. There is but one truth and one good. The broken rationality and morality of fallen man do not excuse him from responsibility in his dealings with the ultimate rational and moral structure of things.

The line of continuity is to be established in human experience from the perspective of special revelation, not from the perspective of general revelation. For the knowledge by general revelation is always wrongly put together by man-as-sinner. Whenever he systematizes it he distorts it because the mind is in the service of a morally rebellious will. This should be carefully differentiated from the existential view which holds to the fallacy that the moral command cannot be rationally grasped, and that when it is cast in rationally consistent form it is always and necessarily misconceived. Whether some men desire it this way or not, the fact is that human beings do order their religious and moral experience by guiding principles that are inevitably reflected in their conduct. An attack upon the rationality of morality is in the last analysis an attack on morality itself. In the historic Christian view, the moral command can be rationally and propositionally expressed. Man's finiteness limits his understanding of the moral law. Man's sin conceals and distorts that law. But special revelation expresses it with rational consistency.

The continuity of general ethics with the ethics of special revelation is not the straight-line continuity that natural theology would have in the Thomistic tradition of confident rationalism or in the more modest position of Butler and the "probablists." The continuity between the two appears broken from the standpoint of the natural man. Indeed he is prone to attack and repudiate revealed ethics rather than hail it as the fulfillment of his higher ideals. But redemptive revelation uncovers the point of connection as it attacks man's pride and unmasks his pretense and the arbitrary speculation with which he has enshrouded the *imago*. It shows that man has reduced the moral claim of the *imago* to something less than itself, and quite other than itself. He can no longer be comfortable in the presence of the Divine moral claim. And to escape its demands, he remakes it more to his liking. The product of the remade *imago* is always an ethics beyond animalism, and yet one not oppressively out of reach. But this reduction of the moral ideal increases man's prospect for soul-discomfort when the sinner is unmasked as the moral rebel he is.

Pride and rebellion color his speculative reconstruction of the moral claim of the *imago*. Hence, the connection of revealed ethics with the content of the moral *imago* is apparent to the sinner only in the light which special revelation sheds. The natural content must be reinforced by special Divine confrontation that is objectively and irreducibly given in the biblical revelation. In a dramatic unmasking of fallen man's pride and rebellion for what it really is, the acknowledgment of his sinful pretensions is an indispensable element in his participation in the benefits of redemption.

It is true that by formal logic one can objectively present the Christian world-life view over against competitive views. But the construction of systems of ethics by the unbeliever is his most formidable defense against the Christian view since it gives him a somewhat consistent refuge from the demands of Christianity. However, an abiding point of contact with the *imago Dei* remains in the conscience. The moral content which man always bears because of the *imago* enters into the stuff of which ethical theories are made. By using internal criticism, Christian ethics may demonstrate the inner weakness and deficiency of competitive moral positions. The superior consistency of the Christian view can be seen once its presuppositions are granted. Revealed ethics best saves significance for the highest objectives of competitive views. But not until the whole man — guilty and proud — repents will Christian ethics be openly admitted as a live option for life. Nor until then will the truth and absoluteness of the ethics of creation, redemption, and the future judgment be acknowledged.

The ethics of redemption is not a new morality that reflects a fundamental change in the will of God regarding the essential content of the good. It preserves in full force his rule of righteousness. Calvin did not hesitate to say that "the internal law . . . suggests to us in some measure the same things which are to be learned from the two tables" of the Decalogue.[9] Calvin's discussion of the content of the moral image on the basis of creation is not fully elaborated. Dowey professes to find in Calvin's writings a moral content on the basis of creation which includes the obligation to worship God, honoring of parents and rulers, monogamous marriage, property rights, benevolence to the

[9] Calvin, *Institutes*, II, viii, i.

needy, respect for the aged, and the preservation of human life.[10] Calvin, however, does assign a content to the universal sense of divinity. This rescues it from vague feeling. The content includes the knowledge that God exists, that he is one, that he is a God of glory and majesty, and that he is omnipotent. Alongside this seed of religion universally implanted in men, he finds in conscience the engraved distinction between good and evil and a knowledge-content involving "some notions of justice and rectitude . . . implanted by nature in the hearts of men. . . . For though they have not a written law, they are yet by no means wholly destitute of the knowledge of what is right and just."[11] The sense of shame which accompanies wicked deeds clearly shows the survival of this imprinted knowledge of right and wrong. "Why were they ashamed of adultery and theft except that they deemed them evils? . . . They have thus indeed proved . . . that adultery, and theft, and murders are evils, that honesty is commendable. . . . It matters not whether they permitted the coveting of another man's wife, or of his possessions, or of anything which was his, — whether they connived at wrath and hatred; inasmuch as it was not right for them to covet what they knew to be evil when done."[12]

E. Doumergue proposes a fuller list. But it is not clear whether he restricts these to an *innate content* of conscience, or to what conscience approves in experience. The detailed reconstruction of the principles of piety and charity on the basis of the *imago Dei* is too speculative a task for fallen man. And it is unnecessary for redeemed man. Redemption clarifies the will of God for man and grants him power to conform more and more to its intense claims. Calvin's interest in the content of the *imago* in fallen man is that it renders him guilty and without excuse. He does not attempt a full speculative reconstruction. This is also the New Testament standpoint.

The possibility of an *imago*-content is assailed by recent spokesmen for Christian ethics who hold to a dialectical theology. The admission of any moral knowledge simply on the basis of the Divine image in man, they contend, would compromise the depravity of man, and hence, the doctrine of justification by faith alone. The possession of any

[10]Edward A. Dowey, Jr., *The Knowledge of God in Calvin's Theology* (New York: Columbia University Press, 1952), p. 71.

Dowey's treatment of revelation is confused. He asserts special revelation to be only the revelation of God in the person of Christ and not what is contained in Scripture. But Calvin looks upon Scripture itself as special revelation objectively given. The general revelation discloses God as Creator, the biblical revelation both as Creator and Redeemer. As Calvin asserts, the knowledge of God is manifested "both in the structure of the world and in the general tenor of Scripture simply as the Creator, and afterwards . . . in the person of Christ as Redeemer" (*Institutes,* I, 2, i). But this distinction provides no basis for identifying special revelation only with the revelation through the historical Jesus, nor for assimilating the doctrine of Scripture apart from the revelation of the Redeemer to general revelation.

[11]Calvin, *Commentary on Romans,* 2:14.

[12]*Ibid.,* 2:15.

glimmer of knowledge of the truth is disparaged as a work of the flesh. It is irreconcilable with the acknowledgment of man's depravity as a sinner. But that every act of every human being is sinful is not at all the point of dispute. Rather, the issue is one of truth and meaning, not of virtue.

The denial that man-as-sinner possesses any knowledge whatever of God and his purposes destroys the basis of moral responsibility which the Scriptures locate in man's knowledge of God.[13] The image of God involves not merely the forms of reason and morality, but also an intelligible content which is addressed to man. Nowhere is this content wholly obscured by sin.

The question arises whether this does not issue in a trustworthy natural morality — an ethics of natural law. This possibility is ruled out because the *imago*-content is distorted by the sinner in the handling. Whatever propositions from general revelation are a part of the sinner's moral venture — and the combination and recombination of elements of general revelation vary with the preferences of the moral agent — they are always incorporated into a frame of reference forged by one who is in moral revolt. Thus the *imago*-content is pressed into the service of alien theories of morality.

What is necessary is a distinction between the moral content of the *imago* and the *systems* of ethical behavior that use elements of the *imago*-content in a non-Christian manner. Truth is a system of propositions, and a given proposition can be declared true or false only in relation to an implicative whole. The *imago*-content is reduced, distorted, and even falsified as it is incorporated into spurious systems of ethics.

These systems handle the *imago*-content in such a way as to conceal man's predicament in sin and his hopelessness apart from supernatural redemption. The more sturdily a rebellious ethics is constructed the more the *imago*-content is likely to be neutralized and refashioned. Only biblical ethics proclaims the terrifying truth that man is condemned already on the basis of light which he constantly seeks to darken and that these other systems are sophisticated means by which he would substitute man-made gaslamps for the imprinted beaconlight of general revelation.

It is not in the *systems,* but in *men* themselves that the point-of-contact with the *imago Dei* is to be found. Man, whether he follows Naturalism or Idealism, bears the image. It is the transfer of broken elements of the *imago*-content into secular ethics which actually leads to the major inconsistencies in those systems. Not even the ethics of self-conscious revolt against God and objective morality can fashion its system of morals without borrowing something, even if inadvertently, from the ethics of creation. And the spokesman for anti-God and anti-

[13]That knowledge is an essential basis of responsibility is supported by such biblical passages as Daniel 5:22, Luke 12:47f., and John 15:22.

morality lives closer to the *imago* than does his system of ethics. For the *imago* is a subjective phenomenon of human life and can nowhere be totally pulled out by the roots.

That is why Christian ethics addresses more than the competitive systems of ethics. It speaks directly to man the moral agent who is lost in sin and accountable to a holy God. It has little difficulty pointing out the inner inconsistencies in the speculative ethical framework. And it can find in them emphases which would be acceptable enough in a proper context. But it is not happy to single out such elements of formal agreement as constituting a welcome natural morality and half-way house to the ethics of special revelation. For it is the system as a whole which determines the intention of the particular elements within it. Those propositions are not two-thirds true and one-third false at any point — but either true or false. From the standpoint of Christian revelation and ethics, it is accurate to say that it is impossible for the ethics of revolt to set up a system without some measure of dependence upon the *imago* which survives in fallen man. But those elements gain their truth and vitality from the *imago,* not from the speculative schemes in which they are developed.

The Christian doctrines of knowledge and of ethics interpenetrate each other. The derivation of the whole of reality and life from a rational God means that any proposition gains its truth only from the Christian system. We shall stress that speculative ethics, even where it wrestles earnestly with the moral question, does so within the context of moral revolt. The essential difference between the ethics of special revelation and the ethics of speculative philosophy is that the former develops the *imago*-content as it was ideally intended. The latter always reflects the determination of the sinner to deny that he is confronted by a holy God who judges him.

5

CHRISTIAN ETHICS AND THE ANTITHESES OF SPECULATIVE MORALITY

ETHICS HAS BEEN characterized, as we have noted, by two broad traditions — Idealism and Naturalism. Each has had its speculative and existential wings. These traditions oppose each other in a struggle to the death. They base their claims on vastly different starting-points. Naturalistic ethics begins with the controlling idea that nature is the ultimate reality. Man is no more than a complex animal. Moral distinctions are relative and fluctuating. They change as perspectives change. Idealistic ethics starts from opposite assumptions. The eternal spiritual realm is logically prior to the space-time world. Man is a compound creature anchored to the natural world. He is superior in essence to the animals by virtue of his capacity for self-transcendence and reason. These implicate him as part of the spiritual world. Truth and morality are not phantoms, but are objective and unchanging.

From another point of view these two life-views are not in ultimate contradiction after all. They represent the two main traditions of *speculative ethics. Revelational ethics* objects to them because both are conceived in sin. They are self-justifying efforts to be morally right while rebelling against God. The one tradition takes the course of animalism. It avoids the truth about man's moral predicament by assimilating man to the world of nature. The other tradition takes the course of deifying man. It conceals the desperate ethical plight of man by assimilating him to the supernatural. The ethics of special revelation unmasks them both as man-made, speculative distortions of the real ethical situation. They are attempts to align sin with fallen conscience. Each can be classified by the extent of moral concession in its system. Martensen refers aptly to "the morality of compromises," of a "continued lulling of the conscience amid light-hearted appeasements," which finds security only by boasting that the morality of forgiveness of sins "belongs to an antiquated and overcome standpoint."[1]

Specially-revealed ethics shows secular ethics to be less than trustworthy in its interpretation of the moral scene. Secular ethics is not an exposition of general revelation; it reflects the distortion that is the result of human sin. Christian ethics refuses to embrace speculative

[1]H. Martensen, *Christian Ethics,* trans. from German by William Affleck (Edinburgh: T. & T. Clark, 1884), I, 107.

ethics as the ethics of the kingdom. Rather, it discerns therein both the broken image of general revelation and the reflection of the moral revolt of man worked out in arrogant pride or servile self-effacement. The very best of rationalistic ethics is not an "elemental Christian ethics," for even that best distorts the true nature of the good.

An effective way of showing the contrast between revealed ethics and speculative ethics lies in the manner in which revealed ethics solves the moral tensions that speculative ethics creates. The problems of ethics are enduring problems. Man has them always with him. Speculative thought grapples with these problems, only to split over the answers. The net result is many conflicting answers to the same moral question. Man may take his pick — but somehow the edge is taken off his moral eagerness. If no one really knows, why should he be earnestly concerned? Christian ethics rises above this party strife, giving an ultimate answer to the moral question.

Rationalistic ethics, as is obvious even from our sweeping survey, fails to overcome antagonisms between the religious and the ethical, between freedom and necessity, between duty and happiness, between egoism and altruism, and between ethical form and content. It is frustrated in the effort to do justice to both elements of these antitheses. Each successive viewpoint issues in an unsatisfactory adjustment of one to the other. The attempt to treat satisfactorily one side of the antimony tends to work a corresponding injustice upon the other. This should be obvious from a glance at the history of speculative ethics. Here the extremes protrude readily into view.

(1) There are the religious views which sacrifice the ethical. This is especially true of the mystical-pantheistic systems which regard God and the ecstatic life as "beyond good and evil." They may retain an ultimate significance for the good and the true, but so make God and man one as to destroy the ethics by regarding the moral "is" as the "ought." At the other extreme stands humanistic ethics, which destroys the religio-supernatural element at the same time it tries to preserve the seriousness of the moral struggle.

(2) There are the libertarian views. They aim to preserve the realities of the moral situation by the doctrine of free will. This leads, in modern theories, to the conception of ethics as autonomous. Man is wholly creative in the moral world. Here one thinks of the influence of Kant upon moral theory and the extension of that influence in Personalism and later phenomenalistic and existential ethics. They emphasize in common that the individual would not be morally free if the moral *ought* were externally addressed to the conscience and if any reality external to him were a factor to be considered in determining his decisions. Opposite to these views are the unapologetic defenders of a necessitarian or deterministic morality, *e.g.*, the Stoic and Spinozistic schools.

(3) Then there are the moral philosophies that emphasize the *form* of ethics, but whose practical value for the man in the street is nullified

by a failure to make clear how any content for ethical living can be determined. There is no guidance for practical decisions in every-day moral situations. For example, the Kantian dictum, "act always so as to treat another person as an end, and never as a means," sounds ideal, but is really very vague. On the other side are ethical schools which conceive their task to be the minute codifying of ethical conduct. They cover as many of the details of life as possible, but fail at the crucial point of relating such deeds to a controlling principle which can give a cohesive moral unity to the whole.

(4) There is contradiction within teleological moral philosophies which gives rise to controversy between egoism and altruism. One wing identifies the *summum bonum* with the happiness of the individual. This is especially true of the pre-Christian world with its numerous varieties of egoistic hedonism. Opposing this group is the utilitarian viewpoint with its identification of the good with the happiness of the greatest number.

(5) There is disagreement between the teleological and the ateleological schools, dividing the whole history of speculative morality. The teleological camp declares that the morality of an act depends upon its consequences, upon its actual production of the end at which it aims. The ateleological camp declares that an act is virtuous if it proceeds from a good motive, regardless of the consequences. This antithesis works out finally into an irreconcilable antagonism between pleasure and duty, and the identification of the good life with one element to the exclusion of the other.

In the long history of moral philosophy intermediary positions have arisen in which these antitheses are not expressed so extremely, but are adjusted in varying degrees to each other. But the characteristic of speculative ethics lies in this: it is always by an adjustment of one of these elements to the other that it seeks solution, rather than by transcending the antitheses in a higher approach.

That each of these elements — religion and morality as a unity, freedom and necessity, duty and happiness, egoism and altruism, form and content — has its indispensable place in an adequate ethical approach, is not under dispute. And the determination of moralists to preserve one or another of these factors comes from a genuine basis which these elements have in the objective ethical order. They are required because of general moral revelation. The *imago Dei* invests these elements with permanent significance for the moral life. The failure of the speculative schemes lies not in their retention of one or another of these elements, but in the manner in which they are retained. In the system of checks and balances some elements are preserved at the expense of others, and therefore those elements which are preserved have a distorted and one-sided significance. Doubtless at some points one theory may be closer to the significance which general revelation and the *imago* require for these elements than will a rival theory. This diversity in dealing with the essential ingredients of the moral problem accounts for the variety of speculative systems. But there is also another way of accounting for them. The revolt of the man in sin against the proper claims of the ethical order expresses itself in many ways. One temperament is prone to give up easily one set of elements; another temperament desires to hold on to those same elements.

Scientific morality differs from popular morality in its attempt to reduce these preferences to a convincing coherence and consistency. The half-heartedness and hesitancies of one school yield, by way of reaction, to the more thorough adjustments of the other. And the frustrating verdict of the long history of speculative ethics is that its energies have been invested in the promulgation of systems which are in impressive contradiction. The survey of non-Christian ethics, Brunner affirms, yields the verdict that "none of these systems achieves a real synthesis," and that while each has its own value and its own weakness, their unsatisfactoriness cannot be eliminated by a recombination of selected elements.[2]

The present disintegration of Western culture represents a considerable inability to reconcile the competing demands of morality. The modern mind is not convinced of the truth of any moral claim due to the babble of voices, each asserting its own "truth." This sense of frustration in defining the nature and content of the *ought* plagues almost every phase of culture. Writing of American education, James Mulhern mirrors the growing disposition to consider social ethics, no less than individual ethics, beyond the possibility of rational synthesis: "Our educational thinking in the present century has been marked by an effort to reconcile the logically irreconcilable notions of freedom and equality, to effect a compromise between the needs of the individual and the needs of society, while preserving the essence of our faith in individualism."[3] Here the pervasive temper is that equality requires the repudiation of freedom, and that the individual good may be secured only at the expense of the social good, and vice versa.

Recent existential thinkers attempt to bridge the antinomies of speculative ethics by disavowing the possibility of a rational synthesis and proposing instead a "faith-synthesis" which perpetuates the tension as a religious asset. This school of thought, of which Niebuhr is the most vigorous exponent, argues that any effort to reduce the claims of the ethical life to rationally-consistent principles destroys the original tension of Christian morality. It asserts that Christian ideals are transcendently related to the historical. But in reality, the abandonment of devout reason as a criterion springs from an extreme view of Divine transcendence. It results in an objectionable antithesis between eternity and time, and a neglect of the rational and moral significance of the

[2]Emil Brunner, *The Divine Imperative,* p. 43.
[3]James Mulhern, *A History of Education* (New York: Ronald Press, 1946), p. 612.

imago Dei which survives in fallen man,[4] and a failure to apprehend the persistent demand of man for a coherent understanding of the whole of his experience. It does violence, moreover, to the fact that the biblical revelation is couched in the form of revealed truths and principles, and is addressed to the whole man through the intellect. There is therefore every reason for avoiding the existential despair of reason.

The ability of Christian ethics to reconcile the competing claims of the ethical situation and to present them with logical coherence and consistency gives it one of its compelling advantages over speculative ethics. Hebrew-Christian ethics is not content simply to take the broken fragments of discordant morality and to blend them into an eclectic whole. Rather, it transcends the antinomies of the speculative systems. It transcends them, not by abandoning the enduring need of man for a coherent grasp of the form and content of morality, but by exhibiting that form and content in such a way as to do justice to all the legitimate claims of the ethical life and neglecting none. It meets head-on the problems which speculative ethics is unable to resolve. Taken comprehensively, truth is on the side of Stalker's declaration that "the answers proceeding from the Great Teacher are directed to the very problem on which the human mind has always been pondering."[5]

The Hebrew-Christian revelation unveils the fact that God and the good are inseparable considerations. Worship of God and devotion to the good of man no longer stand as separable possibilities. Hinduism, or the old Greek and Roman polytheism with their immoral divinities, or Mysticism with its ecstatic union with God coupled with social passivity, is discredited. Also discredited is the modern movement for individual and social justice that builds on non-religious or anti-religious foundations — whether Positivism in the past generation or Humanism and Communism in ours. Each of these fosters a legitimate interest that is carried out in an objectionable and perverse manner. Genuine ethics is theonomous, the good is God-formulated. Pure religion is ethical; biblical Theism requires the love and service of one's fellow-man as an essential expression of the service of God. The ethics of Divine revelation stands against speculative ethics by exhibiting the good as the will of God alone and by insisting upon a holy neighbor-love as an essential expression of love for God.

The summary of the Law, as Jesus Christ authoritatively expressed it, establishes not only the inseparable connection of true religion and ethics, but also the priority of worship. Dean Pike notes in a chapter intriguingly entitled "Worship and Evangelism" that the "first and great commandment" to love God with one's whole being has its parallel in

[4]Niebuhr himself assigns to general revelation and reason an importance for the moral life not found in Barth, and beyond that acknowledged by Brunner, but he nonetheless repudiates its ontological significance as an instrument for comprehending reality.

[5]James Stalker, *The Ethic of Jesus According to the Synoptic Gospels* (New York: George H. Doran, 1909), p. 17.

the first two of the Ten Commandments. He remarks that "Christian ethics unequivocally starts with God; thus our first ethical duty is the exaltation of God in our lives."[6] God is to be adored not simply as a means to something else, but for his own sake. Such worship leads the heart to neighbor-love, and, in fact, imposes it as a necessity of the moral life. Religion which saps away the fundamental principles of morality certainly gains no tolerance from Jesus Christ. Just as the ethics of Jesus is inseparable from his religion, so his religion demands morality. Man is to will what God wills. Jesus lifted both ethics and religion to new heights from which they cannot recede without decay. Vallings properly reminds us that "Jesus Christ effected an alliance and a permanent reconciliation between religion and morality. . . . He found a moral factor in all religion. He enshrined forgiveness and brotherly love in the prayer of prayers."[7] Therefore Christian ethics rises above those tendencies which would preserve the religious at the expense of the ethical or which would sacrifice God-love for neighbor-love. True as it is that God is to be adored primarily for himself and not as a means, the mood of worship which cuts itself off from neighbor is not a worship acceptable to the Living God. Neither are moral duties toward men to proceed simply from abstract principle. Religion and ethics are inseparable. God-love which does not require neighbor-love, neighbor-love which does not flow from God-love, these are perversions of true religion and sound ethics.

The Gospel raises the debate over determinism and freedom to wholly new dimensions. The biblical revelation that man is a creature excludes absolute liberty, but finds man's freedom is in his proper union with his Maker. Outside that union he falls into bondage. Whatever may be said about man's power of self-determination, he, as an unredeemed man, has squandered the power of acting according to his true or ideal nature. The question of freedom must be answered in the light of the nature of his spiritual life as a whole and such liberty as is inherent in it. One of the ironies of speculative ethics is that so many of its traditions insist centrally upon the freedom of the moral agent, and yet it is so barren of genuine moral achievement. Augustine set the discussion in its biblical context: only that man is free who is free to do the will of God; man as sinner, who revolts against the will of God, is in bondage. "When ye were the servants of sin," Paul writes, "ye were free from righteousness" (Rom. 6:20). Luther's treatise on *The Bondage of the Will* reflects substantially the same viewpoint. The liberty of the flesh, adds Calvin, "so frees us from obedience to God, that it makes us slaves to the devil."[8] The freedom of man is tied up wholly with the Gospel and with the new birth. "If the Son shall make you

[6]James A. Pike, *Doing the Truth: A Summary of Christian Ethics* (Garden City: Doubleday, 1955), p. 99.
[7]J. F. Vallings, *Jesus Christ the Divine Man: His Life and Times* (New York: Revell, n.d.), p. 224.
[8]Calvin, *Commentary on Romans,* 6:20.

free, you shall be free indeed" (John 8:36). "Where the Spirit of the Lord is, there is liberty" (2 Cor. 3:17). Outside redemption there is no release from bondage to sin. In Calvin's words, "no one can be a servant to righteousness except he is first liberated by the power and kindness of God from the tyranny of sin."[9]

But this liberty is a new bondage, an ethico-spiritual service of the holy Lord. Brunner clearly sees that "this freedom is at the same time complete captivity, indeed more than that: it is absolute dependence on God's action."[10] Paul states the fact pithily: "Being then made free from sin, ye became the servants of righteousness" (Rom. 6:18); "now, being made free from sin, and become servants to God . . ." (6:22). But this servitude to Christ is no mechanical determinism. It is rather an ethical compulsion in which liberty and necessity meet in unswerving dedication to the right and good. The life in the Spirit is a life of obedience in which one finds freedom in voluntary service of Christ. It is liberty within the government of the Spirit.

Archibald Alexander once remarked that "a man is never so free as when he is the bondsman of Christ."[11] This echoes Paul's word that "the law of the spirit of life in Christ Jesus hath made me free from the law of sin and death" (8:2). "Christ's cross . . . delivers Christians from what may be termed moral drudgery; they are not oppressed and pined serfs, but freemen and fellow-heirs, serving the Lord Christ with all gladness of heart."[12] Yet Paul was the slave of Christ, "bringing into captivity every thought to the obedience of Christ" (2 Cor. 10:5). "True liberty, in the spiritual as well as the civil sphere," as Fairbairn remarks, "is a *regulated* freedom; it moves within the bonds of law, in a spirit of rational obedience; and the moment these are set aside, self-will rises to the ascendant, bringing with it the witchery and dominion of sin."[13]

The vocabulary of the Pauline epistles is filled with such words as serve, servant, service. The difference "between Saul of Tarsus and Paul the Apostle," as W. G. D. MacLennan has noted, "lies in the nature of the obedience. The old obedience was a bondage in the spirit of servants; the new is a bondage in the spirit of sons. The difference is world-wide. The one is service in the mood of cringing obedience . . . the other . . . of mutual confidence and reciprocal love."[14] Bondage to Christ is the glad response of the recipient of unmerited favor; it is a filial rather than a legal obedience.

[9]*Ibid.*, 6:18.
[10]Brunner, *op. cit.*, pp. 58f.
[11]Archibald B. D. Alexander, *Christianity and Ethics* (London: Duckworth, 1914), p. 96.
[12]Joseph Parker, *Ecce Deus* (Boston: Roberts Brothers, 1871), ch. XVI.
[13]Fairbairn, *The Revelation of Law in Scripture* (Edinburgh: T. & T. Clark, 1869), p. 284.
[14]MacLennan, *Christian Obedience*. Kerr Lecture (London: Nelson, 1948), p. 40.

Much of the difficulty in modern ethical discussions of the problem of freedom and determinism arises because the question of responsibility is already set in a debatable and sub-biblical context. The presupposition of moral responsibility in the Bible is man's knowledge of the good; the ground of his condemnation is his failure to perform the good. But almost all modern ethical theory reflects a wholly different bias: Freedom is the guarantee of the validity of the moral quest, and determines the very shape of ethical realities.[15] The growing skepticism about changeless moral principles doubtless is a part of a movement away from knowledge as a ground of moral accountability. Modern dialectical moralists, faced by the writings of Barth, Brunner, and Niebuhr, have revolted against the optimistic Kantian formula "I ought, therefore I can." They have reverted to the Pauline-Augustinian alternative "I ought, but I cannot,"[16] even though their conception is based on a profoundly non-biblical theory of the fall of man. The philosophical prejudices of the dialectical view require an abandonment of any possibility of knowledge of the will of God by revealed concepts and principles. They also move toward a one-sided discussion of the question of freedom, and discount knowledge as the ground of responsibility.

The only true freedom is the freedom which is born of the new birth. Prior to that dramatic experience, men are free only to choose which false gods they will serve and what priority they will assign to an arbitrary scale of values. This "freedom" is at the expense of the Divine will, since every motive and act is expressive of a margin of revolt against the Living God. After regeneration men are free to do the will of God. Classic theology had a series of Latin phrases by which it emphasized these facts. Before the fall Adam was *posse non peccare* — able not to sin, and not merely *posse peccare* — able to sin. After the fall he was *non posse non peccare* — not able not to sin. After regeneration this servitude to sin is broken in principle by servicing Christ. Not until man gains a glorified nature will he be *non posse peccare* — not able to sin.

Since the regenerate man becomes an agent of the Divine will and by his acts of obedience facilitates the conquest of the Kingdom of Satan and the triumph of the Kingdom of God, he shares creatively in the unfolding plan of God for the age of grace. In a sense the obedient believer helps to shape the "evolving order." Every moral decision and act is aligned either for or against God's purposes. The believer implements the will of God in his life and thus helps to shape the final outcome of things. The decisions and acts of the world of unbelief must

[15]This prejudice is retained by Dean Pike who, while subscribing to the mythical view of the fall, grants that an analysis of the factors bearing upon decision yields a deterministic conclusion, nevertheless argues from the universal feelings of remorse and guilt to an implied freedom, and ignores the question of outraged knowledge (*op. cit.*, 19).

[16]Cf. the writer's *The Protestant Dilemma* on "The Mid-Century View of Sin" (Grand Rapids: Eerdmans, 1948).

always be overruled and judged. But even in the community of faith, the Divine purpose is not suspended upon the decisions and acts of the faithful since they are fallible in their obedience. Yet the Lord's Prayer, "Thy kingdom come on earth as it is in heaven," more nearly describes the actual situation among believers than it does any other area of life, for the eternal ethic breaks into time conspicuously in the regenerate life of the Church.

Christian ethics exhibits both the form and content of morality without sacrificing either to the other. Here another of its superiorities is evident. It does not offer empty formalism from which no practical guidance for the daily decisions of ethical life can be made. It will be recalled that this is a difficulty both of teleological and of ateleological ethics. Egoism and altruism come to frustration as theories because of their inability to estimate with confidence the consequences of an action. Hence, they provide only hesitant and precarious guidance. Kant grounds the morality of an act in its motive rather than in its results. Yet he fails to show how the categorical imperative can supply guidance for practical decisions. It is just a generality of life. Unless ethical theory provides some particularized direction for the vital decisions of daily life it paralyzes effective moral action.

On the other hand, ethical rationalism ventures to discriminate between approved and disapproved acts but characteristically fails to show just why certain actions are right and other actions wrong. This failure to exhibit the form from which virtuous acts flow is a specialty of secular ethics.[17] Kant's formula that the good can be identified unreservedly only with a good will is almost acceptable if it gains the Hebrew-Christian sense. But Kant's metaphysical agnosticism forbids this. The will conformed to the Divine requirement is good. And the will of God is no empty form. It expresses itself in particular moral requirements, in commandments.

One of the major debates in contemporary ethical discussion centers in the question of how generally the content of revealed ethics should be stated. Dialectical ethics, reflecting a modern epistemological bias, shies away from the biblical identification of the will of God with specific commandments and precepts. Rather, it tends to limit the revealed content of ethics simply to the formula of "love for God and neighbor," or "a Spirit-directed life." The historic Christian view is that biblical revelation provides a content of moral principles and precepts that give specific and practical direction. The Christian revelation of the good as obedience-in-love to the revealed will of God combines the form and content of ethics with an inner unity that is not found in the speculative approaches.

The conflict between egoism and altruism, the promotion of self-interest versus the interest of mankind, is lifted to a new orientation by the second half of Christ's summary of the Law: "Thou shalt love

[17]Gordon H. Clark, *A Christian View of Men and Things,* p. 187.

thy neighbor as thyself" (Mt. 22:39). Unrecompensed love is to structure the whole of life as the Divine command. The moral agent will promote at the same time his own best interest and that of his fellow man by doing the will of God. In love the supreme interests of all men coincide.

The failure of secular morality to reconcile individual and universal interests is an obvious blot upon its history. In the ancient world the naturalistic emphasis on egoistic pleasure implied a clear indifference toward altruistic claims. While Aristotle avoided the emphasis on pleasure, his ethic was nonetheless egoistic. In the modern world that has been conditioned by the Christian impact the ancient egoistic attitudes have been insufferable. That is, until this present century. As the writer of *Ecce Homo* remarks, "The selfishness of modern times exists in defiance of morality; in ancient times it was approved, sheltered, and even in part enjoined, by morality."[18] But the modern secular morality moved to the full swing of the pendulum to the utilitarian emphasis on the greatest good of the greatest number. This anti-egoistic morality was often dignified by calling it Christian. This was because it promoted a species of universal welfare and self-surrender. But Utilitarianism was no more an essentially Christian ethics than was the egoism it replaced. Deep down it still failed to surmount the conflict of egoism and altruism. Ewing rather humorously evaluated it: "In sharp contrast to even the higher egoism and still more to egoistic hedonism the ethical view popularly preached in Christian countries has usually been that the primary virtue is unselfishness viewed as the readiness to sacrifice oneself for other men. But this view cannot, any more than egoistic hedonism, be carried to its absolute extreme. A society in which everybody spent his life sacrificing all his pleasure for others would be even more absurd than a society whose members all lived by taking in each other's washing."[19] A major weakness of this stress on self-sacrifice is its lack of assurance that the individual's own interests are really preserved in the promotion of those of others. And the strength of Christian ethics is that it does not attempt to balance and adjust these claims the one to the other. It is both personal and social, and it holds both in an inner unity which rises above any conflict that may be between them.[20] Love holds the interest of the self and of others together. "Rights, in us, are nothing, but just claims to the performance of duties by others," writes Timothy Dwight. Of the religion of the

[18]Sir John Roberts Seeley, *Ecce Homo* (5th ed., London: Macmillan, 1892), p. 151.

[19]A. C. Ewing, *Ethics* (London: English Universities Press Ltd., 1953), pp. 31f.

[20]"Christianity . . . in its essence . . . is both social and personal, and the one aspect of it cannot be rightly understood apart from the other. This becomes evident when we study the teaching of Jesus and the interpretation of it in the New Testament." Ernest F. Scott, *Man and Society in the New Testament* (New York: Scribner, 1946), p. 20.

Scriptures he states that "as it produces the punctual performance of all the duties, so it effectually secures all the rights of mankind."[21]

The ethics of revelation also overcomes the tension introduced into the moral life when pleasure and duty are set in opposition. Secular ethics has issued on the one hand in an ethics of duty at the expense of personal pleasure, and on the other hand in an ethics of pleasure which threatens to negate duty. The failure to exhibit the organic relation of pleasure and duty is the deficiency which allows for such miscarriage in moral theory. From time to time this has unfortunately colored ethical theories which profess to be Christian. In order to guard the clear biblical emphasis on an objective morality over against a mere deference to subjective preferences and desires, some moralists have felt obliged to eliminate from Christian motivation any consideration of individual pleasure and reward. Thus the cold rigor of a devotion to duty is held to exclude the prospect of future reward or even personal spiritual or material blessings as justifiable ethical motives. On the other hand, secular exponents of the ethics of rigorism have censured the biblical outlook as a morality of compromised inducements, since it promises temporal and eternal blessings. Actually Christian ethics shows the path of duty to be also the path of genuine happiness, and true happiness as the service of God and man. It reconciles the two — and here proves itself again to be superior to secular ethics.

The ethics of Hebrew-Christian theistic revelation commends itself to logical thought because its coherence avoids the conflicts which lurk in the speculative accounts of the moral claim. It rises above the interior contradictions of secular ethics and provides a new integration of the legitimate elements of the moral situation.

"Christianity escapes the difficulties and the futilities of other systems," writes Gordon H. Clark, after a survey of revealed and non-revealed ethics. "And such an escape recommends the position."[22]

[21]Timothy Dwight, *Theology Explained and Defended* (Glasgow, Blackie, 1837), III, 120.

[22]Clark, *op. cit.*, p. 187.

6

THE WORLD OF FALLEN MORALITY

THE WORLD of human decision and relations is a fallen world in revolt against the holy will of the Creator-God. The image of God in man is sullied. Man is a moral rebel who is threatened by Divine wrath.

This fundamental premise places the Christian interpretation of the moral life in direct opposition to sin-concealing views. It gives no quarter to pantheistic and idealistic notions that the whole of reality is made up of an indestructible good. Biblically-revealed ethics dismisses as shallow all evaluations of the ethical situation which hesitate to view sin, death, and Satan as determinative categories. Tolerance of depthless views of the moral predicament in sin would only give birth to equally superficial views of man's deliverance. Christianity clearly points out the moral divorce of God and man. Reconciliation is man's most desperate need.

One need not look far to discover why speculative ethics is embarrassed in the presence of these basic moral categories. The admission of sin, death, and Satan as controlling ideas carries with it additional implications which the speculative theorists care not and dare not to acknowledge. These elements determine both the definition and the solution of the moral problem. That is why non-redemptive ethics verges continually toward the sin against the Holy Spirit. Whereas the sin against the Holy Spirit unequivocally designates the Holy Spirit's work as satanic, speculative ethics refuses to view the world as fallen, unregenerate and demonic, and in its higher traditions tends to refer all human activity directly to a Divine agency.

Christianity declares that God is more than the ground and goal of the moral order. Unequivocally it lays stress on the reality of God's judgment of history. It affirms, that is, the stark fact of moral disorder and rebellion: "the whole world lieth in wickedness" (1 John 5:19). By emphasis on the fact of sin and the shattered moral law of God, on the dread significance of death, on the wiles of Satan and the hosts of darkness, Christian ethics sheds light on the treacherous realities of moral decision. Scripture speaks plainly of this "evil and adulterous generation." Unredeemed men are children of Satan. The broken law slays those who look to it for life. Death is man's wages for sin. The Bible pictures the moral world as a fallen realm. It stands in deliberate and responsible revolt against the Holy Lord. It lacks resources of its own to avoid final doom. The biblical setting for the moral struggle includes Satan, the superhuman agent and coordinator of evil. There is also man's moral bankruptcy before the Divine claim, man's enslavement to sin, and his existence under the Divine sentence of death.

The moral drama may be depicted by the threat posed by the creature world to the rule of God in space-time existence. God takes countermeasures to secure the ultimate doom of Satan and unpenitent moral agents. By dramatic and cataclysmic means he progressively establishes his kingdom in its full sway. As the Kingdom of God enlarges in scope and the Holy Spirit is more active in human life, the ultimate doom of Satan draws closer. Victory over death is more assured. The annulment of the law as an unpaid debt-bill is nearer. And an enlarging triumph over sin becomes the experience of the believer.

The stages of this Divine counter-offensive extend from the fall of Satan and the subsequent fall of man to the final subjugation and doom of all the hosts of evil. The Bible develops this movement from Genesis through Revelation. This drama has several scenes: the creation and fall of man, the Divine offer of redemption to sinful man, the coming of the supernatural Redeemer in human flesh to bear the penalty and guilt of sin, and the final judgment and separation of the righteous and the wicked. But everywhere, in Genesis or the Gospels or the Apocalypse, its background is the struggle between the holy Creator and Satan.

It is against the works of the Devil that the plan of redemption is aimed. Jesus Christ himself regarded his task primarily to be the overthrow of Satan. Revealed ethics therefore cannot properly discuss Christ's view of evil without emphasizing the reality of Satan, the superhuman tempter and ringleader of evil in the spiritual world. Denial of actual existence to Satan became a characteristic tenet of modern Western culture in the decades when it was self-deceived over its moral health. It credited itself with transcendent spiritual achievements even while it was swiftly returning to pagan thought and life. The fallen world reaches bottom in its ridiculing of the fall and its deification of spurious values. The ethics of liberal Protestantism built on an idealistic and evolutionary metaphysics. It found the subject of Satan and fallen spirits an embarrassment. It especially did not know what to do with Christ's acceptance of them.[1]

Harnack had set the mood for viewing belief in demons as a sign of degeneration in religion. He traced the extraordinary spread of belief in demons and second-century outbursts of demonic disease to the loss of the element of faith in pagan religion. Since Harnack allows only

[1]D. C. Macintosh's curious predicament supplies a ready example. His argument for the reality of a personal God is developed empirically from the fact of values present in human experience. On the one hand he contends that there is no necessity to argue from the presence of disvalue in our experience to a persônal Satan. On the other, he asserts that Jesus Christ (who defined the whole struggle of right and wrong in relation to God and Satan) is the supreme example of a personality perfectly adjusted to the moral and spiritual world. *The Problem of Religious Knowledge* (New York: Harper, 1940), pp. 197ff.

an "imaginary world of spirits,"[2] the psychological explanation of demons, which doubtless has a considerable measure of merit, is made to cover the whole. As the pagan world deteriorated into chaos, men were left with deceptive supports. The emptiness of satanic idols is seen starkly when they are unmasked and brought to judgment by the living God. But the historical fact of a renewed awareness of the demonic realm agrees with the New Testament emphasis on the fallen spirit world.

The thesis of the essential goodness of man has been so obviously invalidated by contemporary life that its prestige as a ruling tenet in modern scholarship is lost. It is now seen to be a romantic myth. The nineteenth-century overestimation of the unregenerate man was not a distinct gain for ethical thought. Rather, it removed the basis for a proper understanding of the moral dilemma. It enthroned the dogma that human nature apart from special Divine intervention had abundant resources to fulfill all the demands of the moral law. Kant's dictum, "I ought, therefore I can," became the rallying-cry which concealed human rebellion and corruption. The ethical life was viewed as the occasion for manifesting what is most Divine in man's nature.

The liberal attempt to read the Bible "in the light of the new knowledge" proved to be a mythologizing of revealed ethics. It gave special authority to the speculations of the age. The denial of the fall of man worked itself out in a remarkable twist. Things were deliberately turned around. For Hegel and the pantheizing evolutionists, the "emergence" of the guilty conscience signaled man's "rise" from an amoral ancestry. Rosenberg and the Nazis evolved their own doctrine of a "fall." It was the Nordic failure to conquer "inferior" races because of interbreeding with them.

Simone De Beauvoir has noted one of the motivations which underlies existential philosophy is restoring "a real role to evil."[3] This is a reaction against the idealistic metaphysics which reduced evil to a finite illusion and to the humanistic consignment of it to the non-human world.

Much contemporary theology, despite the return to a more "realistic" estimate of man, hesitates to put the moral problem in its biblical setting.[4] Recent dialectical moralists, among them Emil Brunner and Reinhold Niebuhr, admittedly have reinstated the demonic as a decisive ethical consideration. But they contradict the biblical doctrine in two

[2]Adolf Harnack, *The Expansion of Christianity* (London: Williams & Norgate, 1904), I, 157f. Harnack fails to establish his thesis that Paul's doctrine of sin was unfavorable to exorcism. After remarking that exorcists are never mentioned in Paul's letters, he is compelled to acknowledge Paul's assertion of the reality of demonic spirits in 2 Cor. 12:7, Eph. 6:12 and elsewhere (*ibid.*, 161, n. 2).

[3]Simone De Beauvoir, *The Ethics of Ambiguity*, p. 34.

[4]Amos N. Wilder would assure us that "historically sympathetic appreciation of the phenomena of demonology in the Bible removes the scandal from Jesus' acquiescence in the views of his time at this point." *Eschatology and Ethics in the Teaching of Jesus* (rev. ed., New York: Harper, 1950), p. 11. The Fall is treated as a mythical story which objectifies the experience of the race (*ibid.*, p. 23).

ways. They hesitate to return to the biblical view of Satan as a personal fallen spirit and the invisible master-mind of the revolt against God. Instead they regard whatever is created finite and historical as inevitably evil. This renewed emphasis on sin in human experience is sub-biblical. But the new mood in theology and ethics is seen in Brunner's acknowledgment that "where the significance of Jesus Christ is taught as canonical truth . . . dark supra-mundane forces are mentioned."[5] The role of the demonic and satanic has been highlighted by the rise of modern totalitarian powers. The succession of global military conflicts and the mushrooming of barbarism in social and personal life give some credence to the diabolic. But the avoidance of a doctrine of Satanology has weakened human responsibility since moral evil is regarded as an inevitability of finite existence. In contrast, the Bible sees evil against the background of a resistible though powerful invisible demonic spirit world. The dialectical view of evil leads to a misunderstanding of Christ's triumph over the forces of darkness and to a false picture of the nature of the moral conflict in human experience. It is here that striking revisions of biblical ethical theory may be anticipated in these contemporary views that profess to speak from the standpoint of Christian revelation.

Christ did not hesitate to represent the supreme moral temptations of his incarnate ministry as a contest with Satan. The myth-forming trend about Satan is at its worst when Satan is replaced by sophisticated speculation. The invisible Tempter is an undeniable factor that faces all serious ethics. Jesus Christ specifically instructed his disciples in the Lord's Prayer to ask for deliverance from the evil one. The whole biblical witness is one in its affirmation that God sent his Son into the world to combat and overthrow Satan.

The fallen world of ethical rebellion is depicted in Scripture as under the sway of Satan. It is a kingdom of darkness whose creatures are the servants of the evil one. Twice Jesus speaks of the unregenerate as "children of Satan" (Mt. 13:38, Jn. 8:44). He is the spirit that works in the "children of disobedience" (Eph. 2:2). The New Testament pinpoints the background for the stark realities of evil in Satan himself. Thirty-four times that name crosses its pages in the Gospels, Epistles, and the Apocalypse. Synonyms raise the number of references to forty. Satan is described as the god of this world, blinding the minds of the unbelieving (2 Cor. 4:3f.). Apart from the redemptive activity of God, the fallen world is the threshold of hell itself; it "lieth in the evil one."[6] At the outset of human history this original enemy of God plunged the human race into guilt by seducing its representative, the

[5]Emil Brunner, *The Christian Doctrine of Creation and Redemption,* Dogmatics, Vol. II, trans. Olive Wyon (London: Lutterworth, 1952), pp. 134f.

[6]The force of 1 John 5:19, here referred to, is striking. As the believer is elsewhere pictured by the phrase "in Christ" as in organic union with the Redeemer, so a deep relationship is suggested between the unbeliever and Satan as the inspiration and power of those whom he energizes.

first Adam, to sin. The Old Testament refers the rampant wickedness of pagan life not to atheism but to the service of false gods — idolatry.[7]

The doom of Satan, the original enemy of God, is one of the basic objectives of the Kingdom of God. Throughout the old dispensation, beachheads were made into Satan's realm by the Kingdom of God. The promises of redemptive deliverance began with the Proto-Evangelium (Gen. 3:15). Satan's power was not snapped during the Old Testament period. Almost in one nation alone were men and women rescued from his idolatrous service. He had appalling access to believers, as we know from the experiences of Saul and Job. He even ensnared choice servants of God, such as David, in terrible sins. From the opening of Christ's ministry to its close, he was in an ethical conflict with Satan and his hosts. He himself represented his redemptive vocation as the destruction of the works of Satan. His task, as Harnack acutely notes despite his disbelief in demonology, was not simply "to exorcise and vanquish demons in individual life, but to purify all public life from them. . . . Nor was this mere theory; it was a vital conception of existence."[8] Before Christ's public ministry Satan dared tempt in the wilderness. The redemptive ministry of Jesus Christ included the conquest of Satan in principle, and while Satan has never operated outside the permissive will of God, the subjection of Satan is not a full reality. Yet the fact of his defeat is graphically affirmed and illustrated. Jesus summarizes his ministry by the proclamation that Satan is despoiled of his servants and instruments (Mt. 12:29). The disciples enthusiastically report that even the demons are subject to them. The resurrection defeated Satan in his own devices at their peak of wickedness. The consequences of the incarnation and atonement change the orientation of humanity to Satan. Satan remains as the defiant and influential power in the world of unbelief, which is in darkness (Col. 1:13). The cosmos uncommitted to the Christ is ruled by Satan (Eph. 2:2; cf. Mt. 4:16, Lk. 22:53, Acts 26:18, Rom. 13:12, Eph. 5:8, 6:12). But all excuse for ignorance of the real Lord of heaven and earth is removed by Christ's resurrection (Acts 17:30f.). Satan continues to hinder believers, as we know from the instance of Paul's thorn in the flesh (2 Cor. 12:7, 1 Thess. 2:18). If not resisted, he can wreak havoc in the moral life (Acts 5:3, 1 Pet. 5:8). But the believer is delivered from his sway. The power of the evil one is broken in the life of the redeemed to a measure largely unrealized in Old Testament times, although anticipations of such gracious deliverance may be found in the lives of Abraham, Moses, Isaiah and others. To the extent that Christ rules, Satan is deprived of his power. Satan's position has become objectively a compromised one. The world that is dependent upon the dominion of Satan stands convicted by the Spirit of the

[7]The thesis is thus dignified that the gods a man worships serve as an index to his scale of values.
[8]Harnack, *op. cit.*, pp. 160f.

sinfulness of its unbelief, of the holy righteousness of Christ whom it rejects, and of its service to the prince of this world who is already under sentence (Jn. 16:8ff.). The prayer of Christ sustained Peter against Satan's desire to sift him (Lk. 22:31). After Christ's resurrection believers were urged not to give quarter to Satan (Eph. 4:27) and to stand against his wiles (Eph. 6:11). They were assured that Satan will flee when resisted (Jas. 4:7). The progressive and historical nature of the triumph over Satan is clear from the fact that only after the millennial age is inaugurated is Satan bound. This will be an era in which he will pose no problem for the believer. Whatever scope may remain for individual sin, there will no longer exist any organized kingdom of evil, except for that brief season when Satan is loosed. The complete, final, and eternal subjugation of evil comes at the end of the millennial reign (1 Cor. 15:24, Rev. 20:10), when Satan is doomed to the lake of fire (Mt. 25:41).

Death is another controlling category in biblical ethics. The phases of its conquest are similar to the redemptive triumph over Satan.

Wherever death touches human life, whether physical or spiritual, it is given an ethical significance in biblical theology. The "steady march of death" in the human race, to borrow Homer's phrase, is not dismissed as a normal biological phenomenon. It is explained as a consequence of the Adamic rebellion (Gen. 2:17, Rom. 5:12). Man by creation was made for fellowship with God. He is a compound creature, and the whole man has a destiny in eternity. Death began the violated probation of the first man, and is the result of his disobedience.

Death is a three-headed monster, as the Scriptures depict it: physical, spiritual, eternal. Outwardly, physical death is the separation of the spirit from the body. The body then undergoes dissolution (Eccl. 12:7). But the biblical orientation of death in all its types is ethical. Spiritual death ensues when man is cut off from fellowship with God (Eph. 2:1). Physical death cuts him off from the opportunity for repentance (Heb. 9:27). It perpetuates spiritual death into the irrevocable state of eternal death (Rev. 2:11).

Death is an enemy. The fundamental element in the fear of death, according to the Bible, is neither its shortening of the present life, nor an uncertainty about the future. Rather, it is the certitude of Divine judgment (Prov. 11:4). The natural revulsion at the thought of bodily decomposition is not denied by the Old Testament (2 Sam. 22:5f., Psa. 55:4f.). Through dread of it men are in bondage (Heb. 2:15). The brevity and uncertainty of life and fear of death plague the unredeemed world in its efforts to arrive at a satisfactory pattern of living. Because death is not recognized as an abnormal phenomenon linked with the moral rebellion of the race and connected with the prospect of redemption, it is a monstrous tyrant.

The phases of the triumph of redemption over the fallen world through the inbreaking kingdom of God may be charted in the Divine counter-offensive against dread death. Redemption is directed toward fallen men who stand always under the shadow of death. Only because of the gracious salvation of God is the mass of humanity divided into the lifeless and the living. The offer and provision of redemption provides the possibility of spiritual life. The believer is restored to fellowship with God. Even in the Old Testament, the mitigation of the fear of death is the experience of believers who are assured that God is with them to counteract all the consequences of sin (Psa. 23:4, 116:15). This calmness toward death sets the pious Hebrew life in contrast with the confused and baffled attitude of the Gentile world toward death. Old Testament believers did not share the Gentile melancholy in the face of death, but neither did they share the New Testament cheer. The Old Testament saints were aware that the fate of the righteous after death was far happier than the hopeless plight of the unredeemed. But they recognized that the very fact of physical death means that man still endures the consequences of sin despite the promise of redemption. However, its nature as a penalty is removed. During the time man exists in an intermediate state as a disembodied spirit, the effects of his moral revolt are continually evident, and the benefits of redemption have not yet extended "far as the curse is found." This is doubtless why the Old Testament outlook, so much like the New, dwells to such a very little extent upon the intermediary period. But it looks beyond to the day of resurrection. In this regard Job's delight that in his flesh he is to see God (19:26) may be compared with Paul's assurances that the spirit will not be forever naked in eternity (2 Cor. 5:1-2, Rom. 8:23). Separation of the spirit from the body contradicts man's status as a compound creature who was made for fellowship with God. The intermediate period is one of happiness for the believer, but it is also one of incompletion. It corroborates the fact that the work of redemption is not yet completed and that man bears still the scars of his rebellion.

The fact that ethical implications everywhere permeate the discussion of death in biblical theology means that immortality is sketched only in relation to the moral problem. The Bible is nowhere interested in such an answer to the question of immortality that is ready to settle for mere conscious survival. The Greek and Roman speculation about the survival of the soul and the poetic depicting of the gods' lives as moral debauchery is a wholly different mode of thought from the Hebrew-Christian disinterest in any assurances about the life to come which do not supply a solution of the ethical problem. Immortality holds nothing but the promise of dread and doom if sin is not undone. Only an experience of "eternal life" gives indication of the spiritual and moral tone fit for eternity to come. This alone supplies a worthwhile alternative to spiritual death in the present state. And it is the only assurance that man's destiny in eternity includes a vital fellowship of the whole man with God. There is no other hope in the face of physical death.

Jesus Christ is the first to bring immortality to light (2 Tim. 1:10). He becomes lord over death by annihilating it. Death itself is broken by Christ's triumph over it. He is the firstfruits of the resurrection (1 Cor. 15:20, Rom. 6:9, Rev. 1:18). Christ voluntarily laid down his life for sinners only to take it up again beyond the tomb (Jn. 10:18). This made the new community of faith alive with a sense of victory. The subjective spiritual and moral experience of New Testament believers gains profound reorientation from his resurrection. Not only the fear of physical death, but the sting of spiritual death is removed (1 Cor. 15:55), for to depart and be with Christ is preferable (Phil. 1:23). The life of the spirit has a new dynamic through the Resurrection and Pentecost. The redeemed enjoy in this life a spiritual and moral union with the exalted Redeemer. Already, as partakers of eternal life, they are "risen with Christ" (Col. 3:1). The believer has passed spiritually from death to life (Jn. 5:24) and can view the destruction of his body as the transition to an eternal dwelling (Jn. 8:51, 11:26, 2 Cor. 5:1). He yearns patiently for the future bodily resurrection and for complete conformity to the image of Christ which the future glorified state will bring (Rom. 8:23). He is not sentimentally attached to the present body. Those who have "fallen asleep in Christ" share spiritual fellowship with the One who has carried human nature into the eternities. There they await the future resurrection of the body.

The Divine conquest of death moves into another phase with the millennial age. This age starts with the resurrection of the righteous dead (1 Thess. 4:13ff., Rev. 20:6) and their complete conformity to the glorified Christ (Rom. 8:29, Phil. 3:21, 1 Cor. 15:49). It ends with the second death or final doom of the wicked (Rev. 20:14, 21:8). The future resurrection is the antidote to physical death. Consummating the believer's possession of. eternal life in Christ, it completes the redemptive triumph over death. The eternal kingdom is necessarily one in which redemption has fully annulled the consequences of sin for the redeemed ones. The mediatorial reign of Christ extends until the last enemy, death itself, is abolished (1 Cor. 15:25f.). In the new heaven and the new earth "death shall be no more" (Rev. 21:4).

The entrance of the kingdom of holiness into the fallen order of human relations may also be dramatically shown in the changing position of man before the law. The significance of the law requires fuller treatment at a subsequent point. But the rule of God can be seen in the progressive Divine rescue of man from his fallen lot beneath the law. The law stands out everywhere throughout the Old Testament as the instrument of death to fallen men.[9] Even for Old Testament believers, the law remains a debt-bill, except through the

[9]The commandment which God gave Adam in the state of integrity did not, before the fall, possess the character of an instrument of death.

promise of the Redeemer who is foreshadowed in the sacrificial system. The New Testament also views the law as a death-decree for the sinner (Col. 2:14). The believer cherishes the law because it mirrors the holy will of God (Psa. 1:2, 119:11, 44, Prov. 6:23, Micah 6:8), not because he can hope for salvation through keeping it. His only hope for salvation is Jesus Christ.

Christ alone delivers believers from the curse of the law. The sacrificial system did so only by promise,[10] and he supplied the fulfillment of its unpaid pledge. He "blotted out the handwriting of the ordinances that was against us, which was contrary to us, nailing it to his cross" (Col. 2:14). The statement of debt was marked "paid in full." The unfulfilled law had stood in the way of reconciliation to God, retaining a punitive force against mankind. But Christ in death suffered the curse of the law for men (Gal. 3:13) and thus became the end of the law (Rom. 10:4). The law was nailed to the cross in him. It ceased to block us from God. Because of Christ's life and death, the law is already fulfilled for the believer. It is taken out of the way, it is disarmed. The Christian is given right standing with God by faith in Christ. He lives in justification — victory, in justification — being free from the law, being no longer doomed by it. But he is not, indeed, free from ethical law in the absolute sense. He is doubtless free from certain laws, *e.g.*, the law of sin and death. But the moral law epitomizes the will of the God whom the believer loves. His delight now is to please God in conforming himself to that will. In the Old Testament the day is anticipated when the law will be written upon the hearts of men (Jer. 31:33, Ezek. 11:19, 18:31).

While the inwardly cherished law was a reality in the experience of Old Testament saints, the necessity for repeated sacrifices reminded them that complete justification awaited the fulfillment of God's promises (Heb. 9:9f.). Doubtless even Abraham and the patriarchs enjoyed full salvation. But the atonement and exaltation of Christ provided its ground. This reality lifted the believer's experience into a new spiritual relationship with the law. Pentecost marks the writing of the law upon the heart through the indwelling Spirit (Rom. 5:5). From that time "the law of the Spirit" (Rom. 8:2) becomes a significant ethical category. The law written upon the inward parts is not full-bloomed until sanctification passes into glorification. Man will then receive a spiritual body, a body which is wholly in the service of spiritual claims (1 Cor. 15:44).

In summary, the ethics of Hebrew-Christian revelation deals with morality integrally with the Divine counter-offensive to Satan, sin, and death. An actual fall of man, and his revolt against the ethico-religious design of God in creation, is everywhere presupposed. The Spirit of

[10]The point is not that Abraham, Moses, and Elijah had to wait 1,000 years for salvation, however, for Moses and Elijah appeared with Christ on the Mount of Transfiguration.

God, by whom the universe was fashioned, does not strive forever with the impenitence of man in revolt (Gen. 6:3). "Common grace" admittedly refers to the Spirit the fact that unbelievers have had a conspicuous role in the advancement of culture and the restraint of destruction. The Spirit has given men many talents even though they refuse to recognize their talents as gifts from God. But regardless, the words of Jesus picture the immense gulf between the human world in sin and the Spirit of truth: "Whom the world cannot receive; for it beholdeth him not, neither knoweth him" (Jn. 14:17).

Only the intervention of the grace of God spares the fallen world of human relations from utter doom. The establishment of the Divine rule is seen in the progressive conquest of Satan, sin, and death. It is also apparent from the enlarging influence of the Holy Spirit in the world. In the Old Testament the Spirit was with believers in a profounder way than he was with the unbelieving world. In the older dispensation the Spirit came upon individual men for special purposes and ministries (Gen. 41:38, Num. 27:18, Ezek. 2:2, 37:14), even as he does today. But after Christ's conquest on the cross, the Spirit was sent to indwell believers permanently (Jn. 7:38f., 14:16f., Acts 2:4ff.). Since Pentecost the Risen Christ joins believers together into a single body of which he is the head. And the filling of the Spirit becomes a daily personal prerogative (Eph. 5:18). The outpouring of the Holy Spirit at Pentecost was a great intermediary event before the end of the age of grace. It was a milestone in the inauguration of the Day of the Lord (cf. Peter's citation of Joel 2:28ff. in Acts 2:16ff.). This present age of sanctification in the life of the redeemed looks ahead to the future age when the believer will live forever in a society in which God shall be "all and in all" (1 Cor. 15:24-28). All competitive rule and authority and power shall be completely abolished.

The fact that such desperate and far-reaching measures are brought into play to effect man's rescue indicates something of the desperateness of his predicament in sin. The Scriptures picture his condition as one of guilt, corruption, and liability to penalty. The predicament is two-sided — racial and individual. It springs from his involvement in the Adamic fall and from his own personal transgression of the will of God. As a consequence of original sin he suffers from the guilt of Adam's transgression, inherits a defiled nature, and is exposed to penal evils. But this implication does not destroy his moral responsibility in personal decision. The Bible emphasizes man's personal rebellion more than his participation in Adam's rebellion. By his personal transgressions he daily ratifies the Adamic revolt a hundred times over. The Adamic fount of moral attitude and behavior is perverse. And fallen man identifies himself with it in thought and motive and deed. Thus his guilt and penalty increase, each day storing up additional wrath for the day of wrath.

Recent theologians of neo-orthodox and existential persuasion have reconstructed the biblical doctrine of the fall. The orthodox doctrine of the historical fall of the first man from a state of created innocence is replaced by the doctrine of an existential fall. The fall becomes a repeated experience in the life of everyman in which he translates the Divine claim into something less than its requirements. Niebuhr has given the existential reformulation its most familiar statement. Man is a finite creature who stands anxiously at the juncture of the eternal and the created world. Instead of resolving this anxiety by trust in God, he inevitably seeks his security through sinful means. And so he constantly disfigures the Divine ideal, objectionably actualizing it in self-confident pride. The basic weakness of this view is that it considers as normal what is really an abnormal state of anxiety in the experience of man. It also makes man's fall into sin inevitable, and hence jeopardizes his moral responsibility. And it sets man in an environment of ceaseless spiritual tension. This implies life in a universe devoid of providence and teleology, wherein God no longer holds things together by the word of his power.

It is true that sin does presuppose itself and that a complicated structure of evil does penetrate human history, society, and the individual. But this is a consequence of original sin, not the essence of it. When Dean Pike tells us that "actually original sin is not because of Adam and Eve; rather, the narrative of Adam and Eve is because of original sin,"[11] he little realizes the cost of the exchange. If sin presupposes itself as something inevitable in finite existence, then it can hardly be regarded as something which ought to be condemned. Divine justice would not condemn what is a given in divinely made man.

The existentialist reconstruction contradicts the witness of revelation that sin was not inevitable. Man was created in the image of God and was morally good. He deliberately chose to rebel. The existential contention is that the essence of the doctrine of the fall can be retained without holding to a historical fall. This opens the way for a serious perversion of the work of Christ. Why may not the existential results of the atonement be retained without the historical Jesus? That the New Testament does not view the fall existentially is obvious from Paul's emphasis on "one man" who is the ground of our condemnation. He also stresses that the judgment of God comes equally on those who do not sin after the similitude of Adam's transgression (Rom. 5:12-21). Whether Paul's words have a view to infants, to whom the notion of an existential fall or leap of faith obviously cannot apply, or not, his language — "not after the similitude" — excludes an existentializing of Adamic experience.

The biblical account of the fall has the merit of guarding the integrity of man's original holiness. It keeps his responsibility for moral compromise. It maintains the providential orientation of the universe

[11]James A. Pike, *Doing the Truth,* p. 68.

toward those who are spiritually obedient. And it presents the drama of sin and redemption as a coherent unity. It teaches that sin is a foreign, not inevitable element in man.

Man's plight in sin is depicted in the Scriptures in two ways. There are scathing indictments of particular sins. There are also passages which trace sin to a fundamentally corrupt nature.

The list of human vices usually centers our attention on the gross external sins of the flesh. The Apostle Paul presents seven lists of vices (Rom. 1:29ff., 1 Cor. 5:11, 1 Cor. 6:9, 2 Cor. 12:20, Gal. 5:19f., Eph. 4:31, 5:3, and Col. 3:5ff.). Lindsay Dewar has noted that the sin of fornication holds a prominent place in five of the lists, appearing first on numerous occasions.[12] The refusal to whitewash sexual sins is in contrast with the sexual looseness of the Gentile world of that day and of ours. Sexual sin includes fornication, adultery, uncleanness, lasciviousness and effeminateness. Second in prominence is the sin of covetousness or greed. "Idolatry" in the Colossians passage probably refers to this sin. Extortion may be considered as an extension of it. The unusual evil caused by this sin is suggested by its appearance in five of the lists. The greedy desire for material things is a deadly sin, since it stamps out the loftier longings of the spirit. Also conspicuous is the sin of bad temper, sometimes designated wrath. Its appearance in four of the lists suggests the devastating effect upon the soul of uncontrolled outbursts of violence. Related to this evil are anger, passion, bitterness, railing, blaspheming, malice and murder. Paul's lists include also the sins of the tongue, such as reviling, whispering, backbiting, insolence, boasting, shameful speaking, filthiness, foolish talking, jesting, clamor, and deceit. There are sins of quarreling, such as strife, jealousy, factions, divisions, heresies, swellings, and tumults. The term wickednesses also appears, but it is too general to detail.

Of these sins Paul listed, it is noteworthy that Jesus also condemned fornication, lasciviousness, covetousness, railing, clamor and deceit. In fact, it has been suggested that Paul omits only three sins which Jesus specifically indicted: the evil eye (which may be intended by the reference to sorcery in Galatians), foolishness (to which there may be an allusion in 2 Cor. 11), and false witness (which Paul doubtless assumes to be sufficiently interdicted by the second table of the law; cf. Rom. 13:9).

Of greater importance is the place which Paul assigns to pride. It is the font of sin. This suggests at once the emphasis of Jesus laid on the sins of the spirit. The Jewish world avoided the gross sins of the flesh. It took great pride in being so far above the Gentile world morally. But the searching eye of Jesus Christ uncovered sins of the spirit. These terrible sins had become a characteristic of the Pharisees with their mere outward conformity to the law.

[12]Paul is "at one with Christ, who was really the first seriously to challenge this sin in the pagan world, in which it was rampant." *An Outline of New Testament Ethics* (Philadelphia: Westminster, 1949), p. 150.

If it be true that sin holds in no other ethical system the perilous significance attached to it by Hebrew-Christian morality,[13] it is equally true that Christian ethics stresses the importance of inner motivation as does no other moral system. To Jesus of Nazareth above all Christian ethics owes the emphasis that sin is primarily thought or disposition, and that the sins of the flesh are but the working-out of the wicked inner life.

Christian ethics also espouses the biblical view that man's moral predicament may be traced to a corrupt nature that cannot be conformed to the right apart from spiritual rebirth. In both the teaching of Jesus and the epistles this estimate of the sinner's moral plight is foremost. "Make the tree good and the fruit will be good" (Mt. 7:17, 12:33ff.). "Except a man be born again he cannot see the kingdom of God" (Jn. 3:3). Jesus found the key to true morality in the new birth. The Pauline expressions carry forward the same theme. Men are "by nature the children of wrath" (Eph. 2:3), but "if any man be in Christ he is a new creature; old things are passed away, behold all things are become new" (2 Cor. 5:17).

The underlying contention of Christian ethics is that every want of conformity to God is sinful and wicked. This includes both lack of conformity in action and in motive and affection. The deepest recess of the heart is judged equally with any external deed. It is also a basic premise of Christian ethics that the whole race is characteristically rebellious against the God with whom they have to do. "There is none righteous, no, not even one," declares Paul, "all have sinned, and fall short of the glory of God" (Rom. 3:10, 23). Such words are a terse and terrible indictment of fallen human nature. The great Apostle refutes any notion that the picture he portrays is simply his own invention: he draws upon the Old Testament and reiterates a judgment which had been uttered by the Living God. The very opening chapter of Romans sets out with this theme of depravity. The spiritual apostasy of rebellious man is not traced to particular bodily and sensual desires. Rather, as Harless observes, the ". . . tendency of their thoughts to vain imaginings, and a darkening of their hearts in spiritual matters, preceded, according to the apostle, that bondage to the mastery of bodily and sensual desires."[14]

The emphasis on the image of God in fallen man must be aligned with the biblical account of man in sin. The divine image is broken, though not completely shattered. Man continually suppresses, by his

[13]"In the Christian view of man's moral condition and task, *Sin* has a place and significance such as no other ethical system attributes to it. No other scheme of morality sets the fact of human sin in the light in which in Christianity it is defined and condemned. Very decisively did the Founder of Christianity discriminate between moral Transgression and ceremonial neglect or irregularity." George Walker, *The Idealism of Christian Ethics* (Edinburgh: T. & T. Clark, 1929), pp. 32f.

[14]G. C. Adolph von Harless, *System of Christian Ethics* (Edinburgh: T. & T. Clark, 1887), p. 257.

unrighteousness and injustice, the truth which dwells in him. The result is that a process of darkening counteracts the light presented by the *imago Dei* (Rom. 1:18). Paul holds that an ineradicable moral claim is implanted in man's heart (Rom. 2:14f.), and yet because of human corruption man neither comprehends God's desires nor seeks after them. Knowledge of the Creator and of his purposes is dimmed, and the will has no desire for union with him. The Apostle shows this appraisal to be the proclamation of the Scripture itself: "As it is written, there is none righteous, no not one, there is none that understandeth, there is none that seeketh after God" (Rom. 3:10f.).

The moral law therefore is frustrated in fallen man's experience. It no longer can attain its original end of enabling man on the basis of creation to live in conformity with Divine purposes. Now it designates him a transgressor of the will of God. Behind his rebellion, the Divine moral claim continues to assert itself: it is inscribed or engraved upon man's heart. Its function becomes one of condemning man, marking him for judgment through his revolt against its claims. The moral content in fallen man is not known by a mind and will and affection reconstituted by saving grace. Rather, it harasses a man who knows himself to fall far short of its claims. He endures the terrors of his predicament only by converting the ethical claim into a phantom of its real self.

The biblical ethics of transcendent revelation and redemption is perhaps most dramatically pictured in the Greek term *katargeō*. This striking word is used frequently in the New Testament to express the Divine counter-offensive to Satan, sin, and death. The Revised Standard Version translates it fifteen different ways in its twenty-seven occurrences. It is used of Christ's redemptive work in behalf of man in sin, under the law, in the grip of the powers of this world, under the sentence of death, and ensnared by the wiles of Satan. New Testament ethics may be said to revolve around the concept of two ages, the present age which is destined to pass away, and the age to come which is brought in by the counter-measures of redemption. The term under consideration graphically depicts Christ's inauguration of the new age. The first phase of this new age was the Christ-event — his life, death, and resurrection. It has stirred up believers to an expectation of the second phase — Christ's return.

The basic meaning of *katargeō*, "to render inactive or ineffective," might be paraphrased in modern speech "to put out of commission." The hopeless predicament of the lost sinner is dramatically nullified by redemptive rescue. Fallen man as he is swept into salvation is removed from the wrath of God and placed in his service.

Katargeō bears this technical ethico-religious sense with dramatic frequency in the New Testament. Of its twenty-seven uses, all but two (Lk. 13:7 and Heb. 2:14) are by Paul and even in these exceptions ethical implications are present.

The old self is crucified with Christ so that the sinful body might be "destroyed" (Rom. 6:6). The passage clearly avoids the Greek view that the body is intrinsically evil. But translating *katargeō* by "destruction" has unhappily suggested the possibility of sinless perfection in this life. The point is rather that the body of sin has been wrested from its wicked ruler and freed for the use of another. *Katargeō* suggests that Christ changes completely the pattern of living — sin no longer has control over man's nature.

The work of Christ likewise nullifies the ability of the law to condemn the believer to death. The sinner is "discharged" (Rom. 7:6) from the law or "brought to an inactive relation" to it, as the death of a husband relieves the widow of her legal obligations to him. Again, the point is not that the law is destroyed and loses all service in ethical matters. Rather, its capacity to slay the redeemed sinner is abrogated. Christ "abolished" in his flesh the enmity of the law against the sinner (Eph. 2:15). By his death he brought the commandments to idleness. Christ did not destroy the law, but he fulfilled it in behalf of sinners and neutralized its condemning function.

The texts dealing with death that use *katargeō* are equally illuminating. We are told that Jesus Christ "abolished" death (2 Tim. 1:10). Unquestionably during his earthly ministry Jesus had power over death, as we know from the raising of Jairus' daughter, the widow's son, and Lazarus. But the Apostle apparently indicates by the terms "Savior" and "Gospel" that it was by his own death that Christ dealt death to death itself. Death was not absolutely destroyed; it is a fact of present experience. But his victory guarantees for the believer death is a "sleep" from which the body will be wakened in resurrection. Christ has thus made ineffectual the role of death. The final eschatological victory over death is stated in 1 Corinthians 15:26, "The last enemy to be destroyed is death." In this passage the translation "abolished" or "destroyed" is appropriate.

Since the Scriptures assign to Satan the power of death, the nullification of death implies conquest over Satan. The writer of Hebrews declares that Christ assumed flesh and blood "that through death he might 'destroy' him who has the power of death, that is, the devil" (Heb. 2:14). However, the destruction of Satan is not fully accomplished as both Christian experience and the Apocalypse (20:10) attest. But Christ has freed his followers from servitude to Satan.

Man's rescue by God is depicted in still another area. *Katargeō* is used of Christ's triumph over world powers that are hostile to the purposes of God. The complete destruction of this opposition is eschatological: "Then comes the end, when he delivers the kingdom to God the Father after 'destroying' every rule and every authority and power" (1 Cor. 15:24). Paul declares that "the rulers of this age . . . are doomed to 'pass away' " (1 Cor. 2:6). As Christ approached the cross, he assured his disciples, "In the world you have tribulation;

but be of good cheer, I have 'overcome' the world" (Jn. 16:33). Even the Antichrist, the incarnation of evil, will not stand against the risen Lord who will return to " 'destroy' him by his appearing and his coming" (2 Thess. 2:8).

The witness of the New Testament, therefore, is that the whole world of moral struggle is moving toward a cataclysmic day when the forces of evil will be finally and completely subjugated to the purposes of the holy Lord. Jesus Christ, through whom sinners are reclaimed and recovered for a life of holy living, struck the death blow to sin, the condemning aspect of the law, death, Satan, and illicit world powers. But where the fallen world has not turned to Christ, it still lies in the lap of the evil one, waiting to share his doom in the great and awful end-time.

The Christian doctrine of human depravity does not mean that man is as wicked as he can be. Nor does it mean that man has no moral insight or moral striving. Human history is religious and ethical history. The radical naturalistic negation of objective morality which has greatly influenced our generation represents only an undercurrent in the history of thought. The major mood in the history of philosophy and religion has dealt with the moral claim as a genuine reality. And the same is true of human life as a whole. Man assents to the convictions of the good and the right. He strives to adjust life somehow to the moral order, often by denying personal desires and sometimes with sacrificial heroism. But the Christian doctrine affirms that none of these factors is incompatible with a solemn view of sin. Rather, moral striving gives sin an added element of tragedy. Instead of acknowledging his dread predicament of moral failure and seeking Divine rescue, man seeks by his own tainted efforts at righteousness to reverse his plight. Even the life of higher idealism and humanitarian effort is often compromised by wicked motives. Despite ethical endeavor in human affairs, the verdict of revelation is that man falls under judgment. "For whosoever shall keep the whole law, and yet stumble in one point, he is become guilty of all" (Jas. 2:10). Every part of the whole of man's life needs to be transformed and changed. The fountain must be fed by new waters.

In revealing the world of human relations as a fallen world, Hebrew-Christian ethics stresses the disparity between life as it is and life as it ought to be. The world is in the grip of Satan and his hosts. Man's fall and rebellion have darkened the whole of human history with sin and death. The moral law stands over against man as a threatening lawsuit. For one reason only does the Bible proclaim the absolute necessity of a "salvation ethics" centering in a Divine initiative. There just is no other way out.

7

TRANSCENDENT REVELATION AS THE SOURCE OF CHRISTIAN ETHICS

THE HEBREW-CHRISTIAN ETHIC is transcendently revealed. Its source is a special Divine disclosure to man. In contrast with the ethics of human insight and speculative genius, Christian ethics is the ethic of revealed religion. In the preface to the Ten Commandments stands a dramatic and momentous phrase that is characteristic of revelational ethics: "And God spake all these words" (Exod. 20:1). From this source it gains an eternal and absolute quality. It communicates to man commands and norms that are unaffected by society or by time or by place.

Any ethical viewpoint which discounts this supernatural source cannot represent itself as being genuinely Christian in character and composition. For Christian ethics derives its content and sanction and dynamic and goal from God — not from some inference from anthropology or sociology. It does not approach the problem of morals from the manward side and attempt to work its way to God. It is not only super-social and super-national, but supernatural.

More is meant by the statement that the distinctive ground of Christian ethics is transcendent than that it is philosophically and metaphysically oriented. It is indeed a *metaphysical ethics.* And so it has scant sympathy for Kant's optimistic effort to make metaphysics dependent on ethics, rather than the reverse. But while the Christian ethic does have a specific metaphysical background, it is not enough simply to say that it cannot be elaborated as a life-view apart from a metaphysical basis. "Our view of God and of the world, our fundamental *Welt-Anschauung,* cannot but determine our view of man and his moral life. In every philosophical system from Plato to Hegel, in which the universe is regarded as having a rational meaning and ultimate end, the good of human beings is conceived as identical with or at least as included in the universal good."[1] So wrote Archibald Alexander, and with point.

But if one has a naive view of morality, if he professes disinterest in all "metaphysical sophistries," one may be just as naive if he reverences anything and everything which passes by the name of philosophy. Least of all, can Christian ethics show favor for a metaphysics which

[1]Archibald B. D. Alexander, *Christianity and Ethics,* pp. 18f.

makes no room for the supernatural. And yet even out of Christian divinity schools such moral philosophies have come. Henry Nelson Wieman's unabashed naturalism is an example. Idealistic metaphysics has often appeared in a role hostile to specifically Christian ethics because it has gnawed away at the specific metaphysical foundations on which Christian morality is based. Supernaturalistic metaphysics, no less than naturalistic metaphysics, may be antagonistic to the foundations that furnish the indispensable support for revealed Christian morals. E. S. Brightman's speculative ethical personalism illustrates the point. Metaphysical, moral and spiritual realities are ultimately one for Christian ethics. The error of ancient Greek speculation was its notion that ethics can be sustained independently of religion, and made to walk on its own feet, or that it can be enforced adequately by philosophical considerations alone. This error is again gaining wide currency. The tragic collapse of Greek culture should provide a sober warning for those who are reactivating such views.

The distinctiveness of Christian morality requires at very least that it be conceived as *religious ethics.* As Ramsey observes, "The first thing to be said concerning Christian ethics is that it cannot be separated from its religious foundation."[2] The Scriptures, as Alvah Hovey remarks, "enjoin upon men the duty of supreme love to God. Here . . . it is noteworthy, that the duty of honoring abstract right, eternal order, or natural law is never urged by them as tantamount to honoring God . . ."[3] Christianity takes its place as formal religious ethics against the widespread modern effort of secularism to secure the "independency" or "autonomy" of morality. The idea of the good must be identified with the will of God. The classic Greek world, for all its metaphysical hunger, left the relation between ethics and the religious Reality in ambiguous suspension. The abstract principles of the True, the Good, and the Beautiful served as norms from which an ideal moral code could be deduced. Since Kant's day the moral theory of modern postulational Idealism has championed an ethics that is only marginally related to religion and the religious. It has attempted to make religion dependent upon morality rather than to acknowledge that the moral is based on the religious. Kant, Lotze, and Bowne were influential champions of this point of view.[4] Thus while protesting the *complete* segregation of morality and religion and insisting on religion as the complement and implication of the moral life, supernaturalistic metaphysics nonetheless loses religion as the enforcing schoolmaster and, equally important, as the determinative source of right, when it is speculatively forged.

[2]Paul Ramsey, *Basic Christian Ethics,* p. 1.

[3]Alvah Hovey, *Manual of Systematic Theology and Christian Ethics.* (Philadelphia: American Baptist Publication Society, 1877), p. 368.

[4]E. S. Brightman, in his *Moral Laws,* contended that norms are theonomous but values are autonomous. Thereby the ethical life was deprived of all sanctions transcendent to the intrinsic moral demand of human nature.

Humanism takes the next step. It not only finds the basis for morality in human nature, but it also considers the appeal to the supernatural wholly unnecessary and even false.

Whatever else may be said about systems of morality that discuss the problem of conduct with no necessary religious reference and project a science of ideal behavior on the ground of inherent worth alone, it must be said that such abstractions of ethics from religion have little in common with the ethical teaching of Jesus or with the Bible as a whole. The moral goal lies beyond morality, it lies in religion itself. C. J. Barker rightly observes: "Herein lies one differentiation of Christian ethics — they are through and through religious ethics. No ethics that are not religious can be satisfying. They can be descriptive, illuminating, and persuasive: but they cannot give the final ground of their own precepts, nor answer the questions to which they inevitably give rise."[5] C. H. Valentine expresses the same thought in equally striking words: "The foundations of morality . . . are to be found in the bedrock of religion. . . . The power to lead the moral life and reach the moral goal is the power which comes into morality from religion. . . . Morality is bankrupt and cannot meet the claims of life unless it draws upon the resources of religion. . . . The true authority of morals comes from the religion which reveals the nature and purpose of God."[6]

Christian ethics gave fair warning to the experiment with the ethical life which sought a sufficient basis for the absoluteness of morality in an appeal to human nature alone. Such an experiment was doomed to failure. Nor is there any surprise that this undertaking is sagging today before the onslaught of naturalistic ways of thought and life. The verdict of Luthardt on the pagan life of antiquity is finding a new and disastrous fulfillment in our own era: "Religion was severed from morality, and morality from religion, and the outcome of the ancient world was an immoral religion and an irreligious morality." Doubt that moral distinctions have a basis in what is profoundest and most durable in reality corrodes the vitality of ethical living. The only effective solution is in the exhibition of the inner connection between ethics and the supreme religious Reality. As Henry Nash observes, "Nothing save a sense of deep and intimate connection with the solid core of things, nothing save a settled and fervid conviction that the universe is on the side of the will in its struggle for that whole-hearted devotion to the welfare of the race without which morality is an affair

[5]C. J. Barker, *The Way of Life; A Study in Christian Ethics* (London: Lutterworth), p. 13.

[6]C. H. Valentine, *Moral Freedom and the Christian Faith* (London: SPCK, 1932), pp. 17, 85, 118, 137.

of shreds and patches, can give to the will the force and edge suitable to the difficult work it has to do."[7]

It is God who demands the moral life, not merely the moral life that demands God. Christian ethics by its very nature is opposed to every species of anthropocentric ethics, and asserts the indispensable connection between religion and ethics. Hence it resists every attempted secularizing of morality and every sentimental "Christianizing" of prevailing modes of conduct. The foundation of biblical morality is found in the bedrock of religion: that much must be said. Ultimate moral reality is one with ultimate religious reality. The distinction between ethics and religion is only a contingent one, for they cannot be dissociated. Jesus shared the moral traditions of Israel in insisting that ethical behavior is never performed in a religious vacuum. Instead, religion supplies the very presupposition of the moral. As Ernest F. Scott comments, "For Jesus . . . religion was no mere shell, enclosing an ethic, which was the kernel. He thought of morality as growing out of religion, and existing for the sake of it. The idea that you may discard the religion of Jesus and still retain his pure morality is utterly mistaken, for without the religion you have nothing at all."[8] But there is more.

Christian ethics cannot be represented merely as a religious ethic. For Christianity stands in moral judgment upon much that passes by the name of religious ethics as well as upon anti-religious ethics and non-religious ethics. A simply religious ethic may be backslidden and therefore corrupt. There is much to be said for Henson's characterization of revealed religion as "revolts of morality against degenerate religion."[9] False conceptions of God will lead to false conceptions of the moral life. Even pagan moralists voiced deep indignation of the

[7]Henry Nash, *Ethics and Revelation,* p. 50. Nash writes elsewhere: "Nothing short of an impassioned belief in the unity and sincerity of the universe, nothing but a solid and enduring conviction that the whole heart and meaning of things is in solemn league and covenant with humanity's deepest and holiest desire can give birth and breeding to a mighty common purpose waiting for, and working toward, the uplifting of the lowly. Therefore, faith in duty, when it is followed home, leads conscience into the Old Testament, into the prophetic view of the divine life as a unity, of the eternal good as creative, and of history as a sacred process, leading toward a moral goal" (*ibid.,* p. 232). New York: Macmillan, 1899). Nash's approach goes too much in debt to the idealistic emphasis on man's direct moral continuity with the Divine, but the deeper stress on a comprehensive moral order is to the point.

[8]Ernest F. Scott, *Man and Society in the New Testament,* p. 59. Scott's failure is his tendency to speak of religion as a general concept, and hence to miss the unique basis of biblical theism in special revelation. Hence we read: "Here we see the meaning of religion, and the necessary place it must always have in man's life. Each lower authority depends on a higher one, and ultimately there must be one which is absolute. It cannot be found on this earth, for there is no earthly judgment which cannot be called in question. There needs to be present in us the faith in a higher power to which we can appeal; we must learn to see our lives and the things around us as God sees them. This is what we seek from religion, and without this no real life is possible" (*ibid.,* p. 237).

[9]Herbert H. Henson, *Christian Morality.* Gifford Lectures (Oxford: Clarendon Press, 1936), p. 15.

epics about the ancient polytheistic gods who exulted in a lower level of behavior than their human contemporaries, as if Divinity provided exemption from moral responsibilities. Professor W. P. Paterson once remarked, and pointedly enough, that "a religion without grace is ineffectual . . . a religion without morality, contemptible." From anthropology we can call forth ready examples of so-called primitive behavior in which religion is seen to promote immorality. The Old Testament repudiates the pagan rite of prostitution in the sacred temples as a corruption of religious ethics. It is prosaic to say that many religions are concerned more about external conformity than about internal virtue, and thus share in the neglect of the weightier matters of the Law. More distressing is that the knowledge of the Law has been concealed and distorted by large segments of the religious enterprise. Often their ethical schematizations represent compromise adjustments of the absolute Divine claim. Moreover, only monotheistic religion can sponsor a dominating and authoritative unity in ethical demands and avoid degenerating the ethical into personal or community etiquette.

Because Christianity does not give up its basis in a transcendent revelation it need not surrender its moral requirements to the cultural prejudices and corruptions of the day. A religious ethics may simply endorse the accepted patterns of behavior. If its gods are already a reflection of the social environment, the religion serves as a cosmic basis for individual conformity to the prevailing social code. Only the ethics of special revelation dares stand in judgment upon much that passes for the "highest morality" of the age. Only Christianity dares oppose the status quo. Only Christian ethics dares pronounce final doom upon the prevailing religion and its gods. True religion does much more than to furnish a cosmic support for ethics: it cuts the support from beneath inadequate patterns of behavior and from beneath false religions.

Luthardt was right when he insisted that "that alone is true religion which produces a vigorous morality, and that alone is a vigorous morality which arises from true religion."[10] Seen in this context, Christian ethics is anything but a merely religious ethics. It does not have its roots in ecclesiasticism nor in some humanly contrived creed or theology. It does not seek a basis in some common denominator which may be abstracted from the world's religion, nor is its ethics simply a distillation of elements most universally present in the so-called higher religions. Christian morality holds to the priority of the religious metaphysical, and in doing so it exhibits a distinctive Divine command. Man is naked under the penetrating gaze of his Creator-God and moral judge. This God has clearly published his absolute moral requirements in the Law to Israel. The whole of biblical ethics is under the sway of revealed religion, so that a specific view of God conditions the ruling

[10]Christian Ernst Luthardt, *Apologetic Lectures on the Moral Truths of Christianity,* trans. Sophia Taylor (4th ed., Edinburgh: T. & T. Clark, 1872), p. 19.

conception of life. "The God they worshipped was to the Jews the source and sanction of the moral law. . . . Morality is to them the embodied will of God. . . . The ethics of the Bible from one end of it to the other are religious."[11]

The Christian ethic is a specially revealed morality — not merely a religious ethics. It gains its reality in and through supernatural disclosure. Biblical behavior is not based solely on human values and ideals. Its fountainhead is the will of God. It is received in the Divine confrontation of man by commandments, statutes and laws, and face-to-face in the incarnation. "The Christian system takes as its point of departure the revelation of God, and the manifestation of man's possibilities, in Jesus Christ. The Christian ethic is, so to speak, theocentric. Its foundation is laid not so much in the study of man's nature, functions and capacities, as in revealed truths respecting the purpose and character of God."[12]

"The prophetic movement in Hebraic religion," Niebuhr notes, "offers an interesting confirmation of the thesis that a genuine faith in transcendence is the power which lifts religion above its culture and emancipates it from sharing the fate of dying cultures."[13] Christian morality presupposes a view of life anchored in special Divine disclosure and defined uniquely in harmony with an ideal that is nowhere found in man outside this sphere of revelation.[14] Christian ethics appears as the ripe fruit of the Divine movement which shaped Hebrew-Christian monotheism in contrast to the other religions and moral outlooks of the world. Hence it has the highest base for enduring vitality in duty and virtue. Ethical Idealism was uncertain that the moral realities

[11]T. B. Strong, "Ethics," in Hastings, *Dictionary of the Bible* (New York: Scribner, 1911-12), 1, 777f.

[12]R. L. Ottley, *Christian Ideas and Ideals* (New York: Longmans, Green, 1909). p. 18.

[13]Reinhold Niebuhr, *An Interpretation of Christian Ethics,* p. 30. Ethical Existentialism today reimports into ethics the notion of Divine judgment and transcendence but, within the requirements of its anti-metaphysical approach, means by this something quite foreign from a transcendent revelation. So Jaspers writes that "the judgment that is ultimately decisive" for the ethical man "is not even that of the men he respects" but that "only the judgment of God can be decisive" (Jaspers, *Way to Wisdom,* p. 68). A closer reading, aware of the indebtedness of the existentialist movement to Kant, will disclose, as Kimpel readily observes, not the viewpoint of traditional Christian faith, of the legislation by a transcendent Divine authority of a moral law binding upon all mankind, but rather the notion that "authentic being" serves as a Divine voice to the individual, that internal to an individual's own experience the distinction must be made between what is universal and valid and what is relative (Kimpel, *Faith and Moral Authority,* p. 64). No authority external to the self is allowed to define for man the nature and content of the good, on the approach of philosophical Existentialism; the claim of the higher, or universal self, a distinction interior to human experience, alone legislates the form of morality.

[14]"I have made the whole difference between Christian and pagan ethical speculation turn upon the presence in Christianity of a new vital force, whose activities form the subject of a new ethical theory. And my further contention is that this essential difference saves Christian ethical theory from the failure which haunted speculations of this kind under the old conditions." T. B. Strong, *Christian Ethics.* Bampton Lectures (New York: Longmans, Green, 1896), p. 706.

which it professed to find implicit in man's personal and social experience actually structured the world as a whole. This uncertainty led the era inaugurated by Kant in which a heroic effort was made to constitute the metaphysical world in moral dimensions. But it is really biblical ethics that can overcome this uncertainty by its confident proclamation of the doctrine of creation and the self-revelation of the will of the holy Lord of creation and history.[15] The self-revealing God unveils himself as the supreme moral tribunal before whom all creatures must bow in every age and place, and from whom none can flee.

Several factors, then, conserve a dynamic ethic and guard against sacrificing ideals to impulse. These are religion, an understanding of the spiritual world as it really is, and submission to God who is the source of moral law and the judge before whom all will one day stand.

Whoever has studied firsthand under distinguished champions of the Platonic-Kantian-Hegelian-Lotzean tradition in moral philosophy cannot forget the poignant, the almost pathetic, determination to eradicate the cleavage between the real world and the ideal world. Who can soon forget the complexity and the ingenuity of these attempts to show that the analysis of human moral experience implies or requires the predication of an ultimate and absolute moral reality? Those of the Plato-Aristotle-Hegel school try to prove it by rational demonstration; those following Kant by a faith-postulation. Others attempt it by a volitional "leap" rather than an intellectual argument. And who can overlook the fact that in this type of argument the force of the leap from man to God depends upon the force of the assertion of man's moral continuity with God? Often this assertion is made to imply that man has metaphysical continuity with God as well. The argument preserves the objectivity of the moral order by a device which requires the denial of the sinfulness of man and of his fallen condition. This is really its prime weakness — it preserves the reality of the good by obscuring the reality of the bad.

Yet the conscience of man cannot distinguish the good without some reference to the bad. Hence man is always ready to revolt against idealistic ethics. Indeed, he must do so if he is to affirm his creatureliness or even his essential animality, rather than to accept the lie of his divinity. Speculative ethics may stress with good reason that it is necessary for the moral sensitivities of man to find a cosmic home. It may also emphasize the fact that the universe must sustain and fulfill the good life, instead of being antagonistic to morality. It may contend with trenchant force that if the world is not constituted morally, man is

[15]Those who hold, as does J. Clark Murray, that Christian ethics is "essentially a religious system" because morality "by a necessary movement of thought . . . passes over into religion" misunderstand the indispensable basis of biblical morality in special transcendent revelation. *A Handbook of Christian Ethics* (Edinburgh: T. & T. Clark, 1908), p. 3. The arbitrary rejection in the uniqueness of Christian ethics grows out of a reconstruction and assimilation of the biblical view to a philosophy of "the general evolution of intellectual and moral and religious life in the world" (*ibid.,* pp. 39f.).

contradicted by his environment and demoralized. Then the objective validity of all his judgments of moral value and the significance of what seems of ultimate worth to him evaporate. The universe itself is devoid of meaning. The sense of the ought-to-be is reduced to a psychological abnormality which swindles man out of the animal satisfactions which would otherwise be his.

Christianity can admit no ultimate distinction between the course of the universe and the requirements of the moral life. The same God who created the universe sets the moral standard. So Christianity regards the whole creation as disposed toward moral interests. That the universe is neither hostile nor indifferent to moral realities is implied in the Hebrew-Christian revelation that the space-time world is the creation of an absolutely moral being.

But speculative ethics is projected by man from the shadows of moral revolt. So it does not — and dare not — admit that the moral order is as real as the will of the Living God and that man is a responsible rebel who is doomed on account of his sins. The Hebrew-Christian revelation spectacularly unfurls man's true moral state. By holding together the fact of creation and the fact of redemption in their unitary moral demand it gives the sinner no escape. It allows him no flimsy excuse for animal behavior as a means of avoiding the pretense of divinity. Man's only comfort is to hold in one single acknowledgment the graphic reality of the moral claim and the terrible reality of his guilt in sin. And here comfort is in redemption, not just in the acknowledgment of his terrifying state. Christian ethics is not the moral agent searching the inner recesses of his ethical life for every possible evidence that he is on speaking terms with the Deity, rendering at last the happy verdict that at all essential points he and the larger Spirit are in unanimous agreement. Rather, Christian ethics is the holy Lord addressing man by his Word, revealing himself at once as the God who speaks already in man's conscience, serving an advance summons to appear before his judgment throne, and is God requiring from man the abject confession of his guilt as an indispensable element of his forgiveness. Thus the fact of transcendent revelation displaces the realistic leap to God by a twofold certainty: it is really God who addresses man on the basis of creation; this same God has unveiled his face in the Redeemer Jesus Christ.

An approach to a theological status for Christian ethics as a whole is made by Jacques Maritain in his *Science and Wisdom,* in which ethics is subordinated to theology.[16] But Roman Catholic scholars have protested against the derivation of the principles of ethical science from special Divine revelation rather than from natural human experience.[17] Thomas Aquinas carried forward essentially the Aristotelian definition

[16]Jacques Maritain, *Science and Wisdom* (London: G. Bles, 1940), p. 81.
[17]Cf. Vernon J. Bourke, *Ethics: A Textbook in Moral Philosophy* (New York: Macmillan, 1951), p. 81.

of the Good not as the will of God, but as that which perfects human nature.[18] One weakness of Thomistic ethics is its failure to deal realistically with the fact that human nature is fallen. Nature as sinful is split, and does not lead by an unbroken path to conformity to the will of God.[19] But even if this were not the case, the primary reason the creature is obliged to perform the good is not that man's moral dignity requires it, but that God commands it.

Without doubt Christian ethics is related to general ethics. The denial that it belongs to the genus of philosophical ethics generally rests upon two errors: one defines special revelation in an anti-rational, anti-conceptual spirit; the other implies that philosophical ethics is justified in its repudiation of the principle of special revelation. All ethics is in a sense revelational, that is, it has general revelation as its foundation. But general ethics is ethics in revolt. And the Hebrew-Christian revelation unmasks that revolt. The real antithesis has its ground in this: Christian ethics insists on the necessity of supernatural redemption; secular ethics denies the fall.

From what has been said already about the theoretical relevance of specially revealed ethics, as well as about the ethical implications of the Divine moral image in fallen man, it is apparent that this relationship must not be artificially severed any more than carelessly maintained. We must not hurriedly surrender the field of ethical battle to the relativists if they fail to tolerate a specially revealed ethic. If the revelational viewpoint is discarded, there are yet the lessons of history and sociology that are arguing points against immorality and promiscuity. There is also a moral law within man that indicts him whenever he proposes to live as an animal.

The Christian ethic is transcendently based, and it also presupposes an immanent basis. Because of this, Christian ethics is related to both speculative and religious ethics. Christian ethics proclaims a universal and general Divine revelation. It holds to an inherent moral element in every man. Even the fall into sin has not been able to eradicate that moral element. Rather, it remains as the backdrop for man's continuing revolt against the will of God, and it makes possible the Christian appeal. Dewar reminds us that "Our Lord appeals to the natural law as bearing witness to the essential goodness of God."[20]

The speculative and religious competitors to specially revealed ethics are constructed out of human initiative and speculation. They do not

[18]This is doubtless at the root of R. A. Tsanoff's statement that "the ethics of St. Thomas is the rationalistic naturalism of Aristotle, but seen through a stained glass window." *The Moral Ideas of Our Civilization* (New York: Dutton, 1942), p. 68.

[19]Ernest F. Scott suggests the priority which the Bible assigns to God in relation to self-knowledge: "We come back here to the principle which determines all the New Testament teaching on human personality. It is only through knowledge of God that men know themselves, and the more he knows God in his true nature the more does each man know himself" (*op. cit.*, p. 106).

[20]Dewar, *An Outline of New Testament Ethics*, p. 34, cf. p. 116.

have the perspective of man as a fallen creature. One and all, they are immanentistic, that is, they come from human reason unenlightened by special Divine revelation.

Christian ethics is distinctive in being something much more than a higher version of other views. It gains its reality because of a unique Divine inbreaking. If we allow its own witness to be heard rather than forcing alien views upon it, the Bible portrays ethical monotheism as the result of Divine revelation to history from above and without. Ethical monotheism was not a gradual emergence from inferior views. This is not a popular theory in an evolutionary age, but it remains nonetheless the constant testimony of the biblical outlook. If special historical revelation is a reality, it becomes the cardinal consideration in the interpretation of life. It must dominate our view of human aims and values. It is our primary and central point of reference. The first principle of ethics then is at once metaphysical and religious and theological. And Christianity affirms this assuredly in view of special Divine revelation.[21]

The transcendent basis of biblical ethics in special Divine revelation is the consistent affirmation of the whole sacred literature of the Hebrew-Christian movement. "Practically all the Loci of Christian Dogmatics and Christian Ethics pervade and ramify one another, and can be distinguished only in thought. Every dogma has its ethical aspect or quality."[22] In Hovey's words, "In the order of logical study, Christian ethics must follow Christian theology. For theology treats of God under the influence of that grace; the former deals with the Giver and the giving of true moral life; the latter with the growth and expression of that life. . . . The grand distinction of Christian conduct is this: it is rooted in faith, and sustained by divine grace. Faith works by love. The former receives; the latter gives. The former sustains; the latter acts."[23] From Genesis to Revelation the connection of this particular form and content of morality with the monotheism of Divine disclosure is everywhere asserted as a fundamental notion. The whole of Scripture carries forward the correlation of ethics with the God of creation, of the summons to repentance and of the judgment to come.

The Jew knew that morality must be theological. In fact, as Dewar points out, "The very word *torah* — *i.e.,* revealed instruction — ever

[21]The ethics of liberal Protestantism had its basis, as Reinhold Niebuhr remarked, in "a devitalized and secularized religion in which the presuppositions of a Christian tradition have been rationalized and read into the processes of history and nature, supposedly discovered by objective science" (*op. cit.,* p. 10). Its error was twofold: the repudiation of a transcendent-revelation basis for Hebrew-Christian ethics, and the baptism of a semi-secular, semi-Christian speculative ethic as divine. When the ethical content of Christianity is speculatively regarded as anticipated by a general movement or evolution of morality, the distinctive elements of Christian morality are usually dismissed as speculative accretions.

[22]Leander S. Keyser, *A Manual of Christian Ethics* (Burlington, Ia.: Lutheran Literary Board, 1926), p. 29.

[23]Hovey, *op. cit.,* pp. 367, 374.

reminded him of that."[24] The Decalogue is bound up with God's election of the Hebrews. All its elements are "theologically conditioned," even the duties to men in the second table appearing as "moral duties . . . to be fulfilled . . . to the glory of God, as divine commands."[25] The supreme way of the good life centered in the Living God. This is explicit in the Decalogue from the very first words, emphasizing, as Patrick Fairbairn notes, "His *being,* His *worship,* His *name,* and His *day."*[26] Luthardt remarked that "the first commandment is to recognize Jehovah as God, as He has revealed Himself in the history of salvation, and as Israel has experienced Him as Redeemer in His grace and power. This is an act of *faith.* In this all else is grounded and comprehended, so that what follows is only an unfolding of it. Thus all morality is rooted in religion, all moral action in faith, and all moral conduct of man in God's relationship of grace."[27] And again, "There is not in the literature of any nation such a summary of morality as we possess in the Decalogue, that briefest yet most comprehensive compendium of morals. But morality, as here required, is reduced to love to God and love to man; these are designated by our Lord as the two chief commandments, and we accordingly divide the law into two tables. In so doing we express the connection of religion and morality."[28]

Of the division of the law into two tables, so that the duties of religion precede the duties to men, Calvin wrote: "The first foundation of righteousness is certainly the worship of God; and if this be destroyed, all the other branches of righteousness, like the parts of a disjointed and falling edifice, are torn asunder and scattered. For what kind of righteousness will you pretend to, because you refrain from harassing men by acts of theft and rapine, if at the same time you atrociously and sacrilegiously defraud the majesty of God of the glory which is due to him? . . . It is in vain . . . to boast of righteousness without religion; as well might the trunk of a body be exhibited as a beautiful object, after the head has been cut off. Nor is religion only the head of righteousness, but the very soul of it, constituting all its life and vigour; for without the fear of God, men preserve no equity and love among themselves. We therefore call the worship of God the principle and foundation of righteousness . . . We assert also that it is the source and soul of righteousness . . . In the first table . . . he instructs us in piety and the proper duties of religion . . . in the second he prescribes the duties which the fear of his name should excite us to practice in society."[29] Elsewhere he commented: "The second table of the law . . . sufficiently instructs us in the duties we owe to men for

[24]Lindsay Dewar, *op. cit.,* pp. 18f.
[25]*Ibid.,* pp. 14f.
[26]Patrick Fairbairn, *The Revelation of Law in Scripture.* Cunningham Lectures (Edinburgh: T. & T. Clark, 1869).
[27]Luthardt, *op. cit.,* pp. 46f.
[28]*Ibid.,* pp. 22f.
[29]Calvin, *Institutes,* II, viii, xi.

the sake of God, on regard to whom the whole rule of love depends. The duties taught in this second table, therefore, we shall inculcate in vain, unless our instruction be founded on the fear and reverence of God."[30]

W. J. Henderson finds a permanent reminder of the God-based moral law in the appointments of the tabernacle. "Morality is under Divine protection: are not the tables of the law in the Ark that occupies the most sacred place in Jehovah's shrine?"[31] And the same viewpoint dominates the wisdom literature: "Even in the sapiential Books . . . the wisdom of man is found in the fear of the Lord and in obedience to His law."[32]

This viewpoint is also found in the Old Testament prophets: the inseparability of pure morality from pure religion is their consistent assumption. The Hebrew mind never entertained the idea that religion and ethics can be separated. The 'Torah' controlled Hebrew life in detail. It revealed God the Creator as the author of the moral law. Religion and ethics were indissolubly fused. Religion without the ethics was inconceivable, and ethics unintelligible and impracticable without the religion.

Jesus did not modify the theological orientation of ethics. He reinforced it. Neither expediency, nor considerations of pleasure or prudence, nor the utilitarian concern with the greatest happiness of the greatest number, nor the appeal to the constitution of man and his ideal self-fulfillment gave him the fundamental touchstone of morality. Hirst remarks that a "distinctive feature in Jesus' attitude to morality was the definitely *religious setting* in which He placed conduct. Strictly speaking, Jesus was not a moralist; His primary mission was to reveal God as the Father and Redeemer of mankind."[33] The moral claim of God and the disclosure of his will is the center of ethics. In disentangling the inner meaning of the Law from the accretions of tradition, Jesus correlated the ethical claim with the Word of God. The inseparability of piety and morality is reinforced in his summary of the commandments. Whoever does not love his fellow man is deficient in the love of God, and whoever lacks love of God does not properly love his fellow man.[34] As a distinguished Lutheran theologian remarked, "The Christian morality cannot be surpassed, for it centers in the command: 'Thou shalt love the Lord, thy God, with all thy heart and with all thy soul and with all thy mind,' and 'Thou shalt love thy neighbor as thyself.' "[35]

[30]*Ibid.*, II, viii, 1.

[31]W. J. Henderson, "Ethics," in Hastings, *Dictionary of the Bible,* 241a. Cf. Ex. 40:20, Dt. 10:5, 1 Ki. 8:9, Heb. 9:4.

[32]T. B. Strong, "Ethics," in Hastings, *Dictionary of the Bible,* I, 788.

[33]Edward Hirst, *Jesus and the Moralists: A Comparative Study of the Christian Ethic.* Fernley-Hartley Lecture (London: Epworth, 1935), p. 18.

[34]"No man fulfills all the duties of charity, unless he really fears God" (Calvin, *Institutes,* II, viii, liii).

[35]F. Pieper, *Christian Dogmatics* (St. Louis: Concordia, 1950-53), I, 34f.

Liberal Protestantism fails to see this inseparability of the theological and ethical. Its rallying cry was "retain the Sermon on the Mount, but away with all creeds and metaphysical affirmations." But the ethics of Jesus cannot be "salvaged" in this manner, since its dependency on the theological is its characteristic feature. The Sermon is thoroughly religious. Any reinterpretation as "pure ethics" completely changes its intention.

Marshall says if we abstract Jesus' ethical maxims from their religious bases, they are "rendered practically useless" and "theoretically unintelligible."[36] The validity, cogency, and practicality of the ethical content are then surrendered. Those who recognized that Jesus' teaching was functionally dependent upon his beliefs grasped only half the facts, although an important half. The other phase is the inseparability of this functional from the objectively real spiritual and moral world as he set it forth. None of the moral principles of Jesus is separable from its theological basis because, as Marshall asserts, "all the ethical teaching of Jesus is rooted in His religion, in God."[37] Marshall acknowledges that some utterances seem purely ethical and almost anti-religious. For example, there is the rebuke to long prayers by unethical men, or the regard for befriending the distressed more important than temple worship, or his own befriending of the irreligious (harlots, tax-gatherers, sinners), or the condemnation of religious leaders. Yet all this is but a commentary on Jesus' teaching that false religion yields unethical fruit, while true religion yields the highest ethics. This position is far removed from an exaltation of ethics above religion.

In Dewar's words, Jesus "contrived to weld ethics and religion into such a unity as had never been previously known."[38] Plummer points out that in the Lord's Prayer "as in the case of the Decalogue and of the Two Great Commandments (xxii.40), the first part refers to God, the second to man."[39]

The Pauline ethic bears the same theological stamp. If some attempt a non-theological Pauline ethics, others claim that he was concerned mainly with the theoretical and not with the practical sides of life. "No charge brought against Paul," W. G. D. MacLennan astutely answers to that charge, "can be more absurd than that which accuses him of being so concerned with this faith-union that he relegated morality to the fringe of things important. His teaching is ethical throughout and his call is for a life of obedience to Christ in every relationship."[40] That the moral life is conceived of as the spiritual

[36]L. H. Marshall, *The Challenge of New Testament Ethics* (London: Macmillan, 1946), p. 14.
[37]*Ibid.*, p. 12.
[38]Dewar, *op. cit.*, p. 20.
[39]Alfred Plummer, *An Exegetical Commentary on the Gospel of Matthew* (Grand Rapids: Eerdmans, reprint, 1953), p. 96.
[40]W. G. D. MacLennan, *Christian Obedience,* p. 40.

reign of God in the lives of believers is evident from an objective study of his letters. Marshall has contended with sufficient force that while Paul's ethics is "not inseparably united with the term 'Kingdom of God' " nevertheless "the *idea* of God's rule in the heart is as central in his teaching as in that of Jesus," and that only a difference of vocabulary creates the impression that the Kingdom idea is peripheral in Paul's thought.[41] The theological character of Paul's ethics is obvious from the fact that he traces the moral degradation of the pagan world to desertion of the knowledge of God (Rom. 1:28). It can easily be seen in his derivation of moral obligation from the great Christian doctrines of the incarnation (Phil. 2:4ff.) and atonement (Rom. 12:1ff.). It is equally clear from his declaration that morality crumbles if the resurrection is a fiction rather than a fact (1 Cor. 15:13ff.). For the denial of the resurrection, in Paul's view, not only subverts the Gospel, but it strips the moral claim of force, voiding its truth and reality, by deteriorating men to the level of perishing beasts. The theological and the ethical everywhere cohere. When Paul declared the law "holy and just and good" (Rom. 7:12), he "conjoined the one great word of religion and the two great words of ethics."[42]

Not only is morality grounded in the character and will of God, but the moral objective cannot be seriously approximated apart from Divine grace. Both the revelation and the realization of the ethical life have God as their vital presupposition. Marshall notes that "Paul's views about the 'Good' are most clearly revealed in his account of the Fruits of the Spirit . . . and thus provide a striking demonstration of the complete fusion of religion and ethics in Pauline thought."[43]

What is true of Pauline theology and ethics is likewise true of Johannine. "Morality is based upon religion, and ethics upon dogma. Dogma treats of communion with God, ethics of likeness to God. Communion with God is the prerequisite of likeness to Him. Such is the moral standpoint of Christianity. We find it in all parts of Holy Scripture, but perhaps it is nowhere so definitely expressed, or so consistently carried out, as in the First Epistle of St. John."[44]

Christian ethics presupposes God's covenant with man, a covenant which exists in view of God's determination to write his will on the hearts of a company of redeemed persons. Revealed ethics is specifically an *ethics of Divine covenant*. It does not gain its place in the Hebrew-Christian community as a mere prophetic ideal that can be explained by a special genius for religion or a gifted spiritual intuition. In sharp contrast with speculative systems, the biblical code and ethic rest upon a covenantal foundation that is progressively renewed by Divine revelation and reaches maturity in Jesus Christ. God has entered into covenant-relation with man, and in his grace he is the God of

[41]Marshall, *op. cit.*, pp. 247f.
[42]Dewar, *op. cit.*, p. 122.
[43]Marshall, *op. cit.*, p. 290.
[44]Luthardt, *op. cit.*, p. 23.

continuing covenant. While salvation is no longer suspended upon works, the perpetual significance of the divinely-imposed rule of duty remains. The covenant into which the holy God enters with man involves his gracious provision of salvation for man from his dire predicament in sin, and it includes the publication from age to age of the specific form that obedience to the Divine will is to take.

The deliverance of Israel from Egyptian oppression is depicted as a fulfillment of covenant with the patriarchs Abraham, Isaac, and Jacob (Ex. 6:4-8). This covenant was ratified in blood by the circumcision. God's intention was to raise up "a kingdom of priests and a holy nation" that should keep covenant with him (Ex. 19:3-6). The covenant was divinely initiated; man-lost-in-sin is in no position to enter into negotiations with the Holy Lord. It is not man's obedience that inaugurates the covenant-relation, but the covenant-relation comes out of mercy and shapes man's conduct to conform to the will of God. As Luthardt remarks, "The Covenant is the point of view under which the relationship of God to His people is put from Gen. ix.9 to Jer. xxxi.-xxxiv. It is not like a bilateral contract among men, but it proceeds exclusively from God and His initiative as a unilateral institution of God into which man, and therefore Israel, only enters. . . . The spontaneity and activity of God, presupposed in the formation of the Covenant, are given expression to in the accentuation of God as the subject of the Covenant."[45] Christian ethics is the cherished ethics of those standing in covenant relation with God, those who by faith are children of promise (Gal. 4:28). The covenant is beyond doubt rooted in God's election-love, and centers in the gracious Divine provision of redemption for man lost in sin. J. C. Wenger emphasizes that all the covenants of the Bible find their continuity in salvation by faith which results in holy obedience to the Lord.[46]

Divine covenant declares at once the grace and the righteousness of God. Divine revelation and redemption seek to produce holiness in men, *i.e.,* obedient conformity of sinners to the Divine image. Abraham's forsaking of kindred and home in Ur of the Chaldees was an initial move of faith predicated upon promises regarding the land (Gen. 12:7), a posterity (Gen. 15:1ff.), and an everlasting covenant with Isaac (Gen. 17:19). As seen in relation to the covenant, the Decalogue has a dramatic importance. It states the moral law of God comprehensively in propositional form. The God who redeems in grace is "the faithful God, who keepeth covenant and loving kindness with them that love Him and keep His commandments to a thousand generations" (Dt. 7:11). The determination of God to raise up a righteous people through gracious redemption stands at the center of covenant ethics.

[45]Christian Ernst Luthardt, *History of Christian Ethics,* trans. W. Hastie (Edinburgh: T. & T. Clark, 1889), p. 42.

[46]J. C. Wenger, *Separated Unto God* (Scottdale, Pa.: Mennonite Publishing House, 1952), p. 7.

The covenant hope is vivid in the prophetic message about worship and conduct. The certainty of God's covenant promises and their importance as a determining factor in the moral outlook of Israel are highlighted by Jeremiah (33:6ff., 20ff.). Moses told Israel "Thou art a holy people unto Jehovah thy God: Jehovah thy God hath chosen thee to be a people for His own possession, above all peoples that are upon the face of the earth" (Dt. 7:6ff.), and Peter reiterated this confidence to the early Christian believers: "Ye are an elect race, a royal priesthood, a holy nation, a people for God's own possession, that ye may show forth the excellencies of him who called you out of darkness into his marvellous light: who in time past were no people, but now are the people of God; who had not obtained mercy, but now have obtained mercy" (1 Pet. 2:9ff.). The covenant of grace enters upon a second mode of administration with the coming of Christ and his fresh interpretation of the moral law. The covenant ethic now centers in the teaching and example of Christ as the authoritative interpreter and fulfiller of the law.

Obedience enters as a requirement in all stages of God's covenant relations with men. The God of covenant is the God of holy commandment. And the covenant people are the people "called to holiness." The obligation to the life of specially revealed ethics rises because God has chosen a people in covenant-love.

Because Christian ethics is the ethics of special and not of universal revelation, it is not immanently accessible to all men on the basis of creation. Rather, it is an actuality within a company of people to whom God has specially addressed his Word. It is *the ethics of the believing church.* It is the moral inheritance of a fellowship of men and women "separated unto God." The church is a spiritual, ethical, and vital creation that is divinely called into being with Christ as its head. It is the household of God, whose mission is to hold before the world the realities of a redemptive morality. It has a Gospel to proclaim and a new life to live. The whole of human interests, individual and social, may be transformed under the influence of the Spirit of God. The irresistible logic of the Christian life includes this organic relation to God and the dramatic conformity of human affairs to the will of God.

The ethics of revealed religion therefore divides mankind into two radically opposed groups: the followers of the broad way and those of the narrow way. In the Old Testament the chosen people proclaimed an urgent message to their pagan neighbors. In the New the believing church has a globe-girdling mission to an unbelieving world. Rather than being a mere derivative from or intensification of a universal ethical impulse, Christian ethics made the church the light of a dark world and the salt of a putrefying earth. P. T. Forsyth said in *The Cruciality of the Cross* that "there is no issue so vital to human society as righteousness. A society rises in the scale in proportion as righteousness is felt to be central and supreme."[47] The burden of responsibility that such a judgment places upon the Christian community is patent. The first chapter of Romans is Paul's picture of the extreme moral debasement of the Roman empire. The first Corinthian letter is his reminder to that church that it is set against the world and that Christianity passes a harsh judgment of moral disapproval on pagan immorality. Christianity was at war with the so-called civilized morality of pagan Graeco-Roman society. Christian ethics is not borrowed from the world, but proclaims a "nonconformist" morality over against the "ethics of the world." It is an ethics which divides the world in two. It stands "in the midst of a crooked and perverse generation" (Phil. 2:14f.) and offers it a way of escape. The height of Pauline indignation could only have been reached in 1 Corinthians 5 where he deals with a believer guilty of a sin "not so much as named among the Gentiles." Instead of tolerating it, let alone approving it, he would "deliver such an one unto Satan for the destruction of the flesh" (5:5).

The believer finds a climate for moral growth in the believing church. His membership in the body of Christ supplies a telling motivation and energy for the avoidance of sin and for the realization of the virtuous life. The biblical conception of the union of believers in Christ has in modern times acquired overtones of a doctrine of corporate life and personality that is more Hegelian and idealistic than Pauline and theistic.[48] The New Testament clearly speaks of a new ethical brotherhood based on redemption. It is a community of grace with a unique social solidarity, and it has striking significance for moral achievement. A church with no living Christ as its sustaining presupposition and with no Holy Spirit as its dynamic could give no exemplary ethics to the world. It would then lack the very personal and social power of ethical living supplied by union with Christ. As the head of a new race, Christ is the supreme personality who shapes the motives and conduct of all who are organically united with him.

Believers make up the mystical body of which the Risen Christ is the living head. This is a determinative ground for avoiding idolatry (1 Cor. 10:14ff.) and adultery (1 Cor. 6:15). In the latter passage Paul dramatically asks whether those who are "limbs" of Christ shall be made the members of a harlot.

But the significance of union with Christ is far from a merely negative one. The fellowship of believers in the corporate life of the church is essential for personal growth and collective maturity. H. A. A. Kennedy writes wisely that "the Christian community affords the best

[47]P. T. Forsyth, *The Cruciality of the Cross* (London: Hodder and Stoughton, n.d.), p. 142.

[48]The metaphor of the body and its parts has a non-Christian as well as a Christian connotation; one finds it in Plato and Hegel as well as in Paul, and it became a favorite notion of modern absolute idealists who, although professing to write Christian ethics, profoundly miswrote it. The expression for Christianity belongs to the community of faith, not the body politic, nor the social organism as a whole.

training in ethical discipline."[49] This concept that the believing church supplies an ideal and indispensable environment for moral maturity cuts across two biases that are gaining wide support today. One is the notion that superior moral earnestness and moral worth are to be found outside the church. There is without doubt wide disparity in professing Christendom between its ideals and its attainments. And the modern mood has projected vigorous ethical movements on an humanistic base. But when the *believing* church and the world are compared, the long witness of history is still an indisputable testimony to the source of genuine and enduring ethical vitality — the church. A. B. Bruce's remark, that "many . . . have left the church in order to become Christians,"[50] can only be regarded as the vocabulary of temporary and uncharacteristic reaction. Where genuine believers are gathered in the unity of living fellowship with Jesus Christ, the church has no occasion of uneasiness through whatever ethical concern may be implemented by secular movements. It will always find that the highest elements of that concern represent broken reflections of the Christian ideal. A second notion that is equally objectionable is that the isolated local church, out of effective contact with the larger Christian fellowship, or that the isolated believer, maintaining his personal devotions in independence of a local church, is ethically self-sufficient. In numerous evangelical circles this mood gained ground as a reaction to the inclusivistic temper of ecumenical movements and to the control of many local churches by the liberal philosophies of religion at the expense of revealed theology. But a surer instinct motivated believers who affiliated with biblically-oriented churches and who sought out larger associations of such churches, than those who reacted to this invasion by liberalism with a private Christianity and who reflected thereby the secular accentuation of individual life. This accounts in part for the ease with which Fundamentalism, which often took a bold and commendable stand against worldly evils, settled ethical questions by a short-shrift legalism.

While the redeemed life always begins with a personal response to Christ, ethical discernment and maturity are furthered by a *mutual* deliberation and appropriation of the biblical revelation to the demands of modern life. The English "you" with both singular and plural sense, obscured in the King James Version the Scripture's frequent mention of the ministry of the Holy Spirit to believers in their collective life. But it is especially in the creation of a new spiritual and ethical fellowship, the *koinonia,* that the Spirit's most characteristic activity is seen. H. Wheeler Robinson refers us to the familiar words of benediction, "the fellowship of the Holy Spirit," by way of reminder that "the gifts and graces of the Christian life are all pointed towards mutual

[49]H. A. A. Kennedy, *The Theology of the Epistles* (London: Duckworth, 1952), p. 145.
[50]A. B. Bruce, *The Kingdom of God* (4th ed.; New York: Scribner & Welford, 1891), p. 144.

service; they are all created within, and primarily for, the Christian community by the Holy Spirit."[51] The best spiritual gifts are available to all, but God also gives diversities of gifts, administrations, and operations with a view to the whole company of believers (1 Cor. 12:4ff.; 28ff.). No believer can live to himself. The unity of believers in Christ involves such a close sharing of life that the New Testament uses such metaphors as the Vine and the branches, the Head and the body, the Chief Cornerstone and the temple, and Christ and His bride. Christian ethics is no Robinson Crusoe venture; it is a redeemed company of believers bound together in the confident investment of their lives in the ethics of revelation. And if believers need each other for moral maturity, it is true in an immensely greater measure that the world must leave its presuppositions and adopt those of the believing church if real moral earnestness and stature are desired.

There is more. Christian ethics is the ethics of revelational metaphysics, of redemptive religion, of Divine covenant, and of the believing church. It is all of these because it is anchored in the nature and will of the God who disclosed himself in the Bible. The standard of perfection for ethics cannot be defined apart from reference to the living God. "Be ye perfect as your Father in heaven is perfect" is no mere call to eternal Ideas which are striving for a full manifestation. It is a declaration that the moral ideal binding on man is eternally actual in the God of the eternities. Christian morality is not the revelation of an ideal that exists eternally in the Divine mind and to which man is summoned. It is the revelation of a perfection realized eternally in the Divine nature that is validated forever by the Divine will. It is the ethics of the Holy God. "The moral law, as the norm and goal of our life, obtains its validity and obligation for us not because it is an arbitrarily-given command, but because it is of the very character of God."[52] For this reason Christian ethics is supremely a theocentric ethics. And because Christianity makes an ultimate affirmation that Jesus of Nazareth is the supreme revelation of God, the ethics of revelation is called Christian ethics. Otherwise it might have been called "the Divine imperative" or "covenant morality." The term "Christian ethics" shows clearly that this ethics is rooted transcendently within the Godhead.

And yet such designations as "covenant morality" may be used properly to signify Christian ethics as appropriately as is the term "biblical ethics," provided they are not intended as alternatives to the latter. Christian ethics is ultimately "biblical" since it is found in God's specially-revealed Word that was spoken by chosen prophets and apostles and written for our instruction. The content of Christian ethics is safeguarded from a spiritual mysticism by the biblical rule of Chris-

[51]H. Wheeler Robinson, *Revelation and Redemption* (New York: Harper, 1942), p. 287.
[52]Alexander, *op. cit.*, p. 27.

tian conduct, and it is safeguarded from legalism by the New Testament setting forth of the essential significance of the Old Testament revelation. Hence it is properly designated the *ethics of the Bible.*

Christian ethics is also connected to dogmatics. Because it contains the Divine communication of truths about God and his purposes, the Bible fulfills its role as the trustworthy rule of faith and practice. The attempt during the nineteenth century of moralists like Haering, Martensen, Dorner and Wuttke, who sought to treat ethics separately and independently of dogmatics, finds a subtle parallel in the theology of crisis. This theology professedly champions an ethics of special revelation. At the same time it repudiates entirely the historic Christian confidence in revealed doctrinal and ethical truths. Actually Christian ethics receives its formative principles and normative standards from dogmatics that is based on a revealed theology.

The transcendent metaphysical basis of Christian ethics has been pushed into the background of interest since Kant's day. This narrowing of interest in the metaphysical side of morality by assigning priority to the ethical life itself has involved more and more the construction of "Christian" ethics with metaphysical scaffoldings provided by the speculative philosophies. But such constructions have invariably required a new version of the ethical content as well. This is because the Christian life view cannot be blended with any and every world-view, or in other words, because alien metaphysical outlooks require an alien morality. The Christian life view will not long survive a combination with any metaphysics other than that of transcendent revelation. For a time the two positions may exist side by side as unreconciled neighbors, but sooner or later the tension will work itself out in open injury. The inspiration and power and the reality of Christian ethics is drawn from its basis in special revelation. Apart from that basis its significance as the supreme norm of human conduct can never be maintained.

Speculative ethics knows nothing of the moral life in relation to the Kingdom of God, to Jesus Christ and his Church. For secular philosophers the moral life is anchored only in natural facts or distilled autonomously from human nature. Or it may be rooted in an unseen metaphysical world with no sense of Divine revelation.

The morality which is merely philosophical is an arbitrary abstraction, a speculative reduction of the fullness of reality. What to the secular moralist is the crown of the evolutionary process in the mundane order — an ethical standard deduced from the world and the conscience of contemporary man — is to the Christian moralist the shadow of reality. He would relate man's search for the good to God's revelation of his Divine will. He would contrast the changing face of human insight with the changeless God. He would meet man's desire for moral growth with Christ's summons to be "perfect as your Father in heaven is perfect" (Mt. 5:49).

The content of the moral "ought" for the Christian is transcendently derived. This is in contrast with all idealistic efforts to distill moral principles from the nature of mankind viewed as an aspect of the Divine. The Christian ethical standard is based on God who is man's judge and redeemer.

The Christian ethic, then, is a given or revealed ethic. Its basis is transcendent, not an immanent possession of man as fallen in sin. It is a metaphysical and religious ethic. But it is also the ethic of the specially-revealed God. Indeed, it is a covenant-ethic. It is the ethic of the believing church whose task is the rescue of a morally-crippled world.

8

THE GOOD AS THE WILL OF GOD AS LORD

AN OXFORD TUTOR recently acknowledged that only by a return to the Hebrew-Christian belief in the will of God as the foundation of ethics can we gain "assistance in the elucidation of an otherwise insoluble problem" — that of "achieving a real union of the two fundamental concepts of moral philosophy, duty and value."[1] Thrust into the ethical stalemate of our age, his judgment is a pertinent reminder of the uniqueness and importance of the biblical view that the good is what God does and wills.

"To the Israelites," L. A. Garrard remarks, "God is the ultimate source of all moral obligation. The only absolute duty is to do his will."[2] Hebrew-Christian ethics unequivocally defines moral obligation as man's duty to God. "The conception of moral duty and moral value as founded *in the nature of man* may have been implicit, but it was not developed as the primary foundation of moral conduct. Man's chief duty is to obey God. . . . The emphasis is placed on *obedience.*" So writes Clifford Barrett of the Hebrew-Christian ethic.[3] And in this acknowledgment he is decidedly correct. The good in Hebrew-Christian theistic ethics is not that which is adapted to human nature, but it is that to which the Creator obliges human nature.

The doctrine that the good is to be identified with the will of God cuts across secular ethics at almost every point. It protests against Utilitarianism, and its validation of the good by an appeal to consequences alone. It indicts Kant's supposition that duty and obligation rest upon a wholly immanental basis. According to Kant, the human will alone imposes man's duties upon him and affirms for him the categorical imperative.[4] This theory of morality mediated to the modern

[1]L. A. Garrard, *Duty and the Will of God* (Oxford: Blackwell, 1938), pp. 51f.
[2]*Ibid.*, p. 58.
[3]Clifford C. Barrett, *Ethics* (New York: Harper, 1933), p. 49. Barrett suggests that since an authoritarian standard was accepted, and the concepts of morality not analyzed independently of religious foundations, the inherent significance of the good life was unexplored. But it was just this refusal of biblical ethics, as against the Greek anthropocentric approach, to investigate the good life primarily from within the standpoint of the fallen man, as that which most adequately expresses and develops human nature, which attached a distinct significance to the moral life, refusing to disjoin it from the questions of sin and redemption, of justification and sanctification. Above all other considerations, the moral agent is duty-bound to God.
[4]Kant's anti-metaphysical philosophy ruled out consideration of an objectively real God. The moral life gains a religious aura, he indicated, when the demands of conscience are regarded *as if* they were the commands of God. But, for Kant, this religious interpretation moves in the sphere of postulation, not revelation.

man the artificial hope that the objectivity of the moral order could be maintained by a deliberate *severance* of duty and the good *from* the will of God. The Hebrew-Christian ethical perspective also challenges the many species of humanistic ethics so influential in the Western world today. Biblical ethics discredits an autonomous morality. It gives theonomous ethics its classic form — the identification of the moral law with the Divine will. In Hebrew-Christian revelation, distinctions in ethics reduce to what is good or what is pleasing, and to what is wicked or displeasing to the Creator-God alone. The biblical view maintains always a dynamic statement of values, refusing to sever the elements of morality from the will of God.

That the essence of true morality is to be found primarily in complete obedience to the sovereign Lord provided the climate of thought which Hobbes secularized and perverted in the *Leviathan.* His contemporary, Ralph Cudworth (1617-1688), who wrote *Eternal and Immutable Morality,* sought to place all men, including Hobbes and his sovereign, under an obligation to act for the common good. Cudworth argued that the distinction between right and wrong does not depend upon sovereign will, but on the moral order which confronts the whole of reality. Cudworth did not hesitate to insist that the principles of morality are addressed even to the Divine will and hence are determinative of it. By moralists under Cudworth's influence, man's obligation to obey the injunctions of Scripture was no longer suspended exclusively on the fact that God commands obedience, but correlative reasons for man's conformity were introduced, *e.g.,* that obedience involves the common good. British moralists especially contributed to this Platonic rather than Hebraic orientation of values. The erroneous notion gained ground swiftly that the best device for thwarting political Naturalism, and for protecting the idea of duty from arbitrary perversion, is to assert the independent existence of moral values, rather than to defend the good as the will of God. God is himself thereby assertedly obliged to uphold these values, and hence precluded from acting in an arbitrary way. Hence the detachment of the content of morality from the will of God became the optimistic basis of a reply to political Naturalism and all forms of moral autonomy.

Thereafter, the phrase "I ought" no longer means "the sovereign Lord commands." Rather, it is informed by self-evident truths or by intuitions of the moral order, as by the Cambridge Platonists, and finally it loses its connection with a transcendent moral order no less than with the sovereign Divine will. Thus the Christian West enters into a non-Christian orientation of the account of duty, and the outcome of this transition is that the doctrine of obligation is sketched independently of both the will of God and of theism. At first it was thought that, while separated from the will of God, moral obligations were as secure as mathematical axioms. They were safeguarded by universal and necessary implications of conscience or by some other immanentistic device. In place of the God-spoken moral imperative there arose a categorical imperative. This endured as an effective rallying point for ethical Idealism for less than a century. When the empirical and evolutionary movements in modern thought were felt, the attempt to secure the absolute obligation to perform every duty within an autonomous ethics dissolved, and with it the absoluteness of duty. Instead of exhibiting the inner unity of duty and goodness in their ultimate basis in the will of God, it lost the sanctity of moral obligation.

Yet the failure to identify duty and the good with the will of God is characteristic of idealistic ethics both in ancient and in modern times. Even those moral philosophies that professed hostility to an autonomous ethic and championed the transcendent objectivity of the moral order regarded the good as something given to God. They viewed the good as something to which God was bound rather than as something legislated by him. This prepared the way for an objectionable doctrine of the "good in itself." The good then is superior to God. It is a content which is externally addressed to him as it is to us. This thesis runs through Oriental religion as well as early Western philosophy. It underlies the Zoroastrian notion that Ormazd becomes supreme through his furtherance of the good. This view assumes the existence of an ethical law superior to God himself. It is found also in the Hindu conception of the law of Karma. God is the author of sovereign causality in an impersonal moral universe. Yet not even he can interfere with its autonomous operation now that it is in movement.[5] The same idea becomes influential in Western thought through the moral philosophy of Plato, as expressed in the *Euthyphro*. Plato did not clearly identify the Idea of the Good with God, but it stood at the apex of the Divine Ideas. Hence the good can only be regarded as confronting the eternal spiritual world.

This notion of an "intrinsic good" is alien to biblical theology.[6] The God of Hebrew-Christian revelation is the ground of ethics. He is the supreme rule of right. He defines the whole content of morality by his own revealed will. It is not merely because "in God is the perfect realization of the Ideal Righteousness,"[7] but because God legislates the nature of the good that biblical ethics is a radical departure from the pagan view of the moral order. The distinction between intrinsic and instrumental goods may be a grossly misleading distinction. In the proper context it is quite acceptable. Scripture would solidly back the

[5]Vinjamuri E. Devadutt, in *Biblical Authority for Today,* Alan Richardson and Wolfgang Schweitzer, eds. (Philadelphia: Westminster, n.d.), p. 67.

[6]Gordon H. Clark writes: ". . . in non-Christian systems God and man both face an independent good, and if their minds function normally neither judgment is superior to or different from the other. In Christianity, however, no such comparison is possible, for God's thinking makes a thing so and man's thinking merely discovers that it is so." *A Christian Philosophy of Education* (Grand Rapids: Eerdmans, 1946), p. 123.

[7]George Walker, *The Idealism of Christian Ethics,* p. 30.

idea that the good is not to be prized merely for the sake of consequences or for the rewards it gives. That is an unacceptable variation of an instrumental good. The fear of punishment and the desire for reward may be acceptable as secondary motivations in the ethical life, but they can hardly bear the whole weight of a healthy moral outlook. The good must be good for an intrinsic reason that is apparent from an analysis of the nature of the good.

This artificial view of an instrumental good is overcome by showing clearly that the will of God is the only intrinsic good. Since the good is divinely-willed, and since God attaches rewards to its fulfillment, it is both intrinsically and instrumentally good. The good is not prized more highly if its instrumental aspects are disparaged and it is viewed as a purely intrinsic good. It is the will of God that defines the nature of intrinsic goodness. There exists no intrinsic good that is distinguishable from the will of God and to which God must conform.[8]

Therefore the good must be conceived in wholly personal dimensions. The good-in-itself is none other than God-in-himself. Keyser remarks, "Christian Ethics goes back to God as the ultimate ground and source of morality."[9] Kant's insistence that there is nothing good in the last analysis but a good will is formally right. His error was his displacement of the Divine by the human and his staggering moral optimism about human nature. The will of God is the source of the ethical law and supplies the content of morality. It alone is intrinsically good. Man's life is not to be oriented to impersonal eternal values,[10] to objective norms, to ethical laws, to principles of conduct, to abiding virtues, viewed abstractly or independently of the Divine will. These place obligation upon men only insofar as they may be traced to the will of God. The human race is "under personal orders and command." In the Christian view ethical categories are not "the realm of ends," but are "the Kingdom *of God.*"

The question whether the good is to be conceived as identical with the nature of God has supplied fuel for theological debate in numerous Christian controversies. Sometimes this discussion rises out of speculative theories of the Divine nature, especially those about the troublesome question of essence and person. It is possible to hold a view that transcends the conflict, yet it is important to rule out dangerous and

[8]Alvah Hovey quotes from Secretan: "To suppose moral order pre-existent and supreme would be to make moral order God. To suppose them eternally simultaneous would be to divide the sovereignty of the universe between abstract law and the Being consenting to it." *Manual of Systematic Theology and Christian Ethics* (Philadelphia: American Baptist Publication Society, 1877), p. 369.

[9]Leander S. Keyser, *A Manual of Christian Ethics,* p. 31.

[10]The preference for the term "value" in ethics over the term "good," often arises today from a revolt against the absolute and unquestioned characteristics with which the latter is identified, whereas the former "enables us, without any difficulty, to recognize *degrees.*" J. S. Mackenzie, *Ultimate Values in the Light of Contemporary Thought* (London: Hodder & Stoughton, 1924), p. 93.

misleading views.[11] It is obvious enough that unless there is an ultimate ethical tension in the being of God, the Divine nature and will cannot be thought of as in competition with each other, but as morally identical. From this standpoint the good is conformity to God's being and to his will. But the nature of God must not be regarded as necessarily good in the sense that it gains its goodness independently of his will, nor that his good nature determines his will so that the will bows to the good by a sort of pantheistic inevitability. The good is what God wills, and what he freely wills. The good is what the Creator-Lord does and commands. He is the creator of the moral law, and defines its very nature.

At the same time no suggestion is conveyed that the good is arbitrary or a matter of Divine "caprice." That term frequently suits the propaganda purposes of those who caricature Divine sovereignty. Biblical morality itself has supplied a perspective from which the capriciousness of the polytheistic gods of Greek mythology may be judged. The moral activity of God is a closer definition of his nature.[12] It is the constancy of God's will in its ethical affirmations and claims that supplies the durable basis for moral distinctions.[13] Hovey declares, "The moral law is a free expression of his will to others, and therefore in the fullest and strictest sense it is from him, under him, dependent on him, and immutable only as he is immutable; while the same law comes down upon us from his mind and will, imposing itself on our consciences, and therefore is over us, and independent of us."[14] In stipulating the moral law, the Creator-God lay under no necessity other than to form it according to his own pleasure, and hence in conformity with his real character and purpose. The will of God so reveals his character that the man who conforms to his commandments will exhibit the image of God in his life. The Hebrew-Christian knowledge of God is a knowledge of the Righteous One. The commandments are mani-

[11]"The Right is grounded in both the *nature* and the *will* of God. God must be good in His very being, or He could not be good at all. At the same time, He must be free, or He would not be a moral being. Yet, if there ever was a time when He was not free, He never could have become free. Whatever God is now, He must have been from eternity" (Keyser, *op. cit.*, p. 37).

[12]W. E. H. Lecky, in *History of European Morals,* describing the collapse of morality in "The Pagan Empire," says of the ancient civilizations that "the moral ideas had at no time been sought in the actions of the gods, and long before the triumph of Christianity, polytheism had ceased to have any great influence upon the more cultivated intellects of mankind." (New York: Appleton, 1929).

[13]R. F. Weidner stresses that "His will is not like that of a man, subjected to a 'must' and an 'ought' which has to be fulfilled by a temporal development and effort. His will cannot be altered like that of a man, it is unchangeable, the same yesterday, today, and forever. This thought not merely calls us to humility, but at the same time breathes into us hope and consolation. We are comforted and strengthened by knowing that there is One who is good—that above all the confusion of the world, above all the fickle and changing will of man, above folly and sin and misery, there yet exists a will essentially good." *A System of Christian Ethics* (Philadelphia: G. W. Frederick, 1897), p. 22.

[14]Hovey, *op. cit.,* p. 369.

festations of his character, and righteousness is what he prizes as his special glory (Ex. 33:18f., 34:6f.).

One need not throw doubt upon the moral earnestness of the long tradition of moral philosophy from ancient Greek to modern times by observing that their independency of this Hebrew-Christian ethical perspective has resulted in vacillation about men's virtues and doubt about their duties. There is a growing uncertainty in modern thought that personal happiness and goodness can be reconciled. This tension of duty and value, of goodness and happiness, rises from an unconvincing and unstable exhibition of their inner nature and relationships.

This problem has plagued the whole history of philosophical ethics. Much of the moral fervor that motivates speculative morality springs from the conviction that alternate expositions of conduct threaten to reduce our duties to illusions. Duties may be sacrificed to personal or universal happiness. Or happiness may be banished by a life of rigorous duty. Or a virtuous life may be insisted upon with no apparent reason why men are obliged to pursue it. The end result is 'oughts' that are not clearly moral.

The question what makes an act a duty has been answered ambiguously throughout the whole history of ethics. The view that finds in consequences or good results the obligatory basis of our actions, and conceives the ethical act merely as instrumentally good is inadequate. The view that regards an action itself as intrinsically good with total indifference to its consequences, and derives goodness from obligation, is equally inadequate. Both views fail to grasp the fact that obligation and virtue, goodness and happiness, find their common ground in the Divine will. They also fail to recognize that the notions of duty and goodness cannot be analyzed so as to enforce their interlocking nature when this fundamental reference is ignored. Why should man be obliged to do what is regarded as intrinsically good without regard to the consequences? Why is he obliged to do what leads to good consequences if he is in doubt regarding the basic rightness of his action? Speculative ethics furnishes a running commentary on this tension and fails to resolve it.

Modern hedonism is not as crude as its ancient counterpart. It equates the term 'pleasure' or 'happiness' with the 'good.' The 'good' is a term whose moral status is then suspended in doubt. Is it self-evident that our duty ought irreversibly to aim at the greatest happiness of the greatest number? May it not in point of fact consist at times in something quite different from this? Does duty never benefit the minority? May not one be called upon repeatedly to do that which will lead to unhappiness, his own as well as that of a majority of others, in the very course of duty? May there not exist an ethical imperative which discredits Utilitarianism as sub-moral? If it can be shown that a certain act would produce the greatest happiness for the greatest number of people, does that automatically establish one's obligation to perform it? How does one make the transition from an 'if I do . . ., then . . .' to the 'therefore, I ought . . .'?

On the other hand, it is equally difficult to hold that an action is good simply because it is motivated by the sense of duty. Granted that a sense of duty is an essential element in the performance of a good act, how can it be argued that just the presence of this sense of duty defines an act as good? Is it self-evident that whatever acts flow from a sense of duty are for that reason, and that reason alone, good? If the sense of duty alone establishes the morality of an act, then it makes no difference what the particular act might be, since it is motivation alone that gives it its moral tone. Are there not other elements to consider than a sense of duty in defining right action?

The attempt to define moral obligation either by ethical consequences or by ethical motivation thus ends indecisively. "It appears," Garrard commented as he surveyed the frustration to which the major ethical movements have come on this problem, "that it is no more possible to derive goodness from obligation than obligation from goodness, and that each must be regarded as *sui generis*."[15] If this is the verdict to which the ethical quest is driven, the baffling question of the relationship between duty and goodness is still unresolved. Some contemporary moralists are dissatisfied to leave the problem there. They seek a unity of duty and goodness by appeal to some higher law, that assigns to duties a determining quality beyond the mere obligation to perform them. Thus provoked by the predicament into which moral philosophy has fallen, a contemporary interest has arisen in the will of God as the supreme source of ethical claims.[16]

However, these speculative attempts to base ethics on a theonomous instead of an autonomous foundation by emphasizing that duty cannot be separated from the will of God halt short of the Hebrew-Christian ethical perspective. For example, Martineau contends against Kant that " '*obligation*' is a relative term, implying somewhere a corresponding *claim of right*: i.e. it takes two to establish an obligation."[17] The ought, then, has God as its indispensable presupposition. Garrard agrees with Martineau, "there seems . . . no other view that explains all our thoughts about claims," they "are otherwise left hanging in the air."[18] This is hardly a return to the Hebrew-Christian emphasis that the good is known in and through Divine initiative in which the Living

[15]Garrard, *op. cit.*, p. 17.

[16]It is revealing how many treatments of Christian ethics, colored either by Kantian autonomy or by the excessive Divine immanence of Hegelianism, fail to work out the content of Christian ethics convincingly from the will of God as its source.

[17]James Martineau, *Types of Ethical Theory* (3rd ed. rev., Oxford: Clarendon Press, 1891), II, 107.

[18]Garrard, *op. cit.*, p. 49. The same idea is found in R. L. Ottley: "An absolute morality implies the existence of a divine will and personality behind it; the idea of good cannot be dissociated from the idea of God." *Christian Ideas and Ideals*, p. 39. For biblical ethics, however, the connecting link between morality and religion is supplied from the Divine side, by the self-disclosure of the Divine will.

God in a special once-for-all historical disclosure makes known his will in the form of precise commands. Whatever may be said of Garrard's alternative to the categorical imperative of Kant, the principle that "we ought always to do the will of God,"[19] offers us no revival of Judeo-Christian ethics. Rather, it is a speculative reconstruction that borrows certain features from biblical theistic ethics. In the borrowing, it empties them of much that is distinctive, and in the end it proposes under the general category of an "ethics of the will of God" something that is a subtraction from the original. True enough, the ethical claim finds no real support on an autonomous basis only. The appeal to the Divine better explains man's feeling about his moral duties, so that "as soon as we come to regard our duty as a fulfillment of God's will, we begin to see a value in it that was previously hidden, and indeed to understand how it may have a greater value than any alternative act that is possible."[20] Moreover, such a concept formally achieves "a real union of the two fundamental concepts of moral philosophy, duty and value."[21]

But Garrard's appeal to the will of God actually retains but one feature from a much more inclusive realm of revealed truth. No solid case can be made for maintaining the will of God as the distinctive category of morality apart from the historic biblical concept of special Divine revelation. Garrard states that he would "never dream of suggesting" that the advantages from equating duty with the will of God "could constitute the sole, or even an adequate reason for believing in the Christian God. All that I would contend is that those who believe in God will find some satisfaction in the reflection that their belief is of assistance in the elucidation of an otherwise insoluble problem."[22] But one does not believe in the Hebrew-Christian God as an independent fact apart from the self-revelation of the Divine will. It is in and through God's disclosure of himself and his purposes that the Hebrew-Christian movement has come to the knowledge of God. The Hebrew-Christian God-concept is not a philosophical device which is used as leverage to extricate philosophical ethics from an insoluble inner difficulty by furnishing a supernatural sanction for a speculative ethics. The reality of the self-revealing God and of the good as the will of God stand or fall together in biblical revelation. God reveals himself in a once-for-all prophetic and apostolic disclosure of his purposes. And he declares a specific moral content which shows his will for man. He summons men to obedience. For Garrard, the will of God is incompatible with external revelation. It is defined by immediate inner illumination. Moreover, it is emptied of all of its specific biblical content and is confined to the purely formal rule of love of God and neighbor. The biblical revelation of the Hebrew-

[19]*Op. cit.*, p. 47.
[20]*Ibid.*, p. 50.
[21]*Ibid.*, p. 51.
[22]*Ibid.*, pp. 51f.

Christian God knows no such purely formal delineation of the will of God. So Garrard's reconstruction must be dismissed as a speculative device that he uses in an attempt to find a way out of the insoluble difficulties that confront general moral theory. "The law was given to us from heaven to teach us a perfect righteousness," writes Calvin, and "in it no righteousness is taught, but that which is conformable to the decrees of the Divine will. . . . It is therefore vain to attempt new species of works in order to merit the favour of God, whose legitimate worship consists solely in obedience. . . . Any pursuit of good works deviating from the law of God is an intolerable profanation of the Divine and real righteousness. There is much truth . . . in the observation of Augustine, who calls obedience to God sometimes the parent and guardian, and sometimes the origin of all virtues."[23]

Hebrew-Christian ethics centers in the Divine revelation of the statutes, commandments, and precepts of the Living God. Its whole orientation of the moral life may be summarized by what the Holy Lord commands and what he forbids: what accords with his edicts is right, what opposes his holy will is wicked.[24] In his Gifford Lectures H. H. Henson appropriately noted the fact that it was from Judaism that Christianity "inherited the conception of a moral law expressing the will of a Righteous God and, in its essential contents, declared in the Decalogue."[25]

The moral law that lays an imperative on the human conscience is nothing more or less than the manifested will of God. For man nothing is good but union with the sovereign holy will of God. Sin therefore must not be defined primarily as social irresponsibility. Rather, it is repudiation of a Divine claim. David's words "against thee only have I sinned" (Psa. 51:4) echo the penitent's confession at its deepest level. Since God fashioned man to bear his moral likeness, nothing other than the fulfillment of this Divine purpose is man's supreme good. This purpose of God is the moral standard by which man throughout all history will be judged. Society in all its breadth and depth is responsible to the will of God. According to Christianity, to be morally good is to obey God's commands. The performance of God's will alone constitutes man's highest good.[26] The rule of life is to "seek first the kingdom of God and his righteousness" (Mt. 6:33).

The stress Jesus placed on the spiritual aspect of the Kingdom of God as the rule of God in the lives of his subjects reinforces this idea

[23]Calvin, *Institutes,* II, viii, v.

[24]"The good is what God rewards and the bad is what He punishes." Edward John Carnell, *An Introduction to Christian Apologetics* (Grand Rapids: Eerdmans, 1948), p. 154.

[25]Herbert H. Henson, *Christian Morality, Natural, Developing, Final* (Oxford: Clarendon Press, 1936), p. 137.

[26]The Reformation marked a reassertion of this truth, obscured by mediaeval Romanism. "Calvin substituted for the obedience due to the Roman Church and its clergy an absolute obedience to God which was a great return to truth." W. G. D. MacLennan, *Christian Obedience,* p. 100.

that the good life is submission to the sovereign God. MacLennan singles out as "the most important conception in His teaching . . . the living of life in wholehearted loyalty to God and unquestioning obedience to His will in this world here and now. He is urging upon men the seeing and accepting of the rule of God in their daily living. If they see and grasp that central reality of life, all else will fall into line and life will take on a power and a peace and joy which can be found in no other way."[27] The point is enforced even more emphatically: "It is clear that the rule of God as taught by Jesus demands an obedience of a nature which is nothing less than a complete subordination of the human will to the will of God. The motto for any son of the Kingdom, as for Jesus Himself, is: 'Not what I will but what Thou wilt.' It is a demand quite as rigorous as was ever made under the Law."[28] Christian obedience is the rule of God in the lives of his creatures.

The Apostle Paul's perspective is the same. The teaching of Romans 12:2 is that "the good, the acceptable, and the perfect is the will of God."[29]

In summary, the man who does the will of God does what is intrinsically good. At the same time he does that which will yield to him his greatest personal happiness as well as best promote the general welfare. He finds that obedience is not a dread chore. He delights to do the pleasure of his God. The conflict between duty and happiness is resolved by the grace of God at work in the heart of the believer, "for it is God which worketh in you both to will and to do of his good pleasure" (Phil. 2:13).

[27]MacLennan, *op. cit.*, p. 16.
[28]*Ibid.*, pp. 18f.
[29]G. Chr. Adolph von Harless, *System of Christian Ethics*, p. 63.

9

LOVE, THE DIVINE IMPERATIVE IN PERSONAL RELATIONS

CHRISTIAN ETHICS IS, as we have indicated, the ethics of the church against the world; it is not a living possession of the unbelieving community, but of the community of faith. The church has this ethic for a directive of its behavior among the redeemed. It is also a guide for the church's dealings with all men, and it is an example of the divinely-approved pattern for living. The church is morally obligated to humanity as a whole, and her duty to men is a part of her duty to God. She does not possess this way of life to condemn the world, but to be a witness to all mankind. She is to be an instrument of rescue as well as a reminder that God wills to reign socially and universally.

Only those who understand that Christian ethics is the ethics of the church in contrast with the ethics of the world, and not simply a higher level of the world's behavior pattern, can appreciate the social urgency of revealed ethics. One who sees the world with idealistic prejudices may repeat the entreaty "Thy will be done" (Mt. 6:10), but like Bosanquet, in his small volume *What Religion Is,* he will omit the phrase "in earth as it is in heaven." J. S. Mackenzie points out that he will do this because for him the whole of reality is regarded as standing already in an inner harmony. But Christian ethics is an ethics of service. It is an ethics that gains solicitude from the fact that God orients the prayers and lives of his followers toward the Kingdom to come. He moves toward his determination to bring the whole human enterprise within the Divine orbit. The contrast between the is-now and the ought-to-be preserves the transforming dynamic of Christian ethics.

No other religious ethic has been tempered by this awareness that it is "evangelistic ethics." Others may seek to recover society from its moral collapse by calling for a relatively higher standard than prevails in the *Zeitgeist.* Christian ethics must protest that a culture raised only on such adjustments will soon again decay. It proclaims instead the changeless absolutes of revealed morality. Social relevance is written on its every word. "Christianity carries the fortunes of mankind," Henson remarks, "and . . . its failure would mean nothing less calamitous than the spiritual suicide of humanity."[1] Christian ethics is a rescue mission

[1]Herbert H. Henson, *Christian Morality,* p. 31.

located on every pathway of moral decision in society. "This new life that came into this world with the Christ is essentially multiplicative — destined to multiply and expand in an innumerable company of renewed men, redeemed by His saving power and quickened and organized and unified by His outpoured Spirit."[2] Pentecost marked the beginning of the Spirit's dispensation in which the body of believers are the crucial segment of humanity for the course of earthly history. With this realization, the necessity for Christian social ethics arises.

The distinctive feature of Christian ethics is its operation on a principle of universal love — love that is extended alike to believers and unbelievers. It is service in a new spirit (Rom. 7:6), based on the apostolic rule: "Let no man seek his own; but each his neighbor's good" (1 Cor. 10:24). The Christian stands at the crossroads of the petition "Thy will be done on earth as it is in heaven." He may stand indebted to others for only one debt — the debt of love (Rom. 13:8). And this is one beneath which he always stands, and which is forever due (1 Cor. 13:8).

In view of his permanent assumption of human nature, the Divine incarnation of Christ is a spectacular declaration that humanity is not finally doomed without opportunity for repentance and decision. Were humanity already irrevocably doomed and did the possibility of rescue exist no longer for any of the fallen race, the second person of the Trinity would not have taken on himself human nature. His incarnation-name is Immanuel, "God with us." *Jesus Christ* is "with" mankind in its predicament of sin. He is dramatically identified with the race by his incarnation. His advent not only guarantees that he will some day reappear as man's judge (Jn. 5:27), but it also assures the present offer of salvation (Acts 13:38f.). Whoever upholds Christian ethics champions also the truth that God has not yet finally abandoned the sin-gripped world to face judgment. God yet extends his call to repentance and his offer of pardon. He still embraces the world within his holy love (Jn. 3:16).

What then is the moral responsibility of the believer to the unbeliever? Of the friend of God to the man of the world and the enemy of God? The world scorns the will of God. The community of faith eagerly embraces it. The will of God in its broadest sense still encompasses the revolt of the wicked, and God's ultimate purposes are so worked out that even the wrath of men is made to praise him. But the Divine will is not accomplished on earth as it is in heaven. The world is bitterly opposed to it in temper and deed. Even the believing church does not perfectly carry it out, though she is committed to it in principle.

The phrase "enemy of God" is not too strong to apply to the unbeliever. Such he is. And so the Scriptures label him (Rom. 5:10, Phil.

[2]David S. Adam, *A Handbook of Christian Ethics* (Edinburgh: T. & T. Clark, 1925), p. 68.

3:18, Col. 1:21, Jas. 4:4). He is pictured as a stranger or alien to the covenants of promise (Eph. 2:12) and to the household of the faithful (Eph. 2:19). Jesus stressed that faith calls a new family into being. It is the household of God, and it is distinguished from the natural groupings of ordinary social relations in the world. "Who is my mother? and who are my brethren? . . . whosoever shall do the will of my Father who is in heaven, he is my brother, and sister, and mother" (Mt. 12:48, 50).

But in social relationships the unbeliever is never automatically designated as an enemy in the New Testament. In fact, it is right at this point that the believer is called upon most conspicuously to live "to the glory of God," to "show forth the image of God" in his daily walk. And Christian ethics is not satisfied here with a pious mouthing of technical phrases, such as those we have just placed in quotation marks. It becomes distressingly explicit about their meaning for motive and action. The whole moral law is summarized in the two great commands, "Thou shalt love the Lord thy God with all thy heart, and with all thy soul, and with all thy mind, and with all thy strength" and "Thou shalt love thy neighbor as thyself" (Mt. 22:37, Mk. 12: 30f., Lk. 10:27). This is the very first principle of Christian ethics.[3] The surpassing magnitude of the commandment of love lies in this: love is the very essence of the law; it is the fundamental reality that performs and includes the whole of the law. "On these two commandments hang the whole law, and the prophets" (Mt. 22:40). Love to God must fill the whole of the inner life. It must determine desire, thought, and will. It must rule the outer life as well. The absolute and uncompromised simplicity of the man's moral might is to be channeled in devotion to God.[4]

This love for God is to be worked out in love to all men as a fundamental motive of human action. According to the summary of the law, the love of God is to be expressed by serving him through the service of man.[5] Genuine piety and service are correlative. To love God and

[3]The connection between the ethics of unrequited love and the principle of special revelation must not be lost. The greatest of the commandments is "Thou shalt love Jehovah thy God," *i.e.*, the God of covenant-love, of redemption, and hence of the incarnation. It is significant that, after his reply to his questioners (who may have phrased the question about the greatest of the commandments in the expectation of eliciting "Thou shalt have no other gods before me," and along with it an implicit disavowal of Jesus' unique sonship), Jesus, having stressed the requirement of total love for the redemptive God, interrogates his questioners in turn about "the Son of David" (Mt. 22:41ff.).

[4]The fact that only two passages in the Synoptic Gospels (Mt. 22:37, Mk. 12:30ff., Lk. 10:27, and Lk. 11:42) and five Pauline passages (Rom. 8:28, 1 Cor. 2:9, 8:3, 16:22, Eph. 6:24) speak of man's love for God, is to be explained, doubtless, by the standpoint of redemptive revelation. It is from God's love to man that love derives its impetus and character in the life of the sinner.

[5]Felix Adler points out that Confucius' version of the Golden Rule meant "Keep the balance true between thyself and thy neighbor," whereas Jesus' version is "Look upon thy neighbor as thy other self; act towards him as if thou wert he." *An Ethical Philosophy of Life* (New York: Appleton, 1918), p. 32.

keep his commandments, to love and serve him, to love him and walk in his way are ethical exhortations which recur with untiring regularity (Ex. 20:6, Dt. 5:10, 12, 11:13, 22). The Apostle John appeals to the explicit teaching of the Redeemer to show the inseparable connection between love of God and love of neighbor: "If a man say, I love God, and hateth his brother, he is a liar: for he that loveth not his brother whom he hath seen, how can he love God whom he hath not seen? And this commandment have we from him, that he who loveth God love his brother also" (1 Jn. 4:20f.). "God is love, and he that dwelleth in love dwelleth in God, and God in him" (4:16). The love of God is the service of man in love.

Whether this high ethic shall be applied by a Christian to a particular person is not based upon the character of that person nor upon the relationship that exists between the Christian and that person. Love is rather a fundamental principle of Christian ethics, and one which places it over against pagan morality. Jesus specifically condemned the Gentiles for confining love to their brethren. He blamed the publicans for exhibiting love only for those who loved them in return. He repudiated the prevailing Jewish limitation which confined love to one's neighbor but denied it to one's enemy (Mt. 5:43ff.).

From the viewpoint of Greek and Roman moral philosophy, Jesus' ethics of love is extreme and immoderate. It is well known that the Christian failure to "observe distinctions," in fact, their distaste for the prejudices of social classes and Greek and Roman ideals of social life, was one of the main provocations for persecution in the Roman empire.[6] The pagan renunciation of the ideal of unrequited neighbor-love (love that freely serves the interests of others and asks nothing in return) on the ground of national, racial, or class distinctions once again reared its ugly head in the neo-paganism of the twentieth century. The Nazi glorification of the Nordic race and the repudiation of the dignity of the Jews are too recent and too terrible to be soon forgotten. Communism's philosophy of hatred and violence threatens the whole morality of love.

The retrograde social mood of our day more and more senses that the inherited Christian view of neighbor-love is inseparable from the whole framework of special revelation and redemption. So there is a growing secular compromise of the Christian ethic which, now and then, flares into open hostility. In a recent study (*Protestant-Catholic-Jew,* 1955) Will Herberg reports on a poll of the attitudes of citizens of the United States toward the law of love: 90% said they obey it toward those of other religions, 80% toward those of another race, and 57% toward those of a dangerous political party. In the name of a delicate moral sense we are now and then told that the law of neighbor-love is an idealization and exaggeration of the moral sentiments, and that it

[6]Sir William Ramsay, *The Church in the Roman Empire* (10th ed., London: Hodder and Stoughton, n.d.), pp. 200, 239, 246, 347.

expresses "an aspiration to a moral perfection that can never be attained rather than a practical counsel that is applicable in real life."[7] This simpering note should occasion no surprise to a moral awareness that is alert to the lessons of history.

Nietzsche condemns the Golden Rule as a prudential evasion, which calculatingly acts towards others so they will reciprocate as desired. Thus he misunderstands its intention, negatively, to cut us off from all right to complaint if, when we treat others as means to our ends, they so treat us; and positively, that we fulfill the Divine moral requirement as stipulated in the law and the prophets only when we deal with men on the principle of genuine neighbor-love. Nietzsche strikes against the doctrine of equality. He affirms the inequality of men in their right to the opportunity to fulfill their potentialities (not merely in physical and intellectual capacity, material circumstances and vocational gifts). He regards the herd as of low dignity, the Superman who lies ahead of the present age as alone worthy. This involves him in scornful contempt of the notion of "neighbor." Love to those who stand nearby is disparaged; "love" for the far-away and distant, the Superman, replaces it. Love of enemies and love of kinsmen and family are all repudiated as elements of a slave-morality. Nietzsche understands neighbor-love to be grounded in human weakness, and calls for its elimination through an enlargement of self-love.[8]

The premise on which Christian love operates is that of fullness and abundance, rather than out of a sense of personal deficiency and weakness. The ancient Greek idea, that love has its birth in a subjective need which can only be resolved through another who is indispensable to one's own inner strength, was not far in the background of Nietzsche's thought, who appealed for the restoration of the classic pagan morality and yet repudiated the Christian doctrine of neighbor-love as integral to a slave-morality and springing from weakness rather than self-assertion. But it is just this weakness which the Christian doctrine of neighbor-love transcends, since it flows from the plenitude of grace. The natural self-love of the fallen man is inverted, not into an anti-moral arrogance, but into *agape*.

From two sides it has been asserted even within Christian circles that the believer is not obligated to practice love toward the world, only toward the household of faith. A distinction is thus set up among the recipients of the moral act. This distinction determines the relevance or irrelevance of revealed ethics for an action.

In earlier centuries the Anabaptists contended that there was no obligation to consider those who were not regenerated as brethren. The Anabaptist emphasis on the distinctive reality of spiritual brotherhood by the new birth is a necessary one. The modern liberal doctrine

[7]Gaetano Mosca, *The Ruling Class,* trans. Hannah D. Kahn (New York: McGraw-Hill, 1939), p. 120.
[8]Nietzsche, *Thus Spake Zarathustra,* I, xvi.

has reduced Christian brotherhood to an ethical association of unregenerate men dedicated courageously to the motive of love. The New Testament emphasis stands against the superficial doctrine that Jesus accepted all men as his spiritual brethren simply on the basis of creation. Rather, supernatural regeneration is the necessary prerequisite for admission to the Christian brotherhood. The Fatherhood of God means a divinely-established sonship through repentance and spiritual rebirth. But the Anabaptist view is one-sided. It commits a grave error when it denies that sonship to God and a human brotherhood exist among men as sinners on the basis of creation. The consequence is a distortion of Christian moral responsibility to the world. The world is surrendered entirely to the control of Satan, and the believer is excluded from relations with the unregenerate. If the believer withdraws himself completely from the world, he has no opportunity to apply the law of love to man. This automatically limits the application of Christian ethics to the household of faith. It is ironic that the liberal ethic missed the redemptive content of Christian revelation but asserted the universal relevance of the motive of unselfish love, while the Anabaptists missed its universal reference through indifference to the brotherhood of man on the basis of creation.

In more recent times, the doctrines of election and reprobation have sometimes been invoked to justify a distinction in the application of Christian ethics. Unrequited love is appropriately exhibited toward the elect, but it is irrelevant in relationships with the reprobate.[9] In this view one's ethical attitudes as a believer depend upon the spiritual outlook of the object of one's actions. Is he a brother in Christ or a reprobate soul? This position presupposes that the believer is able critically and infallibly to discern the identity of the elect and the non-elect. But it commits also a worse error: it arbitrarily limits the requirement of neighbor-love imposed on the believer, and commits him to a double morality — one for believers and one for unbelievers. The Bible does not enjoin a universal love on the basis of the Decalogue, and a quite different love, limited to believers, on the basis of the New Testament. Our Lord declared that "none other commandment" is "greater than" the two tables of the Law (Mk. 12:31). He assured the essential unity of neighbor-love and believer-love.

Both the foregoing views violate the clear emphasis of the New Testament that the Christian life is distinguished by an ethics of love which is to be applied universally, and not confined only to those who reciprocate that love. The beauty and exaltedness of evangelical character is in loving God with the whole heart, and in neighbor relations

[9]For a current conflict over this view, cf. James Daane's reply to the "two camp ethics" of the Protestant Reformed leader, H. Hoeksema: "Christian Ethics and the Doctrine of Election," *The Reformed Journal,* IV, 2 (Feb., 1954), pp. 4ff. The controversy is important also for its reflection of the fact that Christian ethics corresponds with its theological base.

in which the believer loves his neighbor as himself — without further qualification. The Scripture furnishes no encouragement for using some arbitrary standard to determine the "eligibility" of the recipient of one's ethical attitudes and conduct. Indeed, it protests against this as a violation of the fundamental biblical idea. "The whole human race, without any exception," wrote Calvin, "should be comprehended in the same affection of love, and . . . in this respect there is no difference between the barbarian and the Grecian, the worthy and the unworthy, the friend and the foe; for they are to be considered in God, and not in themselves. . . . If we wish to adhere to the true law of love, our eyes must chiefly be directed, not to man, the prospect of whom would impress us with hatred more frequently than with love, but to God, who commands that our love to him be diffused among all mankind; so that this must always be a fundamental maxim with us, that whatever be the character of a man, yet we ought to love him because we love God."[10]

The doctrine of love to strangers outside the circle of faith is a doctrine of revealed ethics in Old Testament and New. There is an ocean of depth in Kierkegaard's reminder that "no poet has ever sung about loving one's neighbor, any more than he has sung about loving him 'as one's self.' "[11] But this is the love which Christ commands. "The Christian teaching is to love the neighbor, to love the whole race, all men, even one's enemy, and to make no exception, either of partiality or of dislike."[12] Love alone fulfills the law. This was reaffirmed and expounded by Jesus over and against the perversion of the law by the religious people of his day. He dramatically eliminated the prevailing distinction between neighbor and non-neighbor as the basis for determining the content of ethics. It has sometimes been questioned whether Jesus originated the summary of the Law. The fact that the rich young ruler quoted the formula (Lk. 10:25ff.) has been taken as evidence that it may have enjoyed something of a wide circulation in devout circles. There can be no doubt that Jesus gave to the formula the full authority of his messianic office in opposition to competitive interpretations of the Law. It is doubtful that the young lawyer knew only the principles of Jesus. The scribes were required to repeat the first resumé of the Law (Dt. 6:5) morning and evening, and its general familiarity is beyond doubt. It is unlikely that the lawyer would have joined Leviticus 19:18 to Deuteronomy 6:5 unless Jesus steered him that way with his questions or unless it was tradition for them to be joined.

[10]Calvin, *Institutes,* II, viii, lvii.

[11]Kierkegaard, *Works of Love* (Princeton: Princeton University Press, 1946), p. 16.

[12]*Ibid.,* p. 17.

But the formula enjoyed already the authority of the Old Testament.[13] The two great commandments are to be found in the Law: the first occurring in Deuteronomy 6:4f. immediately after the rehearsal of the Ten Commandments, and the second in Leviticus 19:18. In Leviticus we learn that Moses instructed the Israelites: "Thou shalt love thy neighbor as thyself" (19:18). The term neighbor was not limited to the believing Hebrew, nor for that matter to the Hebrews at all. It embraced also the stranger sojourning in the land: "And if a stranger sojourn with thee in your land . . . the stranger that dwelleth with you shall be unto you as one born among you, and thou shalt love him as thyself" (19:33f.). Strangers were to be loved as though they were covenant-members, but they were prohibited from sharing in the covenant until they obeyed its demands.

The Old Testament *'ahebh,* the usual Septuagint equivalent of which is *agapē,* is used of Divine love, human love to God and to human beings. The root *rhm* appears expressing sympathy for those needing help, hence pity or mercy. Love is thus disclosed in the Old Testament as "fundamentally a spontaneous feeling which impels to self-sacrifice . . . "[14] Of interest is the fact that in translating the word neighbor, the Septuagint used *ho plesion sou* meaning "anyone around you." Thus it understood a Hebrew's neighbor to be anyone living next to him.

The enlargement of the native meaning of Greek words through a coloring gained from the Septuagint translation of Old Testament ideas is forcefully illustrated by the term *adelphos.* In classic literature the word bears the ordinary sense of brother. But the Septuagint translators used the term in a multiple sense: for brother; for neighbor, in Leviticus 19:17; and for a member of the same nation, as in Exodus 2:14 and Deuteronomy 15:3. In the New Testament the term was even more expanded in the teaching of Jesus. It looked beyond membership in the same family or nation to membership in the spiritual family of Christian faith; and in Matthew 7:3 it gained the widest sense of neighbor, one who belongs to the human race.[15]

The later Jewish leaders introduced the distinction between neighbor and enemy, and justified having one ethical attitude toward one's

[13]Claude G. Montefiore, the learned Jewish New Testament scholar, has found in Jesus' emphasis on love for all men, and not simply fellow Jews, a specific example of the superiority of the teaching of Jesus to that of the rabbis. Montefiore, however, is reluctant to trace the narrowed concept of human love only to the rabbis, but finds it grounded in the Old Testament. "If one were to take the Old Testament as a whole, I am not so sure that one can honestly say that its general teaching is very definite on the love of enemies, even of Israelite enemies." *Rabbinic Literature and Gospel Teachings* (London: Macmillan, 1930), pp. 62f. But Christ's teaching authoritatively exposits the Law, that had been virtually nullified in its guidance on the matter of love for enemies by his contemporaries. Cf. Vincent Taylor, *The Gospel According to Mark* (London: Macmillan, 1953), pp. 487f. for evidence that the command to neighbor-love was held to have a universal range by some rabbinic sources.

[14]Kittel, *Bible Key Words* (New York: Harper, 1951), p. 12.

[15]H. A. A. Kennedy, *Sources of New Testament Greek* (Edinburgh: T. & T. Clark, 1895), pp. 95f.

neighbor and another toward one's enemy.[16] The classic "love your enemies" passage (Mt. 5:43ff.) is our Lord's rebuke to this degeneration of the spirit of revealed ethics into a political morality comparable to that of the Gentiles.[17]

"One of the major points of contrast between the Greek and Christian conceptions of ethics is found," Patterson remarks, "in the emphasis which is given by the latter to the idea of the equal worth of all human beings."[18] The Greek virtue of moderation was characteristically developed to emphasize interest in the welfare of one's own class, but slaves and barbarians were despised in contrast to free citizens.[19] The humanitarian ideal of Christian ethics reached far beyond the limits of national and class distinction. Its moral force encompassed the popular and even the philosophical conceptions of morality. It addressed its message both to the sunken rabble of Corinth ("such were some of you," 1 Cor. 6:11) and to the haughty philosophers of Athens (Acts 17:18f.). Racial and national prejudices were decried by Stoic philosophy and Roman jurisprudence, but it was only through the Christian abolition of class distinctions that the doctrine of neighbor-love became a living premise. Christians believed this destruction of prejudice to be the will of God and their duty to man. The affirmation of the oneness of humanity — by creation, in the fall, in the offer of redemption, in the prospect of judgment — brought a spiritual force to Christian ethics that produced a universal sympathy and an organized philanthropy not known in pagan Greece.

Viewed with the biblical perspective, neither the Gentile nor the prevailing Hebrew attitude approached a serious morality. Jesus' story of the Good Samaritan (Lk. 10:30ff.) enforces this point: the fact that the subject was a Samaritan lends a touch of irony, since no love was lost between Jew and Samaritan. While the priest and Levite

[16]"The love of neighbors of which Judaism speaks generally halts at the frontier" (Kittel, *Bible Key Words,* p. 41). The weakness of conceiving love as "what does no harm" is seen in Hillel's summary: "Do not unto thy neighbor what is hateful unto thee; that is the whole Law. All the rest is commentary."

[17]Philo writes: "The Jew must first show love to his fellow Israelite: he stands at the center; round him are proselytes and resident aliens; then follow enemies, slaves, beasts, and plants in ever-widening circles until at last we arrive at the love of all creation" (*De Virtut.,* 51ff.). This very arrangement shows the prevailing structure of Jewish love for neighbor.

[18]Charles H. Patterson, *Moral Standards* (New York: Ronald Press, 1949), p. 199.

[19]It is curious that Socrates, while he did not arrive at a satisfactory formulation of the content of the good life, in Plato's *Republic* quite unmercifully disposes of the view of Polemarchus that the nature of a good man's acts is to be determined by whether or not the recipient is a friend or an enemy. Polemarchus is unable on his thesis to find a way out of the difficulty that we cannot always distinguish seeming friends and enemies from real friends and enemies. With regard to the ethical agent, moreover, Socrates argues that the skill requisite for performing justice is not given an individual simply in his capacity of being the friend of another; that would amount to an "extra-moral" grounding of the ought. The moral man cannot desire the injury of any man, whether friend or foe. Yet Socrates defines the good life only in terms of justice; he is a stranger to justification, and hence to *agape.*

passed by, the Samaritan compassionately ministered to the half-murdered victim without first making a distinction because of race or religion. Christ elicited from the Pharisees the admission that the Samaritan, who was really not as close to the victim of assault as were the priest and Levite, demonstrated himself to be a neighbor by showing mercy. The point is that true neighbor-love seeks its opportunities of service. Kierkegaard rightly observes that Christianity has made it forever impossible to be mistaken about the identity of one's neighbor: "You can never confuse him with another man, for all men are the neighbor. If you confuse another man with your neighbor, then in the last analysis there is no mistake, for the other man is also your neighbor."[20] In Kittel's words, Christ demands an "absolutely unsentimental readiness to help."[21]

There is no one simple reason set forth in Scripture to enforce the requirement of a universal love. There are numerous factors. The requirement of unrequited love is demanded by the whole structure of the moral situation. Appeal is made to the fact of the solidarity of the race on the basis of creation, to the fact of God's common grace, to the fact of Divine redemptive love, and to the fact of future judgment.

The universal fatherhood of God and the corresponding brotherhood of man is one ground for universal application of the principle of love. The Bible assumes that all men have a claim on neighbor-love because they share a common human nature in creation. Man is involved with neighbor in a brotherhood which sin has not entirely eradicated. The sanction for the love of strangers in the Mosaic legislation is the fact that every man is obligated before God to deal with every other man according to this principle of love. The Israelites were to love the stranger "for ye were strangers in the land of Egypt" (Lev. 19:34). The Christian is to do "good unto all men" (Heb. 13:16), whether deserving or undeserving, through a regard for them as bearers of the *imago Dei*. The stranger or the enemy in need of assistance is not to be despised, but because of the Divine image in him, he is to be embraced by the Christian's affections. The injuries men inflict are to be repaid with kindness (Mt. 5:44), and their curses with blessings (Lk. 17:3f.). In his humiliation Jesus assumed in fact the human nature of all humanity on the basis of creation, and in that sense our Lord "became everyman's Neighbor, for he is the Man with whom all men have to do."[22] The incarnation makes Jesus' redemptive love accessible to the whole human race. The Apostle Paul refers to the unbelieving Jews as his brethren according to the flesh, and acknowledges a love for them on that basis that is of such staggering

[20]Kierkegaard, *op. cit.*, p. 43.

[21]Kittel, *op. cit.*, p. 48.

[22]James Daane, "St. Paul's Brother," *The Reformed Journal,* IV, 3 (Mar., 1954), p. 9, where he adds: "Denial of the brotherhood which is according to the flesh, is a denial that Jesus in the incarnation became one with the human race."

magnitude that he could wish himself "accursed for their sakes" (Rom. 9:3).

The common grace of God to fallen man buttresses the universality of the claim on love. Jesus' repudiation of the "hate your enemy" credo contained this dramatic statement: "That ye may be the children of your Father which is in heaven: for he maketh his sun to rise on the evil and on the good, and sendeth rain on the just and on the unjust" (Mt. 5:45). Hence the fact of election does not set aside the universality of love. As an act of grace, election is uniquely a Divine act. Man is not qualified nor entitled to imitate it by exercising discrimination between men. The human act of love is not electing in character, but is bound by God's common grace to a non-discriminatory manifestation.

The nature of redemptive love makes it morally impossible for the believer to limit his love only to friends and equals (1 Jn. 3:16ff.). God has loved him, though he was unlovely and unworthy; how can he pretend superiority to any man? In Paul's letter to Philemon about the slave Onesimus, the appeal to have mercy for love's sake supersedes all other appeals (Philem. 9; cf. Rom. 12:10, Phil. 2:4). Nor is love to be shown only to those who are on good terms with us. For the Gospel is the message of God's self-giving for those at enmity with him (Rom. 5:10), for those to whom he is under no antecedent obligation to extend anything but his wrath. The supreme glory of the Godhead is the exercise of this disposition of love to the unworthy neighbor. The successive generations of the age of grace unfold the dramatic fact that God is love. Christ is the original autograph of the Father's love for the lost, and his disciples are to be living commentaries on that love. "As my Father hath sent me, even so send I you" (Jn. 20:21), he instructs them. The implications of this reciprocal relation between redemptive love and love expressed in the life of the believer will be considered more fully in the delineation of love as a Christian virtue.

The believer's love for strangers no less than to neighbors is enforced by our Lord's appeal to future judgment and reward. Perhaps no more sobering passage in this regard can be found than Matthew 25:34ff.: "Come, ye blessed of my Father, inherit the Kingdom prepared for you from the foundation of the world: For I was . . . a stranger, and ye took me in. . . . Then shall the righteous answer him, saying, Lord, when saw we thee a stranger, and took thee in? . . . And the King shall answer and say unto them, Verily I say unto you, Inasmuch as ye have done it unto the least of these my brethren, ye have done it unto me. Then shall he say also unto them on the left hand, Depart from me, ye cursed, unto everlasting fire, prepared for the devil and his angels: For . . . I was a stranger, and ye took me not in. . . . Then shall they also answer him, saying, Lord, when saw we thee . . . a stranger, . . . and did not minister to thee? Then shall he answer them, saying, Verily I say unto you, Inasmuch as ye did it not to one of the least of these, ye did it not unto me. And these shall go away into everlasting punishment: but the righteous unto life eternal." Note also Matthew 5:46: "For if ye love them which love you, what reward have ye? Do not even the publicans the same?" The force of this passage can only be that the wicked are those who show love only to those who requite it, while the godly are those who extend love also to strangers. Whoever is accessible to me, hungry, thirsty, naked, sick, imprisoned, though a stranger, has a claim on my affection.[23] The Johannine epistles rule out a neutral attitude toward the world by their reiteration of the alternatives of love or hate. A relationship that does not embrace one's neighbor within the circle of one's love neglects or abandons that one. Beyond that, it brings him within the sphere in which love is absent, and hate prevails. It is ironic that John alone has become known as the apostle of love. Actually, that is every disciple's badge of identification (Jn. 13:35). The early Christians astounded their pagan neighbors. Unbelievers could not get over the bond of love between believers: "See how they love one another" was their comment.

This biblical ethic of love stands as the impetus for the church's missionary service and for her cultural concern over a doomed world. The Christian moral consciousness reacts in protest against the concept that love is to be reserved only for those who stand within the circle of faith. The enthronement of neighbor-love in personal relations is a strong impetus to a dynamic social ethics, as William Newton Clarke acknowledged of the life of Jesus. "His example in the ethical life is a social example as well as an individual one, for what example in social practice can compare with his devotion to the good of men?"[24] The apostle Paul's missionary burden came from his dedication to the biblical view of love for those in need.[25] His Christian concern stands out in stark contrast with the traditional Jewish hostility to the Gentiles. Paul evidently regards the proclamation of the Gospel to the unbeliever as an indispensable element in the Christian manifestation of love.

Christian love is only half biblical when it deteriorates into a concern only for the souls of men and is indifferent to the needs of the body. What believer ministers to himself only in this way? It is scarcely biblical at all when it degenerates into a mere humanistic concern for the social side of life to the total neglect of the life of the spirit (2 Cor.

[23]More than this, such love is a mirror of the Divine, is indirectly a displaying back to Christ, as in his name, of an undeserved love he has shown us. An added reference is found in Hebrews 13:2, "Forget not to show love to strangers, for thereby some have entertained angels unawares," where Christian hospitality suggestively is pictured as inclusive of a concealed Divine guest.

[24]William Newton Clarke, *The Ideal of Jesus* (New York: Scribner, 1915), p. 23.

[25]"I am debtor both to the Greeks and to the barbarians; both to the wise and to the unwise. So, as much as in me is, I am ready to preach the gospel to you that are at Rome also" (Rom. 1:14f.; cf. Rom. 13:8).

4:2f.).[26] The believer is obligated to bring every blessing into the life of another that lies within his power to communicate. This implies the weakness of Kierkegaard's observation that a man living on a desert island could be said to love his neighbor by renouncing self-love and developing his mind in harmony with the commandment.[27] For love ferrets out a neighbor to impart a blessing to him, even in a distant land or another world. So the incarnation has defined it for us.

Had God conducted himself toward his enemies with vengeance and hatred, he could have exercised no love toward sinners who held enmity for him. Then the whole plan of redemption would have been excluded. The Logos could have assumed only the garment of a vengeful judge, trampling an entire rebellious race in his fury, finding pleasure only in the death of the wicked. The sun would have been darkened from rising on the unjust, and the rains withheld from the evil and thankless. The love of God would never have been unfurled in the display of grace to men caught in the misery of sin and guilt.

Love to neighbor involves interest in his behalf to the same extent that we take interest in our own behalf. It includes the fulfillment of all good deeds which we are capable of exerting for his benefit. It employs itself in beneficent acts rather than a merely philanthropic speculation that easily discourses on distant suffering and neglects the need that is at hand. Our response to those in need near us tests the reality and spontaneity of our love, whereas the practical impossibility of ministering to those far removed from us easily excuses us from a sense of obligation and appears to justify self-complacency. A professed love that languishes and dies in one's own neighborhood is no neighbor-love. Even a priest and a Levite, should they have been bound for a religious convention built around the theme of *agape,* had no justification for bypassing the destitute victim.

The Golden Rule, in its Christian exposition, is not mere abstinence from injury to another. Nor is it the calculating morality of mutuality, or fair play to others so they will reciprocate in kind. Neither is it the mere sentiment of benevolence found in modern humanitarianism, although here at least the anticipation of the return of one's love is removed. The Golden Rule must be taken along with Jesus' full teaching on neighbor-love. It involves aggressively seeking the good of others independently of merit and reciprocation, and all other considerations, except that God has exemplified such a love.

[26]Ernest F. Scott detects the essentially individual and spiritual approach to the problems of mankind which distinguishes the Bible: "The truth is that in the New Testament there is no social teaching, as we commonly understand the term. Christianity is not an ethic or a political system but a religion. It knows nothing of society in the abstract but thinks only of persons, so related to each other that every one of them may fulfill the higher ends of his being." . . . "The present writer is convinced that the true solution of most of our urgent problems is to be found in the New Testament, but he feels strongly that its social teaching is often grievously misunderstood." *Man and Society in the New Testament,* pp. 7f.

[27]Kierkegaard, *op. cit.,* p. 18.

We shall have to derive the content of this love from the larger teaching of Christ and the New Testament. But its radical nature is brought to view by two passages in the Sermon on the Mount. They are to be coupled with Jesus' warning that the flush of anger is murder-in-the-making, and point to the indispensability of reconciliation to the neighbor-love relationship. The lone portion of the Lord's prayer on which Jesus commented was on intercession for forgiveness. "If you forgive not men their trespasses," he warns, "neither will your heavenly Father forgive your trespasses" (Mt. 6:15). Whoever really understands what is involved in God's forgiveness of the sinner cannot cut off a neighbor from forgiveness. The second reference goes further; it shows neighbor-love as even more aggressive. It requires the interruption of an act of worship in order to restore harmonious relations with another person where such a relationship has been fractured. Here neighbor-love takes precedence even over the worship of God, because God is glorified in the fulfillment of the two great commands, and dishonored in the disregard of the one. Neighbor-love becomes therefore an aggressive instrument for the extension of social peace.

The neighbor-love of which the Scripture speaks abstains from any voluntary injury to others; it initiates no falsehood, fraud, slander, sophistry, quarrels, oppression, plunder. The fruits of love are of a holy order. Love to neighbor not only abstains from evil, but promotes the welfare of our fellows, whether it be instruction or advice, reproof or defense of their good name, or special aid in their afflictions. Love does not ask whether it shall express itself but how and when and where? It stands ready to promote with vigor the good of others. It does not hesitate to feed the hungry nor to clothe the naked without reference to reward. And it has a view not only to their bodily good, but to their spiritual good, seeking to reconcile them to God. "Our life will . . . be governed according to the will of God, and the prescriptions of his law," wrote Calvin, "when it is in all respects most beneficial to our brethren."[28] The life of neighbor-love lets no opportunity pass to benefit another.

While the believer's obligation is as wide as humanity, no denial of the propriety of a love particularly addressed to his brethren in faith and to the members of his own household is intended.[29] But such love is not in the spirit of a *discriminatory* neighbor-love that renounces in practice the universal claim upon it. John's first epistle is replete with

[28]Calvin, *Institutes,* II, viii, liv. "Self-sacrifice for the sake of others, as a means to social good, is the central idea of Christian morality." L. H. Marshall, *The Challenge of New Testament Ethics,* p. 35. This "central idea," however, must not be separated from the love of God in which it is grounded, nor from the principle of a specially-revealed ethics.

[29]"I do not deny, that the more closely any person is united to us, the greater claim he has to the assistance of our kind offices. For the condition of humanity requires, that men should perform more acts of kindness to each other, in proportion to the closeness of the bonds by which they are connected, whether of relationship or acquaintance, or vicinity; and this without any offence to God, by whose providence we are constrained to it." Calvin, *Institutes,* II, viii, lv.

statements that love for the brethren is a sign of genuine faith in Christ, and its absence a warning of a spurious faith (1 Jn. 3:16ff.). He that does not love his brother is a child of the devil, not of God (1 Jn. 3:10), abides in darkness (2:9, 11; 3:14), cannot love God and is a liar if he professes love for God (4:20). "Honor all men. Love the brotherhood," writes Peter (1 Pet. 2:17). John stresses that he that loves his brother "abideth in light, and there is none occasion of stumbling in him" (1 Jn. 2:10); he knows that he "has passed from death unto life" (1 Jn. 3:14). The lack of love for fellow-believers is therefore a sign of an empty profession. For Christian love for Christians is a spontaneous concomitant of regeneration into God's family, and involves none of the adjustment of love to the animosities of the world. "Beloved, let us love one another: for love is of God; and every one that loveth is born of God, and knoweth God. He that loveth not, knoweth not God; for God is love" (1 Jn. 4:7f.).

Yet love for the family of faith and for one's own immediate family is not exempted from the Christian principle of love for others "as one's self." To the contrary, it too must be brought under that criterion. Husbands are to love their wives as themselves (Eph. 5:28, 33), and wives and husbands alike to find the pattern of their self-giving in Christ's love for the church (5:24f.). And the Christian conception of neighbor, as we have already emphasized, precludes limiting the command to love to the circle of one's own family, relatives, friends, or fellow-believers. The basis of discrimination lies in the special obligation of the believer to his family which calls for a higher measure of the love shown to others. The family circle, the fellowship of believers, afford a fuller opportunity for neighbor-love (Gal. 6:10); but they provide no excuse for any evasion of the law of love in its widest claims (Jas. 2:8). The fact that a brother-love attaches to the fellow-believer does not annul the general human duty expressed in the command of love toward all members of the great human family on the ground of a creation equality before God.

The connection between marital love and family love, on the one hand, and neighbor love, must not be lost. On the one hand, neighbor-love finds its most zealous and intimate expression in marital love and family love. In this circle of relationships, above all, neighbor love is purified more and more of the remnants of egoism. But precisely because of the discipline which neighbor-love undergoes in the climate of marriage and the home, marital love can bring to neighbor love in its larger responsibilities a new dynamic and sacrifice. "Love of neighbor which is all-inclusive and whole-hearted requires an extension to all men of the kind of love normally found only between the members of a family. Neighbor love means brother love for every man. . . . The unselfish love . . . normally confined within its [family] limits is to flow forth to the family of all mankind."[30]

[30]G. F. Thomas, *Christian Ethics and Moral Philosophy*, p. 78.

That God wills to reign socially, and that he obligates men to live in love for others unspoiled by inordinate self-love, can only mean that the believer must not allow himself to be drawn out of the world. To stand obediently within the will of God is not, as Mysticism would have it, the absorption of the individual ineffably in the All so that distinctions of time and space and self-consciousness and good and evil are transcended in the mystic contemplation of an Absolute that itself transcends all finite existence and concerns. To define the love of God by such quietism that ignores humanity in its act of worship is to misconceive the will of God and the content of love. "It is the Christian love which discovers and knows that the neighbor exists, and, what amounts to the same thing, that everyone is a neighbor." So Kierkegaard has well phrased the outgoingness of regenerate love.[31] The incarnation and the atonement define the unique love of God for man. They constitute a Divine outreach to the lost, a redemptive mission. To be caught up in the love of God is to be set aflame with that same mission. God's will has humanity specially in view, and to be stationed obediently inside the will of God is to adopt God's will for the world. It is to become absorbed in his purpose for mankind, to seek the recovery of the lost. As with the two tables of the Law, so with the two great commandments, the love of God appears as the foreword to the love of man.

The promise of a society in which evil will be subjugated and righteousness will reign is implicit in God's will to reign socially. It is basic to the concept of the "Kingdom of God" which looks for the ultimate triumph of righteousness and judgment upon wickedness. Christian redemption is nothing if it is not an ethical redemption, and as such it comprehends more than the restoration of the individual to the image of God. It aims at more than a moral transformation of sinners and their possession of a new ethical character. It looks ahead, in and through the church as a partial manifestation, to the Kingdom of God as the most complete and far-reaching social order known. The expression "the Kingdom of God" reminds us that the Christian moral ideal has a social aspect, as well as an individual aspect. It anticipates a reign of love established in the hearts of men on the basis of the redeeming love of God. The kingdom motif is characteristically central in Jesus' thought and teaching, and in it religion and ethics meet.[32] The rule of God in the lives of men under the sway of his holy will — that is its central idea. The Kingdom exists socially only as individuals are brought within the orbit of that will. The "Kingdom" terminology is not nearly so conspicuous in Paul's thought and writings, but the idea is nonetheless central. The phrase "Kingdom of God" has a rich fullness, and is comprehended as present and inward as well as future

[31]Kierkegaard, *op. cit.,* p. 37.

[32]Marshall asserts that "all the ethical teaching of Jesus is simply an exposition of the Kingdom of God, on the way . . . men inevitably behave when they actually come under the rule of God." *Op. cit.,* p. 31.

and outward. But even in the eschatological concept the righteous rule of God in the lives of men remains.

This need not imply the optimistic view that the Kingdom of righteousness will emerge in history as the capstone of the efforts of the church.[33] Nor does it demand the pessimistic theory that excludes a millennium in history on the ground that the historical is inevitably sinful, and that in history conflict must always rage between God and the demonic.[34] A historical fall and a historical redemption would combine to suggest the reign of Christ at some point in history for a complete exhibition of his triumph. Such an expectation has its roots both in Old Testament prophecy and in New Testament teaching, *e.g.*, Revelation 20. The kingdoms of this world are to be the kingdoms of our Lord and of his Christ (Rev. 11:15). This implies a transformed humanity, both in its personal and social dimension, a new spirit infused into family, labor and governmental relations, and into literature, music, the arts and the whole domain of culture. But the prospect of such a climax to history, ushered in by the cataclysmic return of Christ, dare not diminish for the sensitive Christian spirit the ethical urgency of human life. That the victory of right is assured, even if at an indefinite moment in the future, provides no occasion for moral holidaying. In fact, it guarantees that there is no escape from the dread doom of immorality and wickedness, and it adds another vivid reason for lighting the darkness of men's hearts. To live inside the will of God is to serve him in the service of mankind, to love him and, for his sake, all others as earnestly as ourselves.

[33]James Orr shared the post-millennial viewpoint: "What did Christ come for, if not to impart a new life to humanity, which, working from within outwards, is destined to transform all human relations — all family and social life, all industry and commerce, all art and literature, all government and relations among peoples — till the kingdoms of this world are become the kingdoms of our Lord and of his Christ (Rev. 11:15)? Whether more slowly or more rapidly, whether peacefully or, as Scripture seems to indicate, by a succession of crises, surely this grand result of a kingdom of God will be brought about. . . . Christianity is a power also for temporal and social salvation, a leaven which is to permeate the whole lump of humanity." *The Christian View of God and the World* (Grand Rapids: Eerdmans, reprint, 1954), p. 329.

[34]So Emil Brunner, Reinhold Niebuhr and existential theologians generally.

10

THE DETERMINATION OF THE CONTENT OF THE MORAL LIFE

RECENT VIEWS DEFINING the moral life tend to use the term "Christian ethics" in such a way that it means something other than "biblical ethics." They do retain two basic ideas from biblical revelation: God's will is the source and dynamic of moral endeavor, and a distinctive ethics arises out of a distinctive relation to a distinctive Deity. But when the effort is made to become more specific, the theories fall into conflict. This is true of their expositions of the nature of God, of the moral relationship between God and man, and of the ethical implications of this relationship. The common denominator in recent works on Christian ethics is their revolt against an authoritative biblical criterion and their effort nonetheless to find a confident pattern of life.

W. G. D. MacLennan quotes approvingly Brunner's repudiation in *The Word and the World* of scriptural authority as "false, blind" and as involving "suicidal idolatrous obedience."[1] Reinhold Niebuhr strikes at the same thing when he protests that "Orthodox Christianity, with insights and perspectives in many ways superior to those of liberalism, cannot come to the aid of modern man, partly because . . . its morality is expressed in dogmatic and authoritarian moral codes."[2] Niebuhr said in his Gifford Lectures that to use the Bible as an authority in ethics is to make it "a vehicle of sinful sanctification of relative standards of knowledge."[3] C. J. Barker sounds a similar note: "For Christianity, ethical conduct is . . . not adherence to a closed book of rules and regulations."[4] Paul Ramsey declares that "God *now* enters into cove-

[1]W. G. D. MacLennan, *Christian Obedience,* p. 101. Brunner claims the Reformers repudiated biblical authority, while MacLennan contends, more accurately, that they restored it; Calvin called for an absolute obedience to God, and "the rules for that obedience were written words of the Bible interpreted in their literal sense. The result was, if not immediately, at least in the following centuries, a new servitude to the written Word which was alien to the obedience to which Jesus called men, and which Paul had found 'glorious liberty' " (*ibid.,* p. 100). Whatever their disagreement on the facts, they unite in the prejudice against an authoritative scriptural ethics.

[2]Reinhold Niebuhr, *An Interpretation of Christian Ethics,* p. 4.

[3]Niebuhr, *The Nature and Destiny of Man* (New York: Scribner, 1943), II, 152.

[4]C. J. Barker, *The Way of Life,* p. 15. "No supposed exegesis must ever be allowed to force upon man a doctrine repugnant to his moral and religious convictions" (*ibid.,* p. 14). Barker apparently assumes the normality of the moral and religious sentiments of the natural man or, at any rate, that biblical instruction affords no basis for revising them. And yet he professes to write Christian ethics, though not New Testament ethics: "This is not a book on New Testament

nant with man, overcoming . . . all Do and Don't morality whether in the form of an external law *once* valid for the Jews or an inward law *once* valid for the Gentiles."[5]

When one asks what alternative is offered, what is the nature and content of the unique moral claim made by the will of God, the answer of these moralists in revolt is apparent. No unanimity remains, but rather the widest diversity. Christian ethics is embarrassed today by scholars who profess to set forth the nature of revealed ethics by appealing to the will of God, and yet who fall into frustration in defining its content.

When the traditional link between the Bible and the revealed will of God is severed, where is knowledge of the Divine will to be found? Ernest F. Scott appeals to man's "inward sense of the will of God."[6] Ramsey declares that "Paul believed that God actually revealed Torah to Moses" but contends, consistently with the modern bias against biblical revelation, that what God is doing in Jesus Christ "ought now to become the one and only center of man's existence before God."[7] Brunner tells us that no man, not even an Apostle [and he might have added: not even the historical Jesus], can indicate the will of God to another in advance. He repudiates any formulation of the Divine will by commandments, principles, or moral teaching.[8]

One view borrows more from evolutionary dogmas than from biblical theology and argues that Divine revelation is progressive. Hence the content of Christian ethics advances in tone, and must not be equated rigidly with a past standard.[9] An absolute Divine moral claim is thus held to be inconsistent with an objective revelation that reaches its peak in Jesus Christ and the New Testament. In the name of ethical progress, the theory curiously prevents any generation from laying hold of an absolute morality. Another view argues that the details and particulars of biblical ethics are inadequate guides for *our*

ethics in the sense that it is based on the exegesis of New Testament texts. Yet it is hoped that the spirit breathing through the New Testament has neither been badly missed nor through ignorance badly misinterpreted. Where New Testament texts are quoted it is rather to acknowledge the source that inspired the idea set down than to produce corroborative evidence. The Christian revelation authenticates itself to our own moral judgment" (*ibid.*, p. 12).

---

[5]Paul Ramsey, *Basic Christian Ethics*, p. 84f.

[6]E. F. Scott, *Man and Society in the New Testament*, p. 14.

[7]Ramsey, *op. cit.*, p. 84.

[8]Brunner, *The Divine Imperative*, p. 118.

[9]Nicolas Berdyaev declared: "There are no superhuman or non-human ideal values, changeless and eternal. Creative gifts and values are dynamic, and through them the creation of the world is going on. The new ethics rooted in Christianity must go beyond the conception of ideal norms." *The Destiny of Man* (3d ed., London: Bles, 1948). Beneath this, of course, lies the repudiation of the unchangeability of God: "The static conception of God as . . . having no potentiality and completely self-sufficient is . . . not a biblical conception. The God of the Bible, the God of revelation . . . has . . . dramatic developments in His inner life, inward movement . . ." (*ibid.*, p. 28).

moral problems. We must look to ethical principles rather than to any code of particulars to supply us with a divinely-approved plan of behavior. The difficulty here is that the details of the ethical life to which this theory refers appear in the Bible as particularizations of the larger principles. Moreover, it is difficult to understand what use principles may have if they are not readily applicable to the practical situations of life. Another theory declares that the teaching of Jesus, in contrast with that of the prophets or the apostles, is to be received authoritatively. It simply ignores the authority Jesus himself assigned to the law. And it neatly overlooks the authority he conferred upon the apostolate. Yet another theory declares that Christianity does not set forth its ethical claim in teaching at all, not even the teaching of Jesus. Rather, ethics lies in an attitude toward life. One must have selfless love toward others. Nowhere is this love so clearly seen as in the life of Jesus. No other event has been such an inspiration for this love as has the death of Jesus. It is the principle of selfless love that is the form of ethics. Content must conform to this principle, yet the content can only be individually determined. This view and the others do not account for the vast detail of content that is characteristic of New Testament ethics.

Beneath these modern speculative attempts to define the will of God lie a number of varying philosophical prejudices. These prejudices do not form a self-consistent system, but their common end is revolt against identifying Christian ethics with biblical ethics. For one school, evolutionary philosophy is the controlling factor. For another, a bias against particularistic revelation. And for another, the critical repudiation of the trustworthiness of the Bible. For still another, an irrationalistic metaphysics that excludes conceptual revelation and propositional ethics, and hence cannot tolerate identifying the transcendent will of God with either a canonical moral code or timeless principles. The revolt against biblical ethics reaches a climax in the dialectical and existential variations as they cut out the last semblance of an objectively valid ethics. They reinterpret special Divine revelation to mean immediate dynamic encounter. This encounter involves man's obedient will, but no Divine communication of ethical principles.

Since Scripture is no longer the determinative source of the content of the moral life, such content must be drawn from some other source. This abandonment of the Bible as the normative source is in direct contrast to the traditional view of Scripture as the only infallible rule of faith and practice. It has caused such a narrow statement of the divinely-approved content, that many contemporary expositors are driven to state Christian ethics only in terms of its form, *i.e.*, love, without dictating any content whatever in advance.

One or two remarks may indicate the revolutionary implications for Christian behavior of such a view. For one school of liberal moralists, love as the form of Christian ethics required absolute pacifism. Many of these expositors have since modified this view in deference to other pressures. For another school, love as the form of Christian ethics meant virtual identification with the socialist-communist formula "from each according to his ability, to each according to his need."

The enthusiasm for love, when expressed as a bare idea lacking in specific definition, therefore requires sharp criticism. It is possible to recognize, in seeking to spell out the formula "love one another," a voice which is quite other than Divine, and to cherish illegitimate schemes as the will of God. The invocation of love, as without further biblical definition exhaustive of the entire moral claim, tends easily to resolve religion itself into little more than the love of man to man. In fact, by loosing *agape* from a divinely-approved content, it may even prove to be a mistaken human sentiment to which Divine sanction is unjustifiably attached. In personal ethics, no less than in social ethics, love as a formal principle detached from authoritative external content gained a fallible internal direction. This placed so-called Christian love in hostility to what had once been regarded as the distinctive expression of Christian ethics.

One recent example may serve to illustrate this well. Dean Pike stresses that God has taken pains to reveal man's purpose. But he repudiates the Hebrew-Christian confidence that reaches back more than 3000 years that revelation is "a matter of direct word from on high." The Scriptures are "secondary in authority" to man's "free and divinely inspired response" to the will of God disclosed in historical events and personal life.[10] Yet when Dean Pike wants backing for his idea that the law of love is pivotal to ethics, he does not hesitate to lean heavily on the fact that it is "the basic law of life in both Old Testament religion and New Testament religion — expressed in the Shema and the 'two great commandments.' "[11] Pike rightly adds that such a broad law does not give us "rules for a given man's life."[12] But instead of finding in the revealed biblical ethic authoritative guidance for the application of love to specific life situations, he regards biblical norms and commandments as "rules of the road." These are generally serviceable, but detours may be taken at any time according to personal conviction. The result is that even the Decalogue and the Sermon on the Mount lose their absoluteness; they no longer supply the definitive content. "It is safe to say that God generally wills that there be no adultery."[13] But because of the existent evil in the world even the commandments against adultery and killing "end up being somewhat less than absolute. All that is absolute is the 100 per cent claim of God on each individual life: that we serve Him with full devotion in the sense of vocation."[14] Christian ethics is "not a set of

[10]James A. Pike, *Doing the Truth,* p. 34.
[11]*Ibid.,* p. 39.
[12]*Ibid.,* p. 51.
[13]*Ibid.,* p. 59.
[14]*Ibid.,* p. 60.

laws, not even a set of noble and lofty norms."[15] In fact, Pike assures us that a reverent skepticism about what God wants the believer to do is an essential element in Christian maturity: "As important as the desire to do the will of God is the recognition of the tentative and contingent character of our judgments as to what is the will of God. But that in all that we do we are bound to seek to do the will of God is fundamental in the light of His all-embracing concern and the all-embracing claim made upon us."[16] Whatever elements of biblical ethics such an exposition may prefer to retain out of the spirit of eclecticism, one fact is obvious. It has deprived revealed ethics of an absolute content with which the form of love is to be confidently filled. In doing this, it has blotted out the first glory of the biblical ethics: that God has intrusted his clearly spoken Word to man. And it looks suspiciously like a compromising of the moral law to "the moral climate of the time."

The problem of finding a confident and significant content for the moral life is therefore a central problem of ethical study.

The major questions about the content of Christian morality are: (1) how serviceable and comprehensive was the moral content of the *imago Dei* prior to the fall? (2) how adequate is the content of the *imago Dei* in consequence of the fall? (3) what is the significance of special revelation in defining the content of morality?

In an earlier chapter the content of the image of God on the basis of creation was discussed, and a protest was raised against the easy dismissal of the innate factors in moral experience. These innate factors dealt somewhat with both the form and content of morality. The standpoint of the New Testament concurs with that of the Old: the moral law is written on the human heart (Rom. 2:14f.). An essential element in the ethical situation of the creation-state was the nature and constitution of the soul. A moral framework was wrought into the inner make-up of man's being. An undeniable claim to duty and goodness structured human nature over against all temptation. The ethics of special revelation is not honored by derogating this natural morality, as if man were fashioned in creation without moral accountability, or as if no inner moral sense survived the fall. Biblical morality is not cast in the guise of the *wholly* other. It is indeed *other,* and not merely the more perfect and the more complete. It goes against universal practice, but it is agreeable to general revelation. In affirming that the law is written upon the hearts of the Gentiles, Paul suggests there is correspondence between the Gentiles' moral instinct on the basis of creation and the contents of the Mosaic law. This need not imply that all the particulars of the Mosaic law could be derived from intuition had man not fallen into sin. But Paul doubtless implies that the content of innate morality had some definiteness, and that the data of the moral

[15] *Ibid.,* p. 61.
[16] *Ibid.,* pp. 46f.

instinct were sufficient in a general way to serve as a guide for moral action.

The moral law of creation has at its roots the same content as the Mosaic law and all revealed morality: at very least, the fulfillment of the law is a total love for God and man. Yet the interior law was not the only exposition of the law of love vouchsafed to man in the state of integrity. Lightfoot is true to the Genesis account of origins in his observation that "the law writ in Adam's heart was not particularly every command of the two tables, written as they were in the two tables, line by line; but this law in general, of piety and love towards God, and of justice and love toward our neighbor."[17] The law imprinted on the soul by creation was simply the submission of the whole man to the will of God. The content of that will had yet to be made definite in its details.

Even though Adam had a certain morality written into his nature, there was still need for specific instruction and commandments conveyed externally by supernatural disclosure.[18] In man's primal state the basic elements of morality that were his by creation were insufficient to define the whole content of human duty. His spiritual nature doubtless bound man to act in the spirit of truth and right, but he could not derive all the commandments of a dutiful life from his inner constitution. The Genesis account contradicts any idea that the law engraved on man's heart gave him detailed content from which he could deduce every factor of the moral claim. Even prior to the fall the rule of life included an immediate intercourse between man and his Creator. In that relationship God clearly told man what he wanted him to do. Man's native moral endowment on the basis of creation was not enough; God supplemented it by positive commandments. Such were the moral laws which were given in Eden by supernatural revelation (Gen. 1:28, 2:15ff.; cf. 3:3, 11, 17). Apart from such moral instruction man could not have clearly discerned the will of God in many of its implications. Right from the start, man stood in Eden not only *in* law, but *under* law.

The spirit of law imprinted internally on Adam's primal make-up was given additional precision by specific outward commands. This was done to give him more specific moral guidance and to test his character. The connection between the fall and a positive external command emphasizes the fact that man as originally structured was not left merely to infer the details of the will of God from the felt presence of a moral law within his breast. He could not find out by an inference from conscience alone what God wanted him to do. The innate moral nature "required, both for its development and its probation," as Fairbairn puts it, "certain ordinances of an outward kind, specific lines

[17]Lightfoot, *Works,* IV, 379.
[18]Patrick Fairbairn, *The Revelation of Law in Scripture,* pp. 35f.

of action and observance marked out for it by the hand of God."[19] In fact, the fall of Adam immediately followed a supernatural revelation of a particular moral requirement, since the Divine judgment upon Adam stresses his transgression of a specific commandment (Gen. 3:17). That Adam might not touch the tree of the knowledge of good and evil without abusing his personal freedom was known to him only because of this closer external definition of the Divine will. The fall occurred at the point where there could be no uncertainty. God had singled out the fruit of a specific tree and said man was not to eat it. Man was required to respect the authority of God. This circumstance itself suggests in a striking way the fact that the whole content of the moral law was not inwardly communicated even before the fall. Rather the moral law was dependent upon supernatural revelation for a decisive content.[20]

That a decisive content of morality was given to Adam is fully confirmed by a consideration of the commands set forth in the Genesis account. It should be kept in mind that the commands in Eden were outward and positive. They were not on that account less moral, for morality is what God commands. But they were particular rather than universal, and hence perhaps outside the range of human inclinations. Adam was not tested by a command not to murder Eve, which he might have obeyed by natural inclination. These outer commands could not in themselves have supplied the fundamental elements of the ethical situation; rather they presuppose them. At every point they relate man's conduct to the will of God; yet they actually are tests of obedience by formal imposition of express Divine enactments. The moral requirement thus gains a fuller definition.

The positive commandments in Eden do not deal with the details of man's behavior, but with the great turning-points of his social existence: procreation, replenishing the earth by geographic distribution upon it, subduction of the earth in conformity with spiritual purposes, the necessity of labor, the keeping of the Sabbath, and the institution of monogamous marriage. A full exposition of the orders of creation belongs more properly to social than to personal ethics. Such a distinction may be pressed beyond proper limits; the sharp modern contrast between the two all too frequently reflects contemporary socialistic propaganda. But the point to be noticed here is that man as a moral agent is dependent upon external Divine command if he is to know what pleases and what displeases God in all the spheres of life. Who cannot sense at once how vastly different a turn might have been given

[19]*Ibid.,* p. 48.

[20]Of the command respecting the tree of knowledge, Fairbairn remarks that "in itself, and apart from the Divine authority imposing it, there was nothing about it strictly moral: not on this account therefore was it given, but as serving to erect a standard, every way proper and becoming, around which the elements of good and evil might meet, and the ascendency of the one or the other be made manifest" (*ibid.,* pp. 56f.).

to the innate moral sense had it not been for the expansion of the content of a divinely-approved life by a revelation fuller than that innate sense of right and wrong?

The first and most general command is that of procreation — mankind was to be fruitful and multiply and replenish the earth. It might be asked, Why was such a stipulation necessary for man? How does he differ from those lower animals whose perpetuation on earth was to be accomplished by sexual reproduction? An answer may be found in the part sex plays in the life of man. Because he possesses certain intellectual, volitional and emotional qualities, he is able to separate sex from pure instinct. The animal is guided by instinct alone in its sexual activity. This instinct keeps it from promiscuity and excess. Man has a strong sex drive and is free to express it when and where he chooses. He is not guarded from excess and looseness by the controlling power of instinct as is the animal. Sex is God-given to man so man may replenish the earth. Man and his posterity are to serve God morally and spiritually. And man's life of sex must not be so used that this goal is frustrated. So the command is given that man may be guided rightly in his sexual experience.

God gave another instruction to man. Man is to subdue the earth and to have dominion over its living creatures and its fruitful production. This implies that man must necessarily be distributed over the habitable earth, not confined to limited geographic areas. He was to govern nature in order to develop to the full its potential for reflecting the glory of God and promote the well-being of man. Nature bore by creation and preservation the impress of the Divine Mind. Man was to bring to play upon it the creative effort of a human mind fashioned in the Divine image. This broad command that man is to subdue the earth gives legitimate standing to the enterprise of science. Yet this birthright of science does not stand alone, but is bracketed by commands suggestive of its perversity whenever devoted to the frustration of other creation ordinances.

This ordinance protests against an asceticism that disdains nature. It rules out an exploitation of nature that withdraws it from a spiritual control either by forcing nature into the service of unspiritual designs or by neglecting to exercise moral dominion over it. The processes and produce of nature are to be subservient to ethico-intellectual interests and are to contribute to social progress. This leads readily to a fuller declaration of man's vocation on earth. This is contained in his appointment to dress and keep the garden.

The third ordinance is an assignment to industrious employment. Man is not to work independently of God. Rather, he is to promote God's benevolent design. The life of indolent and selfish repose is thereby condemned as godless, and man is appointed to vocation. The Hebrew term translated "to till" connotes work in the sense of service. It is the precise word used of the suffering "Servant" in Isaiah 53, and therefore connects the vocation of man with the well-being of the race. That man was both to till and to dress the garden indicates that the earth was to minister to the aesthetic as well as to the practical needs of human life, and that it was admirably suited for such a role.

As man the worker bears the image of God the Worker, so the fact of God's rest seems to have implied from the outset that labor for God was to be complemented by rest in God. The example of God resting from his labors in creation is made the solemn ground of appeal in the Decalogue for the formal enactment of the observance of the day of rest. The interspersing of work by rest in God is thus given a significance that is primarily religious and moral. It is necessary for man as a bearer of the *imago Dei.* The use of the day of rest goes far beyond mere mental and physical recovery by cessation from labor. Man's existence is patterned not only after the Divine will, but after the Divine example. If the standpoint of Genesis is honored, the principle of one day in seven — of creation and rest, of labor and spiritual repose — is a fundamental principle in the Divine intention on the basis of creation. It is not to be referred exclusively to the state of redemption and the struggle against sin. This viewpoint is taken by John Murray in his Payton Lectures soon to be published under the title *Principles of Right Conduct.* This book will develop an effective exposition of pre-lapsarian ethics. Murray contends that the action of God in creation-rest had relevance for Adam before the fall. Just as "days, seasons and years" regulated his life (Gen. 1:14f.), so one day in seven he was to cease from the kind of activity involved on the other days, and to give himself to employment of another sort. The words of the Genesis narrator are compatible with such a view: "And God blessed the seventh day, and hallowed it; because that in it he rested from all his work which God had created and made" (Gen. 2:3). Murray argues forcibly that if the ordinance of the sabbath was obscured during the patriarchal age — an issue rendered obscure by the silence of the Pentateuch — the later sabbath-breaking would reflect a decline similar to the lapse from the original ordinance of monogamy.

Noting that the first and last of the creation ordinances deal with the order of sex — the one with procreation, the other with marriage — Murray makes a pointed appeal to the New Testament to reinforce the significance of these positive commands on the basis of creation. He particularly treats the institution of monogamy. Despite the polygamy of the patriarchal era and the Mosaic consent to divorce because of the hardness of men's hearts, the verdict of Jesus Christ is clear: "from the beginning it was not so" (Mt. 19:8).

Man's mind and will, his movements, his sexual behavior, his toil and pleasure, thus become means of carrying out God's purposes for the creation. The natural is linked to the moral and spiritual everywhere and inseparably by these ordinances of the creation state. Unless God had made his intentions for man clear in these areas, man would have been seriously handicapped in trying to find out the specific implications of the will of God for human behavior.

If God-love is the regulative norm of self-love, as will be contended subsequently, then it is the real starting-point for determining the content of the moral life. Man's ethical obligation to God, and man's knowledge of that obligation on the basis of creation, therefore assume singular importance in any discussion of the content of the moral life. The content of self-love becomes secondary to the definition of God-love. The fact that creation-ethics as much as redemption ethics had in view man's total love for God and neighbor has already been indicated; both the innate content of the *imago Dei* and the external precepts provided in man's state of integrity are anticipative of this ethical objective. The entirety of the creation ethics is a commentary on the two great commandments.

If the *imago Dei* alone was not enough to give unfallen man the whole content of morality necessary to please God, how much more is it insufficient as a moral guide for fallen man. If unfallen man needed God to tell him what he wished of man, how much greater the need of fallen man for revelation of God's will. Man in revolt could never ferret out of nature the precise content of the will of his Creator. In this fallen condition, man lends himself quickly to satanically-inspired doubts that God had addressed him externally by specific command on the basis of creation (cf. the "yea hath God said" of Gen. 3:1). Indeed, he characteristically seeks to thwart and suppress the law written on his heart and to silence the voice of conscience within him. That man in sin is a moral rebel has already been stressed sufficiently so that it is necessary only to mention it here. The content of the *imago Dei* condemns him in his revolt. Conscience continues to plague him in his prodigal course, and to judge him in anticipation of his final judgment. But conscience no longer supplies him with even that modicum of trustworthy guidance that it gave to unfallen man. Man desperately needs an authoritative external revelation of the moral law.

At this point a protest is sometimes raised by those who emphasize that a trustworthy content for moral behavior is given to fallen man by the surviving *imago*. Appeal is made to the law of love. This law assertedly so structures the human personality that not even the corruption and active moral hostility of the sinner dims its adequacy for providing moral guidance.

In its moderate form, this theory does not deny that God has spoken clearly and propositionally to man in the Bible. In fact, it would even grant the need for such a revelation. What it does deny is that man has been so corrupted morally and spiritually by sin that he no longer possesses any trustworthy norm for moral behavior apart from revelation. Christ himself affirmed the existence in every man of a principle of self-love that is to be the criterion of an acceptable neighbor-love:

"Thou shalt love thy neighbor as thyself" (Lev. 19:18, Mt. 22:39).[21] Love is self-instructing, interpreting the inner meaning of the Law. The "as yourself," it is contended, presupposes a trustworthy moral content within the experience of the unregenerate man. It is a content not determined by exegesis of the biblical revelation, but exists rather as a psychological given. Man has a progressive insight into his duty independent of the biblical revelation. The content of this element cannot be codified, since it presumably belongs to the non-propositional mystery aspect of life. Yet the creature, even in sin, aims at his own happiness and good. This very drive of self-love condemns him, for he does not love his neighbor with equal concern as he loves himself. It is even argued that those who reject such content have not matured to "the mystery of the self." A measure of support seems to be given this view by Jesus' sketch of the good Samaritan. The Samaritan, who had grave theological errors, showed a commendable neighbor-love. It flowed from his immediate self-consciousness. And those whose general doctrinal beliefs were sounder, *i.e.,* the priest and Levite, failed to show such love. The Bible doctrine is not merely that Christians are obligated to love their enemies, but that unregenerate sinners are also bound to love one another. The biblical view of man nowhere justifies him if he withholds his love in personal relations from his fellow man. There is no room for a justifiable hatred, or for conscientious personal revenge. Man must love all with whom he comes in contact — family, friends, countrymen, enemies (Lk. 10:27), the whole of mankind (Mt. 5:42. Lk. 6:32, 35). Everyman is neighbor.

That a natural self-love exists in man is not at all in dispute. To hate one's flesh is obviously averse to nature and contradicted by general experience. In fact, this natural self-concern supplies the background for Paul's statement that the lack of love by a husband for his wife is as unnatural as the lack of self-love. "So ought men to love their wives as their own bodies. He that loveth his wife loveth himself. For no man ever yet hateth his own flesh; but nourisheth and cherisheth it, even as the Lord the church" (Eph. 5:28f.). It is significant, however, that whereas Paul negatively excludes self-hatred, he affirmatively asserts nothing more than that man strengthens and renews himself through food ("nourishes") and protects and preserves ("cherishes," literally, "warms," as a mother's tender solicitude) his life. The phrase "even as the Lord (nourishes and cherishes) the church" warns us against understating what is of universal validity. More is implied here than that man nourishes his body to maturity and fosters it with clothing and externals, although sound scholarship may be adduced in support of the view that Paul has in mind here only the elementary needs of food and raiment. The fact that Paul elsewhere finds it necessary to warn against a false asceticism that deprives the body of its necessities (Col. 2:23) may indicate that the "cherishes" has a wider meaning. It

[21]New Testament reiterations may be found in Rom. 13:9, Gal. 5:14, Jas. 2:8.

is obvious that love for one's own body cannot be annihilated. It is also quite consistent with human nature that false views regarding the nature of one's love for his body will gain wide acceptance. It is not strange therefore that asceticism should be so popular, since man may expect great personal advantage and reward from mortifying his flesh.[22]

Paul does not say that husbands are to love their wives "as they *love* their own bodies," but they are to love them *"as being* their own bodies,"[23] as Christ loves the church. The Apostle does not measure the husband's ideal love for his wife by his love for his own body.[24] Yet he does assert that the husband must love his wife *"for* no one ever yet hateth his own flesh." Each is concerned for his own welfare.

Kierkegaard remarks that in the command of neighbor-love the starting-point comes last: "the presupposition that every man loves himself."[25] But the italicized words in "Thou shalt love thy neighbor *as thyself,"* as in the similar constructions in Ephesians 5:28 and 5:33,[26] need imply nothing more than "as being yourself." This interpretation would not assign to the words the sense of "as you actually love yourself." For that would imply that fallen man can know a moral content from within his fallen nature. The love he naturally has for himself would then serve as the acceptable standard and norm of neighbor-love.

There is no question that every human being has feelings of self-regard, of self-respect, and of personal worth. The question is the propriety of asserting that the kind of love fallen man has for himself is wholly approved by God and can be the norm of neighbor-love. There is no doubt that self-regard is a law of man's rational nature. No man can desist from a psychological self-regard for preservation,

[22]There is no express command "Thou shalt love thyself." Some expositors see in this confirmation that every man does so naturally, by the law and light of nature. "God has put a principle of self-love and of self-preservation into all His creatures, but especially in man" (W. Burkitt, quoted by Lange, *Commentary on Matthew,* 22:39). On the other hand, Calvin remarks: "Since men are born in . . . a state . . . entirely governed by an immoderate self-love . . . there was no need of a law which would inflame that love, already of itself too violent. . . . The Lord, in order to give us the best expression of the strength of that love, which we ought to exercise towards our neighbors, has regulated it by the standard of our self-love because there was no stronger or more vehement affection. . . . For God does not appoint our self-love as the rule, to which our love to others should be subordinate; but whereas through our natural depravity, our love used to terminate in ourselves, he shows that it ought now to be diffused abroad; that we may be ready to do any service to our neighbor with as much alacrity, ardour, and solicitude, as to ourselves" (*Institutes,* II, viii, liv).

[23]It does violence to psychological fact to regard man's love for his wife as but a compliance "with the universal law of nature by which we all love ourselves," or as but a hallowed phase of self-love, if we may recall Chrysostom's notions. But no such assertion is intended here.

[24]Cf. Charles Hodge, *A Commentary on the Epistle to the Ephesians* (New York: Robert Carter, 1868), 5:28.

[25]Soren Kierkegaard, *Works of Love,* p. 15.

[26]Cf. B. F. Westcott, *St. Paul's Epistle to the Ephesians* (Grand Rapids: Eerdmans, reprint, 1950). It can hardly be said that Christ loves the church as he loves himself, but he loves the church as his own body.

comfort, and enhancement in life. Thus far we have spoken only of a psychological disposition and not of a moral obligation. There is no need to stop here. It may, and indeed must, be affirmed that on the basis of creation man is endowed with a proper self-love. Even in sin he knows on the basis of the *imago Dei* not to harm himself and others. His instinct of self-regard is reinforced by reflection and is guarded by the sense of duty.

The duty of neighbor-love as well as that of self-love is stamped on man by creation. And it is not true that men in sin have no natural sense of either. Jesus spoke of neighbor-love as it survives in fallen man in the intimacy of family relations: "Ye . . . being evil, know how to give good gifts unto your children" (Mt. 7:11). It is an exaggeration to say that sin erases every last vestige of self-love and of neighbor-love. There is nowhere a human being whose conscience has not required him to deny himself what he wants in deference to another person's good. And in doing so he has known the rightness of his action. This is doubtless far from *Christian* love for neighbor, but it does show that the virtue of self-denial was not wholly eradicated by the fall. Every missionary has discovered that even the most degraded heathen show some response to the law of neighbor-love.

Yet there is no biblical substantiation for any view that man has perfect self-love or perfect neighbor-love. Nowhere is man's natural love said to be so good that God whole-heartedly approves of it. Nor can it be said that it is always of such a high quality that it is the ideal standard of conduct. Man has repeatedly hated himself and others. He is weighted with a sense of guilt and longs for integration and reconciliation.

Those who believe that fallen man's self-love serves as a standard for acceptable neighbor-love fail to see that normative self-love and neighbor-love are never out of balance. Self-love that is not at the same time motivated by God-love and neighbor-love is inordinate. Kierkegaard asserts: "To love one's self in the right way and to love one's neighbor are absolutely analogous concepts, are at bottom one and the same. . . . The law is: 'You shall love yourself as you love your neighbor when you love him as yourself.' "[27] The concept of neighbor is precisely "the middle term of self-abnegation, which enters between the I and I of selfishness, but also between the I and the other I of earthly love and friendship."[28] The distorted moral judgment of man in sin gives an objectionable direction to his natural self-love. It gives him a bent neighbor-love. He wonders who his neighbor is; he seeks his own advantage to the disadvantage of others. Apart from sanctification, self-love cannot be a trustworthy criterion of behavior. Love to self, in the climate of unregenerate men, is very vague, and has little content, and even that content stands in need of revision.

[27]Kierkegaard, *op. cit.,* p. 19.
[28]*Ibid.,* p. 45.

This judgment is supported by the apostolic writings. They consistently speak with disapproval of man's self-love. The epistles depict history moving toward an apostate future. Indeed, they indicate that inordinate self-seeking will disclose itself under the Christian banner. Men will be "lovers of self" (2 Tim. 3:2). This phrase is listed with a number of vices, and recalls a similar description of the moral depravity of the heathen (Rom. 1:28ff.). Hence it can hardly be said that the natural man aims in every action at his own real happiness and good. This would tend to trace his moral failure to his ignorance of what is truly conducive to his moral and spiritual welfare. The fact is that a content of moral insight survives on the basis of the *imago,* but man compromises it. Despite his knowledge that his own good and happiness are inseparable from love for God, he perversely seeks happiness in moral revolt. The mysterious characteristic of the self in sin is that it fluctuates between knowing that the true good and happiness are in God, and grasping for that good and happiness in spurious alternatives that involve an inordinate self-love. So it is necessary to enforce by precept the avoidance of this inordinate love which leads to judgment.

Kierkegaard acknowledges that the command of neighbor-love does not imply that everyone "loves himself best" nor that self-love is to be held in honor. The intention of the command is "to strip us of our selfishness."[29] Christianity, he tells us, must presuppose that every human being has a selfish love for self, which only neighbor-love can eradicate.[30] Neighbor-love proceeds from man's admitted self-love to "the proper kind of self-love,"[31] approving only that self-love which is embraced in "love your neighbor 'as yourself.' "[32]

Historical exegesis supplies a reliable clue to the sense of the commandment. Leviticus 19:18 sets love for neighbor as one's self in opposition to vengeful ill-will and hatred for him. Hence it means the active promotion of his good, as we would promote our own good. Vincent Taylor suggests that Jesus interpreted the command in this way. He equated love for neighbor with "unselfishness, compassion, and succour" in the parable of the good Samaritan.[33] The New Testament carries forward this idea that such love fulfills "the whole law" (Gal. 5:14; cf. Rom. 13:9).

The New Testament supplies the highest form of the motive for neighbor-love by appealing to God's commands and the superlative manifestation of love in Jesus Christ. Believers ought to "love one another, even as he gave us commandment" (1 Jn. 3:23); "We love him, because he first loved us" (1 Jn. 4:19).

Once we dispose of the notion that in his self-love the sinner possesses an innate standard for proper neighbor-love, the door is open

[29]*Ibid.*, p. 15.
[30]*Ibid.*, p. 37.
[31]*Ibid.*, p. 16.
[32]*Ibid.*, p. 18.
[33]Taylor, *The Gospel According to Mark,* p. 488.

to attach a regulative significance to self-love. It now has a condemning function in the moral situation. No man hates himself; yet man in sin may be designated as hateful to God (Rom. 1:30) and to his fellow-man (Tit. 3:3). This indicates that man is always partial to self as he judges the ethical situation. Despite his fall into sin and his perversion of the moral claim, man shows by this fact that his discrimination against God-love and neighbor-love involves his personal preference. In view of its regulatory character, self-love does not supply man with information on the problems of conduct, nor does it supply him with a fixed and trustworthy norm of action. It is a sliding scale that confronts him in all his actions with the reminder that he is selfish in them all. Hence it fulfills a condemning role in the service of the negative conscience. The "as yourself" of the commandment does not measure the quantity of neighbor-love man is to have, but rather the quality of neighbor-love that is to be bestowed constantly, freely, readily, sincerely, unfeignedly, compassionately.

It may be effectively argued that a Divine standard is necessary to know what proper self-love and proper neighbor-love consist of.[34] Two elements of Jesus' summary of the law point in this direction. The first is the possibility of understanding the commandment of neighbor-love to mean: "You shall love your neighbor as you ought to love yourself." The imperative force of the "Thou shalt" is brought to bear upon neighbor-love and self-love alike. Taken in this sense, it means that man ought to love his neighbor not as he does love himself, but as he ought to love himself, or in H. A. W. Meyer's words, "as thou shouldest love thyself."[35] Pike thinks the injunction may be rephrased, "Love your neighbor as you ought to love yourself, and, Do unto others as you ought to want them to do unto you."[36] Kierkegaard, too, admitting that a man may "call that love which is really self-love," implies that all true love "is grounded . . . in the love of God."[37] This leads to the second element that suggests that love gains its only approved standard from God. Godet well expresses the feeling of many scholars that the second part of the summary is a corollary of the first, and "cannot be realized except in connection with it. Nothing but the reigning love of God can so divest the individual of devotion to his own person, that the ego of his neighbor shall rank in his own eyes exactly on the same level as his own."[38] Bengel also remarks that "he who loves God will love himself in a proper degree, without

[34]It would be far less risky to find the point of the parable of the Good Samaritan in the teaching that genuine neighbor-love draws no distinctions, not even of nationality and religion, in its objects, than to find in it a basis for the notion that a trustworthy moral content is actualized by the unregenerate man on the basis of creation. Any human being in need, and to whom I can respond, is my neighbor.

[35]H. A. W. Meyer, *Commentary on Matthew,* 22:39.

[36]James A. Pike, *Doing the Truth,* p. 167.

[37]Kierkegaard, *op. cit.,* pp. 7f.

[38]F. Godet, *Commentary on Luke,* 10:27.

selfishness."[39] The replacing of fallen self-love by a regenerate self-love thus becomes a purpose of sanctification. As Screwtape writes to Wormwood, "He [God] wants to kill their animal self love as soon as possible; but it is His long term policy, I fear, to restore to them a new kind of self love — a charity and gratitude for all selves, including their own; when they have really learned to love their neighbors as themselves, they will be allowed to love themselves as their neighbors."[40] Here we may recall one of the most sobering utterances ever to fall from the lips of Jesus: "He that loveth his life shall lose it; and he that hateth his life in this world shall keep it unto life eternal" (Jn. 12:25). Even the intimacy of family-love may be improperly oriented to the love of God, and so may defraud an individual of a destiny fit for eternity: "He that loveth father or mother more than me is not worthy of me: and he that loveth son or daughter more than me is not worthy of me" (Mt. 10:37). An over-regard for others must be placed alongside selfishness or a want of regard for others. Both these evils are precluded by love for God who commits every man to the love of neighbor as himself. The moral principle that welds all man's duties into a unity is the love of God with which the summary of the law starts. Christian self-love fulfills the antecedent and correlative requirement of love to God.

Hence, when both neighbor-love and self-love are ideally expressed, they are but love for God redirected and reflected. The effort to make fallen self-love define proper neighbor-love inverts the biblical perspective. "Ultimately love to God is the decisive thing; from it stems love to the neighbor, but paganism never suspected this. They left God out; they made earthly love and friendship into love, and abominated selfishness. But the Christian commandment of love commands men to love God above all else, and next to love the neighbor. In earthly love and friendship partiality is the middle term. In love to the neighbor, God is the middle term; if you love God above all else, then you also love your neighbor and in your neighbor every man. Only by loving God above all else can one love his neighbor in the other man."[41]

The notion that natural self-love is to be used as the standard by which neighbor love is to be externally measured overlooks the fact that self-denial is in no sense the law of fallen human nature. Christ alone induces it. Hobbes located the ultimate source of action in self-preserving and self-gratifying principles. The tension of much modern ethics has been that of creating a neighbor-concern alongside these basic drives.[42] Comte sought to merge selfish and unselfish interests on the ground that the subordination of egoistic to altruistic motives

[39]John Albert Bengel, *Gnomen of the New Testament* (Philadelphia: Perkenpine & Higgins, 1862), I, 258.
[40]C. S. Lewis, *Screwtape Letters* (New York: Macmillan, 1946), p. 74.
[41]Kierkegaard, *op. cit.*, p. 40.
[42]Reginald A. P. Rodgers, *A Short History of Ethics* (London: Macmillan, 1911), pp. 257ff.

best secures personal interests. This is no subordination at all. Utilitarianism avoided strict egoism by assuming that if each sought the good of the whole he would seek his own good. This presupposed a harmonious world of moral relations that evolutionary Naturalism after Darwin and Spencer easily toppled. Modern Naturalism insisted on both egoistic (self-preserving) and altruistic (race-preserving) impulses and motives, deriving their origin and value from natural evolution. Herbert Spencer argued that nature seeks the preservation of the type rather than the individual; at the same time he held the ultimate goal to be the welfare of individuals. He believed evolution was gradually removing the tension between individual and social good. He optimistically proposed a compromise between egoism and altruism which the forces of natural evolution, constantly working toward a more perfect adaptation of egoistic and altruistic requirements, would achieve on one hand through deepened personal sympathy and on the other through improved social conditions. Yet his naturalism allowed no moral or spiritual or rational end to shape the whole. The attempt to make natural self-love the well-spring of neighbor-love belongs to secular ethics rather than to biblical ethics.[43] Not a single word is to be found in the New Testament championing the cause of *eros*. Kierkegaard notes, "What heathendom . . . called love, as distinguished from selfishness, was partiality. But a passionate partiality is essentially another form of selfishness."[44] Love for neighbor is not simply a higher form of self-love; instead, both mirror God's love for man.

All that we have contended for in principle — that the moral content of the *imago* nowhere comes into being in the experience of fallen man in such a way that it supplies a trustworthy norm of moral action — is admitted by some recent expositors who insist upon a transcendent reference for Christian ethics. But they hold it in a highly objectionable context. Because of their bias against the admission of Divine revelation in conceptual form, they tend to understate the rational significance of the image of God in man renewed in redemption. They obscure the clear emphasis of Scripture that the unregenerate man is guilty because he has knowledge of God and his will that he spurns, and that this knowledge is reinforced by special revelation. And, because of the same bias, they tend to regard the Spirit-directed life of *agape* as the all-sufficient rule of conduct for the believer. They find the whole of the ethical life in the principle of submissive obedience. This exposition of Christian ethics tends to define Christian virtue simply as the life of love in action. Based on such passages as "love fulfills the law," it excludes an objective authoritarian ethic entirely. Setting aside all

[43]"Even the term 'philanthropist' has fallen into disrepute," as J. S. Mackenzie observes, because "many people who appear to be aiming at social welfare are found, on closer examination, to be really aiming at their own glorification, or else have very imperfect conceptions of what is really for the benefit of the society in which they live." *Ultimate Values,* p. 169.

[44]Kierkegaard, *op. cit.,* p. 44.

positive commandments as legalistic, it accepts as ethical norms only "the readings of love's dictates." There is much talk, indeed, in these circles, of the revealed will of God, and of faith and love as tests of an unreserved obedience. But there is also a lack of detail in defining the content of moral and positive obedience. Their assumption that undefined love is the law finds no basis in the teaching of Jesus and the apostles.

Man's original moral constitution as a creature who bears the Divine image must not be compromised. Man has moral knowledge that is not totally eradicated. It is, indeed, weakened by sin. Because of the darkness of the mind this knowledge even ministers to corruption, since the voice of conscience no longer has the support of true religion. Man's lust even schools his conscience to tolerate a loose and debauched morality. But the internal moral element gains fresh force, being renewed in redemption, a force that unregenerate man does not have. One acquires from this fact a new appreciation of the significance that the Apostle gives to the work of the law inscribed on man's heart by creation. The ethics of special revelation includes a republication of the law written on the heart. The renewal of the *imago* by redemption gives such new vigor and firmness to the interior moral endowment that its significance has frequently been exaggerated by those who would make the regenerate conscience the only necessary guide for ethical living. The whole content of the moral life is derived from the redeemed conscience. In our times, this view is often joined to the emphasis on love as the essence of revelational ethics. It is held that love supplies its own law and that the renewed conscience is a self-sufficient monitor of conduct.

If this position is not resisted, "Christian ethics" easily becomes what is really a false mysticism. Christianity changed not only the vocabulary but the content and nature of love. In contrast with the modern assignment of an emotional meaning to love, the medieval tradition assigned it a volitional meaning, conceiving it in terms of decision rather than of sentiment. And Christ gave this decision its only Christian direction: "If ye love me, keep my commandments" (Jn. 14:15).

The New Testament affirms that Christ exhibited the perfect moral image of God, but that is far from asserting that this perfect image is to be found also in the ethical sensitivities of redeemed sinners. Indeed, the Apostle exhorts believers to "prove" what the will of the Lord is (Rom. 12:2). Even though the inward "thou shalt" is filled with new meaning by the experience of regeneration, it is not sufficient to discriminate all the issues of good and evil in itself. Some clear direct Word from God is desperately needed.

The studied observation of those Christian norms that can be derived from such internal criteria should be enough to cast doubt upon the sufficiency of the view that depends upon these criteria alone. Even if the effects of the fall were wholly undone in this present life of faith, the theory ends in practical confusion because sanctification is a progressive experience. On any theory of regenerate moral life, the believer's conscience needs constant education as part of his growth in grace. Unless one is ready to grant that the moral content of all regenerate conscience is equally good — a position which would soon reduce to absurdity because different believers react to the same moral problem in different ways, all in clear conscience — the theory must be abandoned. Left to itself without further guidance, love would not know how to decide spontaneously and creatively the proper mode of its expression.

Only because biblical modes of behavior have been formed in believers by the Holy Spirit is it easy to think that love abstracted from special biblical revelation can prescribe its own law. The content of even the law written on hearts has been revealed to us in Scripture. The believer does not gain special revelation from the *imago Dei,* but the content of the *imago* is stated clearly and supplemented in special revelation.

Love is the power that fulfills the commandments, and without it any attempt to keep the commandments will be defective. Jesus has so stamped the history of ethics with the concept that only inward righteousness is genuine righteousness that Sidgwick asserts this to be a distinctive feature of Christian morality: "an inwardness not merely negative, tending to the repression of vicious desires as well as vicious acts, but also involving a positive rectitude of the inner state of the soul."[45] The "law of love" is assuredly a controlling principle of Christian ethics. This cuts the ground from under all theories of the moral life that exclude love to God as basic. In this sense, love indeed "fulfills the law."

Love is even designated by Jesus the "new commandment" (Jn. 13:34). But the sense in which it is new must be carefully defined, lest it be thought that it displaces all other Divine commands. Rather, it fulfills them in the right spirit. Neighbor-love was no new commandment to the disciples. It had already been pointed out as a duty by Jesus, and before that it was commanded in the Old Testament. It is unlikely that Jesus designated it as "new" simply to single it out as *the* way of excellence (cf. 1 Jn. 2:7, 3:11f.). What was new was that a fellow-believer is to be loved as a blood brother because of his faith, since redemption established a new family on the basis of a common prospect for eternity (Jn. 19:26f.). This was not required by the command of neighbor-love, but is now seen to be contained in it. At the same time, the "new commandment" revived with a new vigor the duty of neighbor-love that had been neglected by the Jews.

When love has no specific content, it is an abstract and ethereal law that lacks definition. When no content is given, the appeal to love reduces to a denial that there is a trustworthy rule for the believer's

[45]Henry Sidgwick, *History of Ethics* (New York: Macmillan, 1896), p. 114.

conduct. Those who say the Gospel is their rule are often confused: the Gospel is a message of grace; by itself it is no rule of conduct, except in the larger sense that the "whole counsel" of God includes precepts. The life of love is not self-instructing and self-directing. Love does not spontaneously and automatically disclose how it is to come to self-expression. If it fulfills the law, it neither obliterates the commandments nor is it their source.

Love, as the Bible exposits it, is not something as nebulous as moderns would have us think. The New Testament knows nothing of lawless believers in Christ. No believer is left to work out his moral solutions by the principle of love alone. He has some external guidance from Divine revelation. The early believers were not delivered from an obligation to obey the precepts of the law. The life of love which Christianity proclaims is centered in love for the Living God who has revealed his will, and only to the extent that love impels the believer to fulfill God's revealed will is it genuinely of the Holy Spirit. Love is in accord with the biblical ethic when it devotedly seeks to obey fully the Divine commands.

The content of love must be defined by Divine revelation. The biblical revelation places the only reliable rule of practice before the community of faith. What the Bible teaches gives trustworthy direction to love of self, of neighbor, of God. The pages of the Bible are filled with an interest in good fathers and children, good husbands and wives, good neighbors and friends, good rulers and subjects, good states and the good life, and the feeling of love even in the regenerate believer is inadequate to chart the whole implication of the moral life.

This relationship between love and law that we have just developed is resisted and repudiated by a number of recent writers who assert that the life of love and the life of law are antithetical. The life of love, it is said, cannot be commanded, and the life of conformity to commandments is necessarily legalistic and not spiritual.

It is true, of course, that command does not and cannot of itself generate love.

But it does not follow from this that love cannot be commanded. The fact is that the Ten Commandments and the Law in its entirety and the two commandments in which Jesus summarizes the Law are cast in the "thou shalt" form. Love to God and love to neighbor are commandments. Love is a requirement of the Law, not an alternative to it. "He that loveth his neighbor hath fulfilled the law" (Rom. 13:8). "Love is the fulfillment of the law" (Rom. 13:10). As the Apostle indicates in this context, love alone keeps the divinely enjoined commandments in the right spirit and hence belongs itself to Divine command. Jesus himself supplies the precedent for this emphasis. The life of Christian love is a life of obedience to the will of God as articulated in a specific manner and addressed to men as creatures bearing his image.

Moreover, the *desire* to keep the commandments is a necessity of a biblically-approved ethic — and not the by-product only of a "legalistic misunderstanding." It is more. It is the very means by which man expresses his love for God. From the very outset of human history God has sought man's obedience to objectively revealed precepts and commands. Determination to keep the revealed law of God is not a concession to the principle of works at the expense of the principle of grace. The intention to fulfill the Law is one which biblical ethics clearly vindicates. This is apparent from Old and New Testament alike. The righteous man meditates in God's law day and night (Ps. 1:2); the law of God is in his heart (37:31). The Apostle Paul indicates that this view is his: "The law is holy, and the commandment holy, and righteous, and good . . . the law is spiritual" (Rom. 7:12ff.). It is not the Law as such which troubles Paul but rather it is his lack of conformity to the Law.

It is the Apostle of love who stresses commandment so greatly that he equates love to God with keeping the commands of God. "He that keepeth his commandments abideth in him, and he in him. And hereby we know that he abideth in us, by the Spirit which he gave us" (1 Jn. 3:24). "This is love, that we should walk after his commandments" (2 Jn. 6). And behind this joining together of love and commandment stands the teaching of the Master from whom the Apostle learned. Jesus himself, addressing his disciples, made obedience to his commandments the very evidence of their love for him: "If ye love me, keep my commandments" (Jn. 14:15; cf. 15:14). The Great Commission, itself a command, included the injunction that the apostles teach their converts "to observe all things whatsoever I have commanded you" (Mt. 28:20). Even more impressive is the fact that the incarnate Son characterized his earthly ministry by his obedience to Divine command: "that the world may know that I love the Father, and as the Father gave me commandment, even so I do" (Jn. 14:31); "I have kept my Father's commandments, and abide in his love" (15:10). Devotion to the commandments is not antithetical to the life of love, but gives evidence of it, and even contributes to it. To the regenerate believer, who does not look to the Law as a means of justification, love is generated by a whole-hearted response to the Law.

The modern misunderstanding of the relationship between law and love comes from false views of the nature of man and of the nature of revelation.

It has often been suggested that the sense of ought is a phenomenon only of the bad conscience, *i.e.*, of the experience of man who stands inordinately related to God. But to assert that the good cannot be experienced as a command from without, but only by an inner compulsion, is merely to assume what needs to be demonstrated. The Genesis narrative confirms the view that unfallen man was under Divine command, and that the sense of duty and of love for God were complementary and natural. The period of probation was intended to confirm man in the integrity of obedience to the Divine moral commands. God did not impose commandments as the result of sin, or merely as a provision looking to redemptive grace, but he did so as part of creation itself.

Beneath this feeling that there is an antithesis between love and commandment stands the modern dialectical misunderstanding of revelation. According to this non-biblical theory, God does not reveal himself in conceptual and propositional form; he is said to reveal "himself," *i.e.*, in a mystical supra-cognitive encounter. Such a theory is required if obedience to commandment is to be set over against obedience to God. A commandment becomes nothing more than a human statement of the Divine will. Being human, it is necessarily not wholly true, and hence is misleading. One can know the Divine will only in direct mystical revelation. The cost of such a distinction is staggering. It leads to the surrender of the historic Christian conviction that the Old Testament commandments are the will of the Living God divinely imposed in propositional form (Ex. 20:1ff., Dt. 4:13). This conviction is based on the teachings of Jesus (Mt. 5:17) and Paul (Rom. 2:17f., 3:1f.). The new theory would substitute the immediately-experienced "command" of God, requiring total obedience, but communicating no rationally coherent direction for moral action. Fortunately, this theory is not required by biblical revelation. The necessity for it comes only from the modern revolt against revealed doctrine that involves at the same time a revolt against revealed ethical commandments. This revolt prospers by carrying forward a definition of revelation that had been given currency by Schleiermacher — God communicates redemption, not doctrine. But this can hardly be said to be the historic Christian point of view.

The dialectic theory of revelation is driven to regard the Ten Commandments simply as a fallible human witness to a single command. The Decalogue is just a verbal symbol pointing to the Divine summons to personal obedience. Just as revealed doctrine, or the disclosure of religious truths about God, is ruled out by this anti-propositional theory of revelation, so revealed ethical propositions or commandments are ruled out. If a revealed world-view is excluded, a revealed life-view is also ruled out. The loss of the propositional significance of the Law and the repudiation of a systematic ethics is part of the price paid by the dialectical moralist.

When the higher critical view of the Scripture is coupled with an existential philosophy, as in Brunner's development of Christian ethics, the Law in its propositional form is reduced to a psychological device that propels the soul into moral crisis before God. It makes the person a tension-filled candidate for grace. Its significance is not that of revealed commandments. The commandments become "Divine Command" only to faith, in an encounter of obedient response to God, rather than being what they are — the commandments of God, faith or no faith. The Decalogue is not "a systematic and comprehensive arrangement of the whole sphere of collective life."[46] "The Commandments of Scripture are not intended to secure the ethical tension of life by inclusion in something universal, in a law which is always applicable"; rather they "are intended to show very plainly that the absolute demand for union with God and with our neighbor cannot possibly be deduced from any such universal law."[47] Such statements clearly show Brunner's anti-systematic and anti-conceptual approach to ethics.

Actually the Law does more than humiliate man in his sinfulness; it is more than a psychological forerunner for the Gospel. The Law is a schoolmaster to lead men to Christ. It prepares the way to the Gospel by confronting him with the actual content of the moral law in the form of demand. The reluctance to define the will of God by specific commands gains its motivation from the modern revolt against the connection of revelation and reason, and consistently results in a loss of interest in the ethical teaching of the Bible, the ethics of Jesus included. For Brunner there is no universal ethic — only what God commands the individual in a given instant.[48] This command is assumed to be the same for anyone who is in the same instant. Not even an apostle (Brunner might have added, not even Jesus of Nazareth) can tell us God's will in advance.[49] Yet in reality both the Old Testament and the New are very careful to define in great detail the content of Christian ethics.

An extremely artificial contrast between love and law sometimes appears in contemporary ethical discussions. Its effect is to minimize the relevance for the Christian life of principles as well as specific commandments. In modified expression, this viewpoint conceives the Christian under grace to be free from any responsibility to an ethical code. Grace is in contrast with Old Testament obligation to the Law. This representation will be evaluated later, and our attention now given to the broader claim that principles of conduct necessarily define the good in legalistic terms and hence exclude the kind of morality that proceeds from a spiritual basis.[50] If the Christian ethic were defined as

[46]Emil Brunner, *The Divine Imperative,* p. 137.
[47]*Ibid.,* p. 136.
[48]*Ibid.,* p. 120.
[49]*Ibid.,* p. 118.
[50]Schleiermacher is the champion of this life of sanctification in the spirit which is free of outward rules. "Something like legislation will always exist in Christian life in order in certain spheres to guide the actions of those who lack insight. . . . But to law itself we can concede no value in the sphere of sanctification, for love always is, and does, much more than law can be or do. . . . The goal of sanctification can only be behaviour exhibiting in all its details the strength and purity of inward disposition, and law, as a collection of separate precepts, can never let us see this. . . . To call propositions expressive of the inward spirit commandments is a most inaccurate form of language." *The Christian Faith* (Edinburgh: T. & T. Clark, 1928), p. 523. The underlying ideas are that law in propositional form is inescapably unspiritual, and that genuine spiritual experience is supra-conceptual. To the former we reply that the Ten Commands were divinely spoken and divinely

a system of law and principles, of propositions, Brunner tells us that would mean "the Good would be defined in legalistic terms."[51] That which is done on the basis of principle is legalistic.[52] This trend of argument follows not from the facts of the ethical situation, but rather from the requirements of Brunner's philosophy of revelation.[53]

Thomas, curiously, belabors the prevalent antinomian and nominalistic tendency that over-emphasizes the uniqueness of each moral situation and act so as to deny the relevance of ethical principles and moral rules. The assumption that love, unaided by moral rules, "can discover in each situation what it should do" he considers "unrealistic."[54] The Christian life requires not only the inspiration of love and the assistance of the Holy Spirit, but the guidance of moral laws. Biblical laws, he insists, can "furnish guidance" in the different relationships of life. That we cannot lay down laws for every situation in life does not mean that no laws can be stipulated for many or none. In fact, Thomas repudiates the notion that conduct performed in fulfillment of the commandments is necessarily legalistic: "There is nothing about moral laws or rules that necessarily leads to a neglect of motives and the whole inward side of morality," he writes; and again, "a meticulous observance of all the details of the written and oral law was quite compatible with love of God as one's primary motive."[55] Thomas refuses to contrast the motives of love and duty, regarding them as complementary.[56]

All this is well and good. But if one looks next for an identification of the content of the law of love with what God has commanded in the Scripture he is disappointed. Thomas acknowledges that the long sweep of Christian history avoids a contrast between love and law. There is no depreciation of law, nor of the essential continuity of Old and New Testament ethics, in Augustine, Aquinas, Luther, Calvin and Wesley. Yet the Anabaptists are praised, in contrast, for recognizing Jesus'

---

written on stone, and that the Apostle Paul declares "I had not known lust, except the law had said, Thou shalt not covet" (Rom. 3:20, 7:7), so that it is by the law that the Spirit convinces of sin; and to the latter that Schleiermacher falsifies biblical doctrine in deference to an arbitrary philosophy of revelation.

[51]Brunner, *op. cit.*, p. 91.

[52]*Ibid.*, p. 117.

[53]This is clear from Brunner's "straw man attack" against verbal inspiration and biblical inerrancy. The argument is that this doctrine involves a rationalistic, legalistic misunderstanding of biblical ethics (*ibid.*, p. 101). But the Sermon on the Mount is hardly aimed against the authority of the Scriptures; cf. the emphasis on fulfillment and "not one jot or tittle." That God's will is objectively communicated through the Law and the prophets and hence in Scripture is our Lord's characteristic assumption; cf. the formula "it stands written" used in the wilderness temptation, and Jesus' reply to the rich young ruler in which there was no rebuke because he thought the written Law requires a complete obedience, but the issue was whether or not he had fulfilled it. While Brunner may avoid a legalistic understanding of ethics, he does so by a rationalistic misunderstanding which evaporates its objective and specific content.

[54]George F. Thomas, *Christian Ethics and Moral Philosophy*, p. 131.

[55]*Ibid.*, p. 128.

[56]*Ibid.*, p. 130.

"radical ethic of love." Thus Thomas prepares for a disjunction of the ethic of love and the biblical command. Commandments are said to have only a general validity, *i.e.,* they give us "right directions," while the law of love alone is absolute. The notion that Jesus gave "absolute rules" is repudiated as legalistic, and the counter-notion that he gave only "illustrations of the central principle of love," or "indications of the way love will lend one to act in certain kinds of situations" defended.[57] "Thou shalt not kill" is true only "on the whole and for the most part."[58] The ideal of monagamous marriage should take cognizance of the remnants of sin in the lives of Christians; hence divorce is sometimes justifiable.[59] Thomas does not go on to say that adultery presumably is also. Nor does he hasten to point out another possibility, that it may sometimes be right to violate all the commandments.

Thus Thomas virtually reinstates the contrast between law and love. And he involves Christian ethics in insuperable tensions and inconsistencies. For he declares that "the law of love as interpreted by Jesus" alone possesses "absolute and universal validity."[60] Yet Jesus excludes any conformity of the commandments to the climate of the times, but rather intensifies their claim (cf. Mt. 5:17ff., 19:8). Thomas' adjustment of the biblical precepts to human circumstances and conditions involves him actually in an abandonment of that "primary ethical principle" of Hebraic ethics which "sets the ethics of the Old Testament sharply apart from all forms of the humanistic ethics which has so deeply influenced Western moral philosophy."[61] For he finds himself driven to repudiate the notion of moral precepts "binding on men simply because they were commanded by God."[62] The validity of commandments is to be determined in part by "their relation to personal fulfillment and social welfare," criteria which apparently are to be regarded as independent of what God commands.

The biblical commandments, moreover, are said to represent differing levels of "insight." Not only is the universal validity of some precepts doubtful, but others are of "very little" value.[63] Sometimes a commandment is distorted by the religious zeal of the writer.[64] Even the Gospels likely contain misrepresentation of Jesus' ethical teaching.[65]

If one asks what controlling idea underlies the hesitancy to identify the content of the law of love with precepts, the answer is not far away.

[57]*Ibid.,* p. 59.
[58]*Ibid.,* p. 134. It is one thing to assert that the commandments are universally valid where they are intended to apply, another to attack their universal validity. Thomas here appeals to war and self-defense as compromising universality of this command. But Jesus indicated its inner meaning; to kill out of the motive of hatred is wrong even in war and self-defense.
[59]*Ibid.,* p. 237.
[60]*Ibid.,* p. 135.
[61]*Ibid.,* p. 3.
[62]*Ibid.,* p. 134.
[63]*Ibid.,* p. 133.
[64]*Ibid.,* p. 134.
[65]*Ibid.,* p. 237.

Thomas remarks that "a difference of attitude than the traditional one towards the moral laws of the Bible is essential" if the disjunction is to be maintained. "The traditional attitude represented by Aquinas and Calvin," he writes [and he might equally have asserted, by Jesus and the apostles, and by the whole Hebrew-Christian movement previous to Schleiermacher], "was a product of a pre-critical conception of revelation" according to which "revelation was an external communication of truths in propositional form by God."[66] There is every evidence that the critical and anti-intellectualistic view of revelation actually dictates the refusal to accept the biblical precepts as expressive of the Divine will, rather than that, as Thomas seems to indicate, the looser view of the commandments (which assuredly is not postulated in a vacuum wholly devoid of assumptions) encourages the new view of revelation. In the last analysis, Thomas not only elevates love and subordinates moral law, but he quotes approvingly (what he elsewhere repudiates) Brunner's emphasis that there is but one invariable Divine command, love, whose content is variable according to circumstances.[67] The moral laws of the Bible cannot tell us "ahead of time and without question what we have to do."[68] Thus another earnest exposition of the moral situation, by its disjunction of love from the fixed biblical content, unwittingly opens the door to a spontaneous and unprincipled morality. For we are given no external criterion for determining the ideal content of moral love in the face of competing claims.

Biblical ethics does not exhibit love and law or principles as mutually exclusive categories; the good life is the life of love, and sin is lawlessness and the unprincipled life. To love God is to do the will of God or to keep his commandments. Every statement of the love of God in terms either of Old Testament or of New Testament ethics equates it with the fulfillment of specific commandments. The Psalmist was able to declare "The statutes of the Lord are right, rejoicing the heart" (Psa. 19:8); and Jesus, whatever may be said about the major differences between Old and New Testament ethics, declared "If ye love me, keep my commandments" (Jn. 14:15). Doubtless the legalistic attempt to fulfill the Law by regarding it the way of salvation for fallen man is the great perversion of Judaism. Against it both New Testament and Old Testament strike out when they are properly understood. But it is one thing to assert, as biblical ethics must, that the will of God is revealed in specific commands and principles which may be kept either formally in the disastrous spirit of legalism or spiritually in the power of love, and quite another to advocate the dubious view that love and command-or-principle negate each other because fulfilling the latter inevitably involves legalism. Such a misinterpretation of biblical ethics can only involve the misunderstanding of Christ's relationship to the

[66]*Ibid.*, p. 134.
[67]*Ibid.*, p. 137.
[68]*Ibid.*, p. 138.

Law, and of the believer's as well, since it empties the Divine command of its specific content on the pretext of doing justice to love as the supreme principle of Christian morality. Another ethical theory attempts to reduce the content of Christian ethics simply to action shaped by the form of love as a higher species of morality bound to no law-code, yet it does not hold to the thesis that commandments and principles inevitably involve legalism. In a subsequent chapter the faithfulness or unfaithfulness of this antinomian view to the New Testament picture of conduct will be discussed.

If the sense of duty and the spirit of love stood in no essential conflict in man before the fall, the object of redemption is to secure once again their perfect complementation. The tension between command and love in the life of man as sinner is due to their disjuncture in the moral life. Man in sin seeks artificially to justify himself by law-keeping, though he does not really love God; hence he neither fulfills the commands externally in his actions, nor internally in the spirit of love. In the regenerate life that is motivated by love for God and is self-assured of a gracious redemption, the tension is set up by the awareness that incomplete obedience springs from imperfect love. Perfect love fulfills all the commandments. The complete elimination of this tension waits for the life of glory, but even in the present life of sanctification the tension is transcended in principle in the realization of the fact of the filial relationship of the redeemed believer to his heavenly Father.

In this chapter we have been concerned to show the plight of ethics in a fallen world, even though it emphasizes that the good is what God wills and makes a plea for special revelation, when it seeks to define the content of the moral life independently of the biblical norm. By a sort of philosophical shell game it is possible by concealed dependence upon tradition to import a greater or lesser directive content without acknowledging the debt.

The ethics of Niebuhr is cast in the existential mode and supplies us with a supreme illustration of the curious contradiction into which a truncated Christian ethics may come at last. On the one hand, the fall of man is interpreted existentially: Adam is everyman, living at the juncture of the world of nature of which man is a part, and of the Divine world, since as a spirit he bears also the Creator's image. Everyman in every moral act yields to anxiety; instead of accepting his finite and dependent creaturehood and trusting the future to God as the true center of life, he independently seeks his own security and hence falls into the life of pride and self-seeking. Christ alone teaches us the true law of life — the law of love. He discloses sacrificial and forgiving love. Salvation, also existentially interpreted, is a response to this love; it is no once-for-all, final experience, but a repeated response in dependent contrition. Every fall requires a new "justification by faith." The vulnerable point in Niebuhr's existential ethics is the contradiction with which it handles the revelation of the love of Christ. On the one hand, he sets out with the view that history is inevitably sinful, and that sacrificial love negates history. Hence the revelation of sacrificial love in history is impossible. But unless the historical Jesus is regarded as having actually unveiled sacrificial love in history, Niebuhr's ethics can in no sense of the word be dignified with the title Christian. If *agape* is an abstraction suspended above the historical Jesus and not a reality exhibited in the historical stratum, we are dealing not with Christian ethics but with a gnosis quite distinct from the New Testament insistence that Divine revelation has reached its high point in the incarnate God. On the other hand, the admission of the historicity of Jesus' sacrificial love is devastating to the whole existential structure. If *agape* is an actual historical achievement, then the position that history and human nature are inevitably sinful is bankrupt. Niebuhr is driven to a choice between Christian or existential ethics. If *agape* is objectively unveiled by the historical Jesus, we have Christian but non-existential ethics; if not, we may have existential ethics, but it is far from Christian.

The loss of the objectivity of biblical ethics has meant more than the loss of a sure content of the moral life. It has meant, even among distinguished expositors of Christian ethics, the loss of *agape* as an achievement even in the life of the historical Jesus.

11

THE BIBLICAL PARTICULARIZATION OF THE MORAL LIFE: THE OLD TESTAMENT

IN STATING THAT God only is the ground of the good and that the Divine will itself is the rule of right, one must immediately ask the question, On what ground can we possibly make these declarations? On this point the Hebrew-Christian faith is clear in its reply: What God has revealed in the inspired Scriptures defines the content of his will.

We have already noted that even unfallen man needed supernatural revelation in order to have some content of an approved morality. The ethics of external revelation did not simply duplicate what was already in man on the basis of creation, but it supplemented as well as enforced his moral intuitions. From the very outset of human life, the ethical situation was defined by duties and convictions that were not accessible from natural reason alone. How much greater, therefore, would be man's dependence upon supernatural guidance and direction once his moral integrity was sacrificed and the inner moral intuition clouded by a recalcitrant will.

The ethics of special revelation answers a dual condition of human nature — its essential finiteness and its contingent sinfulness. Its uniqueness does not lie in any contradiction to the innate moral sense of the *imago Dei,* but rather in its intensification and expansion of that very sense, and in its simultaneous opposition to various false ethical perspectives man has developed out of his moral revolt. The special disclosure after the fall transcends the law written on men's hearts in a twofold way: it is intended to make known the way of obedience, and to make known the way of recovery from disobedience.

From these facts we may infer what is actually the case: that Divine revelation will not take the form merely of generalities, but will have practical implications for the whole life of motive and behavior. It goes beyond the so-called "beggarly elements" of moral science, and orients the whole man and his conduct to the holy Lord. And from the very dawn of history God has not left the creatures of his image to grope in blind darkness, but has illumined their path with the light of Divine commandments. There are revealed sign-posts in Eden, and these sign-posts were multiplied and given a fixed objective and written form after the fall, lest man be overwhelmed in sin by the maze of conflicting demands impelling him from without and within. That God has been pleased to reveal his will, and that he has done so in express commands, given to chosen men through the medium of human language, and available to us as the *Word* of God in written form, is so clearly the historic conviction of the Hebrew-Christian movement as to be virtually an indisputable characteristic.

The abandonment of this biblical orientation for the will of God is a characteristic feature of recent moral theories. They speak for Christian ethics, but are frustrated in exhibiting its content. In the Middle Ages the Roman Catholic Church began to remove the Bible from a place of prominence in defining faith and practice. It supplanted the revealed ethic by a scheme of works. The newer views profess a return to grace alone, but continue to sketch the content of the Christian life objectionably because they do not identify the will of God with what the Bible requires of man.

The abandonment of the Bible as the inspired and authoritative rule of life means much more than the loss of the details of approved Christian behavior. For the only claim Christian ethics has left is that some man asserts segments of it. This emotional, perhaps nostalgic, preference may retain a few chosen elements of the traditional ethics, but mostly it holds them in a truncated and distorted form. That the ideal morality is inseparable from a distinctive metaphysics of revelation, and that the content of ethics is defined by the will of God alone, are propositions that stand at the heart of biblical revelation.[1] From the standpoint of revealed ethics, the Divine moral claim is a unitary whole that does not lend itself to arbitrary selection. The theological ground of Judeo-Christian ethics and its basis in the Divine will are inseparable from the specific content of ethics mediated by the unique revelation of God known to us in the Bible. To lose the Bible as the authoritative norm of the knowledge of God's will is to lose the confident assertion that God's will is the rule of right. Revealed Scripture remains the central and controlling factor in man's conception of the moral life.

The Bible is the superlative propositional revelation of God; in defining man's duties it is the repository of the world's noblest ethical ideals. It is the supreme evidence that God has not withheld from individuals and nations the moral instruction they need for the perfect fulfillment of their calling. Those who exhibit its moral claims assert them to be more than human representations; indeed, they do not

[1]An example of a Christian moralist who repudiates an authoritative biblical ethic and who then treats the Bible authoritatively where it suits his purposes, is provided by MacLennan: "The dominant note of Old Testament religion is obedience to the declared will of God. That will was set forth in the Covenant relationship which is glimpsed far back in history, and which was plainly set forth by Moses. From the side of man his duties under the Covenant are set forth in the Ten Commandments, and in all additions to and deductions from that code." *Christian Obedience,* p. 10.

hesitate to identify them as the very will of God, revealed and written.[2] The Torah gained its hold on Hebrew life because it was considered to be revealed instruction. The reverence Jesus held for the Law in its written form is clear from the famous phrase, "not one jot or tittle shall pass away" (Mt. 5:18). This implies that he appealed to the Old Testament as authoritatively containing the Divine command. Paul declares the glory of the Hebrews to be that they alone knew God's will (Rom. 2:17f.), possessing the very oracles of God.

The fact is that those expositors of revealed ethics who would reconstruct what earlier generations of Christians conceived the will of God to be can only conclude that for them the Bible was the precise delineation of the Divine will for man. Treat the Scripture though they may as only a record of what previous ages thought of the will of God, or as the advancing insight of men of faith into the nature of moral realities, or as the highest mirror of the ethical in all successive ages, yet the fact remains that it is in and through the conviction that the absolute requirement of God is here unveiled that the Bible gained its existence. Every unbiased summary of the Hebrew-Christian understanding of the Divine moral claim must reflect this confidence that the will of God has been focused for men in and through a special activity of intelligible revelation and inspired writings.

The Genesis account of paradise and the fall, T. B. Strong notes, contains "all the elements of the ethical idea as it presented itself to the Jews. God gave a command which man disobeyed. . . . The sin which led to the Flood was disobedience or rebellion against God. . . . The sin of Sodom is represented as an outrage upon God. . . . The special covenant is based on the readiness of Abraham to accept the guidance of God. . . . The sin of Esau consists in the neglect of this covenanted right of access to God. . . . The Commandments come with the *imprimatur* of God . . . the covenant-relation is alluded to in the prefatory verse . . . in Ex. 20:2. . . . In regard to the . . . [priestly] legislation . . . the whole order is rested upon the covenant-relation with God, and, more than this . . . the character of God is placed in definite connexion with the rules laid down. The holiness of God requires this elaborate ceremonial order to preserve it from the contamination of hasty and unfit intruders, and to retain the condition of the people at a level high enough to enable them to use their covenant privileges. This is proved by the refrain which recurs at intervals . . . —'I am the Lord'; and by such marked phrases as . . . 'Ye shall not profane my holy name; but I will be hallowed among the children of

[2]"Everywhere in the Bible the high ethical standard is upheld. Somehow, you feel at once, in reading the opening chapters of the Bible, that you are in the presence of an absolute law of right. The bars are nowhere let down. Already in the forbidden tree we see clear moral distinctions. In the treatment of Cain 'sin croucheth at the door.' The antediluvians were punished because 'every imagination of their heart' was evil. And so on through the Bible." L. S. Keyser, *A Manual of Christian Ethics*, p. 70.

Israel.' . . . In the book of Deuteronomy . . . there is a more pronounced insistence on . . . the close relation of God to the people in view of His moral character. . . . Enough . . . has been said to establish the truth . . . that morality for the Jew meant that which God had commanded; immorality, that which God forbade. . . . The characteristic note . . . is that God takes command over life as a whole . . ."[3]

The Old Testament disclosure itself requires from the outset a distinction within revealed ethics between perpetual obligations and temporary obligations. Some great principles of obedience are of perpetual obligation, and others binding at one period and abolished in another. What is forbidden on the basis of the *imago Dei* by natural law is wrong perpetually. Even the Apostle does not hesitate to relate Christians to this general revelation: "Whatsoever things are true . . . honest . . . just . . . pure . . . lovely . . . of good report; if there be any virtue . . . think on these things" (Phil. 4:8). But some divinely-promulgated laws concern things that in themselves are morally indifferent. God has expressly enjoined certain requirements as evidence of obedience in a given period or age, in addition to those implanted in some measure in the minds of men on the ground of creation. God alone can inaugurate them with religious sanctions, as God alone can abrogate their requirement.

The distinction between interminable and limited obligation is required by the content of ethical revelation at the creation, of the Divine establishment of Israel, and with the New Testament disclosure. But this does not imply approval of the contrast sometimes made between moral obedience and positive obedience. According to that objectionable view, only what is perpetually binding is moral. Moral obedience is perpetually binding; positive obedience may be required in one dispensation and abolished in another. Moral obedience arises from the nature of God, and cannot be altered without altering our conception of the Divine character. The one is of Divine appointment because it is forever right, the other is temporarily right because of Divine appointment. The objection to this view is that it conceals the basis of all revealed morality in the will of God. Both the notion of changeless norms, echoing popularly-held theories inconsistent with basing morality on God's will, and the notion that temporal obligations are on that account not fully moral, need to be avoided. If the essence of morality is that God commands it, both that which is of perpetual obligation and that which is not are moral. The difference between obligations is not that some are less moral than others, but that God decrees some obligations to be perpetual. The principle of temporary obligation is established in the Old Testament dispensation by that body of "carnal ordinances imposed on them until the time of reformation" (Heb. 9:10). In the New Testament, baptism is imposed as a precept of positive obedience.

[3]T. B. Strong, "Ethics," in Hastings' *Dictionary of the Bible*, I, 777ff.

Obedience to the revealed will of God, whether to perpetual or temporary obligation, is required by Scripture as evidence of genuine faith and love. Comprehensive devotion to God and our fellow-man requires fulfillment of the entire moral law.

The fact that the fall itself comes by the violation of a positive commandment against eating the fruit of a given tree enforces from the outset the truth that the will of God is decisive for the moral order. Man stands answerable to the holy Lord, the living ground of ethical distinctions, and to natural morality, the innate moral sense given him by the holy Lord. If this unitary source of morality is kept in view, it is permissible to distinguish within revealed ethics between that which is commanded because it is eternally right, and that which is right in a given age because it is commanded. Such a distinction is necessary in setting forth the ethical situation before the fall. The commands externally addressed to Adam involved more than a fuller elaboration of the content of the moral image of God, but added a specific prohibition not explicitly contained therein. The fact that the redemptive revelation is addressed to a sinful society, therefore, leads to the expectation that new complexes of special conditions will govern man in the predicament of sin that touch both the form and manner of his obedience.

It is this correlation of the absoluteness of God's moral claim with his command of what is eternally right and with what is temporally right because divinely commanded that ties the revealed will of God dramatically to special revelation. Whoever objects because the content of biblical ethics is historically communicated, insisting that it then cannot bind the conscience universally, nor be regarded universally as a ground of moral culpability, has failed to grasp man's condition in sin, and has missed the pattern of redemptive rescue in special historical revelation. The biblical portrayal of the Divine moral claim is not just an abstract system of moral principles; it is deliberately tied to various positive commandments and forms of obedience that were given in specific situations in history. These historical features are the warp and woof of special revelation. God redeems *in* history and time, not apart from them. Critical morality has often sought to use the historical element in revelation as a wedge to weaken the essential morality of that revelation. The historical actually makes more vivid an interest in the changeless moral will of God, and it focuses dramatic attention on the responsibility of faithful believers to obey it.

Though it unveils changeless ethical verities, the moral revelation itself has a history. The Old Testament definition of the content of divinely approved behavior requires a distinction between "carnal ordinances imposed . . . until the time of reformation" as well as perpetually-legislated norms of right and wrong. This history, however, is also a progressive development toward a fixed goal. The particular stages of the ethical revelation have a distinguishable role within the larger whole.

The difference between the Old Testament and the New Testament is not absolute. It is a matter of degree. The faithful in the old economy of promise and in the period of prophetic types were doubtless bound to a large number of detailed commandments that were interwoven with the lines of permanently valid morality. While the Old Testament forms are wholly done away in the New Testament economy, yet the New Testament era is not free from positive enactments of its own. It need not be insisted that all the facets of Christian morality are included in the Decalogue in order to maintain the constant validity of revealed morality. In both Testaments there is the moral law that is binding upon all men in all circumstances and places; there are also commandments of temporary significance. During his earthly ministry Jesus Christ sometimes addressed commands to his disciples that are not applicable in the present church age. The Ten Commandments do not contain the whole content of Christian obedience. They specify neither baptism nor the Lord's Supper as elements of obedience, and yet these are specifically enjoined by Jesus Christ; a believer who withholds himself from them is disobedient to his Lord. Our Lord commissioned the apostles to baptize all converts, and to teach them "to observe all things whatsoever I commanded you" (Mt. 28:20).

The nature of the revealed ethic is progressive. A later age is always called upon to "fulfill" the continuing moral claim, although God may supersede certain positive laws in the newer era. Each period has its characteristic features and special arrangements by which it may be readily distinguished from the others. Yet the great whole of God's movement in history is never obscure. The Psalmist and the prophets appeal confidently to the revelation of duty given in the Law; Jesus did not come to destroy but to fulfill the Law and the Prophets (Mt. 5:17); Paul found the ancient revelation profitable for doctrine, reproof, correction, instruction in righteousness (2 Tim. 3:16; cf. Rom. 15:4, 1 Cor. 10:11). The essential is a unitary whole that runs through all the circumstantial of the several dispensations, and it has vital bearing on our present decisions and actions.

The Ten Words enunciated on Sinai contain the essential principles of a righteousness that truly mirrors the pure character of the holy God. Their explicit definition of man's religious and moral duty unveiled with one bold stroke the holy nature and purpose of the Living God and a morality of permanent universal obligation. They stand apart from all temporal injunctions in the scriptural revelation; they are valid for all men in all places and at all times.

The giving of the Law is a peak in Old Testament history. It towers above that long stretch of events that reach back through the patriarchal period beyond the flood, behind the fall in the garden. Biblical history makes it clear that man was morally accountable to God before the Law was given at Sinai despite the fact that during the patriarchal age there is no clear testimony to the existence of authoritative Divine law addressed externally in the form of definite imperative commandment. In lieu of objective and formal law, man was to be guided morally by the directive light of conscience and the tradition of moral duty in paradise that had survived into the fallen situation of man. The principles of moral duty on the basis of creation bear witness from Eden to Egypt in the absence of formal law. Expelled from Eden, man had a fresh and intense moral knowledge that survived the fall. It included the positive enactments of God and the penalties resulting from the fall that intensified the sense of the immediate moral authority of God. The will of God had not yet been given written form in the lengthy patriarchal era. But the days of man were long at that time. Adam was alive at the time of Lamech, father of Noah — if we dare assume that no broken links occur in the genealogies of Genesis. This longevity kept alive the moral situation, it enunciated clearly the decisive landmarks of truth and right, and it quickened for the time the responsible knowledge of duty surviving in man after the fall. At the same time, the principle of evil worked itself out in growing hostility to the good; fallen man lacked the moral power to enforce the higher sentiments of his conscience, and the rent in human nature had given it a bent toward sin. The first murderer is Cain, and a principle of violence introduced into society gains an increasingly appalling magnitude until it invites at last the Divine interposition of the flood. Not even the new state of things after the flood restrained men and nations from their wayward and iniquitous course.

Yet the patriarchal period is not entirely lacking in evidence of a special Divine intervention for the moral and spiritual guidance of man. The sacrifices cannot be referred merely to conscience nor to tradition, for in any event the tradition would require explanation. And obvious illustrations of formal legislation are the post-deluvian law of blood for blood and the Abrahamic covenant of circumcision which was the sign and seal of the covenant of grace.

God in redemptive grace singled out a people who were to be the channel of the Redeemer's advent. They were appointed a witness to the world of the blessings that come from obedient service to the holy Lord, and the repository of his specially-revealed oracles. The catastrophe of the deluge and the revelation of Sinai complement each other; the destruction of a wicked humanity on the one hand, and the covenant preservation of a chosen nation on the other. But in each case the uncompromised proclamation of the Divine passion for holiness and the heinousness of sin tighten the bonds of moral obligation. But the Sinai pinnacle comes also as the climax of a whole series of gracious promises that reach back to the protevangelium of Eden, to the covenants of blessing with Noah and Abraham, that aimed to preserve a living piety on the basis of a gracious redemption.

The law given through Moses reinforced the creation ordinances established in paradise. The immediate object of Sinai was to establish the covenant into which the Almighty had entered with the representatives of the chosen people in which he redeemed them from bondage in Egypt and now constituted them a unique nation. The deliverance itself, however, had been predicated upon the Lord's disclosure of himself to Moses as the God of Abraham, Isaac and Jacob, the God of covenant-promise, who delivered Israel out of Egypt. And they were to be constituted "a kingdom of priests and a holy nation" (Ex. 19:6). Even though grace occupies the foreground, redemption has as its implication conformity to the spiritual and moral order. There is unrelieved sternness in the list of thou shalt not's. The law clearly pronounces stringent prohibitions against transgression, and in doing so it does not presume to give a wholly new statement of man's moral duties. Rather, it implies and republishes and expands the morality of creation. That the formal revelation of the law was given through Moses to the covenant people — "the law came by Moses" (Jn. 1:17) — does not deny, but presupposes that the human race stood from its original state under obligation to Divine command.

Fairbairn long ago observed that the Ten Words hold a peculiar prominence in the Mosaic legislation because of several circumstances — "being not only the first in order, and in themselves a regularly constructed whole, but the part which is represented as having been spoken directly from Heaven in the audience of all the people, amid the most striking indications of the Divine presence and glory — the part, moreover, which was engraven by God on the mount, on two tablets of stone — the only part so engraven — and, in this enduring form, the sole contents of that sacred chest or ark which became the center of the whole of the religious institutions of Judaism — the symbolical basis of God's throne in Israel." There can be no reasonable doubt, Fairbairn goes on to infer, that these distinctions were intended "to secure for this portion of the Sinaitic revelation the place of preeminent importance, to render it emphatically THE LAW, to which subsequent enactments stood in a dependent or ancillary relation."[4]

The double form of the Decalogue (Ex. 20:1-17, Dt. 5:6-21) of itself poses no difficulty, since the substance and order of the commands are identical in both accounts. The schematization of the commandments, however, has been arranged in various ways. While the Scripture itself speaks of "two tables" of the law, it does not precisely divide the commandments. Perhaps this is because of their interior religio-ethical unity that is enforced also by the law of love as the summary of the law. It is obvious that the first four commands contain duties that are directed especially toward God, and the subsequent commands, duties

[4]Patrick Fairbairn, *The Revelation of Law in Scripture*, pp. 82f.

toward neighbor. The fifth word, "honor thy father and thy mother," forms the transition and in some respects may be attached either to the first or the second table. Respect for parents is built on the principle that they represent God. The parents exercise a borrowed authority over the young in their period of training; hence respect for parents is respect for God. Beyond this, the discussion of the schematization of the commands is not of great moment. The fact that the commandments are cast in negative form indicates that they are addressed to man in the state of disobedience, and have a view to the fires of evil that burn in the heart of fallen man. Implicit in each negative form is the affirmative, as the Mosaic emphasis on the requirement of love for God and for man places beyond doubt. The existence of the positive call to duty on the basis of creation is assumed, and is made certain by Jesus as the inner spirit of the law.

In summary:

(1) Thou shalt have no other gods before me.
(2) Thou shalt not make unto thyself any graven image.
(3) Thou shalt not take the name of Jehovah thy God in vain.
(4) Remember the sabbath day to keep it holy.
(5) Honor thy father and thy mother.
(6) Thou shalt not kill.
(7) Thou shalt not commit adultery.
(8) Thou shalt not steal.
(9) Thou shalt not bear false witness.
(10) Thou shalt not covet.

It may not be possible to exhibit an inner connection at every point between the ten words and the ethical situation before the fall. But one can hardly read the commandments without immediately recognizing certain terms and themes: *imago,* labor and rest, marriage and procreation, coveting.

The first three commands suggest at once the background of the narrative of the creation and the fall. Man is himself the unique bearer of the Divine image (Gen. 1:26) and to fashion any competitive image would threaten the great truth that God is Spirit; it would reflect on the dignity of man, and it would ultimately encourage sinful man to overlook the incarnated image of God in Jesus Christ. The Law, by its uncompromising prohibition of graven images, fixes attention on the Living God to whom man in sin reflects a shattered image. The tolerance of false gods could only make light of the fact that man's peculiar glory is his image of the Living God, and that man's tragic shame is the sullying of that image. The name of Jehovah stands for the revelation of his character and will. That magnificent name was taken in vain by Adam and Eve who, when they violated the Edenic command, were not held guiltless, and who involved the race with them. From the penalty of death attached to profaning God's name (Lev. 24:16), it appears likely that the commandment looked to the avoidance of blasphemy, in thought and deed.

The fourth command implies the perpetual significance of man's original appointment to cultivate the earth and to place it in the service of spiritual ends. His vocation was not annulled by the fall, but he was still responsible to work and rule for God in the lower world. That this conviction survived the fall is evident from those outlines of the history of the race from Eden to Sinai that reflect fallen man's struggles to dominate the earth. While the commandment enjoins the sabbath rest, its appeal to the creation ordinance brings into view at once the original appointment to labor and rest: "Remember the sabbath day, to keep it holy. Six days shalt thou labor, and do all thy work; but the seventh day is a sabbath unto Jehovah thy God; in it thou shalt not do any work . . . for in six days Jehovah made heaven and earth, the sea, and all that in them is, and rested the seventh day: wherefore Jehovah blessed the sabbath day, and hallowed it" (Ex. 20:8-11). The primeval sanctification and blessing of the seventh day at the completion of the creation reappears as the ultimate sanction for the sequence of labor and rest in the life of man who bears the Divine Worker's image.[5] The relative silence of the patriarchal record about the early forms of religious worship is quite compatible with the exercise by the faithful of special devotion to God on this particularly hallowed day. At the same time, enlarged opportunity for spontaneous worship could constitute an added embarrassment for unregenerate man. The spiritual impulses that survived the fall and the memory of the sabbath ordinances supplied the background of the early institution of animal sacrifice as a divinely approved mode of access filled with spiritual and ethical lessons.

The foundations of family life come to the fore with the fifth commandment, honor for parents. It is an ordinance that, from the very nature of the creation happenings, one would not expect to be explicitly formulated among the external commands addressed to Adam, although it may be regarded as implicit in the light that the creation narrative sheds on domestic life. Explicitly, the narrative anticipates more directly the seventh commandment against adultery. The creation of a single male and from his side a female companion as his helpmeet, is to provide a permanent spiritual and moral basis for monogamous marriage. As in origin, so in life, the man and his wife are to coalesce into the unity of one being. "Therefore shall a man leave his father and his mother, and shall cleave unto his wife, and they shall be one flesh" (Gen. 2:24). But in an incidental manner, the passage, by its reference to father and mother, renders an implicit

[5]The fact that Deuteronomy 24:17f. stresses God's redemptive deliverance of Israel from bondage, and does not adduce the Divine procedure in creation, in enforcing the commandment of rest, does not exclude this larger lesson from the creation history. It reflects rather the existence of additional sanctions for obedience.

support also to the view that honor for parents was a duty enjoined by creation from the beginning of family life. The suggestion that an intimacy of attachment and mutual self-interest exist between man and his father and mother is clearly the underside of the passage. The fifth commandment, as the New Testament emphasizes in reiterating it (Eph. 6:2), is the first to which a specific promise is attached. Obedience to it would bring the younger generation prolonged well-being in the land which the God of covenant had given them. Hence the Decalogue underwrites the soundness of the thesis of social ethics that a well-ordered nation has its roots in a well-ordered home. Reverent obedience to responsibly constituted authority is part of that home structure.

To return for a moment to the seventh word, the one against adultery, we have the remarkable witness of Jesus Christ that this prohibition was implicit from the very first in the concept of monogamous marriage. His stern words against adultery and divorce appeal to the Divine purpose in marriage on the basis of creation. "So then they are no more twain, but one flesh. What therefore God hath joined together, let no man put asunder" (Mk. 10:8f.). "Moses for your hardness of heart suffered you to put away your wives: but from the beginning it hath not been so" (Mt. 19:8). The enduring significance of marriage was not formally set forth in the creation narrative by specific Divine prescription, yet it is nonetheless clearly the original purpose of God for human life. Even the so-called "Mosaic tolerance" of divorce, which occurs not in the Decalogue but in the judicial statutes and directions of the law, is brought under scrutiny from the standpoint of creation. Murray has argued with considerable strength the position already charted by some of the older divines that the Mosaic reference (Dt. 24:1ff.) is intended to restrict abuses accompanying divorce, not to justify divorce in such cases, and that the comment of Jesus agrees with such an interpretation.[6] At any rate, the creation account and the Decalogue, and alongside them, the teaching of Jesus, enforce monogamous marriage as the Divine intention for man.

The sixth word, the one against murder, may also be shown to have a basis in the earlier constitution of the moral order. The evil of murder is already implied in the fact that man uniquely bears the Divine image. The law of blood for blood, introduced immediately after the flood (Gen. 9:6), guarded the sacredness of human life even in the fallen state. How much more intolerable must the sin of murder have appeared before the fall!

The sixth commandment, as does the whole law, gains its fuller meaning only when the law is perfectly summarized by the law of love. On this ground Calvin refused to limit the force of the sixth commandment to an injunction merely to abstain from injury to others, or from the desire to inflict such harm. Implicit in the command, he asserted,

[6]John Murray, *Divorce* (Philadelphia: The Committee on Christian Education, Orthodox Presbyterian Church, 1953), pp. 3ff.

is the requirement to assist our neighbor by every means within our ability. Hence the law enjoins not alone the protection of the lives of others, but it commands the protection of the wife or daughter's chastity and honor, and of the neighbor's property and character. Here it becomes increasingly plain that the law is a law of love to neighbor. That the Decalogue itself has in view the interior life of motive and thought, and not merely external conduct, is brought to the fore especially by the last commandment, the one against coveting. Even in this word we may find another connection with the creation narrative. The term used in the Decalogue is *chamad*. This very form occurs in Genesis 3:6 in connection with the fall: "The woman saw that the tree was . . . *to be desired* to make one wise and she took of its fruit and ate, and gave to her husband by her, and he did eat." The coveting of the illicit, of the divinely prohibited, leads at the very dawn of human history to the distrust of God's commandment and then to a disregard of it. Hence the central importance of all desire and motive, of a genuine love that stands sentinel against lust after the illicit, appears as the summarizing emphasis of the Decalogue.

The commandments, therefore, stipulate the precise course of action for human life involved in the great law of love. In the Old Testament dispensation, many statutory directions are added for the practical life. There are also the rites and ceremonies belonging to the Levitical code of worship. While not sharing the permanence of the moral law, these nonetheless were binding upon the consciences of those who placed themselves in the service of the Living God in the theocratic nation. These statutes were not automatically to be considered a part of civil government generally. The ceremonial law had, likewise, only a dispensation-long validity. Any broad treatment of biblical ethics must give full consideration to these enactments peculiar to the dispensation of promise. They serve to enforce the larger principles of truth and duty, and to maintain a virile anticipation of the Messiah to come.

It is not necessary here, however, to do more than sketch the broadest outlines of the fuller requirements in the Old Testament era. Statutes or judgments, called the *mishpatim* (Ex. 21:1), illustrating the commands in their bearing upon particular untoward circumstances, have an enduring worth since they set forth basic lines of application. The law of retribution — "life for life, eye for eye, tooth for tooth" (Ex. 21:23ff.) — is easily misunderstood; it fixed *limits* of punishment in a barbarous era, and the principle underlies every worthy criminal code. The ceremonial law governing the ritual of the Levitical system takes up a large part of the Law. The tabernacle itself has the ark of the covenant as its center of interest. The ark is the repository of the Decalogue where Jehovah distinctively manifests his glory (Ex. 25:21f.). The ceremonial law therefore maintains the centrality of the revelation of truth and duty afforded by the moral law. It should be no surprise, therefore, that the teaching in the Levitical code presupposes and enforces the Decalogue in its emphasis that access to God exists only for the righteous, and that the unrighteous are excluded. The Levitical institutions at the same time stressed that in view of the universal sinfulness of man all access was on the basis of mediation alone, and that the great glory of Israel was the Divine promise to her of a Mediator.

One need only read the rest of the Old Testament to note that the Decalogue is supplemented by comprehensive ethical principles that are worked into the warp and woof of a revelation at once progressive and propadeutic, that is, adopted to the moral growth of a reclaimed people. Yet W. Robertson Smith one-sidedly reflected a critical bias, as is now widely admitted, when he pronounced the opinion that the acknowledged laws of social order are largely identical in all parts of the world, and that the Hebrew religion holds no fundamental superiority in this sphere. Yet Smith may be taken as a more competent guide when he says that the Hebrew religion uniquely ascribes absolute sovereignty and absolute righteousness to God, displaying a wholly consistent character and ethical standard in his rule over Israel. "The heathen gods are guardians of law, but they are something else at the same time; they are not wholly intent on righteousness, and righteousness is not the only path to their favor, which sometimes depends on accidental partialities, or may be conciliated by acts of worship that have nothing to do with morality."[7] Israel knew from the first days of the nation, in fact, that the heathen religions held wrong conceptions of the Godhead. The Hebrew system had, in John Paterson's words, a foundation "wholly ethical."[8] The prophets dared to find in a righteous nation, and not simply in isolated lives, the supreme reflection of the righteousness of God and of his government of the world.

The commandments of the Law are fundamental to Old Testament ethics. Alongside them stand the moral principles set forth in the Psalms, Proverbs and prophets. The emphasis of the Psalmist often falls on the permanent ethical principles that structure the whole of history and life. This submergence of the specific in the ethical universal causes no little perplexity for those scholars who seek to date these writings by internal considerations alone.

The prophetic ministry was a dual ministry. Primarily it was forth-telling God's word so as to shape the course of history by moral decision, and secondarily it was foretelling the Messiah who was to come. The prophets spoke God's will afresh to each generation, and hence they were aware of the temper and feelings of their times. They dared to find in the religious nation, and not simply in isolated individual lives, a reflection of the righteousness of God and of his government of the world. They shaped the ideals of the nation, and mourned over her

[7]W. Robertson Smith, *The Prophets of Israel and Their Place in History* (new ed., London: Adam & Charles Black, 1895), pp. 72ff.

[8]John Paterson, *The Goodly Fellowship of the Prophets* (New York: Scribner, 1948), p. 198.

apathy in attaining them. They were intensely patriotic, but their patriotism was based on the claims of religion and morality. They cried out against mere formal religion or ethical behavior. They guarded worthy temporal interests best by stressing the eternal ones.

The moral truths uttered by the prophets stretched like threads from the Decalogue and the larger Mosaic legislation through the loom of their times, and produced, under the impulse of the God of the prophets, the fabric of moral conviction that continued to distinguish Israel at her best from all the nations of the world. It has been rightly noted that the first of the eighth century prophets, Amos, "does not identify morality with religion but he will not accept a religion that excludes morality."[9] Thus he prefigures Christ's protest against a ritual that had supplanted the moral.

The connection between moral rectitude and national survival is nowhere voiced with greater power than by Isaiah, declaring that "if only the rulers in Jerusalem would listen to and obey the God of their fathers, their beautiful city, at least throughout the Assyrian period, would remain inviolate as a divine signet in the Holy Land."[10] And when the nation went into captivity in her disobedience, a prophet was still at her side. The glory of Israel's future in the splendor of the millennial age when righteousness would be the very heartbeat of men was glowingly sketched by Ezekiel.

As part of their forthtelling ministry, the prophets applied the changeless Word of God to specific moral problems of their own time. In many ways they were primarily social moralists, for they spoke to the theocratic nation as a whole and spoke of oppressing social evils. Yet they were also very practical personal moralists. They knew the nation could change nothing unless individual members of the nation changed inside themselves. So the prophets called upon individuals to trust God, repent from sin, and serve the Lord by obeying the revered Torah. They took a general ethical principle from the Torah and gave it flesh and bones as they pointed out the specific application of the principle to concrete moral situations in their own society.

Thus the prophets stood between Moses and the greater than Moses, enforcing the validity of the older revelation, supplementing it, applying it, and clarifying the expectation of the coming Redeemer. They contribute, both as forthtellers and foretellers, to the real inner unity of the two testaments. The continuity of the Mosaic, prophetic, and New Testament ethic shines lucidly through Jesus' constant appeal, to "the law and the prophets," and through his tendency to employ the term "the law" when referring to the Old Testament as a whole. The New Testament identifies the prophets dramatically with the tradition of redemptive revelation: they were men "of whom the world was not worthy" (Heb. 11:38).

[9] *Ibid.*, p. 25.

[10] John Adams, *The Hebrew Prophets and Their Message for Today* (Edinburgh: T. & T. Clark, 1928), p. 14.

12

THE BIBLICAL PARTICULARIZATION OF THE WILL OF GOD: THE SERMON ON THE MOUNT

WITHOUT QUESTION, the best known fact about Jesus Christ is that he gave the Sermon on the Mount. People may not have the vaguest notion of what the Sermon on the Mount is all about, but they invariably connect "Jesus Christ" with "The Sermon on the Mount" and add what a "good thing" they think it is. Actually it is his fullest treatment of morality. For those who have read it and felt its impact, it is his most debated utterance. It has exercised enormous influence both inside and outside organized Christianity because of the revolutionary character of the ethics it contains. But how its moral content is to be integrated with the whole of biblical theology and ethics, on the one hand, and correlated with contemporary life, on the other, is a central problem.

The famous archbishop of York, Dr. Magee, once remarked that "a Christian State carrying out in all its relations literally the precepts of the Sermon on the Mount could not exist for a week," to which a Gifford lecturer appended the comment that "as much could be said with equal truth of a Christian individual."[1] By others the Sermon has been proclaimed the only divinely-forged pattern of national and individual survival.

C. W. Votaw, in his classic article on the Sermon in the extra volume of Hastings' *Dictionary of the Bible,* says: "The words of Jesus in this Sermon present an ideal of human life, founded upon religious truth and ethical principles, which has been and is intuitively recognized as the highest standard of life yet conceived, or even as the ultimate standard to which mankind can and must attain. . . . The kind of life which He here describes has been the guiding star of civilization."

At least seven competitive appraisals have been made of this manifesto of morality. Namely: (1) humanistic; (2) liberal; (3) dispensational; (4) interim-ethic; (5) existential; (6) Anabaptist-Mennonite; and (7) Reformed. The immense influence which each of these theories has had, especially in the present century, makes it necessary to sketch out and evaluate their central positions.

Hans Windisch, in *The Meaning of the Sermon on the Mount,* wisely instructs us to ask three questions of every interpretation of the

[1]Herbert H. Henson, *Christian Morality,* p. 253.

Sermon on the Mount in order to bring to the fore its fundamental intention: Does it hold that literal fulfillment of the Sermon is intended? Does it hold that such fulfillment is possible to man? Does it hold that the Sermon is relevant to the contemporary moral situation?

(1) Strictly speaking, there is no "humanistic interpretation" of the Sermon on the Mount. Rather, there is a "humanistic repudiation" of the Sermon which rises by way of reflex out of a naturalistic view of life. Denying the reality of the supernatural and repudiating changeless and universally valid norms of morality and truth, Humanism, as the devout expression of Naturalism, frequently sought to exist within the fold of the Christian church. In this environment, it was forced to interact with the moral teachings of Jesus.

Humanism endeavors to sever the Sermon from any connection with the supernatural, from the sinfulness of man, and from many of its inner demands. It argues in self-convinced fashion that modern man has better ideas about "God" and "being" than did medieval man. The philosophy of religious development and cultural evolution means that Jesus, who stands behind (and hence below) us, may and must be by-passed. We may cull from his teachings insights of ethical worth, but must recognize as well that he was a creature of his times. Humanistic moralists either dismiss the Sermon on the Mount as the passé ethical prejudice of a past age which, in common with all early traditions, must be superseded, or they attack it as inadequate for the complexities of contemporary life.

The humanistic formula asserts, therefore, that a literal fulfillment of the Sermon was intended by Jesus; that it is hypothetically possible of fulfillment today; but that it is an unrealistic code, irrelevant to the complexities of the present-day ethical crisis.

Some variations of humanistic thought do not give so harsh an appraisal. But in the long run the position, as worked out by its more consistent expositors, reduces to this ground. Unquestionably, Jesus is frequently adulated in a most superlative manner. The John Herman Randalls declare that "Jesus was beyond question a truly great moral genius," perhaps the greatest ethical teacher in our tradition.[2] And humanist writers, in the spirit of Charles Francis Potter, sometimes latch onto the ethics of Jesus whenever a verbal similarity of objectives is found: "Jesus raised his voice again and again on behalf of broad Humanist ideals such as the spread of altruism, the brotherhood of man, and peace on earth. . . . Humanism, then, holds that certain of the teachings of Jesus possess an ethical import that will always be pertinent for the human race, and that the Jesus portrayed by the gospels represents one of the supreme personalities of all history, a fighter against the hidebound Philistines and Pharisees of his day and

[2]Randall and Randall, *Religion in the Modern World* (New York: Frederick A. Stokes Co., 1929), pp. 213, 216.

a radiant martyr . . ."[3] What humanists find of value in the Sermon is its recognition of certain ideals which they themselves consider to be primary, especially the love and service of man (Mt. 5:43ff., 7:1ff.) and peace (5:9).

Nevertheless, the dogma of evolutionary Naturalism prevails as solidly in the ethics of the Randalls and of Potter as with humanists who begrudge every good word about Jesus and the Sermon. Supernaturalism is scathingly rejected, and all confident basis surrendered — so it would seem — for holding that any ethical principles "will always be pertinent," whether those of Jesus or of his would-be modern supplanters. "The danger of looking to Jesus as the final moral authority," the Randalls write, "lies not in what men find in his teachings, but in what they do not find. They imagine those teachings are sufficient in themselves. . . . The Jesus whom modern research has placed in his social environment . . . is not able to offer completely adequate moral guidance for today."[4] The mood of such a passage may be less violent, but its final verdict concurs with that of Harry Elmer Barnes that "we can never have an intelligent and satisfactory modernized religion until the Jesus stereotype is forever laid at rest."[5] What is implicit in his humanist associates, Barnes formulates with explicit precision: "Once we make a candid examination of the actual teachings of Jesus, in so far as we know of them, it must be admitted that they are not only archaic, but even destructive of any advanced civilization. . . . If the teachings of Jesus as they exist were applied to contemporary society, nothing less than anarchy and the destruction of the civilized order would inevitably follow."[6]

Humanist ethics denies the liberal Protestant claim that personal religious and ethical integration is most effectively achieved through attachment to the example of Jesus and participation in the historical movement he initiated.[7] It goes on to repudiate his ethics as inadequate to the present social situation and, if imposed upon it, dangerous and harmful. "Could a simple carpenter in Galilee two thousand years ago have uttered the final word on human relationships? Granted his ethical insight, is there nothing more to be learned? . . . Can we regulate marriage today, with all its complex problems, by insisting that man shall not put asunder what God hath joined together?"[8] "The moral precepts of Jesus show little concern with what have become the necessary conditions of human existence today. The disinterested investigations of the scientist, the thinking of the philosopher, the art of the painter, the sculptor, the writer, the dramatist, the poet, the

[3]Charles Francis Potter, *Humanism* (New York: Simon and Schuster, 1930), p. 14.

[4]Randall and Randall, *op. cit.*, pp. 215f.

[5]Harry Elmer Barnes, *The Twilight of Christianity* (New York: Vanguard Press, 1929), p. 388.

[6]*Ibid.*, p. 419.

[7]Edwin A. Burtt, *Types of Religious Philosophy*, p. 356.

[8]Randall and Randall, *op. cit.*, p. 82.

musician, the practice of one's vocation, the perpetuation and education of the race through family life, the devotion of marriage, political and economic reorganization, international cooperation, — to all these vital concerns of today the words and practices of Jesus are either irrelevant, or profoundly out of harmony with the convictions of modern men. There is not one of these forms of our life in which Jesus can be imitated, or his words obeyed literally, without the downfall of the whole structure of modern civilization."[9]

Elsewhere the controlling ideas of naturalistic ethics have been stated and criticized. If supernatural being and revelation are arbitrarily excluded, if all truth is tentative and all moral judgment relative, it would be impossible for Jesus — or anybody else — to have uttered the last word on anything. But no naturalist has ever convincingly exhibited the whole of reality to be, fundamentally, the non-mental whirl to which he would reduce it, and every attempt to do so raises more difficulties than. it relieves. When the humanist makes it a cardinal point of objection to Jesus' teachings that they are everywhere permeated by his belief in the supernatural, the objection presupposes what the naturalist has failed to demonstrate. To the ancient naturalistic bias, contemporary Humanism adds the appeal to evolutionary progress, implying that new and more relevant values are in process of emergence. But distinguished modern partisans of evolutionary theory insist that biological evolution need not imply the relativistic view that truth and morality are subjective and changing. And biblical theism makes it clear that evolution is not the ultimate category in either biology or ethics, but rather it is Jesus Christ, as Creator and Redeemer. The definition of the true and the good does not depend upon the passage of time, else they must remain undefined until the whole process has run its course, in which case they will no longer be serviceable to mankind. Doubtless Jesus spoke to his times and in the idiom of his day. But with the same voice he spoke to all ages, for he uttered the idiom of eternity. Never was the highest moral achievement of a morally-conscious generation brought under such severe scrutiny and judgment as was the generation to which Jesus spoke. Yet it was not to his generation alone, but to all generations, that Jesus addressed his ethical deliverances. He dealt with universal human nature in its essential state and in its predicament conditioned by sin, and for that reason his moral teaching is timeless. It will be found that Jesus brought all the personal relationships of life into focus by seeing motive and conduct with a clear eye. When men fulfill the stringent requirements of the Sermon in their personal relations, it will be time enough for them to supplement its demands on the premise that they are not sufficiently exacting to contribute to cultural and social stability. An ethics predicated on changeless norms of truth and morality would seem to guarantee stability more than a view which insists upon constant revision.

[9]*Ibid.*, p. 219.

And as Marshall aptly phrases it, "in Jesus of Nazareth ethics reaches its climax and crown, so that any higher ethical ideal cannot . . . be conceived by the mind of man."[10]

It is untrue that modern man has outgrown the Sermon on the Mount. The claim that it is irrelevant to the contemporary cultural crisis, and that its fulfillment, even if possible, would result in absurdity, reflects the arbitrary temper of humanistic ethics, rather than the actualities of the moral situation. Modern man may evade the requirements of the Sermon, but it remains to condemn him as a transgressor.

(2) The liberal view regards the Sermon on the Mount as setting forth those moral imperatives upon whose fulfillment salvation depends. In place of the "good news" of redemption by Divine atonement and rescue, it propounds the "brave news" of salvation by human works. In the spirit of liberals who identify the ethics of the Sermon with "the gospel in a nutshell," H. S. Brewster titled his volume on the Sermon *The Simple Gospel.* He asserts that here Jesus "offers a sane, wise plan of civilization building."[11] Adolf Harnack thinks the Sermon suspends man's salvation wholly upon his personal fulfillment of these ethical requirements: "He [Jesus] . . . goes . . . through the several departments of human relationships and human failings so as to bring the disposition and intention to light in each case, to judge man's works by them, and on them to hang heaven and hell."[12]

Whether regarded as an ethics of personal or of cultural salvation, the Sermon was widely championed as the way out of man's moral slough. In this regard, the modern view does not depart significantly from the ethics of a first-century spiritualistic Judaism devoid of the expectation of a messianic Redeemer. In the twentieth century this same general pattern was hailed as a Christian program for cultural survival, exclusive of personal regeneration and redemption by grace, under the formula of the "social gospel." The liberal view holds that literal fulfillment of the Sermon was intended by Jesus, that such fulfillment is possible to human beings in their present condition, and that the Sermon remains a practical ethical program for the ideal development of mankind.

A slight variation of the liberal view is the view of the Sermon as an exposition of those practical regulations by the observance of which an individual may now obtain personal righteousness, and hence eschatological salvation. Such a view is held by Hans Windisch. He tells us that the Sermon is the rule of life for repentant individuals who have entered God's kingdom through repentance and individual obedience. "The message of salvation in the Sermon . . . is based wholly upon

[10]L. H. Marshall, *The Challenge of New Testament Ethics,* p. 215.

[11]H. S. Brewster, *The Simple Gospel,* p. 194.

[12]Adolf Harnack, *What Is Christianity?* (New York: G. P. Putnam, 1901), p. 72.

the experience of salvation under the old covenant,"[13] which Windisch describes as fellowship with God resting on the certainty of the devout Israelite that his sins are forgiven, and hence that he is not cut off from God. "The Sermon is a message for those already converted, for the children of God within the covenant of Israel or the Christian community."[14] Jesus' radical confidence that the demands of the Sermon may be realized by devout believers is to be explained by his own consciousness.[15] "The religion of the Sermon . . . like . . . Judaism, is predominantly a religion of 'works' and of eschatological salvation. It is not to any marked extent a religion for sinners."[16] The Sermon assertedly carries forward what Windisch supposes to be the Old Testament emphasis — that all salvation issues from obedience.[17] "The doctrine of salvation in the Sermon on the Mount stands in sharpest contradiction to that of Paul . . . in Romans, chapters three to eight. There is a gulf here between Jesus and Paul that no art of theological exegesis can bridge."[18] "The way to be saved is to do and to keep the commandments of Christ . . . is to trust him as the divinely commissioned prophet and world judge."[19] Hence the "gospel" in the Sermon is almost as pre-Pauline and pre-Christian, we are told, as that of "deutero-Isaiah" and the Psalmist.

The social gospel formulation of the Sermon on the Mount, while emphasizing cultural social salvation rather than individual eschatological salvation, shares with the approach just sketched an indifference to the place of imputed righteousness in the experience of the converted. The advocates of the social gospel emptied the crucifixion of all meaning beyond heroic martyrdom and the magnetism of moral devotion.

The social gospel was built upon the foundation of modern idealistic and evolutionary assumptions about mankind and history. So it is no surprise to find the Sermon interpreted so as to present a cultural ethic by conformity to which an ideal state of human social relations may be achieved. By this approach the uniqueness of the New Testament *Kerygma* is sacrificed to the philosophy of developmentalism. The ethical ideals of the Sermon are regarded as the fulfillment of man's longings, rather than as clarifying his desperate need of Divine rescue. "Give the tendencies everywhere discoverable another decade of development," wrote Shailer Mathews a few years before the first World War, "and its truth will be less open to question."[20] He regarded the Sermon as a summary of Christ's Gospel: it "contains the ideals which the

[13]Hans Windisch, *The Meaning of the Sermon on the Mount,* trans. from German by S. MacLean Gilmour (Philadelphia: Westminster, 1951), p. 177.
[14]*Ibid.*, p. 111.
[15]*Ibid.*, p. 103.
[16]*Ibid.*, p. 168.
[17]*Ibid.*, p. 101.
[18]*Ibid.*, p. 107.
[19]*Ibid.*, pp. 169ff.
[20]Shailer Mathews, *The Gospel and Modern Man* (New York: Macmillan, 1910), p. 262.

gospel presupposes as the final ideals of the spiritual life it undertakes to beget."[21] The Sermon does not presuppose the supernatural redemption of man in sin, nor is it to be confined only to neighbor relations. It is an ethic for all men, Christian or non-Christian, in world relations. By thinkers who move somewhat within the orbit of Christian theology, such as E. Stanley Jones,[22] the social gospel as a cultural ethic is coupled with an emphasis on the need for spiritual rebirth on the part of men (although Jones' relatively optimistic view of human nature and deliverance from sin nonetheless crowds out the full doctrine of redemption).

The social gospel appeals to the Sermon at the expense of the remainder of the New Testament and its supernaturalistic theology; the Golden Rule alone became its sufficient guide for life and for the solution of all problems of the social order. But J. Gresham Machen was quick to point out that for historic Christianity the Golden Rule was not addressed universally, but only to Jesus' disciples in whom a great change had been wrought, and whose ethical judgments therefore were hardly reducible to those of the world at large.[23] Actually, the social gospel approach accepted certain of the Sermon's moral principles not primarily because they belonged to the teachings of Jesus, but because they were in agreement with contemporary social ideals. Jesus was not concerned primarily to perpetuate the cultural enterprise in its character of deliberate hostility to the redemption which he himself came to offer mankind. His concern, in the Sermon as elsewhere in his discourses, was for the kingdom of God, not the provision of a cultural ethic. The Sermon itself implies the loftiest possible view of Jesus as "a new teacher who claims a personal right to set his interpretation over against the prevalent tradition,"[24] as the authoritative interpreter of the supernaturally-communicated Decalogue, and as the judge of all the race. It is implicit in the Sermon that Jesus views himself to be far more than even the most revered of the prophets. Windisch, who finds no warrant for a Chalcedonian Christology here (the historic church has never proposed to find that warrant here *alone*), admits "an element of tension between a proclamation that has no place for a mediator and a self-consciousness that tends to include mediation as a function."[25] Jesus related the content of the Sermon not only to his own authority, but to faith in his own person. As Edersheim remarked of the Sermon, "it is the voice of God which speaks to us."[26] And yet, to regard the

[21]*Ibid.*, p. 256.

[22]Cf. E. Stanley Jones, *Is the Kingdom of God Realism?* (New York: Abingdon-Cokesbury, 1940).

[23]J. Gresham Machen, *Christianity and Liberalism* (Grand Rapids: Eerdmans, reprint, 1946), pp. 37ff.

[24]T. B. Strong, *Christian Ethics,* pp. 20ff.

[25]Windisch, *op. cit.*, pp. 210.

[26]Alfred Edersheim, *The Life and Times of Jesus the Messiah* (Grand Rapids: Eerdmans, reprint, 1953), I, 525.

Sermon in this larger sense as the sum of the Christian religion, or of Christian ethics, would be to commit a grievous error.

If the Sermon provides the basis of salvation, personal or cultural, historical or eschatological, on the ground of works and apart from a divinely-provided atonement, then all to whom it is addressed are doomed. Rudolf Bultmann has here asked the leading question, even if on the way to a false solution: "Will Windisch contend that he fulfills the requirements of the Sermon? Or does he assume that another man does so? Then why not?"[27] The Sermon can have no function but to condemn if it looks for fulfillment in the lives of men, and knows nothing of redemption. J. Gresham Machen incisively saw that this ethical requirement when taken simply as a salvation-program offered the sinner could lead only to desperation and hopelessness. "The new law of the Sermon on the Mount can only produce despair. Strange indeed is the complacency with which modern man can say that the Golden Rule and the high ethical principles of Jesus are all they need. In reality, if the requirements for entrance into the Kingdom of God are what Jesus declares them to be, we are all undone; we have not even attained to the external righteousness of the scribes and Pharisees, and how shall we attain to that righteousness of heart which Jesus demands? . . . Even Moses was too high for us, but before this higher law of Jesus who shall stand without being condemned? The Sermon on the Mount, like all the rest of the New Testament, really leads a man straight to the foot of the Cross."[28]

That the holy requirements of the Sermon must be fulfilled if there be salvation, that the Sermon brings out ethical principles which have a claim upon every human life,[29] that a world or culture in which personal relations are shaped by these principles would be remarkably healthy and virile — these are the solid elements which may be culled from this approach. But even these insights were misshaped and misdirected by the liberal repudiation of the significance of Jesus Christ as Redeemer, of the necessity of supernatural redemption and regeneration. An ethic intended for re-created disciples was thereby distorted into the gospel-less idealism for pagans. The ethics of the Sermon became merely a humanist-socialist attempt to change the cultural pattern. Yet the Sermon itself nowhere implies an optimistic development of human nature. Rather, it stands in universal judgment upon it. The Lord's Prayer, by the petition "thy kingdom come" (6:10), connects the Kingdom of God not with the works of unregenerate men, but with supernatural grace.

[27]Rudolf Bultmann, *Glauben und Verstehen* (Tubingen: Mohr, 1933), p. 199.
[28]J. Gresham Machen, *Christianity and Liberalism*, p. 39.
[29]That the Sermon expects literal fulfilment is clear from the closing parable of the wise and foolish builders (Mt. 7:24), from the concreteness of the Sermon as a whole, from the fact that ceremonial conformity is designated as righteousness (5:20) but of an inadequate kind, from the practical teaching as that on divorce (5:31f.).

In elaborating upon the inadequacy and essential falseness of the liberal "social gospel," the writer does not disclaim concern for social justice nor does he disown personal responsibility in matters of social ill. Christianity stands in full-bodied and extremely relevant judgment upon the twentieth-century world. But such considerations concern more the realm of social ethics than of personal ethics. Suffice it to say, that the regenerated believer who is personally oriented to God and to ethics is in the best vantage-point for a valid Christian critique of society.

(3) The dispensational view of the Sermon denies to it any relevance to the present age of history and identifies it rather as the code of ethics that will prevail in the millennial kingdom. Its significance for the present is at best only secondary. Fulfillment of the Sermon is unintended and, presumably, impossible; its ethical ideals are irrelevant to the present era.

The dispensational system of interpretation arose in England among the Plymouth Brethren, and was taught with widening influence by J. N. Darby (1800-1882) and William Kelley (1821-1906). In America it received the support of James M. Gray, C. I. Scofield, Arno C. Gaebelein, L. S. Chafer, and many others. The view rigidly distinguishes the dispensation of law (Sinai to Calvary) from the dispensation of grace (Calvary to the second advent) both chronologically and in principle and spirit. The principles of the two dispensations are held to be diametrically opposed, and the subsequent dispensation of a thousand-year kingdom-rule is assertedly predicated on law. Christ's teachings are assumed to be divided in their application, some applying to the legal kingdom age and some to the present church age of grace.

Every exponent of dispensationalism develops fully the implications of this view for the Sermon on the Mount. The Sermon is held to be legal in character. The King "sets forth the nature of the proposed Kingdom and the laws by which He will govern the earth when He re-establishes and occupies the throne of David."[30] "As a rule of life, it is addressed to the Jew before the cross and to the Jew in the coming Kingdom, and is therefore not now in effect. . . . The Sermon . . . both by its setting in the context and by its doctrinal character . . . belongs for its primary application to the future kingdom age."[31] "The new rule of life for this age then is the command of Jesus 'that ye love one another as I have loved you.' Nothing is said concerning the Sermon on the Mount as the rule of life whatsoever."[32] "The Sermon on the Mount is the proclamation of the King concerning the Kingdom. . . . It is the millennial earth and the Kingdom to come, in

[30]William L. Pettingill, *The Gospel of the Kingdom* (Findlay, Ohio: Fundamental Truth Publishers, n.d.), p. 58.

[31]L. S. Chafer, *Systematic Theology* (Wheaton, Ill.: Van Kampen), V, 97ff.

[32]*Ibid.*, p. 69.

which Jerusalem will be the city of a great King."[33] "Christian position is not revealed in the Sermon on the Mount. The Sermon is not given as the standard of Christian experience and work."[34] "We are not to make the mistake of trying to force the Sermon on the Mount to a literal fulfillment today. It will be fulfilled literally but not until the age in which we live has come to its close and the Lord Jesus shall be dealing with His people Israel."[35]

A tendency of many dispensational writers is to acknowledge a secondary application of some phases of the Sermon to Christian life in the present age on the theory that the church and the kingdom-to-come have some elements in common.[36] But the Christian is held to be free from the Sermon as such "because the day of . . . application has not yet come to the earth."[37] As part of Scripture it is profitable, and contains many principles eternally operative. Some dispensationalists, who do not develop this matter of a limited contemporary relevance, nevertheless do not assert that it cannot apply. Yet in its primary and literal significance the Sermon is directed to the millennial kingdom as its governing code of laws, and not to Christian conduct in this life.

The dispensationalists argue that the beatitudes seem to be a pattern of works necessary to attain the Kingdom (5:1-12), whereas the believer has already attained access by grace, and his virtues are a reflex of the regenerate life; that mercy is conditioned therein upon the recipient's mercifulness, whereas the believer possesses unmerited mercy; that the child of the Kingdom is to manifest good works (5:13-16), while the Christian is to manifest Christ; that Christ intensifies rather than relieves the Law (5:17-48), stressing what must be done meritoriously "that ye may be the children of your Father which is in heaven" (5:45); that even the Lord's Prayer is not uttered in the name of Christ, and conditions forgiveness upon our forgiving others (6:1-18); that the instruction is generally drastically legal and based on merit; that the Golden Rule does not rise above the level of self-interest; and that the references to hell and hell fire do not apply within a context of grace, but only of law.

The dispensational interpretation turns on several controlling ideas: (1) That the Sermon is solely law, and contains nothing of the Gospel. Since the element of grace is lacking, and its outlook is strictly that of law, it has a view to that future period when grace has run its course. The Christian is not under law, but under grace, hence the Sermon does

[33]Arno C. Gaebelein, *The Gospel of Matthew* (New York: Our Hope Publications, 1910), p. 110.

[34]Gaebelein, *The Annotated Bible,* "The Gospels and the Book of Acts" (New York: Our Hope Publications, 1913), p. 21.

[35]Donald G. Barnhouse, *His Own Received Him Not, But* . . . (New York: Revell, 1933), p. 40.

[36]Cf. Gaebelein, *op. cit.,* p. 21; Pettingill, *op. cit.,* p. 59; F. W. Grant, *The Numerical Bible* (New York: Loizeaux Brothers, n.d.), p. 70. H. A. Ironside, who granted the Sermon a greater application to the Christian life than many others, finally repudiated the dispensational interpretation of the discourse.

[37]Barnhouse, *op. cit.,* p. 38.

not apply. (2) That the Kingdom of heaven and the Kingdom of God are not equivalent. The Kingdom of God is universal, including all moral intelligences subject to the will of God in all ages, it is said, while the Kingdom of heaven is mediatorial, messianic and Davidic, and has as its object the earthly establishment of the Kingdom. (3) That the Sermon is intended for an age of righteousness in which Christ rules, not the present age ruled by the power of Satan.

With regard to the first contention — that the Sermon represents a standpoint other than that of the redemptive Gospel, and that it is therefore not intended for the Christian — it is necessary to make some observations of an introductory nature. The complex question of the Christian's relationship to law is discussed at some length in another chapter. If the risky antinomian view is held that because the believer is saved by grace, he is free of all responsibility to law, then any proclamation of moral laws must of necessity be legalistic and anti-grace. But such a view of the Christian's relationship to law does not fit the teachings of Scripture and is out of accord with the historic Christian consciousness. It is one thing to say — as indeed every Christian must — that the law as an unpaid debt-bill has been paid up in full by the mediatorial work of Christ; it is another thing to say — what Christian ethics in its best expression has deplored — that the biblically revealed moral law no longer has an instructive value for the believer.

If the presence of exhortations to fulfill the moral law are to be taken as a sign that the standpoint of grace is forsaken, the New Testament is thrown into hopeless confusion. Side by side in the Pauline literature one finds the perspective of grace and the declaration of its moral nature (cf. Acts 14:22, Rom. 8:13, 13:9, Gal. 6:9ff.). It is incredible, moreover, that the requirements of the Sermon should so generously correspond with the ethical teaching of the epistles and yet be held to be intended for another age. One can find in the epistles passages which in fact echo specific teachings of the Sermon (Rom. 12:14, 1 Jn. 3:15). Indeed, there is *no principle* in the Sermon which the believer dare not in good conscience seek to uphold. Is anger now justifiable? Is the lustful glance? Is hatred for enemies? Is revenge? Whatever is enjoined by the Sermon accords perfectly with the New Testament requirements for everyday Christian morality.

But if the Sermon can be applicable to the Christian because of its enunciation of moral laws, the absence of the Gospel-motif from it and its essential incompatibility with that motif would be an insuperable objection. The discussion is best broken down into two issues: whether salvation can be regarded as complete without a satisfaction of the principles taught in the Sermon, and whether the Sermon does in fact reflect the standpoint of the Gospel.

If there is one theme which runs the gamut of God's dealings with man, it is his moral earnestness. The man in sin is cut off from God, and if there be redemption, there must be salvation ethics. What God has in view in salvation is man's deliverance not merely from the penalty of sin, but from sin as an element in man's life. Every instance of Divine activity in human relations enforces the validity of the moral law. The fall of man and the lapse of the race into sin is a direct consequence of man's disregarding the divinely-pronounced directives for conscience. Salvation can involve nothing less than restoration to a serious regard for the moral principles which the Creator addresses to his creatures. More than this, in view of the righteousness of God, if salvation is to be a possibility at all, it can come only through the fulfillment of the moral claim. There is no place in the Kingdom of heaven for those whose righteousness does not exceed that of the scribes and Pharisees, however upright their moral posture may be alongside that of the pagan world. There is no solid ground for the dispensationalist claim that the terms righteousness and peace are kingdom concepts opposed to grace and belief. The Sermon bears the dual theological emphasis on the uncompromising righteousness of God and on the absolute necessity that the moral law be fulfilled if man is to contemplate a felicitous destiny in eternity. And this emphasis, of course, is the underside of the biblical doctrine of atonement and mediation and of the work of the Holy Spirit in the sanctification and glorification of the believer. The Sermon contains the principles of holiness which abide through this life and the life to come. The emphasis on the unyielding moral principles of God is not only compatible with the standpoint of grace, but is in fact part of its very essence. Salvation comes through the keeping of the Law and the meeting of its demands; the Bible knows nothing, at any point, of a redemption which ignores the moral claim, of a salvation which bypasses the moral law.

But what is there of grace in the Sermon? Man as sinner has squandered his opportunity for meeting the demands of the Law; is not the Gospel the cheering news that another has met its ultimatum in our stead? And what reflection of this emphasis, indeed what least hint of it, do we find in the Sermon?

Such a question drives us at once to the necessary distinction between historical and theological interpretation. The contrast between John's Gospel and the synoptics is rather striking in this regard. The Fourth Gospel moves constantly within the orbit of faith; from the outset Jesus is hailed as Redeemer, and while there is a progressive unveiling of Jesus as the Christ and Son of God, the selection of miracles and discourses keeps this subject of his redemptive significance in the foreground. It would be foolhardy to dismiss the Sermon as representing a standpoint competitive to that of grace, as it would to dismiss much of the remainder of the synoptics because the suggestions of the atonement occur only here and there within the ministry. Christ's every suggestion that he would die in Jerusalem is turned aside by his disciples; that he would die for sinners would have been a doctrine even more incomprehensible to them before the event than immediately after its occurrence, in view of their peculiar messianic expectations (Lk. 24:21). There must be an atonement to expound before the prophetic intimations gain their full-orbed significance. The Sermon, admittedly, does not deal with the problem of man's ability or inability to live up to its requirements; it sets forth the righteousness which God approves, but does not specify how it is to be gained. The beatitudes do not presuppose a works-righteousness. That there is no place in a true believer's life for mourning; that the similitudes of "light" and "salt" gain from Old Testament prophecy an exclusive application to Israel and must not be applied to the ingrafted branch, the church; that the passages on judging others, fasting and public prayer, and the association of God's mercy with the merciful disposition to others of the moral agent are pure legalism, are gratuitous assumptions.

Even the dispensationalist reference to a millennial kingdom based on law, and not on the Gospel, is inadmissible from the standpoint of biblical theology. The standpoint of grace dominates the whole biblical revelation after the fall. The law is nowhere communicated to fallen man as a means whereby, in his sinful condition, he may attain acceptance with God, although the fulfillment of the Divine command in its totality is on the basis of creation a hypothetical means of salvation. The law of Moses is not based on a covenant of works which offers men salvation on the condition of human merit; rather, it is addressed to Israel by Jehovah its Redeemer. Grace demands righteousness, but also provides it. The Sermon is addressed to Christ's disciples (Mt. 5:1f.), and is not a prophetic discourse. The millennial kingdom likewise reflects the standpoint of grace. The book of Revelation, replete with eschatological detail, maintains the centrality of the crucified Redeemer; there are twenty-seven references to Christ under the familiar sacrificial category of the Lamb, and the emphasis on his death abounds. If the "jot and tittle" passage means the abandonment of the standpoint of grace in a future millennial age, it would surely seem to imply the permanent validity of the ceremonial law. But the reinstitution of blood sacrifices would repudiate the already accomplished sacrifice of the true Lamb of God (Jn. 1:29, Heb. 9:26). Here even the dispensationalists divide in the consistent application of their own principle, some exponents of the view disallowing the restoration of sacrifice.

With regard to the second contention, that the phrase "Kingdom of heaven" in the Sermon assigns it to the millennial era, it may he replied that the argument is fallacious.[38] The gospels frequently use "Kingdom

[38]An able criticism of the dispensational view is set forth by George E. Ladd, *Crucial Questions About the Kingdom of God* (Grand Rapids: Eerdmans, 1952), pp. 122ff. Ladd accounts for "Kingdom of God" and "Kingdom of heaven" by the evangelists' translation of the Aramaic which Jesus supposedly spoke, with Matthew avoiding the Divine name in accord with Hebrew preference, and Mark and Luke using the favored terminology of the Gentiles.

of God" and "Kingdom of heaven" interchangeably. Mark and Luke employ the one term (Mk. 1:15, Lk. 9:2) where Matthew uses the other (Mt. 4:17, 10:6f.). The attempt to assign "Kingdom of heaven" the sense of "Christendom" or professing Christianity, beginning with Matthew 13, also fails. The argument is that Jesus offered an actual restoration of the earthly Davidic kingdom, the acceptance of which would have provided an alternative to his crucifixion. When this overture was rejected the earthly kingdom was postponed and with it the requirements of the Sermon. The Kingdom of heaven was then manifested in a mystery form in this age. But Jesus actually resisted Jewish pressures that he establish an earthly empire (Jn. 5:15). And the Old Testament prophecies (Ps. 22, Isa. 53) concerning the Messiah's sufferings and death suggest that it was necessary, as Jesus himself said, that he die in Jerusalem (Mt. 16:21). That the Kingdom of heaven means Christendom is inconsistent with Jesus' assertion that it is hard for a rich man to enter the Kingdom of heaven (Mt. 19:23; the least of a wealthy man's difficulties would be an entrance into the sphere of professing Christendom). The difficulty arises in Matthew 18:3ff., where Jesus makes conversion the condition of entrance into the Kingdom of heaven.

The third contention, that the Sermon is intended for a millennial age in which evil is subjugated, ignores its reflections of an age of conflict between evil and righteousness, seen here as fully as in other New Testament passages. The moral agents in view are exhorted to search after righteousness, peacemakers are commended, reward is promised for reproach, persecution and false accusation are to be endured for Christ. These facts presuppose an environment in which evil is aggressive. Other elements of the Sermon suggest at once that it is not intended for the age of millennial bliss. An era requiring special principles to govern face-slapping and turning the other cheek (5:39) is hardly one to which the term "millenium" is aptly applied. The presence of enemies who need to be loved, of those who hate the righteous, of reviling, persecution and slander endured for Christ's sake, of a reward which is to be welcomed "in heaven" in contrast to the present deprivations, the implication of the minority status of the faithful in the role of salt and light, combine to overwhelm the thesis of a primary millennial reference.

The dispensational view arbitrarily transfers the significance of the completest statement of ethical principles we have from the lips of Jesus Christ to the remnant of believing Jews in a future age, and leaves us without an extensive statement from him on the ethical principles governing disciples in the age of grace. George E. Ladd remarks, "a system which takes this great portion of Jesus' teaching away from the Christian in its direct application must receive penetrating scrutiny."[39] The largest single corpus of the teaching of our

[39] *Ibid.*, p. 104.

Lord, containing his principal ethical instruction, is thereby deprived of direct relevance to Christian conduct.

The dispensationalist notion that the requirements of the Sermon are irrelevant for this age and legalistic derives largely from positions which most Reformed interpreters who insist on its relevance reject—that the Sermon is designed to cover official as well as personal relations, and that the Sermon seeks only a literal fulfillment of specific command in strict obedience to an ethical code rather than expressing ethical principles which are metaphorically illuminated.

The question of the Sermon's proper interpretation remains. But there is no secure ground for postponing the relevance of the Sermon to a future eschatological age, and asserting that it is not intended for Christians in the present life. While the requirements of the Sermon are impossible of fulfillment, the reason is neither eschatological nor an essential element of human nature, but simply man's conditional predicament in sin. The demands of the Sermon were fulfilled, in fact, by Jesus of Nazareth, else there would remain no hope for the salvation of sinners.

(4) The interim-ethic school viewed the Sermon as setting forth exceptional regulations for a period of end-time stress, based on Jesus' expectation of an immediate eschatological age. Because the Sermon's precepts presumably excluded all interests and values other than those dictated by the expectation of an abrupt and immediate end of the present world order, Johannes Weiss and Albert Schweitzer repudiated the general validity of the ethics of the Sermon. The dramatic summons to repentance and to "superhuman" righteousness, the call to love of enemies, the prohibition of resistance of evil, the negation of the worth of this world's goods, were held to reflect the mistaken expectation that the world denouement was just about to happen. Hence, the Sermon's unyielding demands were dismissed as an impossible guide for the ordinary conduct of life.

The interim-ethic interpretation contends that literal fulfillment of the Sermon was intended, that it is possible but absurd if the world will continue more than a few weeks, and that its ethic is therefore irrelevant to the contemporary moral situation.

The eschatological kingdom is regarded by this view as the fundamental factor in Jesus' preaching. His whole ethical teaching is brought under the conception of repentance as not merely a call to turn from the guilty past, but predominantly to "a moral renewal in prospect of the accomplishment of universal perfection in the future."[40] All present earthly institutions, *e.g.*, the state, fall out of view, either as not existing in the coming kingdom, or having but a sublimated significance. Instead of founding a kingdom, as liberal ethics generally assumed, Jesus waited for it as a future apocalyptic reality through a miraculous Divine

[40]Schweitzer, *The Mystery of the Kingdom of God the Secret of Jesus' Messiahship and Passion* (New York: Macmillan, 1953), p. 53.

irruption which would end human history. The Sermon aims to ready men for that swift and imminent transition.[41]

The Lord's Prayer expresses this future hope: "Thy kingdom come" (6:10), and is a prayer for an eschatological community. The beatitudes define the moral disposition which justifies man's admission into the kingdom; hence the present and future tenses. The content of the Sermon represents the new legislation on which the kingdom will be based. No retaliation, no prosecution nor self-defense, is permitted By the motive of reward alms-giving, prayer and fasting are oriented eschatologically. The Sermon concludes with an admonition, in view of the imminent end, to build a structure that will resist the storm and tempest.

There can be little doubt that the New Testament ethic, from John the Baptist through Jesus and the apostles, is constantly colored by reference to judgment and catastrophe. Without question, Jesus' ethical message was influenced by eschatological ideas; the discourses, the parables, the very language of conversation, is filled with the conviction that he is to be the agent in an all-embracing judgment of mankind. For Jesus no less than for the Old Testament prophets, moral principles do have an eschatological background.

But does this mean that the ethics of the Sermon is thereby invalidated? The modern mind has tended to approach New Testament ethics with two prejudices — belief that a cataclysmic finale of history centering in the return of Christ and the judgment of the race is outmoded (in the view of the past generation because of anti-miraculous and evolutionary views of nature and history) and belief that Christ and the apostles expected the end of the world in their generation and that their eschatological notions are thereby the frenzied imaginings of religious zealots.

To escape a wholly negative consequence for Jesus' ethics, the advocates of interim-ethics sought to separate some elements of his moral teaching from dependence upon the eschatological. Weiss himself was compelled to distinguish as non-eschatological such emphases as the claim of the law, love of God and neighbor, delight in nature and the world of men, and some of the parables. In contrast, the remainder of Jesus' ethic was dismissed as emergency legislation invalidated by the erroneous expectation that the end of the present world order is at hand. Schweitzer followed much the same pattern in *The Quest of the Historical Jesus.* To assert that all these injunctions depended upon the imminent end-time would reduce the ethics of Jesus to absurdity. The teaching about believers as salt and light, spiritual adultery, prohibition of divorce except for unchastity, oaths, forgiveness, the speck and the log, assurance of answered prayer, and the Golden Rule, are

[41]The eschatological orientation is seen in 5:3-12, 19f., 21-26, 27-30, 33-37, 43-48; 6:1, 2-4, 5-6, 9-13, 16-18, 19-21, 22-23, 24, 25-33; 7:1-5, 13-14, 21-23, 24-27.

hardly valid only on condition that the world order would end suddenly.[42]

This method of carving up the ethics of Jesus has been criticized along two lines in our century.

One school has sought to separate the ethics of Jesus wholly from the eschatological, dismissing the latter as culture-bound and acknowledging that it must be discarded, but insisting on the permanent validity of the moral teaching. So Marshall, for example, thinks the eschatological teaching has been shown to be false, but contends that the ethical teaching of Jesus and Paul does not rest upon it.[43] E. F. Scott[44] and H. J. Cadbury[45] have taken the ground that the apocalyptic elements only intensify the moral demand of Jesus, but do not shape it.

To refer Jesus' stringent ethical demands to apocalyptic enthusiasm, protests Marshall, is to make nonsense of his position. "It is difficult to find a single ethical precept in the gospels which can fairly be regarded as intended, and therefore valid, only for the brief interval" suggested by the interim-ethic school.[46] He notes Wilhelm Herrmann's remark that even the one passage which lends itself most to the position is doubtful: "Lay not up for yourselves treasure upon earth . . ." (Mt. 6:19f.). Dean Inge stresses that the values of Christianity are eternal and "do not depend for their validity on temporal happenings in the past or in the future."[47] The truth in this position is, of course, the emphasis on the permanent validity of Jesus' ethical teaching. But the theory has two fatal weaknesses. The New Testament representation of Jesus leaves little doubt that the ethical and the apocalyptic stood not only side by side with equal ultimateness, but are inseparably interwoven. Moreover, the complete disjunction of the content of Christian ethics from all temporal happenings can only imply its independence of the tradition of special revelation and of the ministry of the historical Jesus. If the validity of Christian ethics is to be maintained in its historic sense, that validity must not imply the irrelevance either of special revelation nor of the eschatological.

The attempts of those like Marshall, who would detach the whole of Jesus' ethic from eschatology, and those of the interim-ethic school to detach some elements of his ethics from such dependence are exceedingly vulnerable. Modern biblical scholarship has reassessed the place of the eschatological element in the New Testament, and has come to the conclusion that it not only permeates the whole of the ethics of

[42]Elements of the Sermon in which no eschatological reference is necessary are 5:13, 14-16, 21-26, 27-28, 31-32, 33-37, 38-42, 43-48; 6:2-4, 5-6, 14f., 16-18, 24. 25-33, 34; 7:1-5, 6, 7-12, 15-20.

[43]L. H. Marshall, *op. cit.*, p. 195.

[44]E. F. Scott, *The Ethical Teaching of Jesus*, p. 195.

[45]H. J. Cadbury, *The Peril of Modernizing Jesus* (New York: Macmillan, 1937), p. 128.

[46]Marshall, *op. cit.*, p. 193.

[47]W. R. Inge, *Christian Ethics and Modern Problems* (New York: G. P. Putnam, 1930), p. 23.

Jesus, but constitutes one of its characteristic sanctions. The humanists were nearer the truth in holding that the teachings of Jesus are everywhere interpenetrated by his belief in his supernatural messianic being and in the coming kingdom of God (while they wrongly repudiated his ethics on that ground), than those idealists who think that his ethics is easily and everywhere separable from his eschatological views, and who retain his ethics on this erroneous ground. Whether the eschatology is to be taken literally or existentially, whether it constitutes only a formal or also an essential sanction[48] — these are the problems over which contemporary scholarship is divided. But that the ethical and the eschatological belong together, there is now little dispute.

The note is even sounded today that it is because of its eschatological significance that the ethics of Jesus has permanent validity. Instead of "destroying Christian ethics the eschatological element gives a genuine emancipation from worldliness which leads to prophetic witness," writes Don E. Smucker. He points out that "unless the Christian community grasps something of life's contingent quality, the teachings of the Sermon on the Mount appear to be foolishness."[49]

Along with the humanistic and dispensational views, the interim-ethic view dismisses the Sermon as irrelevant, but it does so for radically different reasons. The humanists argue on evolutionary assumptions that the gradual emergence of the spiritual kingdom simply makes the earlier ethic out of date; the dispensationalists contend that the deferment of the earthly kingdom postpones the relevance of the Sermon; the interim-school asserts that the nature of eschatology in the Sermon destroys the ethic of the Sermon.

But many students of Christian ethics regard this easy dismissal of the Sermon as artificial and unjustifiable. If there is a permanently valid ethics, one will not go wrong in seeking it here. And to seek it here drives one also to a quite different appraisal of eschatology. The division of the elements of the Sermon into "eschatological" and "non-eschatological" already reflects a bias inherited from the interim-ethic school. The whole of Christ's ethics is eschatological in the sense that it has final judgment as its premise. And the whole is non-eschatological in the sense that its validity is not suspended at any point upon the immediate end of the historical order. The dismissal of the relevance of the Sermon by the interim-ethic school is a reflex of a highly debatable premise — that the eschatology of Jesus and Paul finds its center in the declaration that world-history would be cataclysmically ended within their lifetime.

[48]The evaluation of Amos N. Wilder's theory of a merely formal, rather than essential, eschatological sanction for ethics, is considered separately because it does not turn especially upon the Sermon on the Mount, but rather bears on the whole of Christian ethics.

[49]Don E. Smucker, *The Theological Basis for Christian Pacifism* (Mennonite Conference on Church and War, Detroit, 1950).

(5) The existential interpretation holds that the ethics of the Sermon is valid for all who share the disposition of mind and will it illustrates. The Sermon does not give concrete ethical instruction and is not to be taken as an authoritative exposition of normative laws and concrete ethical demands. Rather, it orients life "eschatologically" to the absolute-claim of God, and depicts the proper attitude by which the believer experientially resolves the time-eternity tension.

The teaching of the Sermon is valid therefore only as an ethos or ethic of attitude. Only in respect to the inner will or disposition is its fulfillment intended, is it relevant to the moral crisis, and is it conditionally possible. As an objective exposition of moral actions it is neither valid nor intended for fulfillment, hence irrelevant.

The "eschatological" element is thus regarded as essential to the ethical teaching: the Christian believer exists always in the "last day" — at the borderline of two worlds. The eschatological aspect in its literal sense is repudiated. But instead of a dismissal of the eschatological as entirely fallacious, that element is reinterpreted existentially. No longer does the eschatological serve in any sense as a time concept distinguishing a chronologically future age from the present. Rather, it becomes experientially a concept of being and value in personal experience. The tension of the present moment in relation to an end-time judgment is displaced by the tension between the is and the ought involving the necessity for continuous repentance and faith. To use the motif popularized by Friedrich Overbeck, the end of the world is at hand existentially. An eternally valid "new being" is suspended constantly above present experience. The demands of the Sermon are concerned only with the production of a right attitude, its extreme examples making vivid the realization that God desires complete and uncompromised obedience.

Early traces of this view may be found in Herrmann's writings. An approximation of the view is found in many expositions which insist that the Sermon does not aim to set forth commandments that are to be fulfilled literally. Rather, by the imposition of impossible demands Jesus seeks to drive us to an experience of Divine mercy and to the spirit of absolute dedication involved in the approved moral life. The distinctive feature of existential ethics, however, is to be found in the repudiation of the idea that content for ethics is propositionally expressed in terms of self-consistent principles. Instead, there is a restatement of ethics in terms of subjective ethical experience, and in the reinterpretation of eschatological motifs in the existential mood.

Gerhardt Kittel took the position that none of Jesus' teaching taken as individual precepts is absolutely original, but that the novelty of his ethics is to be found in its absolute intensity. This intensity was intended to cast man into moral despair. The ethics of Jesus does not purpose to give practical guidance, but to confront man with an impossible demand: ". . . a demand exaggerated to the point of paradox and nonsense."

For Kittel, the impossibility of meeting the requirements of the Sermon, or of salvation by works, has as its goal a resort to salvation by grace, to a way of salvation beyond command and precept. Hence the Sermon anticipates the Pauline doctrine of the cross and of a divinely-provided justification by faith. The Sermon loses entirely its significance as practical ethical legislation; it serves only as prolegomenon to a contrite surrender of spirit.

The existential view is reflected in the writings of Martin Dibelius. He shares the position that the Sermon is given pedagogically to convict us of moral failure, to awaken in us the consciousness of sin, to prod us on to ethical obedience. It was not given as a rule of life. Jesus intends by his teaching, we are told, to place the individual in a predicament requiring decision, to compel the hearer to pass a condemnatory judgment upon himself. He does not, according to the theory, communicate valid ethical doctrine, but "paradoxes" designed to shock and to stimulate his hearers to action. Though Jesus speaks in the form of commands, he gives no commands. Rather, he aims to propel his listeners into a vivid spiritual encounter with God that will issue in a "new being" through unconditional surrender and obedience. The commands are pointers to the eternal kingdom and its total claim; they are not authoritative commandments that demand compliance. They urge us on as invitations to the Divine likeness and the new being.

Rudolph Bultmann in 1941 carried forward this existential motif by assigning a decisive role to the category of myth in interpreting the *Kerygma*. Bultmann said that the whole New Testament message was in myth form, but defined the *mythos* as expressing a particular understanding of man's existence which must be interpreted existentially. Even the cross and the resurrection become meaningful, he contended, only as they drive us to decision, to a re-understanding of the moral situation, to the new life.

The existential interpretation is favored by numerous exponents of dialectical theology who, as noted earlier, hold that revelation cannot be expressed in concepts and propositions, and hence that there is no revealed moral and theological doctrine. The scriptural teaching is regarded as a witness to a present encounter in which God addresses the will in personal revelation with a claim to total submission. Brunner tells us that "None of the commandments in the Sermon on the Mount are to be understood as laws, so that those who hear them can go away feeling, 'Now I know what I have to do.' "[50] The Sermon "is not intended merely to 'intensify' or to 'spiritualize' the divine law, in order that now we may better know—beforehand—what God wills from us . . ."[51] "The commandments of the Sermon on the Mount hold good today just as at all other periods in history: not as a law but as a guide to the Divine Command."[52]

[50]Emil Brunner, *The Divine Imperative,* p. 136.
[51]*Ibid.,* p. 137.
[52]*Ibid.,* p. 434.

The difficulties raised by the existential view of the Sermon are many. The broadest objection, no doubt, is that the view surrenders the *Kerygma* and biblical theology as a whole to the dictates of the modern speculative presuppositions of existential philosophy. Beginning with a decidedly prejudiced view of the tension between the eternal and temporal, it finds an artificial relief of that tension only by an existential leap of faith. The centering of faith-experience in this mystical encounter with God moves far away from the Hebrew-Christian confidence in a historically-mediated revelation.

Moreover, the depreciation of the literal and historical leads to an allegorizing of the essential features of biblical history and to treating them instead as religious psychology. This tendency is most fully observed in Bultmann's writings. Once the existential premise is granted, any attempt to assess the historical significance of any element of the *mythos* is fraught with difficulty. If the doctrine of the fall can be existentialized in subjective experience quite independently of the historical Adam, the doctrine of redemption may be similarly divorced from any dependence on the work of the historical Jesus. The Bible is asserted to have a myth framework, and its core is to be found simply in understanding our existence in a new way, *i.e.,* in God's confrontation of us in our existential situation. Then the atonement and the resurrection may become "concrete contemporary experiences," but they no longer constitute the decisive turning-point of world history. The confrontation of man by God and man's new life in the Spirit have a specific historical background in biblical theology. Apart from this objective, historical setting, the emphasis on the experiential side of the religious and moral life is capable of easy and grotesque distortion. Whatever theory of ethics Existentialism may evolve, it cannot do justice to the biblical view of time and history, and it runs the danger of handling essential elements of that history in the spirit of docetism. The existential view, therefore, lends itself to a new mythology, however sophisticate and intellectual, maintaining a connection with Christian ethics through secondary points of connection.

The notion that Jesus' ethics elaborates an intense inner demand for obedience which is to be contrasted with propositional biblical ethics is an overstatement. Doubtless Jesus sharpened the inwardness of the moral claim, and did so as one who authoritatively interpreted the law. The emphasis on attitude, intention of heart and *agape* belongs to the core of Christian ethics. The call for a radical or intensely inner moral obedience is not peculiar to the New Testament, but was already a feature of Hebrew ethics, not only in the great prophets but in the earlier period. The Sermon on the Mount makes no greater demand than does Deuteronomy 6:4f.: "Hear, O Israel, Jehovah our God is one Jehovah: and thou shalt love Jehovah thy God with all thy heart, and with all thy soul, and with all thy might."

If the New Testament ethic is paradoxical, the Old Testament ethic must be regarded as having the same aim. That the ethical requirements of Scripture addressed to man as sinner serve to awaken guilt and constitute a call to repentance is not in dispute. The question is: Is the basic intention of the Sermon merely to convict hearers of incomplete obedience? Does it in any sense state the ethical imperatives that constitute God's will? It is clear from such passages as Matthew 23:3ff. that Jesus' ethic has a view to specific works, to an observation of ethical precepts by doing them. If Jesus did not mean to extend a concrete summons to obedience, it is difficult to understand why he couched his instructions in the form of commandments. And if Christ gave no commands, how could we be convicted of disobedience? Can it be shown that an actual fulfillment of his commandments would betray the intention of the Sermon? Is it a ludicrous misunderstanding of Christian ethics to seek to keep literally such commandments as those against adultery and murder? Does Jesus not specifically warn against teaching men that even the least of his imperatives may be broken in its form of commandment (5:19)? Jesus is assuredly dealing with a righteousness of doing as well as a righteousness of being, even though the latter is fundamental. Is it not, in very fact, only non-Christian ethics that could be indifferent to the fulfillment of the commands of the Sermon?

Jesus gives the inner meaning of the commandments. Hence, if the Sermon is irrelevant as commandment, so is the Old Testament law. But to regard the Old Testament law in this light is to reduce to nonsense the sense in which the prophets, and not alone legalistic Judaism, understood it. The spiritual significance of the law did not mean that the commandments were to be ignored as practical legislation. Jesus does not assail the attempt to keep the Old Testament law, but the failure to keep it, and the consequent mistaken expectation of salvation by works on the part of those who have broken it. Jesus did not "redeem" men from the law by altering the fundamental character of the Jewish revealed ethic of obedience.

It is clear that Jesus understood the law to be the will of God in propositional form. He so interpreted it in the Sermon.

It may be that the position that views the ethical teaching of the Bible and Jesus as something other than practical legislation actually reflects an objectionable doctrine of man, rather than a false view of revelation. The prejudices of modern theology impose an arbitrary restriction on the function of the Sermon. If human nature, as the theology of crisis insists, is inevitably sinful, then it would indeed be foolhardy to look here for ethical principles and commandments to be the rule of life for man. In view of such a definition of human nature, the Sermon could not under any circumstances be regarded a practical ideal; its only significance could be to throw man into critical despair. But if human nature is not by creation inevitably sinful, if it is conditionally rather than essentially sinful, if ideal human nature ought to live in absolute conformity to the Divine ethical commands, then the Sermon as a practical rule of life becomes at once a live option. This immediate relevance of the Sermon to life can be defended, as we shall see, without falling into the errors of Pelagianism. The fact of man's self-estrangement doubtless is a proper and essential element in Christian psychology which deals realistically with the fall and sin of man. But the existential views wrongly depict this as complete estrangement from the moral-rational *imago Dei.* The emphasis that the new being is shaped by decision alone caters to evolutionary modes of thought which depreciate man's unique status on the basis of creation. Against Descartes' "I think, therefore I am" and Kant's "I ought, therefore I am," biblical thought knows how to insist also "I am, therefore I think and therefore I ought." The new being of redemption is continuous with the created being.

In fact, few of the Sermon's demands carry any suggestion of absurdity or that rigorous impossibility which existentialist moralists tend to find there. The question is not whether man as sinner, or even as redeemed, can by his own effort fully keep the requirements, but whether such conformity can be conceived for man in the state of ideal obedience, and whether, more particularly, such obedience may be predicated of Jesus Christ. Windisch is doubtless right in his protest[53] against Brunner's "overemphasis on 'impossibility' as its essential characteristic" in the appraisal of the sermon in *The Mediator.*[54]

There are evidences within the Sermon, moreover, that indicate that the evangelists understood the Sermon in its propositional form to be universally valid. We do not question that the ethics of Jesus has in view man's subjective conviction of moral failure, intending to awaken within him the consciousness of sin. Nor do we question that its impact should turn the will of man to the disposition of absolute surrender and obedience in a new spiritual creaturehood. Nor are the conditions of this new being here set forth. But a passage like Matthew 7:12 — "All things therefore whatsoever ye would that men should do unto you, even so do ye also unto them: for this is the law and the prophets" — indicates that if Jesus taught merely an ethos, or an inner disposition, Matthew misunderstood the teaching to include also an ethics of general validity.

This suggests that the antithesis which the existential school elaborates between ethos and ethics, attitude and obedience to commands, being and doing, is an unnecessary and artificial one. Jesus, in announcing as his aim the fulfillment of the Law, meant at the very least that he would meet its provisions and requirements (5:17). His disciples were to display good works before men (5:16). Those who "do and teach" all the commandments "shall be called great in the kingdom of

[53]Windisch, *op. cit.,* p. 121.
[54]Emil Brunner, *The Mediator* (Philadelphia: Westminster, 1947), pp. 418ff.

heaven" (5:19). The disciples' prayer is that God's will "be done on earth as in heaven" (6:10). And entrance into the Kingdom of heaven is restricted to him "that doeth the will" of the Father (7:21). We have already ventured a criticism of contemporary views that Christian love is to be contrasted with spiritual obedience of Divine commandments. Here we are insisting, from within the structure of the Sermon itself, that Jesus did not break with the casting of ethics in the form of Divine law and commandments. The reiterated "but I say unto you" does not presuppose a criticism of the earlier statement of the content of ethics in the form of law and commandments. It is a criticism of the reduction of the content of those commandments, either by relaxing their stringency, or by giving them a merely legalistic and subspiritual significance.

Christian ethics admittedly gets the classic formulation of its inner disposition — the principle of love — from Jesus Christ. Not merely from his teaching, but from his example and, primarily, from his substitutionary sacrifice. But Christian ethics is not left to chart its course of divinely-approved conduct by self-reflection alone, or by an immediate spiritual impression traced to "encounter." The believer, though renewed in disposition, is not perfect, and still is subject to erroneous impulses. He does not stand related to God in an immediacy identical with that of the chosen prophets and apostles, and assuredly not Jesus. So it is through an objective Divine outline alone that he can discriminate between right and wrong directions of love in action. The biblically revealed ethic of principles, commandments, examples, and applications provides such a content. Obviously, the Sermon does not contain "thou shalt not" commandments as its characteristic pattern. Some negations do appear. But the prohibitory form is not necessary to commandment (although it is specially suited to man in the state of sin), and it seems unnecessary therefore to contend that the Sermon gives us only principles but not specific commandments. Its declarations do not deal directly with the lesser matters; nor is the whole of life covered in the outward pharisaic sense. But it includes commandments as definitely as does the Decalogue, as we shall see.

The inner life is a unity; God the Father is the center of the spiritual life; moral and spiritual values have primacy over the material; love is the fundamental social law; righteousness has its roots in the inner man; fulfillment is the final test of life — these are principles which the Sermon upholds. And, in a sense, the whole Sermon may be regarded as a series of concrete enforcements of these principles. But it is a gross oversimplification to assert on that ground that Jesus sets forth only ethical ideals implicit in the believer's relationship to God and accepted by those in the kingdom, but he does not set forth specific commands. Marshall makes this mistake. Doubtless, love with one's total energy for God, and for neighbor as for self, condenses "into one simple statement . . . the whole law with its 600 commandments."[55] And equally true is it that the Sermon reflects at points an oriental imagery that cannot be taken literally, yet without implying the non-literal nature of the whole. But the Sermon does not stop there. The two great commandments are not left to a finite definition of their own proper course of action. Love for God is assuredly a great moral dynamic, and love for man "the clue to the overwhelming majority of the problems of conduct,"[56] but something more than clues to the approved life are given. It is not sufficient to say that Jesus adds to general principles (as doubtless he does) "lightning sketches of a non-vindictive spirit in actual operation."[57] Such emphasis on general principles and avoidance of the idea of commandment takes away from the Sermon something of its absolute quality of *oughtness.* This is especially clear in revolts against the idea that Jesus set forth rules, and not merely an exemplary spirit. "To claim that He was laying down rules for His followers in some later age threatens us with the tyranny of Mohammedanism, permanently fettered to standards which reflect the political and moral conditions of Arabian society in the sixth century."[58]

The expression of Christ's spirit is said to be normative for the Christian life. "Rather by redeeming our attitudes and lifting us into a world of new insights than by giving us positive guidance in detail about the moral demands of Christian living" is Christ said to be relevant. The question of details aside, the real issue is: Does the guidance which Jesus gives us reach beyond attitudes and insights into specific commandments? Windisch claims to have demonstrated — and his case is a forceful one — that the imperatives of Matthew 5 are commandments, and that it is a false alternative to say that Jesus brought a new attitude but not law, precepts and commands. Obviously, Jesus requires a determinative attitude, but the attitude itself emerges in a characteristic relation to the individual commands. The exhortations to right behavior nowhere imply a disparagement of precept in deference to attitude as the sole interest. Even the "tree and fruits" passage does not lessen the value of individual acts (Mt. 7:17ff.). The discussion of alms, prayer, and fasting contrasts right and wrong behavior, and not disposition over against behavior, as if the two were antithetical. Refusal to perform the requisite deeds ends in doom: "Everyone therefore that heareth these words of mine, and doeth them, shall be likened unto a wise man . . . and everyone that heareth these words of mine, and doeth them not, shall be likened unto a foolish man, who built his house upon the sand . . ." (7:24ff.). The contrast between spiritual obedience and the fulfillment of moral precepts has a shallow basis. Can one read the Sermon and fail to detect in the reiterated "but

[55]Marshall, *op. cit.,* p. 104.
[56]*Ibid.,* p. 107.
[57]*Ibid.,* pp. 125f.
[58]Frank Russell Barry, *The Relevance of Christianity* (rev. ed.; London: Nisbet, 1952), p. 74.

I say unto you . . ." the enunciation of formal rules which are to be kept? As Windisch remarks, "Jesus was not conscious of any tension between principle and precept. He never thought of attitude as something superior to commandment, or of the latter as but a limited and isolated application of the former. . . . Even when he gives ethics a very general formulation (Matt. 5:48, 7:12), he phrases it as an imperative from which behavior in an individual, concrete instance is to be deduced as an individual prescription."[59]

The radical and artificial interpretations of the ethics of the Sermon to which both the interim-ethic and existential schools have been driven by their adjustments of its eschatological elements provide sufficient reason for inquiring whether historic Christianity has not grasped the spirit of those elements in its creeds better than the theories fashioned from the modern standpoint. The eschatological factor is clearly interwoven with New Testament ethics. But that its essence was the false expectation of the end of the historical order in the lifetime of Jesus and Paul, or that it is a new being which hovers constantly above the present life as a prospect through existential decision, is far from obvious. Were the former the case, it would be difficult to explain those elements in the New Testament ethic that are not conditioned by a doctrine of momentary destruction, *e.g.,* the final great commission to carry the Gospel to the ends of the earth. Does the New Testament ethic really disclose no positive concern whatever for the earth-world, and does it rule out all consideration of earthly interests and values? And do the elements of interim-ethic, properly so called (*e.g.,* Jer. 16:1ff., 1 Cor. 7:25ff.), depend for their force upon apocalyptic misexpectation? Conceding the eschatological element to be intrinsic, may not the data be more satisfactorily handled by the traditional view Jesus and Paul held that the consummation of all things is already under way, but that neither affirms its dramatic climax to be immediately due?[60] Both Jesus and Paul share the belief that the Kingdom of God has already impinged upon history in a supreme and decisive way through the incarnation and Christ's conquest over Satan, and both look to a future superlative climax applying the consequences to the whole human race.

The Sermon ethic does not actually lose its practical significance through the existential failure to grasp its propositional significance. The Sermon remains valid not only in the disposition it intends, but in its precepts and commandments. Doubtless its requirements awaken

[59]Windisch, *op. cit.,* p. 86.

[60]Against those who contend that Paul's eschatology stymied the integration of his ethics with social institutions, the state, and international relations, stands the fact that he did apply his ethics to the state (Rom. 13:1ff., 1 Tim. 2:1f.). The wild claim that Paul favored celibacy because the human race had "no future" is met by the fact that he did not forbid marriage nor did he deny a future for the race. Against the view that Paul held earthly goods in contempt because of the expectation of world-end stands the more sober judgment that he saw material things in balanced perspective (2 Thess. 3:6ff.).

repentance in man as sinner. But those requirements hold permanent significance also for man as redeemed. They reflect, in fact, a Divine requirement for man on the basis of creation.

(6) The Anabaptist-Mennonite view is that the Sermon was addressed to the church to be obeyed in this age both in so-called official and in personal relations. In all the areas of life — personal, social, business and political — it stipulates the morality which is to distinguish regenerate believers. The words are to be taken in the natural literal sense, and their claim is not superseded in any of the relations of life.

A second distinctive feature of the Mennonite interpretation is that the Sermon is held to replace the ethics of the Old Testament. The emphasis on "progressive revelation" is held to imply not, as contended by the Reformers, that Jesus abrogated the ceremonial law and exposited the inner meaning of the moral law, but that he raised the moral law itself to higher ground. The Reformers contended that God required the same moral standard in the old and new dispensations, but that he tolerated more in the old. The Mennonites contend that he requires more in the new than in the old. What he explicitly commanded in the old, he explicitly forbids in the new. Speaking of the Old Testament moral code, Guy F. Hershberger asserts that "in Matthew 5 Jesus definitely rejects the civil code of Moses because it did not measure up to the standards of the Kingdom and the higher moral law."[61] The Anabaptist view is that the Old Testament ethic is done away as inferior, outdated, and overruled, and that the whole Christian ethic is suspended upon the New Testament alone.

The next distinctive Mennonite emphasis is that the use of force and the infliction of human punishment are inconsistent with the New Testament law of love. The resistance of evil by force and the meting out of punishment are held necessarily to involve an inward disposition of vengeance and hatred or lovelessness.[62] Hence participation in warfare is ruled out and pacifism endorsed. Don E. Smucker writes: "Nonresistance is applied agape. . . . The supreme contribution of Christian pacifism is to insist that agape-love requires the ethics of Christian pacifism in order to be agape-love. . . . The eight beatitudes are eight steps incompatible with war . . ."[63] Hershberger affirms: "The Mennonite Church . . . believes that war should be avoided by the state, but also insists that war is morally wrong now, and that it always was wrong because it is a violation of God's moral law. There-

[61]Guy F. Hershberger, "Peace and War in the New Testament," in *Mennonite Quarterly Review,* XVII (Apr. 1943), pp. 59ff.

[62]Calvin, to the contrary, argued that judicial proceedings in no way violate the Pauline "Avenge not yourselves, beloved, but give place unto wrath: for it is written, Vengeance belongeth unto me: I will recompense, saith the Lord" (Rom. 12:19) provided the Christian's conduct toward his opponent is as kindly as if the matter in dispute were transacted and solved amicably.

[63]Don E. Smucker, "The Theological Basis for Christian Pacifism," in *Mennonite Quarterly Review,* XXVII, 3 (July, 1953), pp. 163ff.

fore the individual actually sins when he takes any part in war at all."[64] Moreover, the commandment not to kill includes, in the Mennonite view, the prohibition of capital punishment. The taking of human life under any circumstances is considered a sin.

The corollary of this renunciation of force is the emphasis on a complete disjunction of believers and the state. The church and the state are regarded as essentially adverse to each other. "The state cannot be Christian in its methods," writes John C. Wenger, "because it does not control its citizens by the proclamation of the Word of God but by the arm of the law, which is ultimately the method of force."[65] Edward Yoder interprets Jesus' attitude toward the state to be "one of essential indifference."[66] The state is a divinely ordained order of preservation in a sinful society, but it belongs to a wholly different order than that of regenerate believers.

To argue at length the subject of the Christian view of the state and of social ethics would carry us far afield from the Sermon on the Mount. The necessity which the larger New Testament imposes, as well as the fuller teaching and example of Jesus, for an application of the Sermon to personal rather than to official relations, will be argued in connection with the Reformed view.

Here is may be noted, however, that the Sermon is not decisive for the subjects of war and capital punishment. Jesus' emphasis on the sixth commandment unveils the inner spiritual attitude of hate as a wicked sin. But to the Old Testament command he does not add that capital punishment and war are wrong. If that is the sense of the commandment, it must belong to the Old Testament conception. But the Old Testament record cannot be reconciled to this alternative. God punishes Israel for idolatry, for adultery, for disregard of the sabbath, but not for resort to war in self-defense. In fact, he often commands their participation in such a war.

An obvious difficulty which the Mennonite view faces is that the issuance of contradictory moral commands by God in different ages seems to imply moral development in God. The Mennonite attempt to escape this difficulty, by contending that God in the Old Testament commanded men to do what was against his will,[67] creates more problems than it solves. For one thing, morality is then no longer

[64]Hershberger, "Mennonites and the Modern Peace Movement," in *Mennonite Quarterly Review,* II, 2 (Apr., 1928), p. 163.

[65]John C. Wenger, *Separated Unto God,* pp. 249f.

[66]Edward Yoder, "Christianity and the State," in *Mennonite Quarterly Review,* XI, 3 (July, 1937), pp. 171ff.

[67]Hershberger writes of the Hebrews: "When they thus willfully turned their backs against God, He commanded their leaders to let them have their way, not because it was his will . . ." and "Because of the hardness of their hearts, God commanded the granting of divorce which was, however, against His own divine will." "Peace and War in the Old Testament," *Mennonite Quarterly Review,* XVII, 1 (Jan., 1943), pp. 5ff.

identical with what God commands. For another, the absolute character of Divine commandment is undermined.

The most serious indictment of the Mennonite interpretation is its under-estimation of the essential continuity of biblical ethics. Jesus does not in the Sermon impose upon his hearers a morality which is qualitatively different from the Old Testament claim.

What he criticizes is not the Law itself, but contemporary formulations of the Law. This is supported by an examination of the quotations which he cites, by the verbal formula by which he introduces them, and by the contextual remarks which prepare for the discussion. Having asserted that he came to fulfill the Law and the prophets, indeed, to vindicate the validity of the previous ethical revelation down to the very least commands, he would have exposed himself at once to the charge of self-contradiction had his real purpose been to set them completely aside. He had not come to nullify Moses, and to set himself in antagonism to the Decalogue. Rather, he showed the strict conformity between the Old Testament disclosure and his own view of the moral law. Christ does not begin his ethical teaching *de novo*. He takes his starting point as the law of Moses. There may be an element of overstatement in the contention of the New Testament scholar Gerhard Kittel that "there is not a single one of Jesus' ethical teachings of which it could be said, a priori, that it has any claim, as an individual precept, to absolute originality."[68] But of the fact that Jesus' teaching harmonized with the Old Testament there can be no doubt. In the broad context, he sets aside any intention of destroying the Law (5:17); its very details must be fulfilled (5:18). Those who disparage even its lesser requirements are to be held accountable. To relax the hold of the commandments involves a reduced place in the kingdom (5:19), and one who measures his righteousness by any lower principle cannot enter heaven (5:20). The standards of the scribes and Pharisees were defective, lacking in stringency, both in teaching, attitude, and performance.

Passing from this larger context of discussion to the formula by which the series of sayings is introduced, it must be admitted at once that the indecision over a dative or ablative Greek construction leaves us unsure whether Jesus remarked "Ye have heard that it was said *to*" or "*by* them of old time." In addition to similar constructions which require the former, both in Matthew's gospel wherever it occurs and on numerous occasions elsewhere in the New Testament, it may be observed that the latter translation would inject a contrastive emphasis on the personalities involved ["it was said by them of old . . ." "but I say unto you"] whereas the point of contrast appears to be what is taught — the weakening of the intention of the Mosaic law contrasted with its actual claim. Yet even the rendering "to them of old" might possibly mean that *God* said this *to* Moses and the prophets, while "by

[68]Cited by Windisch, *op. cit.*, p. 60.

them of old" rules out God as the giver or sayer. Not only is the translation "to them of old" most natural but, as Fairbairn points out, all the leading Greek commentators adopted it, as did the Syriac and Vulgate, whereas the first resort to "by them of old" was made by Beza.[69] Five times Jesus declares "Ye have heard that it was *said*" (5:21, 27, 33, 38, 43), not "that it was *written*," but when he rebukes the religious leaders, he asks them, "Have ye not *read*?" (12:3, 5; 19:4, 21:16, 42; 22:31). The Golden Rule, the very climax of the Sermon, is identified as an Old Testament rule (7:12). The contrast is not between the teaching of Moses and the teaching of Christ, the phrase "of old" being omitted four times (5:31, 38, 43 and also 5:27 in the best manuscripts); it is between the illicit additions to and reductions of the revealed law, and its true requirement as Jesus expounds it.

Hence the view is here resisted that Christ placed himself in absolute antagonism to Moses, as Manichaeanism taught, and also that he criticized the Mosaic law as imperfect and carnal, and hence expanded and revised it, as most Greek and Roman Catholic theologians, and after them Socinian and Arminian writers generally, have contended. Augustine already faced this view and placed himself squarely in opposition to it in controversy with the Manichaeans.[70] Luther and Calvin stand with Augustine, and the more recent writers on their side include Stier, Meyer, Olshausen, De Wette, Bleek, Ewald, Tholuck, Liddon, Fairbairn, and many others. In our decade, Murray has ably championed the same position.

Even where the quotations of the law are repeated without an unjustifiable addition on the part of his contemporaries (5:27, 33), the meaning was improperly reduced. All the precepts of the law with which our Lord deals involve, therefore, his critical appraisal and repudiation of the rabbinic interpretations, which either halted with an outward regard to the letter, or ventured to add supplementary comments which moderated the force of the commandments (5:21, regarding murder; 5:33ff., regarding oaths; 5:43, regarding neighbor love). This is confirmed by his indictment of the scribes and Pharisees later in the gospel for — in the words of Isaiah — "teaching as doctrines the commandments of men" (Mt. 15:9).

The specific references make it apparent that Jesus is not changing the Law, but rather unveiling its inner requirements. The prohibition against murder (21ff.) and adultery (27ff.) apply to the life of thought as well as of deed; the moral obligation they impose is spiritual, and not merely external. Jesus does not set forth a higher law of his own to discredit the Old Testament law, but declares that the requirement of Old Testament law was more exacting than the current tradition taught. This interpretation fits the facts in every instance in which the formula occurs in the Sermon. The only difficult passage is

[69] Fairbairn, *The Revelation of Law in Scripture*, pp. 228f., n. 1.
[70] Cf. Augustine, *Contra Faustum*, L, xvii, vi; xix, xxvii.

that bearing on divorce (31f.). Murray's discussion of this subject shows that no necessary exception exists in this case.[71] The remarks about oaths (5:33ff.) and the law of retribution (5:38ff.) do not take exception to the Mosaic legislation, but to the prevailing abuses of the biblical commandments. The command to swear in God's name (Dt. 6:13, 18ff., Ex. 22:11) had deteriorated into a justification of ambiguity in speech by modulated oaths (Mt. 23:16ff.). The law of retribution, which regulates the maximal penalties in graded proportion to the offenses committed, and which is in force wherever civilization prevails, had deteriorated into the negation of the law of love, so that men were regarded as receiving their due without reference to the principle of neighbor-love.

(7) The historic Reformed view is that the Sermon is an exposition of the deeper implications of the moral law, and hence a statement of the practical way in which *agape* is to work itself out in daily conduct here and now. The Sermon expresses therefore the only righteousness acceptable to God in this age or in any. As such, the Sermon condemns the man in sin, is fulfilled by Christ's active and passive obedience, and serves as the believer's rule of Christian gratitude in personal relations.

The Sermon has for its intention the same as did the Torah: that it be fulfilled. The difficulty of carrying out a given command may be granted, but Jesus refuses to tolerate such concessions to inner obduracy as those made by Judaism. He sets forth the only righteousness by which man gains access to the Kingdom of God. The Sermon does not deal directly with how a man might meet its requirements. But its presupposition is none other than that of Scripture in its entirety: that it is impossible for man as sinner to justify himself before the law, and that he can meet the Divine requirement of righteousness only through the Mediator. The Sermon is relevant as the standard of life and conduct which convicts men of sin and which restrains wickedness, and as the rule of daily life for the Christian believer.

The existential view errs in holding that the Sermon is not intended as practical legislation clearly defined in propositional form. The dispensational view errs in holding that the Sermon was given as practical legislation to be fulfilled primarily in the future millennial age. The humanist is wrong in holding that it has been outmoded by evolutionary progress; and the interim-ethic school is wrong in its position that the Sermon is discredited by its eschatological factor; the liberal is wrong when he treats the Sermon as an ethic independent of supernatural redemption; the dispensationalist is wrong when he assigns it only a secondary relevance for this age; and the existentialist is wrong when he finds its relevance only in the sphere of attitude and not at all as practical legislation. The humanist, liberal and interim-ethic views are

[71]John Murray, *Divorce,* pp. 19ff. Christ in Matthew 19:9 indicates that the Mosaic legislation recognized the Divine ideal on the basis of creation: Moses *suffered* (hence recognized the action as less than an absolute ideal); his legislation was *permitted* (with Divine approval).

wrong in supposing that man in his present state can fulfill the requirements of the Sermon, although they differ in that two of these views regard such fulfillment as absurd and socially irrelevant, while the liberal view regards it as socially desirable. Some dispensational writers imply that during the millennial age, when the Sermon is relevant for the Jew under the law rather than grace, some will attain salvation on the basis of fulfillment. This is despite the emphasis of the Gospel that the salvation of sinners is solely on the ground of grace. The existential view proclaims, and rightly so, the impossibility of the man in sin himself fulfilling the Sermon's requirements, although it erroneously dismisses the propositional nature of the teaching.

By way of contrast, the Reformed view maintains certain important emphases in interpreting the Sermon: it sets forth at the same time the moral claim of the Creator addressed to man on the basis of creation, the Decalogue, and the future judgment. The Sermon is a closer definition of the constant-Divine ethical requirement.

As the Sermon reflects the experience of Jesus, the bearer of ideal human nature, it reflects an absolute moral claim that is fully natural. Its extreme and radical impression upon its hearers is due to man's predicament as a sinner, but from the point of view of Jesus, the speaker, the Sermon has no paradoxic and radical elements. The Sermon has in view God's rule over human life; he alone defines the nature of the right; and apart from the satisfaction of his ethical stipulations there is no acceptability with him.

The sermon marks no departure from the creation ethic, nor from that of the Old Testament. It lays stress on the inwardness of the law's demands with even more exactness than do the prophets, although this is not a difference of emphasis.

A major tenet underlying the Reformed view is the unity of the Divine covenant with man.[72] As God is uniform in his nature, his revelation likewise does not change over time nor does it contradict itself. The ethical norms he addresses to man are constant ones. These ethical norms constitute the one law of God, eternal, unchanging, authoritative for all men at all times in all places. The moral law, as revealed in creation, in the Decalogue, in the discourses of Jesus, and in the criterion of the final judgment, is an organic unity. This fact is substantiated by the exegesis of Matthew 5:17-20, and this passage determines the approach to the Sermon as a whole. Not even Christ can improve the moral law, for he is its ultimate source. Jesus declares the Mosaic ethic to be eternally valid and to exhibit the righteousness requisite for entrance into the kingdom. Instead of reversing it or revising it, Christ declares the whole law, including its least commandment, to be eternally binding. Hence he asserts the basic harmony and

[72]Calvin writes: "The covenant of all the fathers is so far from differing substantially from ours that it is the very same; it only varies in the administration." *Institutes,* II, x, ii.

continuity of his ethic with the Old Testament ethic. The fact of "progressive disclosure" in revelation-history does not involve a change in the essential meaning of morality. The later manifestation is implicit in the earlier and develops harmoniously from it within an organic whole. True, the New Testament moral revelation is characterized by certain differences, but these are differences of mode, not substance.[73] The Sermon brings into clear relief the eternal oneness of the law.

The Sermon presupposes the realizability of the ethical demands of God in human nature. The will of God is presented as genuinely capable of actualization by essential human nature, and that will is nowhere reduced nor accommodated to the moral limitations of man as sinner. The dictum "I ought, therefore I can" is not without its truth, even though Kant and liberal moralists after him reduced its meaning to make human ability the measure of human responsibility. Its biblical sense, rather, is that human responsibility, established on the basis of the revelation of the will of the Creator, measures the ability of human nature on the basis of creation. Man's inability to fulfill the Divine demand must be traced not to his essential humanity but to human nature conditioned by sin. There is no salvation that does not obediently fulfill God's commands; this is the teaching of Old Testament and New Testament alike (Lev. 18:5, Rom. 10:5, Gal. 3:12).

If we survey the Sermon itself — conscious that it is not the whole of the ethical teaching of Jesus — we shall find all the evidence we need of his profound regard for the authority of the Decalogue.

Jesus elsewhere expresses in the all-inclusive commandment of uncompromised love for the Living God that men are to have no other gods than Jehovah. Here, the same thought appears as the constant presupposition of the Sermon. The Lord's Prayer crowds out all other reference-points for this world and the next (6:9ff.); it is God's kingdom that will prevail (6:13), and that men are to seek above all else (6:33); their perfection is to mirror his (5:48), their works are to glorify him (5:16), and they are to hunger and thirst for the righteousness he prescribes (5:6); he sees them in secret (6:4, 6, 18), and rewards sincerity in almsgiving, prayer, fasting, while denying a reward to ostentation (6:1ff.).

The commandment against graven images is not reflected as explicitly as the first commandment. Israel had learned well the evils of idolatry. She had spent long years in captivity — a judgment upon her for bowing down to false gods. Never again had she given herself over to a pagan deity. But what Jesus elsewhere states so forcefully — that "God is spirit" (Jn. 4:24) — is clearly implied in the prayer address "our Father which art in heaven" (6:9).

[73]Calvin's list of the five differences may be summarized: The New supersedes the Old by completing what was partial, by exhibiting the substance instead of only the shadows of figures, by a spiritual doctrine written on the heart rather than in literal and external form, by liberty through deliverance from former bondage, and by its universality in contrast with the older limitation to one nation.

God's name must not be taken in vain. This commandment is echoed in the condemnation of frivolous and ambiguous oaths (5:33, cf. Lev. 5:4, 19:12). Perjury was severely condemned by the Mosaic law, as was any vain and needless use of the name of God. The Jews sidestepped the letter of the law by swearing in the name of the creaturely. Their intent was the same as an oath that used the name of God — to transfer the aura of the sacred to the dubious. The Old Testament term *shav,* used in Exodus 20:7 and Deuteronomy 5:11, carries the dual connotation of vanity and falsehood. It may not be too far amiss to find a link to this commandment in the prohibition of vain repetition in prayer (6:7), and in the exhortation implicit in the instruction for prayer: "hallowed be thy name" (6:9).

In suggesting points of continuity between the Sermon and the Decalogue, we shall postpone discussion about the fourth commandment, the sabbatarian commandment, until last in order to give it the full discussion it requires.

Concerning the fifth commandment, regarding honor toward parents, the Sermon has nothing to say. However, it does take cognizance of special parental care for the young (7:9f.). And it implies in using the term Father when speaking of God that an earthly father is a responsible authority deserving of obedience. But elsewhere in the gospel of Matthew we learn of Jesus' vindication of the commandment. He strikes out against the way in which the Pharisees and scribes neglected or perverted it: "He answered them, 'And why do you transgress the commandment of God for the sake of your tradition? For God commanded, Honor your father and your mother, and, He who speaks evil of father or mother, let him surely die. But you say, if anyone tells his father or his mother, what you would have gained from me is given to God, he need not honor his father. So, for the sake of your tradition, you have made void the law of God. You hypocrites!" (Mt. 15:3ff.). The background that provoked this comment is interesting. By a legal maneuver, a Jew could dedicate his possessions to the temple, and thereby evade the necessity of supporting his parents while he himself could continue to benefit from the proceeds. The commandment is thus given a very practical interpretation: small children owe their parents obedience, and adult children owe their parents assistance. To profess to honor God by devoting one's substance to him while neglecting the support of needy parents is regarded as a dishonor to parents. This, in turn, disregards a fundamental duty of life.

The commandment against murder is one of the two which Jesus analyzes at some length. In doing so, he emphasizes its inner spirit. And this provides a pattern of interpretation that guards against casting the law as a whole into a lower form. The Greek word for kill used here means "the taking of human life." The force of Jesus' teaching is that before the stage of outward violence is reached sin has been committed in inward intention. This renders a man equally guilty with the actual murderer in God's sight. The first flush of anger is murder. Charles Gore writes: "Our Lord raises deliberately allowed sins of thought and feeling to the level previously occupied by overt acts."[74] Geoffrey Stafford comments, "According to the ethics of the Sermon on the Mount the intention ranks with the act, the desire to destroy with the deed."[75] The commandment against murder is not kept even by the mere abstinence from the intention to injure another. Before a believer can present an offering to God, all must be right between himself and his neighbor. The believer must settle all matters of grievance amicably. In fact, the command against murder is seen at last to have its basis in the principle of love, and hence requires the actual benefitting of the neighbor. Whatever withholds from him a blessing which we are empowered to impart deprives him of life.

The Sermon brings a remarkable confirmation and vitality to the seventh commandment, against adultery, and to monogamous marriage as the Divine purpose in creation. The commandment had always been violated in outward unfaithfulness to the marriage bond. Now Jesus intensifies this by saying it is violated in the lustful glance. "Whosoever looketh upon a woman to lust after her hath committed adultery already in his heart" (5:28). Arthur Pink writes, "Our Lord here declared that the seventh commandment is broken even by a secret though unexpressed desire."[76] The Pharisees had extended the commandment no further than the outward and physical act, supposing that God would be indifferent if the iniquity were restricted to the mind.

It is quite natural that Jesus would treat the nature of the marriage bond at the same time he spoke about adultery. The easy dissolution of formal marriage ties in order to change bed-partners is adultery *de facto*. In another passage (19:8), Jesus said that divorce was not something inherent in marriage from the start. On the basis of creation, there was not an escape-hatch from the marriage bond. Marriage was "for keeps," not "for trial."

Moses had been appealed to by those wanting a divorce as an authority giving them leave to put away their wives. Jesus clearly counters reading easy and quick divorce into Mosaic legislation by categorically stating that unchastity is the only possible grounds for divorce.

There is reason to hesitate over the assumption that Mosaic legislation approved a basis for divorce other than adultery. The decisive passage (Dt. 24:1ff.) is equally consistent with the idea that Moses imposed restrictions on injustices that characteristically attended divorce from a wife for reasons less than infidelity. The object of the passage is to guard the dignity of the marriage relationship by preventing a

[74]Charles Gore, *The Sermon on the Mount* (London: John Murray, 1907), p. 60.
[75]Geoffrey Stafford, *The Sermon on the Mount* (New York: Abingdon, 1927), p. 214.
[76]Arthur Pink, *An Exposition of the Sermon on the Mount* (Grand Rapids, Baker, 1951), p. 82.

man's remarriage to a woman he had divorced and who had married again. Why had Moses allowed a written bill of divorce in circumstances not involving adultery? Jesus replies that he suffered this. There is no necessary implication that Moses approved such extension of the grounds of divorce. Nor is there any indication that the standpoint of the Decalogue did not consistently reflect Moses' own position.[77] The widened liberties that tradition gave to divorce were repudiated by Jesus. He asserts here that monogamous marriage is basic to creation ethics. Marriage again becomes a commitment in which both partners strive to make it work and succeed at the highest level, rather than a legalized way to get sexual gratification and have a housekeeper.

The eighth commandment, against stealing, does not come directly into view in the Sermon, although stealing is implicitly condemned in the reminder that "thieves break through and steal" earthly possessions (6:19), whereas heavenly treasure cannot be looted. But the application of the principle of inwardness, already insisted upon, would find a violation of the command not only in the outward misappropriation of another's property, but in a selfish use of it, whether by violence or deception.

The prohibition of false witness, likewise, is not directly introduced in the Sermon. In the treatment of murder, an insult heaped upon another is prohibited (5:22). Moreover, such judging of others so that their faults are exaggerated is specifically condemned (7:1ff.). It is from such distortions that false witness frequently springs.

The commandment against coveting is not explicitly treated either. Yet it is strongly reinforced by the inwardness of the Sermon as a whole. Certain isolated evidences of its validity are readily detected: the poor are blessed (5:3); earthly treasure is not to be amassed (6:19ff.); anxiety over things is the root of many evils (6:25ff.); one cannot worship both God and mammon (6:24). The propriety of finding such a connection is quickly gleaned from the larger teaching of Jesus. A covetous request by a man seeking an inheritance brought a stern rebuke and warning: "Take heed, and beware of all covetousness; for a man's life does not consist in the abundance of his possessions" (Lk. 12:15).

If the principle we have followed thus far is sound, it will be impossible to dismiss the sabbath commandment as belonging to the ceremonial law alone and therefore as wholly abrogated by Jesus. It is equally impossible to deny all point of continuity between the sabbath and the Lord's Day. Nowhere in the teaching of Jesus do we find any declaration that the sabbath is to be abolished, nor is there any questioning of its validity on the basis of the Divine command. Rather, there is always an implicit recognition that the distinction of the six and one days has a Divine authority. Six are for work; one is for rest and worship. Nowhere does he argue for the relaxation of its authority.

[77]Fairbairn, *op. cit.*, p. 127f.

But, as in the case of other commandments, he vigorously defends the sabbath against the misconstructions and appendages of the legalists and traditionalists. The sabbath is treated in two aspects in the New Testament. One is the ceremonial aspect that finds its origin in the creation sabbath of the Lord God. It is a prefiguring of the eternal rest of believers. The other aspect is sabbath as it was viewed by the Pharisees and legalists among the Jews of Jesus' day. The elders had added tradition upon tradition to make the sabbath a burdensome religious requirement. Its ceremonial significance was fulfilled and abrogated in Christ. The legalist encumbrances were swept away by Christ. The ceremonial significance was valid only until the Lord of the sabbath himself came, yet the sabbath-principle itself has permanent validity. The Christian exposition of the sabbath adds nothing essentially new to the Decalogue, but teaches merely that its temporary features fall away. It is infused with an enlarged inward significance in the era of fulfillment. It refocuses upon a dramatic spiritual content in the present age that had been concealed in part by the accretions of tradition, the legalistic spirit of observance, and concentration on its ceremonial side.

The essential purpose of the sabbath is not in conflict with the preservation and maintenance of life. Jesus permitted his disciples to satisfy their hunger by plucking grain as they passed through a cornfield (Mt. 12:1ff.; Mk. 2:23f., 3:1ff.; Lk. 6:1ff., 13:10ff.; Jn. 5:9). The sabbath existed for the good of man, not man for the sabbath. This basic principle had already been enforced when David ate the shewbread in an emergency, and when Jesus taught that a sheep could be rescued from a pit on the sabbath. The principle that the sabbath was spiritual could be seen from the fact that the sacred rite of circumcision was permissible on this day no less than others, and extended services could be conducted in the temple. The sabbath did not therefore imply simply an absolute rest. Rather, it implied the cessation of ordinary labor imposed by the demands of man's vocation in order that the higher claims of life might be brought unrestrictedly into view. The prohibition of labor had a view to the enlarged life of fellowship with God, and not alone the observance of the ceremonial law and the benevolent rest from labor requisite for physical renewal. In unusual circumstances, work could be justified; but whatever robbed the sabbath of its holy and gracious purpose was to be resisted. The real aim of the sabbath is the wellbeing of man, and from the beginning its outward observance was intended to implement that design. The sabbath is an instrument of the spiritual rule of God in the life of man. "The Son of Man is Lord of the sabbath." Fairbairn tells us: "He is Lord of the Sabbath, and, as such, has a right to order everything concerning it, so as to make it, in the fullest sense, a day of blessing for man — a right, therefore, if He should see fit, to transfer its observance from the last day of the week to the first, that it might be associated with the consummation of His redemptive work, and to make it, in accordance with the impulsive life and energy thereby brought in, more than in the past, a day of active and hallowed employment for the good of men."[78] It points beyond the Logos' creation-rest to his redemption-rest.

The Sermon itself provides, as we have noted, its own broad contact with the ethical teaching of the Old Testament in Jesus' declaration that he came not to destroy, but to fulfill the law and the prophets (5:17). And the point of connection with specific commandments of the Decalogue is obvious. Not only does the teaching on murder and adultery immediately recall the sixth and seventh commandments; there is a considerably broader connection. The commandments occupied a most conspicuous place in the Old Testament economy, even though they were not the whole of revealed morality. Jesus maintains their crucial relevance. If we turn to the ethical teaching of Jesus as a whole we find, even if in summary form, remarkable evidences of Jesus' assertion of the permanent validity of the commandments. In a classic passage Jesus asserts that the real cause of all moral impurity is internal; he brings into view at least five of the commandments in a single sentence: "From within, out of the heart of man, come evil thoughts, fornication, theft, murder, adultery, coveting, wickedness, deceit, licentiousness, an evil eye, slander, pride, foolishness" (Mk. 7:21f.). The conversation with the rich young ruler leads directly to the validity of the commandments. And in one gospel the commandments are conjoined with the principle of neighbor-love, as Jesus already had done in the Sermon. The meeting of the divinely-required righteousness is made the condition of salvation: "If thou wilt enter into life, keep the commandments . . . thou shalt not kill . . . commit adultery . . . steal . . . bear false witness. Honor thy father and thy mother, and, thou shalt love thy neighbor as thyself" (Mt. 19:19; cf. Mk. 10:19, Lk. 18:20). The difference between the legalistic and the spiritual way of keeping the commandments is brought into clear contrast by the rich ruler's insistence: "All these I have observed; what do I lack?" (Mt. 19:20). The reply made obvious the principle that the law of neighbor love, which fulfills the second table of the Law, involves an active concern for the blessing and good of others. The besetting sin of this ruler lay in his attitude toward his wealth. Jesus made it crystal-clear that every violation of the commandments derives from a flaw in the life of love. And every such violation brings man to the threshold of the judgment to come. The ethic of Eden and the ethic of Sinai and the ethic of the Mount of Beatitudes and the ethic of the future judgment of the race stand in essential unity and continuity.

The essential continuity between the law of Moses and the ethical teaching of Jesus in and through their common basis in special Divine disclosure does not exclude the unique contribution that Jesus brought to Hebrew-Christian ethics. Indeed, it is a violation of the facts to

[78] *Ibid.*, p. 238.

represent the Mosaic law as carnal in order to enhance the ethics of Jesus. That Jesus introduces an important advance into the whole tradition of revealed ethics is beyond question. But the Old Testament itself repudiated an external and narrow conception of moral obligation. The Golden Rule itself is followed by the assurance that "this is the law and the prophets" (7:12). What has been called "the elevation of morality into the sphere of the Spirit" involves no radical break with the Mosaic and Old Testament conception. Rather, it is a break with the enslavement of ethics by the mere letter and by the particular rules of conduct of Jesus' contemporaries. Jesus' attitude toward the Old Testament is at all points the very highest; he regards it and appeals to it as an authoritatively inspired literature, the veritable Word of God communicated through chosen men. The tradition of Moses and the prophets was never intended to serve as a mere outward regimen, and that with no responsibilities outside of national bounds. In criticizing the mere legalistic observance of the Old Testament ethic (Mt. 12:9f., Mk. 2:21ff.), Jesus shares the spirit of the Hebrew morality of revelation. Whatever must be said about Jesus' abrogation of the Old Testament ceremonial law, which he did in fulfilling it, his fulfillment of the moral law is directed at preserving intact the ethical revelation of Sinai in its claim upon mankind. And he insisted that that claim had to be fully met if there were to be redemption.

The Sermon is the final and deepest statement of the Law. In this exposition of the Law we come upon one of the ways in which Jesus registers an advance upon the past. He claims for himself an authority every bit the equal of the Old Testament; the reiterated "but I say unto you" implies an authority on his own account which makes an appeal to Moses and the prophets unnecessary. Alongside his regard for the Old Testament as inspired stands the confidence that he enters authoritatively into the depths of its inner meaning. He assigns to himself the right to criticize the Law itself, not in the sense of destroying it, but of fulfilling it by bringing out its inner moral demand and by exhibiting its higher intent. The Sermon doubtless follows "the best traditions of Hebrew religious thought," T. B. Strong avers, but "in its emphasis upon the spiritual as opposed to hollow externalism . . . it goes deeper into things . . ."[79] The Mosaic law is exhibited "in its deeper import," Tholuck has somewhere remarked, as the moral norm of Christ's kingdom.

This advance may be seen in the intense inwardness of the Sermon. The flush of anger constitutes murder, the lustful look is adultery. The act resides in the intention. Alongside this analysis of negative behavior stands the equally vivid analysis of the positive: love alone fulfills the whole of the commandments. It alone embraces the entire content of moral obligation. The Mosaic law, as we have noted previously, gave no mere marginal consideration to the whole-souled love for God and to

[79]T. B. Strong, *Christian Ethics*, pp. 20f.

neighbor. And it even protested the reduction of the latter to a narrow nationalist prejudice. But it was Jesus who brought together in a single utterance these disjoined Mosaic emphases on love, and exhibited their inner unity as the first and second commandments which contain the spirit of the whole. The whole emphasis on inwardness characteristic of the Sermon demonstrates in many ways the fact that the essence of the Law, even when stated in the form of negative prohibition, is love. Although the sabbath command is not repeated in the Sermon, elsewhere Jesus brings it under the same principle. None of the commands can be invoked so that disservice to one's neighbor is justified, not even that of the sabbath: "Is it lawful on the sabbath day to do good, or to do evil? to save life, or to destroy it?" (Lk. 6:9). The spirituality of the moral law of God, reaching in its precepts behind all words and actions to the very thoughts and intentions of the heart, is raised to the highest plane.

Implicit in Jesus' exposition of the law and the prophets and in his rejection of the interpretations supported by contemporary spokesmen for Judaism is his unyielding claim to be the authoritative expositor of the exact significance of the revealed law. He repudiates the oral tradition of Jewish Torah, singling out for special criticism its prescriptions concerning relations with the Am-ha-Arez (Mk. 2:15ff., Lk. 7:29, 15:1ff.), sabbath observance (Mk. 2:23ff., 3:1ff.; Lk. 13:10ff., 14:1ff.); fasting (Mk. 2:18ff.), and ceremonial purifications (Mt. 15:1ff., Mk. 7:1ff., Lk. 11:37ff.). Six times in succession he places himself over against the prevailing official interpretations of the law and in correction of the received tradition declares: "But *I* say unto *you*" (5:22, 28, 32, 34, 39, 44). The "for verily I say" (or "I tell you") is found in 5:18, 20, 6:2, 5, 16, 25 and 29, until we hear the astonished crowds recognize that "he taught them as one having authority" (7:29). The legalistic emphasis on the letter of the Mosaic law without the spirit of love, and worse yet, the relaxation of the letter by devious twisting of tradition and interpretation, fell not only below his requirement, but also below that of the law and prophets.

This is reflected further in Jesus' annulment of the ceremonial law, a dramatic development of vast importance in the religio-ethical outlook of the Hebrew Christian revelation. The Mosaic legislation incorporated at once the revelation of the eternal moral law and those positive commandments which were to be observed during the Old Testament dispensation of promise and messianic anticipation. It did not so clearly distinguish between the permanent and temporary validity of these elements, since both were imposed as absolute requirements. Priority is doubtless assigned to the Decalogue. And the prophets lash out against those who conform to the ceremonial law in order to compensate for despite done to the moral law which it is actually intended to serve. Still, the Old Testament view bounded the whole of life necessarily by the ethical-ceremonial. The distinction between the two is laid bare by

Jesus. He fulfills and thereby abrogates the ceremonial. He fulfills and thereby validates perpetually the ethical. The most forceful statement of the contrast, from his lips, is to be found in Mark 7:14-23. The Revised Standard Version makes clear that Jesus claimed in his own person the right authoritatively to abolish the ceremonial law: "Whatever goes into a man from outside cannot defile him. . . . Thus he declared all foods clean" (Mk. 7:18f.). Such a passage makes it impossible to exegete the "jot and tittle" declaration to imply the permanent validity of the ceremonial law. The only consistent exegesis is to subjugate this declaration to the many other New Testament verses that bear upon the believer's fulfilled relationship to the ceremonial law.

In Jesus' abrogation of the ceremonial system we are led to his personal significance as the Messiah of Old Testament prophecy and the Redeemer of the doomed souls of sinful men. He himself stands at the center of the Sermon in a way in which Moses never stood related to the Old Testament law. This is evident in several ways.

He criticizes the current scribal and pharisaical interpretations of the revealed law. He claims the right authoritatively to discriminate the inner, neglected meaning of the law of Moses. Those who fail to "do these sayings" are foolish, imperiling their destiny in the life to come (7:24ff.).

He even goes further. He actually sets aside a Mosaic judgment indicating that it involved a concession to the low condition of society which was not tolerated in man's condition of integrity before the fall. Divorce was not right even though Moses had reluctantly allowed it. The moral will of God was otherwise. Even in a sinful society, the believer is called to the Divine ideal in creation, *i.e.*, monogamous marriage (Mt. 19:8f.), except for the one sin which is destructive of monogamous love — adultery (Mk. 10:1ff., Lk. 16:18). The Sermon proclaims an ethic of absolute obedience; it exhibits the norm of the judgment of the human race. Windisch rightly affirms that the Sermon "presents a doctrine of righteousness whose fulfillment guarantees acquittal at the Day of Judgment and admittance to the Kingdom of Heaven (Mt. 5:20, 7:21, 5:3ff.) . . . the righteousness laid down in the Law . . . given a stricter interpretation" and "this righteousness is the new doctrine of Christ Jesus."[80]

He indirectly draws attention to himself as the sinless one who alone meets the requirements of perfect righteousness. The discourse, as Hogg and Watson remark, is his "self-portraiture"; he "lived the Sermon for thirty years before He preached it."[81] He speaks as an authority independent of the law, conscious of his own righteousness. He has come not to destroy even the minutiae, but rather "to fulfill" (5:17). Not only does he exhibit the radical inner demand of the law in his own

[80]Windisch, *op. cit.*, p. 168.
[81]C. F. Hogg and J. B. Watson, *On the Sermon on the Mount* (London: Pickering & Inglis, 1947), p. 12.

teaching, but he meets that demand in the way he lived. The perfect is now manifested not alone on the teaching level, but is spelled out in the flesh. His own personal purity is the drama of the purity of God.

He represents himself as sitting on the judgment seat of God determining the eternal destinies of all men. The judgment will discriminate the obedience or disobedience to his commandments of "everyone which heareth these words of mine" (7:24). The wicked will hear him say "I never knew you; depart from me" (7:23). There is more about hell in this sermon than in any of his other discourses. He clarifies the inner intensity of the law's demand, and enforces it with new and more powerful sanctions, including his personal agency in the judgment to come.

He regards himself as the climactic goal to which the whole movement of Old Testament revelation is directed. He confirmed and completed the Old Testament disclosure. Whoever reads the Sermon carefully cannot but be impressed, as Samuel J. Andrews was, by the intimation that all who receive him are exposed to reproach and persecution, which attaches to them "for my sake" (5:11).[82] He claims the right to interpret the Old Testament as the Coming One, setting himself in the context of the messianic promises: "I am come" (5:17).[83] Basil F. C. Atkinson is quite right in insisting that "Jesus fulfilled the law in His life by perfectly keeping it, in His teaching by promulgating an ethic of love which fulfills the law . . ., and in His death by exhausting its sanctions."[84]

If the Sermon on the Mount commences with blessing, in the initial beatitudes, the role that grace plays in it is not without some parallel in the law of Moses. The Decalogue contains also its underlayer of grace, shining forth in the preface to the commands and in the gracious promises interwoven among the successive prohibitions and injunctions. The two revelations differ in degree, not in kind. While the stern requirements of righteousness occupy the forefront, the background is grace. The Sermon, like the Decalogue, was given by the Redeemer-God.

The Sermon does not rule on the question of the possibility of human fulfillment of the Sermon in man's present condition — an issue which the New Testament epistles answer unequivocally in the negative. It may be profitable, nonetheless, to ask whether the Sermon contains any suggestions or anticipations of an answer. Some commentators have ventured to find in "narrow is the gate and hard the way to life, and few there be that find it" (7:14) an indication that some, at least, will meet the Sermon's requirements by their own efforts. But the saying does not settle the question, for it is equally applicable and true within the context of grace. Moreover, certain elements of the Sermon weigh

[82]Samuel J. Andrews, *The Life of Our Lord* (Grand Rapids: Zondervan Publishing House, reprint, 1954), p. 273.

[83]Cf. the Johannine "He that should come."

[84]Basil F. C. Atkinson, in *The New Bible Commentary* on Mt. 5:17 (Grand Rapids: Eerdmans, 1953).

against such a theory, the most impressive being the phrase "if ye then, being evil" (7:11). Here Jesus seems to endorse the view later expressed in the doctrine of original sin. In this passage occurs the emphasis on God's provision of "good things" tapered to the special needs of his creatures (7:11). The disciples' prayer, moreover, incorporates the reference to the forgiveness of sins (6:12). And the phrase "I am come" (5:17) suggests that the messianic redemptive standpoint is presupposed.

And yet it can hardly be said that the doctrine of the cross, let alone of substitutionary atonement, is overtly presented. Indeed, one will search the gospels as a whole for more than occasional passages in which the atonement is brought explicitly into view, and even here the failure of the disciples to grasp its realities before the crucifixion and resurrection is patent. The New Testament assumes that the full explication of the atonement is appropriate and effective only after the event itself is an accomplished fact; once Christ's death furnishes an efficacious atonement, imputed righteousness becomes a central theme.

It would be a risky venture to argue, from the theology and ethics of the Sermon taken in isolation, that the Christology and soteriology of Matthew are non-Johannine and non-Pauline. John's gospel sets out with the significance of Jesus in the familiar sacrificial category of the Lamb (Jn. 1:29). He is identified from the beginning as the Messiah and Son of God (Jn. 1:34). Matthew's gospel reaches this confession only by the time of Caesarea Philippi (Mt. 16:16). It unveils the redemptive Christ as late as the "Son of Man" saying (20:28) and the supper (26:28). But in neither gospel is the significance of Christ's atonement clear to the disciples prior to the crucifixion (Jn. 2:22). And in neither can the least suggestion be found of a disagreement among the disciples and apostles over the significance of Jesus. So too, the Sermon implies no diversity with the developed Pauline perspective. Paul's epistles contain fragments of the Sermon (*e.g.*, Rom. 12:14, 20), not as an ethics of works-salvation, but as instruction for new converts and for the moral edification of believers saved by grace.

The Sermon presents Christ in the role of moral legislator. He warns of the judgment to come. Obedience to his words will determine the destinies of men. This is evidence of the fidelity of the narrative to the progressive self-revelation of Jesus. The announcement of the gift of redemption is marginal to the primary purpose of the Sermon. The Sermon does not treat the subject how man possesses the righteousness that is necessary for entrance into the Kingdom; it develops the indispensability of such righteousness. Hence it cannot be represented as occupying a position contrary to Paul's doctrine of justification by faith alone. At most, it may be regarded as taking "the last step" before the actual proclamation of that gift (7:11). A righteousness superior to that of the scribes and Pharisees for outward conformity is necessary for entrance to heaven (5:20); even the lesser violations place one in danger of judgment and hell fire (5:22); many go to destruction (7:13); rather than break the law, it is better to pluck out an eye or cut off a hand (5:29f.); trees that do not bring forth good fruit are cast into the fire (7:19); even many who call Jesus Lord, prophesy in his name, cast out devils, and do other remarkable deeds will be repudiated as workers of iniquity (7:23).

Could there be any more direct introduction than this to the proclamation and admission of the necessity of Divine redemptive rescue? J. Gresham Machen remarks: "The Mosaic law requires already more than man as sinner can fulfill; the deeper law of Jesus asks even more, and before it all are obviously condemned. Like the rest of the New Testament, the Sermon leads straight to the Cross, to a divine means of salvation."[85] The standard condemns all men as sinful, and "aside from the truth of the divine person and redeeming work of Christ, it would fill the heart of the hearer with bewilderment and despair."[86]

With reference to the soteriological question, therefore, it might be said that the liberal view was right in finding no overt teaching about salvation by atonement in the Sermon, but wrong in repudiating the doctrine on that basis. The existential view is right in asserting that the moral requirement drives the hearer to despair, rather than to confidence in the ability of the natural man to fulfill it personally and culturally. But this view errs in suggesting that fulfillment is inevitably impossible for human nature as such. The Sermon basically provides a closer definition of the law. Christ fulfills the law efficaciously for all who put their trust in him, and it remains the rule of gratitude for Christian behavior.

The validity of the Sermon as a rule of practice for the regenerate believer who shares in God's redemptive grace is recognized by two important evangelical Christian traditions, the Anabaptist and the Reformed. But these traditions differ sharply over the question of the applicability of the Sermon to all the ethical relationships of life. The Anabaptist-Mennonite tradition holds that the Sermon provides a revealed guide for both official and personal relationships; the Reformed tradition confines its significance to personal relations.

The impracticability of the Sermon as an exhaustive rule of social ethics has been voiced by many. Humanists have complained of its inadequacy for grappling with problems of the economic and political order. However, it is fair to remark that even if such social ethics were clearly expressed, the naturalistic bias would still discriminate against any absolute ethics. Yet there is force to the question: "Is simple uncalculating compassion, is purity of heart, is brotherly love, enough with which to face the intricate network of modern industrialism? Are we to live our social life by taking no thought for the morrow?"[87] The

[85]Machen, *Christianity and Liberalism,* p. 38.
[86]Charles R. Erdman, *The Gospel of Matthew* (Philadelphia: Westminster, 1920), pp. 45f.
[87]Randall and Randall, *op. cit.,* p. 82.

question was aimed, of course, at the liberal social gospel expectation that the Sermon constitutes a cultural ethic for unregenerate man. Humanism shared the optimitic view of human nature, but doubted the social adequacy of the Sermon. If pacifism appeared to some humanists for a time as a workable solution for the problems of war and international tensions, the law of love was admittedly not without utility in the economic world. Yet the admonitions of the Sermon appeared visionary and impractical as an exhaustive criterion of morality in the social orders.

The Anabaptist-Mennonite tradition insisted that the Sermon is a New Testament code for all the relations of life, not as a cultural ethic for mankind generally, but for Christian society on the basis of regeneration. It viewed the New Testament as surpassing the Old Testament by internalizing conduct generally, and especially by prohibiting the believer's participation in war. The relevance of the Sermon was restricted to believers, who were to withdraw themselves socially from the world. They were to orient all the social duties of life to its demands. Hence a policy of pacifism and non-resistance, of refusal to take oaths, came to characterize the Anabaptist and later Mennonite groups in their strategy of withdrawal from the world. The price of maintaining the social relevance of the Sermon as a cultural ethic was not simply an insistence on a regenerate expression of conduct. It involved the removal of the Christian community from the world. This separation became an ideal to strive toward. The pursuit of utopianism in history became the goal of Christian achievement.

The Reformed view, insisting equally on a regenerate basis for Christian experience and life, was suspicious of the attempt to withdraw believers out of the world and to establish a utopian society. It was convinced that the former attempt was based on a misconception of the church's relation to the world, and the latter on an optimistic view of regenerate but unglorified human nature. The Reformed interpretation does not deny the contemporary relevance of the Sermon, but vigorously resists the attempts to crowd its claim exclusively upon every life. But it finds in the Sermon the Divine rule for neighbor relations, which is to be supplemented by biblical ethics in the larger sense if an adequate ethics in official and social relations is to prevail. Just as the epistles unfold the implications of the atonement, consistently with the more meager statements bearing on this doctrine from the lips of Jesus, so they enlarge upon the implications of Christian ethics for social action.

The importance of this distinction may be brought out by an illustration from everyday life. In Christian businessmen's circles it is often said that the Sermon on the Mount is the superlative code of ethics for success in business. But the fact is that a big businessman who conducts his trade by the ethics of the Sermon — giving two garments when one is asked free, not resisting violence — would soon find himself hopelessly in debt or completely out of business. Brunner remarked pointedly,

"It is unfair and absurd to require a Christian business man to conduct his business 'according to the laws of the Sermon on the Mount.' No one has ever conducted business on these lines or ever will; it is against all the rules of business itself. The 'office' of a business man belongs to a specific order which is not that of the relation between one person and another."[88] What is said here of the order of economics applies equally to the order of the state. A nation which runs its affairs by the law of neighbor relations — acting only on the principle of unrequited love, giving twice as much as its enemies demand, and committed to nonresistance of aggressions against it — is in process of national suicide.

The Reformed view thus approaches the Sermon with the presupposition that it does not negate the validity of civil government, not only because of the Sermon's failure to exclude such loyalties explicitly, but because only such an understanding of the Sermon appears consistent with the remainder of New Testament ethics. The example and teaching of Jesus in other passages bear this out. The Kingdom of Christ is not hostile to the civil order. The believer is involved in his relations to the state in certain social, political, and economic duties. But the Sermon does not reach beyond the person-to-person sphere with the consequent annulment of all other social and official relationships.[89]

The Sermon does not deal with the believer's official relations in the broader social sphere, according to Reformed sphere ethics. And hence, it does not bear on the questions of war or public oaths. No ethics of the individual's duties to community and state nor of the official relationship imposed upon men by the state and other social organisms is set forth. The Sermon utters the will of God irrespective of the difficulties raised by necessary secondary loyalties due to life in the world.

The Sermon is a guide in the immediate "one-and-one" neighbor relationships of life. This can be demonstrated from the circumstance that Jesus nowhere in his teaching expressly prohibits military participation, but has recourse to the subject for illustrative purposes (Lk. 14:31); he did not always apply the Sermon as the only rule of conduct, since by using the words "thou sayest" before Caiaphas the

[88]Brunner, *The Divine Imperative,* p. 434.

[89]The Mennonite interpretation argues that sphere ethics results in a necessary bifurcation of the ethical experience of the individual in the matter of personal and official duties, and that the "impracticality" of person-ethics in official relations is no disproof of relevance, since even in immediate neighbor-relations the personal ethic of the Sermon appears at times quite impractical. But the prime issue is not practicality in any event, but rather the Divine will and the whole gamut of ethical obligations this imposes upon man. The tension of the Christian ethical life in a fallen world is not confined to the adjustment of personal and official duties. Even the level of immediate neighbor relations involves us at times in a tension not wholly dissimilar from that involved in bearing arms in war, while loving one's enemy, as when justice requires the use of force in the very course of love.

high priest (Mt. 26:63f.) and Pilate the governor (27:11), he voiced a public oath (in the former case explicitly "by the living God").

The Sermon gives an individualistic articulation of ethics — dealing with my relations to the person at my side, and not with the larger question of my duty to social groups in the order of economics and politics, or to humanity as a whole.

Always it is the believer's relationship with one or two neighbors which is in view: brother, wife, enemy. This is a man-to-man ethic, in which the believer readies himself for the kingdom of heaven. Slavery to mammon, treasuring money and possessions, anxiety for future necessities, are all excluded. They not only detract from due attention to the service of God, but they betray a distrust of the fact that the believer's daily life is fully in God's care. To die by and for these commands is to make a smooth moral transition to the eschatological future.

Do we then compromise and nullify the intention of the Sermon when we add to our conduct official loyalties to the social order that are not mentioned in the Sermon? If the Anabaptists regarded such loyalties as a paganization of Christian ethics, others, *e.g.*, Georg Wunsch, have contended that the morality of the Sermon requires correction by that of God's created order. But there is no need to pose the issue in this form. Windisch argues rightly that even within the Sermon the created order is not wholly ignored. Jesus teaches that the order of creation itself disposes of the propriety of all temporal anxieties. The discourse teaches two spheres of Divine goodness — God's government of nature, in which his goodness is extended even to the wicked, and God's relationships with those in his Kingdom, where men call him Father and participate in view of forgiveness of sins. This recognition of God as creator means that the Sermon is not hostile to the world order, even though it does not delineate the responsibilities imposed on us by that order. Moreover, the fuller teaching of Jesus indicates his interest also in the claim that our social existence makes upon us. While the sinful bent of society constitutes a perversion of the Divine purpose, the present order in which all live falls in some sense within the will of God. And so we sustain positive relations to it. Jesus declares "Render unto Caesar the things that are Caesar's" (Mt. 22:21). While the Sermon prevents us from yielding to any notion of the autonomy of state or society, it does not preclude the recognition of responsibilities to the state and to society.

But any Christian social ethics must be formulated in view of biblical teaching elsewhere. In the Sermon Jesus recognizes only what must be rendered to God, not what must be rendered to Caesar. Our knowledge of the will of God is not to be derived only from the Sermon on the Mount. But the Sermon makes clear that in the Kingdom of heaven —

in contrast to our present social order — God stands in direct and immediate control. Love of God and love of man are involved also in responsibilities to the state, of which we learn elsewhere; love of neighbor requires a service to the state as well. But in official social relations a principle of justice prevails which is hardly to be identified with the one-and-one love of the Sermon on the Mount.

The epistles, those of Paul especially and to some extent those of Peter, indicate how state and society impose upon the believer additional responsibilities to those of neighbor-relations. The neglect of these responsibilities may also involve un-love. They set the ethical problem in its broader dimensions, and expand the implications of Christian ethics for community and economic realms, and exhibit more fully the believer's duty in the nation and in the world of work.

The ethics of sphere-sovereignty is often criticized as illegitimately contrasting personal and non-personal ethics. All our actions are held to be personal, and responsibility for them cannot be transferred to the state or society as an impersonal institution. Both Mennonite and Reformed views agree on the relevance of the Sermon as a rule of personal ethics, but they often fix attention on their differences. Mennonite ethics implies that the Reformed view surrenders the law of love in the social sphere and hence depersonalizes ethics; Reformed ethics accuses the Mennonite of making Christianity impractical by neglecting the larger cause of social justice. The contrast which Reformed ethics has always made between individual responsibility in the personal and social spheres is not intended to indicate an impersonal sphere of action. The question is not one of the transfer of responsibility, but rather of the recognition of legitimate authority to which one is bound to yield an ethical obedience. This artificial contrast is encouraged by the assignment of the Sermon on the Mount to the realm of "personal" ethics only, and even the description of it as an "ethic of neighbor-relations" falls under the same criticism in view of our Lord's emphasis in the Sermon itself that even enemies are to share in our neighbor-love (Mt. 5:44). Hence some such word as "immediate" is necessary to guard the idea from misleading elements. In the intimate, immediately-adjacent circle of daily relations, the larger elements of the social structure enter with less force.

We have said enough to indicate that the whole of Christian ethics is not to be derived from the Sermon on the Mount. Christian social ethics, which must be left for a separate volume, and Christian personal ethics must both be oriented to the biblical revelation as a whole. The larger teaching of Jesus must be kept in view in order to fashion a complete statement of the virtues he approved and the vices he condemned. But the Sermon does not on that account lose its crucial importance as the most comprehensive ethical discourse to fall from his lips. The Sermon remains an "ethical directory" for Christians. It contains the character and conduct which Jesus commends to his followers, the demand which the nature and will of God make upon men, the fundamental law of the Kingdom, and the ideal and perfect standard. It is the ultimate formula of ethics for which ideal human nature was fashioned by creation and is destined in eternity. Fallen nature is justified in Christ in conformity to it, and redeemed nature approximates it by the power of the indwelling Spirit of God.

13

THE BIBLICAL PARTICULARIZATION OF THE WILL OF GOD: THE LARGER NEW TESTAMENT

WE HAVE ALREADY INDICATED that every statement which would do justice to revealed ethics must assume, even if only tacitly, that the Scriptures define the content of the Divine will, and that the precept or law of God is nothing more or less than what the Bible requires of man. It will be said, of course, that a dramatic and important change takes place in the transition from Old to New Testament ethics. But even this can be maintained in conformity with Christian ethics only as it is shown that this is what the Bible teaches. If it be insisted that the ethical instruction of Jesus is the molding influence of Christian behavior and that the apostolic teaching in ethics enters properly into the moral outlook of the early church, this can hardly be defended except as being what the Bible teaches. If it be contended that there is more to the Christian ethical claim than mere precepts, but that the example of the life of Jesus exhibits the ethical ideal realized in human nature, this in turn can be vindicated only as what the Bible teaches. If it be emphasized that without a central and decisive reference to Jesus as Redeemer even his significance as a Teacher and as an Example is grossly misunderstood, this can be effectively maintained only by exhibiting it as the position of the New Testament. If it be asserted that Christian ethics depends directly upon the Holy Spirit as the dynamic of the moral agent's life, this too rests for its adequate warrant upon its conformity to the biblical witness. The revolt against an identification of the content of revealed ethics with what the Bible requires of man does not follow from any argument that to do so conceals essential elements of an ideal morality. The biblical representation of the claim of God and the obedience required of man embraces all of the legitimate elements of the ethical situation.

Since the rise of modern anti-intellectualistic views of revelation the idea of a unitary biblical ethic, of one coherent and consistent moral requirement that lays claim on all men at all times, has more and more been doubted and even assailed. This mood has found it profitable to exploit the differences between Old and New Testament ethics. It represents them as being in conflict over central features of human behavior. The most elementary New Testament standard is critical of practices which the Old Testament is said, if not to have approved, at least to have condoned — *e.g.*, bigamy, polygamy, divorce. These appear in the record without overt disapprobation and with no penalties. The impropriety of viewing the Old Testament in such light should be obvious at once from our earlier discussions of the Decalogue. The condemnation of adultery and of other transgressions is implicit in the creation ethics of man's state of integrity, as well as explicit in the law of Sinai. Without question the level of achievement in certain periods of the Old Testament history falls below others, and Israel went at last into captivity because of ethical disobedience. But the criterion of ideal behavior is never to be defined even by the achievement of the regenerate man, whether as an individual or in the entire community of faith, for man is still imperfect. A coherent Divine standard cannot be distilled from an empirical survey, even though a pattern may doubtless be inferred from the consensus of sanctified moral opinion.

Bigamy, polygamy, and divorce indubitably enter into the story of the patriarchal age, as well as that of subsequent ages. What is of consequence is the interpretation of these facts. A theological "justification" of these practices has even been ventured. The necessity of multiplying the race in its beginnings, and the fact that the Messiah had not yet been born, supposedly justified polygamy in the old dispensation, while the new economy removes every last vestige of approval of it. But nowhere in the Old Testament are polygamy and divorce considered as expressive of the will of God, lack of conformity to which is to be disciplined. Rather, they appear as temporary concessions made to human weakness of what the Old Testament clearly condemns as wrong in its specifically formulated ethical teaching. At most it might be said that polygamy and divorce were tolerated by way of sufferance or forbearance, as a concession to man's weakened condition in sin, in order to prevent a more radical abuse through the hardness of his heart. The New Testament provides some encouragement for so regarding divorce in the older economy (Mt. 19:8). Here again the fact of revelation in the historical flux opens up the possibility of a progressive revelation of the Divine ideal. The ideal existed already on the basis of creation, and subsequent revelation does not frustrate that ideal. Rather, its goal is man's restoration to it through the process of redemptive rescue. From the standpoint of the New Testament, therefore, even such a concession to human infirmity may be criticized. This criticism does not imply an ultimate self-contradiction within the Bible, but it exhibits the single viewpoint of Divine ethics in relation to man in the state of integrity, sin, redemption, and the judgment to come.

That the New Testament marks, as we have yet to observe, a distinct development in ethical revelation is not under dispute. What is denied is that this advance takes the form of a reversal of Old Testament. It is not only the New Testament that views monogamous marriage as the Divine ideal. The biblical revelation, on the basis of creation and the revelation of Sinai and the Sermon on the Mount, provides no ethical validation of either polygamy or divorce as the Divine ideal. There is a growing intolerance of what conflicts with the Divine will in the history of the redeemed. With the progress of redemptive revelation, man in sin was more and more enlightened about the implications of the moral law. At last the moral law was perfectly incarnate in Jesus Christ. Christians are more and more enabled to approximate its requirements through the subjective dynamic of the Spirit following Pentecost.

The New Testament judges transgression more incisively than does the Old. Even though adultery shatters the marriage, the death penalty is annulled (Jn. 8:5). But the reason is that the Old Testament gradations of punishment are transcended, and the sins of disposition rank with those of outward deed in being absolutely condemned (Mt. 5:28, Jn. 8:7). With the manifestation of the Redeemer, unacknowledged and uncovered sin has no plausible excuse (Jn. 15:22); the times of ignorance are ended (Acts 17:30). Not only is the murderer a candidate for the judgment, but "whosoever is angry with his brother without a cause shall be in danger of the judgment; and . . . whosoever shall say, Thou fool, shall be in danger of hell fire" (Mt. 5:21f.).

More than this, by unveiling moral perfection in the flesh, the New Testament removes the last comfort that man may find in his speculation that sin necessarily follows from man's having been made by God the way he was. The New Testament revelation exhibits the higher ideal as one that was in force before the fall and was perfectly realized in the human nature of the Redeemer. The New Testament pictures transgression against the will of God darkly against the provision of the Holy Spirit. In this era inaugurated at Pentecost God has made possible high moral performance through the moral dynamic of the Holy Spirit.

Yet the New Testament advance in ethics does not involve a basic disagreement with the Old Testament about the ultimate norms and standards of morality. There is a diversity in the degree in which these norms were realized in history. The public punishments of the various transgressions are relaxed in the church age with its greater emphasis on inwardness. But basic agreement between the two may be found in the biblical criteria of right and wrong.

The New Testament as a whole, as do Moses and the prophets and Jesus Christ, views the Decalogue as being a peak in ethical revelation. Jesus is not alone in his insistence that the Torah has a permanent duration. It has, in fact, a basis firmer than the stability of the space-time universe (Mt. 5:18). "The moral law, as revealed in the Old Testament, had with the apostles of our Lord a recognized place in the Christian church," Fairbairn remarks, "and was plainly set forth by them as the grand test of excellence, and the authoritative rule of life. They recognized and appealed to it thus simply as it stood in the written revelation of God, and *because so written.*"[1] The biblical reve-

[1]P. Fairbairn, *The Revelation of Law in Scripture,* p. 275.

lation in its entirety enforces the impression that the Ten Commandments are a perpetually valid summary of the moral law. The Pentateuch itself makes clear by the narrative of Cain and Abel (Gen. 4:8ff.) that it was wrong to kill long before Sinai. It has always been wrong to erect false gods, as wrong for Satan and his hosts as for man. To make a graven image of God, to take his name in vain, to desecrate the sabbath, to dishonor parents, to kill, to commit adultery, to steal, to bear false witness, and to covet are eternally wrong.

An examination of the epistles will show that the New Testament summarizes the whole of moral obedience by the law of love, which fulfills all the commandments. The commandments retain their force by clearly defining the will of God. The force of the commandments as individual precepts is stipulated by James, the brother of the Lord. The breaking of a single commandment, and that but once, is sufficient to mark man as a violator of the law of God. "For whosoever shall keep the whole law, and yet offend in one point, he is guilty of all. For he that said, Do not commit adultery, said also, Do not kill. Now if thou commit no adultery, yet if thou kill, thou art become a transgressor of the law" (Jas. 2:10f.).

The first commandment is everywhere interwoven in the New Testament reconciling of faith in the deity of Christ with the virile monotheism of the Old Testament. The command may not be repeated formally, indeed is not. But what more impressive acknowledgment of its validity can be found than in the fact that the passion for monotheism fills the inspired Christian writings, and that the Son is everywhere represented as the unveiled Creator-Redeemer God of the Old Testament? Paul dismisses the eating of idol-meat with reference to this point: "We know that an idol is nothing in the world, and that there is none other God but one. For though there be that are called gods, whether in heaven or in earth, . . . to us there is but one God, the Father, of whom are all things, and we in him; and one Lord Jesus Christ, by whom are all things, and we by him" (1 Cor. 8:4ff.).

The shame and corruption of the Gentile religion includes its fashioning of gods in images "made like to corruptible man, and to birds, and fourfooted beasts, and creeping things" (Rom. 1:23). Paul asserted to the Athenians with their passion for statues and idols of the gods: "We ought not to think that the Godhead is like unto gold, or silver, or stone, graven by art and man's device" (Acts 17:29). Thus the epistles reiterate the emphasis of the gospels on the invisibility (Jn. 1:18) and spirituality (Jn. 4:24) of God.

The Pauline condemnation of both Jews and Gentiles as sinners includes the repetition of the verdict of the prophets against the Hebrews: "The name of God is blasphemed among the Gentiles through you" (Rom. 2:24). The name of God is not to be blasphemed at all (1 Tim. 6:1, James 2:7).

The New Testament respects the sabbath in the spiritual, non-legalistic sense, and gives it, as it does the previous commandments, a Christological orientation. If the New Testament affirms the deity of Christ (Tit. 2:13) and declares that he bears the essential image of God (2 Cor. 4:4, Col. 1:15), and if it magnifies the name of Jesus Christ, then it emphasizes also that the Son of Man is lord of the sabbath (Mk. 2:28). Jesus singled out the sabbath, not only for performing what was contrary to the encumbrances of tradition (Mk. 2:23, Jn. 9:14), but for some of his miraculous works (Jn. 5:9, 9:7) in order to emphasize that the purpose of the day was to minister to spiritual purposes. It was not to be used for the oppression of the spiritual life: "Moses therefore gave unto you circumcision . . . and ye on the sabbath day circumcise a man. . . . Are you angry at me, because I have made a man every whit whole on the sabbath day?" (Jn. 7:22f.). If the sabbath was introduced in Eden, it did not from the first bear the ceremonial significance attaching to it in the Mosaic economy. Even in that economy, its spiritual purpose was not obscure. The rite of circumcision could be performed on the sabbath when that was the eighth day, and temple services were held. The sabbath was not a day for passive inactivity, but for deeds of love and grace. The creation cycle of six and one according to the Mosaic principle attached to the day special ceremonial responsibilities peculiar to the Old Testament economy. But the principle of the new dispensation commemorates the resurrection of Christ and the fulfillment of the Old Testament. The New Testament observance of the Lord's Day maintains the ratio of one to six in a new order. It declares thereby that creation itself was conceived of on redemption lines and that the Lamb was slain from the foundation of the world (Rev. 13:8). The epistles mention the keeping of the sabbath merely ceremonially with terms of strong disapproval (Col. 2:16). The first day of the week replaces it in the redeemed community (Acts 20:7, 1 Cor. 16:2).

In the Old Testament dispensation of promise the moral law was joined with a ceremonial law that defined the religious pattern of the old dispensation. The sabbath commandment stands as a bridge between the old and the new. It has a permanent validity, but in the Old Testament it is in a temporary form that is no longer valid now that the whole ceremonial law has been abrogated. The Christian, like the Jew, cannot earn salvation by keeping the commandments. Moreover, since Christ has come, the Christian can no longer keep the ceremonial law as his rule of life, lest by doing so he deny that Christ has fulfilled it. The Christian therefore keeps the sabbath commandment only in the sense that it mirrors the eternal moral law of God. The sabbath is freed of its connection with the ceremonial system; it continues nonetheless to be a special day, hallowed by our Lord's resurrection, for the assembling of believers and for unimpeded special devotion to the things of God; it perpetuates the right of man as a worker to a day of rest from his labors; and it serves as a figure of the spiritual rest that remains for the people of God. The Christian observes the day as he does all the commandments, on the principle of grace which runs through both Testaments, but in such a way as to emphasize the resurrection-day displacement of the seventh-day laden with ceremonial laws which waited for their fulfillment.

The fifth commandment, the one to honor parents, is likewise reasserted in the New Testament. "Children, obey your parents in the Lord: for this is right. Honour thy father and mother; which is the first commandment with promise; that it may be well with thee, and thou mayest live long on the earth" (Eph. 6:1ff.). This includes several significant emphases. Parental obedience is to be pursued not simply out of natural affection, but it is the will of God, a spiritual service. The commandment, moreover, is related specifically to Christ: obedience is to be rendered in the fear of the Lord. This suggests that even this command cannot be carried out in its full intention apart from spiritual grace and power. The specific attachment of promise to this particular commandment is noted, although Paul makes it universal by omitting those words that gave the promise a special theocratic form in the old dispensation — prosperity and length of days in the promised land. The commandment of parental reverence, like that of the sabbath, is valid outside the Hebrew theocracy. This commandment is seen again in Colossians 3:20: "Children, obey your parents in all things: for this is well pleasing in the Lord" and in 1 Timothy 5:4: "If any widow have children or nephews, let them learn first to show piety at home, and to requite their parents: for that is good and acceptable before God." The latter passage vindicates the propriety of the support of dependent parents by their children. This Christian duty ought not to be shunted to the church or society in general. Such support is guarded from abuse: where parents are not needy, another Pauline principle comes to play: "Children ought not to lay up for the parents, but the parents for the children" (2 Cor. 12:14). Elsewhere Paul admonishes parents against a harsh, nagging, or capricious spirit of child control (Col. 3:21). In the graphic Pauline portrayal of Gentile corruption, disobedience to parents is singled out as one of the pagan vices (Rom. 1:30).

The fifth word, concerning parental honor, is the first of the commandments relating to man's social duties. Among the remarkable features of New Testament social ethics, which we can only touch upon in this volume, is the fact that the Apostle Paul emphasizes that all the believer's duties to the state are comprehended in the law of love. He stipulates especially that love expedites the fulfillment of the last four commandments. "Owe no man anything, but to love one another; for he that loveth another hath fulfilled the law. For this, Thou shalt not kill, Thou shalt not steal, Thou shalt not bear false witness, Thou shalt not covet; and if there be any other commandment, it is briefly comprehended in this saying, namely, Thou shalt love thy neighbor as thyself. Love worketh no ill to his neighbor: therefore love is the fulfilling of the law" (Rom. 13:8ff.). And the Apostle Peter clusters the social commandments together in a similar way: "Let none of you suffer as a murderer, or as a thief, or as an evildoer, or as a meddler in other men's affairs" (1 Pet. 4:15).

The command against murder, like the whole moral law, is retained in the New Testament with that intense inward emphasis found in the Sermon on the Mount. "Whosoever hateth his brother is a murderer," writes the Apostle John (1 Jn. 3:15). Thus he insists that from the Divine perspective the essential element in murder is the inner attitude. The deed only gives shape to the attitude already there. Both murder and war are traced by James to inner passion (Jas. 4:1f.). There is no need, in view of the New Testament defense of monogamous marriage, to argue about its attitude toward the wickedness of adultery. Paul fearlessly lays bare the unrighteousness of the Hebrews by exposing the fact that, while proclaiming the wickedness of adultery and of stealing, they did not fully honor the commandments (Rom. 2:21f.). In a passage in the Ephesian letter the Apostle pleads for true holiness; he pleads for an end to stealing, to lying and evil talk, and to the inner sins of the heart from which outer transgressions flow. "Wherefore putting away lying, speak every man truth with his neighbour. . . . Be [righteously] angry but do not sin; do not let the sun go down on your anger, and give no opportunity to the devil. Let him that stole, steal no more. . . . Let no corrupt communication proceed out of your mouth, but that which is good to the use of edifying, that it may minister grace unto the hearers. . . . Let all bitterness, and wrath, and anger, and clamour, and evil speaking, be put away from you, with all malice . . ." (Eph. 4:25ff.). In the matter of false witness, the New Testament introduces a dramatic inversion of the whole concept of witnessing. The Greek term *martus,* or witness, came to mean "martyr," because the early believers in such great numbers preached the Gospel, giving witness to its truth to the unregenerate. Instead of bearing false witness, they bore the true, at the cost of their lives. They were determined above all not to be found false witnesses to God (1 Cor. 15:15) nor to the reality of Christ's deity and resurrection (1 Jn. 2:22f., 27), which they proclaimed even in the face of death.

It would be little less than pedantic to labor the New Testament presupposition of the permanent validity of the tenth commandment. The term gains a positive sense, that of coveting spiritual gifts (1 Cor. 12:31), through the desires that the Holy Spirit plants in regenerate hearts. But the wickedness of coveting for selfish reasons is echoed with all the disapproval of the Decalogue. "The law . . . said, Thou shalt not covet," writes Paul (Rom. 7:7), and hence the commandment doomed him from any hope of salvation by works. To the Ephesians he writes: "But fornication, and all uncleanness, or covetousness, let it not be once named among you, as becometh saints. . . . For this ye know, that no whoremonger, nor unclean person, nor covetous man, who is an idolater, hath any inheritance in the kingdom of Christ and of God" (Eph. 5:3ff.). From the New Testament standpoint, coveting involves the worship of false gods. A striking commentary on this fact is provided by a verse in the epistle to the Hebrews. It exhorts believers to live without covetousness "and be content with such things as ye have; for he hath said, I will never leave thee, nor forsake thee" (Heb. 13:5). The believer's contentment expresses his confidence that he is not alone in the providences of life, but has the greatest treasure of all. Three times in the first Corinthian letter Paul indicts the covetous (1 Cor. 5:10f., 6:10). In his letters to the Romans (1:29), Corinthians (2 Cor. 9:5), Ephesians (5:3), Colossians (3:5) and Thessalonians (1 Thess. 2:5) he writes with sharp disapproval of the sin of *pleonexia,* the desire for more than what is properly one's own. And in 1 Timothy 6:10 he penned those classic words about the love of money as the root of all evil, "which while some coveted after, they have erred from the faith, and pierced themselves through with many sorrows." The coveting of worldly things leads men astray from the faith and damages their souls.

The Bible defines what it means to fulfill the law of love for God with our whole being and for our neighbor as ourselves. It sets forth the righteousness that aligns man's life to the pure will of God. For this reason no man need be in doubt about what inner attitudes and pursuits are approved by God, and what are condemned. The inspired Scriptures place before him the universal rule of life by which his duties may be properly determined. The Ten Commandments unfold more fully in the two tables of the Law, what Christ's two great commandments summarize.

To love God with one's whole being is to worship the self-revealing God alone, to give no adoration to idols, and not to take God's name in vain but to hold its majesty inviolably sacred. Calvin classed the innumerable duties to God which flow from these commandments under four heads: adoration, trust, invocation, and thanksgiving. The fourth commandment requires the day of rest from the labors of the week to be devoted specially to worship, to spiritual meditation on God's mercies and the eternal rest to come, and piety.

The duties men owe to each other are outlined in the last six commandments: parents are to be reverenced, murder is prohibited, as are adultery, stealing, false witness, and coveting.

The force of the last commandment is to exclude every desire from the heart that is incompatible with and prejudicial to love for neighbor as for self. Its end is to promote attitudes and acts of piety that will serve only to benefit others. The heart full of love for God and neighbor fulfills these commandments; the transgression of the commandments mirrors a lack of love for God and man. The two tables of the Law are a unitary whole; the duties owed to men are not independent of those owed to God, but are an essential phase of the rule of love that God wills, and that men owe for his sake. Together, the two tables require all the powers of the soul in love for God and man.

These same commandments are valid in the future eschatological age. This can be shown from the New Testament writings apart from an appeal to Jesus' parables and eschatological teaching. The judgment, like the creation and the giving of the Law, proceeds in view of the eternal righteousness of God. There will be no excuse permitted for having degraded the moral majesty of the Creator and Redeemer. The heavy woes awaiting society for having tolerated these gross sins should enforce with the eloquence of terror the unity of God's moral revelation — in creation, redemption, and judgment.

The living God is the agent in judgment, as he was in creation and redemption. The false gods are then fully unmasked. The false beast worshipped in the Apocalypse tolerates images and identifies himself with the image (Rev. 13:14f.), but those who "worship the beast and his image . . . shall drink of the wine of the wrath of God" (14:9ff.). The judgment completes victory over the beast and his image (15:2, 16:2, 19:20), while those who have not worshipped the beast and his image are vindicated and rewarded (20:4). In the perilous last days before the end-time, blasphemers are particularly singled out as headed for doom (2 Tim. 3:2). It is the beast of the Apocalypse who bears the name of blasphemy (Rev. 13:1, 17:3), and who blasphemes the name of God (13:5f). Men exposed to the terrible wrath of God will blaspheme him (16:9, 11).

The entrance into the sabbath rest that remains for the people of God when they cease from their works is assured (Heb. 4:9ff.), while those who come under the wrath of God "have no rest day nor night" (Rev. 14:11). "Blessed are the dead which die in the Lord from henceforth: Yea, saith the Spirit, that they may rest from their labors; and their works do follow them" (14:13). That the judgment will also enforce the universal validity of the fifth command may be gathered from Paul's insertion of the trait "disobedient to parents" in the list of vices that will characterize the last days (2 Tim. 3:2). The social commandments are also oriented to the judgment and the life to come. "Ye know that no murderer hath eternal life abiding in him" (1 Jn. 3:15). "The fearful, and unbelieving, and the abominable, and murderers, and whoremongers, and sorcerers, and idolators, and all liars, shall have their part in the lake which burneth with fire and brimstone: which is the second death" (Rev. 21:8). The Apocalypse here reflects the standpoint of the Corinthian letters: "Be not deceived: neither fornicators, nor idolators, nor adulterers, nor effeminate, nor abusers of themselves with mankind, nor thieves, nor covetous, nor drunkards, nor revilers, nor extortioners, shall inherit the kingdom of God" (1 Cor. 6:9f.). In the words of the epistle to the Hebrews: "Whoremongers and adulterers God will judge" (Hebrews 13:4). The Revelation speaks of the wrath of God addressed against those who repented neither "of their murders, nor of their sorceries, nor of their fornications, nor of their thefts" (Rev. 9:21). It speaks also of the millennial vindication of those who were "beheaded for the witness of Jesus, and for the word of God" (20:4), and of Jesus as "the faithful witness" (1:5) and "the faithful and true witness" (3:14). "Lying wonders" are ascribed to the Antichrist, whose coming is after the working of Satan (2 Thess. 2:9). The Apocalypse closes the gates of the heavenly Jerusalem to liars: "And there shall in no wise enter into it any thing that defileth, neither whatsoever worketh abomination, or maketh a lie: but they which are written in the Lamb's book of life" (Rev. 21:27). And coveting, which the last commandment expressly forbids, will be common in the last days before the world's hour of judgment: "Men shall be lovers of their own selves, covetous . . ." (2 Tim. 3:2).

The eternal destiny of men is based upon what their disposition toward the Divine commandments has been: "Here is the patience of the saints: here are they that keep the commandments of God, and the faith of Jesus" (Rev. 14:12). Perhaps there is no more sobering and awesome part of the Revelation than the warning that Christ will return to reward men according to their works, and the stern reminder that access to the city of life will depend upon one's relation to the commandments: "Blessed are they that do his commandments, that they may have right to the tree of life, and may enter in through the gates into the city. For without are dogs, and sorcerers, and whoremongers, and murderers, and idolaters, and whosoever loveth and maketh a lie" (Rev. 22:14f.).

It may be thought that the referring to the Ten Commandments as a comprehensive reply to the question "What ought I to do?" is rather artificial and naive, especially when the complexity of modern life is considered. But who cannot sense at once what a morally refreshing world this would be, were human relations restored to the closely knit affection of children and parents; were there no murder of human beings, with the accompanying grief and hardship in the lives of men; were the world of marital affairs immune from the triangles of illicit love, and homes unbroken by divorce and strained affections; were the theft of goods and money an unknown phenomenon; were false witness touching another person unthinkable; were the coveting of another's things resisted with might and main; were only the living God worshipped, and never false gods and graven images; were men to labor creatively six days and give their day of freedom from work in unrestricted devotion to the claims of the spiritual world? And lest it be thought that such external conformity alone comports fully with the commandments, let the issue be posed with larger fidelity to biblical ethics. Who can but acknowledge that the imagination itself is staggered in attempting to weigh the moral force of a world in which the ethical inwardness sought by the Decalogue would be realized, and in which all men would love God with their whole being and their neighbors as themselves? Once the commandments find a hold in the lives of sinful men, and are fulfilled, not merely externally — which of itself would mark an astonishing change in human conduct — but internally, then it will be time enough for skeptics and rationalists to scoff the Decalogue.

And yet, the content of the ideal ethical life is not limited by the Old Testament or New Testament simply to the Decalogue. Formally the commandments include all obedience that may be rendered to God, since our Lord interpreted their inner spirit as the love of God with one's whole being, and love of neighbor as one's self. In this sense, the commandments embrace the entire revealed will of God. But Jesus himself added to the Law specific requirements for Christian obedience. Neither the Decalogue, nor the Sermon on the Mount alone, nor even the teaching of Jesus apart from the apostolic literature, defines the morally right in its fullest expression. Christian morality is not, in the usual sense, reducible to "the ethics of Jesus." In fact, what is usually passed for the teaching of Jesus turns out to reveal a selectivity that actually warps that teaching, eliminating the redemptive factor from Jesus' ethics. Felix Adler singles out as the original contributions of Jesus' teaching the thesis that inner purity is spiritual power whose by-product is love, an emphasis that in fact Jesus shares with the Old Testament, and the regard for evil in others as a means of self-purification by its provocation to self-emancipation from similar impulses, an emphasis indeed remote from the Christian view of sanctification. But when full justice is done to the teaching of Jesus during his public ministry, the whole of Christian ethics is still not in view. Even the tendency to picture Christian ethics as simply an extension of "the example of Jesus" errs because this is not the whole of New Testament ethics. Sometimes this "imitate Jesus" ethics simmers down to little more than an enthusiastic spirit that lacks all specific guidance as to what constitutes moral obedience, as when Bushnell exhorts: "Follow without question the impulse of love to Christ's own person; for this, when really full and sovereign, will put you along easily in a kind of infallible way, and make your conduct chime, as it were, naturally with all God's future, even when that future is unknown; untying the most difficult questions of casuistry without so much as a question raised."[2] Such formulas tend to reduce ideal Christian character to new feelings and impulses produced by a guiding enthusiasm for the Master and miscalculate the need for an objectively stated moral content, and hence miss the force of the biblical revealed ethic. The ideal itself, though embodied in the historical Jesus, could soon fade away into faint outline and sink into the remoteness of the distant past were it not

[2]Horace Bushnell, *Sermons for the New Life* (New York: Scribner, 1864), pp. 127ff.

for two facts: its content is authoritatively fixed in the scriptural record, and Jesus though invisible is alive today by the Spirit, maintaining his hold upon the lives of his followers. The Christian life finds moral force in the authority of Christ's teaching, his example, the special ministry of the Holy Spirit, and the authoritative teaching of the inspired apostles (Jn. 14:26, 15:26f.). The biblical revelation as a whole is the comprehensive exhibition of the content of the good life.

The obligation to obedience includes more than a regard for the Decalogue. Man as sinner is obliged to believe the Gospel and to accept Christ as his personal Savior; not to do so is a violation of specific command. When Jesus was asked, "What shall we do, that we might work the works of God?" he replied pointedly, "This is the work of God, that ye believe on him whom he hath sent" (Jn. 6:28f.; cf. 15:22, 16:9). More than this, special acts of obedience are imposed in the new life. The believer ought not to fear to own Christ's cause, or blush to speak his name; indeed, he is under orders to help propagate the Gospel and to support the cause of missions; he is required to be baptized in the name of the triune God, since the Great Commission includes both the instruction and baptism of converts (Mt. 28:19f.). The ethical disobedience of men in sin includes their rejection of the Gospel. The ethical obedience that God approves includes baptism, witnessing, gathering with fellow believers (Heb. 10:25), and partaking of the Lord's Supper. The believer does not comprehend these duties under the category of law as a means to salvation. They are the means of grace. He gladly responds to every Divine provision of mercy and strength. But nonetheless he is obligated to the moral law, and to those positive commands that control the life of obedience in the church age.

Complete obedience to the will of God in the twentieth century includes the personal acceptance of Jesus Christ, participation in the ordinances of baptism and the Lord's Supper, and a witnessing to the Gospel by word and deed. These remain us that the knowledge of the Divine will, in this age as in earlier ages, is tied directly to special redemptive revelation. Man as sinner cannot reliably intuit the will of God from his inner moral sentiments. The redemptive disclosure of God publishes his will, both the eternal moral law and those positive commands applicable in the various dispensations of grace as evidence of man's grateful and obedient response to redemption. The believer knows, for example, that to marry an unbeliever is disobedience to the will of God, and therefore sinful (2 Cor. 6:14). Thus, alongside the commands of the Decalogue stand other biblical precepts that articulate the will of God. This content of morality is not limited to the express precepts but embraces all they imply — building churches, establishing Christian schools and seminaries, endowing hospitals, printing and circulating the Bible, keeping the Lord's Day, holding family worship.

It is little wonder Christianity seems deficient as a practical guide for life when the clear principles and directions it has laid down are expressly repudiated as legalism by some who profess to speak for Christian ethics. A spiritual ethics forbids the reduction of the good life to the mere fulfillment of moral rules; it throws its emphasis instead upon moral renewal, from which alone great virtues spring. Christian ethics cannot thereby be reduced to simply a nebulous feeling of good will toward others, lacking direction. Admittedly, the New Testament is no mere law book like the Institutes of Justinian or the Code Napoleon, nor was the Old Testament ever intended to be such a book. The New Testament does set forth the law of love in the form of the two greatest commandments. This law itself rules out granting any degree of adequacy to mere legal conformity to the commandments and precepts of revealed ethics. Yet the New Testament is an authoritative guide, an inspired record that gives us concrete ethical instruction. The implication that a book or record or prescription of right conduct necessarily comes between the Saviour and his disciples is ill-founded. To be "in Christ" means that he seeks to establish his authority within us, and not merely to speak to us from without. Much of the emphasis that the moral teaching of Jesus is not to be taken literally, and that the New Testament tradition in no sense is a reference for ethical decision, comes from the high-sounding but mistaken notion that the inner life of love by the Spirit requires the abandonment of all external example and of all statement of the content of ethics in propositional truths.[3]

From the will of God as a general fact to the particulars of Christian living is a transition that recent ethical theory, even where it professes to be revelational, makes with awkwardness and difficulty. Current treatises on the ethics of revelation show generality and indefiniteness in detailing the will of God.

And yet there can be no doubt that the Hebrew-Christian movement in earlier ages was assured that it knew the will of God not merely in a broad and general sense, but in its bearing on the details of personal ethics. All the duties of piety and love came distinctively into view. The will of God embraces all the particularities of life. It does not provide certain preliminary principles merely, but goes on to give man specific guidance for ethical decision and to escort him through a "well" regulated life with a good conscience before the righteous Lord.

There is actually no ethical decision in life which the biblical revelation leaves wholly untouched and for which, if carefully interpreted and applied, it cannot afford some concrete guidance. The biblical teaching is not always explicit. Yet the broad scope of life that it does cover in its specific terms is such as to give biblical ethics an immense advantage over all other moral theories in the attempt to define the content of the ideal life. The ethical problems to which the Bible speaks explicitly are many. The questions to which it gives no explicit answers may be considered under large principles and examples.

[3]Cf. Hugh Martin, *Morality on Trial* (London: SCM, 1933), pp. 54f.

It is true that Jesus himself did not exegete for us all the commandments. But he placed before his followers instruction of how love fulfills certain of the commandments, and a personal example of how love fulfills them all. His pattern of interpretation, the primacy of inner motivation, is full of implications for the whole of ethical decision and life. Moreover, he encouraged his followers to grow into a mature obedience. They were to seek within the fellowship of the Holy Spirit to apply the commandments and other precepts, and to apply the biblical principles to the practical affairs of life on the moving front of human experience. God by the Spirit makes relevant some rule of life in the Bible, personalizing it to the everyday life situation. Jesus Christ sanctions the "search" of the Scriptures for the instruction they afford (Jn. 5:39). In the ethical dilemmas of life there is never a real conflict of duty, even though the mind and heart may be torn between apparent conflicts that are as yet unresolved. The Spirit is a source of subjective guidance in the sense that the relevant biblical principles are applied in such a way as to bring about an inner dedication and response to the will of God in the particular ethical situations. It is true that the believer at no point perfectly incarnates the will of God. Yet the regenerate life is now placed consciously within the Divine orbit, and the will of God becomes the determinate reference point for the believer.

That God intends his will to be known concretely by men and to be performed is one of the first principles of Scripture. The New Testament summary of the life of David is that he was laid to rest "after he had in his own age served the will of God" (Acts 13:36). God's tribute was that he had "found David, the son of Jesse, a man after my own heart, which shall fulfill all my will" (13:22). Jesus has left the Christian community the supreme example of dedication to the Divine will. In his case he deviated not one whit from what God desired. "My meat is to do the will of him that sent me" (Jn. 4:34). His whole mission in life was to do "the will of him that sent me" (Jn. 5:30, 6:38). The verse that the epistle to the Hebrews writes over his incarnation, "Lo I come to do thy will, O God" (Heb. 10:7), has its counterpart in the Garden of Gethsemane, "My Father, if this cup may not pass away from me, except I drink it, thy will be done" (Mt. 26:42). Indeed, it was "according to the will of our God and Father" that Christ "gave himself for our sins, that he might deliver us out of this present evil world" (Gal. 1:4), and "according to the good pleasure of his will" that he "foreordained us unto adoption as sons through Christ Jesus unto himself" (Eph. 1:5). The Almighty refuses to hear those who are in rebellion against his will: "We know that God heareth not sinners; but if any man be a worshipper of God, and do his will, he heareth him" (Jn. 9:31). Only a horrible destiny in eternity awaits such rebels: "Not everyone that saith to me Lord, Lord, shall enter into the kingdom of heaven; but he that doeth the will of my Father who is in heaven" (Mt. 7:21). The inheritance of everlasting blessedness is pledged to those who perform God's will: "Ye have need of patience, that, doing the will of God, ye may receive the promise" (Heb. 10:36). Franz Delitzsch appropriately remarks that "the doing the divine will and the receiving the promise are . . . thought of . . . as the one the direct cause of the other, which accompanies and crowns it; and the will of God is not the primary original divine counsel fulfilled by Christ . . . , but a secondary will and purpose concerning us, the redeemed, viz., our stedfast perseverance in faith and hope . . ."[4]

Two of the most sobering parables ever to fall from the lips of Jesus show in contrast the attitude of the two sons toward the will of God (Mt. 21:28ff.) and the attitude of the faithful and unfaithful servants (Lk. 12:47f.). Elsewhere he declares: "Whosoever shall do the will of my Father who is in heaven, he is my brother, and sister, and mother" (Mt. 12:50). In a dramatic passage the Apostle John remarks: "The world passeth away, and the lust thereof, but he that doeth the will of God abideth forever" (1 Jn. 2:17).

God has taken all the initiative required to make his will clearly known by man in sin. The distinction of the Hebrews is that they, in the midst of the world of Gentile depravity, had the will of God in written form (Rom. 2:17f.). The prayer Jesus taught his disciples contains the petition "Thy will be done in earth, as in heaven" (Mt. 6:10). The Apostle John writes that "this is the confidence that we have in him, that, if we ask anything according to his will, he heareth us" (1 Jn. 5:14). Paul desired that the Colossians would be "filled with the knowledge of his will in all wisdom and spiritual understanding; that ye might walk worthy of the Lord unto all pleasing, being fruitful in every good work . . ." (Col. 1:9f.), and Epaphras prayed that they would "stand perfect and fully assured in all the will of God" (4:12). The benediction of the epistle to the Hebrews longs that God will "make you perfect in every good work to do his will, working in you that which is well-pleasing in his sight" (Heb. 13:21). The believer is to "prove" the will of God, which is good, acceptable and perfect (Rom. 12:2). If anything is certain about biblical theology, it is the assurance that God has removed every last obstacle to the knowledge of his will.

God has objectively published his will in the Hebrew-Christian Scriptures, where it stands propositionally expressed for all to read and know. The glory of the Hebrews was that they "knew God's will, and approved the things that are excellent, being instructed out of the law" (Rom. 2:18). The will of God was made known by the Old Testament law, and then in turn by Jesus Christ and the apostles.

One of the remarkable features of New Testament ethics is the manner in which the apostles leap from the will of God as a general concept to the approval of a particular act or to the disapproval of a

[4]Franz Delitzsch, *Commentary on the Epistle to the Hebrews,* 10:36 (Grand Rapids: Eerdmans, reprint).

particular vice. For them, the will of God is not a general but undefined sentiment, identified only by an inner disposition. Rather, it is a particular manner of life (1 Cor. 15:33). The New Testament concept of "the Way" is assuredly broader than a merely ethical pattern. It embraces the assurance of eternal life. Yet it includes also the idea of an ethical outlook and content that is quite specific.

"Be not foolish," the Apostle Paul urges, "but understand what the will of the Lord is" (Eph. 5:17). From this, he points to a single vice as outside the will of God: be not drunk with wine. Over against this, he states the will of the Lord: "be filled with the Spirit" (5:18). That the Decalogue did not contain all man's ethical duties is clear from the Old Testament, and here we have in the New the recognition that the other moral precepts, such as temperance, justice, truth, beneficence, have a claim upon man. In fact, if one combs the Old Testament teaching, he will find in the Law little in the way of a positive prohibition of drunkenness, the strongest statement being an implied censure in Deuteronomy 29:19. It is clear from the prophetic denunciations that the Old Testament frowns upon the vice, however, and Paul shows here that man is made to be inspirited (cf. Gen. 2:7, Jn. 14:17), not to be intoxicated. Both phenomena are strange in appearance to the natural man, involving a certain excitableness and disorder compared with the "normal" state of things (Eph. 5:19f.). Believers are no longer confined to the conversational language of ordinary life; filled by the Spirit, they speak to each other in psalms, hymns and spiritual songs. They are given to praise of God, singing and making melody in their hearts to the Lord. And thanksgiving is constant. The inseparability of the spiritual and the ethical returns to view here, since in his preface to the picture of Gentile corruption in Romans one, Paul summarized the depravity of the pagan world in these words: "Knowing God, they glorified him not as God, neither were thankful" (Rom. 1:21).

By "walking as wise, not as unwise" Paul does not mean that the Christian life involves only certain outward singularities. To be filled with the Spirit means "subjecting yourselves to one another in the fear of Christ" (Eph. 5:21). All social relationships are tempered by the Christian's communion with his Lord. Christ, the head of the Church, gave himself in love for the salvation, sanctification and glorification of the body. In this he is a pattern for the relationship of husbands and wives, fathers and children, masters and slaves. In fact, the first terms in these couplets — husband, father, master — are all designations applied to God, while the companion terms — wives, children, slaves — are applied to believers as the objects of his love. This remarkably affects the relationships of believers with those about them (5.22ff.).

The wife is to submit herself to the husband as her head; this is analogous to the relation of the Church to Christ as its head and Saviour. And the husband is to love his wife as Christ gave himself for the body, the Church. The husband's love for his wife is to be a husband's love for himself, since monogamous marriage constitutes them one flesh or body (5:29ff.). The bond between parents and children is likewise deeply affected by this God-ward relationship, as the references "in the Lord" and "of the Lord" (6:1ff.) make clear. Children are to obey and honor their parents in the Lord; fathers (who bear the responsibility of rule) are not to provoke them, but to "nurture them in the chastening and admonition of the Lord." When the relationships of life are lived out in Christ, the motivation for morality is of the highest order. As children reflect obedience to God in their obedience to parents, so fathers are to be instruments of the Lord's training and correction of children. Lastly, the master-servant relationship is transformed when the moral life is oriented to God. Servants are to obey their masters "as unto Christ . . . as servants of Christ, doing the will of God from the heart; with good will doing service, as unto the Lord, and not unto men" (6:5f.). Here the slave's duties are at once enlarged and reduced to that alone to which the Divine Master obliges him. Masters are to forbear threatening because of this same orientation of their duties: "he who is both their Master and yours is in heaven, and there is no respect of persons with him" (6:9). The force of these passages is that to be filled by the Spirit is to do the will of God. The social relationships between husbands and wives, parents and children, master and slave, employer and employee, mirror on the level of human affairs the relationships between Christ and his bride, the Father and his earthly children, and the Master and his bondservants. Here the husband stands in the bride's place, the father in the children's, and the master in the slave's. What far-reaching changes would result for our social order, plagued by adult irresponsibility and juvenile delinquency, marital resentments and infidelity, and employer-labor tensions, if these relationships were brought into conformity with the will of God!

In Paul's very first epistle we find a similar transition from a general reference to the will of God to its particular implications for daily life. "This is the will of God, even your holiness" he writes (1 Thess. 4:3). Then he adds a series of exhortations for which Divine sanction is claimed. The apostle exhorts these early Christians "in the Lord Jesus, that, as ye received of us how ye ought to walk and to please God, even as ye do walk,—that ye abound more and more" (4:1). This appeal for moral earnestness in the Christian life is based on the consciousness that God is the ultimate source of the instructions: "he that rejecteth, rejecteth not man but God" (4:8).

What sanctification means for specific areas of life is set forth in full detail: negatively, abstinence from fornication (4:3); positively, the honorable and chaste satisfaction of sexual impulses (4:4); negatively, the avoidance of a covetous and fraudulent taking advantage of neighbors (4:6); positively, the increase of brotherly love (4:9), the pursuit of a quiet living, mindfulness of one's own concerns, fulfillment of the responsibilities of work (4:11). The purpose of this divinely-willed manner of life is that believers may walk becomingly in relation to others, and not be thrust upon others because of wants and needs which labor would have supplied (4:12). The moral force of this passage is at once obvious when one recalls that lust and covetousness, frequently mentioned together in Paul's letters, were the cardinal heathen vices, and that it was the fidelity of the Thessalonian converts to Christian standards that inverted their former manner of life and made holiness characteristic of the Gentile Christians.

One can also show from passages in both Peter and James that they too move from the Divine will to specific implications for daily life and conduct. For them, as for the biblical tradition as a whole, the appeal to "the will of God" was no mere generality that lacked practical consequences.

The early Christians were often maligned as evil-doers. Peter exhorts them to silence such criticisms by good works. "For so is the will of God, that by well-doing ye should put to silence the ignorance of foolish men" (1 Pet. 2:15). By right conduct in the various relationships of life the believers were to prove themselves blameless before the non-Christian world. "Having your behavior seemly among the Gentiles; that, wherein they speak against you as evil-doers, they may by your good works, which they behold, glorify God in the day of visitation [*i.e.*, of final blessing or judgment]" (2:12).

The passage deals especially with the matter of the believer's relationship to constituted social authorities. The subject of personal holiness, often in the forefront of the epistles, has already been touched in passing: "Beloved, I beseech you as sojourners and pilgrims, to abstain from fleshly lusts which war against the soul" (2:11). Thus the will of God in relation to authorities is developed. Peter stresses that the believer is not to invoke his liberty in Christ tyrannically because of the Divine ordinances regulating man's social life: "Make yourselves subject to every ordinance of man for the Lord's sake: whether to the king as supreme" (2:13). The Greek term *ktidzein,* to ordain, is always used of Divine agency, not of human. The state is a Divine order of preservation in the social realm, and the believer is duty-bound to the sovereign power. This obligation extends also to subordinate officials, who share in the political power's task of supporting good and restraining evil: "or to governors, as sent by him for vengeance on evil-doers and for praise to them that do well" (2:14). The believer's freedom does not exempt him from submission to heathen authorities constituted to enforce the right: "as free, and not using your freedom for a cloak of wickedness, but as bondservants of God" (2:16). Their submission was not that of slaves, but of those who were inwardly free, bound only to the will of God, and who recognize these offices as divinely appointed for moral ends.

This principle carries over into all the social relationships: "Honor all men. Love the brotherhood. Fear God. Honor the king" (2:17). Living in the holy awe of God, the believer does not deprecate others because in his own dignity he recognizes their dignity and worth. He loves believers who share a special community of divine life, and he accords the supreme power the respect due him.

Exhortations follow addressed to slaves (2:18ff.), to wives (3:1ff.), and to husbands (3:7). "Servants, be in subjection to your masters with all fear, not only to the good and gentle, but also to the froward" (2:18). The domestic servant is not to condition his behavior upon his earthly master's character. Rather, he is to shrink from disobedience, and is to endure patiently undeserved suffering in view of the example of Christ. The Christian wife (doubtless one who has become a convert after marriage) is to be subject to her husband even though he is an unbeliever, seeking to win him to obedience to the will of God through her reverent and chaste bearing rather than through a nagging type of preaching: "Wives, be in subjection to your own husbands; that even if any obey not the word, they may without the word be gained by the behavior of their wives; beholding your reverent and chaste behavior" (3:1f.). Instead of the vain self-adornment of worldly women who delight in the empty game of eye-catching by perishable external adornment, the Christian wife finds her indispensable adornment in a meek and quiet inner spirit which has value in the eyes of God. "Let not yours be the outward adorning with braiding of hair, decoration of gold, and wearing of robes, but let it be the hidden person of the heart with the imperishable jewel of a gentle and quiet spirit, which in God's sight is very precious" (3:3, 4). The husband, to whom the wife is to be subject, is to honor the wife, because she is the weaker sex, because they are heirs together of grace, and because a deviation from this will hinder prayer: "Husbands, live considerately with your wives, bestowing honor on the woman as the weaker sex, since you are joint heirs of the grace of life, in order that your prayers may not be hindered" (3:7). Finally, touching the relations of Christians with others, we have a final exhortation to "unity of spirit, sympathy, love of the brethren, a tender heart, and a humble mind" (3:8).

The epistle deals also with the believer's relations to a hostile world (3:9ff.). The law of love is to prevail; even evil and reviling are to be repaid by blessing. The words recall the Lord's Prayer and the Sermon on the Mount (Mt. 5:10): "Do not return evil for evil or reviling for reviling; but on the contrary, bless, for to this you have been called, that you may obtain a blessing" (3:9). The believer is to be zealous to do good, since God is gracious to the righteous, but angry with the wicked. Those who suffer for righteousness' sake will be divinely blessed (3:14), suffer for doing right rather than doing wrong (3:17), shame their abusers (3:16), are in a position to give a reason for their hope (3:15). They have before them the example of Christ's sufferings (3:18ff.) which supremely illuminate the suffering of the innocent.

We would miss the ethical force of the Petrine teaching if we failed to consider how vastly different our own society would be if Christian teachings had never taken root. How different was that world of raw paganism to which Christian theology and ethics was first addressed. However, the borrowed light of Christianity is getting dimmer. The mood of social anarchy is rife today; and a growing skepticism regarding constituted authority can be discerned, whether it is in government or the home. This is largely because these areas of life are no longer oriented to the will of God. Especially in our time when the beauty of woman consists so generously in the outward, the Petrine emphasis that beauty of character must have the priority would work a sweeping transformation in sexual emphases.

One more passage, this time from James, indicates that the will of God is not a mere generality in biblical ethics, but bears fully on the practical issues of life. In some of the early church services, those who appeared wearing a gold ring and fine clothing were given conspicuous seats, while the obviously poor were assigned inconspicuous locations (2:2ff.). To the Apostle, this was a shameful violation of the law of love: dishonor to the poor man, and unjustifiable catering to the rich (2:6f.). James catalogues this sin of deference to particular persons along with murder and adultery as a violation of the law of love sufficient to shut off any hope for heaven on the basis of a works-righteousness. This is his judgment were it a man's only transgression. To despise the poor, or to court the rich, is a sinful infringement of the Mosaic law (Dt. 1:17). A person who believes he will not be welcome in church, or will be looked down upon if his "Sunday best" is shabby, reflects to the discredit of the congregation. To be rich toward God is man's chief distinction; poverty toward God ought to be regarded with disdain. This is the mood that makes for a virile church.

It would be possible to continue at length with examples from the Bible of practical applications of the will of God to the ethical requirements of everyday life. But enough has been said to show that the Scriptures contain much more for man's ethical direction than the Ten Commandments in their clear and vivid stipulation of what God wills.

While the Bible does not give us ready-made a system of ethics, the growing distrust of a systematic biblical ethics is unjustified. The principle of progressive historical revelation does not allow the possibility of a completed system of ethics before the completion of the revelation. And the fact that the biblical revelation has reached its climax and is complete therefore removes any hesitancy about a systematic schematization of biblical ethics. While the Bible is no systematic ethics text, it contains revealed ethical truths capable of systematic correlation. There are also whole blocks of extended moral instruction, in New Testament as well as Old. Not only are these passages capable of reconciliation, but they form a unitary whole, mirroring the revelation of a single Divine will for man.

The hostility to systematic revealed ethics grows out of some of the following biases: a rationally consistent ethics would mark a return to legalism and a code-ethics that does violence to spiritual morality; or the newer view of revelation precludes revealed doctrine, whether theological or moral, so that all statement of the content of ethics in intellectual form is rationalistic; or metaphysical agnosticism, which requires a religious concern only with results in character and conduct, excluding a careful definition of right morality beyond disposition and intention. All such objections are raised from alien philosophies; they do not breathe the spirit of the New Testament. They may accord well with the temper of this decade that has been set by the prevailing forms of speculative thought, but they sacrifice much that is integral to the character of biblical morality.

The biblical revelation of the will of God is a three-fold guide.

There is (1) the statement of comprehensive moral principles that furnish safe guides for the course of duty. The Old and New Testaments alike share in this treasure of fundamental ethical precepts from which are to be drawn the approved ethical patterns of outlook and behavior. By devoting full attention to these principles, we gain a closer definition of the will of God. Alongside the exhibition of general commandments and comprehensive principles, the biblical revelation of the will of God includes (2) special rules and the application of Divine ethical principles to some particulars or details of life. Without setting before us an exhaustive codification of every activity possible in life, as if obedience to God were a matter of a mechanical and legal outward conformity, but by outlining the ultimate principles of righteousness, and by applying these principles in certain particular instances, the content of the Divine will is propositionally defined for man in the Bible. The scriptural revelation sets before man a divinely-willed content of morality, and exhibits the possibility of the filial bond that remains to the sinner through Christ Jesus. It unveils also (3) the life of Christ as the one perfect example of conduct for man. Thus, the Old Testament appeals to the character of God as the model of the believer's ethical life,[5] and the New Testament adds the drama of the incarnation with its subsequent appeal to the God-man as the will of God manifest in flesh.

The biblical revelation does not stand before us as a systematic ethics, any more than as a systematic theology, although its cardinal ideas radiate from a central unity and are capable of consistent and coherent exhibition. That the Bible cannot be equated with an ethical system is true enough, but ethical ideas underlie the whole, and these are capable

[5]It is the Psalmist's appeal to the Divine character as exemplary, to sacrificial love and to wrath, which leads to the imprecatory psalms. Psalm 18:25f. provides an example of a derivation of the moral ideal from the character of God.

of systematic presentation. The loss of confidence in a unified biblical ethics during the past century has been due to a naturalistic bias in liberal Protestant thought that ruled out miraculous revelation and led to uncertainty about the dating and authorship and order of the sacred books. This bias encouraged a view of the late origin of ethical monotheism and a suspicion of trinitarian theology and ethics. In humanistic circles, so-called Christian ethics was stripped of every vestige of the supernatural. More recently, the revolt against a systematic biblical ethics has sprung out of the dialectical or existential prejudice that the spiritual and moral world cannot be grasped rationally or cognitively. These views do not have their basis in biblical ethics, but in speculative principles drawn from the changing philosophic dogmas of the day. The Christian tradition is then accommodated to the philosophic fad.

The rule of right defined by the will of God is fully and authentically revealed to man in revolt in the sacred record. The Bible is the only infallible rule of Christian practice no less than of Christian faith or doctrine.[6] In the matter of divinely approved conduct, it is the first and last word, the ultimate court of appeal. Whatever knowledge of moral realities enters into man's outlook from other sources, the Bible will confirm and complete what is of genuine worth. It will also rectify the moral sentiments and convictions of the natural man. The brilliance of its ethical light discloses the flagging moral zeal of the unregenerate man. It reveals that his ethical insights are impaired both by finiteness and by sin, that his moral judgments are warped by evil propensities, so that their clarity and fullness are diminished and their character marred.

Nevertheless, the connection between the biblical precepts and the pressing decisions of modern life is not always apparent, even though the controlling ethical principles are inscripturated. And even consecrated Christians, devoted to the will of God, and seeking the guidance of the Holy Spirit in applying the ethics of inspiration in their immediate situation, have had to confess at times that some other biblical principle should have been applied, or that a mistake was sincerely made. The distinguished pastor who puts out a fleece, accepts in good conscience the presidency of a seminary, and then reverses his commitment; the missionary on furlough who learns of a business opportunity which will enable a larger effort, and then loses his meager savings when the venture goes bankrupt — such illustrations could be multiplied.

These difficulties of personal decision do not in any way minimize the fact that the glory of the Scriptures is their specific articulation of the moral order. Even though the Bible does not settle all the decisions of life beyond the possibility of subjective miscalculation and error, it

[6]As L. S. Keyser said, "It is the business of Christian Apologetics to vindicate the divine inspiration and authority of the Holy Scriptures, while Christian Ethics accepts the findings of its sister theological discipline and builds upon them. On the other hand, the high standard of morality inculcated by the Bible becomes, in turn, a cogent apologetic for its divine inspiration." *A Manual of Christian Ethics,* p. 21.

explicates the demands of the moral order compellingly and comprehensively. And even where there has been indecision, or an acknowledged mistake, those involved have had to add their witness to that of the Christian community at large that the Spirit and the Word have given to Christian living a practical direction for life that can be found nowhere else. It is not the ordinary but rather the unusual experience of the consecrated Christian believer that in the ethical decisions of life he is stalemated as to what to do. The final word is not one of indecision and uncertainty about the will of God. In a time of almost universal fluctuation and relativism of standards, where the Bible prevails as a lamp unto the feet of the devout, they walk with sure step.

At the same time, there need be no pretense about infallibility of Christian life anywhere on earth. Not even for the popes is such claim made by Romanism. The Christian life is a growth, not an automatic machine; it is a spiritual walk, in which one advances in insight into the claims of revealed ethics, a walk in which conscience, still fallible even in the lives of the regenerate, is progressively conformed to what is good and right. It is one of the features of Christian growth that the devout spirit recognizes some thoughts and deeds to be wrong today that passed as acceptable but yesterday — an experience repeated often through the tomorrows of life. It is not that the standard has changed, but that the true and the good are more fully perceived, and devotion to them is enlarged. In the Christian life, grace and conduct are everywhere correlated. When the believer is aware of his failure before the moral standard, he is not doomed by the Law, since he knows salvation by grace. In the midst of his shortcomings he looks to the shed blood of Calvary and is thankful. He knows how to make the Law minister to the Gospel. The regenerate heart does not gain acceptance with God by good works, but rather expresses gratitude to God for the forgiveness of sins by doing them.

14

THE LAW AND THE GOSPEL

PERHAPS NO PHASE of the study of Christian ethics is shrouded with such confusion today as the treatment of the Law in its relation to the Gospel. The controversy over the relevance of the Law for the believer has been complicated still more by Karl Barth's use of the term "law" in a non-biblical sense. He contends that only through the Gospel does the Law become significant for us. Emil Brunner further confuses the issue by coupling the general moral law with a non-historical notion of "by creation" and "after the fall" amounting to a psychological tension of the "ought" and the "is." Such existential ethics deals with Law and Gospel mainly as symbols of inner moral strife. What is often ignored is that this existential conflict, detailed to conform to modern presuppositions about the whole man in all his tensions, can really be explained only by the old concept of biblical predications that elaborate more fully what it means that man is a sinner before God. In addition to this, new difficulties have grown out of the dualism of law and love, out of the revolt against a systematic ethics in any form, and out of the modern reconstruction of the doctrines of revelation and inspiration that professes to find elements of error in Scripture itself and is uncertain how much of it comes from the traditional sources. The role of the Law has thus become one of the most difficult questions of contemporary study in Christian ethics.

Instead of arguing at length the case for Mosaic communication of the Law, we simply state our confidence that liberal scholarship has not succeeded in its attack upon the tradition. The priority of the Mosaic to the prophetic tradition is increasingly acknowledged, even in circles once hostile to this viewpoint.

The significance of the Law is that it inscripturates God's command in propositional form as a fixed rule of life. As such, it is an expression of God's eternal moral will, grounded ultimately in the very being of God. The Law tells what the eternally righteous Creator and Lord requires of his creatures. Since it is based on the nature and purpose of the changeless God, the Law can never be abolished, but remains forever. Not even Christ abrogates the Law taken in this sense, nor is the Divine salvation of sinners by grace accomplished in violation of the moral law or in disregard to justice.

These suggestions involve a number of important considerations: that the Law is propositional in its form; that the Law is not an arbitrary legislation of the will of God; that God secures the salvation of the elect only in the course of justice and righteousness. Each of these factors provides a major turning-point in contemporary ethical discussions.

Concerning the Mosaic law, one must say in agreement with the biblical witness that it has been in some respects abrogated, in others fulfilled, and yet properly understood, retains a perpetual and undiminished moral relevance for the community of faith. The significance of the Law is to be located between two extremes: one would bind the believer to the Mosaic law even in some aspects of Old Testament administration (*e.g.*, the observance of the seventh day as a sabbath); the other would thin out moral obligation by freeing the believer from any responsibility to law whatever.

Beyond question, the ceremonial customs and observances belonging to the law under the Old Covenant have fallen away. The Jewish dispensation is at an end; the Christian era has begun. The ritual aspect — meats and drinks and carnal ordinances (Heb. 9:10) — was typical in character. It has lost its relevance now that the reality, the Saviour whom the shadows prefigured, has appeared. As ceremonial law, the Mosaic prescriptions have been abrogated.

The ordinances pertaining to the Old Covenant have no binding authority on the Christian church. The Gospel did not destroy their purpose, but it fulfilled that purpose beyond the competency of ceremony. The Holy Spirit made clear that Gentile and Jew now receive the Divine gifts on equal terms, irrespective of ceremonial observances (Acts 13). The Jerusalem Council settled the dispute about conforming to the law of Moses for salvation by declaring the legal observances to be no longer binding (Acts 15). The apostle to the Gentiles, addressing the Judaizers, declared that neither circumcision nor uncircumcision was profitable for salvation, and that whoever trusted anything alongside the work of Christ for sinners made his faith in Christ of no effect (Gal. 1:6ff., 2:14). The ceremonial law lost its binding force even upon Jewish Christians through Christ's fulfillment of the provisional and typical economy, as the epistle to the Hebrews teaches. The manifestation of Christ is the end of the temporary observances.

The appointments for worship, so important in the era of type and shadow — the special place, the form of service, the official leaders — have only a secondary notice in the New Testament era from Jesus and the apostles. Even the ordinances of baptism and the Lord's Supper, despite their continuing place in the church, may be contrasted to circumcision and the passover. They are not sketched in typical Old Testament detail. Their central purpose is given. The Christian community has fallen into conspicuous disagreement over administrator, candidate, mode, and time. There is an avoidance of the ritualistic, and a centrality for the spiritual; Paul guards the Lord's Supper against certain abuses, but he makes a point of the fact that he did not personally baptize great numbers (1 Cor. 1:14ff). The essential element of the ordinances is not to be found in anything outside their spiritual significance.

But the New Testament goes beyond this. It also affirms the believer's unlimited freedom from the law in its Mosaic system and schematization, done away with by the epochal events narrated in the gospels. The law in its Mosaic form of administration is fulfilled by Jesus Christ. The Christian is "not under law" (Rom. 6:14f., Gal. 5:18), he is "dead to law" (Rom. 7:4ff., Gal. 2:19), he is "redeemed from under law" (Gal. 4:5). The law as part of the Mosaic economy, whether ceremonial or moral, has no claim against the believer. Its requirements are met for him, and his salvation is secured for him by the merits of Jesus Christ.

What then are we to say of the permanent and universal moral obligation of the believer? If he is loosed from obligation to the Mosaic law, is he on that account freed of responsibility to moral law entirely? The answer requires a statement of the connection between the Mosaic law and the eternal moral law of God. Jesus himself stressed that he came not to destroy the law and that not even a jot or tittle of the law would pass away (Mt. 5:17f.). How can the believer be loosed from the Mosaic law and yet its imperishable moral significance be maintained?

The Mosaic law as moral, as non-ceremonial, is the revelation of the righteous will of the immutable God, a Divine declaration of holy will which directs and bounds all men in all times and all places. It constitutes their whole duty toward God. Yet it obviously was not the first transcription of the Divine mind and will for man. It was rather the republication of God's will for mankind from the very beginning in classical form and under new sanctions along with the divinely-willed ceremonial elements of the Hebrew cultus. The Mosaic law must thus be comprehended as a crucial phase of a larger unity. From one viewpoint, it reinforces what is inscribed as moral law upon the hearts of all men (Rom. 1:19f., 2:14f.). This elemental law, which initially supplied the basis of a covenant of works, is objectively restated by the law of Moses and confronts man as sinner with the Divine expectation and command. Nor was the Mosaic law the last transcription. God does not desire a mere external regard for his commandments; the Mosaic law itself looks ahead to the moral law reinscribed upon the hearts of men by the Spirit of God (Jer. 31:33). The law of Moses was not given as the way of salvation by works; it presupposed the Abrahamic covenant of grace, and it was addressed to the children of promise, to the chosen people. The cardinal significance of the Sermon on the Mount has already been discussed. The unity of the moral law is thus to be found in the righteous will of the changeless God, written upon men's hearts, obscured but not obliterated by sin, republished in the Mosaic revelation, made subjectively vital through regeneration.

The Divine will was not for the first time disclosed in the Mosaic law (Gen. 2:16f., 8:15ff., 9:1ff.). Had there been no law from Adam to Moses, there would have been neither sin nor death (Rom. 5:12ff.). To murder, to commit adultery, to steal, did not first become wrong with the proclamation of the Decalogue. Nor did it initially become wrong to steal and murder and covet when the Creator made known statutes and commandments to the original pair in the garden (Gen. 2:16). It had always been wrong to murder, to commit adultery, to steal, to covet. These are fundamental and universal principles that flow from the nature and will of God.

Because the believer stands forever under the rule of God, he is obligated to God's moral demands. As the revelation of God's will, the moral law obliges the Christian, granted that its Mosaic form is not primarily addressed to him. The eternal moral law is binding not on the believer in its Mosaic form, but the Old Testament moral law rather retains its force because it is a part of the righteous will of the immutable God. The Sermon on the Mount makes plain that the Decalogue, rather than losing relevance for Christ's followers, is intensely relevant in a radical inwardness. The moral precepts of the Decalogue were elevated by Jesus. "Christ then, beyond all question," wrote John Smith, "teaches this: that, with whatever temporary accommodations to an infantile stage of moral development, the law contained the norm, the essential principle of the Divine unveiling, having . . . imperishable validity for all time."[1] The Mosaic commandments are strengthened in their moral significance by Jesus' declaration that their inner meaning is total love to God and man (Mt. 22:37-40). This is also the perspective of Paul ("For this: Thou shalt not commit adultery, Thou shalt not kill, Thou shalt not steal, Thou shalt not bear false witness, Thou shalt not covet; and if there be any other commandment, it is briefly comprehended in this saying, namely, Thou shalt love thy neighbor as thyself," Rom. 13:9) and John ("Whosoever doeth not righteousness is not of God, neither he that loveth not his brother. For this is the message that ye heard from the beginning, that we should love one another," 1 John 3:10b, 11). Their point is not that love displaces the commandments, but that love to God and man fulfills them.

The eternal moral law of God is binding on believer and unbeliever alike. To the believer, this is not a predicament of terror for the sole reason that the Saviour has met the full demand of the law and is the ground of his salvation. But believer and unbeliever alike are answerable to the Divine moral demand. God condemns one because the law's demands are not met by him; he spares the other because they are met in a substitute.

The biblical revelation of the moral law was never communicated with the intention of providing man in sin with a possible scheme of

[1]John Smith, *The Integrity of Scripture* (London: Hodder & Stoughton, 1902), p. 104.

works-righteousness. It was given as a corollary to grace. The object of the revelation of the Law even on Sinai "was not to *give,* but to *guide* life."[2] Even as a key element of the Mosaic revelation it was not intended to serve as a means of justification or salvation. The biblical viewpoint is that of the dependence of the Mosaic law on the Abrahamic covenant of grace (Gal. 3:17ff.). To Israel, the chosen people, the Law was not given as a covenant of works, but as subordinate to the promise.

It is an erroneous idea, therefore, that the Law as such annuls grace. The purpose of the Law within grace was to act as a molding influence of Hebrew character. Apart from grace, the Law led to legalism, to the idolatry of the Law, and to false self-righteousness. The redeemed sinner is warned against such bondage to the Law that comes from seeking life from it. The believer is not under the Law as a covenant of works (Gal. 3:13), nor as a source of terror (Rom. 8:1). It is a perverted view of the Gospel that seeks life in whole or part through compliance with the Law, since man as sinner is precluded from finding justification on the ground of works. The Law cannot justify a man who has violated the least of its commands (Jas. 2:10) ; it grants no pardon, it has no power to cover sin and reclaim the sinner. But it is an equally perverted view that represents the Law as thrown into utter oblivion and insignificance by grace.

A balanced statement of Christian ethics must avoid the distortion of both Law and Gospel, protecting the former from the perversion of legalism, and guarding the latter from the perversion of antinomianism. Taken in the right sense, the Law ministers to grace, and grace to the Law. The classic text used by many who misconstrue the relation of law and Gospel is Romans 6:14: "For sin shall not have dominion over you: for ye are not under law, but under grace." This passage gives no comfort to any antinomian interpretation of the theme "free from the law, O happy condition." Rather, it emphasizes that no excuse remains for sin's domination of the believer's life. The Christian is no longer in hopeless bondage to a moral law he cannot fulfill, binding his conscience to a scheme of behavior beyond his reach as a sinner, and exhibiting him as a slave mastered by sin. Now the law's power against him is broken. God's free grace to the sinner has shattered the condemning power of the Law and has inspired moral endeavor with the liberty and assurance of spiritual life. Whoever ventures to turn this text into a comprehensive account of the believer's moral situation and to represent him as detached from all responsibilities to the Law does violence to the very context in which the verse occurs, and from which it must not be separated. The apostle proceeds to emphasize that the liberty of the Gospel is not a license to sin. The Gospel, while it shears the commandments of their terror, does not reject them with contempt. Rather, it elevates them to a higher moral plane. They become the veritable mirror of love in action.

[2]Fairbairn, *The Revelation of Law in Scripture,* p. 276.

The ministry of the Law may be comprehended in three roles. Doubtless it held yet another meaning for unfallen man — that of summarizing the righteousness that, had man conformed to it, would have given him continued and uninterrupted fellowship with his holy Maker. But for man in sin the law holds out no hope whatever as a means of justification before God. Its three-fold significance is political, pedagogic, and didactic.

Political. Even where there is no saving faith, the Law serves to restrain sin and to preserve the order of creation by proclaiming the will of God. The law written upon the heart, which constitutes man as morally responsible to God and neighbor, is republished and clarified to the sinner in the Ten Commandments. The natural knowledge of the law that man retains after the fall on the basis of creation is enforced, and purified from distortion by the special biblical revelation. By its judgments and its threats of condemnation and punishment, the written law along with the law of conscience hinders sin among the unregenerate. It has the role of a magistrate who is a terror to evildoers. By its proclamation that God approves conformity to the law's demands, it provides additional sanctions for rectitude. The Law thus promotes order in the domain of common grace. It fulfills a political function, therefore, by its constraining influence in the unregenerate world.

Pedagogic. The Law escorts unregenerate men to Christ by exposing their moral failure. Since they are impotent to fulfill its demands, they are encouraged to realize their need of Divine grace and salvation. "The law is become our tutor to bring us to Christ, that we might be justified by faith" (Gal. 3:24). As a looking-glass that mirrors man's actual condition in sin, and as a ceremonial type that emphasizes the dire need of sacrificial atonement, the Law compels recourse to the mercy provided in the Redeemer. A conspicuous Pauline theme is that the Law brings a curse, not justification. "Cursed is every one that continueth not in all things that are written in the book of the law, to do them" (Gal. 3:10). The first three chapters of the epistle to the Romans develop the emphasis that the Law brought fallen man under guilt (Rom. 3:20). Since he must be freed from the claim of the Law, the Law is serviceable on the road to grace. It is a pedagogue that brings men to Christ.

The Law therefore becomes a means of grace, disclosing the actual nature of sin and man's need for redemption. This instructive work of the law is not automatic — as if the Law by itself were a means of sanctification, rather than a universal instrument of condemnation. It performs this task only in conjunction with special grace. Where this grace is resisted by the sinner, the Law — not indeed as its essential intention but as an accidental result — may excite sin to more malignant expressions. Christ is, as Paul affirms, the "end" or object of the law

(Rom. 10:4). The Law does more than to disclose man's moral immaturity;[3] it unmasks him as a moral rebel in the bondservice of sin.

Didactic. The Law serves as a standard of obedience to God. The fruits of the Spirit are weighed in the balances of the Law. It remains valid for the believer as the rule of Christian gratitude. The fact of salvation by grace gives no license or inducement to sin to the believer. Rather, grace implements the moral life, "What then? Shall we sin, because we are not under law, but under grace? God forbid" (Rom. 6:15). The Law is the divinely disclosed manual of what constitutes the life that is "hidden in Christ." The life of ideal Christian conduct is godly conduct that is epitomized in the Law.

The conscience of believers does not gain assurance of justification from seeking to keep the Law, but from embracing God's mercy in Christ. The Law has no legal obligation to which the conscience of believers is answerable before the tribunal of God. No longer does it stand over the believer saying "Do this and thou shalt live . . . in the hour that thou eatest thereof thou shalt surely die."

But the Law is a reminder to the Christian of his call to sanctification; it is an impetus to the fulfillment of his duties in voluntary obedience to the will of God. While believers are not justified before God by their personal obedience to the moral law, they are, as the Scottish principal, George Hill, expressed it, "as much bound to obey it as if another method of justification had not been revealed to them."[4]

In the context of salvation by grace, the Law serves as the external criterion of virtue, as the rule of moral good and evil for the believer's walk and conversation. It sets forth the will of God in terms of what ought to be accomplished and avoided. "For the commandment is a lamp; and the law is light; and reproofs of instruction are the way of life" (Prov. 6:23). The whole preceptive word of God thus becomes the believer's rule of conduct: "Do we then make the law of none effect through faith? God forbid; nay, we establish the law" (Rom. 3:31). The impotence of the Law to justify the sinner, and the fact that he experiences justification by faith, does not imply that the Law and the commandments are destroyed. The Bible refers to the Law as perfect (Ps. 19:7), imperishable (Mt. 5:17f.), holy and good (Rom. 7:12),

[3]L. H. Marshall does not go far enough when he tells us that the Law presented "a high ideal of conduct . . . of supreme importance, especially for the ethical development of the immature." *The Challenge of New Testament Ethics,* p. 226. This implies too low a view of the Law, too high a view of fallen man. His verdict should occasion no surprise, then, when he adds that "when they ceased to be mere moral minors and had attained their moral majority, they no longer needed a tutor" (*ibid.,* p. 227), for it depends also upon this optimistic assumption about human nature. When the Apostle Paul speaks of the Law as suited to man's condition of childhood, as assuredly he does (Eph. 2:14ff., Col. 2:14ff.), it is especially the observances which fall away with the coming of the Gospel to which he refers.

[4]George Hill, *Lectures in Divinity,* ed. from ms. by Alexander Hill (New York: R. Carter, 1862), p. 629.

and as spiritual (Rom. 7:14). In the gospel dispensation, it remains as the criterion of the life of spiritual obedience.

While it is the New Testament emphasis that the law of love sums up all the commandments, the apostle Paul — in the very course of stressing this fact — details various commandments. He does this not to draw a contrast between love and commandment, but to emphasize that the commandments are relevant to Christian behavior as the canons of the good life (Rom. 13:8ff.). John Murray remarks that the concrete principles of the Decalogue have relevance to the believer as the criteria of that behavior which love dictates.

The Law does not lose its force against the Christian because commandment is an inferior and faulty form of ethical demand, but because its requirements have been fully met for him by Christ. The Law ceases to terrify the believer as an unpaid debt bill when once the debt is paid for him.

The New Testament nowhere asserts that the Law ceases to be an expression of the will of God. The growing hostility in contemporary statements of Christian ethics to keeping the commandments is profoundly in error. Their argument is that such obedience necessarily involves subethical motivation. This has its basis in a twofold deficiency: an alien philosophical bias that superficially contrasts the Law and the Gospel, and a lack of knowledge, and even distortion, of the plain teaching of the New Testament.

It is true that Brunner acknowledges that "the commandments form *part* of the revelation of the Divine will,"[5] and even remarks that they are authentic expositions of the will of God. Yet he robs this concession of all force by denying that revelation is propositionally expressed, and thereby denying that the commandments communicate the content of God's ethical demand. The commandments become, in his view, merely "witnesses to His revelation . . . revelation indirectly."[6] Revelation itself is identified instead with "The Command," an immediate spiritual confrontation in which Christ personally demands full submission. Partitioning this one command into many commandments is derogated as a sinful tendency that reduces the command. The implicit contradictions that are here latent — the commandments make the command authentically concrete, yet sinfully reduce it; the commandments are a part of revelation, yet the content of revelation cannot be expressed in principles and propositions — are not to be found in the New Testament view of the Law. They are due to the bent of the dialectical theology toward anti-intellectualistic views of revelation. The biblical principles themselves condemn legalism in ethics. These revealed commandments constitute, in fact, God's personal articulation of his will. If the propositions and commandments are only humanly formulated, if they are only fallible attempts to give body to a superior mystical revelation,

[5]Brunner, *The Divine Imperative,* p. 134.
[6]*Ibid.,* p. 134.

then the step is not a large one that views all precepts as rigid, lifeless substitutes for love. But such a view accords poorly with the biblical view of law. It is not the Old Testament alone that regards the Decalogue as of Divine origin, indeed as dictated verbally by Jehovah. For Jesus, the Law contains all God's will and man's duty. In its concrete form the Law is imperishable; it is easier for heaven and earth to pass away than for one tittle of the Law to fail (Mt. 5:18, Lk. 16:17).

Brunner has no biblical sanction for asserting that "the Law itself is not what God wills."[7] God wills the Law, not "legally fulfilled" but fulfilled in love. Love does not do away with the Law by destroying the propriety of conduct by obedience to revealed precepts. Legalism is not due to the law and commandments, but to a misuse of them. The biblical contrast is between law or commandment "fulfilled" legalistically and a spiritual fulfillment as an expression of spiritual devotion. In an ultimate sense the contrast between Spirit and command, between love and law, is artificial. Jeremiah's revelation of the New Covenant should settle this: "I will put my law in their inward parts, and in their heart will I write it" (Jer. 31:33). This is the standpoint of the New Testament as well. "If ye keep my commandments," said Jesus, "ye shall abide in my love" (Jn. 15:10). That the Law in its propositional form breaks the tension of moral responsibility and decision is a complaint[8] which should be silenced easily by an appeal to the biblical assumption that the propositional form of the law *secures* its dynamic. "Cursed be he that confirmeth not the words of this law to do them" (Dt. 27:26). The fact that the Divine will is given in articulate propositional form gives it an irreducible force.

Conduct based on precepts does not necessarily divert attention away from God to actions; only a scheme of morality that wrongly contrasts revelation and precepts can fall into that error. Behavior is sub-ethical when it flows from wrong principles. It is not sub-ethical because it is bounded by precepts recognized as the revealed will of God. What love destroys is conduct under the chafing constraint of the revealed "ought." Love devotes itself in gratitude to the will of God enunciated in the moral precepts of revelation. The contrast between Spirit and commandment grows out of the modern revolt against objective authority in ethics, and out of the rise of theories that seek instead for inner expressions of the moral claim. Marshall asserts that the Christian believer can "follow what his heart desires without transgressing what is right."[9]

[7]Brunner objectionably presupposes that unless the content of God's will is conveyed *only* by subjective encounter, "the absolute and binding character of the Divine Command would be weakened, the sense of responsibility for decision would be broken, the electrical charge of the moral moment would be released, the act of decision would gain a false sense of security by having anticipated decision" (*ibid.*, p. 136). The command is in fact weakened, and responsibility likewise, when the will of God is deprived of articulate expression.

[8]*Ibid.*, p. 142.

[9]Marshall, *op. cit.*, p. 69.

The inner sway of the Spirit in the heart is "an adequate ethical guide. . . . The Spirit is a source of moral insight vastly superior to the law."[10] In such formulations, the Spirit not only illuminates the biblically-revealed ethic to the mind, but becomes an independent source of the content of the moral life. The revolt against authoritarian ethics leads often to a statement of inner sanctions for ethics in which the difference between "Christian" and idealistic ethics is more one of vocabulary than of fact. It is true enough that only the performance of acts which man himself acknowledges to be his duty is ethical, but it is untrue that external authority *always* involves the moral agent in blind dependence. The great aim of Hebrew revelation and redemption is clear: "He is a Jew, which is one inwardly; and circumcision is that of the heart, in the Spirit, and not in the letter; whose praise is not of men, but of God" (Rom. 2:29).

The modern philosophical ethics of inwardness has its roots in part in a secularized rebellion against the medieval Roman Catholic ethics of elevation of a priestly hierarchy to supreme power over conscience and life, against its scheme of sacraments or impersonal grace, against its indulgences and the other paraphernalia of moral outwardness. The place of individual conscience, of the purity of morals, of personal religious relationship, of inward morality, needed to be vindicated. But the tragic feature of modern philosophy is that, rather than return to a purer Christian ethic, it ventured upon a more subtle revolt in the speculative ethics of Kant and Hegel and their successors. "An inwardness," in which the soul was no longer regarded as radically sinful, was held to be competent to elaborate adequate ethical ideals. The individual conscience could now furnish all needful moral illumination. The false veneration of the church as an infallible external authority led to the disregard of the authority of the self-revealing Christ and his written word.

The Roman Catholic view of justification regards the sinner as accepted in God's sight not on the ground of the sufficiency of the atonement, but, in addition to Christ's death, of the infusion of a new nature by the priestly rite of baptism. This denial of justification by faith alone works against the spiritual and ethical by the mechanical and legal scheme of confession, absolution, masses, indulgences, merit — a procedure that often works more for the repetition of sin than for abandonment of it. The moral contrast between Protestant and Roman lands is a commentary on the direction each gives to Christian ethics. A visit from England, Scotland, the Netherlands, to France, Spain, Italy, Peru, Latin America, discloses remarkably different attitudes toward personal morality.

Christian ethics assuredly pleads for inner sanction and controls, restored in the life of the regenerate man under the sway of the renewing Spirit. Yet it does not rid the moral life of an objective ethic whose

[10]*Ibid.*, pp. 220, 232.

content was mediated through prophets and apostles, supremely illuminated by Jesus, and inscripturated in the Bible. It is the New Testament standpoint, penned by the apostle Paul near the close of his great ministry, that "all scripture . . . is profitable . . . for instruction in righteousness . . . that the man of God may be perfect, thoroughly furnished unto good works" (2 Tim. 3:16f.). The rule of the Spirit does not remove man from the will of God objectively revealed in the Bible, and emancipate him to moral self-sufficiency. The Spirit rules in and through the written word, which he has inspired. The spiritual discernment of the regenerate man is not relieved of the need for ethical instruction and guidance.

The difficulties posed by the artificial contrast of love with law have driven the "Spirit-ethics" schools to some obviously untenable positions. Marshall plainly reflects the attempt to impose a biased view upon Pauline ethics, "Paul abandoned the Code-method for the Spirit-method . . . he had scrapped the Ten Commandments, and all the rest of the Law."[11] To deal with those elements of Pauline literature that stand in stark contradiction to this dismissal of the ethical relevance of biblically revealed precepts, Marshall argues that Paul "occasionally lapsed into legal language . . . (and) spoke of a law that is binding on the Christian, and of an external moral standard. . . . Paul had not completely abandoned his earlier Jewish modes of thought. He was partly accommodating his teaching to the Old Testament standpoint and to Jewish ideas."[12] But an examination of Paul's teachings, given the untenable thesis that obedience to divinely-revealed commandments is unspiritual, will accord better with a conclusion that Marshall refuses to draw — that Paul does not arrive at a "Spirit ethics." Surely the Apostle declares that the Gentiles are "not . . . without law to God, but under law to Christ" (1 Cor. 9:21), that love fulfills the revealed commandments (Rom. 13:8f.), that the words of Jesus constitute precepts which bind the Christian (1 Cor. 7:10). The notion that Jesus repudiated the biblical commandments, and was concerned only about ethical attitudes, is not only superficial, but grossly misleading. It is not surprising, given such a misconception, that Marshall should feel compelled to reduce some of Jesus' moral instruction to "urgent advice."[13] The contrast of reverence for commandment to spiritualistic ethics would require that notion that Jesus himself promulgated an ethic less spiritual than that championed by our modern protagonists of Spirit-ethics. His parting commission to his followers is "Go and make disciples . . . , baptize them . . . , and teach them to obey all the commands I have laid on you" (Mt. 28:19, 20).

The spirit of New Testament ethics is anti-legalistic, in the sense that it gives a searching criticism of any mere outward conformity to

[11]*Ibid.*, p. 230.
[12]*Ibid.*, p. 231.
[13]*Ibid.*, p. 102.

moral claims. It is not on that account anti-legal. The Law was to be written by the Spirit upon the hearts of men, but what the Spirit was to write remained the Law. The Spirit does not reject the commandments, but rather insists upon and implements their spiritual fulfillment.

The early fathers did not "understand" that Christian ethics implies the repudiation of ethical claims in the form of commandment and precept. References to "commandments" of Jesus Christ may be found in Clement, Polycarp, and Ignatius. Granted that Romanism gradually developed the idea of obedience to the commands into a system of merit, that in the post-apostolic period "Paulinism was ere long displaced by the prevailing moralism of the incipient Catholic Church,"[14] the fault was not with the interpretation of Christ's teaching by the idea of commandment. "The declension from the joyous Pauline conception of the gospel as an emancipation from law and of the Christian life as a life of freedom and spontaneous, obedient service in the power of a living faith and boundless gratitude"[15] was brought about because the fulfillment of those commands was sought once again in a legal rather than in a filial way, because the significance of the Gospel was obscured.

The question is not, therefore, one of the relevance of the Decalogue in which the moral law of God is known to us, and of the more precise exposition of it given by Jesus Christ in the Sermon on the Mount.[16] The real issue is whether any other moral scheme is relevant, whether all others are not at once unmasked alongside it as second-rate and man-made competitors, whether in the presence of any other moral demand we would not sense ourselves to be deteriorating into ethical reduction.

The paramount and ineradicable message of Sinai gains rather than loses force as the cultural crisis intensifies. It remains as a beacon, illuminating the righteous and immutable will of God which directs and binds all men, in all times and places, to their whole duty toward God. It finds the basis of a durable society not one-sidedly in the rights of the individual, nor in the strategy of political representatives to whom these rights have been delegated in part, but in the sovereignty of the holy God and in an individual relation to him, and through him to other men. This alone is the secure foundation of social organization. It proclaims the ultimate theocentric origin and basis of all law, supreme over the rulers and lawgivers of earth as well as over all people in general; nowhere does a soul have inherent rights against God. The Law has a religious preface, indeed the first commandment serves as its

[14]James MacKinnon, *From Christ to Constantine* (New York: Longmans, 1936), p. 230.

[15]W. G. D. MacLennan, *Christian Obedience,* p. 50.

[16]When Brunner recognizes that God's personal command takes the form of law, he introduces an inconsistency which requires the discard of his contrast of love and law, or he is using ambiguous language: "The commandment of love, taken as a law — the requirements of the Sermon on the Mount regarded as a law — is and remains . . . the standard for man, wherever he may be . . ." *The Divine Imperative,* p. 227.

basis. It is not the intrinsic dignity of human nature that occupies the forefront of the moral question; rather, it is man's obligation to the Creator and Lord and to his fellow men in view of the realities of creation and redemption.

From this fact it is obvious that the Law does not have for its object conformity to a collection of abstract rules, but is intended as a means to know God, and to obey his will. The authority of the Law is not impersonal and mechanical. No mere formal observance, even if it could be given, would suffice. While it is true that the obedient will can act in view of law or principle, it is equally true that conduct regulated only by abstract principles can never be good. One must be personally related to the Law-Giver to obey the law rightly. Obedience must be within the family. What the New Testament deprecates is the unpromising and self-deceptive regard for the law as a basis of salvation for sinners on the ground of works and exclusive of reliance upon grace (Rom. 4:12ff., Gal. 2:21, 3:10ff.). It was Schleiermacher's failure to see this that misled him into the position that since "the Law lacks the power of the Spirit from which the Christian life must flow, . . . it cannot well be maintained that the Law was inspired by the same Spirit of which the same Apostle says that it is no longer communicated through the Law and its works but God sends it into our hearts only through our connection with Christ."[17] This failure is perpetuated by liberalizing views of Christian ethics in our own times. They all — whatever grounds they may profess to adduce for it, and whatever ingenious theological formulas they may bring to its side — erect an unnecessary antithesis between law and Gospel, and they depreciate the inner moral significance of the Law and the commandments of God. True as it is that biblical ethics may be "fulfilled" legally, which is really to reduce its claim to a "bargain counter" morality, yet a vital fulfillment of the commandments is not possible. Indeed, adequate Christian living requires an orientation of the whole of life to these revealed principles of conduct. The forgiven Christian is not a lawless Christian. Grace enables him to conform more and more to the image of the changeless Law-Giver.

[17]Schleiermacher, *The Christian Faith*, p. 608.

15

CHRISTIAN ETHICS AS PREDICATED ON THE ATONEMENT

THE CHRISTIAN LIFE is a living commentary on the Pauline "therefore." This word usually marks the transition from the exhibition of God's redemptive act to the life of moral earnestness that is expected because one has been redeemed. Brunner remarked in *The Divine Imperative* that Christian ethics is a "wherefore" ethics, and Dean Pike characterizes his own recent volume titled *Doing the Truth* as "an extended footnote on the 'therefore' which is St. Paul's transition between the recital of the mighty acts of God and the charge to live as becomes them."[1]

The indispensable background for the doctrine of the good life, if forged in Christian dimensions, must always be the fact of a divinely-provided redemption. Ethics is not primarily a matter of human relationships, but is fundamentally a man-to-God relationship. The question which Christian ethics poses in view of man's failure in sin is not "What works must we do to become righteous?" Such an inquiry can only come from a profound misunderstanding of the moral situation. Rather, the question is, "How can we as sinners be considered righteous?"

The Christian answer is that by redemption man becomes rightly related to the will of God. In looking for a foundation of ethics, Calvin rightly finds in the atonement "the main difference between the Gospel and philosophy." "Though the philosophers speak excellently and with great judgment on the subject of morals," he observes, "yet whatever excellency shines forth in their precepts, it is, as it were, a beautiful superstructure without a foundation; for by omitting principles, they offer a mutilated doctrine, like a body without a head. . . . Paul lays down . . . the principle from which all the duties of holiness flow, even this, — that we are redeemed by the Lord for this end — that we may consecrate to him ourselves and all our members."[2] This dependence of the life of virtue upon its redemptive base is well-worded by James Orr. Christianity, he writes, is "a great Divine economy for

[1]James A. Pike, *Doing the Truth*, p. 9. The fact of forgiveness predicated on the atonement is, as Dean Pike remarks, one of the "great theological premises about the nature of God on which the system of Christian ethics rests. He takes up the slack between His righteousness and our actual behavior, if we repent. He takes the burden and the hurt of our sins unto Himself" (*ibid.*, p. 87).
[2]Calvin, *Commentary on Romans*, 12:1.

recovery of men from the guilt and power of sin — from a state of estrangement and hostility to God — to a state of Holiness and blessedness in the favour of God, and of fitness for the attainment of their true destination. . . . And Redemption here includes, not merely delivery from existing evils, but restoration of the Divine likeness which has been lost by man, and the ultimate blessedness of the life everlasting."[3] Bishop Moule succinctly voices the same thought: "For the life of Christian virtue, Christian grace is the living requisite."[4]

Many persons in the twentieth century, and doubtless even some who consider themselves believers, would consider it theological exaggeration if they were told that the most significant and tremendous occurrence of all man's tragic history is the death of Christ. They might indulgently smile if told that this most monstrous crime in the range of values outweighs in gravity and portent all that men or nations ever have done or will do, and that it was decisive for the moral destiny of all mankind. But there Christ "brought evil to a moral head and dealt with it as a unity."[5] Precisely because Christianity locates its center where no other religion finds it — that bloody cross whereon the Saviour atones for the sins of men — it provides a wholly different orientation for the ethical life. The passionate ethical character of the New Testament, as Denney reminds us, is "condensed and guaranteed in that atoning work of Christ which is in every sense of the word its vital centre."[6]

The notion that the evangelical doctrine of propitiatory sacrifice is fundamentally immoral and beyond justification is published with increasing frequency in our generation. The complaint is not a new one, although the extent to which it is voiced seriously within the professing church itself is. Horace Bushnell had already formulated, with classic simplicity, the complaint that substitutionary atonement is revolting to the moral sense and dishonoring to God. The theology of substitution, it is contended by those who share his complaint, inverts the moral poles of the universe. "To allow the guilty to escape, and the punishment to fall upon the righteous" — as the protest may be phrased — "encourages the transgressor to sin with impunity, and remits that penalty which is at once an educational and reformatory necessity for him."[7] In his volume titled *What Is a Mature Morality?,* H. H. Titus asserts that "To many people it seems immoral to picture God as . . . one who needs to be appeased by the blood of a victim. We cannot think . . . of atonement as the propitiation of an angry monarch God. We feel a moral revulsion at the thought of sinners in the hands of a wrathful God. . . . Many conceptions which are set forth in terms such as blood

[3]James Orr, *The Christian View of God and the World,* pp. 287f.
[4]Handley C. G. Moule, *Grace and Virtue* (London: Cassell, 1913), p. 13.
[5]P. T. Forsyth, *The Cruciality of the Cross,* p. 117.
[6]James Denney, *The Death of Christ* (New York: Hodder & Stoughton, n.d.), p. 327.
[7]Junius Remensnyder, *The Atonement and Modern Thought* (Philadelphia: Lutheran Publishing Society, 1905), pp. 98f.

atonement, expiation, ransom, substitution, satisfaction . . . and the like, have not only lost much of their meaning, but they offend the enlightened moral sense of today."[8]

Some offense which the moral sense takes over the statement of Christian doctrines is justified. The doctrine of atonement is sometimes understood merely as a legal fiction that requires a grotesque view of God. This impression has been given credence by unfortunate sermonic illustrations in which the essence of the doctrine of atonement is depicted as a judge's arbitrary decision to punish an innocent third party while the guilty defendant goes scot free. Such a representation seems to underlie the protests against substitution voiced by Hastings Rashdall,[9] Leslie Weatherhead,[10] and many others. And did this accurately represent the historic Christian doctrine, such a conception of the atonement would have to be repudiated from the standpoint of biblical theology and ethics. The Psalmist stresses the impossibility of one man atoning for another: "None of them can by any means redeem his brother, nor give to God a ransom for him" (Ps. 49:7). When Titus, for example, understands the doctrine to involve "a God . . . practicing deceptions or who permits the shifting of moral responsibility . . . a peevish King,"[11] he singles out elements against which any sensitive conscience must rebel. But the doctrine of atonement has been vindicated against such misconceptions by the ablest expositors of the biblical view.

It is one thing to say that the Christian doctrine of atonement is repugnant to the moral sense, and another to assert that it must be so. Doubtless there are elements in the biblical concept that will always irk the self-righteous sinner who thinks himself justified by his own works. But such a moral sense in its protest against the doctrine of substitution wrongly assumes its own infallibility, and the conception of God that it evolves has its roots in speculation rather than in the Divine self-revelation. The Hebrew-Christian Scriptures assert the reality and indispensability of propitiatory atonement, and pronounce judgment upon the fallible ethical sense of fallen man. J. B. Champion has noted that man as sinner is inclined to a speculative revision of the idea of God rather than disposed to conform his moral sense to the determinations of revealed ethics. "When progress in the ethical conception of appeasement has reached the point where God is thought too good to require appeasement, there is need then for an equal advance in our thinking on the ethics of appeasement. All natures, even the ethical, have their fit and rightful appeasements. The higher our ethical conception of God, the higher must be our ethical conception of the appease-

[8]Harold H. Titus, *What Is a Mature Morality?* (New York: Macmillan, 1943), pp. 146f.

[9]Hastings Rashdall, *The Idea of Atonement in Christian Theology* (London: Macmillan, 1919), p. 423.

[10]Leslie Weatherhead, *The Transforming Friendship* (London: Epworth, 1933), p. 143.

[11]Titus, *op. cit.*, p. 146.

ment which his nature will demand."[12] Yet it will not do to allow any suggestion to prevail that an absolute antithesis exists between the biblical and the intuitive conceptions of justice. It is not man's instinctive notion of justice at all that is in conflict with the scriptural representation; rather, it is the direction that sentiment takes in contemporary thought. "The Gospel of the Cross as presented in the Scripture," Hall well reminds us, "neither antagonizes the intuition of justice, nor affronts the moral sense."[13] The means of man's moral rescue are themselves ethical; they do not wave aside the eternal justice and holiness of God, nor do they explore an avenue of forgiveness that bypasses the righteous requirements of the Divine nature, nor do they purchase a moral holiday for the pardoned sinner.

The subtle and perverse effect upon the moral sentiment that comes from excising the biblical representation of the atonement from one's outlook upon sin and redemption has been stressed too little. Thomas H. Hughes reminds us that "to make forgiveness cheap and unconditional is to do an injustice and a moral injury to the personality of the forgiven, for it wrongs his moral sense, undermines the stability of his moral universe, and works moral and spiritual degeneration in his being."[14] And while Dr. Hughes is no uncritical advocate of the traditional theory of the atonement, it is in this safeguard of the transcendent significance of good and evil that one facet of its strength is to be found.

H. E. Guillebaud's chapter "Is Substitution Immoral?," in his volume *Why the Cross?*, points out the misunderstandings involved in the critical misconceptions of the substitutionary view. The biblical doctrine of atonement is not open to the weaknesses that caricatures of it are. The antagonists of substitution can quickly dispatch some straw-doctrine, but they cannot so easily dispense with the revealed account. It affirms that God, the righteous Judge of a fallen world, himself assumed human nature in Jesus Christ in order to bear the penalty of his broken moral law in the nature of the guilty offenders.[15] The irrelevance of Martineau's objection is at once apparent: "The transference of guilt from one individual to another, standing on the same plane, involves a contradiction of the first principles of morality."[16] The God-man serves, in the historic view, as the subject of an intimate union and identification with the Godhead on the one hand, and with all of the human race who turn to him by faith on the other. Where theology has declined so that deity is no longer ascribed to Christ, and where the identity of the vicarious sufferer with the holy Judge is obscured, there

[12]John B. Champion, *The Living Atonement* (Philadelphia: Griffith & Rowland, 1910), p. 196.

[13]Charles C. Hall, *The Gospel of Divine Sacrifice* (New York: Dodd, Mead, 1897), p. 169.

[14]Thomas H. Hughes, *The Atonement* (London: Allen & Unwin, 1949), p. 203.

[15]H. E. Guillebaud, *Why the Cross?* (London: Inter-Varsity Fellowship, 1937), pp. 147ff.

[16]James Martineau, *Theories of the Work of Jesus*, p. 479.

the doctrine of atonement can but appear immoral. But such a view has no right to speak for the standpoint of Christian ethics. Charles Hodge reiterates that "guilt can be removed only by punishment. Either the sinner himself must bear it, or a substitute must be provided to assume the guilt, and bear the punishment, and so freedom of guilt is secured for the offender. This is the fundamental idea of Atonement or satisfaction as presented in the scriptures."[17]

The repudiation of the biblical doctrine of atonement involves, whether intentionally or not, an attack upon the objective reality of the moral order, and for that reason conditions the ethical question at every turn. Anselm emphasized centuries ago that the deletion of the atonement inflicts a blow on the moral government of the world, weakening and discrediting it.[18] Smeaton remarks that "a scheme of thought which runs counter to the atonement, if carried out to its logical consequences, is destructive to religion, and subversive of morality. . . . The position too widely maintained at present, that God is nothing but a fountain of goodness, who sacrifices everything to the happiness of His creatures, destroys all religion, because it takes no account of the subjection, love, and reverence due to God."[19] If the necessity of atonement is traced by revealed theology to the uncompromising righteousness and justice of God, and to the unrelieved heinousness of sin, then the dogma that the atonement is dispensable makes God out to be less holy, and deals tolerantly with sin. The Cross is the center of the moral universe, unveiling God's absolute refusal to suspend his law of holiness. The sanctity with which penal theory invests the moral law is one element of its strength. It stands as the supreme obstacle to making sin relative, to reducing the justice of God to anthropomorphic projections, to concealing his moral indignation and ethical anger. That the moral law cannot be defied with impunity is dramatically clear from the fact that "God spared not his own Son." The moral world is one in which holiness reigns absolutely and uniformly. Whatever tampers with this undermines respect for the fact that the moral claim reaches to every last motive and act of the responsible being. If the claim of the law or the punishment of sin is relaxed in but a single province of the moral universe, the Divine ethical government is to that extent dishonored and weakened. What fact more fully enforces the majestic righteousness of God than the conviction of the inviolability of his moral law published by the atonement of the Cross?

The atonement and a right conception of the character of God are inseparable. God is "of purer eyes than to behold evil, and . . . look upon perverseness" (Hab. 1:13) and he is pledged to inflict "indignation and wrath upon every soul of man that doeth evil" (Rom. 2:6f.).

[17]Charles Hodge, *Systematic Theology* (Grand Rapids: Eerdmans, reprint, 1952), II, 532.

[18]Anselm, *Cur Deus Homo*, I, xii.

[19]George Smeaton, *The Doctrine of the Atonement as Taught by Christ Himself* (2d ed., Edinburgh: T. & T. Clark, 1871), pp. 408f.

The Bible looks upon sin not merely as an infraction of positive Divine enactments or commandments, but as the violation of God's moral law grounded in his character. The essential attributes of the Divine nature call for the appeasement of God's wrath if the sinner is to be spared. The remark of P. T. Forsyth, "There is only one thing that can satisfy the holiness of God, and that is holiness — adequate holiness,"[20] will forever hold true. Those who repudiate the necessity for the atonement ignore God's holy aversion to sin, his condemnation of it, and his determination to punish it. The first principle of Divine government is that God demands and vindicates his rights in the intelligent universe; he cannot recede from his moral claims, nor can he witness rebellion without inflicting due punishment. The atonement is the recognition and enforcement of this principle. "Those who deny the necessity of a penal substitutionary atonement, by implication also disown the strict punitive justice of God, in virtue of which he must necessarily punish sin," writes Berkhof.[21] "If the law is regarded as an expression of the moral character of God, and therefore as a necessary revelation of the will of God for the guidance of His moral creatures, it becomes utterly impossible to assume that the Judge of all the earth might have pardoned sin without any adequate atonement."[22] Scripture itself finds in the atonement alone the vindication of God's righteousness and justice if the guilty sinner is to be forgiven: "God hath set forth . . . a propitiation through faith in his blood, to declare his righteousness . . . that he might be just, and the justifier of him who believeth in Jesus" (Rom. 3:25f.). Without those ethical satisfactions provided by the atonement, the moral nature of God could not have allowed the forgiveness of sins.

The assault on the doctrine of atonement has also led to flimsy evaluations of moral evil. To declare that sin does not lead to death and doom is to question whether holiness and justice are attributes of God as well as to misrepresent as tolerable to God what is actually opposed and abhorrent to his nature. Belief in the atonement therefore keeps the general respect for morality from deteriorating into an ethics of convenience. One of the sources of the power of Christianity lies in the fact that, as Edward J. Hamilton notes, "the death of Christ reveals not only the love of God but also the divine hatred for sin."[23] The sufferings of Christ declare that hatred; they are the supreme reminder that the wages of sin is death. Nowhere is it so apparent that Divine love cannot be reduced to mere benevolence, and that the love of God is high and holy. The Father-love of God is answerable to

[20]P. T. Forsyth, *The Work of Christ* (New York: Hodder & Stoughton, n.d.), p. 126.

[21]Louis Berkhof, *Vicarious Atonement Through Christ* (Grand Rapids: Eerdmans, 1936), p. 51.

[22]*Ibid.*, p. 64.

[23]Edward J. Hamilton, *The Moral Law* (New York: Funk and Wagnalls, 1902), p. 437.

righteousness and justice; it is consistent with severity and judgment. Even the barren fig tree may be spared another year, but it is to be cut down in final judgment if it bears no fruit (Lk. 13:8, 9). Canon Gore has put it, "mercy, rejoicing against judgment, must prepare for judgment at the last." Denney assures us the atonement "is a homage paid by Christ to the moral order of the world established and upheld by God; a homage essential to the work of reconciliation, for unless men are caught into it, and made participant of it somehow, they cannot be reconciled . . ."[24] In that ancient world to which Christianity addressed its Gospel and which had lost hold of personal morality, the early church vindicated the existence and authority of a moral law. It stamped a shaming sense of sin upon the conscience of that pagan environment by its incessant proclamation of the death of Christ for sinners. No mere re-identification with the moral law by those who have rebelled against it is sufficient to rub out the consequences of the guilty past. For God maintains a relationship to his rational and ethical creatures not only of a beneficent Father, but also of a righteous moral governor, with a concern for the authority of his laws and the rectitude of his creatures. The guilty sinner owes more than future obedience; his debt includes satisfaction for past sin. Our Lord's mission included the payment of man's penal debt; he met the Divine displeasure against sin, and to be our Redeemer, it was not possible that the cup of death should pass from him, though he had lived a sinless life. Hence the Christian community has always recognized it to be a perversion for one to regard his work as that only of a moral example.

Faith in the atonement of Christ is the supreme moral act of which man is capable. It does not by-pass the ethical verdict against moral evil, but enforces it. It is the over-emphasis on the moral *effect* of Christ's death that does not see in the atonement an objective work directed primarily to satisfy the outraged holiness of God. Such an over-emphasis leads sooner or later, as Denney did not hesitate to say, to hedonistic rather than ethical estimates of life. "We cannot dispense with the ideas of propitiation, we cannot dispense with a work of reconciliation which is as objective as Christ himself, and has its independent objective value to God, let our estimate of it be what it will. The world with Christ and his Passion in it is a different place from the world without Christ and his Passion in it. It is a different place to God, and God's attitude to it is different. Is there any other way to express this than by saying that Christ and his Passion constitute an objective atonement, and that it is on the basis of this that men are reconciled to God?"[25] The Cross is beyond doubt the most poignant disclosure of the forgiving heart of God. But it discloses at the same time the most drastic condemnation of human sin possible.

[24] James Denney, *The Christian Doctrine of Reconciliation.* Cunningham Lectures (New York: George H. Doran, 1918), p. 235.
[25] *Ibid.*, p. 236.

What can so infuse human life with the awareness of its high calling and with the dread of sin as a right view of the atonement can? According to such a view only the substitute of infinite dignity can stand between the guilty sinner and the Divine wrath. What can lay bare the bitter memory of past sin, stripping away its false allurements, more than the realization that they contributed to the agonies of Christ? "The more you abolish the significance of Christ's redeeming death once for all," writes Forsyth, "the more you are doing to lower humanity morally, and make it a less precious thing than the cosmic world around us."[26] "The very dignity of man himself is better assured if he were broken upon the maintenance of that holiness of God than if it were put aside arbitrarily, just to let him off with his life. . . . Any religion which leaves out of supreme count the judging holiness of God is making a great contribution to the degradation of man."[27]

Christian ethics and the atonement are inextricably bound together. To deplore the atonement, whether it be simply dismissed as superfluous or decried as barbarous, is to deplore Christian ethics. There is no Christian ethics which does not flow directly from the atonement.

Schleiermacher and liberal Protestant theology have had a baneful influence upon Christian ethics by concealing the Divine wrath, and by suppressing the judicial aspect of the ethical. The faulty liberal conception of human nature lent itself to a faulty conception of its moral recreation. Wherever this influence has prevailed, it has misstated the outlines of moral redemption by professing to nurture spiritual life without expiation, and ethical renewal without propitiation. The essence of Christianity was shriveled by this liberalizing theology into being merely the teaching and example of Jesus. And even these were considerably truncated (since his metaphysical teaching entered inevitably into his example and the liberals arbitrarily considered his metaphysics as invalid). The significance of the incarnation and the atonement for Christian faith was largely missed. Biblical theology has little sympathy for narrowing redemption to the life of fellowship with Christ. Rather, it depicts the moral life of the spirit as being the result of the objective fact of atonement.

Only in recent decades have Divine justice and punishment due man for sin come back into vogue in theological thought. Indeed, the necessity for a proper substitution and for expiation and for imputed righteousness is now a popular doctrine. The liberalizing versions of Christian ethics, according to which Christ redeems men simply by incorporating them into the fellowship and vitality of his life, operated with false views of God, of sin, of redemption, and of the well-spring of Christian virtue. The flaw in such views is that they conceal the wrath of God, and they fail to grant that sin involves punitive justice. The biblical view of atonement, to the contrary, takes for granted that the sinner

[26]P. T. Forsyth, *The Work of Christ,* p. 114.
[27]*Ibid.,* p. 128.

not only forfeits fellowship with God but stands in need of redemption from guilt, penalty, and corruption; and apart from Christ's expiation there is neither remission of sins nor a restoration to fellowship with God.

The dialectical theology of crisis, now so stylish, re-emphasizes the expiatory work of Christ. At the same time it denies any propitiatory and forensic significance to the atonement. This view revives an emphasis on the Divine wrath, but it does so only with half-seriousness, and in the final analysis subordinates God's wrath to his love. That God goes to the Cross to secure man's forgiveness doubtless reveals the very nature of God. "The characteristic feature of the ethics of the prophets," T. B. Strong says, is their continual representation of God as "longing to pardon — rising up early and sending His prophets — that men may come back to their allegiance, and realize the blessings of the covenant-union."[28] But it is equally true that the biblically-revealed God forgives only in view of the satisfaction of Divine justice and righteousness by the atonement, and by personal appropriation of its benefits. The tendencies toward universalism in Barth's theology, the confidence of Niebuhr that God ultimately will forgive all men, and Brunner's equal aversion to the traditional doctrine of eternal punishment, are elements of the recent theology that reflect the hesitant role assigned to the atonement. Niebuhr especially appeals to the centrality of the Cross, yet for him it is alternative to the shed blood of Christ. It is not by the atonement as a substitutionary act that men are saved in his system. They are saved by their existential perseverance within the tensions of the dialectic.

The clear doctrine both of the gospels and of the epistles is that Christ died in the stead of sinful men. This doctrine is not drawn only from the Pauline letters, as the older liberal theology contended it was in an effort to discredit the doctrine of substitution. It is found with equal directness in the Petrine[29] and Johannine literature, and belongs to the warp and woof of the Synoptic Gospels as their consistent presupposition.

First Corinthians 15:3 makes it obvious that the presupposition of all primitive Christian preaching was Christ's atonement for sinners. Hence the early Church held to a soteriological view of the Messiah. Alongside this was the conviction that man's attempted observance of the Law was inadequate to secure justification before the holy Creator and Lord. All sacrifices of man's devising, all man-made temples and worship were

[28]T. B. Strong, "Ethics," I, in Hasting's *Dictionary of the Bible,* 780f.

[29]James Denney remarks, on 1 Peter 2:21ff., that "the apostle does not raise the question whether it is possible for one to assume the responsibilities of others in this way; he assumed . . . that the responsibilities of sinful men have been taken on Himself by the sinless Lamb of God." *The Death of Christ,* p. 70. F. W. Dillistone adds that "readers of this epistle found nothing strange or abhorrent in believing that Christ actually took upon himself the burden of their judgement and made it possible for them to be vindicated by God." *Significance of the Cross* (London: Lutterworth, 1946), p. 53.

futile. The Old Testament sacrificial system is not a half-barbarous rite appropriated from pagan sources, for then the New Testament must be divorced from it as an embarrassment. Rather, it was an elemental form that expressly anticipated the great spiritual fulfillment to come; it was a reminder of the sinfulness of sin and of an efficacious atonement fully and finally available for the remission of sin. There is no ethical handling of sin without expiation, without the juridical character of the Cross, without the vindication of God's righteousness. Speaking about ethics, it is simply not enough to say of Jesus that he lifted the moral elements of Judaic religion to new heights, that he infused Hebrew ideals with a profound spirituality and widened them to universal application. He did all this, and infinitely more. Because his teaching and example are quite misunderstood in their importance if the atonement is hid, it is best to emphasize the significance of his role as Redeemer first. He is not merely the revealer of God — else he is ground for man's despair — but the Redeemer of sinners.

Only an ethical scheme that balks at the whole biblical plan of redemption and shies away from the significance of the atonement on rationalistic grounds can maintain that salvation by substitutionary death is a late and unforeseen development of Christ's ministry, an afterthought that was not a part of his original intention. The high conception of Jesus as the promised Redeemer of doomed sinners fills the view our Lord had of himself in the gospel narratives. It is not confined to the teaching of the New Testament epistles.[30] The whole modern liberal effort, to make the pattern of the salvation of the many through the deliverance of a suffering remnant the key to the vicarious death of Christ, cannot arrive at a satisfactory ground-spring of redemptive life because it inadequately depicts the profound implications of the Redeemer's death. Under this view, Christ's passion loses its uniqueness except as the supreme instance of the general principle. Likewise, even though Wilder says that "Jesus thought of Himself not merely, like John, as the proclaimer of the Kingdom but as its bearer," the force of Christ's death in its biblical significance is evaporated by his notion that Jesus offered "His death to the cause of the Kingdom" with a confidence that God "would use it in some major way toward the coming of the Kingdom."[31] "In the Passion," we are told, "Jesus was inevitably led to take upon Himself the sole burden of the Kingdom of the future; to become its door . . ." Wilder's notion is that atonement is simply Paul's interpretation of the Cross. Wilder backs away from a high view of the uniqueness of Jesus' death: "in the teaching and action of Jesus . . . the new work of God comes *most* plainly into view and is *most* effectively mediated to men."[32] The italics are sup-

[30]Arnold T. Ohrn, *The Gospel and the Sermon on the Mount* (New York: Revell, 1948), pp. 33f.
[31]A. N. Wilder, *Eschatology and Ethics in the Teaching of Jesus*, p. 181.
[32]*Ibid.*, p. 188.

plied to emphasize how far from Paul's view of the atonement Wilder stands.

The emphasis of evangelical ethics on the objective significance of the Cross has led to the charge that it neglects the significance of subjective moral decision in the life of the believer. Evangelicalism tends to make men indifferent to personal morality because it stresses their justification before God on the ground of another's sacrifice. But actually the neglect of the objective element leads to inadequate and fallacious views that do not really meet the need of the guilty conscience and that do not fulfill the high ethical promise with which they set out.

Perhaps the most conspicuous example of the delicate connection of moral earnestness with the propitiatory doctrine is supplied indirectly where one would least expect to find it — from a study of the fortunes of the so-called "moral influence" theory of atonement. The "moral influence" theory deviates from the biblical doctrine of the atonement as a vicarious satisfaction, and instead stresses only the subjective effect of the Cross upon sinners as a manifestation of Divine love. It was characteristic of the champions of this view to lampoon the theory of propitiatory atonement as involving an unethical transfer of guilt from the wicked to the righteous, a complaint with which we have already dealt. Professedly to safeguard the ethical import of the atonement, the advocates of the moral influence theory assigned to the doctrine of justification the notion "to make just," rather than its biblical forensic sense of "to declare just." The experience of justification was thus given a "vital" turn, becoming an aspect of the process of renewal or sanctification. But such a theological transaction costs more than it saves. By giving justification a subjective turn, it takes away the sinner's assurance of absolute acceptance with God on the basis of Christ's death. It thus violates the biblical position that in the work of justification God alone acts on the condition of faith in Christ, whereas in the work of sanctification the regenerate sinner coöperates with the renewing activity of the Holy Spirit. But internally it faces an equally profound difficulty. The theory views the death of Christ as the supreme example of Divine displeasure against sin, calculated to move the minds of men to an abhorrence of evil. But that the sinless Christ should be made such an object of displeasure seems a violent contradiction of the nature of God and an intolerable anomaly in his moral government of the world.

It is indeed ironic that, after presenting the moral influence theory of the atonement as a desirable alternative, Bushnell conceded its inferior ethical dynamic unless it is given the literary cloak of the traditional theory of satisfaction. "In the facts, outwardly regarded, there is no sacrifice, or oblation, or atonement, or propitiation. . . . The agony is eloquent of love, and the cross is a very shocking murder triumphantly met; and if then the question rises how we are to use such a history so as to be reconciled by it, we hardly know in what way to begin. . . . Plainly, there is a want here, and this want is met by giving a thought-form to the facts which is not in the facts themselves. They are put directly into the moulds of the altar, and we are called to accept the crucified God-man as our Sacrifice, an offering or oblation for us, our Propitiation. . . . Without these forms of the altar, we should be utterly at a loss in making any use of the Christian facts that would set us in a condition of practical reconciliation with God."[33] The devastating force of this concession, that greater ethical motivation comes from this view when it is disguised in the ideal forms of expiation and sacrifice of the traditional view of propitiatory atonement, was too obvious to escape attention. "According to the confession of its ablest expounders," remarked A. A. Hodge, "that moral effect which the theory in question maintains is the sole aim of the redemptive work of Christ is at least as well produced by our view of the work of Christ as by theirs."[34] Underlying the moral influence theory one can frequently detect the assumption that salvation is universal as well as by works, a premise which holds little incentive to moral exertion, for if the works of all are sufficient, no one need exert himself more. There are other weaknesses of the theory. It presupposed that a display of love deliberately calculated to move man to moral obedience would have the same effect as a voluntary and spontaneous sacrifice issuing from the motive simply of love. It did no justice to the biblical emphasis that the atonement is efficacious for those who died before Christ's advent as well as for those who came afterward.

The moral influence theory was predicated upon a radical denial of the revealed view of Divine law and justice through the rejection of sacrifice and of forensic justification. Hence it was the virtual negation of the theory of morality that rests on biblical principles. Over against the moral influence view stands the consistent emphasis of Scripture that the atonement is no mere declaration of Divine love, but rather is a satisfaction to placate the wrath of God toward man as sinner. Without the appropriation by faith in the atonement man stands exposed forever to the terrible doom that is the reward of unbelief (Jn. 3:18, 36; Rom. 2:4f.; 1 Cor. 6:9f.; Heb. 10:29).

If the relation between Christ's death and the life of virtue is not adequately worked out in many treatises on Christian ethics, that is not a failure of the New Testament. On its pages the moral life gains its birth from faith in Christ's atonement; it is sustained from moment to moment by its inspiration. To the complaint that the substitutionary doctrine is "immoral in its practical tendencies, since Christ's obedience takes the place of ours, and renders ours unnecessary," Strong replies fitly that the objection ignores not only the method by which the benefits of the atonement are appropriated, namely, repentance and faith, but also the regenerating and sanctifying power bestowed upon all who

[33]Horace Bushnell, *Vicarious Sacrifice* (New York: Scribner, 1877), pp. 533ff.
[34]A. A. Hodge, *The Nature of the Atonement* (Grand Rapids: Eerdmans, reprint), p. 322.

believe. Faith in the atonement does not induce license, but 'works by love' (Gal. 5:6) and 'cleanses the heart' (Acts 15:9)."[35] The doctrine of redemption does not relax the believer's obligation to the Divine commandments, nor weaken his motives to observe them. The motives and ideals of the believer are to be found in that Cross. H. Wheeler Robinson reminds us, "In the most comprehensive survey of the Christian life which the New Testament affords — that of Romans xii - xv. 13 — the feature of supreme importance is the point at which it begins. The life to be described is essentially a redeemed life, and from that characteristic both its dynamic and its peculiar and essential qualities are derived. We cannot hope to be good Christians in character and conduct without sharing in the essentials of the Christian faith. The redeemed life cannot be lived in anything like its fulness without experience of the Christian redemption."[36]

The common objection that substitution exempts men from the earnestness of personal morality is aptly repudiated by the New Testament assertion that the atonement supplies the supreme motive for bringing glory to God through ethical obedience. It is also refuted by the fact that the world has been lifted above the level of pagan morality by the influence of the Christian community filled with this confidence in the atonement and living out its ethical claim in the Western world.

Christianity is a religion of redemption, and it is equally an ethics of salvation. Christian salvation is no unmoral and unspiritual scheme. From start to finish, in and through the atonement, its ideal life is a life of vital ethical experience through a living union with Christ. While it may be true that examples can be found of those who presume on Divine goodness by living a life of unholiness while they fool themselves with the hope that they will escape the consequences of their sins through Christ's sacrifice, this is not characteristic of the evangelical temper. Note the sobering word of James: "show me your works and I will show you your faith" (Jas. 2:18). The atonement is regarded as God's counter-stroke to sin. While the penal theory does not start out with the subjective significance of the atonement, nonetheless it firmly insists that the atonement must directly touch and transform the moral life of man.

The vital connection between the atonement and morality may be sketched with equal force from the teaching of Christ (Jn. 6:51) or from the New Testament apostolic literature (Rom. 6:4, Gal. 2:20). The epistles constantly hold up the fact that the Cross is meant to supply believers with a guiding principle of behavior on the ground of their purchased deliverance. The appeal is not to prudence, nor to self-respect, but to the fact of redemption. Since the redeemed are bought with a price, and are not their own, they are directed to glorify God with

[35]Augustus H. Strong, *Systematic Theology* (Philadelphia: Griffith & Rowland, 1907-09), p. 770.

[36]H. Wheeler Robinson, *Revelation and Redemption,* pp. 281, 283.

body and spirit (1 Cor. 6:20). "The ground and motive for holy duty, for inflaming and increasing the true fear of God, and for expelling misleading aims and tendencies, as seen in almost every point of practical religion, will be found in the apostolic epistles, traced up to the atonement of Christ."[37] The acceptance of the atonement carries with it a demand for personal holiness.

In Romans 6:1-7 Paul deals with the objection that the satisfaction of Divine justice by the atonement of Christ has a tendency to make man rest in what has been done by the substitute and then to be indifferent to the purity of heart. Paul here clearly teaches that those justified by faith through grace cannot deliberately continue in sin. The reason is two-fold: theological and psychological. In the first place, the reason a repentant sinner turns to Christ is to get away from sin and its consequences. Whoever would intentionally continue in sin after such a resort to Christ has not understood what is involved in coming to Christ for redemption. In the second place, it is psychologically impossible to serve two masters; one will be the servant either of sin or of the Lord. The same movement from belief to a holy life may be found in the Petrine emphasis (1 Pet. 2:21-24) that Christ's atonement means not only that our sins and their consequences are cancelled but, as F. W. Dillistone stresses, "the further outcome . . . that we may live to righteousness — may live, in other words, the justified life under the sovereignty of God."[38] Smeaton observes, "the participation of the saving benefits flowing from the atonement yields the strongest of all motives that can influence the human heart, not to dishonor, but to glorify the ineffably gracious Giver of such blessings."[39] The New Testament constantly moves from the atonement as a motive to the life of holiness as an anticipated result. Because of the Divine provision of redemption, *therefore* (probably the most important pivotal word in biblical ethics) sin is not to reign in our mortal bodies (Rom. 6:12), *therefore* we are to present our bodies a living sacrifice as our reasonable service (Rom. 12:1), *therefore* we are to glorify God in our bodies (1 Cor. 6:20), *therefore* we are to display right conduct toward a fallen Christian (1 Cor. 8:11), *therefore* we are to faint not, but to renounce "the hidden things of dishonesty, not walking in craftiness, nor handling the word of God deceitfully; but by manifestation of the truth commending ourselves to every man's conscience in the sight of God" (2 Cor. 4:1ff.), *therefore* we have a dynamic that obliges us to live not unto ourselves but unto him (2 Cor. 5:15), *therefore* we are to imitate him and walk in love (Eph. 5:1f.), *therefore* we are to bear abuse for him (Heb. 13:13), *therefore* we are to be ready to suffer for doing God's will (1 Pet. 3:16, 4:19), *therefore* we are to follow in his steps (1 Pet. 2:21).

[37]Smeaton, *op. cit.*, p. 413.
[38]F. W. Dillistone, *The Significance of the Cross*, p. 53.
[39]Smeaton, *op. cit.*, p. 408.

The forensic theory of atonement establishes an organic relation between the Cross and redemption, since without that sacrifice an insuperable obstacle to man's forgiveness would have existed in the nature of God; and it establishes a causal connection between redemption and the good life. The spiritual development of the justified sinner and his "growth in grace" is an extension of perfect reliance upon Christ, whose death gains our pardon and whose resurrection life in man imparts those influences of the Spirit which are basic to sanctification. "If . . . we were reconciled to God through the death of his Son," the great Apostle writes, "much more, being reconciled, shall we be saved by his life" (Rom. 5:10). The one unitary outflowing of supernatural grace secures both the justification and the sanctification of the sinner. Faith in Christ involves union with him, union with him in his deliverance of us from the Father's wrath, and union with him as the inward principle of the Christian life. "I am crucified with Christ; yet I live," writes the Apostle; "yet not I, but Christ liveth in me" (Gal. 2:20). "He died for all, that they which live should no longer live unto themselves, but unto him who for their sakes died and rose again" (2 Cor. 5:15).

There is a world of truth in Gamertsfelder's comment that "the key to moral philosophy is the cross of Christ."[40] Small wonder then that it may be regarded as furnishing the strongest of moral forces, as the inspired writers themselves anticipate and illustrate by their own lives.

Smeaton, in his classic work on the atonement, is constrained to devote an entire section to "The Influence of the Atonement, Correctly Understood, on the Whole Domain of Morals and Religion." And Christian moralists have always been aware that ethics is but the power of that Cross over the life of redeemed man. The manner in which faith in the atonement colors the quality of Christian virtue is now and then noted by writers on ethics. For example, Smeaton contrasts the ethics of Epictetus and Kant with delineations of Christian ethics, remarking that moralists who plume themselves on merit apart from dependence on the atonement are frequently hard and arrogant, while those who stand perpetually before a holy God in a Mediator's virtue tend to humility. "When St. Paul bids the Corinthians find a pattern of liberality, it is in the Lord of Heaven, who, though He was rich, for our sakes became poor. When he would teach the Philippians the humility of Jesus, and urge them to cultivate the mind that was in Him, it was not of the washing of the disciples' feet he spoke, but of the descent from highest heaven to this world of men. And when St. Peter sought the encouragement of the Lord's example for His followers, it was to His mysterious sufferings and death upon the Cross that he pointed, to that sacrifice which none might copy but whose spirit all might find."[41]

[40]S. J. Gamertsfelder, *Systematic Theology* (Harrisburg, Pa.: Evangelical Publishing House, 1938), p. 320.

[41]R. H. Fisher, *Religious Experience*. Baird Lecture (London: Hodder & Stoughton, 1924), pp. 191f.

Delete from New Testament ethics the great facts of the incarnation and of the atonement and one is left with a wholly inadequate view of Jesus. It is these great facts that supply the well-springs of Christian action in the biblical appeal that Christ be enthroned as Lord of life.

The crucifixion has awakened unprecedented moral stirrings and efforts. It has lifted redeemed human nature to self-sacrifices higher and purer than any which the pages of history elsewhere record. In a deteriorating society it loosed an immeasurable gusher of refining and elevating influence, and raised up a succession of men and women of the loftiest zeal for the welfare of others. The Cross has brought a new center to civilization by which civilization itself is now measured. It has inspired literature and the arts, so that in their best expressions they have become a vehicle of the eternal. It has inspired benevolence and compassion, so that the impotence and need of men has called forth neighbor-love. It has infused ordinary believers with a sense of missionary duty, sending them to the pathless wilds of distant lands. "It has been believed in by millions as the propitiation for the sins of the world," D. W. Simon writes, "and as such has stimulated thought, awakened hope and love, strengthened volition, and restored life to an extent unparalleled within the known existence of humanity."[42]

Not without good reason does Henry Oxenham close his treatise on the atonement with an excursus "On Certain Ethical Contrasts of Christian and Heathen Civilization," in which he traces the moral gulf between the world of Aristophanes or Juvenal and that of post-Christian Europe in the centuries of faith to the influence of the Cross. "The foolishness of that preaching of the Cross overcame the world; it subdued the pride of philosophy, and tamed the fire of lust," he writes.[43] It is true that in the best moral yearnings of the pagan world we find confirmation of the fact that God has nowhere left himself without a witness, and it is equally true that even within so-called Christian cultures the Sermon on the Mount has gained only an approximate realization; yet wherever the atonement has long been proclaimed "the cruelty of the old civilizations" has given way to "the tenderness of feeling, the scrupulous thoughtfulness for others, which has always been more or less a characteristic of Christian society."[44] The disappearance of human sacrifice, the public provision for suffering and sickness, care for the poor and neglected, the rise of a new era of sympathy and consideration which we take for granted today under the notion of Christian humanitarianism, the wave of conviction that led slowly but surely to the abolition of slavery, all these reflect a changed temper of

[42]D. W. Simon, *The Redemption of Man. Discussions Bearing on the Atonement* (Edinburgh: T. & T. Clark, 1889), pp. 393f.

[43]Henry N. Oxenham, *The Catholic Doctrine of the Atonement: An Historical Review* (3d ed., London: W. H. Allen, 1881), p. 311.

[44]*Ibid.*, p. 391.

society which, as Oxenham reminds us, is related to the fact of Calvary by "a sequence of causation, as well as of chronology."[45]

"It is the attraction of the Cross that has wrought through all ages of the Church, alike in the conversion of sinners and unbelievers, and in moulding the choicest specimens of heroic sanctity; beneath the shadow of the Cross the afflicted, the bereaved, the brokenhearted, the world-wearied and heavy-laden have found their rest. Out of the Passion has come the sanctification of our sorrows, and the deepening of our joys, the realization of the divine antithesis exhibited in the Beatitudes, 'as sorrowful yet always rejoicing.' . . . The Cross is the sustaining power both of the active and contemplative devotion alike of individuals and communities."[46]

The atonement teaches the spirit of genuine self-sacrifice. "All genuine nobility of character springs from self-oblivion, and self-oblivion is the spirit of sacrifice. The toil of the mission, the zeal of the apostle, the varied ministries of bodily or spiritual consolation, the meekness of endurance, the heroism of action, the patience of confessorship, the courage of martyrdom — all these are fruits and tokens of the Cross. It is the source of their energy, and the rule of their fulfillment."[47]

No less an appraiser than the distinguished church historian F. J. Foakes-Jackson is authority for the verdict that not only the life of personal virtue, but also the impetus for social reforms touching slavery, women's rights, working conditions, and the plight of the suffering and needy, are all to be traced to the confidence in the atonement so conspicuously championed by evangelical Christianity. "No branch indeed of the Western Church can be refused the honor of having assisted in the progress of human ideas, and non-Christians have participated largely in the work of diffusing the modern spirit of kindness," he acknowledges. "But the credit of the inception of the movement [of social reform] belongs without doubt to that form of Protestantism which is distinguished by the importance it attaches to the doctrine of the Atonement. . . . History shows that the thought of Christ on the Cross has been more potent than anything else in arousing a compassion for suffering and indignation at injustice. . . . The later Evangelicalism, which saw in the death of Christ the means of free salvation for fallen humanity, caused its adherents to take the front rank as champions of the weak. . . . Prison reform, the prohibition of the slave trade, the abolition of slavery, the Factory Acts, the protection of children, the crusade against cruelty to animals, are all the outcome of the great Evangelical revival of the eighteenth century."[48]

[45]*Ibid.*, p. 393.
[46]*Ibid.*, p. 322.
[47]*Ibid.*, p. 327.
[48]F. J. Foakes-Jackson, "Christ in the Church: The Testimony of History" in H. B. Swete, *Cambridge Theological Essays* (New York: Macmillan, 1905), pp. 512ff.

The Christian movement therefore has good reason to beware of all pleas for morality which start out with the rejection of penal and substitutionary conceptions. Though it be a thousand times interdicted by speculative moralists who misrepresent it as morbid and mechanical, the atonement alone meets the requirements of biblical theology and alone evokes adequate sentiments of respect for the Divine and of self-surrender. The direction of the good life is determined and fashioned by the expiatory Cross as its center and quickening power. The contrary notion, that God forgives and redeems without the atonement, soon leads to moral speculations, in which forgiveness and redemption are no longer relevant to ethics, and in which the ethical life is but a phantom of the Divine ideal.

The moral perfection of Jesus sustains an ambivalent relationship to men. On the one hand, hope for an atonement for sin is possible because of his perfection. He is constantly the example of true piety to the Christian community. His perfection also fulfills the periodic craving for a moral ideal in the heart of the unregenerate man. We all share a propensity to imitate others, and the importance of a right example, of a perfect model, is never far out of conscience. At the same time, the realization that moral perfection has actually been achieved in the flesh strikes conviction into the sensitive life. There is ironic truth in Mark Twain's barb that "few things are harder to put up with than the annoyance of a good example." The sense of appalling inferiority which overtakes us in the presence of moral perfection is often forgotten in the superficial quotation of "Lives of great men all remind us we may make our lives sublime." The sight of the ideal not only may discourage, but accuse and condemn. So an awareness of the sinlessness of Jesus, as the New Testament itself so clearly shows, does not by itself inspire men around him to strive for moral heights. That is why the proclamation of Christ's superlative example does not provide adequate incentive to follow in the ethically-sensitive steps of the Son of Man. Small wonder that Guthrie once exclaimed: "To rise to His example, to attain to His holy and blameless life, ah! that seems as impossible as to climb the ethereal heights where that bright orb is shining, as it shone on Eden, and shall shine when the judgment of this world is come. We say, Who is sufficient for these things?" It is awareness of his atonement for sinners that enables his followers to draw near to him as "holy, harmless, undefiled, and separate from sinners." "Every scheme that looks for Christian faithfulness from a bare imitation of the Master is wrecked on this — that the sight of holiness appals as much as it attracts; and unless we know that He has suffered for us to win an atonement with God, it is useless to point to His example that we should follow in His steps."[49] Whoever acknowledges only the sinlessness of Christ, and not his work as Redeemer, strips Christianity of its good news, and reduces the incarnation to sheer condemnation of human nature. Where the

[49]R. H. Fisher, *op. cit.*, p. 193.

ethical quality of Jesus' life is held in view simply so it may be imitated, it is inevitably reduced by accommodation. It remains true, however, that when the significance of Christ's atonement for sins has been properly held, his moral example has remained the proper aspiration of those who trust him. But only the experience of redemption can "produce that moral crisis in the soul which is the death of sin and the life of righteousness."[50]

Of far-reaching experiential importance in the doctrine of substitutionary atonement, over and above its theological significance, is its significance for the believer's filial relation to God. The believer thereby knows that his acceptance with God is not conditioned upon his own moral successes or failures, but that he has been incorporated into the family of God on the basis of Christ's sacrifice. He is related to God as to a Father, and his existence is that of a son, embracing a filial spirit inspired by trust and love (Gal. 4:6f.). Access to God in the Old Testament is more an aspiration and longing; in the New Testament it becomes a reality because forgiveness is now possible, because the promised atonement has actually taken place. The writer of Hebrews notes that the Old Testament sacrifices were powerless to cleanse the believer's guilty conscience; this was done by Christ's atonement. "The starting point for *Hebrews* is the axiom 'that man cannot worship God with a (guilty) conscience.' . . . As the Old Ritual 'cannot, as touching the conscience, make the worshipper perfect,' 'the way into the holy place hath not yet been made manifest,' and there is no open access to God in worship. The coming of Christ, however, puts an end to this dilemma. . . . In principle it is now possible for man 'to serve the living God' entering, with serene confidence, into *the holy place*. . . . The Christian life moves steadily away from the pain of conscience."[51] Without the consciousness of the atonement, the spiritual man lapses quickly into the unfilial spirit. Where the guilt-complex remains, it paralyzes moral effort — modern psychoanalysis is right in this insight. The atonement supplies the only recreative bridge over the dark chasm of guilt, and holds the key to psychological and ethical renewal. The need of it continues throughout the life of moral effort on this earth, and it provides a guarantee against moral catastrophe in an unknown tomorrow. If the ethical life is to have a controlling motive, means, and goal it must be rooted in confidence in the atonement. The atonement makes possible imputation of man's sins to Christ and of Christ's righteousness to sinners, so that man is deemed righteous in God's sight. The Christian life is one of assured forgiveness of sins, and presupposes the removal both of the sense of guilt and of guilt itself. The believer is taken up into the positive fellowship of eternal life with Christ in the consciousness of an intimate sonship.

[50]Henry Yooll, *The Ethics of Evangelicalism*. Hartley Lecture (London: C. H. Kelly, 1906), p. 114.

[51]C. A. Pierce, *Conscience in the New Testament* (Chicago: Alec R. Allenson, 1955), pp. 100f. The references cited are from Heb. 9:8ff. and 10:19.

As an example of the moral influence of an objective atonement, note the appeal Paul makes for purity in 1 Corinthians 6:13ff. He does not say, "If you commit fornication you are accursed." Indeed he does say many times that fornicators and murderers will never enter the kingdom of God. However, passages relating to this (*e.g.,* 1 Cor. 6:9, 10) refer to unbelievers, not believers. These passages simply do not say that a believing man is accursed if he falls into sin. Such a statement would be false. Paul does not appeal, therefore, to the principle of condemnation when exhorting the believer, for it just does not apply. Rather, he says, "Do you not know that you were bought with a price?" (1 Cor. 6:19f.). It is granted that fornication is utterly opposed to God's holy will. But the highest reason to abstain from such an abominable act is not fear of condemnation. It is love for Christ.

The Cross stands therefore at the religious and moral center of history. The whole of human decision and life and destiny is tied to Christ and his atonement. To lead man before that judgment-seat of sin, and in so doing to the grace of God in Christ, is the supreme task of the ethical quest. For the Cross demonstrates that the crucial fact about the history of man is not simply the ethical quest; it is the moral problem finding a religious solution in the atonement. There it is made clear that victory over evil cost the incarnate God his life. The righteousness of God is maintained with mercy and forgiveness for the sinner only by the self-emptying of one of the three persons of the Godhead. The blood that flowed from Calvary was, as the great Apostle of redemption reminds us, "the blood of God" (Acts 20:28). Nowhere in the history of the race has the moral quest found a truer center, nor a more vigorous motivation for holy living than in the atonement.

16

CHRISTIAN ETHICS AS THE MORALITY OF THE REGENERATE MAN

EVERY SCHEME OF ETHICS has a latent anthropology. Naturalism reduces the moral agent to an interesting variety of the animal species, Idealism to a creaturely embodiment of Divinity. Both types of secular ethics do not deal adequately with a fact of human experience that is a fundamental premise of revealed ethics: man is a sinner bearing a fallen nature. He really does not take the moral quest with all seriousness unless his nature is regenerated. Even where human nature is unregenerate, man's responsibility and guilt are ineradicable, but only where man is "born again" does the life of moral virtue move toward God-likeness.

Christian ethics demands the crucifixion of the old nature and the birth of a new. By this insistence it sets itself against the whole tide of speculative ethics, which seeks salvation through the gradual perfection of the old nature. The Christian exposition of the moral life starts from a new character, a divinely given existence that man possesses "in Christ." As William Childs Robinson has remarked pointedly, the world's "way of salvation" is the fiction of justification by sanctification, whereas biblical ethics unveils the great reality of sanctification by justification.

"There is one fundamental difference between the pagan and Christian theories," writes Gordon H. Clark, "which makes all other differences appear subsidiary. According to Greek philosophy, the chief end of man was the perfect development of his natural abilities. Aristotle made contemplation the height of man's attainments because he regarded reason as man's highest function. The Stoics . . . said, 'nature herself never gives us any but good inclinations.' Epictetus says, 'You are a distinct portion of the essence of God and contain a certain part of him in yourself,' cultivate therefore the god within you. And the other schools say similar things. But Christianity has not merely a totally different aim but a radically opposed one. In the New Testament instead of the development of the natural abilities the desirable thing is found to be the death of the natural man and the birth of a new and supernatural man."[1]

[1] G. H. Clark and T. V. Smith, *Readings in Ethics,* pp. 114f.

A distinctive emphasis of biblical ethics therefore is that it roots the moral life in the putting to death of the soul's natural bias for sin. As Calvin notes, the pagan moralists, when exhorting others to "the sublimest virtue, . . . advance no argument but that we ought to live agreeably to nature"; that is, "in the recommendation of virtue," they "never rise above the natural dignity of man." The Scriptures, to the contrary, teach that "we are degenerated from the original state in which we were created," and seek our conformity instead to a pattern that is unveiled in human nature by Jesus Christ who becomes the supernatural Head of the body of the faithful.[2] "Of this transformation, which Paul styles a renovation of the mind, though it is the first entrance into life, all the philosophers were ignorant. For they set up Reason as the sole directress of man; they think that she is exclusively to be attended to; in short, to her alone they assign the government of conduct. But the Christian philosophy commands her to give place and submit to the Holy Spirit; so that now the man himself lives not, but carries about Christ living and reigning within him."[3]

No representation of Christian ethics is true to its name that does not teach that the old man must be put off, for it is corrupt, and that Christ must be put on (Eph. 4:20ff.). Unless Christ possesses the soul, transforming and pervading the whole of life and penetrating the inmost desires and affections, there is no new nature. It is Christian ethics alone which centers the moral controversy in the emphasis that human nature is radically altered from its original state through corruption, and that it is capable of an equally radical transformation through redemption. The firm belief that a new creation of human nature is necessary and possible is peculiar to revealed ethics. Its corollary is that fallen man has involved human nature in an abnormal predicament. Regeneration alone returns man to a position of ethical normality. The necessity for the new birth stems from the corruption of human nature through man's implication in Adam's original sin and the consequent alienation of his life from God (Ps. 51:5, Rom. 5:12ff., 8:7f.). This corrupting rot of sin has penetrated the whole, conditioning all his faculties (Eph. 2:3). Only such a drastic rescue from spiritual death and quickening to eternal life as the new birth affords will suffice. And no lesser dynamic than the Holy Spirit can avail to bring it to pass (Jn. 3:3, 5). Whoever does not grasp the radicalness of this contrast is foredoomed to misunderstand also the way in which Christian ethics transcends the conflict between egoism and altruism, as well as what revealed morality means by self-denial and self-sacrifice.

The "new man" is a central motif in Pauline ethics. It is the characteristic phrase for the regenerate man of Christian experience, the

[2]Calvin, *Institutes,* III, vi, iii.
[3]*Ibid.,* III, vii, i.

individual born from above by the Spirit of God.[4] The only relevant non-Pauline passages are in 1 Peter 1:3, 23; the other pertinent references are in Paul's epistles (2 Cor. 5:17, Gal. 6:15, Eph. 2:10, 4:24, Col. 3:10, Tit. 3:5). The Greek language of Hellenistic times contained two different words for the adjective "new": *kainos,* or new in respect of quality, unmarred by service or age (Mt. 27:59f.), and *neos,* or new in respect of time, recently come into existence (hence "young" in Lk. 15:11f., 1 Tim. 5:1f.). Both words occasionally are applied to the same noun, as when Christ is designated as the Mediator of a "new covenant" — *kainos,* novel, in Hebrews 9:15, and *neos,* or recent, in Hebrews 12:24.

The "new man" is both *kainos* and *neos*; each epithet gives predominance to a different notion.[5]

That the believer is a *neo-anthropos* registers several truths. Paul writes to believers as "having clothed yourselves with the *new* (man), who is ever being *renewed* unto discernment after the image of the One who created him" (Col. 3:9f.). The regenerate man is newly or freshly created; he does not find his essential principle in the old nature; but like the primal man, he is fashioned by the Spirit after the unsullied Divine image. Jones remarks, "The new man is a creation of God, and is renewed according to that ideal of man which was originally in the mind of the Creator."[6] Moreover, the new man is "in process." Lightfoot concurs, "the new birth was a recreation in God's image; the subsequent life must be a deepening of this image thus stamped upon the man."[7]

This growth-aspect of the new life we shall consider subsequently, for the new man does not long remain a "babe in Christ." The aim of regeneration is that he shall be a *kaino-anthropos,* a man whose moral nature is renovated and built over.[8] "Put off the old man . . . and be

[4]There is a striking absence of discussion of the subject of the new man in recent books on Christian ethics. Even Ramsey, in *Basic Christian Ethics,* makes no obvious reference to the new man, or the texts relating thereto, even in the longest chapter entitled "This Human Nature."

[5]R. C. Trench, *Synonyms of the New Testament* (Grand Rapids: Eerdmans, reprint), p. 220.

[6]J. Ithel Jones, in *The New Bible Commentary,* p. 1049.

[7]J. B. Lightfoot, *St. Paul's Epistle to the Colossians and to Philemon* (London: Macmillan, 1897), p. 214.

[8]Trench remarks: "Take . . . the *neos anthropos* of Col. iii.10; and the *kainos anthropos* of Ephes. ii.15. Contemplate under aspects of time that mighty transformation which has found and is still finding place in the man who has become obedient to the truth, and you will call him subsequently to this change, *neos anthropos.* The old man in him, and it well deserves this name, for it dates as far back as Adam, has died; a new man has been born, who therefore is fitly so called. But contemplate again . . . the same mighty transformation; behold the man who, through long commerce with the world, inveterate habits of sinning, as the snake its shrivelled skin, coming forth 'a new creature' (*kaine ktisis*), from his heavenly Maker's hands, with a *pneuma kainon* given to him (Ezek. xi.19), and you have here the *kainos anthropos,* one prepared to walk 'in newness of life' (*en kainoteti zoes,* Rom. vi.4) through the *anakainosis* of the Spirit (Tit. iii.5)" (*op. cit.,* pp. 223ff.).

clothed with the new man (*kainon anthropon*), created like God in righteousness and holiness of the truth" (Eph. 4:22ff.). The apostle emphasizes the qualitative newness of the regenerate man much more than its temporal aspect. The qualitative aspect endures throughout the transition from infancy to maturity in the new life. The *kainos*-concept is expanded, by the conjunction of the word with other nouns, to stress the new quality of life (Rom. 6:4, 12:2, Tit. 3:5, 2 Cor. 5:17, Gal. 6:15) especially in its ethical bearings. Charles Hodge remarks that "The idea of purity is associated with that of newness . . . a new heart, a new creature, a new man. Newness of life is a life that is new, compared with what is natural and original; and it is a holy life, springing from a new source."[9]

The two references in Peter's first epistle (1:3, 23) provide a fitting capstone for the discussion of Paul's doctrine of the new man. The one refers to the temporal aspect of the new birth, corresponding to Paul's *neos anthropos*; the other to its qualitative aspect, or to Paul's *kainos anthropos*. Who, then, is the new man? In R. A. Webb's words, he is "not a theological transubstantiation: a being whose substance has been supernaturally converted into some other sort of substance. . . . He is not a scientific transmutation: a species of one kind which has been naturally evolved into a species of another kind. . . . He is not a metaphysical reconstruction: a being with a new mental equipment. . . . He is an evangelical convert: an 'old man' with a new regnant moral disposition, an 'outward man' with a new inward *fons et origo* of moral life; a 'natural man' with a new renovated spiritual heart."[10] Or as John Gill puts it: he is "altogether a new work; it is called a creature, being a work of almighty power; and a new creature, and a new man, consisting of various parts, and these all new: there are in it a new heart, and a new spirit, a new understanding. . . ."[11]

Secular moralists in the post-Christian era have found ways and means of striking back at the Christian demand for regeneration. Their caricature of the new birth has found an echo even within professing Christian circles through the invasion of idealistic and humanistic schemes of morality. The fact that the Spirit of God is everywhere active in human life has been made to support the fiction that every concern for moral endeavor presupposes the new birth. Shailer Mathews stated the argument in characteristic extreme: "To doubt that God is working in extra-ecclesiastical efforts at social betterment is to come dangerously near the sin against the Holy Spirit. . . . God brings in His Kingdom by any man who is working in the spirit of Jesus

[9]Charles Hodge, *Commentary on the Epistle to the Romans* (Grand Rapids: Eerdmans, reprint, 1953), p. 195.
[10]R. A. Webb, "Man, New," in *International Standard Bible Encyclopedia* (Grand Rapids: Eerdmans, reprint), III, 1975.
[11]John Gill, *Body of Divinity* (Atlanta: Turner Lassetter, reprint, 1950), pp. 529f.

Christ."[12] Humanistic writers were not always as blunt as Harry Elmer Barnes. He frequently stated with explicit candor what was latent in their position, the complaint that to require man's rebirth was tantamount to disrespect for human personality. Barnes wrote that "One can discover in the teachings assigned to Jesus passages which are destructive of any dynamic conception of personality and would lead to self-effacement if not to self-destruction."[13] All humanists repudiated the contention that personal ethical integration is "most effectively achieved through attachment to Jesus and participation in the historical movement which he initiated."[14] The humanist, while far from accepting any thought of depravity of the human race, recognizes that something is wrong that needs to be set aright. That the world is not a "bed of roses" is, for the most part, man's own fault. But God is unnecessary for man's redirection. Reese optimistically asserts "man can reshape himself."[15] Randall concedes that selfishness is the cause of the trouble in the world. "No one who reflects can doubt that selfishness is the root-cause of practically every sin and misery and ugliness in human life, and that if only selfishness could be utterly and completely destroyed as Jesus hoped to destroy it, the Kingdom of Heaven would indeed come on earth, as he declared it would come some day."[16] While Randall endorses Jesus' indictment of selfishness, his own view of selfishness conspicuously reduces Jesus' view, both in regard to the malady and to its cure. Randall paraphrases Jesus' teaching: "If any man would find his Self that is one with God and with all men, he must absolutely lose, that is destroy, eradicate, die to, wipe out of consciousness, his superficial, unreal and selfish self. And he who thus dies to this separate, private and selfish self (in his own consciousness), has indeed found or awakened to (in his consciousness), his real and permanent and divine Self."[17] Any thought of the corruption of human nature or the necessity of supernatural rebirth is cavalierly dismissed, yet Randall appeals to Jesus for corroboration. The only change of human nature that modern secular ethics tolerated was based on evolutionary assumptions. While it made the stupendous claim that man had emerged from non-mental and non-moral life through a wholly animal ancestry, and while it looked for an earthly millennium that would be achieved by man's unaided ingenuity, it nonetheless shared with the whole movement of speculative ethics a controlling idea that biblical ethics repudiates. That idea is that man in his present state represents an essential con-

[12]Shailer Mathews, *The Gospel and the Modern Man,* p. 321.
[13]Harry Elmer Barnes, *The Twilight of Christianity,* p. 410.
[14]Edwin A. Burtt, *Types of Religious Philosophy,* p. 356.
[15]Curtis W. Reese, *Humanism* (Chicago: Open Court, 1926), p. 48.
[16]John Herman Randall, *The Spirit of the New Philosophy* (New York: Brentano's, 1919), p. 196.
[17]*Ibid.,* p. 203.

tinuity with the Divine.[18] Hence he is not exposed to the wrath of God nor in need of supernatural regeneration as the condition for a positive relationship to the moral world.[19] Greek philosophy as well as Hebrew revelation based true moral living on a good nature. Plato's *Republic* made clear that true righteousness requires an inner bent of soul. But it was thought to be within man's reach by a reordering of the immanent claims of the soul. William James could speak of a "higher part . . . co-terminous with a More of the same quality" but not Christianity. Heredity and environment are key words of philosophic reform and they are important ethical categories, but they do not go deeply enough into the human problem. The more powerful factor is Christ. Rebirth can overcome them. Nor are they ever so favorable as to annul the necessity for that supernatural transformation. The regenerate man does not simply regard the higher part of himself as the ideally spiritual. He is, in his total being, born from above. That man's ethical condition is one of imperfect development and that human nature requires revision and elevation — this much is widely admitted. What secular ethics denies is that man is a fallen and doomed sinner, that human nature in this condition is alienated from God and the good, and that the new birth alone reinstates him harmoniously to the will of God. The attempt to solve the moral problem while ignoring the light of redemptive revelation is bypassing human wisdom for sheer foolishness.[20]

At the same time, it should be emphasized that regeneration does not mean that man acquires a super-human or quasi-Divine nature. Not only is the line between man and the supernatural firmly fixed on the basis of creation (the Christian church has expressed this by the doctrine of the *two* natures in the incarnation), but so is the essential continuity of human nature. Christian ethics avoids the myth of man's animal past and of his future deity. And because it does so, it maintains the tense

[18]The theology of crisis marks a half-hearted compromise with this position insofar as it regards human nature on the basis of creation as inevitably sinful. Such an anthropology, which implies that man lacked the image of God by creation, accords poorly with a theology of Divine wrath. It need not surprise anyone, therefore, that the "wrath" of God, by this school, is characteristically enclosed by the love of God, and loses its biblical force.

[19]Note L. H. Marshall's erroneous verdict: "Jesus did not conceive of man as by nature separated from God — this idea was Greek in origin and reappears in Barthianism today." *The Challenge of New Testament Ethics,* p. 20. Marshall's acknowledgment that Jesus "always attacks the disease not its symptoms" (*ibid.,* p. 68) should have led him in the direction of such statements as "if ye then, being evil" (Mt. 7:11) and "a corrupt tree bringeth forth evil fruit" (7:17).

[20]"Self-wisdom is the negation of all higher wisdom, for the reception of which, however, the spirit of man itself is organized: it is the negation of God, as of Him who alone is wise (Rom. xvi.27, Jude 25); the negation of the wisdom which comes from above (Jas. iii.15); the negation of conscience which wishes to exalt the consciousness of man above the limits of the Ego, and which convicts the Ego, while persevering in its egotism by the antagonism of its thoughts, of folly. With this self-wisdom the heart becomes foolish (Rom. 1:21); with it commences the darkening of the consciousness with respect to conscience, which, by various stages and degrees, finally leads to that hardening of the heart which the Apostle Paul describes as the prevailing condition of nations (Eph. iv. 17-19)." G. C. Adolph von Harless, *System of Christian Ethics,* p. 91.

predicament of man as a sinner. The regenerate soul is not new-created, lacking all point of connection with man as he was first created, or even as he is fallen. The whole man is renewed, but the soul which is then brought into God's service has as much a connection with the fallen self as does the body (Rom. 6:13, 12:1). The new does not stand in *essential* contradiction to the old. It is the ideal expression of what the old was originally meant to be. This the Holy Spirit alone accomplishes. "What is new forms no contradiction to the old nature 'omnis natura in quantum natura est, bona est,' says Augustine (*Enchirid.* ch. xiii.), but, if one may so speak, to the nature which has become hostile to nature. Were it not so, the apostle could neither reject that which is opposed to God as opposed to nature (Rom. i.26), nor could he assert that nature teaches us what is due to God and what is becoming (1 Cor. xi.14), or that men do by nature the things contained in the law (Rom. ii. 14)"[21] Regeneration imparts to man a new character, in which God stands at the center of his motives, decisions, and acts. It does not give him a new metaphysical substance. Man did not cease to be man in the fall, nor does he become a superman through redemption. He becomes partaker of the Divine nature (2 Pet. 1:4), not by an infusion of the essence of God constituting him a *tertium quid,* but by living a spiritual and moral life in organic union with Christ.

The new birth is that life imparted by the Holy Spirit to man on the condition of repentance and faith in the propitiatory atonement of Christ, whereby the whole man — volitional, intellectual and emotional — is rescued from the dominance of sin and restored to the spiritual and moral lordship of the Living God. The new birth is not an achievement of human effort, but the work of God in the lives of those who believe on the Saviour (Jn. 1:12f.). In these terms, the biblical conception marks a sharp contrast with the loose notions of "conversion" that prevail both in liberal and humanistic circles. Liberal theology denuded the concept of any reference (1) to a transcendent supernatural agency, (2) to the Holy Spirit as a distinct person of the Godhead, and (3) to the substitutionary atonement of Christ as its presupposition. The "new birth" or ethical change that Liberalism championed was an integration of personality and ethical dynamic that could be achieved by wholehearted surrender to Jesus Christ as supreme moral example. The acceptance of Jesus as the ethical ideal, especially in his example of love, gave the moral life a direction and finality that resolved the inner tensions and discords that come from the competitive instincts and inclinations of the human personality.

Humanism was perturbed over this account of conversion because it was too absolutistic and finalistic; biblical theologians were distressed because of its bias against the supernatural, against the deity of Christ and his atonement, and against the unique person and work of the Spirit. Humanistic moralists pointed out that although Liberalism

[21]G. C. A. von Harless, *op. cit.*, p. 8.

professed to adopt the modern scientific method as the sole reliable criterion of knowledge (and on that account had discarded the miraculous), it still attached a finality to Jesus Christ that was intolerable for a methodology yielding only tentative results subject to constant revision and requiring validation in present experience. The humanist proposed instead to define the moral ideal, or "God," in view of moral effects in the life of man. Man's moral predicament is the inner disharmony and conflict of interests; whatever best integrates the personality and delivers it from this tense and frustrated condition — whether it be the example of Buddha or Jesus, or devotion to some ethical ideal such as pacifism, or to some noble cause such as the Red Cross or to social service in general — is "God," and hence worthy of unreserved devotion and moral dedication. Note that there would then be as many gods as there were workable solutions for individuals. In these speculative reductions there remained little connection with the biblical view of regeneration other than the employment of the same terms and words. Because they already held a hallowed meaning, they carried overtones which strategically concealed from the uninitiated the apostasy from Christian ethics which was under way even by those who professed devotion to its concepts.

The futility of the attempt to adjust the claims of the natural self, individually and collectively, is attested by the cleavage between egoism and altruism which secular ethics has been impotent to transcend. The competition between self-assertion and self-repression, between self-affirmation and self-negation, and the ingenious but unsatisfactory proposals for limiting and compromising both the self-regarding and the benevolent tendencies of man, stand as central but unresolved problems of the history of secular ethics.

What has been said of self-denial, within this secular framework, is, predicated on a fallacious anthropology and ethics alike. Johnston is formally right: "Self-denial cannot be the ultimate moral ideal. For self-denial as the absolute moral end would involve the abnegation of the *whole* self; and that is impossible."[22] But the profounder fact is that neither self-denial nor altruism, cultured upon unregenerate human nature, can yield a stable adjustment. "The world will never be transformed by calling forth or organising new forms of selfishness to redress the balance of the old."[23] Reese shares the vulnerable humanistic bias, proposing to displace the supernatural by the concept of the sacredness of society. "The humanizing of human nature consists in the gradual organization of instincts or impulses or original tendencies in harmony with the growing conception of individual and social worth, i.e., in harmony with community of interests. . . . As the human race progresses its conception of individual worth grows apace. . . . Society,

[22]G. A. Johnston, *An Introduction to Ethics* (London: Macmillan, 1915), p. 193.
[23]J. Scott Lidgett, *The Spiritual Principle of the Atonement.* Fernley Lecture (Cincinnati: Jennings & Graham, n.d.), p. 416.

too, becomes a sacred thing. . . . So we must organize our fear, our hunger, our pugnacity, and our love around the will to responsible living, i.e., the will to self-hood in harmony with the self-hood of our fellowmen and the interdependence of all."[24] Dewey's assurances anticipate the egoistic-altruistic clash: "Interest in the social whole of which one is a member necessarily carries with it interest in one's own self. . . . To suppose that social interest is incompatible with concern for one's own health, learning, advancement, power of judgment, etc., is literally nonsensical. Since each one of us is a member of social groups and since the latter have no existence apart from the selves who compose them, there can be no effective social interest unless there is at the same time an intelligent regard for our own wellbeing and development."[25] And Potter adds what is really latent in both of the above statements in his discussion of "self-giving." "The person who found himself growing by correct moral choices finds that growth is increased by self-giving to others. . . . His ideal becomes not merely the development of his own individual personality but the growth of all persons. . . . This self-giving is not to be confused with self-sacrifice . . . nothing of an expiating nature. . . . For the giver of self for the benefit of others derives benefit himself in several ways. Not only does he get better drinking water when securing a better water system for the town, but also he will be thought of more highly by his associates."[26] The basic motivation here remains a selfish desire for self. The way to get along in the world and to make it a desirable place to live is to fit one's self into the whole, to become a part of the group, to work for the betterment of the whole, since in doing so you will better your own lot in life. But what is one to do when the betterment of the whole seems in effect to be detrimental to me, the individual? If betterment of the whole is effected basically from a selfish desire for self, would it be logical to maintain that self should yield when the group's betterment apparently threatens that of the individual? History bears out the fact that in real life the individual will not do this. As long as the individual is blessed by benefits from the whole, as long as the ideals and the goals of the whole are his ideals and goals, he is one of them. But the moment his goals, ideals and purposes in life run counter to that of the whole, he will go along with himself and not the whole. Christian ethics is the replacement of egoism by the voluntary acceptance of the rule of God.

The naturalistic emphasis on self-development, the idealistic emphasis on self-realization, spawn an ethic that ignores the fact of the corruption of human nature through sin. In place of this optimism about unregenerate nature, Christian ethics requires self-denial, the crucifixion of the old nature, the identification of the ethical life with the new (not simply the "higher") man.

[24]Reese, *op. cit.*, p. 49
[25]Dewey and Tufts, *Ethics* (New York: Henry Holt, 1908), p. 303.
[26]Charles F. Potter, *Humanism*, p. 27.

The biblical orientation of the ethical problem to the inner life of the spirit gives prime impetus to the study of personality. The doctrines of Trinity, of the Incarnation, and of Christ indwelling the believer, have had an important influence in the development and discussion of the concept of the "person." As Strong notes, "The distinctive feature of Christianity in the ethical regard is . . . the new importance assigned . . . to personality. . . . In the ethical, as well as the metaphysical region, the idea of personality is the gift of Christianity to human thought."[27] The doctrine of the new birth has guarded against idealistic and pantheizing correlations of the human with the Divine Spirit. In modern ethics the loss of interest in the doctrine of the new birth was in part a consequence of the invasion of theological ethics by post-Hegelian notions of man as a part of the Absolute. Such a system of morality could not accommodate the biblical conception of self-denial. It made room only for the contrast of part and whole, of finite and infinite, but not for the contrast of the unregenerate sinner and the holy God who dooms him apart from the new birth.

The Christian teaching on the worth of human personality must be seen through the eyes of the doctrines of creation, redemption, and destiny. Otherwise it is easily misconstrued in the secular sense of the "infinite value" of the individual.[28] Christianity resists the naturalistic and totalitarian depreciation of human personality, but it is equally cautious about pantheistic and idealistic excess.

Man has a value above all the other creatures of the space-time world. This is clear from the circumstances of creation. God fashioned him at the apex of the movement of creation, in his own image, for eternal fellowship with himself. Man's value is nonetheless finite, although lifted above that of other finite creatures because of the Divine image. The worth of man is to be vindicated. The fact that in the incarnation the Logos permanently identified himself with human nature indicates that fallen human nature has value as a candidate for redemption. But the new birth aside, the value of man — in his rational and moral accountability — is vindicated further by the peculiar destiny to which he is consigned as a consequence of impenitence. He will not cease to be; nor will he exist in a state of felicity; but he will live in a state of conscious punishment. Man in hell still has the value of vindicating the righteousness of God, though under wrath. Here again it is plain that it is the "new man" above all who mirrors the highest worth of human personality;[29] while a creature of finite value, nonetheless he becomes

[27]T. B. Strong, *Christian Ethics,* pp. 129ff.

[28]"Christianity . . . teaches that each individual as such has infinite value." Reginald A. P. Rodgers, *A Short History of Ethics,* p. 221.

[29]Christianity has asserted "the supreme value — not of the individual, but of the Christlike person. It has always condemned to final punishment . . . all individuals whose private judgment and life were not in accordance with the Word of God. The *absolute* value of the individual in hell . . . is not an *absolute* value of any worth. It means alienation from the *Kingdom* of God, the Church triumphant." J. Macbride Sterrett, *The Freedom of Authority* (New York: Macmillan, 1905), p. 13.

the object of an infinite love, and moves in the society and fellowship of infinite personality.

The difficulties of the notion of man's "infinite value" are apparent. Rodgers seeks to resolve the tension between personal wellbeing and social duties thus: "If each person is of infinite worth he is entirely justified in pursuing his own good; and, for the same reason, he should sacrifice himself for the good of others, since they likewise are of infinite worth."[30] But can a person of "infinite worth" so easily be placed under absolute obligation to others? Does not the doctrine of human rights and worth depend in the first place upon the infinite worth of God alone, and next upon the fact that man bears his image, and hence man has rights and duties on the basis of creation?

The Christian insistence on the new birth accords with the emphasis that the moral problem must be stated in terms of *being* rather than only of *doing*. The formula "I ought, but I cannot," summarizes the predicament of fallen and unregenerate man. It fixes attention on the inability of the sinner to meet the demands of the moral law because of the corruption of his nature. Secular ethics, because it ignores this insight, continues to ask: What shall I do to be good? But Christian ethics, aware that man's nature and the deeds which spring from it are sinful, asks the more fundamental question: What ought I to be? Indeed, it anticipates the answer, asking: "What must I do to be saved?" (Acts 16:30). The speculative notion that conduct determines character, that the habit of good actions begets virtue (Aristotle), must therefore give way to the biblical disqualification of that possibility for man, and the converse position that character determines conduct. From the good tree alone one is to look for good fruit; the corrupt tree will bear evil fruit, and is doomed to be hewn down and cast into the fire (Mt. 7:17ff., Eph. 2:3).

The new life is also stated in the New Testament as the life of belief in Christ. "I believe" occurs more than ninety times with reference to belief in Christ in the Gospel of John. Belief was not mere mental assent; it involved a way of life. The test of a child of God is not mere descent from Abraham, but belief in his Son, a complete resting of oneself on Christ as the Saviour of the world. The only "work" for the would-be servant of God is to believe on Christ. This one moral act is the basic act from which all actions derive their value. "He who believes is not condemned" (3:18).

Believers are children of God, being "born again" through the moral transformation and renewal of their entire spiritual nature by the Holy Ghost. The phrase denotes the origination of a new or second life in man. It is a life he does not enter by natural birth.[31] Only by redemptive ethics is the moral predicament of fallen man fully dealt with. "If any man be in Christ, he is a new creature . . ." (2 Cor. 5:17).

[30] *Op. cit.*, p. 289.
[31] Alvah Hovey, *Manual of Systematic Theology and Christian Ethics*, p. 243.

The doctrine of crucifixion of the old self is to be paralleled by the doctrine of the realization of the new self. Where the latter emphasis is absent, the Christian life deteriorates into a morbid and repetitious resort to the altar rail in defeat and repentance. Christian ethics proclaims more than the doom of the old nature; it affirms the birth and growth of the new man in Christ. Where the new self is not brought to fullness, the essential dignity of Christian living is obscured, and the tension over the crucifixion of the old nature occupies the forefront of interest which belongs properly to delight in the achievements of the new self.

The goodness attained by the regenerate man is never independent of the grace of God at work in him. Only the new self can see the radical need for self-denial; it is then for the first time fully apparent. "The regenerate man has the centre of his life no more in himself, nor in the world, but in the crucified and risen Christ."[32] Only where supernatural regeneration is experienced is a decisive blow dealt to the old nature. "For ye are dead and your life is hid with Christ in God" (Col. 3:3; cf. Gal. 2:20, 6:14f.). Only as the new man is put on is the old man put off (Eph. 4:22f.). And only one who loves God and his fellow men in this context can govern his life by the evangelical moderation of the self, since it now becomes obvious — as formerly it was not — that the love of God and of neighbor as one's self is the exact equivalent of biblical self-denial. The Scriptures do not merely hint at this position, but they state it plainly in the strongest possible way. To "find" one's life on the basis of the old nature is ultimately to "lose" life; to lose the old life is really to gain life by the new. To exalt the old self means ultimate self-humiliation; to humble the old self leads to a self-exaltation fitting one for a felicitous destiny (Mt. 20:16, 23:12; Mk. 10:31; Lk. 14:11, 18:14, 22:27). One of the great lessons that Jesus taught his disciples was personal humility, a virtue nowhere so impressed on human experience as by the new birth. The disciples were greatly concerned on one occasion about their rank in the Kingdom of heaven (Mt. 18:1ff.). Jesus set a child in their midst and spoke of conversion.

The ethical doctrine of God-love and neighbor-love calls for nothing less than the eradication of the self-love of the natural man, and the birth of a new self who finds his place in the world of existence by devotion to the will of God. Whatever is motivated by the old self-life contributes nothing to the fulfillment of duty, but comes under the judgment of God. No mere self-abasement that actually promotes in principle the survival of the old nature, but a self-crucifixion, is at the heart of the biblical view of the moral life. Such a doctrine is the stumbling block of every idealistic view of human nature which regards man on the spiritual side as, at the deepest level of being, an aspect of God, or where this is avoided, as morally continuous with the will of

[32]H. Martensen, *Christian Ethics*, I, 154.

God. No wonder the doctrine of the new birth is a scandal to speculative morality.

Christian ethics requires the renunciation of the self, the laying aside of the old nature, the birth of a new man, the exhibition of a new character. Even the external discharge of all the obligations of love, were it possible to the natural man, would not include the fulfillment of one's whole moral duty to others, since it would not flow out as a sincere or self-denying principle.

Yet this renunciation of self has nothing in common with Mysticism, and its advocacy of the absorption of the self in the Absolute, so that self-consciousness disappears. Neither the Christian doctrine of creation nor the fall, nor redemption, could tolerate such a view. It is incompatible also with biblical regeneration. The regenerate self is not taken out of the space-time world, nor out of the world of finite selves. Its duties are love to God *and neighbor.* This self has legitimate rights, and may seek its own place alongside all other selves. We are not called to neighbor-love so that our self may be destroyed, but that we may enjoy our highest good. But the self that lives selflessly in the world of persons is not the old self; the second great commandment stands after the first: the self which finds its own place in neighbor-love is the self devoted unreservedly to God. It is no longer inordinately inclined to an exclusive love of self, and disposed to inferior consideration of others. Only this self, however, is free to act out of disinterested love, and can place the good of others above one's own advantage, and to hurry to another's assistance with that same impulse of mercy and humanity as we would to our very own. From the biblical viewpoint, all moral endeavor that proceeds from the old nature, even where it reaches out to others, is tarnished by an excessive and objectionable self-love.

That men are to seek the will of God with their whole being and to love their neighbors as themselves, can only mean that self-denial in this context is a crowning virtue. The repudiation of the doctrine that men need to be born again is a repudiation of the biblical summons to self-denial. And the rejection of the biblical summons to sanctification, to set one's self apart to God, is also an attack on this doctrine.

The temptation that we can best serve God, or neighbor, through the amassing of wealth, or power, or the prestige of some human office, is a dangerous one. He best serves God and man who loves them above all else, and does not make his affection for them a reflex of a deeper love for money, glory, or whatever else. When love for God is second, it is not love for God at all. An idol then stands at the center of life, and all other motivations, love of man included, are endangered.

The will of God as the rule of life means more than a long-range dedication. It can be achieved only in and through a constant reference of one's whole outlook and bent of mind to God, so that those vices which spring from an inordinate self-love will be given no opportunity to thrive in thought or deed. From whence comes pride, greed, luxury, but from an immoderate self-love?

Not that the new man exists only where there is subjective moral perfection, for not one of the regenerate from the Apostle Paul onward has reached that mark in this life. But the believer is committed in principle and in the bent of his life to the will of God. For that reason he is engaged in a life of spiritual progress in which even his failures are turned propaedeutically and therapeutically to good. The real Christian practices virtue voluntarily on the ground that it is God's will. He does not do God's will involuntarily, or only for the sake of something higher to which it leads. "Show me if you can," challenged Calvin, "a single individual, who, unless he has renounced himself according to the command of the Lord, is voluntarily disposed to practice virtue among men. For all who have not been influenced by this disposition have followed virtue merely from the love of praise. And even those of the philosophers who have ever contended that virtue is desirable for its own sake, have been inflated with so much arrogance, that it is evident they have desired virtue for no other reason than to furnish them occasion for the exercise of pride."[33]

But the new man does not become the glorified, sinless man in this life. The era of sanctification, which begins with regeneration, constitutes a perpetual crucifixion of the old nature which is not eradicated once-for-all. The society of the saints is composed of crucified initiates, and Jesus bids each of his disciples daily to "take up his cross" (Mt. 16:24) as a feature of the Christian walk. The shadow of that cross, which speaks of the death of the old man and the birth of the new, hangs continually over the believer's life in this world. The Christian fellowship is the discipline of the cross. It is by the cross that men are taught to live by the will of God instead of by their own inordinate desires.

There is a difference, however, between this cross which men carry through life, and that crucifixion that accompanies the new birth. Believers carry different makes of crosses — adapted to remedy the deficiencies and peculiarities of their own spiritual outlook and needs. The first crucifixion remedies a need common to all mankind — an initial change in the governing disposition and moral relations of man, whereby he is enabled to desire a life conformable to the will of God. The subsequent crucifixions carry this new disposition into the whole scope of life's decisions.

The love of God, or self-denial, is the antidote to ungodliness. Either God is affirmed and the man-in-revolt is denied, or God is denied and hostility to him perpetuated. Consequently, the love of God requires a self-denial that gains its primary definition from the holy Lord who stands over against the preferences of man's mind and will. In yielding himself to ungodliness man denies the claim of God upon him; he must

[33]Calvin, *Institutes,* III, vii, ii.

honor that Divine claim to deny ungodliness. Calvin comprehends in the New Testament term "ungodliness" whatever is repugnant to the serious fear of God. Hence we are driven to the first table of the Law, and a decision for or against it. Are we to be united in holiness to the Living God? Or are we to be separated from him by alien entanglements?

Only by self-denial in relation to men can the law of love to neighbor be fulfilled. The bestowal of honor and preference on others, the promotion of their advancement, the recognition of their superiority, and esteem for their gifts, these can exist sincerely only where the natural tendency to self-honor and self-exaltation, ambition and the desire for pre-eminence are renounced by the Christian. They must be gently forced out of the life by the Holy Spirit. The Spirit will displace the evil with the good, the harsh with the gentle, the self-seeking with the self-denying. Man is no longer to exist as though God were not. Man must submit himself to God who is Creator, Redeemer, Lord. Then he will truly live. But he has lost his life to find life.

Christianity has its own criterion, therefore, to screen candidates for the title of "the higher man." Far above Nietzsche's Superman, and even above Plato's Philosopher-King, it ranks the God-man, and regenerate believers who prize his image. Nietzsche's words, "I am not a man; I am dynamite," find their Christian contrast in the sinner who has experienced the Gospel of Christ as the Divine *dunamis* unto salvation (Rom. 1:16) and the Holy Spirit as the power of sanctification. Human nature restored to its intended intimacy with God is the key to the higher man. Whoever has experienced rebirth knows that among Nietzsche's greatest blunders is his denial that Christianity involves a "yea-saying to life," in contrast with his monster of immorality, *Uebermensch.* Man is but a bridge to superman, for Nietzsche, and the mass of men are doomed to slavery, which he regards as one of the essential conditions of a "high" culture. But the regenerate man of Christian experience is already superman, not a "new species" bred by eugenics and assenting the limitless rights of the individual and the sovereignty of the human ego over all moral ties, but the representative of a higher and superior manhood ennobled by the Spirit of God. John Figgis calls us away from *Thus Spake Zarathustra,* and to the central message of the New Testament, "I am come that they may have life, and may have it abundantly" (Jn. 10:10) as a genuine "yea-saying to life," indeed, as a "yea-saying" to that fullness of life which Nietzsche fled.[34]

[34]John Figgis, *Will to Freedom* (New York: Scribner, 1917), pp. 123ff.

17

JESUS AS THE IDEAL OF CHRISTIAN ETHICS

MUCH OF THE FASCINATION which Jesus Christ has held for scholars comes not simply from his supernatural works, nor from his supernatural teaching, but from his supernatural moral life. The conviction that he is the "personal revelation of the holiness of God"[1] is a prime reason for the great number of *Lives* about him. He was more than the great Teacher of ethics. He was its great Liver.

Nowhere else does human history show the moral glory of the Divine in human life. Nowhere else has the world found such inspiration for moral earnestness. Christ stands behind what D. M. Ross has called "the singular moral heat" of the early Christians.[2] "From Thomas a Kempis' *The Imitation of Christ* to Charles M. Sheldon's *In His Steps*," Hillyer Straton remarks, "Christian ethics has been centered in Jesus."[3] And the sweep of his moral influence does not stop with Christian writing. "The track of His footsteps is seen," Pressensé writes, "wherever there has been any real progress in good, in love, in right, in the moral elevation of men."[4] L. H. Marshall affirms that "beyond Jesus of Nazareth . . . the moral stature of humanity can never go" and that Jesus is "the last word on all the great issues of right and wrong."[5]

We are told that "his biography may be summed up in the words, 'he went about doing good' ";[6] that he lived "the only perfectly Unselfish Life ever seen on earth";[7] that the "grand outstanding characteristic of Christ's work" was his "absolute submission to the will of God";[8] that the uniqueness of Christianity consists in "his utter realization of

[1]H. Martensen, *Christian Ethics*, I, 143.

[2]D. M. Ross, *The Christ of Faith and the Jesus of History* (London: James Clarke, n.d.), p. 79.

[3]Hillyer H. Straton, *Thinking Where Jesus Thought* (St. Louis: Bethany Press, 1945), p. 59.

[4]E. De Pressensé, *Jesus Christ: His Times, Life and Work* (London: Hodder & Stoughton, 1879), p. 506.

[5]L. H. Marshall, *The Challenge of New Testament Ethics*, p. 214.

[6]Seeley, *Ecce Homo*, p. 177. "The story of his life will always remain the one record in which the moral perfection of man stands revealed in its root and its unity, the hidden spring made palpably manifest by which the whole machine is moved. . . . All lesser examples and lives will forever hold a subordinate place, and serve chiefly to reflect light on the central and original Example" (*ibid.*, p. 302).

[7]Cunningham Geikie, *The Life and Words of Christ* (New York: D. Appleton, 1880), p. 6.

[8]Alfred Edersheim, *The Life and Times of Jesus the Messiah*, I, 298.

the immanence of God in this present life";[9] that he is "the moral law incarnate. . . . The law of the 'Good' is in His person a reality."[10]

The magnificent feature of Jesus Christ is that he not only proclaimed a superlative ethic, but he lived it out to the full. In common with the earlier Hebrew prophets he held a morally majestic view of God. He supplemented this view in his own teaching. Granting the holiness of their living, the life of Jesus stands apart from them and from the whole of humanity as a brilliant lightning flash in the dark night. His pure walk is the wonder of our world of mixed motives and deeds. Alongside him, even the best of men must confess unholiness. Schleiermacher agrees that the "entire history of humanity" supplies no analogy for this one whose "whole conduct . . . deeds . . . addresses, have a supernatural character. He must be a divine ambassador." Here the moral life is unveiled with no discordant note, with nothing that is less than ethically superlative.

Whatever may be said about him, whether as a teacher or as a redeemer, his sinlessness is unique in the stream of human life. Nowhere does history show a fountain of righteousness like the ethical pureness which ever lives in him. He presented the ideal of the Kingdom not merely in word but in deed and fact. He is the word of truth and of goodness become flesh. What he taught he uncompromisingly exemplified. "The whole of the active work of Jesus," Wendt writes, "was an exposition of His teaching through His own example."[11] In him the Kingdom itself appeared on earth, in that "the perfect human life, the moral ideal for man, was perfectly realized."[12] "No miracle of Christ equals the miracle of His sinless life," remarks H. R. Mackintosh, in a chapter devoted to the features which set apart "the one quite unspotted life that has been lived within our sinful race" as "solitary and incomparable."[13] Jesus Christ, even if more remains to be said, is the faultless exemplar of virtue, "a self-determining will, perfectly bent on perfect ends,"[14] the lone exhibition of ethical excellence to be found in the history of the fallen race.

Christ's moral perfection has given to Christian ethics one of its choicest weapons against speculative ethics. It sets Jesus not only against the champions of moral Naturalism, from Epicurus to Dewey

[9]William Wallace, *Lectures and Essays on Natural Theology and Ethics.* Gifford Lectures (Oxford: Clarendon Press, 1898), p. 43.

[10]Theodor von Haering, *The Ethics of the Christian Life* (London: Williams and Norgate, 1909), pp. 174f.

[11]Hans Heinrich Wendt, *The Teaching of Jesus* (New York: Scribner, 1899), I, 114.

[12]David S. Adam, *A Handbook of Christian Ethics,* p. 68.

[13]H. R. Mackintosh, *The Doctrine of the Person of Jesus Christ* (New York: Scribner, 1942), pp. 400ff. "To be holy in all thought and feeling; never to fail in duty to others, never to transgress the law of perfect love to God or man, never to exceed or to come short — this is a condition outstripping the power of imagination and almost of belief. Here is a casement on a Diviner world" (*ibid.,* p. 403).

[14]J. F. Vallings, *Jesus Christ the Divine Man. His Life and Times,* p. 216.

and Sartre, but also against the most earnest idealistic moralists, from Socrates, Plato, and Aristotle to Kant, Hegel, and Fichte, or to Hocking, Brightman, and Flewelling. Indeed, none of the founders of the other world religions binds his followers in such personal moral dependence. Whether one looks to Buddha or Confucius, to Laotze or to Mohammed, to Mary Baker Eddy or to Joseph Smith, he finds this ethical teaching to be higher than their own ethical living. In this they do not differ from the philosophers of ethics. The life of Jesus thus gives authoritative power to his ethical teaching, since his life accords to it an atmosphere of personal earnestness and realization.

The point is not that all other religious ethics and moral philosophy are the work of scoundrels. Man really does wrestle with moral claims in human experience. His very death marked Socrates as an ethical martyr. Plato is passionate in his call for social and individual justice. Kant gave a dramatic centrality to the moral life. But Jesus is not related to his teaching simply as Socrates and Plato and Kant were to theirs. His life was comprehensively "the example of His own words."[15] As MacLennan observes, "The life of Jesus differs from that of all other great teachers of religion and morality in that He lived out His teaching Himself to the full. . . . What Jesus taught He was."[16] And this fact of itself makes all the other religious and philosophical moralists seem tame and drab, if not ethically shabby, alongside Jesus Christ.[17] Indeed, they may be men or women whose teaching here and there strikes our fancy. They may even give us some significant insight. But they do not lay upon us the duty of following them. And if they did, we could not do so with good conscience. Where does the study of philosophy or of religion, we may well inquire with Hovey, "recall the name of any saint or sage whose temper was so sweet and just, so holy and pitiful as his? whose word was so luminous and penetrating and vivifying; whose endurance of wrong was so meek and heroic; whose work was so beneficent and God-like?"[18] Where is even one other who has not been victim of the conditioned ideals of his own day? who by his self-giving love and supreme virtue has challenged and placed on the defensive men of all ages, notions, temperaments, and stations of life? Where else is a flawless and imperishable pattern for behavior to

[15]Thomas B. Kilpatrick, *Christian Character. A Study in New Testament Morality* (Edinburgh: T. & T. Clark, 1899), p. 18.

[16]W. G. D. MacLennan, *Christian Obedience,* p. 19.

[17]H. H. Henson, in his Gifford Lectures, remarked: "The history of religion provides no parallel to the personal influence of Jesus. . . . In none other is the historic Founder recognized as the norm of personal morality. . . . The founder of Buddhism was no model for normal men: the founder of Mohammedanism was no model for any man. The problem of their modern disciples is to explain away, rather than explain, their personal record. Jesus alone is able to offer Himself as the sufficient illustration of His own doctrine. . . . In every other case the religion is separable from its founder, having its title to men's acceptance in the truths which it expresses." *Christian Morality,* pp. 301f.

[18]Alvah Hovey, *Studies in Ethics and Religion* (Boston: Silver, Burdett, 1892), p. 68.

be found? Where else is one who stands in no need of ethical renewal from without? Christ did not simply venture to define the moral ideal. He manifested it. The private lives of the great secular moralists are relatively unknown even where their ethical works are well-known.

How are we to account for the lack of dynamic in speculative ethics? The moral philosophers of antiquity and their modern successors ignore the tragic factor of sin in the life of man. How account for their relatively lower ethical claims? They formulate objective standards for morals and religion without any dependence on special Divine disclosure. And they assume that man can fulfill the will of God by works. They do not see that he needs special redemption. On every side they betray the pride of reason.

True as it may be for Socrates that the doctrines of providence, prayer, and immortality were controlling principles in his philosophy, his conviction that he had "never deliberately wronged a single person" shows dim understanding of the law of love in practice. It also shows the classic moral philosophers were wrong when they said it is impossible to have knowledge of the good without acting upon it. One cannot think of Plato without recalling that he was not taken seriously as the philosopher-king he idealized in *The Republic*. Seneca, the lofty mirror of Stoic ethics, praised the poverty of those around him while he lived in luxury. He even wrote the shameful document in which Nero defended the treacherous murder of his own mother.[19] The moral achievement even of the greatest ethical philosophers falls under the biblical verdict that all have sinned and fallen short of the glory of God.

All the excellences of the best men are seen in Jesus, undiminished and unceasing. His spell over the science of ethics, therefore, is not simply that of an attractive, balanced, and deep personality. He does not simply command the respect due a sage. He presents the ideal not only in his teaching but in the flesh. He speaks to the moral dilemmas of life as One who, though sharing the temptations and the burdens of men, nevertheless is a true representation of the Divine nature. "For Christians, the true standard of life exists, not in the dream land of some ideal realm, but concretely embodied in a human life."[20] The Christian ideal is not left to abstraction, but is manifested in the person of Jesus of Nazareth. He is the pattern of perfect living.

Even those who hesitate to make the highest religious claim for Jesus Christ, and whose philosophy leads them in quite other directions, have acknowledged his peerless character. The distinguished personalist, Edgar S. Brightman, said that "in Jesus . . . the ideal of personality had its highest historical illustration."[21] Whoever has learned of Christ can be satisfied with no lesser ideal of humanity. And whoever disregards him will fruitlessly search for a superior ideal. Christ brought ethics at

[19]F. W. Farrar, *Seekers After God* (New York: Macmillan, 1942), pp. 141f.
[20]*The Inner Life* (by Members of the Church of England), Second Series (London: Hodder & Stoughton, n.d.), p. 99.
[21]E. S. Brightman, *Moral Laws,* p. 244.

the summit and lived out its most exacting demands. David Smith said: "He is never worsted in the moral conflict," but "passes through the daily ordeal stainless and blameless."[22] That is why the proud Greek, the noble Roman, the barbaric tribes of the early West, the heathen of the Orient, and the modern pagan and sophisticate are halted in his presence. Here, indeed, is "God living a human life."

It was to be expected that the life and ideals of Jesus would be assailed vigorously by rationalistic ethics. To admit that Jesus authoritatively forged and achieved the moral ideal is the death-blow of speculative morality. The anti-supernaturalism of the nineteenth and early twentieth centuries, later to emerge as a world cultural force in Communism, damned the moral attitudes and example of Jesus as obsolete. The bolder and more radical critics, such as Bruno Bauer, rewrote history in order to do away with Jesus Christ as a historical person, but the Nazarene could not be erased so easily.

The new spirit assails Jesus as a damaging example, attacking such virtues as humility, self-sacrifice and self-abnegation. It proposes to add modern ideals from contemporary science, art, and socio-economic interests. The complaint of the American humanist is zealously worded by Harry Elmer Barnes and Edwin A. Burtt. Nels Ferré, a professing supernaturalist, attacks the moral purity of Christ, declaring that "sinlessness is a bloodless category, making an anaemic saviour."[23] He charges Jesus with "unnecessary sharpness," "moods of undue and exaggerated joy," "impatience." He was "almost neurotically self-concerned and invidious of others."[24]

Felix Adler denies that Jesus has "spoken the last word in ethics," and that "finality appertains to the ethical teachings of the Gospel." Instead, society has become more complex and has forced new problems upon the race beyond the scope of Christian solutions.[25] Jesus' life should not be allowed to obtrude into the mores and problems of our century because he is too little interested in our practical world of affairs.

Thoreau had already voiced a similar complaint from the side of New England transcendentalism. Jesus "taught mankind imperfectly how to live" because his thoughts "were all directed towards another world." But this sort of complaint is heard less and less. It is all too plain that the Master dealt constantly with "men's present needs, their sins, their sorrows and their sicknesses."[26]

But moralists who would not allow themselves to be counted in the tradition of theological ethics have acknowledged the excellence of

[22]David Smith, *The Historic Jesus* (New York: Hodder & Stoughton, n.d.), p. 66.

[23]Nels Ferré, *The Christian Understanding of God* (New York: Harper, 1951), p. 201.

[24]*Ibid.*, pp. 187f.

[25]Felix Adler, *An Ethical Philosophy of Life*, pp. 38, 42.

[26]Sydney Cave, *The Christian Way* (New York: Philosophical Library, 1949), p. 158.

Jesus' example. John Stuart Mill superficially reduced Christianity to the Golden Rule. Yet he said an unbeliever would find it difficult to locate a better example of the rule of virtue than that given by Jesus. His example of mercy, compassion and service admits no comparisons. Said C. E. M. Joad: "We know, in fact, that we ought to live very much as Christ enjoined. We may say that Christ's prescription for good living is wholly impracticable or is much too difficult; but that does not alter our conviction that it is the right prescription."[27] And the agnostic J. Middleton Murry senses that, in the end, human life will be measured by the Nazarene's: "That beauty of Life apprehended in all manner of ways has been the chief dynamic influence upon mankind. . . . Keep our heads as high as we can, they shall be bowed at the last" (before Jesus).[28] Even those who are loudest in their repudiation of Christian ethics have borrowed from it more than they know. "While they have been undervaluing the inner worth of Jesus Christ, they have actually been living on the virtue which came out of the hem of his garment."[29] One need only contrast modern to pre-Christian Naturalism to discern the debt contemporary Humanism owes to the coming of Christ into the world. Even Communism cannot escape his influence. The best elements in its concern for social justice are ultimately rooted in his example. Martineau has noted[30] that Comte propounds as the single maxim which should guide the whole of Positivism the words "It is more blessed to give than to receive." Comte did not even know the source of these words. Yet he deliberately loosed his religion of humanity from the theological fetters of Christianity. But he could not escape the influence of Jesus Christ. So in eclectic outlooks which are openly hostile to Christianity there are unacknowledged debts to Jesus and the prophets who spoke of him.

The older attacks on Jesus' life are fast disappearing. He is no longer accused of ill-temper or disrespect for human personality. Those protests stemmed from philosophies which tended to make human nature Divine. Therefore they concealed the wrath of God. William Ellery Channing spoke for early Unitarianism of "his spotless purity, his moral perfection, his unrivalled goodness." Jesus was "perfect, spotless in virtue, the representative and resplendent image of the moral goodness and rectitude of God."[31] His displeasure arose, as Karl Adam has put it, "from a wounded love of truth and honesty," and he never surrendered moral control in manifesting it.[32] "His anger is detached from all selfish interest; he is enraged against those who have had

[27]C. E. M. Joad, in *Science and Ethics,* C. H. Waddington, ed. (London: Allen & Unwin, 1942), p. 28.

[28]J. Middleton Murry, *Jesus* (New York: Harper, 1926), pp. 161, 316.

[29]*Ecce Deus,* p. 373.

[30]Martineau, *Types of Ethical Theory,* I, 475. What remains of ideality in Nietzsche's writings is largely borrowed from similar sayings of Christ.

[31]William Ellery Channing, *Works* (Boston: American Unitarian Association, 1873), IV, 186f.

[32]Karl Adam, *The Son of God* (New York: Sheed & Ward, 1940), p. 104.

opportunity and yet remain opponents of the truth and of mercy," writes George M. Stratton.[33] And we may add that this is precisely the anger of the future judgment.

The current trend is simply to ignore Jesus Christ. There is not a single reference to Jesus Christ in Dewey and Tufts' *Ethics* that has pointed significance for the subject. Visit the reserve or stack shelves in the specialized graduate libraries. Comb the indices for mention of Jesus in books on general ethics. One will find such references few and far between. When they do occur, it is often in company with others to whom he is arbitrarily levelled. The tendency is simply to overlook the historical Jesus with indifference, and to assume that no significant ethical system — indeed, no ethical system at all — can be associated with his name.

Strangely enough, even Christian scholarship of the past century encouraged this nonchalance toward Jesus. It argued that we do not know enough about Jesus to justify any estimate of his character. The higher critical assault on the New Testament not only undermined confidence in the inherited picture of Jesus but also filled the gap it left in the records with highly fanciful reconstruction. The implication of a verdict like Wundt's was all too plain: "With the exception of a few incidents in the narrative of the Passion . . . the outward life of Jesus is a tissue of legends." The inward life would be even more difficult to recover. The result of such doubt was well expressed by Warner Fite: "It would be not too much to say that for the part of the world called Christendom the life of Jesus is history's greatest problem."[34] Such critical uncertainties prepared the way for varied appeal to "Jesus' example." The great majority of critics credit Christ with infallibility only where he agrees with their conclusions.[35] The next step is to separate the discussion of the Christian moral ideal from a necessary dependence on the historical Jesus.

Modern theology, after having mistakenly "rescued" the "ethical Jesus" from the "biblical Jesus," today sketches his example only in the most cautious and skeletal manner. The significance of Jesus Christ to the progressive revelation of the plan and character of God is placed "behind the historical." A curtain intrudes between the life and teaching of the historical Jesus and the exact content of revelation. One of the marks of the current dialectical theology is that both the teaching and example of Jesus lose their central and authoritative significance for the ethical life.

[33]George M. Stratton, *Anger: Its Religious and Moral Significance* (New York: Macmillan, 1923), p. 129.

[34]Warner Fite, *Moral Philosophy. The Critical View of Life* (New York: Dial Press, 1925), p. 174.

[35]Leo Jacobs, for example, appealed as spokesman for the Socialist, to Jesus' "good will towards man," and declares that Christian and Socialist are united in this approval. *Three Types of Practical Ethical Movements of the Past Half Century* (New York: Macmillan, 1922), p. 19.

Rudolf Bultmann denies that Jesus regarded himself as Messiah. He finds no essential relationship whatever between the Kingdom of God and the historical person of Jesus. Barth complains that "Jesus Christ . . . the Rabbi of Nazareth [is] historically so difficult to get information about, and when it is got, one whose activity is so easily a little commonplace alongside more than one other founder of a religion and even alongside many later representatives of His own 'religion.' "[36] So, too, Brunner treats the historical Christ. He locates Christ's moral authority wholly outside history.[37] The believer cannot learn the content of Christian behavior from the past, either from the Bible or the historical example of Jesus, but only in immediate revelation-encounter with God.[38] Niebuhr rejects the conviction that the historical Jesus is the incarnation of absolute perfection. "The Christian believes that the ideal of love is real in the will and nature of God, even though he knows of no place in history where the ideal has been realized in its pure form."[39] Niebuhr never satisfactorily resolves the tension between the Jesus of history and the Christ of Christian faith in his writings. There is little light in the verdict that "the Jesus of history . . . created the Christ of faith in the life of the early church, and . . . his historic life is related to the transcendent Christ as a final and ultimate symbol of a relation which prophetic religion sees between all life and history and the transcendent."[40]

All such reconstructions neglect the connection between Christian faith and morals and the conviction that the historical Jesus was the embodiment of absolute and sinless morality. Because of this confidence the followers of Christ find their moral example in him. Where else can they turn? Lecky noted that Christianity has been "the main source of moral development of Europe, and . . . has discharged this office not so much by the inculcation of a system of ethics, however pure, as by the assimilating and attractive influence of a perfect ideal. The moral progress of mankind can never cease to be distinctly and intensely Christian so long as it consists of a gradual approximation to the character of the Christian Founder."[41] And this vital connection between his historical manifestation of the Divine holiness and motivation for Christian conduct has been widely recognized. J. Clark Murray states that the moral supremacy of the historical Jesus supplies an irreplaceable motivation for the life which the Christian considers ideal. "From

[36]Karl Barth, *The Doctrine of the Word of God* (Edinburgh: T. & T. Clark, 1936), p. 188.

[37]Emil Brunner, *The Mediator,* pp. 244f.

[38]Cave protests that Brunner, in *The Divine Imperative,* left unanswered the question of the significance of the teaching of Jesus for modern life (*op. cit.,* pp. 5f.). Cave might have added that Brunner likewise assigns the ethical example of Jesus no permanent significance insofar as the content of ethics is concerned.

[39]Reinhold Niebuhr, *An Interpretation of Christian Ethics,* p. 8.

[40]*Ibid.,* p. 120.

[41]William E. H. Lecky, *History of the Rise and Influence of Rationalism* (New York: Appleton, 1903), I, 307.

whatever point of view Christianity may be regarded, even one that is purely historical, the fact forced upon us is the creative power of a great Personality entering into the current of human history, and by His pre-eminent spiritual force giving a direction to the moral life of men. But this means that the moral life of Christendom can be understood only by reference to the creative power of this Personality."[42] John Stuart Mill states that "the most valuable part of the effect upon character, which Christianity has produced by holding up in a Divine Person a standard of excellence and a model for imitation, is available, even to the absolute unbeliever, and can never be lost to humanity. . . . . Religion cannot be said to have made a bad choice in pitching on this man as the ideal representative and guide of humanity; nor even now would it be easy, even for an unbeliever, to find a better translation of the rule of virtue from the abstract into the concrete than to endeavour so to live that Christ would approve our life." As Newman Smyth puts it plainly, "The Christian Ideal has its source and its realized example in the Jesus of the gospel history."[43]

This connection between Jesus and Christian morality has not only been recognized across the centuries. It comes from the New Testament witness itself. It is inseparable, as Smyth observes, from the apostolic picture of the moral life. "The ethical example of Jesus as an object of faith was clearly and positively given in the apostolic witness to him, and it is a known and distinct Light in the Christian consciousness."[44] But that is not all. Jesus himself implied it — more, he explicitly taught it — to his earliest followers. Our Lord's invitation "follow Me" implied a discipleship in the ethico-religious sense. He is "the Way" (Jn. 14:6). The Christian is to walk in him. Jesus consciously knew that he gave man the ideal pattern of behavior, or more accurately, that he fulfilled the requirements of true human morality in his own life. Jesus regarded the life of moral perfection which he lived as the normal way of living for ordinary men who had not broken from obedience to the will of God. He not only knows the moral issues of the great and final judgment, but also says that he is to judge all men.

He washed his disciples' feet. In this he showed humility. He said, "I have given you an example" (Jn. 13:5ff.). This incident may be taken as the summary of his entire humiliation and the ideal of ethical obedience.

He has not the faintest trace of consciousness of personal sin. Everywhere we sense his consciousness of perfect conformity to the Father's will (Mt. 5:20, 12:50; Jn. 4:34, 5:19, 8:29, 14:31, 16:38). He moves among men as the perfect revelation of God, as the unity of the Divine word and deed, as the perfect and unique embodiment of the Father's will. Nowhere does any remark by his disciples suggest that he had

[42]J. Clark Murray, *A Handbook of Christian Ethics*, p. 7.
[43]Newman Smyth, *Christian Ethics* (New York: Scribner, 1903), p. 53.
[44]*Ibid.*

even symptoms of a defiled conscience. There is nothing to compel them to revise their representation of him as one without sin. "No stormy crisis, no breach with His past, lies behind the period of Jesus' life that we know" is Harnack's sure acknowledgment. "In none of His sayings or discourses, whether He is threatening and punishing or drawing and calling people to Him with kindness, whether He is speaking of His relation to the Father or to the world, can we discover the signs of inner revolutions overcome, or the scars of any terrible conflict."[45] The conviction of personal sin is wholly absent from this most sensitive conscience in human life. The penitential confession of the best of Israel's men of God, men like Moses and David, Nehemiah and Daniel, has no parallel in his life. The disciples presuppose the universality of sin. They freely acknowledge their own faults and imperfections. But they never hint anything of our Lord but perfect holiness and the immaculateness of his moral life. "They tell of their little foolish contests for superiority, of their carnality in desiring an earthly Kingdom, and of their cowardice in forsaking their Lord and Master in the hour of extremity; but never do they suggest anything to *his* disadvantage."[46] The New Testament writers candidly confess themselves to be sinners. They are men who have fallen short of the moral ideal. Their hope is redemption. Yet again and again they set Jesus forth as the supreme moral ideal (Eph. 5:2, Heb. 12:3, 1 Pet. 2:21ff.). Their verdict is that Jesus Christ is "holy, guileless, undefiled, separate from sinners, made higher than the heavens" (Heb. 7:26). He is Jesus Christ "the Righteous" (1 Jn. 2:1).

P. T. Forsyth is not amiss in the emphasis that Christ's obedience and trust in God are not the same as that of the disciples. They felt their way through darkness. They lived in moral distance from God. In thought and will they and the Father were hardly one. "He no more confesses his faith than his sin. . . . He possessed the certainty and communion of the Father in himself. And we believe in the Only Son as he believed in none."[47] He was not only conscious of his sinlessness, but he also proclaimed it. He challenged his enemies to prove him guilty of sin. In one of the most remarkable transitions of history he set aside an external morality and put in its place an internal spiritual ethic. "The Pharisee was the Jewish ideal of a holy man, and it is an evidence of the historicity of the Evangelic Jesus," writes David Smith, "that He is so widely diverse from that ideal."[48] The fact is that Jesus spoke with contrariety of ethical spirit, as Vallings puts it, "to all the moral environment of the time, Pharisaic, Sadducaic, Essene, or Gentile."[49]

[45]A. Harnack, *What Is Christianity?* p. 33.
[46]Andrew G. Fuller, *Complete Works* (London, 1837), III, 687.
[47]P. T. Forsyth, *The Person and Place of Jesus Christ* (Philadelphia: Westminster, 1910), p. 133.
[48]David Smith, *op. cit.*, p. 69.
[49]Vallings, *op. cit.*, p. 216.

The Apostle Peter proclaimed to the early believers that Christ left "an example, that ye should follow in his steps" (1 Pet. 2:21). The Apostle John appeals to the Calvary-love of God, and from it argues that "we ought to lay down our lives for the brethren" (1 Jn. 3:16). The author of Hebrews appeals to his example of endurance of contradiction of sinners, "lest ye be wearied and faint in your minds" (Heb. 12:3). The Apostle Paul sets forth Christ's great example in the passage on humility and humiliation: "Let this mind be in you, which was also in Christ Jesus" (Phil. 2:5ff.). Not only the passages which refer specifically to his "example," but those which set Christ forth as the image which believers are to resemble are significant (Rom. 8:29, 1 Cor. 15:49, 2 Cor. 3:18, Col. 3:10). Believers are to 'put on' Christ (Rom. 13:14, Gal. 3:27, Eph. 4:24, Col. 3:10). The Christian is to walk in him. The believer's high destiny is to be made like Christ (Rom. 8:29, 1 Jn. 3:2, 24). Yet he lived the good life as a normal man to be an example for others. He is the example, because he lived the good life.

So it was that the Christian movement in history came by its unshakeable persuasion that the earthly life of Jesus is an index to what God loves and hates, what he approves and condemns. He alone dared say of himself, "My meat is to do the will of him that sent me and to finish his work" (Jn. 4:34), and "I seek not mine own will, but the will of the Father which hath sent me" (Jn. 5:30). He was the living truth and goodness. He was virtue made alive in the flesh. George Walker states what has been the abiding conviction of the Christian movement: "In the ethics of Christianity Christ, its Founder, is held to stand in an unique relation to the mind and will of God, the supremely righteous One. . . . For Christian ethics the life of its Founder is in character, in motive and in will morally at one with the divine and absolute Righteousness."[50] Christ's life remains the unclouded mirror of how human nature ought to be ideally related to the eternal world. As Ramsey acknowledges, "the Bible measures what is required of man against the perfect righteousness of an utterly faithful, savior-God."[51] History now knows virtue, for it has seen Christ. Christian morality is nothing more than Jesus Christ in his followers. They live as he lived, for he now lives in them. The Christian system of morality can be summed up in the person of Christ. For what the Christian means by a virtuous life is really Jesus Christ, as the incomparable example of the Divine ideal realized in the flesh. It is not too much to say that for Christian ethics, virtue is identical with the rectitude and purity of Jesus Christ. What Christianity acquired from Jesus Christ was not merely a widening of the universal scope of ethics in contrast with Hebrew limitations, not only a deepening of moral understanding and obligation, but it was supremely his personal embodiment of the ethical ideal. Henson comments on Paul's exhortation, "Whatsoever ye do, in

[50]George Walker, *The Idealism of Christian Ethics,* p. 21.
[51]Ramsey, *Basic Christian Ethics,* p. 12.

word or in deed, do all in the name of the Lord Jesus" (Col. 3:17). He says that this "cannot mean less than that life, in the totality of its activities, is to be regarded as subject to Christ's law."[52] The moral ideal which Jesus proclaimed is the moral ideal which Jesus embodied. "When we seek the explanation of this unique power which Christian morality possesses, we can but find it in the uniqueness of the Founder of Christianity."[53] He illustrates "personal morality in its completest expression. . . . His precepts . . . the ultimate principles of morality."[54] "He is not the Universal Teacher bringing all knowledge within the reach of His disciples, but He is the Ideal Man."[55] What God has done in Christ, says Cave, became the inspiration and the norm for Christian character. To know what God would have us do, we need to remember what God Himself has done."[56]

The remarkable fact is that the one who ascribed a heinousness alike to sinful thought and sinful act stands before us also as the standard of holiness at its highest peak, and as the sweep of moral law at its furthest reach. In his deeds and in his person the Kingdom of God became entrenched in history. Whoever thinks God is most fully revealed in the impersonal movements of the stellar galaxies must reckon yet with Jesus Christ as the incarnation of righteousness, goodness and love, and with the well-nigh irresistible impression that the eternal God is best seen in his personality and life.

This is not the place to labor the fact that any view of Jesus *simply* as the ideal moral example involves a serious abridgment of Christian ethics. The form and content of revealed morality include the Scriptures, the teaching of Jesus Christ, the redemptive role of Christ, and the work of the Holy Spirit as the dynamic of the ethical life. All these are ethically significant along with the example of the Founder of the Christian religion. "The Christians adopted for their sign," said Bigg, "not a portrait of Jesus, but His Cross." Behind the sinless life of Jesus, as behind all his works, stands the unveiled Saviour of sinners. He is, in W. A. Visser 't Hooft's words, "the main actor in the dramatic history of world salvation."[57] Indeed, he is more. He calls philosophical ethics to a new center. He reorients Hebrew ethics. He exhibits the good life as a consequence of his provision of redemption, rather than as the condition of it. In the moral perfection of Jesus, as H. R. Mackintosh saw, we find at once the guarantee of a genuine incarnation, the essential basis of atonement, the reality of a perfect example, and the outline of our eternal destiny.[58] Regarding Jesus *simply* as the incarnation of a Divine morality soon leads to a "skin and bones" Christian

[52]H. H. Henson, *op. cit.,* p. 145.
[53]*Ibid.,* p. 296.
[54]*Ibid.,* p. 297.
[55]*Ibid.,* p. 305.
[56]Cave, *op. cit.,* p. 43.
[57]W. A. Visser 't Hooft, *The Kingship of Christ.* Stone Lectures. (New York: Harper, 1948), p. 26.
[58]H. R. Mackintosh, *op. cit.,* p. 406.

ethics in which Jesus is exemplary only of a "supreme concern for human values."[59] He is more than the incarnation of obedience and perfection; he is also the incarnation of sacrifice in the sinner's stead.

Yet the true picture of Christian morals is lost whenever Jesus is not taken as the moral example. Then there is only a hazy and nebulous outline. In Jesus, the moral example, the picture is focused sharply. The Christian community has found in him alone the absolute embodiment of moral truth, love and purity. The ideal of conduct is set before us in the concrete reality of human flesh only in the living person of the God-man. The fact that Jesus lived an impeccable life is a constant reminder that believers, in the words of Handley C. G. Moule, "are expected to be *total abstainers* from vice, in a world where indulgence, at least as to the principle of it, was ubiquitous."[60] He stands above the race as the living rebuke to every moral license and to every impurity.

The connection between the imitation of Jesus and evangelical theology has not always been obvious. In some circles so much stress has been placed on the atoning work of Christ that the example of his life was obscured. This tendency is quite as unfortunate as the opposite liberal disposition in our century to study the ethics of Jesus apart from any redemptive issues. Evangelical Christianity has thus risked the loss of Christ as example. "The absolute necessity of following the example of His life is not preached with the same distinctness as that of trusting the atonement of His death."[61] So complained Andrew Murray, and the complaint is sometimes necessary.

There are, of course, reasons for not picturing Jesus as the absolute example of Christian conduct. His redemptive work can be duplicated by none other, and this unique vocation called for singular ways of living. Harnack has a somewhat sobering footnote for the "follow Jesus" moralists. "To 'imitate' or 'be like' Christ did not occupy the place one would expect among the ethical counsels of the age," he writes of early expansion of Christianity. "Jesus had spoken of imitating God and bidden men follow himself, whilst the relationship of pupil and teacher readily suggested the formula of imitation. But whenever he was recognized as Messiah, as the Son of God, as Saviour and as Judge, the ideas of imitation and likeness had to give way. . . . In the early church the imitation of Christ never became a formal principle of ethics (to use a modern phrase) except for the virtuoso in religion . . . ; it played quite a subordinate part in the ethical teaching of the church. The injunction to be like Christ, in the strict sense of the term, also occurred with comparative rarity. . . . The early church did not go the length of drawing up general regulations with regard to the imitation of Christ. For one thing, the Christology stood in the way, involving not imitation but obedience; for another thing, the

[59]H. H. Titus, *Ethics for Today* (2d ed., Boston: American Book, 1936), p. 546.
[60]Handley C. G. Moule, *Grace and Virtue,* p. 83.
[61]Andrew Murray, *Like Christ* (New York: Grosset & Dunlap, 1895), p. 274.

actual details of imitation seemed too severe."[62] Christ could not be imitated in his substitutionary work. He can be copied only where our vocation is the same as that of the God-man. Those who use the life of Jesus as the model for medieval asceticism misread his life. It is true that Christ was unmarried. But he blessed marriage. He did indeed call disciples to renounce domestic claims and thus superseded the emphasis of his disciples that believers care for their loved ones. But he illustrated the nature of the love of God by the intimacy of family ties, father and son, husband and bride. He scathed comfort and advantage. But he did not regard the world as intrinsically evil. His enemies called him a winebibber, as they could not have done, had he been a known ascetic. Henson notes that Paul nowhere appeals to the ascetic side of Christ's life as specifically exemplary for believers. Rather, his three direct appeals point in the other direction: Christians are urged not to repudiate marital responsibilities (1 Cor. 7:10f.). They are urged to pay money to a settled ministry (1 Cor. 9:14), and to give alms. This presupposes private property (Acts 24:17).[63]

If an atonement for man's sin was the exclusive accomplishment of Christ, the efficacy of his atonement gives assurance that the morality which he translated into human life is absolute. The moral authority of Jesus Christ is therefore absolute, and we are to follow him. As representative man he reveals the original Divine intention in the creation of man: "Let us make man in our image." As the obedient Son, he reveals a filial relationship of self-denying submission to God. The chief end of man is the glorification of God in and through spiritual and moral union. Jesus spells this out in human flesh. He exhibits the perfect ideal of humanity. He shows us by his own life what God intended man to be and what man in the fullness of redemption will be.

To be "in Christ" means something quite different from attempting to "be Christ." Shailer Mathews, Francis Peabody, and the liberal school of Protestantism depicted Jesus as "the ideal man, whom all men can emulate, once the persuasive charm of his life has captivated their souls."[64] But the imitation of Jesus must be guarded from such easy misconceptions. It must not be detached from Christ as Redeemer. Nor will monasticism do. Perfectionist delusions of actually duplicating Christ's flawlessness are to be rejected.

Another danger is that the imitation of Christ become mere outward conformity. Jesus becomes the pattern of external habit rather than the moulder of inner disposition. The external copying, if it is the whole of the moral effort of the person, actually reduces to a mockery of Christ's example. He everywhere condemns a "morality" that does not spring from the heart. A literal and slavish conformity which does not flow

[62]Adolf Harnack, *The Expansion of Christianity,* I, 107, n. 1.
[63]H. H. Henson, *op. cit.,* p. 94.
[64]Niebuhr, *op. cit.,* p. 119.

from conformity to "the mind of Christ" fails to grasp the most elemental lesson he taught — the vanity of legalistic morality.

The New Testament commands believers to follow in his steps. It does not belittle the idea of imitation. But such imitation must flow from faith. It results in a reshaping of the inner attitudes, motives, and desires of life. The Spirit now prompts willing conformity. It does not mean asceticism, but it involves an inner death to the pull of the world. It consists primarily in the dedication of the whole personality to the love of God and man as Christ exemplified. "To 'do all in the name of Jesus,' in the sense of the law which has become personal in Him, is to imitate Christ."[65]

Christ faced temptation. He resisted and conquered it. The Spirit succoured him. This makes sure the promise that those who live in him can share in his power over sin. It reinforces the Christian hope that the redeemed soul in its future glory will enjoy an absolute ethical conformity to the nature of God. "In every form temptation was rejected, not because He had no real human faculties to feel its force, but," as Gore states the nature of his obedience, "because His faculties acted simply under the control of a will, which followed unhesitatingly the movement of the Holy Spirit, in other words, which existed only to do the Father's will."[66] His morality is not merely an inference from his Divinity, else its significance for us must be sacrificed. Can only God be moral? Is there no chance for mere man to please God? Christ is the superlative illustration of ideal human obedience. Hence his moral perfection has universal validity. The believer today is not disrobed of his spiritual armor for the moral fray. Men are not left to struggle in their own resources. But a new source of power has been made available to them from their risen and exalted Lord. The old moral inabilities are surmounted. A new moral achievement is possible. Virtue still goes out from Christ. He remains the central and renewing principle of the ethical life, the power which conforms human nature to the Divine law. Christian living centers in his personal presence. He constantly communicates new life to his followers. The imitative life is the life which abides in him. Ethical conduct is for the believer response to a living Person. He was no mere series of moral abstractions to those disciples who walked by his side during those three tremendous years; indeed, his spiritual presence is a dramatic reality among those whose lives are rooted in his. In Haering's words, "Christ is the principle of Christian ethics. . . . The New Testament expresses this truth in the plainest manner by the use of every possible preposition in connection with Christ. 'Of,' 'out of,' 'through,' 'to,' 'according to,' 'on account of,' 'in' Christ all Christian men act, believe, love, live, and die. All the moral action of Christian men is referred to Christ as the

[65]von Haering, *op. cit.*, p. 176.

[66]Charles Gore, *The Incarnation of the Son of God* (London: J. Murray, 1891), p. 166.

personal source of the highest 'Good.' "[67] For the Christian community, this is not only theological fact but it is also experiential fact. "To do all 'in Christ,' eating and drinking, waking and sleeping, praying, troubling, glorifying; in anxiety, in life and in death, — to do this 'in Christ' was not for St. Paul a suitable formula of speech, but a reality."[68] To the company of believers Christ is the Life as well as the Way and the Truth.

For all who would reach the higher moral vistas which Christianity has unveiled to the world, he provides a supernatural escort. The coveted likeness to Christ is approximated through the sacred gift of the Spirit. Thereby he sustains a vital relation to all who follow him, imparting life and power to them. "Christ . . . is the pre-eminent 'Thou shalt' to Christians, because He not only points out the goal, the way and the source of power, but He Himself is all these things."[69]

The example of Jesus defines the will of God in action. "What he loved and hated, what he approved and condemned" both in word and deed dramatically publishes the moral claim. In surveying that life, two dangers must be avoided. One is a tendency to define his morality only negatively, as sinlessness or the avoidance of lovelessness to God. The other is to splinter his life into a number of components and to hold *these* before us as definitive of morality perfectly lived out. So, for example, Henson tells us the three prevailing characteristics of Jesus that are "recognized throughout Christian history as the essential constituents of the specifically Christian morality."[70] They are personal goodness, social service, and self-sacrifice. These are indeed distinguishing elements of theistic ethics. But they easily miss Jesus' great emphasis on the center of the ethical life — absolute devotion to God and man. He unveils in his passive obedience the expanse the love of God has for man. In his active obedience he unveils at its summit man's love for God and man's love for man. Jesus claims much more than the voluntary harmony of his own will with the Father's; indeed, he insists that an eternal and essential relationship of being makes them one. Nevertheless he becomes the norm for human conformity to God. Never was man so moulded to the will of God as was Jesus in the incarnation. He is the revelation of perfect manhood. The inadequacy of all spurious and meager views of the capacity and destiny of man is seen as Jesus shows us in his life what man was meant to be like. Christ convinces us that his precepts and example are beyond man's reach not because his moral faultlessness is for gods only, but because of the rebellion of our race. A holy humanity seems miraculous only because we love our sin too much. Really our lack of holiness is due to rejecting the will of God. The Divine perfections which shine constantly in him mark Jesus of Nazareth as the living law of righteousness. They prove

[67]von Haering, *op. cit.*, p. 126.
[68]*Ibid.*, p. 177.
[69]*Ibid.*, p. 126.
[70]Henson, *op. cit.*, p. 307.

the incarnation to be an ethical as well as a metaphysical reality. Properly W. S. Bruce says that "in the life of the Master, as depicted in the Gospels, we have the Model of manhood and the Ideal of Christian character."[71]

Above all, Jesus summarizes virtue as being love. If ever love was clothed in human flesh — both love for God and love for man — it was in Bethlehem. His love to God supplies an almost interminable theme to religious literature. "The crowning attribute of His human character was Love of God," writes James Stalker. "He never spent an hour, He never did an action, without direct reference to Him. . . . His thoughts were God's thoughts; His desires were never in the least different from God's; His purpose, He was perfectly sure, was God's purpose for Him."[72] His love for men is the bright star in the night of human self-interest, it is the only absolute example of unrequited love.

He condemned the religious pose that professes a love for God, but that ignores man. The Christian life can involve nothing less than sincere love for Christ (Eph. 6:24). The acknowledgment of his Deity, his moral dignity, the grandeur and greatness of his atonement for men, and the strength of his loyalty to God brings out a hunger for communion with him. It infuses a desire for a devotion to the will of God like his. The Christian delights as Christ unsullyingly reflects the image of God. But he will not be loved only because of his Divinity. He wants to be loved for what he was as he shared life with men — he wants love, not as God, but as God-Man. "Love for Christ as a person," Henry C. King remarks, "has, as a matter of fact, proved the mightiest of historical motives to noble living."[73] But the Nazarene gives to this concept of nobility of life an outward as well as an upward reach. His love for men, which inspires theirs for him, he makes a guiding principle for their love for others: "that ye love one another even as I have loved you" (Jn. 15:12). In the parable of the Samaritan and in his own death for men who are at enmity with God, he made clear the comprehensive nature of Christian love.

It may seem an oversimplification to reduce the moral life of Jesus Christ to love. What of the stern side of his nature? the lightning-fierceness with which he assails sin? the sure threat of judgment and hell to come for unrepentant sinners? These emphases guard the definition of love. The gospels know no emotion worthily designated as love, whether applied to God in heaven or to his incarnate Son, which is unconditioned by righteousness and justice.

All Christ's thoughts, words, and deeds are the exposition of that love. Love encompasses all his virtues. "Different manifestations or aspects of His love can each be named a separate virtue: patience, mercy, etc.;

[71]W. S. Bruce, *The Formation of Christian Character* (Edinburgh: T. & T. Clark, 1908), p. 91.

[72]James Stalker, *The Life of Jesus Christ* (rev. ed., New York: Revell, 1891), p. 88.

[73]Henry C. King, *The Ethics of Jesus* (New York: Macmillan, 1910), pp. 19f.

but each is love brought to bear on people whose needs are of different kinds." So writes E. L. Strong,[74] and the appraisal is sufficient to remind us that *agape* — not just any species of love, but *agape* — is the bond which holds together all the virtues.

He clothes the Beatitudes with his own life. Stalker observes that in depicting the blessed man, he himself is the character Jesus describes. Just so he later designated himself as "meek and lowly in heart." Hilarin Felder, in *Christ and the Critics,* sensed the delightful symmetry and proportion of the moral qualities of his life: "We find in him ardent zeal and inexhaustible patience, noble fervour and indulgent leniency, holy seriousness and sunny cheerfulness, an impulse to solitude and yet world publicity, majestic greatness and the deepest humility, inflexible determination and the sweetest gentleness, powerful energy and quiet self-possession, the warmest love for sinners and invincible hatred of sin, compassionate sympathy and strictest justice; irresistible attractiveness and fearless frankness, incorruptible truthfulness and extreme forbearance, mildness and force, resignation and resistance, adamantine strength and motherly tenderness, indefatigable outward activity and inward contemplation . . . and a ceaseless striving to promote the kingdom of heaven."

We catalogue the other upright men of history by their isolated virtues. But when we place them beside Jesus Christ, we quickly observe that the best of humanity "exhibits only the *disjecta membra* of spiritual perfection."[75] Macartney remarked pointedly: "However you take Christ, in what are called the passive virtues — benevolence, compassion, humility, gentleness, patience, long-suffering, or in what are called the heroic virtues — fortitude, daring, courage, righteousness, indignation — it is as impossible to think of any improvement as it is impossible to conceive of any situation in life where He could not be your guide. To compare Him with others is not so much an offense against orthodoxy, as it is against good taste and decency."[76]

To see how to obey the specific commands to pray, to live the life of purity, to exercise a forgiving spirit, to be humble and to serve others, one need only watch Jesus in his daily walk. He is the believer's perfect pattern of resisted temptation (Heb. 3:1ff., 12:3ff.); the supreme example of merciful forgiveness (Eph. 4:32, Col. 3:13, 2 Cor. 2:10); of humble self-denial (Phil. 2:5ff., 2 Cor. 8:9, Rom. 15:2f., 7); of meekness (2 Cor. 10:1, Col. 3:12, Eph. 4:2); of suffering love (1 Jn. 3:16, 2 Cor. 4:10); of holy purity (Eph. 4:20ff., 1 Pet. 1:15). "The conscience of the Church must be educated to understand that the humility, and self-denial of Jesus, His entire devotion to His father's work and will, His ready obedience, His self-sacrificing love and kindly benef-

[74]E. L. Strong, *Lectures on the Christian Character* (London: Longmans, Green, 1923), p. 4.

[75]R. L. Ottley, *Christian Ideas and Ideals,* p. 145.

[76]Clarence E. Macartney, *Twelve Great Questions About Christ* (New York: Revell, 1923), p. 61.

icence, are nothing more than what each believer is to consider it his simple duty as well as his privilege to exhibit, too. There is not, as so many think, one standard for Christ and another for His people. No, as branches of the vine, as members of the body, as partakers of the same spirit, we may and therefore must bear the image of the Elder Brother."[77] Whether one thinks of prayer, of freedom from anxiety, of attitudes toward money, of almsgiving, it is Christ's life of faith and dedication to the will of God which alone supplies the pattern of the right.

If the greatness of prophet and psalmist lay in what was done "by faith," Jesus manifested from first to last an absolute trust in God. His trust in God is seen most clearly as he committed his spirit into the Father's hands in that terrible hour. Never has it been made more clear than by the example of Jesus, nor indeed can it be, that faith supplies the whole foundation of all morality. It is the basis of the ethical life. "He knew," writes Stalker, "that the worst that could happen to Him was His Father's will for Him; and this was enough."[78]

Francis Paget wrote of Christ's calm and steadfast appraisal of the complexities of earthly life as he, the Eternal One, saw them. "He Who so loved the world that He came down to die for it, yet moves among its interests, and displays, and agitations, and disasters, with a tranquility of judgment which might almost be mistaken for indifference. He corrects its axioms, reverses its standards, forecasts its revolutions, disposes of its claims; its highest powers and its most appalling terrors fail alike to affect the steadiness of His penetrating insight. . . . Despised and suffering, weary and deserted, still He speaks at times as though He were already seated on the throne of judgment, with all nations there before Him, waiting in awful, passive, concentrated expectation for His separating Voice."[79] And lifted above the perturbing agitation of the world, his followers are to share this quiet confidence: "Fear not, little flock; it is your Father's good pleasure to give you the kingdom."

He taught truthfulness in speech and life. He lived it. "I am the Truth," he declared, and he promised to send the Spirit of Truth to lead men into the Truth. The great fact that truth is deed as well as word shapes the whole of Christian thought. And Christ is Truth the Deed.

Instead of the spirit of revenge so common to men, Jesus enthroned that most difficult of virtues to cultivate, the virtue of forgiveness. Even when betrayed to death, and when suffering, he forgave.

"The characteristic of humility and submission," Lotze observed rightly, "lacking even in the most mournful expressions of this sense of finiteness in antiquity, was brought for the first time by Christianity into the heart of men."[80] This virtue of humility, now recognized as a

[77]Andrew Murray, *op. cit.*, p. 268.
[78]Stalker, *op. cit.*, p. 89.
[79]Francis Paget, *Studies in the Christian Character* (2d ed., New York: Longmans, Green, 1902), p. 29.
[80]Lotze, *Microcosmus* (4th ed., Edinburgh: T. & T. Clark, 1899), II, 271.

hallmark of Christian ethics, stands over against the high-mindedness and pride which speculative ethics approved. Jesus pictured humility as the only true road to exaltation. The incarnation and crucifixion clothed this virtue with his very life. And they are indeed a prelude to his glorification.

The virtue of patience is likewise inscribed on his daily outlook on life. "He was divinely patient under every form of suffering, — a homeless life, hunger and thirst, craft and violence, meanness and pride, the taunts of enemies and betrayals of friends, ending in an ignominious death. Nothing of all this for a moment turned Him from His chosen path of love and pity. His last words, like His whole life, were a prayer for those who returned Him evil for good."[81]

Honor for parents was one of the commandments of the Decalogue that the New Testament emphasized. The promise of reward came with it. Where do we find greater solicitude for a parent than the concern Jesus showed for Mary his mother even in the hour of his passion?

The Christian community is inspired by much more than Christ's example. It has the inner sense of duty. It has faith's conviction that the lives of the redeemed belong to the Redeemer. It has the promise of future reward. But with the model of Christ's life before it, it rests unsatisfied until his virtues prevail in the hearts of those who love him. Because Jesus begets in his followers a genuine likeness to himself, they in turn may mediate examples to others. They are to be the light of the world (Jn. 8:12, Mt. 5:13ff.) in contrast with the bad example of the scribes and Pharisees (Mt. 23:1ff.). But only as the believers followed Christ were they an example to be followed. The Apostle Paul asserted, "Be ye followers of me, as I am of Christ." The New Testament stresses the importance of Christian example (Phil. 2:15, 1 Thess. 1:7f., 1 Cor. 7:16, 1 Tim. 6:1, 1 Pet. 2:11ff., 3:1f., 15f.). Paul made at least eight direct appeals to Christians to copy his own conduct.

The power of the Christian life has been in every age a powerful confirmation of apostolic doctrine. Marshall points out that the world had never seen any wide realization of character on the "Christian" level before Christ's coming.[82] In a world of rife licentiousness and vice, which condoned sin as natural and normal, there appeared the remarkable phenomenon. A company of followers of the Nazarene arose, devoted to a singular purity of life. They avoided adultery and fornication, life on the carnal level, lying, slander, rapacity and false witness, greed, coveting other's property, treating others as they were disposed to treat the Christians, seeking malice or revenge. They prized spiritual above material possessions. They were kind to enemies. They gave special consideration to widows, orphans and homeless strangers.

[81]Cunningham Geikie, *op. cit.*, p. 6.
[82]Marshall, *op. cit.*, pp. 1f.

They loved all men in a world of racial and national hatred. They regarded slaves with brotherly love and accorded them equal rights. They cared for the sick and poor. And they extended into the course of human history the sublime ethic of self-denying love to which Jesus of Nazareth first gave living content.

18

NEW TESTAMENT PRINCIPLES OF CONDUCT

WHAT SHALL I DO in this situation? Where can I find light on what choice to make? Is this the Christian thing to do? These are questions each Christian asks himself repeatedly each day. He must live the whole of his life so that he pleases God. Life confronts him with decision and he must act. Often he must choose one of several alternatives. Most of the time he does not have the ease of deciding between a moral black or white. Usually all he sees are varying shades of gray. Where can he find some guidance so that he will choose what pleases God?

The New Testament does not give a rule to cover every possibility in life. The Pharisees tried to expand what they knew of the character and will of God into a rule-book that outwardly regulated every hour of the day and every situation that could possibly come up. Jesus stood against such legalism. He knew that true morality comes from the heart.

External conformity to the letter of the law does not necessarily prove a person is acting morally. He may not *want* to do the right. He may conform only because of social pressure. The law may not really be applicable to this particular situation. There may be two laws bearing on this situation that tell him to act in different ways. Which shall he choose? Jesus clearly saw that there are two decisive weaknesses to moral legalism. One is that even if there were a law, man can keep it outwardly as he sins inwardly. The other is the impracticality of making a law corresponding to every situation that might occur.

So the New Testament sets forth a number of basic Christian principles. In addition to general principles, the New Testament indisputably contains several "rules," *e.g.*, "forsake not the assembling of yourselves together" (Heb. 10:25), "pay ye taxes" (Rom. 13:6), "be not drunk with wine" (Eph. 5:18), etc. But it does not endeavor to specify rules for the whole of life. If there are principles, as undoubtedly there are, these should assuredly be applicable to particular cases. These are to guide the Christian in the choices he makes. He must see himself, his motives, and his desires clearly. He must know the New Testament principles for conduct, which apply here, which do not, and why. Then he must decide and act. Thus, by this terrifying and responsible process, he matures ethically. There is no other way.

This chapter will develop a number of the New Testament principles of conduct that the Christian must use to guide his life.

1) The believer's life is one of *Christian liberty* in grace. He is not bound to the Law as a means of salvation. He is not burdened with a legalistic conscience. Christian liberty is the guarantee of the believer's peace of mind. His conscience is to be guarded from unnecessary and unspiritual obligations. The Law no longer whips it.

This Christian liberty extends to the whole of life. "All things are lawful" (1 Cor. 6:12, 10:23) is the primary principle of Christian ethics. This is a summary of the disciple's morality (cf. 1 Cor. 9:19).

Nothing God has created is unclean in itself. Nor does it become unclean when it is used in accord with the design of the Creator. Since God created all things, all things can be properly used. The only limitations are ones God, the Creator, himself sets. "To us there is but one God, the Father, of whom are all things, and we in him; and one Lord Jesus Christ, by whom are all things, and we by him" (1 Cor. 8:6). "For the earth is the Lord's, and the fulness thereof" (1 Cor. 10:26).

The believer, because of his faith in Christ and his sanctification, is uniquely related to the Divine purpose of creation. The conscience of the regenerated person rejoices in that purpose. What God has created is to be "received with thanksgiving of them which believe, and know the truth. For every creature of God is good, and nothing to be refused, if it be received with thanksgiving: for it is sanctified by the word of God and prayer" (1 Tim. 4:3-5). Hence a basic characteristic of the Christian life is an approach to the whole of experience with the proper perspective: the Divine purpose in creation — reaffirmed in redemption.

The world is evil only as a fallen world. It is not evil intrinsically. This view strikes out against negativism in Christian ethics. Christian ethics is not blind to the corrupting leaven of sin in every area of life. But neither is it world-denying. It must be world-affirming because it is an ethics that presupposes creation and redemption.

The requirements of the law have been fulfilled in the Christian's behalf by Christ. Therefore, the believer *must* resist any effort to impose the Law in whole or in part as a means of salvation. "For freedom did Christ free us: stand fast therefore, and be not again entangled with the yoke of bondage" (Gal. 5:1). So urges Paul as he opposes those who demand circumcision for salvation. Against these early Judaizing perverters of the Gospel, as against the semi-works Roman Catholicism of today, the believer is reminded that he is "called unto liberty" (Gal. 5:13f.). This principle also condemns much of what is called "Fundamentalism" in America today. For Fundamentalism in practice requires the believer to abstain from certain "social evils" in order to be acceptable with God[1] — and with other Fundamentalists. Christian ethics thereby becomes an index of legalistic "don'ts." One who is truly born again, it is insisted, does not smoke, dance, go to the theater, gamble, drink.

[1]Cf. the writer's *The Uneasy Conscience of Modern Fundamentalism* (Grand Rapids: Eerdmans, 1947).

Without question, genuine regeneration issues in a marked change in character. But this negativism in Fundamentalist ethics may conceal the fact that one who abstains from the proscribed may be every bit as carnal as one who indulges. Arbitrary legalism is a poor substitute for an inner morality. Not only this, but such legalism emphasizes the less important issues in life, and ignores or excuses the weightier matters of the Law. Smoking can be a subject of legislation; pride cannot.

Not only does legalism bypass the sins of the spirit, but it gives the impression that the Christian life is one of staying out of trouble. If the believer "keeps his nose clean," he will get by with God. But Christian morality is not just negative abstinence. It is positive virtue flowing out from the regenerated core of the person. Sanctification is not a mere abstinence, it is the Lordship of Christ and the rule of the Spirit. It issues in love and kindness and compassion and good works humbly done. There is grave danger in Fundamentalism that sanctification will be misunderstood as mere legal abstinence if "Christian ethics" makes the negation of certain mores the grounds for acceptance with God. Salvation, then, would in spirit be by grace *and* works.

It has often been pointed out that the believer does not live his life "facing God" in quest of approval. That is how the world seeks to please God by works. The believer knows that nothing he can *do* will put him in right standing with God. Rather, grace is his starting-point. He lives his life "from God outward," and has assurance that he is accepted by God through Christ. There is indeed moral earnestness in the believer's walk in grace. But it is an earnestness that seeks guidance and help, not one that strives for initial favor from God. Clarence Bouma forcefully spoke of the Christian life as being the "rediscovery of the moral law." The Godward look and the moral law are hardly lost in the Christian life. But the law is no more a terrifying demand whose satisfaction is the only hope of salvation. It becomes the rule of life which the Christian embraces with devotion.

Believers do not always see the full implications of their Christian liberty. "There is not in every man that knowledge" (1 Cor. 8:7). There is a principle in the New Testament that the conscience of the weaker brother is to be honored. Yet his conscientious objection does not in itself have final validity. Christian conscience is not infallible. It requires growth and education. It may be the conduct of the stronger believer is definitely to be approved and vindicated. All are enjoined to do the same thing, and the objection of the weaker rests on false or inadequate grounds.

In 1 Corinthians 10 Paul treats the subject of offended consciences. He is speaking about buying meat from the public market that had previously been used in sacrifices to pagan gods. He says that such meat has lost its sacrificial character. "Whatsoever is sold in the shambles, that eat, asking no questions for conscience' sake" (v. 25). To interpret this to mean that one is to ask no questions so that he will not know if the meat is sacrificial — and hence avoid a troubled conscience — is to miss the point. There is no question of conscience in the matter at all. Rather, the over-scrupulous conscience of the weaker brother needs enlightenment. He may be wrongly applying some prohibition of the Mosaic code. Here the conscience is not to be stifled but to be educated.

There is nothing in this situation that conscience is to condemn. What belongs to God is not evil, and "the earth is the Lord's and the fulness thereof" (v. 26). There is no God but the Living God, so that the pagans sacrifice their meat to no god at all (8:4ff.). If an unbelieving friend or relative invites a believer to a feast where idol-meat is served, and the believer goes, he may eat without an offended conscience (10:27). He is hardly obligated to sever relationships with that person (5:9ff.). And what is more, the believer's liberty is not to be "judged by another conscience" (10:29). Grosheide comments that "the fact that one may have objection to the eating of sacrificial meat has no significance for another who is strong. The conscience of the strong need not feel burdened just because the conscience of the weak is burdened. On the contrary, such conscience remains free. . . . The strong is not obliged to abstain from sacrificial meat for his own sake . . ."[2] Nor is the strong to be criticized by the weak (1 Cor. 10:30). The weak, too, must recognize the principle of Christian liberty, and not offend the strong.

Moreover, this protest against eating meats may not always come from an over-scrupulous conscience. It may come from a "conscience seared with a hot iron" (1 Tim. 4:2f.). Paul here points out that God made food to be enjoyed with thanksgiving. Hence the purpose of creation is fulfilled only in thankful participation. The great lack of the Gentile world was that "when they knew God, they glorified him not as God, neither were thankful" (Rom. 1:21). Christian living may well be summarized as devotion to the glory of God and thankfulness to him in everything. Even when eating idol-meat, the Christian voices gratitude to God (1 Cor. 10:30).

There is in this a warning to evangelical Christianity. Certain actions may be condemned for inadequate reasons, and the discerning Christian is called upon to protest. The Fundamentalist attitude toward dancing, movies, and wine often takes an extreme form. These are by nature evil, some say; they are always and everywhere to be resisted. This attitude is "world-renouncing" in its presuppositions. It wrongly regards as intrinsically evil that which is in fact not so. What it condemns may indeed be used evilly, but that does not mean that it is evil in and of itself. There is nothing intrinsically evil about the camera or dancing or wine. The Old Testament speaks of a sacred dance. The Preacher mentioned that there is a "time to dance" and a

[2]F. W. Grosheide, *Commentary on the First Epistle to the Corinthians* (Grand Rapids: Eerdmans, 1952), pp. 243ff.

time for mourning (Eccl. 3:4; cf. Ps. 30:11, Mt. 11:17, Lk. 7:32). Those who have watched or done folk dancing find little or nothing to which a sensitive conscience can object. Cicero is no more right when he says "no one dances unless he is either drunk or mad" than are the extreme Fundamentalists when they say the same thing. Indeed, early Christians used dancing as a part of their public worship. They borrowed from the sacred processions of the Jews and combined their dancing with the singing of hymns.

What has been said of dancing can likewise be said of wine. The Bible points to the bountiful Hebrew vineyards as evidence of the blessing of God. The argument that "wine" in the Bible means unfermented grape juice except for the instance where fermented juice is to be used for medicinal reasons (1 Tim. 5:23) is a weak and unconvincing argument. Yet we shall need to speak later of the way in which prevailing cultural vices intervene to shape special Christian attitudes of protest. It is far more realistic, however, to recognize that the Bible speaks of moderate wine drinking, while it always indicts drunkenness. Otherwise one is embarrassed by the presence of Jesus and his disciples at Cana, and especially by what he did there.

However, the believer's liberty is not liberty to license. This principle of Christian ethics is open to gross misinterpretation and misapplication. Sacrifice and love move in as Christian virtues to take their place alongside liberty. The Christian does not live his life to himself alone. He is a member of a community of redeemed society. He lives his Christian life in the context of other people. What he does will have its effect on them for good or ill. "All things are lawful" may be taken alone and may lead to abuse. It cannot be taken as a self-sufficient principle of Christian action. Its adequacy as a principle depends upon the presence or absence of other circumstances. They may legitimately condition the direction of the person's liberty (Gal. 5:13, 1 Pet. 2:16). The eating of idol-meat is a matter of ethical indifference. But there may be situations in which eating it may be wrong. The believer's freedom in Christ is not the only rule of conduct. Grosheide notes that "a Christian's liberty shall not govern his conduct. This is a point which the apostle has stressed throughout the epistle."[3]

2) Christian liberty is for the purpose of *glorifying God,* and not for purposes of sin. That God forgives the sins of his children cannot be an excuse for moral laxity. The believer has liberty on the ground of redemption. Hence he is "without law to God, but under law to Christ" (1 Cor. 9:21). Whatever he does is to promote the glory of God. Nothing in life is excluded from this purpose — "whether ye eat, or drink, or whatsoever ye do, do all to the glory of God" (1 Cor. 10:31). "And whatsoever ye do in word or deed, do all in the name of the Lord Jesus, giving thanks to God and the Father by him" (Col. 3:17).

[3]*Ibid.,* p. 195.

Christian liberty resists license. Rather, it should make men alive to virtue. It does not give a "free pass" to conduct that is displeasing to the will of God. Calvin aptly says that "being Christians under the law of grace consists not in unbounded license uncontrolled by any law, but in being ingrafted into Christ, by whose grace they are delivered from the curse of the law, and by whose Spirit they have the law inscribed on their hearts."[4] He adds that "a pious man considers this liberty in external things as granted him in order that he may be the better prepared for all the duties of charity."[5]

This liberty is given with the understanding that whatever is expressly forbidden in the Scriptures cannot be practiced to God's glory. The Corinthians pressed "all things are lawful" to mean tolerance for fornication. Here is an example of the principle stretched to include too much. While the Corinthians did not try to justify murder and idolatry from the principle of liberty, they did tolerate sins ranging from quarreling to fornication.

"All things are lawful." This is true. But, from Paul's letter to the Romans, it is clear that sin is not lawful for the Christian. "What shall we say then? Shall we continue in sin that grace may abound? God forbid! How can we that are dead to sin live any longer therein?" (Rom. 6:1ff.).

The "lawful" is never to carry the believer outside the will of God. Lawfulness is bounded by Divine authority. "It is the Christian standing under the command of his Lord who says: all things are lawful to me."[6] "When Christian liberty is elevated to the status of a governing principle, the danger is great that things which are forbidden under all circumstances are thought to be permissible."[7] What is in truth lawful to the Christian never is what has been excluded by the will of God as sinful. Christian liberty offers no basis for infringing the holy law of God. For the believer, "all things are lawful" equals "ye are Christ's, and Christ is God's" (1 Cor. 3:22f.).

To misconstrue Christian liberty means to exchange that liberty for slavery. It is slavery to sin and lawlessness. The believer ought not "be brought under the power of any" but Christ. But a miscarriage of the liberty he has in Christ actually means slavery to sin and his consequent loss of liberty.[8] The believer's conscience is not answerable to human authority, but it is to God. Not even acts which have aspects that God would approve are lawful if they also include elements of wickedness and sin.

As Christian ethics must stand against poor reasons for abstaining from certain practices, it must also stand against bad reasons for indulging in other practices. The Scriptures draw up a rather imposing

[4]*Institutes,* II, viii, lvii.
[5]*Institutes,* III, xix, xii.
[6]Grosheide, *op. cit.,* p. 195.
[7]*Ibid.,* p. 145.
[8]Cf. 1 Cor. 6:12, 3:23, 6:20, 7:23, 9:21, Jn. 8:34, Rom. 6:16, 20.

list of sinful actions and attitudes. This ruling out of certain actions and attitudes as sinful is consistent with the principle of Christian liberty, for we have seen how sin is to be excluded from the area where liberty is to be practiced.

The Pauline list of pagan vices is as conspicuous in his letter as is his tally of Christian virtues. Christian and non-Christian characteristics are seen in vivid contrast to each other. Christian character is born of the grace of God; the non-Christian is under his wrath. Paul makes it plain that the acts of the non-Christian exclude him from citizenship in the Kingdom of God: "Now the works of the flesh are these" — here he lists a frightening number of sins ranging from adultery and fornication to drunkenness and revellings. His closing comment on them is "of the which I tell you before, as I have also told you in time past, that they which do such things shall not inherit the kingdom of God" (Gal. 5:19-21).

Nor does the Pauline index of pagan vices exhaust what is specially forbidden to the believer. The Sermon on the Mount is a disciple's ethic. It goes far beyond mere avoidance of gross pagan acts. A "higher righteousness" is here set forth. This "higher righteousness" is in contrast to the legalistic interpretation of the Mosaic law espoused by the scribes and Pharisees — those self-righteous men who prided themselves on their abstinence from pagan excesses. The ethical teaching of Jesus excludes as sin much that the Pharisee (and the Christian believer) would be prone to excuse in himself. Not only the act of adultery, but also the lustful look; not only murder, but also the flush of anger come under his condemnation. He also considers as sinful the ambiguous oath, hypocritical religious observances, and pretentious charitable acts.

It is quite revealing to compare the ethical teaching of Jesus and Paul with the code of Fundamentalism. Jesus and Paul require moral integrity from within the heart of man. The code of Fundamentalism emphasizes external adherence to a few arbitrary customs and external abstinence from a few arbitrarily prohibited things. When a Fundamentalist is pressed with this analysis, he will, of course, deny it. He, too, is vitally concerned with inner moral integrity. *But* one cannot escape the impression that his main interest is in his code. After all, that is where he focuses attention, that is the subject of his preaching and writing, that is the criterion for fellowship. What other conclusion can an observer draw from hearing so much sound and fury? His impression is that the Fundamentalist is more concerned with his code than with the vast spiritual issues in life — love, kindness, patience, tolerance, pride, self-righteousness, bitterness, or humility.

The Fundamentalist catalogue of "sins" is small and specific: commercial movies, dancing, gambling, card-playing, drinking beer or wine or liquor, and smoking. No "spiritual Christian" will presumably do any of these things, and generally will have little to do with anyone who does do them. Everyone who grows up in this tradition finds that it has a vise-like grip on him. His conscience has been made sensitive to these things by the never-ending tirade against them. If he "weakens" and indulges, he is filled with guilt-feelings as automatically as Pavlov's dog salivated when the bell rang.

Many valid arguments can be marshalled against some of these practices. A thoughtful analysis of all factors involved may lead a person to abstain from smoking. He may not like the taste of a cigarette. The smoke may bother his wife. He may not be able to afford the cost, or he may wish to use the money for some other purpose. He may not like the looks of a person smoking. He may be aware that others about him are sickened by the foulness of his wet cigar. He may be fearful of the possibility of lung cancer. He may feel that the possibility of harm to his respiratory system would be dishonoring to God. He may not like the smell of tobacco clinging to all his clothes. He may not like the possibility of staining his teeth. For any or all of these reasons he may choose not to smoke. But this is a wholly different story from condemning smoking as sin because — well, it's sin, that's all. And from the presupposition that it is sin, the Fundamentalist mind-set will use the above reasons to prove that indeed it is sin. The answer to its moral rightness is already in mind before an investigation of the moral issues is made.

It is against this mind-set in Fundamentalism that the writer wishes to protest. He is not arguing for drinking, for smoking, for dancing, for gambling, even for movie-attendance. But he is concerned lest Christians confuse ethical living with an arbitrary legalistic bondage. He is concerned lest externals become so prominent that internal virtues and vices are not treated at all. A proper emphasis must be restored to ethical thinking in evangelicalism so that the vicious sins of the spirit are seen as Jesus saw them.

The preferable approach to Christian conduct is to see how New Testament principles applied to the problems of the early church. Then, one must apply the principles in the Spirit to contemporary problems. What is clearly sin must be so recognized. It is never right. It is well that the believer know why it is prohibited. But prohibition merely because of an inherited bias involves two dangers. One is the legalizing of the Christian life. The other is a blunting of ethical maturity. The believer must come to ethical manhood himself by justifying his activity and motives constantly to a clear conscience before God and his word.

3) The believer is to beware *defiling his conscience*. Since the physical world is morally neutral, it can be used for good or for evil. The conscience of the believer is under no prior legislative bondage as he approaches this world. But what is permitted generally may not be permitted in the life of a particular believer in a particular situation. Without question Christian liberty is a possession of great moral gain for the believer. Yet whatever disrupts his communion with God, or weakens his appetite for the Bible, or dulls his concern for others, must

be set aside. "All things are lawful for me, but not all things are expedient" (1 Cor. 6:12). The spiritual health and well-being of the person takes its place alongside the glory of God as a major consideration in Christian ethics. Hence, the principle of inward intention and inner consequences becomes vital for ethical living.

This has broad implication in modern life. No two people are the same. This is a truism. That may be why we tend to forget it. Much energy is spent trying to mass-produce Christians off the same assembly line so that they will all come out liking and disliking the same things, approving and disapproving the same things, doing and avoiding the same things. There is little recognition of the individual. And yet it is each individual person who is to grow into ethical manhood. Each person is tempted according to the bent of his character. And he must cope with his temptation from within his own maturity in the process of sanctification.

What is the proper amount of food for one person may be gluttonous for another. What is proper toil for one may be overwork for another. What is a matter of sexual indifference to one may be sexual temptation for another. In any case, it is clear that no external laws can be passed that will prescribe what will defile a conscience and what will not. What may be harmless to one may be sin to another. Some are prone to certain temptations, others not so. The same temptation will appeal to the same person more at one time than at another.

The Christian who is maturing in his relationship with God finds that he constantly sees the world with new eyes. He sees dangers he did not see before. He discovers that there are areas in his life which are not yet under the lordship of Christ. He yields more of what he is to the sanctifying Spirit. This means that he never views the ethical problems that arise in his life as identical problems. He never sees them in the same perspective — for he has changed.

Therefore, he — and only he before God — can judge when his conscience is defiled. He must decide for himself what will be the inner spiritual consequences of his participation in any given action or program. He — before God — must pass judgment on his motives and desires.

The Christian is to have a "good" or "pure" conscience. Paul took great care to "have always a conscience void of offence toward God . . ." (Acts 24:16). He endeavored to live "in all good conscience before God" (23:1). As he closed his ministry, he wrote to Timothy mentioning that he served God "with pure conscience" (2 Tim. 1:3). This idea recurs throughout his letters. "For our rejoicing is this, the testimony of our conscience, that in simplicity and godly sincerity, not with fleshly wisdom, but by the grace of God, we have had our conversation in the world . . ." (2 Cor. 1:12). "Now the end of the commandment is charity out of a pure heart and of a good conscience, and of faith unfeigned" (1 Tim. 1:5). He urges deacons to be chosen from among those "holding the mystery of the faith in a pure conscience" (1 Tim. 3:9).

This concern for a pure conscience is not found only in Paul's epistles. The author of Hebrews requests his correspondents to "pray for us, for we trust we have a good conscience, in all things willing to live honestly" (Heb. 13:18). Peter connects salvation with "the answer of a good conscience toward God" (1 Pet. 3:21).

The benefits of cultivating the pure conscience are cumulative. Each time temptation is resisted the spirit is tempered more. There is stronger resistance to the next temptation. But when the believer yields to temptation against the protests of his conscience, the seeds of moral decline are planted. Ethical deterioration in a Christian's life always has a "case history." And an invariable element in his decline is the surrender of the pure conscience and repeated defiling of his conscience by known sin.

The believer is to be a pilgrim in the world. If he makes the world his home, the result will be a defiled conscience. He abides in God as he gives witness to the world. If he abides in the world, he loses his ambassadorship to it. He is to be as Christ was — the friend of sinners who was not conditioned by their sin, but who disclosed it to them by his purity.

However, some of the world's activity is decisively closed to the Christian at all times. Adultery is never an option of Christian liberty. The believer cannot excuse a professional visit to a prostitute by saying he is there to witness to her. Other departments of the world will be closed to some Christians because of their conscience. The believer who cannot visit the world without making it his home has no right to visit it at his weak points. His Christian life withers when he dwells in the world. His conscience becomes defiled and he is the only one to know when this takes place.

This warning against defiling the conscience concerns the Christian in his relation to the *adiaphora,* i.e., those things which are neither commanded nor prohibited in the Scripture. Defilement may come from that which is not strictly sinful. Excessive attachment may convert an otherwise innocent attachment into idolatry and profitless bondage. The believer who "cannot live" without his "hi-fi" collection has become the servant of "hi-fi" and has defiled his conscience. The believer who can enjoy "hi-fi," who can praise God for the pleasures it brings, who can do without it when circumstances of the Lord's doing dictate, continues to live in all good conscience before God.

4) The believer should *place no "stumbling-block" before weaker believers.*[9] "Take heed lest by any means this liberty of yours become a stumbling-block to them that are weak" (1 Cor. 8:9). Paul continues that "all things are lawful: but not all things edify" (1 Cor. 10:23).

Liberty is therefore limited by the principle of expediency. Action must be judged good or bad in the light of its effect on the moral and

[9]Cf. Rom. 14:1, 3, 15:1, 1 Cor. 8:9, 10:23, 25, 29, 32, Gal. 5:13.

religious life both of the doer and of all those whom he may influence. The believer cannot do what is innocent for himself if his action will have a harmful effect on others. There is no such thing as an isolated Christian; he belongs to the redeemed community. He has binding responsibilities to all other members of that community. He cannot disregard the weak from his superior position of strength (if strength it be). He exists, in one sense, for his neighbor's good. ("Let no man seek his own, but every man another's," 1 Cor. 10:24.) He is not to use his "liberty for an occasion of the flesh, but [he is] by love [to] serve . . . another" (Gal. 5:13). He will exercise his freedom in conformity to the higher law of love. Love does not insist upon its own rights when that means trampling upon another's conscience. Love will not act so as to dull another's spiritual sensitivity. Love will not knowingly draw another into sin. Love smoothes out the path for the other person; it does not place stumbling-blocks before him.[10]

The illustration in 1 Corinthians 8 is graphic. A weaker brother sees a believer eating meat in an idol's temple. This may be an official ceremony which would be held in the temple as part of the normal routine of pagan city life. The weaker believer concludes that it is right for believers to eat meat offered to idols, but in doing so he is led back into idol worship. Or it may be he still thinks that the idols are real gods, and his conscience is defiled by his "worshipping" of the idol as he eats. Disregard for the scruples of the weak may mean he perishes. It is sin against him (v. 11) and against Christ (v. 12).

Therefore Paul practices what is consistent with liberty held in love: *forevermore* he will eat no idol-meat whenever this would seduce a brother to sin (1 Cor. 8:13). This principle is reinforced in 1 Corinthians 10:28. The believer may attend a pagan feast with clear conscience, *but* "if any man say unto you, This hath been offered in sacrifice, eat not, for his sake that showed it, and for conscience' sake: conscience, I say, not thine own, but the other's." The context here is not clear whether the protest is voiced by a weaker Christian or by an unbeliever. If it comes from a weaker brother it may be to remind him that idols are supposed to be an abomination to him; if from an unbeliever, it may be to embarrass him over his attendance at the feast. In either case, the believer is to affirm his faith in the Living God and to abstain from eating the meat. He voluntarily suspends his freedom to eat lest the other person be offended or misled. This is honoring the conscience of the other.

How far is one to go in self-denial for the sake of a weaker brother? When does honoring the weaker brother's conscience really confirm him in a false interpretation of ethical living? If he pleads "weak conscience" to further his own will to power, what then?

[10]"Our liberty should be used, if it conduces to our neighbor's edification; but if that be not beneficial to our neighbor, it should be abridged." Calvin, *Institutes,* III, xix, xii.

Paul stressed that some practices are not a matter of conscience at all. Other Christian leaders objected. In the clash of opinion and argument, Paul firmly held the precedence of Christian liberty. For instance, Paul withstood Peter before the Church at Galatia when Peter weakened and tried to bring Christians again under the bondage of the Jewish system. There was more than a matter of conscience at stake here. Some would not hesitate to charge Peter with hypocrisy. The principle of salvation by faith alone was in jeopardy. This principle was far more important than the erroneous conscience of one man.

Again, the Christian will need to distinguish between the weaker brother who is genuinely offended and the cavilling brother who uses an appeal to conscience as a tool to serve his own ends. Jesus sharply rebuked the religious hypocrite (Mt. 15:14), and none can be more hypocritical than one who pleads "conscience" to further his own cause. Christian judgment faces one of its most demanding tasks when the performance of an act harms someone, while its omission would harm someone else, as is sometimes the case in questions of Christian liberty.

The weaker brother is not to be looked down upon as narrow. He is fully a person in his own right — indeed, he is one for whom Christ died. And so he is to be respected. He is not to be engaged in "doubtful disputations" nor in debates that deal only with vain reasonings (Rom. 14:1). Nor is the weaker to be baited into protest by a deliberate course of action which the stronger pursues. The weaker believer may have an overly sensitive conscience from universalizing his own ethical predicament. The stronger may realize this, and may desire to snap him out of it. And so he sets about to force the weaker to participate in some action in which his conscience at present condemns him. This provocative conduct by the stronger may be quite sinful since it may be motivated more by "right" than by love.

Neither is the weaker believer to be offended by a false impression that the stronger is ethically indifferent or insensitive. Such conduct by the stronger that would lead the weaker to entertain such thoughts is dangerously close to sin. The weaker may suspect the stronger of hypocrisy. Rather, the stronger believer is in love to enlighten the conscience of the weaker, and to lead him from service of false scruples to service of the living God in liberty.

Nor can the believer continue in a practice which offends the conscience of another believer, even though it does not lead that one into an act of sin. In commenting on Paul's statement that "when ye sin so against the brethren, and wound their weak conscience, ye sin against Christ," Godet remarks, "Every violence done to a brother's conscience, even though he should not thereby be drawn into a deed of unfaithfulness, is a sin committed against Christ." Grosheide says, "A Christian need not allow his liberty to be curtailed by somebody else. But he is obliged to take care that that other person does not fall into sin and if he would hurt that other person's conscience he has not fulfilled that obligation." With this perspective, Paul summarizes the whole law as neighbor-love: "For all the law is fulfilled in this: thou shalt love thy neighbor as thyself" (Gal. 5:14). A lack of neighbor-love becomes a lack of love for God.

A practice which is contrary to the dictates of a brother's conscience can be carried on only alongside of an enlightening of that brother's conscience. This education is to be done with love. Love would not allow a brother to continue bound by a sub-Christian view of the freedom he has in Christ. But love is also committed to self-denial for the sake of the brother. So the Christian must lift him to a higher morality, not cause him to stumble by prematurely forcing his conscience.

The weaker brother's pitfalls are two: wrongly considering an innocent or indifferent act as intrinsically evil, and as a result of this overscrupulousness, neglecting his responsibility as a Christian witness in certain cultural enterprises. Because he may view movies as being "of the world" and therefore evil, he may fail to see their value as a means of spreading the Gospel, let alone of cultural uplift.

The stronger believer must avoid two dangers: he may so greatly react against the immaturity and prejudice of the weak conscience that he moves into areas that are in fact objectionable, and he may exercise his liberty in such a way that he leads the weaker one into sin or into a defiled conscience. He may, for instance, be convinced he has the liberty to drink wine with his dinner; and in his reaction against the prejudice of the weaker Christian, he may become defiantly proud of his "right." Or he may persuade the weaker to "share this liberty" and drink wine with him — and so cause the weaker to defile his conscience.

The lordship of Christ does not work itself out into the life as a vague religious feeling. Rather, it expresses itself practically by a whole-soul love for God and love for neighbor as one's self. These are the guideposts of the distinctive New Testament morality. The believing church will always be made up of weaker and stronger members. Paul pleads for good will and understanding between them: "We that are strong ought to bear the infirmities of the weak, and not to please ourselves. Let every one of us please his neighbor for his good to edification" (Rom. 15:1-2). The church must not be splintered over questions of conscience. Instead, Christians are to live in love and peace with one another regardless of these differences. They are to live above antipathy and strife. Rather than live in strife, they are to strive for mutual understanding and for each other's good. "Now the God of patience and consolation grant you to be likeminded one toward another according to Jesus Christ: that ye may with one mind glorify God, even the Father of our Lord Jesus Christ. Wherefore receive ye one another, as Christ also received us to the glory of God" (Rom. 15:5ff.). The Greek word translated "receiving" is "taking to oneself with tenderness," as Godet points out. Our Lord so receives believers in Romans 15:7 and John

14:3. And with like words in Romans 14:1 Paul urges the believer to reach out in love to the weaker brethren: "Him that is weak in the faith receive ye (take to yourselves with tenderness)."

The stronger believer is free to change his conduct. He can exercise his right or he can waive it. Wisdom may dictate one course or the other, and he has liberty to adapt himself to circumstances. But the weaker has no options. He is bound inwardly. Paul does not expect initiative from him, for he is incapable of flexibility. Rather, Paul looks to the stronger believer to live with a sense of give-and-take. There are to be no attitudes of superiority or inferiority, no contempt for the weak, no condemnation of the strong.

Both the weak and the strong are equal before God and before the law of love. "But why dost thou (the weak) judge thy brother? Or why dost thou (the strong) set at nought thy brother? For we shall all stand before the judgment seat of Christ" (Rom. 14:10). It is against this setting — the judgment of all on equal terms — that Paul develops the obligation of all Christians to live with understanding and affection for each other. "For one believeth that he may eat all things; another, who is weak, eateth herbs. Let not him that eateth despise him that eateth not; and let not him which eateth not judge him that eateth: for God hath received him. Who art thou that judgeth another man's servant? To his own master he standeth or falleth. Yea, he shall be holden up: for God is able to make him stand" (14:2-4). Each must come to conviction of right and wrong before God, and then he must avoid an inevitable temptation — to despise those weaker than himself, and to judge those who exercise more liberty.

"One man esteemeth one day above another: another esteemeth every day alike. Let every man be fully persuaded in his own mind. He that regardeth the day, regardeth it unto the Lord; and he that regardeth not the day, to the Lord he doth not regard it. He that eateth, eateth to the Lord, for he giveth God thanks; and he that eateth not, to the Lord he eateth not, and giveth God thanks. For none of us liveth to himself, and no man dieth to himself. For whether we live, we live unto the Lord; and whether we die, we die unto the Lord: whether we live, therefore, or die, we are the Lord's" (14:5-8). And so all conduct must spring from one central motive — to honor the Lord. But the individual Christian may have greater or lesser liberty in his conduct, depending upon the freedom his conscience grants him in honoring the Lord.

The tension between abstaining and partaking is therefore resolved by acknowledging the liberty Christ grants the believer as well as the claim Christ has upon him. Legalism is ruled out as a solution. But casuistry, or the application of revealed general principles to particular cases, is not. Conduct must be forged by spiritual decision before the fires of motive and judged by conscience. May I as a believer partake in this activity or that pleasure? If my conscience will allow me to do it "to the Lord" and give thanks for it, then most assuredly I may. If my conscience does not give me liberty, then I may not. For it is to God and not to men that we must give account for our conduct.

5) The believer's liberty is *not to be misused lest the cause of the Gospel is reproached by unbelievers.*

"Sanctify Christ as Lord in your hearts . . . having a good conscience; that, whereas they speak evil of you, as of evildoers, they may be ashamed that falsely accuse your good conversation in Christ" (1 Pet. 3:15f.). The Christian's walk must not give the lie to his confession. It is rather to buttress the witness of his mouth. The accusations of his enemies are to be shown to be slander by the purity of his life. "Their life was . . . to keep pace with their speech."[11] No comfort is to be given the enemy's camp through moral neglect or misbehavior.

The principle of abstention for the sake of others covers more than the single instance of eating sacrificial meat. Paul broadens it into a general application. The believer will place no block or needless offense in the path of anyone wherever he meets him. This includes non-Christians. "Give no occasion of stumbling either to Jews, or the Greeks, or the church of God; even as I also please all men in all things, not seeking mine own profit, but the profit of many, that they may be saved. Be ye imitators of me, even as I also am of Christ" (1 Cor. 10:32f., 11:1). Christian liberty is concerned to rescue men from sin, and hardly to encourage them in it.

6) The Christian is *not to make common cause with the unbeliever,* but is prohibited from an entrance into pagan life for a mutual effort and aim.

Believers are not to be "unequally yoked together with unbelievers" (2 Cor. 6:14). This prohibition applies to more than just marriage. It also precludes any association "in which the unbelieving partner forms the standard which determines the mode of thought and action of the Christian partner."[12] There can be no intimate relationship between lives based on such divergent premises. Two cannot walk together closely unless they are in agreement. The believer has Christ, righteousness, peace, and the prospect of eternal glory. The unbeliever lives in revolt against God. The two mix together in close unity no better than oil mixes with water.

7) The believer may in special times and places be *answerable to an interim code as a temporary or local expedient.* This phrase, "interim ethics," is here used in an altogether different sense from that of Albert Schweitzer, who makes the phrase stand for Jesus' ethics as a whole conditioned by apocalyptic expectation. But interim ethics, as the writer employs the term, is only a small part of the whole of New Testament ethics. And it does not arise out of an apprehension over the nearness

[11]W. H. Griffith-Thomas, *The Apostle Peter: A Devotional Commentary* (Grand Rapids: Eerdmans, 1946), p. 209.
[12]H. A. W. Meyer, *Commentary on II Corinthians* 6:14.

of the eschatological climax. Nor does it imply that God could not have looked ahead and made laws binding throughout all history; indeed, no revisionary standpoint is here implied with reference to revealed moral principles and commandments. The necessity for temporary or interim ethics arises from the particular direction which godlessness and sin take in a particular place and time. It is in this light that we are to interpret a passage like 1 Corinthians 11:1-16, which indicts women who go out into the street with uncovered heads. In Corinth at that time, the bared head in public was a mark of a whore. Christian decency and modesty therefore required that Christian women be covered in Corinth. The basic principles are modesty, propriety, and order. These may express themselves in numerous ways, depending upon the varying social customs of differing cultures. But never is the principle, regardless of how it is expressed, to be violated. To make long hair mandatory for all women of all times is to miss the point. To insist upon decorum and modesty at all times is to rightly apply the passage.

It is here that church manuals gain significance. They go beyond church covenants or laws imposed upon believers as the decrees of religion and morality in the name of the church pointing out what is commanded or forbidden in Scripture. Rather, they contain "counsels" giving earnest advice for Christian conduct in the light of the customs of the world about. The danger lies in this: that adherence to them will become the criterion of the true believer. This leads directly into a deceptive legalism and invites a false self-assurance. However, these "counsels," as they are interpreted against the broadened background of New Testament morality, aid in the application of biblical principles to the climate of the present age. These counsels will have to be revised periodically as the culture itself changes.

An example is the attitude of the churches toward alcoholic beverages in the face of the liquor traffic in America. Arnold Toynbee has noted the prominent connection between the vice of drunkenness and the internal decay of sixteen out of the nineteen civilizations preceding ours. The liquor traffic has made alcoholism a major blot on American life. Only where evangelical Christianity thrives does this traffic face serious obstacles today. The liquor commerce tolerates alcohol education and temperance campaigns, but fights prohibition and opposes politicians favorable to local option. Alert to the special viciousness of the liquor traffic in our generation, Baptist churches frequently include in their church covenants a pledge of abstinence from the sale and use of alcoholic beverages.

Here also is an appropriate place to discuss "separation." This word is a shibboleth among Fundamentalists. "Come out from among them and be separate" may be used as a biblical excuse for cantankerous divisiveness, for a falsely pious withdrawal from non-Christian friends and their activities, or for an evasion of civic responsibilities. On the other hand, inclusivistic churchmen sometimes carry on as if an apostate and idolatrous church were an impossibility in the twentieth century. And some worldlings in the churches act as if "Christian broadness" requires whole-souled indulgence in the spirit of the age.

The biblical doctrine of separation includes man's separation *unto* God as fully as his separation *from* the world. The initial idea of separation in Genesis 12:1ff. is of Abraham's enlistment in the Divine purpose. The idea of separation from evil is only implicit. Israel is separate from the other nations only in and through God's choice of her as his own special people (Dt. 7:1ff., 14:2).

The great purpose of God in separating for himself a people is not that they develop a negative or passive attitude toward certain areas of life. Rather, it is that they be conformed to the character of the Living God. Jesus reserved some of his most scathing denunciation for those whose separation was only legalistic negativism. Separation unto God does not imply that separation from evil is unimportant, but only that separation from evil is the correlate of an intimate personal fellowship with the Living God.

Granting that separation is primarily unto God, not from evil, how much of the culture of the world about shall the Christian assimilate? It is, of course, impossible for him to escape from being greatly influenced by his cultural setting. Culture does much to make him what he is as a person. The question is not, Shall he withdraw from his culture in protest against it? for he can no more withdraw from it than can the fish from water. The question is rather, From what areas of his culture shall he withdraw?

Modern art, for instance, may show the inner mind-set of a culture in revolt against God. This may be equally true of music, sculpture, and writing. Yet, if the grace of God is operative in cultural expression restraining sin in its worst manifestations and making possible classic expressions of the temper of the culture, there is a legitimate field of interest for the believer. If the believer is limited only to those areas of the culture which deal directly and adequately with the claim of Christ upon that culture, he is limited indeed. The newspaper, the literary magazine, the scholarly journals, radio, television, the symphony, and baseball are all closed to him. In fact, he can no longer be a modern man; he must transform himself into a *homo medievalensis*. Because man is personally involved in his culture, Christian personal ethics has an expanding front that soon is Christian social ethics.

But this is no mere plea for acquiescence in the cultural setting. There is vital need for the Christian to beware of defiling his conscience. He must scrupulously examine his inner life and his motives. He must exercise his Christian liberty with the utmost care. One who has no appreciation for art may find in art little more than sexual stimulation; one who has no taste for great literature may find only smut in the classics. And what defiles the conscience is sin.

It was a famous quip of the preacher Blumhardt that man requires two conversions: one from the natural life to the spiritual, and then, to avoid asceticism, from the spiritual to the natural. One who has a concern to find in cultural expression the best achievements of common grace and who has a desire to infuse into the general life of humanity the higher motif of redemption can walk in the midst of what may defile a weaker conscience. And he can be an ambassador.[13] Designation of what aspects of the cultural enterprise are open to the Christian can never be a matter of legislation. All things are pure to the pure. But one must take care that he does not become the slave of some cultural practice. Any aspect of the cultural setting, music or art or writing or sports, can easily become lord and master of even a believer's life. He is to have only one lord and master, God.

[13]An instructive dissertation is Gerard L. Ellspermann's *The Attitude of the Early Christian Latin Writers Toward Pagan Literature and Learning* (Washington, D.C.: The Catholic University of America Press, 1949). The experience of Jerome stands on one side; his heart given to his pagan library, he confessed himself "a Ciceronian, not a Christian," and, after his regeneration, declared "O Lord, if ever again I possess worldly books or read them, I have denied thee" (*ibid.*, pp. 160f.). Augustine too could ask: "What did it profit me that I, the base slave of vile affections, read unaided, and understood, all the books I could get of the so-called liberal arts" and again, "I learned, indeed, in them many useful words; but these may be learned in things not vain, and that is the safe way for youths to walk in" (*ibid.*, pp. 196, 198), but he could also say that "the Christian, when he separates himself in spirit from the miserable fellowship of these men, ought to take away from them" the branches of heathen learning and influence, "and to devote [them] to their proper use in preaching the gospel. Their garments also — that is, human institutions such as are adapted to that intercourse with men which is indispensable in this life — we must take and turn to a Christian use" (*ibid.*, pp. 182f.).

19

THE HOLY SPIRIT, THE CHRISTIAN ETHICAL DYNAMIC

THE SPIRIT IS THE dynamic principle of Christian ethics, the personal agency whereby God powerfully enters human life and delivers man from enslavement to Satan, sin, death, and law. The Spirit of God is not listed under "others" in the *dramatis personae* of redemption. He is a main character whose role is crucial for the life of holiness in all its phases.

What immense consequences follow from this is soberingly disclosed when the moral failure of paganism is set side by side with the moral achievement of redemptive ethics. "Pagan philosophy," Henson noted in his Gifford Lectures, "was morally powerless to cleanse and elevate the habits of pagan society."[1] The Gentile world lay irrecoverably in the grip of that wickedness which the New Testament sums up in its index of vices. The worst features of that pre-Christian way of life are too shocking even to describe. "The golden age of ancient philosophy was in some important respects morally infamous, and the grosser scandals of antiquity — slavery, infanticide, sexual perversion, suicide, and the bloody shows of the arena — flourished in a society which held philosophers in high regard."[2]

Despite the crude charges about Christian conduct circulated at first by hostile Jews, opponents of Christianity stood with its friends in attesting to the purity of life it engendered, and to the "new world of moral power, of earnestness, and of holiness" in which believers moved. Pliny felt compelled to inform Trajan that his examinations, instead of finding anything criminal or vicious, disclosed the Christian gatherings to be concerned with self-confirmation in conscientious and virtuous living. "Even those who consider all religions, including Christianity, to be merely idiosyncracies, and view progress as entirely identical with the moral progress of mankind — even such observers must admit that in these days progress did depend upon the Christian churches, and that history then had recourse to a prodigious and paradoxical system of levers in order to gain a higher level of human evolution."[3] The early apologists knew they were on secure ground when they stressed that by embracing the Gospel the ignoble rose to moral strength and worth, and that the weak and poor were remarkably changed by a Divine power.

[1]H. H. Henson, *Christian Morality*, p. 129.
[2]*Ibid.*, p. 131.
[3]A. Harnack, *The Expansion of Christianity*, p. 260.

It was the Holy Spirit alone who had transformed the inescapable and distressing "I ought" which philosophical ethics was compelled to acknowledge and the tormenting "thou shalt" which Hebrew religion adduced as its complement into the "I will" of New Testament ethical dedication and zeal. While other religions and moral philosophies have pursued ethical ideals, it "remained for Christianity to offer, and to provide, the secret of the doing." It is characteristic of the religion of Christ to say not simply you *must,* with an absolute sanction and validity absent outside Hebrew-Christian revelation, but you *can,* and to show how the amazing quality of the Christ-life can be shared and approximated even before it becomes a fully accomplished fact in the life to come. Plato's ethical synthesis, Aristotle's plea for discipline and habit, the Stoic inhibitive controls, and whatever else the world of philosophical ethics resorted to in an effort to supply an objective dynamic for moral achievement — all these failed to sustain any comparable moral energy and enthusiasm. By purifying the motives of men redemptively, and making available to them a superhuman power of achievement, Christianity flooded its mission fields with a tide of ethical vitality.

The arena of Christian ethics also displayed a moral requirement vastly higher than that of its pagan alternatives. Infanticide, slavery, religious prostitution, which are for us incomprehensible, were by them unquestioned. The speculative moralities, despite lower standards, and a conditioning of salvation on works, were unable to achieve any extensive realization in human life of the higher ideals they championed. Christianity holds before man the absolute perfection of a revealed ethics, and through the power of redemption and the Spirit-sustained life it supplies man with hitherto-unknown reservoirs of moral energy. Pentecost marked the beginning of a distinct era in the moral history of man. Outside Christianity one might find occasional mention of God the Father and indefinite references to the Spirit of God. But the Christian movement alone uncovered a new life in the Holy Spirit grounded in the Son. Its moral horizon, consequently, was nothing less than an absolute ethical perfection, conformity to the will of God.[4]

Not only in respect of standards and of dynamic did Christian ethics contrast favorably with even the highest moral philosophy of its day, but also in the matter of the enlistment of the masses. The great Stoic moralists, whom Lightfoot likened to "professors without any students," were not alone in the ancient world in their failure to "influence the mainstream of pagan life and society."[5] Because of its one-sided "upper

[4]Lindsay Dewar remarks that "the Christian ethic was from the first in a real sense an ethic of the Holy Spirit. . . . He is . . . the generating power and the moral criterion of the first Christians." *An Outline of New Testament Ethics,* p. 102.

[5]The world need not be conscious of a staggering transformation actually under way in its very midst. Most sinners close their eyes deliberately to Christian influences, until one day they find men of their insensitivities no longer in the vanguard of leadership, but on the defensive morally and spiritually. The power of a vital morality does not depend upon a counting of professional noses. The

class" orientation, the classical world did not suspect that a moral revolution was already in progress and was making remarkable gains. A striking evidence of supernatural power was found by the early Christian movement in the circumstance that not the wise and the noble were the characteristic center of its ethical endeavor; rather, poor and weak and underprivileged men were divinely transformed into morally robust leaders.

Henson is right that "the collapse of the distinctive Christian morality would imply nothing less formidable than the moral bankruptcy of the human race."[6] "There has been nothing less than a revolution in the moral sphere, and that revolution is the achievement of Christianity."[7] It stands vindicated as the only moral force that can raise ethically bankrupt individuals and a corrupt society to a higher plane. Therefore it holds an indisputable relevance today. "That old world ended in irredeemable collapse," wrote John Smith, of the civilizations of ancient times. "Despite the periods of ascent under the spell of great religious leaders, in such nations as Greece and Rome, India and China, the traces of degeneracy over wide areas and through long centuries are unmistakable. What arrested that collapse, and breathed into corrupt peoples life from the dead, and built up the modern world on new ethical foundations, was the spiritual force which entered the world in Judaism when it had reached full expression in Christianity."[8]

In *The Expansion of Christianity,* Harnack observed that "if the early Christians always looked out for the proofs of the Spirit and of power, they did so from the standpoint of their *moral* and *religious* energy, since it was for the sake of the latter object that these gifts had been bestowed upon the church. . . . Moral regeneration and the moral life were not merely *one* side of Christianity to Paul, but its very fruit and goal on earth."[9] While one might hesitate to adopt Harnack's judgment that the Christian mission is adequately described as simply the labor of "awakening and strengthening . . . the moral sense,"[10] there can be no doubt that "Christians of the sub-apostolic age . . . the apologists and great Christian fathers like Tertullian and Origen" everywhere exhibit "the ethical demands occupying the front rank.

pagan world was unconscious of the significance of Christianity for three whole centuries. "The greatest religious change in the history of mankind," wrote Lecky in his *History of European Morals,* took place "under the eyes of a brilliant galaxy of philosophers and historians" who disregarded "as simply contemptible an agency which all men must now admit to have been, for good or for evil, the most powerful moral lever that has ever been applied to the affairs of men" (I, 338).

[6]Henson, *op. cit.,* p. 56.

[7]*Ibid.,* p. 134.

[8]John Smith, *The Integrity of Scripture,* p. 206.

[9]Harnack, *op. cit.,* p. 258.

[10]*Ibid.,* p. 259.

They are thrust forward almost with wearisome diffuseness and with a rigorous severity."[11]

The New Testament depicts the ethical as the supreme and permanent work of the Spirit. Paul begins his survey of the ideal life by characteristic references to its redemptive foundation, and he repeatedly concludes his practical exhortation to godly living with a reference to the power of the Spirit (cf. Rom. 15:13). Miracles, tongues, and prophecies appear as temporary phenomena, expedient for superior purposes; the moral ministry of the Spirit in the on-going life of the people of God is indispensable. Prophecy is superior to glossology, but transcending all 'charismata' is the grace of love (1 Cor. 12:31 - 14:1). The other elements pass away (13:8), but faith, hope, and love abide forever; the abnormal yields to the normal and ethical as the permanent center of Divine interest. The infant Christian communities learned from Paul that "the genuine action of the Spirit . . . is a power for worthy living. For those who assimilated the apostle's teaching, the Spirit became the normal principle of Christian life and conduct."[12] The distinctive Christian graces are grounded in the Spirit. The Spirit's work is not to be contrasted with moral transformation. Rather, the ethical renewal of the people of God is his central concern. Paul states bluntly: "God hath not called us to uncleanness, but to holiness" (1 Thess. 4:7). Phillips, in his *Letters to Young Churches,* renders the subsequent verse: "It is not for nothing that the Spirit God gives us is called the *Holy* Spirit."

Men may complain of the lackadaisical ethics of the Christian community today, and their grumble is not wholly without basis. The real reason, however, is not the absence of a superlative dynamic from Christianity, but "the large number of 'Christians' whose religion is almost entirely second hand, and who know next to nothing of a day-by-day friendship with God. . . . Christ can and does actually give Himself to, share His mind with, put His Spirit into" those who really seek the will of God for their lives.[13]

Ethical mediocrity is ignoble for the believer because contentment with an average moral life is a renunciation of the rule of the Spirit and a resignation and deterioration to a grade of ethics beneath the dignity of the New Testament. Life without the Spirit's fullness is ethically dwarfed. Morality divorced from the new life in the Spirit deteriorates to the shadowland of worldly ethics.

The salvation of the sinner is primarily ethical. Jesus' purpose in the incarnation is to "save his people from their sins" (Matt. 1:21), and

[11]*Ibid.,* pp. 259f. Justin Martyr was able to describe the moral earnestness of the Christian believers: "The disciples of Christ die daily, torturing their desires and mortifying them according to the divine scriptures; for we have no part at all in shameless desires, or scenes impure, or glances lewd, or ears attentive to evil, lest our souls thereby be wounded" (Apol. xxvi).

[12]H. A. A. Kennedy, *The Theology of the Epistles,* p. 91.

[13]E. S. Woods, in *The Inner Life* (by members of the Church of England), pp. 112f.

his atonement had in view man's redemption "from all iniquity, and [to] purify unto himself a people for his own possession, zealous of good works" (Tit. 2:14). Its end is not simply deliverance from hell and its misery, but predominantly an "ethical rescue and recovery" and "the impartation of a holy principle into the life, the restoration of the Divine image of purity, the re-establishment of communion with the holy God. . . . The whole Christian conception of soteriology centers in the fact that men are to cease to be and to do evil, and learn to be and to do good. . . . Salvation is therefore an ethical recovery and restoration, or it is not Christian."[14]

The decisive criterion of Christian living is the place of the Spirit in the believer's life.[15] The new moral power and ethical vitality are grounded in the "life-creating Spirit" (1 Cor. 15:45). As in the first creation man is distinguished by the Divine inbreathing of the "breath of life" (Gen. 2:7), so in regeneration the Holy Spirit supplies the dynamic of the believer's new existence. Pentecost affords a graphic fulfillment of the Old Testament prophetic conjunction of an extraordinary visitation of the Spirit with the promised Day of the Lord (Joel 2:28f.), enforced by Jesus' references to the gift of the Spirit. Thereafter the transforming moral enthusiasm and energy of the infant Christian movement were traced invariably to the Spirit. He was represented as Divine wind and fire carrying forward the ethical energies of the faithful with a vivid warmth and purity.

The New Testament doctrine of the good life, therefore, can no more be elaborated without decisive reference to the Holy Spirit than can its doctrine of sin and evil without reference to Satan.[16] What is good in human life has its inseparable source in the operation of the Spirit. Paul not only holds that morality is grounded in the righteous being and will of God, but that "the moral objective cannot be reached, or

[14]L. S. Keyser, *A Manual of Christian Ethics,* pp. 151f.

[15]Harnack thinks that the gradual adaptation of the Christian movement to a worldly life came in part through a vanishing discipline in view of the easier church attitude toward post-baptismal sins. Numerous passages in Tertullian's and Origen's writings indicate that "the Christian churches, together with their bishops and clergy, were no longer what they had previously been, from a moral point of view" and yet the apologistic replies to enemies of the Christian movement (cf. Origen vs. Celsus) make it apparent that "their morals still continued to excel the morals of other guilds within the empire and of the population of the various cities." But the decisive turn, Harnack suggests, is that whereas "the churches hitherto had been societies which admitted people under the burden of sin, not denying entrance even to the worst offender, but securing him forgiveness with God and thereafter requiring him to continue pure and holy, now they had established themselves voluntarily or involuntarily as societies based on unlimited forgiveness." Alongside baptism developed a second sacrament, the sacrament of penitence, and then the distinction of a two-level morality, one for the perfect, and another morality adequate for others. Harnack is right in contrasting this with the Gnostic thesis that a qualitative distinction of grades of human beings exists according to moral capacity, but wrong in finding in Paul "evident traces" of the two-level theory of morality because of his distinction of children and the mature or perfect.

[16]Hence the Spirit appears as the believer's ally in his warfare against sin and Satan (Gal. 5:16ff., Eph. 6:17).

even approached, apart from the help (or, to use the Pauline term, 'grace') of God . . . without this man is helpless."[17] The power to attain Christian ideals is not inherent in man's will as sinner, but requires the determinate activity of the Spirit. True morality is no mere mechanical result of even the regenerate disposition of the believer. He must be continually confirmed in grace. The sinner delivered from guilt through the acceptance of Christ no doubt can attain a higher moral expression and dignity through an awakened conscience. But redemption places an ethical power that is supernatural at his constant disposal. The moral ideal Christ set in the flesh is not to be realized merely by imitation, but by a Divine spiritual reign in the lives of believers. God must communicate to them the dynamic for the transformation of character and the realization of the new life.

Where the Holy Spirit is not the empowering agent of ethical effort, where he is neglected or excluded, the result is either a mottled morality that cannot fully claim to be Christian, or a grafting of some features of Christian behavior on an essentially unregenerate base. "No duty can be truly performed," wrote Keyser, "unless it has as its source and motive power the fact and consciousness of redemption by Christ and regeneration by the Holy Spirit. All other ethics is merely natural ethics under certain influences."[18] How sadly in error, therefore, are those interpreters of the ethical situation who reduce the Spirit to the *esprit de corps* among believers, or to a mere metaphor for the posthumous influence of the historical Jesus. The Spirit is the preserver as well as the inaugurator of the Christian life. The believer is born of the Spirit (Jn. 3:5f.), and he can perpetuate the new life only in the Spirit. Strong remarks, "Man now and here lives his true life in a spiritual atmosphere, in a spiritual society. The springs of his life rise in heaven, where Christ is: and there too is to be found the goal of all his striving. But on earth no less than in heaven this same society exists and operates, transcending all the human bases of division that exist here, political or national, unmodified in its absolute unity, even by the impenetrable veil of death."[19] Called to a life of ethical consistency before God and the world, the Christian can narrow the gap between profession and practice and escape the perils of moral inconstancy and inconsistency through dependence on the Holy Spirit.

Christian ethics can never, of course, be anything less than "the ethics of Jesus," for the significance of the Nazarene as the ideal of Christian morality is a crowning glory of biblical ethics. But it should now be obvious that Christian morality must also be much more. The ethics of redemption is no mere appeal to the example and influence of Jesus, as it has been often misrepresented by liberal expositors who regard neither the atonement of Christ nor the influence of the Spirit

[17]Dewar, *op. cit.*, p. 127.
[18]Keyser, *op. cit.*, p. 237.
[19]T. B. Strong, *Christian Ethics*, pp. 66f.

as essential elements in the ethical life. The Holy Spirit is no mere synonym for the example of Christ, nor even a mystical metaphor for the Indwelling Christ.

But an opposite danger, that of representing the Christian life as "Spirit-centered" rather than "Christ-centered," must be equally avoided. It is by the Spirit that the Risen Christ maintains his rule and reign in the lives of his followers. The ministry of the Spirit implements and facilitates his Lordship.[20] While the redeemed life rests on the historical work of Christ, it is not fulfilled there; Christ died for us on Calvary, and dwells and works in us by the Spirit.[21] The ministry of the Spirit is not to be differentiated from the post-ascension activity of Christ, who is present and immediately active in his followers in the Spirit. The Risen Christ gives to humanity a new moral power. That power is Christ himself, by the Spirit, as the inward energy of the moral life which flows from regenerate human nature. While it is improper to speak of an "extension of the incarnation," since Christ does not become the exclusive personal center of consciousness of the human race, nor does redeemed humanity become his body in the metaphysical sense, yet the new union with Christ is the guarantee that the life of the Incarnate One has not wholly vanished from the earth. The energy of the Spirit, as a new spring of moral activity, actualizes the mind and will of Christ in the experience of his followers, sharpening the perceptions of conscience and conforming the believer to the example of Christ. Strong observes, "the type of life which is set before the Christian as his ideal is indifferently described as the work of the Spirit, and as the interpretation of the example of Christ."[22] The Spirit-filled life leads to the life of Christ-like conduct. Therefore, while the Christian life is a life in the Spirit, it is as such an extension of the power of the Risen Lord, reigning by the Spirit in the lives of his followers.

Through the Spirit the believer stands already in a certain end-time, or eschatological, relationship to Christ. Pentecost has ushered in a new age, wherein the follower of Christ participates in a vital way in the resurrection life of heaven from which place the ascended Lord rules. This heavenly setting, and the believer's union with the Risen Christ by the empowering Spirit, stand at the heart of Paul's representation of the new life.

[20]Many Christians expect an experience of the Spirit subsequent to, and separate from, an experience of Christ, whereas Calvin, in line with Scripture, shows that a richer knowledge of the Spirit cannot be mediated apart from a richer knowledge of Christ. No doctrine of the Spirit is commendable which derogates in the least from the glory of the Person of Christ." Gwyn Walters, *The Doctrine of the Holy Spirit in John Calvin,* unpublished Ph.D. dissertation, University of Edinburgh, 1949, p. 340.

[21]"In the great majority of instances in which he uses 'spirit,'" writes H. A. A. Kennedy of Paul's letters, "he thinks of the Spirit of God (or of Christ) as dwelling in the Christian, or of the inner life of the Christian as recreated by the Spirit . . ." *Op. cit.,* pp. 89f.

[22]Strong, *op. cit.,* p. 65.

From such portrayals of the moral life as those in Ephesians 2 and Colossians 3 — unique in the history of moral philosophy — we can sketch the dramatic and living framework from which Christian morality draws its vitality. "God . . . hath quickened us together with Christ . . . and hath raised us up together, and hath made us sit together in heavenly places in Christ Jesus" (Eph. 2:4ff.). "If ye then be risen with Christ, seek those things which are above, where Christ sitteth on the right hand of God. Set your affection on things above, not on things on the earth. For ye are dead, and your life is hid with Christ in God. When Christ, who is our life, shall appear, then shall ye also appear with him in glory" (Col. 3:1ff.). Justice cannot be done to these passages by suggesting that the believer is linked to the Risen Christ merely positionally, and not at all in actuality. For both here and in related biblical passages an actual participation of the believer in some significant measure in the powers of the new age and of the end-time is straightforwardly affirmed. This is not a literary figure only, but a formulation of the realities of the believer's moral situation. This age-transcending relationship sustained between the new creature in Christ, whereby the believer abides in the Risen Christ and Christ indwells the believer, is reiterated in the Pauline epistles. We are instructed that "like as Christ was raised up from the dead . . . even so we also should walk in newness of life" (Rom. 6:4) and that "if the Spirit of him that raised up Jesus from the dead dwell in you, he that raised up Christ from the dead shall also quicken your mortal bodies by his Spirit that dwelleth in you" (Rom. 8:11). The believer's ethical existence is qualified by our Lord's resurrection life.

The whole discussion of the Kingdom of God is lifted to a new dimension by the fact that the present age involves the lordship of Christ, by the Spirit, in the corporate life of believers. One need not imply evolutionary, nor rule out entirely cataclysmic, features of the Kingdom, to acknowledge an enlarging and progressive manifestation of the Kingdom. The conquest of the law as an unpaid debt-bill, of death and sin and Satan, a conquest registered by dramatic advances in the history of redemption, must surely be regarded as the underside of the enlarging inbreaking of the Kingdom.

The Kingdom of God has, in all its history, both a personal and a social significance. In the Old Testament it existed symbolically in the form of the theocracy: first the direct rule of God over his chosen people in their exodus from Egypt and the wilderness wanderings; then his rule by judges, and then by earthly kings who were to be his agents. The Old Testament monarchy vanished with the captivity, but it looked for a consummation of the prophetic idea of the rule of God. This rule of God was to be both external and genuinely internal, and would culminate in the manifestation of the Messiah. From the standpoint of Old Testament prophecy it can also be said that a new age was anticipated with the advent of the Messiah involving an intimacy of relationship between the believer and the Holy Spirit. The prophets reiterated that the Spirit would be poured out on all flesh at the Messiah's coming. The prophet Ezekiel voices the Divine promise of a more intimate spiritual union: "I will give them one heart, and I will put a new spirit within you; and I will take the stony heart out of their flesh, and will give them a heart of flesh" (11:19f.). Again, "A new heart also will I give you, and a new spirit will I put within you: and I will take away the stony heart out of your flesh and I will give you a heart of flesh. And I will put my Spirit within you . . ." (36:26f.). Alongside this emphasis on an intimate inner relation to the Spirit are those passages that suggest a new abundance and fullness; they speak of a "pouring out" of the Spirit. "Neither will I hide my face any more from them: for I have poured out my Spirit upon the house of Israel, saith the Lord God" (Ezek. 39:29). In relating the events of Pentecost, the book of Acts represents the descent of the Spirit as a fulfillment of Joel 2:28-32: "And it shall come to pass afterward, that I will pour out my Spirit upon all flesh . . . in those days will I pour out my Spirit . . ." (cf. Prov. 1:23, Isa. 32:15, 44:3). Not only from the reference in Joel, but from passages like Psalm 72:6 and Zechariah 12:10, it appears likely that a fuller and final eschatological fulfillment, in an even profounder sense, is intended. Yet it remains an incontrovertible fact that the New Testament consciousness is one of participation in some vital and dramatic way in the enlarged spiritual and ethical realities foretold in the Old Testament.

Old Testament prophecy associates the coming Kingdom with the Day of the Lord. That the promised Kingdom had not previously come, but was a future expectation, is the presupposition of John the Baptist. But he preached its nearness (Mt. 3:1). Jesus Christ from the opening of his public ministry preached the "gospel of the kingdom." The evangelists note in frequent conjunction with this message his healing of the sick, both of general illnesses and special torments, and the casting out of demons. This interest in those whose bodies were diabolically possessed as seats of satanic operation (Mt. 4:24, 9:34, 12:26), sometimes as organs of multiple demonic personalities (Mk. 5:9, 16:9), is a conspicuous feature of the gospels.

The characteristic correlates of the Kingdom were the containment of Satan, repentance and faith in Jesus as Messiah, and regeneration by the Holy Spirit (Jn. 3:3). That the Kingdom has come, in some preliminary form, in the very presence of Christ, is affirmed in Matthew 12:28: "But if I cast out devils by the Spirit of God, then is the kingdom of God come unto you." The displacement of demonic rule by the enlarging rule of God is a primary aspect of the Kingdom.

The kingdom of the Messiah is an actual consummation of the prophetic idea of the rule of God, although participation in that Kingdom is no longer tied to national limitations but simply to faith in Christ (Jn. 1:29). The Kingdom came in a preliminary form with the first advent of the Messiah. Since the consummation of the Kingdom is a future event, and its present form is anticipatory, it is proper to regard the Kingdom of the Messiah as initiated by the Day of the Lord, and reaching from the ascension and Pentecost through the future millennium, or to regard the future second advent of Christ as closing the pre-messianic era. The fact that the Holy Spirit links the believer already to the Risen Christ in a certain end-time relationship is what requires the emphasis that the larger Kingdom is in some preliminary sense already under way.[23] The Kingdom exists now in a mystery form. Not even the future millennial Kingdom is depicted as the final and perfect form of the Kingdom for which the blessings of glorification are stored up. The subjugation of the powers hostile to God is not completed at the *parousia,* nor until the end of the millennium. The millennium co-exists with undestroyed enemies; death is not destroyed until after Revelation 20:1-6, Satan is not finally bound, the final judgment of sin is still future; and the attempt of Gog and Magog to deceive the nations indicates that sin occurs while the millennial Kingdom is in progress. There comes at last an end of the present age of the world, a final consummation and closing, an absolute consummation in which Christ, his mediatorial work ended, gives over the Kingdom to the Father.[24]

[23]There is no need on this ground, however, to spiritualize the millennium, or to regard it simply as the "first thousand years" of the eternal Kingdom, in its supra-historical form. The New Testament suggests these elements: (1) There is a future inheritance of which at present we experience only the earnest of the coming age (Jn. 18:36, 1 Cor. 6:9f., 15:24, 50, Gal. 5:21, Eph. 2:7, 5:5). The *parousia* will unveil Christ's power to subdue all things to himself; nothing can withstand that manifestation of his power. (2) The political aspect of his reign is not excluded. The idea of an earthly messianic Kingdom is deeply rooted in the prophets, and has a New Testament basis (Matt. 11:3, Acts 1:6f., Rom. 9-11, Rev. 20). The lordship of Christ in the believer's life then assumes a fuller millennial form, involving a people and a land, and cannot be reduced simply to the invisible church. The idea of world-rule, of a renewal of the earth, is not excluded. The saints are to reign with Christ a thousand years (Rev. 20:1ff.). (3) The historical, earthly form of the Kingdom is implied by the nature of man's revolt and of God's rescue. An historical fall and an historical redemption imply an historical triumph. The idea of Divine reign, and not merely of Divine rule, is biblical. "The Lamb has made us a *dominion* and priests unto God; and we shall reign on the earth" (Rev. 5:10). (4) But the concept of the rule of God is fundamental, pervading all forms of the Kingdom, even the millennial. The messianic Kingdom is not simply one in which a people are invested with regal authority, but the fulfillment of the anticipation of a future earthly reign by those who at present are a manifestation of the Kingdom of God in its form of Divine rule.

[24]Christ received his power from the Father (Mt. 28:18, 1 Cor. 15:24ff.). He reigns until all enemies — every hostile dominion, power and might — are put beneath his feet; not a single power is exempted from the Divine subjection of all things to him. The last enemy destroyed is death, at the second resurrection terminating the millennium. The mediatorial work is completed; Christ no longer reconciles in the sphere of grace. The messianic reign is ended, Christ's regency ceases, his dominion terminates, his government expires. The Son is willingly subjected to the Father's sovereignty. Then the Kingdom is delivered up to God the Father. While Christ's regency ends, not so his Kingdom, which gains its eternal and highest completion in being given over to the Father as the immediate

It is apparent both from the teaching of Jesus before the events of Pentecost and from the apostles who passed through them, that the New Testament inaugurates at once a new advance of the Kingdom of God and the new ethical era of the Holy Spirit. Jesus spoke of an impending signal gift or impartation of the Holy Spirit in conjunction with his own glorification (Jn. 7:38f.). Then he added that he would send the Comforter to "abide forever" with his followers, and to do so not merely by dwelling "with" but by dwelling "in" them (Jn. 14:16f.). His own presence would abide in his followers in and through that relationship (Jn. 14:18ff.). In the post-resurrection appearances, he instructed the apostles to remain in Jerusalem until they had received "the promise of the Father," or the gift of the Spirit (Acts 1:4).

The author of the epistle to the Hebrews connects the Old Testament prophecies of the spiritual writing of the law on the hearts and minds of men with the era inaugurated by the atoning sacrifice of Jesus Christ (Heb. 10:15f.). Once the law is removed as an unpaid debt-bill, and its fulfillment in the sinner's stead is an actuality and no longer a matter only of sacred promise, the moral requirements of the Old Testament revelation confront man less impressively as an external claim. The Spirit-constrained heart is then able to yield to the moral claim with a sense of inner gratitude that it has been met in Christ.[25] Paul in Romans notes that love for God has been "shed abroad" (the Greek is the more usual "poured out") by the gift of the Holy Spirit (5:5). In Galatians 3:13f. we are told that "Christ hath redeemed us from the curse of the law . . . that we might receive the promise of the Spirit through faith." The indwelling Spirit is therefore the great gift which Christ procures for his followers, and which could not be given until after Calvary and the Resurrection.

All the lines of biblical data therefore converge — Old Testament prophecy, the teaching of Jesus, the apostolic interpretation of Pentecost and of the ethical life-situation of the early Christians — to justify an emphasis on the striking dependence in which Christian ethics stands to the indwelling Spirit and the Risen Lord.[26] The Holy Spirit is depicted in his more intimate presence in believers as the "earnest" of their complete redemption in the final and consummating age. The

---

ruler in the inner life of the Kingdom. Whatever has had no part in Christ's mediatorial Kingdom stands under the Father's rule by way of subjugation and condemnation, not by way of restoration and glorification.

[25]The significance of the crucial forensic element involved in the rule of God in the believer's life is obscured in many recent statements which profess to characterize Christian ethics. It is urged only that external controls be replaced by inner or spiritual controls and the difference between Old and New Testament ethics is sketched in those terms. But this declines easily into that mere interiorization of ethics which, while it throws off legalism, loses all genuine objectivity in ethics, and its supernatural basis along with this. Christian ethics as inner is still Spirit-ethics, and as such enthrones the revealed and inscripturated will of God.

[26]The presence of the triune God, abiding in the believer, received, with the believer's abiding in the triune God, a distinctive New Testament emphasis (Jn. 14:16, 20, 15:4, 7; cf. Jn. 15:5f., 1 Jn. 2:6, 27, 3:6, 24, 4:13, 15).

Greek term indicates a "down payment" which establishes a legal claim in the absence of full possession. In two of the only three uses in the New Testament (2 Cor. 1:22, 5:5, and Eph. 1:14), the word is connected with the resurrection, and depicts that event as already a reality, at least in some measure, in the new ethical life of believers.[27] The Holy Spirit has lifted the family of faith dramatically into the end-time, so that believers share in the resurrection powers of their Risen Lord. They are one with Christ who rose from the dead, in fact, are in him, and he in them, for he is their life. The moral life of believers is a resurrection life; it springs not from the old nature, but has its center in the new life, in eternal life, in and through Jesus Christ.

The Risen Lord's apocalyptic powers impinge upon the present historical order, bringing to believers in advance blessings which are characteristic of the future eschatological Kingdom. In and through the powers he gives to his followers, his Kingdom invades the present world order, so that the future Kingdom is already entrenched in a veiled and mystery form.

This fuller rule of God is graphically depicted by several New Testament texts. The death of Christ incapacitates Satan effectively so he can no longer injure the redeemed. Christ died that he might "bring to naught him that hath the power of death, that is the devil" (Heb. 2:14). Now the eternal life of the regenerate is secure. This is the standpoint of the Pauline letters and of the gospels as well. "Having spoiled principalities and powers, he made a show of them openly, triumphing over them in it" (Col. 2:15). God has rendered powerless those hostile powers that had held sway over doomed humanity. This victory over the forces of darkness has its ground in the atonement of Christ; by his atoning death, God has disarmed them, shamed them, trampled over them. "Now is the judgment of this world: now shall the prince of this world be cast out. And I, if I be lifted up, will draw all men unto me. This he said, signifying what death he should die" (Jn. 12:31ff.). Except for his final public and official humiliation, Satan is actually condemned by the accomplishment of Christ's redemptive work (Jn. 16:11). Jesus himself encouraged his disciples to look upon the exorcism of demons in his name as evidence that the overthrow of Satan was assured: "The seventy returned . . . with joy, saying, Lord, even the devils are subject unto us through thy name. And he said unto them, I beheld Satan as lightning fall from heaven. Behold, I give unto you power to tread on serpents and scorpions, and over all the power of the enemy: and nothing shall by any means hurt you. Notwithstanding, in this rejoice not, that the spirits are subject unto you . . ." (Lk. 10:17ff.). The deliverance from the power of darkness, in H. W. A.

[27]Harry R. Boer, "Life in the Spirit," in *The Reformed Journal,* IV, 3 (Mar., 1954), pp. 3f.

Meyer's interpretation of Colossians 1:13, "has taken place by means of the conversion to Christ, which is the work of God."[28]

Some have resorted to artificial exegetical expedients in order to avoid the dramatic fact that believers are now partakers of the messianic salvation and Kingdom. Commentators have asserted that such passages express what is true only for the Divine foreknowledge, or they are spiritualized interpretations of conversion without a literal sense, or a future hope that faith contemporizes, or a consecrated imaginative picture of our part in the coming eschatological age, an exalted awakening of the devoted consciousness.

Paul declares "God . . . hath quickened us together with Christ, and hath raised us up together, and made us sit together in heavenly places in Christ Jesus." This cannot be reduced merely to an ethical and spiritual quickening in the believer (Rom. 6:4f., 2 Cor. 5:15, Gal. 2:19f.). A believer partakes already in the resurrection and is involved in a present participation in the inheritance of the future Kingdom of God that will be set up at the second coming (1 Cor. 6:9, 15:50, Gal. 5:21, Eph. 5:5, Mt. 25:34). And so, in a sense, believers have been made alive with Christ. Their revivification is included in his because of a dynamic union with the Head of the body (Eph. 1:23). The Christian is conscious of this participation in life with Christ. The change that will occur at the *parousia* is not an actualizing in subjective experience of what has merely been set forth objectively in Christ's resurrection, else Paul would have used the future tense in 1 Corinthians 15:22 and Romans 8:17. The aorist that is used is more than a dramatic exhibition of the apostle's confidence in God's future triumph. The making alive of believers is somehow *now* accomplished with the making alive of the crucified Christ. This is not exclusively a possession in hope (Rom. 8:24) and in some distant future (Rom. 5:10). The believer is involved in Christ's resurrection. God by raising and exalting Christ has in some real sense raised and exalted us with him. The future eschatological age has thus invaded time and history. God has done this to give us an introduction to the Divine riches that will be ours in "the ages coming on." The future parousia will usher in the new age openly — suddenly, in a moment (Mt. 24:27, 1 Cor. 15:52).

But when Paul declares that "our conversation (manner of life) is in heaven" (Phil. 3:20), he intends to convey more than a psychological state. It is more than a dress rehearsal for a future event that has no reality at the present. To reduce his teaching to this level is to do despite to the New Testament doctrine of the Spirit as the vital link between the believer and the Risen Lord.

[28]H. W. A. Meyer, *Commentary on Colossians,* 1:13. Yet Meyer compromises the force of Paul's declaration that we have been "delivered out" of the power which darkness has into the Kingdom of the Messiah by reducing the significance of this to an "as if" translation; he thinks Paul merely conceives the matter proleptically as already consummated: "The kingdom, which is nigh is, by means of their fellowship of life with their Lord . . . as certain to the redeemed as if they were already translated into it."

The eschatological element in the New Testament does not dull spiritual and ethical motivation. Rather, it quickens them with a sense of end-time urgency. The very point secular ethics attacks as unworthy in the morality of revelation constitutes in fact its secret dynamic. The enlarging domain of the rule of God through the overthrow of Satan, the more intimate experience of the Spirit, and now the larger eschatological expectation, intensify concern for all the this-worldly aspects of the moral life. The best safeguard against an autonomous ethic is to judge the decisions of life constantly in the light of God's judgment and ultimate triumph over wrong.

Side by side with this present age which is on its way to its doom co-exists "the age to come" in which the believer also has his existence. The believer's outlook on life is brought into focus by the values of the "age to come." Geerhardus Vos has ably phrased the significance of this new standard of values. "The bond between the believer and Christ is so close that, from Paul's point of view, a detachment of the Christian's *interest* not only, but even a severance of his *actual life* from the celestial Christ-centered sphere, is unthinkable. The latter consideration counts for more than the mere fact that through the appearance or resurrection of Christ the eschatological process has been set in motion. As soon as the direction of the actual spiritual life-contact becomes involved, the horizontal movement of thought on the time-plane must give way immediately to a vertical projection of the eschatological interest into the supernal region, because there, even more than in the historical development below, the center of all religious values and forces has come to lie. . . . The higher world is in existence . . . and there is no escape for the Christian from its supreme dominion over his life. Thus the other world, hitherto future, has become present. Now, if the present world had at the same moment ceased to exist . . ."[29] It is perhaps well to break off the quotation just at this point to retain the "semi-eschatological mood" of the Pauline writings.

It may not be possible to discriminate all the implications for the believer of his life by the Spirit. The Spirit is the principle of knowledge (1 Cor. 2:10), as well as of righteousness. Any study of religious epistemology must provide a full statement of the relation of the Spirit and the written word and the believer. Nothing, not even the secrets of God, is beyond the Spirit's reach or scrutiny. The Spirit reveals to men the findings of his search of the deep things of God. He is the Spirit of Truth (Jn. 16:13). This revelation is committed to believers in the sacred trust that they will preserve it unimpaired (2 Tim. 1:14). The learning and growth of the believer are directly conditioned by his yieldedness to the Spirit. The Spirit comes to the believer's side and shoulders his burdens in prayer when he is unable to formulate his worship and intercession in words.

[29]Geerhardus Vos, *The Pauline Eschatology* (Grand Rapids: Eerdmans, 1952), pp. 37f.

Three of the Spirit's activities bearing on the moral life are especially prominent in the apostolic writings. All are reflections of the primary fact that since Pentecost the permanent indwelling of the Spirit in the bodies of believers has marked a new era of spiritual intimacy between God and his children. Paul inquires of the Corinthians, "Know ye not that your body is the temple of the Holy Ghost which is in you, which ye have of God" (1 Cor. 6:19).[30] There can be no doubt of the presence and activity of the Spirit in Old Testament times. He restrained sin in the world, and rested upon believers (cf. Isa. 59:21, "My Spirit that is upon thee") and even occasionally endowed men with the special requirements of a particular office, *e.g.*, the prophetic. It would doubtless create a false impression to suggest that the ethical activity of the Spirit in the Old Testament is confined to rare incidents. But what can be said is that the Spirit does not infuse the moral effort of the Old Testament as conspicuously nor as vitally as he does in the New.[31] So dramatic is the New Testament change that it is quite proper to say that Pentecost marks the birth of pneumatic ethics; thereafter an ethic of the Spirit is the ideal. The New Testament ethical outlook is everywhere colored by the fact that believers are permanently indwelt by the Spirit of God.[32] By this remarkable Divine presence, the ethical constraint "to love God and neighbor" becomes less external and more internal than in the older dispensation; it is written upon the heart. Fornication acquires the character of sin against one's own body — the spiritual temple of the Living God. The permanent indwelling of the Spirit means both the vivified sense of sin and a quick access to the reserves of moral power in Christ.

The first feature of the Spirit's permanent and universal indwelling of believers is that he baptizes[33] believers into one body, of which the Risen Christ is head. If it is risky to speak in this regard of an "extension of the Incarnation" because of the use of this notion by liberal and

[30]The question "have you had an experience of the Holy Spirit?" is improperly addressed to believers. "No man can call Jesus Lord except by the Spirit" (1 Cor. 12:3) and who is not "born of the Spirit" is no believer (Jn. 3:5). Life in the Spirit is a *conditio sine qua non* of Christian life.

[31]The emphasis "the Spirit was an Old Testament reality too" must therefore not become the basis for clouding the distinctive pneumatic basis of the church's existence. In the Old Testament the Spirit was the "With-Dweller," related to the theocracy and to the individual; in the New, he is the "In-Dweller." In both dispensations, believers have had more potential for ethical realization than appropriated; with us the situation is worse, in view of its expanded opportunities, else the professing Christian fellowship would not be so embarrassingly undynamic.

[32]In John 14:16f., this permanent indwelling is contrasted with the temporal nature of our Lord's physical presence with the disciples in the Incarnation.

[33]R. A. Torrey carefully insisted that regeneration by and baptism with the Holy Spirit be carefully distinguished, on the ground that the former remakes the sinner's intellectual, affectional, and volitional life after the image of God, while the latter constitutes him a member of the body of Christ with its powers and responsibilities of witness. *The Holy Spirit — Who He Is and What He Does* (New York: Revell, 1927), p. 114. Alongside this, emphasis is needed on the simultaneous and once-for-all occurrence of these aspects of the Spirit's work.

immanentist theology, there may be more merit in H. Wheeler Robinson's suggestion of a "Kenosis or self-emptying of the Holy Spirit." The Spirit finds his temple in the bodies of believers, and integrates their lives so that they, in turn, serve on earth as the one body of the Risen Lord. The classic passage is 1 Corinthians 12:12f.: "For as the body is one, and hath many members, and all the members of that one body, being many, are one body: so also is Christ. For by one Spirit are we all baptized into one body, whether Jews or Gentiles, whether bond or free; and have been all made to drink into one Spirit" (cf. Rom. 12:5, Eph. 2:21f., 4:4, 5:30, Col. 1:24, 3:15). The verb *baptize* occurs in the aorist, signifying a completed work and excluding the notion of dismemberment. While the unity of Christ's body is eternal, the unity of fellowship among believers may be broken or hindered apart from the unifying Spirit (Eph. 4:3). "He that is joined unto the Lord is one spirit" (1 Cor. 6:17). This oneness in the body of Christ surpasses the Old Testament unity of believers. The collapse of the temple and the Old Testament ceremonial order, with its centralization of worship in one place where the presence of God uniquely abode, was preparatory to the diffusion of the Spirit (Jn. 4:21ff.) and to the Risen Lord's spiritual headship of the body of believers (Eph. 1:23, 5:23, Col. 1:18).

Christian ethics involves therefore the moral perspective of an organic fellowship within which all walls of partition are demolished; neither Jew nor Gentile, black nor white, master nor slave, rich nor poor, none have any privilege or disadvantage. The dramatic progress of New Testament ethics in this regard is apparent from its larger conception of the circle of believers. Gentile and Jew are on equal terms. They are all members of the organic spiritual body of which the Risen Messiah is the head.

That Christian ethics is the ethics of a body, a community enlivened by the Risen Christ, has implications for the whole moral life. It requires a protest against isolationism in ethical thought and effort. The lone believer does not have adequate reserves for all the ethical demands of life independently of horizontal Christian relations. In ethics, as well as in worship and prayer, Christians need each other for moral discernment, encouragement, and progress. The Christian confronted by decision, and faced by alternatives that seem to require compromise of the ideal, has a right to the prayer and sympathetic understanding and counsel of his fellow-believers. To be a member of the body of Christ means to be mutually involved with all Christians in the moral struggles of each. There must be unfading concern for the suffering of believers in the totalitarian lands, the hunger of those in poverty and need, the anguish of those in physical affliction, the insensitivity of those with unconsecrated wealth or talent, the scandal of those who live in shame. The believer's prayer must include within its scope Russian totalitarianism, Indian poverty, Korean suffering, American greed; it embraces the hospitals, the factories, the service clubs, the prisons, and the brothels.

A second feature is that the Spirit seals the believer. By the Holy Spirit, writes Paul, we are "sealed unto the day of redemption" (Eph. 4:30), "sealed with the Holy Spirit of promise" (1:13). It is in connection with the latter passage that Paul speaks of the Spirit as "the earnest of our inheritance until the redemption of the purchased possession" (1:14; cf. 2 Cor. 1:21f.: "God . . . hath also sealed us, and given the earnest of the Spirit in our hearts"). In the book of Revelation a sealing of the servants of God as his chosen ones takes place before the final judgment of the earth (Rev. 7:3ff.). What then shall we say of this sealing of believers by the Spirit?

A seal fulfills three functions: confirmation, identification, security. The Spirit authenticates believers as children of God, witnessing with their spirits of their genuine sonship (Rom. 8:16, 1 Jn. 5:10). The Spirit, moreover, marks them off as belonging not to the world but to God; cf. John 14:17: "Whom the world cannot receive." Moreover, the Spirit renders their final salvation certain, sealing them "unto the day of redemption" (Eph. 4:30; cf. 1:14, where the language also permits linking the phrase "until the redemption of the purchased possession" with "ye were sealed" in the previous verse). The Spirit is already the down-payment or pledge of an inheritance in heaven, the first-fruits of the great harvest of blessing to come (cf. Rom. 8:23). The Spirit's immanence in believers is therefore to be distinguished from his omnipresence in space and in the lives of men on the basis of creation. His sealing is an operation bounded by gracious choice and which, while it may involve gifts that are temporary and even losable, involves also that baptism and sealing which are permanent.[34] The sanctifying work of the Spirit carries an assurance of a joyful resurrection to come, in which the believer already participates as the Spirit applies the world and will of God in the soul.

The third feature is that the Holy Spirit fills the believer. The Holy Spirit does not direct the Christian's steps nor give him moral power and wisdom automatically. These come from the filling of the Spirit, not merely the indwelling of the Spirit. The life that is not so filled will bear the fruit of the flesh; it has not yet the full spiritual empowerment for life on the highest Christian level.

The indwelling of the Spirit is permanent, and the baptism and the sealing once-for-all, so that the Christian life cannot be spoken of simply as prospective. Paul does not exhort the Corinthians to be indwelt, nor to be baptized, nor does he urge the Ephesians to be sealed by the Spirit; these are once-for-all phenomena accompanying the beginning of the new life in Christ. It is impossible to be a believer

[34]Kuyper, *The Work of the Holy Spirit* (Grand Rapids: Eerdmans, reprint, 1941), pp. 119f.

without being born of the Spirit, indwelt, baptized and sealed by the Spirit.

But "be filled with the Spirit" (Eph. 5:18) is a command addressed to believers with a view to daily renewal. The verb *fill* in this passage is in the passive voice, and the acceptable translation "let yourselves be filled with the Spirit" suggests that the Spirit is eager to occupy us, and that if we are unfilled the fault is ours. This filling is not to be merely a spasmodic last resort in times of moral defeat and ethical exasperation. Rather, it is to be a daily and normal experience.[35] It is the believer's prerogative alone daily to be emptied of all unholy spirits and to be filled with the Holy Spirit. The Spirit is not merely the source of the new life (Rom. 8:2, 6, 2 Cor. 3:6), but the standard by which the believer walks (Gal. 5:16, 25).

The indwelling Spirit and the fullness of the Spirit are therefore, from the New Testament perspective, not necessarily synonymous, although ideally they may be. Offhand, it might seem that one "indwelt" by the Spirit could not be exhorted to "be filled" with the Spirit, even as it might appear that one not filled by the Spirit would not be indwelt by the Spirit. But indwelling is the permanent condition of a Christian life whatever its intensity; the fullness of the Spirit, however, is not self-sustaining nor permanent.

The plea for the Spirit's fullness must not suggest that at regeneration the believer receives only "part" of the Spirit, rather than the "full" Spirit. The Spirit is personal and is not received in parts. The indwelling Spirit means that the believer at the point of salvation receives the whole Spirit (Rom. 8:9-11).

But the full claim of the Spirit may not yet be fully translated into life, and hence the call to the Spirit's fullness perpetually confronts the believer. In this quality of Spirit-filled living, there are no "neutral" experiences for the Christian. Does a given practice further his communion with God? Does it make him alive to the Word of God? Does it promote his growth in grace? Does it fire his passion and concern for those who do not yet believe? Does it further the best interests of his neighbor? The Christian lives positively, not neutrally. The Spirit who has filled him will make him aware of those areas of life that, though good, are enemies of the best.

To deny the Spirit's full sway is to compromise the whole dynamic of the Christian life. The Christian who repeatedly thwarts the Spirit's power may come to question that he is sealed unto redemption. The believer's security is witnessed and confirmed by holiness of life. Where there is little holiness in living, both the world and the believer are thrown in doubt. For the believer unfilled with the Spirit, the world holds a glitter it never held for Jesus, and it appeals to inordinate desire

[35] " 'Be not drunk with wine wherein is excess, but be filled with the Spirit' — is the apostolic counsel. The moral obligation to be 'filled with the Spirit' is as binding as the negative command to shun drunkenness." Henry Yooll, *The Ethics of Evangelicalism* (London: Charles H. Kelley, 1906), p. 122.

in a way that Christ does not. Carnality in spiritual experience may involve also, as it did at Corinth, "envyings, and strife, and divisions" in the body of believers. Not to live by the Spirit's fullness, but to be driven for a sustained period by lesser motives and conformed to the flesh, may even result in uncertainty that one is born of and indwelt by the Spirit.

One may be a believer without this constant filling of the Spirit — a weak believer, not drawing on the spiritual resources at his disposal, but frustrating the Spirit's manifestations, and allowing the old nature to reassert itself in thought, feeling, word, and action. It is possible for a theology which does justice to the Cross and Resurrection as historical facts to choke off a biblical Pneumatology in experience. The work of Jesus in us by the Spirit is the reality for the sake of which the work on Calvary was accomplished. "Know ye not . . . ?" asks Paul, as if to awaken believers to concealed riches, to the indwelling Spirit who yearns to fill them. Spiritual poverty, mediocrity, fruitlessness, discontent, depression, defeat, bondage, are due to ignorance of the Spirit's power. Can he possess more of the believer? Then the believer is unfilled. The carnal man of 1 Corinthians 3, the wretched man of Romans 7, is the believer unfilled by the Spirit. To know Christ in his fullness and to be filled with the Spirit are correlative themes, since the Spirit brings believers under Christ's control.

At Pentecost all who were gathered in prayer were filled with the Spirit (Acts 4:31). Since the Pentecost descent this pneumatic filling normally occurs first at the time of regeneration, although many Christians frustrate the full work of the Spirit. When the filling of the Spirit occurs in conjunction with a later spiritual crisis, the temptation is to regard it as a distinctive second blessing. From the biblical standpoint, however, it is to be succeeded by a third, a fourth and a fifth blessing of a similar kind, and so on *ad infinitum* in daily renewal.[36] This is plain not only from the Ephesian exhortation, but from the fact that in the lives of the apostles we read of successive fillings by the Spirit (Acts 4:8, 13:9). The fullness of the Spirit is the church's daily prerogative. The normal Christian life is that in which this one Spirit alone comes into manifestation. It is possible to have an excess of wine, but not an excessive Spirit-filling (Eph. 5:18); the normal Christian life, in fact, flows from the Spirit as "rivers of living water" (Jn. 7:37ff.). It is this constant infilling that prevents the Christian walk from declining into a feverish obstacle race. The believer is to be "led by the Spirit" (Gal. 5:18), or actually, to be "driven" or "impelled." Moreover, he is to "walk in the Spirit," to regulate his daily life by his guidance (5:16) and orderly control (5:25); indeed, he is to be brimful of the Spirit (Eph. 5:18).

[36]"God's child remains the old man's grave-digger until the hour of his own departure." A. Kuyper, *op. cit.*, p. 484.

Along with the Spirit's baptism and sealing, the filling of the Spirit emphasizes the democratic operation of Christian grace. In an age in which multitudes of persons were regarded of no account, especially slaves and women, it was possible for them to gain a place of importance in the fellowship of believers. They were heirs of all the powers and hopes of the new life. The humblest classes of society were related to what, from the world's standpoint, must have appeared like mysterious powers. The weak, the ignoble, the poor, were indwelt by God's Spirit and accorded all the privileges of full citizens of the Kingdom of God. The Spirit is constantly mentioned in the context of power, of *dunamis,* or dynamic. The Spirit-filled believer is distinguished not alone by his intellectual grasp of spiritual things, but by a Divine power-manifestation. "The kingdom of God is not in word, but in power" (1 Cor. 4:20). "Our gospel came in word, but also in power" (1 Thess. 1:5). Believers are to "be strong in the Lord and in the power of his might" (Eph. 6:10). The evangelist, or minister, or theologian, may continue to proclaim the essential Christian truths, and the church member to "adhere" to them, long after the powerful outflow of the Spirit has been broken in practical life. The disciples were to be clothed "with power from on high" (Lk. 24:49). "Ye shall receive power when the Holy Spirit is come upon you" (Acts 1:8). Alongside the church's confident proclamation of the truth about God and his purposes and its remarkable enthusiasm for holiness, this enduement with power was foremost in its spiritual weapons for reaching out into the lost pagan environment that knew God only at a distance. Jesus returning "in the power of the Spirit" (Lk. 4:14) from the wilderness conflict with Satan was the great Exemplar of his followers, making known the Divine resource for resisting "the prince of the power of the air" (Eph. 2:2). The foes of Stephen were "not able to withstand the wisdom and the spirit by which he spake" (Acts 6:5f., 6:10). To be filled with the Spirit was to be energized by supernatural power. Simon Magus sought to buy the apostolic power with money (Acts 8:18). Whatever must be said, properly enough, about the cessation of certain apostolic phenomena, there can be no doubt that Divine empowerment was intended to be a permanent feature of the believer's relation to the Spirit. A powerless church, no less than a morally languid church, is a sign of a fellowship unfilled by the Spirit; where the Spirit is, there is power. God has never intended the company of believers to stand unarmored against the attacks of the evil one, nor did he plan for them to eke out an undynamic survival in a hostile world. The church sacrifices more than she knows when she loses her dynamic. When there is no effective manifestation of the Spirit in her ministry, her message of redemptive theology and morality is perilously near being merely a philosophical explanation of life. The church that has only theology and ethics, but is powerless, is the church with a stifled Spirit.

But the dynamic of the early church was no magical or occult energy that produced hysteria; the hidden energies which the Spirit loosed in the lives of believers produced a fervent devotion to God and to his will and, hence, a spontaneous ethical enthusiasm. The Holy Spirit transformed moral sensitivities, revolutionized conduct, and set aflame the whole man's love for God. No non-theological, non-moral dynamic was the essence of the biblical religious life. When Paul outlines the effect of the Spirit in man's inner life, his stress does not fall on resultant religious tasks for which men are now gifted, nor on such factors as power in preaching, prayer, and soul winning. His stress is on ethical factors, on the way of the Spirit that contrasts so sharply with the way of the flesh.[37] True, the apostle brings out the charismatic expressions of the Christian life, but his emphasis is on its moral and religious forms also. That the believer's life of devotion is brought within the doctrine and reality of the Spirit means above all a dramatic moral inversion. "It is, indeed, remarkable," asserts C. W. Emmet, "how steadily the New Testament concentrates attention on the inner and less startling gifts of character, which the popular mind would ignore; and if it does not disparage, it certainly does not exaggerate, those which at first sight seemed to give more direct evidence of the presence of the Spirit."[38] The supernatural power that breathed through the life of the early church doubtless aroused the curiosity of the superstition-bound multitudes, and served as an irresistible attraction of an external sort. But none could draw near to the secret of that dynamic without realizing its inseparability from a theological and moral transformation at the very center of human life.

The ethical power of the Christian community was inseparable from Christ Jesus; it was, as indeed it still is, "union with Christ" by the Spirit, and his communication of strength and purity to the disciples. Moral philosophy, moving as it does within the speculative sphere, and remote from the drama of redemption, knows no such setting for the tensions of the moral life. Consequently, it fails to lift the ethical situation reconstructively into the realization of the ideal. Smeaton's observation at this level is succinct and worthwhile.

> "That which enables Christianity to achieve what human speculation fails to accomplish is the fact that it is a life derived from the Spirit of life — not an idea, truth or opinion, — and that as such it cannot but grow. In all systems that are of the earth, we have mere ideas which are as jejune and impotent as their propounders; whereas the last Adam is a quickening Spirit. Whenever Christ is considered as a present fountain of life and Christianity is considered as opening the way to the Spirit of life, it is essentially distinct from the mere influence of philosophical speculation. For

[37]L. H. Marshall, *The Challenge of New Testament Ethics*, p. 291.
[38]C. W. Emmet, "Spirit," in *H.D.B.*, 875b.

where a new supernatural element of life is introduced into fallen humanity, and nature is not left to be wrought upon by a mere idea or a system of thought but animated from within by the Spirit of Him who says: 'I am the life,' — humanity is in connection with the great archetype to whose image we are destined to be conformed."[39]

[39]George Smeaton, *The Doctrine of the Holy Spirit,* p. 248.

20

THE CHRISTIAN LIFE AS A POSSESSION

THE PRESENT REVOLT against the cursory approach to progress indicates a returning to a more realistic doctrine of human nature. Nevertheless, while acknowledging the depth-dimension of sin which sullies all man's motives and acts, it tends to obscure and obstruct the legitimate and related scope of sanctification in the Christian life. The theological atmosphere is replete with interpretations which assert, for example, that even Christian ethical achievement must evidence no specific external distinguishing characteristics within the general tide of comprehensive idealistic morality, or that the Christian life is only a "prospect" and not yet in any sense a "possession," or that the believer's constant reverting to unbelief finds deliverance only in the moment-by-moment existential renewal of relationship with Christ.

Such emphases result from modern speculative assumptions which control the approach to biblical ethics. One dogma insists that the absolute transcendence of God requires an external confrontation of man and disallows an immanent relation to the Holy Spirit within experience;[1] another, that human nature is inevitably sinful (*i.e.*, on the basis of creation) and that the Christian life must be wholly eschatologically oriented and lives in the future alone.

Whatever elements of neglected biblical ethics these recent views incorporate, one thing is sure: they limit the New Testament concept of the growing Christian life. Traditional insistence that the spiritual life exists only where God possesses the believer becomes, rather, an emphasis that the Christian life is not in any sense the believer's possession. Barth, by way of illustration, opposes Augustine's view that the believer becomes the bearer of salvation through the infusion of righteousness. Barth, rather, stresses both the Spirit's presence and the eschatological nature of the Christian life.[2] The conviction, however,

[1]J. Sperna Wieland's complaint against Kierkegaard is quite justified, that "Kierkegaard nowhere takes account of the work of the Holy Spirit" and that this neglect of the Spirit's role in human experience accounts for Kierkegaard's exclusive emphasis on an absolutely vertical meeting of God and man. *Philosophy of Existence and Christianity,* p. 117.

[2]"Everything that is to be said about the man who receives the Holy Spirit, as driven and filled by the Spirit, is in the New Testament sense an eschatological pronouncement. Eschatological means . . . 'related to . . . what from our point of view is still in arrears for our experience and thought, to the eternal reality of the divine fulfilment and completion" (Barth, *The Doctrine of the Word of God* (Edinburgh: T. & T. Clark, 1936), pp. 530f.

that we cannot be Christians here because sin clings to our temporal existence seems contrary to the New Testament concept of Christian growth. Barth's view, with its emphasis on eschatology, tends to minimize the Spirit as a qualifier of the present Christian life. Beneath this, one detects a speculative conforming of the biblical doctrine of sanctification to that absolute discontinuity which Barth asserts to exist between the anthropological experiences even of the redeemed and the Divine claim which impinges on them.

Doubtless the believer's life springs from God alone as a gift of grace, and only in and through the Spirit is this new life perpetuated. The new nature, moreover, is maintained and nourished through a living faith, and hence is bounded by life in God, by an existence dependent upon and dedicated to him. Where genuine faith exists, personal decision and ratification are indisputably essential. Without obedience there is assuredly no saving faith.

But these emphases do not require the denial that the Christian life in some manner is a continuing possession of the believer. That, except for the actual moments of existential decision, the believer ceases to exist as a believer, or that faith exists only in the actuality of decision, so that the believer must continually wrestle himself into existence,[3] is too much a surrender to dynamic psychology. That the new birth is in no sense a "given entity,"[4] that the believer's participation in eternal life is only "for the moment,"[5] that the Christian life is only a "becoming" rather than a "being,"[6] that the believer is always at the same time an unbeliever,[7] are emphases which reflect all too obviously the standpoint of a speculative philosophy,[8] and which do not grasp the fact that behind the dynamic acts of faith in the believer's life stands the continuous disposition of faith born of regeneration. The constant exercise of this faith gradually establishes it into a habit.[9] The Christian life, however important is the necessity for its growth, has an abiding existence on the basis of regeneration, and not merely on the prospect of punctuated renewals. This continuity of the life in Christ may be defended without dependence on the objectionable notion that a new nature is magically infused into the believer. The protest in recent

[3]"The new man exists and continues to exist only in the obedience of faith." Brunner, *The Divine Imperative,* p. 161.

[4]*Ibid.,* p. 86.

[5]Brunner, *Man in Revolt* (Philadelphia: Westminster, 1947), p. 494.

[6]Brunner, *The Divine Imperative,* p. 177.

[7]Brunner, *The Mediator,* p. 618.

[8]The same influence of existential presuppositions is seen in the recent Swedish reinterpretation of Luther's doctrines. The position is defended — in the name of the Reformer — that the believer as egocentric stands under God's wrath, hence that forgiveness has not annulled the judgment of God against the sinner. Sin and grace are regarded not as two chronologically, nor even psychologically, different stages, but as two elements in the same moment of experience, whereby man lives in a tension between judgment and grace. Edgar M. Carlson, *The Reinterpretation of Luther* (Philadelphia: Westminster, 1948), pp. 52f.

[9]Cf. Louis Berkhof, *Systematic Theology* (4th rev. ed., Grand Rapids: Eerdmans, 1949), p. 503; Abraham Kuyper, *The Work of the Holy Spirit,* p. 411.

dogmatics against perfectionist theories of sanctification involves in the service of existential theology a fallacious reconstruction of the biblical view of sanctification, so as to deny to the believer any permanent possession of the Christian life. Dehn even sets himself over against a specific biblical passage (2 Pet. 1:4) to dismiss the possibility of the believer's participation in the Divine nature.[10] Moreover, to meet the requirements of existential theology, he depreciates the concept of the "holy man" as contrary to the New Testament, and reduces the Christian life to such a perpetual struggle as to both minimize the work of the Holy Spirit and to sacrifice the biblical view of the believer's walk. "The Christian is never *in statu,* but continually *in actu,*" we are told. "To be a Christian is forever a process of 'becoming; it is never a state of 'having become.' "[11] But this reduces the believer to an impermanent existence. The denial that sanctification involves an "infused grace" need not involve the denial of any permanent status to the believer as believer, despite the fact that the Christian life is a conflict as well as a walk. The denial of all permanent character to the Christian life does less than justice to those passages which assert that the believer already has eternal life (Jn. 3:15, 6:54), that his judgment has been commuted in view of this (5:24, 10:28), that he has peace (Rom. 5:1) and stands in grace (5:2) and is reconciled (5:10) and is to yield himself to God "as . . . alive from the dead" (6:13).

Doubtless some moderation of the excessive optimism of recent modern ethical theory was called for, especially of pantheistic and of idealistic views which located sin outside the human will, and conceived man as essentially good or as perfectible without supernatural grace. The tendency of current theological ethics is not content to emphasize the effect of original sin upon all human action, both in the world generally, and in the experience of the regenerate specifically. All ethical thought and action is tainted, so it is emphasized, with a compromise which vitiates its purity. Within the sphere of finite and historical effort, even the noblest moral aspiration falls under the judgment of God. But in its contemporary interpretations of regenerate human nature a mood of pessimism hangs over theological ethics which one does not discover to be the characteristic New Testament emphasis.

The Scripture, beyond question, disallows an ethics of sinless perfection in this life. Only they who dilute the hearty flavor of the New Testament concept of sin can escape this. And, while freedom from known sin is its ideal for the believer, the Bible shares no enthusiast's view of regenerate behavior; the deliverance from the thraldom of sin and Satan, while accomplished fully in principle, is a warfare to be renewed daily. And yet, contrary to modern theories, the biblical delineation of the moral life is not clouded in the pall of gloom and despair.

[10]Gunther Dehn, *Man and Revelation* (London: Hodder & Stoughton, 1936), p. 194.
[11]*Ibid.,* p. 197.

The reason is, no doubt, that these theories presuppose a view of the inevitability of sin which in fundamental respects marks a departure from the biblical view and which, while less optimistic than the older liberal theories, nonetheless just as objectionably thwarts the full work of the Spirit in the believer's life. For if, as the current theories presuppose, what is finite and historical is on that account sinful, the ministry of the Spirit can hardly be depicted as seeking to approximate the world of created spirits to that level of moral perfection which was once a created reality. Both an inadequate anthropology and an inadequate soteriology characterize Niebuhr's ethics. Repentance constitutes for him the heart of redemption, and the content of repentance is the acknowledgment that man is a permanent victim of his predicament in sin. Where in such a life of tension and crisis is there room for the quiet trust of New Testament faith? Where is positive fellowship with God? What traces remain of biblical representations of the Christian life as a "walk" with God (Gal. 5:18)?

The New Testament doctrine of the Spirit allows for a possession of the Christian life on the part of the believer precisely because it does not share the pessimistic and relativistic view of the finite, historical order from which current theological ethics proceeds. The life of the Spirit prevails in New Testament morality; its representative ethical mirror is not in 1 Corinthians but is to be found in Galatians, Ephesians, Philippians, and Colossians. A scant margin between unregenerate and regenerate ethics, when appraised by the New Testament evidence, can only be regarded as an accident of the cultural milieu, not as a necessity imposed by the limitations of essential human nature. Any other view works havoc with the doctrine of Christ, rises out of an objectionable anthropology, and inadequately sketches the work of the Spirit in Christian experience. The concept of a God-ethics in the life of the believer is so little foreign to the New Testament that virtues of the Deity are also asserted to be the ideal morality of the Christian life, and actualized in some distinctive measure in the experience of the believer. R. L. Ottley is not wide of the mark in his recognition of the high grade of New Testament morality: "The idea of *perfection* as relatively attainable even within the limits of a human life; the idea of character as an essential unity, combining many different elements in due harmony and proportion — these are peculiarly characteristic of the ethics of the New Testament. Hence, in their descriptions of the Christ-like character, the apostolic writers trace an entire group of virtues to a single course. . . . All virtue implies and issues from a right relationship to God, and in Him to humanity at large."[12] Nor can one reconcile the New Testament emphasis on the believer's position in Christ, and the assertions that in some sense he partakes no less in a standing sanctification as in justification, with those recent reconstructions of the life of faith reducing it to a series of successive crises whose only

[12]R. L. Ottley, *Christian Ideas and Ideals*, p. 167.

connecting link is supplied by the tense leap of faith in existential encounter.

No doubt, Christian life can be seriously frustrated — and not infrequently has been — by excessive claims about sanctification in this life. That glorification waits for the world to come, and that the climax of sanctification is reserved for that future existence, is as obvious an emphasis of the New Testament as that justification and sanctification already now set the believer apart from the corruption of this present world.

Christian perfectionism must be valued for its determination to guard the Christian life from the shaggy dregs of pagan immorality. Perfectionism was preached by John Wesley, although the restrictions which he attached to his doctrine of perfect love are often overlooked: "I do not teach absolute perfection, nor any perfection which does not need a constant application of the blood of Jesus Christ." Today it is the rallying-cry of a number of American denominations, among them the rapidly-growing Church of the Nazarene.[13]

The primacy of man's will, alike in salvation and in sanctification, occupies a central place in all statements of perfectionist ethics. Yet the cooperation of the Holy Spirit, and not simply the determination to reform, is necessary for new motivation toward character transformation. The justified believer is able not to sin, not as a static condition but in view of repeatedly ratified decision and grace. The initial experience of regeneration, however, leaves the sin principle, the carnal nature, as an element with which the believer must contend. A second experience of grace is therefore required to eradicate this sin-principle in the heart. This is a crisis experience of sanctification, in which God meets the longings of the regenerate heart for holiness.[14] The sin principle, the old nature, is now eradicated, and the bias toward sin is gone. Yet the outer world, still under the control of sin, remains a constant source of temptation, and the believer must still vigorously resist external solicitations to sin. As long as he remains in the world, he is on probation. So long as the believer preserves his vital relationship with God he is unable to sin. If, however, he stumbles and perseveres in spiritual indifference, he may lose not merely his sanctification, but his salvation as well.

Recent theology has opposed this treatment of sanctification in terms of sinless perfection, as if "the holy man has undergone something akin to a transformation of substance through his encounter with the

[13]Cf. the volume from this tradition by Lewis T. Corlett, *Holiness in Practical Living* (Kansas City: Beacon Hill Press, 1948).

[14]In the Pentecostal groups this second experience of absolute sanctification is linked with the insistence that apostolic gifts continue in this age, and that the gift of tongues is the evidence of the genuineness of the experience. This connection of absolute sanctification with the framework of miracle is not without its element of consistency. The primary question, however, is the nature of sanctification.

Gospel."[15] Pietism, Methodism, and similar movements of sanctification are dismissed as an effort to give the Roman Catholic figure of the saint a place in the Protestant church. In reply to the perfectionist views, it is pointed out, properly enough, that the New Testament passages which exhibit the nature of regenerated believers as a life of Christian perfection (Rom. 8:1f., "who walk not after the flesh"; 1 Cor. 6:11, "Ye are sanctified"; 1 Jn. 3:9, "Whosoever is born of God doth not commit sin . . . and he cannot sin") are outnumbered by the summons to renewed obedience (1 Jn. 1:8, "If we say that we have no sin, we deceive ourselves"; Gal. 5:17, "Ye cannot do the things that ye would"; Phil. 3:12, "not as though I were already perfect"). The new life is thus man's full possession only in principle. "If the Christians of the New Testament are called 'saints,' " comments Dehn, "this is, as it were, a purely 'forensic' appellation . . . only valid in the judgment of God. They are holy because God has sanctified them in spite of their unholiness, and in the midst of their unholiness. . . . The Christian is always, as the Reformers expressed it . . . 'simultaneously a saint and a sinner.' He is sanctified by God, but a sinner by nature. If he is what he should be in this position, then he is obedient."[16]

The perfectionist definition of sin as limited only to willful transgressions of morality is doubtless thin, although it strikes nonetheless at a realm of moral experience which Christians do not zealously guard. But its easy dismissal of all other aberrations, such as sins of ignorance, as mistakes or errors, indicates that human conduct in its entirety is not adequately interpreted in relation to the fall and to man's depravity.

Alongside the perfectionist has appeared a second view which has been influenced historically by earlier Methodist preaching. Its central emphasis falls on the spiritual man as characterized by the Spirit-filled life. Although this emphasis may lend itself to perfectionist views as well as to more current interpretations of sanctification, it has become specially identified as the doctrine of the Keswick conferences. It is offered as a more satisfactory explanation of the spiritual fluctuation of regenerate life than the previous theory which claims a second work of grace to purify the heart, destroy the body of sin, crucify the old nature and cleanse from all sin, thus completely sanctifying the life and perfecting it in love and holiness, although this work of grace may be lost through neglect or disobedience.

Although shades of variation exist among the exponents of the Keswick approach, the outlines may be taken from the writings of Ruth Paxson.[17] A distinction is made between the natural man or unbeliever, the carnal man or believer who is not enjoying spiritual fullness, and the spiritual man who lives the Spirit-filled life. The

[15]Dehn, *op. cit.*, p. 193.
[16]*Ibid.*, p. 196.
[17]Ruth Paxson, *Called Unto Holiness* (Chicago: Moody Press, 1936), *Life On the Highest Plane*, 3 vols. (Chicago: Moody Press, 1943), and *Rivers of Living Water* (London: Marshall, Morgan & Scott, Ltd., 1935).

natural man is under the uncontested dominance of sin and dead to God. The carnal man is regenerate, but righteousness and sin alternate in dominating his life; while the grosser sins are gone, such characteristics as self-will, self-centeredness, self-conceit, self-love, and false humility continue to assert themselves. In contrast, the spiritual man is under the uncontested dominance of Christ and is dead to the world. The latter step requires awareness of the crucifixion of the old nature which resolves the conflict between the new and old. This crucifixion is not an act of the believer, nor does it occur during his lifetime; rather, the old man was crucified on the Cross at the time of Christ's death. "Assurance of the deliverance from the sphere of 'the flesh' . . . rests upon the apprehension and acceptance of this fact of co-crucifixion."[18] This recognition is the presupposition of vital co-resurrection with Christ. Thus, the believer's sanctification is twofold, both positional and actual. As Christ is enthroned in the believer, complete victory over sin is afforded, and Satan may be reckoned a defeated foe. Perpetual victory requires a life continually renewed and refilled by the Spirit. This is conditioned only upon the believer's conscious yielding and trusting as a voluntary act coupled with faith in God's gift of victory attested by thankfulness and obedience.

Against this "holiness" teaching, as it is sometimes called, the complaint is made that Christians are thereby distinguished as of two kinds. Rather, objectors contend, the distinction between carnal and spiritual is one of degree and not of kind; some traces of carnality attach to the lives of all believers, and likewise, no believer is without some measure of spirituality. Indubitably, some measure of truth obtains here. It must not be allowed to minimize the fact, however, that the New Testament does in truth contrast carnal and spiritual believers (1 Cor. 3:1ff.).

The Reformed theological tradition insists that the roots of sin are so deep in human life that even the regenerate man as sanctified does not in this life actualize perfection at any time. Therefore, a charge of Pelagianism is now and again levelled by this school against the Keswick doctrine of sanctification. Packer asserts that the Keswick teaching is "Pelagian through and through," differing from the Reformed doctrine as chalk from cheese."[19] G. W. Bromiley, however, defends the Keswick view as historically differing not only from Pelagianism and Semi-Pelagianism, but from Arminianism as well, and dismisses the question of an underlying Pelagian exaltation of the will of man as irrelevant. Instead, he avers,[20] the pertinent question is whether or not "in respect of sanctification Keswick allows rather more to the free choice of the will than Scripture warrants?" Even this question Bromiley answers

[18]Paxson, *Life on the Highest Plane,* II, 79.

[19]J. I. Packer, "'Keswick' and the Reformed Doctrine of Sanctification," in *The Evangelical Quarterly,* XXVII, 3 (July, 1955), pp. 158ff.

[20]G. W. Bromiley, "Keswick's Teaching Concerning Sanctification," in *The Life of Faith,* LXXIX, 3458 (Sept. 29, 1955), p. 673.

negatively, pointing to the prevailing Keswick view[21] that the sinner's ability to do the will of God is not natural but supernatural, and that the usual Keswick interpretation of the inability of Romans 7 refers[22] to the carnal believer. The believer's ability not to sin (not his inability to sin) is a possibility which is contemplated wholly within the present action of the Holy Spirit in and by the Word. Moreover, Bromiley urges, the Keswick messages are summonses to decision, addressed to the will not as technical dogmatics but rather, in the spirit of biblical exhortation. But this does not settle the question whether or no the Keswick doctrine places too much emphasis on human activity and response in the work of sanctification.

The precise balance of Divine and human, it must be admitted, is not easy to wrest even from the Scriptures. On the one hand, an abundance of passages justify the verdict of D. S. Adam: "That the spiritual life, and its fruits of knowledge and love and right action, is due entirely to the creative activity of the Holy Spirit of God, immanent and operative in the souls of finite individuals, is frequently affirmed in the Holy Scripture. The Christian life is said to begin with a birth of the spirit, and to be continued and developed under the influence and guidance of the Spirit."[23] On the other hand, the New Testament teaching assuredly vindicates Andrew Murray's emphasis: "The work of Christ is vicarious, that of the Holy Spirit is not. He works *in man,* but not *in his place.*"[24] We must always avoid a conception which suspends the believer's sanctification in this life onesidedly upon supernatural efficiency. Henry Ward Beecher spoke to the point when he emphasized that Jesus did not use the power of miracle to secure the progress of morality in human life, but appealed rather to man's empowerment by the Holy Spirit. "In no instance did he seek to secure moral results by direct power. By his will he changed water to wine, but never pride to humility. . . . The fury of the sea he allayed by a word, but the storms of human passion he never controlled by his irresistible will."[25] The important significance which the gospels attach to the wilderness temptation of Christ emphasizes that, in our Lord's incarnation, the fulfillment of the moral ideal did not come without personal attainment and probation. The tendency of ministers and lay leaders, doubtless earnest, to speak of the necessity of a "second Pentecost" lends itself easily to the error against which we here protest. The Spirit is already with us in his full potentiality. Moral achievement depends mostly upon our appropriation, through the obedience of faith, of the resurrection-life he brings from on high into the redemption-life of man. What is

[21]As set forth, for instance, in *So Great Salvation. The History and Message of the Keswick Convention* (London: Marshall, Morgan & Scott, 1952).

[22]E. F. Kevan defends the view that Paul refers to his pre-regenerate experience.

[23]D. S. Adam, *A Handbook of Christian Ethics,* p. 152f.

[24]Andrew Murray, *The Spirit of Christ* (Toronto: A. G. Watson, 1888), p. 499.

[25]Henry Ward Beecher, *The Life of Jesus, the Christ* (Toronto: James Campbell, 1872), p. 425.

clear is the priority of Divine initiative and the indispensability of human response; man is to "work out" his salvation, but it is God who "works in" him both to will and to work (Phil. 2:12f.).

Pelagianism aside, and granting that in contrast with the monergistic Divine activity in regeneration the work of sanctification is synergistic, the problem to be faced is whether the believer in any act or decision in this life is wholly free of the cloud of sin. The new life consists indeed, as Charles Hodge notes, in a change in "those immanent dispositions, principles, tastes, or habits which underlie all conscious exercises, and determine the character of the man and of all his acts."[26] It involves no change in the substance of the soul, it is no mere change of purpose, but rather, a new and vital principle of life reaching into all the areas of the soul. The new heart, or new character, involves the whole man, whose new thoughts and exercises reflect a delight in the vision of spiritual truths and participation in spiritual realities.

Yet sanctification has, according to Hodge, a progressive side, in which the character is increasingly shaped by this new principle of life. This progressive work requires the cooperation of the believer, although the work itself of sanctification is Divine. It involves "removing more and more" those principles of evil still infecting the believer's nature and "destroying their power," and the "growth of the principle of the spiritual life until it controls the thoughts, feelings, and acts, and brings the soul into conformity to the image of Christ."[27]

In distinction to the Keswick position, Reformed theology insists upon a continuing conflict of the two principles of good and evil in the regenerate soul in this life, while yet allowing the distinct possibility[28] of a progressive displacement of the old by the new nature. Such a theory, assuredly, does not offer the possibility of the believer's arriving at the ability not to sin at all in this life, although deliverance from the dominion of sin as well as the experience of the lordship of Christ as its presupposition are held to be a permanent possibility. "Sanctification is such a change in the state of the soul, that sinful acts become more infrequent, and holy acts more and more habitual and controlling."[29] The new spiritual life "constantly increases in power until everything

[26]Charles Hodge, *Systematic Theology*, III, 85.

[27]*Ibid.*, III, 221. The Westminster Catechism defines sanctification as "the work of God's free grace, whereby we are renewed in the whole man after the image of God, and are enabled more and more to die unto sin and live unto righteousness."

[28]In his *Commentary on the Epistle to the Ephesians* (Grand Rapids: Eerdmans, reprint, 1954), Hodge insists that the sealing of the Holy Spirit is a separate experience subsequent to regeneration. But he does not work out the implications of "united to whom, after ye believed, ye were sealed" for the doctrine of sanctification. Rather, he simply comments: "In Christ, the Gentile Christians had obtained an inheritance, and in him also, they were sealed — after having believed. Whatever is meant by sealing, it is something which follows faith" (*ibid.*, p. 63). It may be recalled that R. A. Torrey asserted that the baptism in the Holy Spirit does not necessarily take place at regeneration, but is a distinct and additional work, which is the prerogative of every believer, and aims especially to equip him for service. *The Holy Spirit*, pp. 112ff.

[29]Hodge, *Systematic Theology*, III, 226.

uncongenial with it is expelled, and the soul is perfectly transformed into the image of Christ."[30] Does the possibility then exist that the believer can be free of known sin? Hodge denies it.[31] The believer does not in actual fact achieve complete victory over sin in this life. Nor does his consciousness permit him to think he has attained perfection. "What the Scriptures teach of the imperfection of the best works of the believer, is confirmed by the irrepressible testimony of consciousness."[32] The believer's works are called good not because the stain of sin no longer attaches to them, but because they are performed with the purpose of complying with the Divine will.[33] Substantially the same view is upheld by John Murray: the believer is never wholly free from sin in this life, hence the conflict in the Christian's life is normal. He would add, however, "there is a total difference between surviving sin and reigning sin."[34] The faith that Christ will exercise his dominion in us supplies the dynamic of holiness.

European Reformed theology expresses a somewhat less optimistic view of sanctification. G. C. Berkouwer presents its contemporary feeling by underscoring actual perfection as eschatological. The church must seek purity not through a second blessing but by feeding "on the first blessing, the forgiveness of sins."[35] "There is never a stretch along the way of salvation where justification drops out of sight. . . . Genuine sanctification — let it be repeated — stands or falls with this continued orientation toward justification and the remission of sins."[36] The New Testament doctrine of sanctification is therefore to be viewed as the regenerate man's *growth "in* holiness" rather than a sudden *leap "into* holiness." Berkouwer denies that holy habits, or that some holy principle, are given to the justified person; indeed, he repudiates such a concept as another expression of the perfectionist error. We are not to speak of the inner actions of the believer as perfections, thereby implying that he has been cleansed or made holy in himself. Like justification, sanctification rests on faith alone. Progress in sanctification is always an increase in the expression of a life positionally sanctified by God. "A sense of guilt is not gradually pushed back by a sense of holiness. Indeed, if sanctification were a process of 'improvement,' a sense of guilt would gradually evaporate. But sanctification as increased

[30]*Ibid.*, p. 229.

[31]The controversy between Calvinist and Arminian at this level reduces largely to the sterner or loose manner in which sin is defined, whether in terms mainly of outward deeds, or especially of inward disposition and motivation. The so-called Oberlin theory of perfection defined sin as voluntary transgression of known law.

[32]*Ibid.*, p. 232.

[33]*Ibid.*, p. 237.

[34]John Murray, *Redemption Accomplished and Applied* (Grand Rapids: Eerdmans, 1955), p. 181.

[35]G. C. Berkouwer, *Faith and Sanctification* (Grand Rapids: Eerdmans, 1952), p. 64.

[36]*Ibid.*, pp. 77f.

immersion in the grace and knowledge of Jesus Christ must result in a deeper sense of unworthiness."[37]

Berkouwer emphasizes that sanctification is not merely a matter of dynamic, but of deepening spiritual insight. It is not so one-sidedly interested in other and greater experiences, but in living out the first experience in its totality. This emphasis should provoke little debate. It does not, however, close the door to new and profounder operations of the Spirit and expressions of grace in the life of the believer. The moral optimism of the New Testament believers took its rise not only from the dark pagan environment of the day, but also from the astonishing approximation of godlikeness in character to which the believer was summoned. We may properly wonder whether a statement of sanctification pessimistic about Christian progress in holiness incorporates all the elements of the New Testament view.

In view of its own moral powerlessness, the predominant contemporary Christian community appends the explanation that the visible apostolic effects of the Holy Spirit belong distinctively to the age of the incarnation and Pentecost. At the same time, it practices an astonishing disregard for those real Divine gifts which are properly the inheritance of believers even in modern times.

The New Testament doctrine, as the writer sees it, admits of no complete sanctification in this life, the gift of justification, rather, guaranteeing the wholeness of Christian experience. Progressive and gradual sanctification is possible, however, although not in the sense of ascent to a level free from all possibility of sudden declension or beyond the realm of further advance. Even for the most mature believer, the possibility of sudden growth remains, either as the crown of moral aspiration, or through God's triumph in the midst of defeat. Sanctification we may define as that gracious Divine work by which the believer, the recipient of holy disposition in regeneration, is progressively renewed to the Divine image, dying to sin and living to righteousness. By sanctification the remaining tendencies to evil are subdued, the godly disposition is maintained and enforced, so that men are delivered progressively from the power of sin and consecrated to the love and service of God.

Furthermore, a certain aspect of this moral process or growth is indispensable to genuine Christian maturity. While the new birth is man's recreation in Christ's image, the subsequent life must be, with the Holy Spirit as helper, "a deepening of this image."[38] In this interim period man is offered time for earnest growth in virtue. The measure of that growth will often turn upon the soul's moral company. In his book *The Marks of a Man*, Robert Speer in an incisive chapter on "The Moral Margin," gives proper warning against a borderline existence of compromise and shame.

[37]*Ibid.*, p. 129.
[38]J. B. Lightfoot, *Saint Paul's Epistles to the Colossians and to Philemon*, p. 214.

If there is one sin which towers above all others as the ugliest of all, it is that sin which Jesus contrasted with all other sins, that sin for which he said there would be forgiveness neither in this world nor in the next, namely, the sin against the Holy Spirit. For other sins the possibility of forgiveness remains; for this sin, none. Christian interpreters have usually agreed that the sin against the Holy Ghost, whose mission it is to testify of Christ, is the rejection of Jesus Christ as personal Saviour. This rejection, if continued, brings one into the life to come without any prospect of a blessed immortality, and with no other promise from the lips of Christ but that of God's abiding wrath upon those yet in their sins. It converts the reversible state of spiritual death into irreversible eternal death. No man can call Christ Lord except by the Holy Ghost, and whosoever commits the sin against the Holy Ghost is forever without the Saviour.

Christian believers congratulate themselves often that apparently they have not committed the sin against the Holy Spirit. They confine this gruesome and abominable rebellion to the world, to those outside of Christ; it is not chargeable to the Christian community. While, however, the Christian community is not guilty of *the sin* against the Holy Spirit, it is guilty of *sins* against the Holy Spirit. This explains why the Church, the organism of believers, is such an impotent and peripheral force in the world today. Those who know their sins are covered by God's merciful atonement upon the Cross, are nevertheless powerless because, while the Spirit is not blasphemed, he is lied to (Acts 5:3), grieved (Eph. 4:30), resisted (Acts 7:51), and quenched (1 Thess. 5:19).

The prominent New Testament concern for holiness was not designated only for the first generation of Christians, or limited exclusively to it. The entire company of believers is separated unto God. The term sanctified used in this sense, is applied to all believers, whatever their degree of holiness (Acts 20:32, 26:18, 1 Cor. 1:2, Heb. 10:14). The Thessalonian letter was to be read "unto the holy brethren" (1 Thess. 5:27). Christians are a holy community with a holy calling (1 Pet. 2:9, 2 Tim. 1:9), a holy temple of God (1 Cor. 3:17, 6:19). Redemption has in view their presentation as "holy and unblameable and unreprovable in his sight" (Col. 1:22f.; cf. Eph. 1:4). That the New Testament believers had not attained holiness is clear, but that they regarded the life of virtue as a Divine expectation and a human obligation is equally clear (Rom. 6:19, 12:1, Heb. 12:10).

The filling of the Spirit does not denote sinless perfection or eradication.[39] But neither does it denote backsliding as a necessary element in the believer's life; that belongs rather to a truncated spiritual experience. The fullness of the Spirit is the only preventative to spiritual decline. Those who make not-yet-sinless sanctification an excuse for indulgence

[39] "Not as though I had already attained, either were already perfect" (Phil. 3:12).

ignore the New Testament emphasis on ethical fulfillment as both the evidence of true sonship and devotion to Christ, and the pathway of spiritual blessing. Salvation is inward and ethical, and therefore can be realized only in moral obedience, in the harmony of the believer's will with God's. "If ye know these things, blessed are ye if ye do them" (Jn. 13:17). "If ye love me, keep my commandments" (Jn. 14:15).[40] "Ye are my friends, if ye do whatsoever I command you. Henceforth I call you not servants . . . but I have called you friends" (Jn. 15:14f.).

While the life of glory remains future for complete realization, by the Holy Spirit's energizing of heart and life the Christian is able to attain a triumphant morality in the present, which not only shames the world but also mirrors the living Christ through continuous approximation of conformity to his image. Man's needs for this life can be met without an indulgent yielding to fleshly appetites and desires. The constant New Testament emphasis on sanctification calls for an existence in the Spirit completely devoid of fulfilling the lusts of the flesh (Gal. 5:16). The relationship between the Spirit and the believer's abiding in Christ is emphasized as the presupposition of "more fruit" and "much fruit"; herein empowerment for witnessing and service finds its spring (Jn. 12:24, 15:2, 5).

[40]Note John 14:16: "And I will pray the Father, and he shall give you another Comforter . . ." The Spirit makes the difference between successful and unsuccessful obedience to the command of love. He is greater than the spirit of the world (1 Jn. 4:4), and is to be in the believer as a river of living water flowing out of his heart" (Jn. 7:38f.).

21

THE DISTINCTIVE NEW TESTAMENT VIRTUES

A JONATHAN APPLE TREE produces Jonathan apples because of the distinctive nature of the tree; a rye plant produces rye grain because of the distinctive nature of the plant. Even so the Christian life produces ethical virtues that are distinctive and characteristic of the Christian life alone. There may be imitations of Christian virtues, but they are no more the real thing than a crab apple is a Jonathan apple. The nature of the fruit depends on the nature of its parent plant. The dramatic about-face by which the early Christian turned his back on the pollution of pagan conduct and set his sights and his heart on a life of moral honor is without any parallel or approximation in the society of his age.

The holiness of the believer results in fruitfulness in his life. In the New Testament, three passages equate Christian ethics with fruitfulness. These passages show the true relationship between Christian ethics and the Holy Spirit. The Holy Spirit is inseparably linked with Christ. The life of the Spirit of Christ in the individual believer is the very life of Christ in him, reproducing the character of Christ by "forming Christ" within his heart. John gives the remarkable teaching of Jesus concerning the vine and the branches; the second is Paul's catalogue of the "fruit of the Spirit"; the third is Peter's list of the Christian graces which he regards as the fruit of the life of Christ within. There is a progressive unfolding and development in these passages.

In John 15 Jesus relates the parable of the true vine. One scans the parable in vain for a reference to the Holy Spirit, yet comparison with Galatians 5:22 makes it obvious that the fruit mentioned in John belongs to the Spirit. Under the figure of a grapevine, Christ speaks of his Church. The primary thought is the union of himself and his people. What sustains this union is illustrated by the life of the vine. Christ himself is the vine; the life is his. While his life-giving energy surges through all the branches, some do not permit free channel. Such branches are the branches that bear no fruit. The larger New Testament teaching instructs us that it is the Spirit who diffuses this life, hence the inference that the fruit which the branches bear is the "fruit of the Spirit."[1] Jesus centers his thoughts upon this fruitfulness, fruit

[1]James E. Cumming, "Through the Eternal Spirit," *A Bible Study on the Holy Ghost* (Stirling: Drummond's Tract Depot, 1891), p. 211.

directly from himself, but he does not specify exactly what the fruit consists of.

Paul takes up in Galatians where Jesus left off in John. He has condensed the parable of the vine into one phrase, "the fruit of the Spirit." Paul then exhibits the excellence of the Spirit's fruit against the contrasting background of the "works of the flesh." The term "flesh" does not mean human nature *per se*. While it is now corrupt, it is not by creation essentially so. The old nature apart from the Holy Spirit "can produce works, but it cannot produce fruit. Works are produced from outward action. Fruit is produced from inward life. Works are wrought. Fruit is grown. Natural man cannot produce fruit for he is dead."[2] We shall examine this fruit of faith in detail shortly.

All men fall into one of the two broad classifications, "in the flesh" or "in the Spirit." When the Spirit reigns inwardly there is a corresponding change of the standards and habits of outward conduct. Paul lashes out against the vices of heathendom that were threatening the infant churches. Such vices were not possible for those who had discarded the old man and were being renewed in the power of the Holy Spirit. "To live by the Spirit, to walk by the Spirit, this was the one safeguard against relapsing into the lusts of the flesh."[3] From and through the indwelling Spirit the spiritual virtues fully ripen.

Peter also has a list of spiritual fruit. The virtues he records will "make you that ye shall neither be barren nor unfruitful in the knowledge of our Lord Jesus Christ" (2 Pet. 1:8). This list is decidedly different from the one in Galatians both in its content and in its order. It contains only two virtues in common with Paul's "fruit of the Spirit." And while Paul begins with love, Peter closes with it. Why this divergence? The one gives the result, the other the process that leads to this result. "Paul stands looking at the harvest; Peter goes through the seasons of spring, summer, and autumn."[4] The regulative condition is diligence. This is followed by the basis of Christian character, faith. Courage of conviction is added to faith. Then comes knowledge, which corrects and guides. Then temperance, or moderation in all things, is added. This is followed by patience which is able to wait with longsuffering. Then godliness, or godlikeness in character. Next comes love of the brethren, and finally the bond of perfection, love.

The believer is like a tree planted by the rivers of water (Ps. 1:3); he bears the fruit of the Spirit (Gal. 5:22). In this respect, he differs from the creature of speculative morality. Secular ethics seeks to draw moral direction and vitality from within the unregenerate nature of man. The world could see a startling difference from its own moral product as it looked upon the virtue of the rank and file of the followers

[2]John B. Kenyon, *The Bible Revelation of the Holy Spirit* (Grand Rapids: Zondervan, 1939), p. 144.

[3]Henry Swete, *The Holy Spirit in the New Testament* (London: Macmillan, 1910), p. 344.

[4]Cumming, *op. cit.*, p. 214.

of Christ. Achievements of the flesh, which Julia Ward Howe's *Battle Hymn of the Republic* aptly characterizes as "grapes of wrath," will be brought under Divine judgment when they are cast at last "into the great winepress of the wrath of God" (Rev. 14:19). The believer's fate will be otherwise. He will be known because of his distinctive fruits (Mt. 7:16ff.). What a man sows, he reaps (Gal. 6:7), and "he that soweth to the Spirit shall of the Spirit reap life everlasting" (Gal. 6:8). From Genesis to Revelation, the Bible stresses in the figure of fruit the inseparability of the moral life from a relationship to the Living God.

The biblical virtues should not be identified superficially with the virtues of other systems of cultural endeavor. T. T. Brumbaugh suggested that the principles of Bushido, a system of Spartan-like virtues that Japanese warrior nobles observed in vocation and daily life, are the equivalent of the Pauline fruit of the Spirit.[5] Bushido was born in Buddhism, Shintoism, and Confucianism. From Buddhism came submission to fate and disdain of life and death; from Shintoism loyalty to the sovereign, ancestral reverence, and filial piety; from Confucianism the ties of personal and neighbor relations. This morality eventually summed up "the Volksgeist of the Island Realm."[6] It stressed justice or rectitude, but had no concept of justification; right reason, without dependence on revelation; courage, wholly that of the brave heart of the natural man; benevolence, yet short of *agape*; politeness, a respect for the feelings and social position of others that evidenced mastery of the unregenerate spirit over the flesh; truthfulness, yet stranger to the Truth; honor, emphasizing the dignity of man and discounting his sinfulness; patience, meekness, loyalty, self-control, all the result of stringent discipline but no new birth by the Spirit of God. The new life in the Spirit is the basic presupposition of virtue for the Christian. Bushido leaves no room for God; its virtues rise out of bent men. Conformity to the Bushido code begets pride; failure to conform results in shame. Christian ethics recognizes that conformity to the will of God is a lifelong process. Failure leads the Christian to ask for cleansing and to call upon Divine help for growth. Moreover, love becomes the moving principle of the whole; it always stands at the head of the virtues. The others are seen in their true light only when they are seen in love. Bushido grants loyalty to superiors the upper place; love is no respecter of persons, and knows no inferior or superior.

The Christian virtues all cohere in a harmonious whole. One is not lifted up at the expense of another; they do not work against each other. It is the Holy Spirit who fits each in place in the good life. "These graces are not said to be the fruits of the Spirit, but the fruit, *i.e.*, if the Spirit is given control of our life, he will not bear one of

[5]T. T. Brumbaugh, *Religious Values in Japanese Culture* (Tokyo: Kyo Bun Kwan, 1934), p. 65.

[6]Inazo Nitobe, *Bushido, The Soul of Japan* (Tokyo: The Student Co., 1905), p. 150.

these as fruit in one person and another as fruit in another person, but this will be the one fruit of many flavors that he produces in each one."[7]

The Spirit is perfectly consistent, and does not contradict himself.[8] A single theme unites the many virtues into a single life of virtue. The life of the Spirit is one in its source; it is many-sided as virtue works itself out on the many fronts of life. The fruit mentioned in Galatians 5 is unitary in the third person of the Trinity, he who bears witness to the Son. Hence, virtue continues to go out from the Risen Christ through the Spirit and so indwells and fills the believer. The distressing pursuit of a "golden mean" between two extremes and the never-ending search for just the right combination of virtues that so haunted class Aristotelian ethics is no plight of biblical ethics. This derivation of virtue from the single source of the Spirit is radically different from Aristotle's adjustment of virtues that can only be laid on a corrupt human nature. The truly virtuous life is not a quasi-harmonious integration of the purely human. It is not the never quite successful attempt to adjust one extreme of action to another. But it is a life in which the good is a unity. Only God is good, and he has now taken residence within the personality of the believer. The single good, God, now becomes expressed in the many separate virtues and graces of Christianity. They are separate only in living expression; they are one in source. Any partitioning of the virtues is an academic partition, made only so we can talk of them.

Because of this inner unity of the moral ideal, the life filled by the Spirit is the best guarantee against ethical one-sidedness. Whether it be virtue in public morals, virtue in the home, a reverence for the purity of others, or the virtue of spiritual controls in one's own life, ethical achievement is correlated by the pervasive influence of the Spirit in the life of the believer. And for this same reason, Christian ethics is delivered from the constant struggle to construct a hierarchy of values. This struggle is one every system of ethics faces when it tries to determine ethical values apart from God. Such a system must find some philosophic glue to prevent the lack of inner unity in values from working itself out in disastrous tension. For Christianity, the virtues reflect interdependence as well as inner unity. "It is not a series of graces, from which one may make a selection, and develop those that accord with his personal preference, while neglecting the others. . . . It is doubtless significant that Paul denotes them as *fruit* of the Spirit, and not the fruit*s* of the Spirit. These gifts constitute one inseparable, coherent harvest of Christian graces. No one of them can flourish without the others. . . . Displace love with hatred, and see how incongruous the entire list becomes . . . in the place of the word joy the term pessimism, and see how absurd the whole aspect of the passage

[7]R. A. Torrey, *The Person and Work of the Holy Spirit*, p. 127.
[8]Kenyon, *op. cit.*, p. 148.

appears. Or substitute conflict for peace, impatience for longsuffering, cruelty for kindness, and see how the beauty of the entire picture is hopelessly marred."[9]

Christian virtue was not born of Greek philosophy, nor of the speculative thought of any age, for that matter. Nor can Christian virtue be wedded to secular philosophy. They mix together no better than oil and water. The medieval schoolmen tried to force an unnatural union between the two — and Christian ethics suffered for it. Ambrose wrote the first treatise on Christian ethics, *On the Duties of the Clergy.* He borrowed his basic Christian virtues — prudence, justice, fortitude, temperance — from Cicero's *De officiis,* and went on to invoke Old Testament heroes as illustrative of them. Aquinas worked out an elaborate merger of Aristotle and Christianity. From Aristotle he derived three intellectual virtues — wisdom, science, and understanding — and the four Platonic moral virtues — prudence, temperance, fortitude, and justice — and to these he added the three theological virtues — faith, hope, and charity. All of these were ruled by reason. But the Christian virtues actually are not natural impulses under the control of reason. As Newman Smyth remarked, we must approach with caution the suggestion that the Christian ideal is "realized in any virtue and in any praise."[10] Augustine referred to the pagan virtues as "splendid vices" because at his best man acted out of the wrong motive of self-righteousness. And so pride corrupted all his efforts. The soul and reason cannot possibly rule the impulses rightly unless they serve God. "The virtues themselves, if they bear no relation to God, are in truth vices rather than virtues."[11] In the same spirit Paulsen remarked that "the ethical virtues of the Greeks . . . are nothing but natural impulses educated and disciplined by reason . . . the more dangerous because they seem good."[12]

This forcible joining of two unlikes has not been confined to medieval scholasticism. Modern Protestant liberal ethics has been deeply influenced by the doctrine of extreme Divine immanence. Indeed, this extreme point of view is regarded both as the foundation for Christian virtue and as its end. Man has no need of a new birth since he is already a part of God. He does not need virtue infused into him; he need only fan to life the innate godly virtue already in him. For example, Marshall says that while Jesus supplemented them, he recognized the four Platonic virtues as cardinal.[13] But such an estimate tends to judge Jesus by Platonic standards, rather than to discriminate the unique biblical virtues. Biblical virtues are not identical with pagan virtues.

[9]Harvey Eugene Dana, *The Holy Spirit in Acts* (Kansas City: Central Seminary Press, 1943), p. 78.
[10]Newman Smyth, *Christian Ethics,* p. 99.
[11]Augustine, *The City of God,* 19:25.
[12]Friedrich Paulsen, *A System of Ethics* (New York: Scribner, 1899), p. 66.
[13]L. H. Marshall, *The Challenge of New Testament Ethics,* p. 90.

Yet pagan virtues are not to be utterly cast out. They are based on a fallacious system — a system that may even be anti-Christian. They result in a certain sinful self-satisfaction and may be a means of work-righteousness. Why then are they so universally acknowledged as good and true? Why is so little argument raised against them? Is it not because they have been formed by man who is stamped with the ethical image of God? The good and the true may come through distorted and stretched. And men everywhere, who also are stamped with the image, acknowledge as good and true what reflects that image, even if sometimes in a crude way.

Jesus appeals to the sense of right and virtue when he addresses unregenerate men. He expects them to respond morally to his ethical statements, for they have some innate standard and judge good and bad. He does say that "none is good, save one, that is God" (Lk. 18:19), and so anticipates Pauline anthropology (Rom. 3:10f.). Yet he denied that goodness was totally destroyed when he said, "If ye then, being evil know how to give good gifts unto your children, how much more shall your Father which is in heaven give good things to them that ask him?" (Mt. 7:11; cf. Lk. 11:13, where the Holy Spirit occurs instead). The essential point is that there is some continuity between Divine goodness and what man acknowledges to be good in his own experience. Some of the judgments of human conscience on fundamental morals are right, for the distinction between vice and virtue has not been totally erased in man. Fallen man lacks love for God, lacks ideal attainment of the good, yet he knows good from evil generally.

Yet, when all of this has been said, unregenerate man and regenerate man are poles apart in the way in which each tries to live the good life. Christianity strives for purity by more than mere embellishment of common moral ideals and practices. It lifts human life on to a higher plane of ethical excellence.

The New Testament introduces a new ethical vocabulary. It effects an actual change in human experience to raise man to a new and abiding life of virtue. And so it gives an actual godlike quality to the moral life of the believer.[14]

In the matter of ethical vocabulary, the distinctively scriptural words unfold new vistas into moral realities. Dean Inge notes that the Gospel introduced a new ethical terminology required by its new ethical content. "The Greek words which we translate love (or charity), joy, peace, hope, humility, are no part of the stock-in-trade of Greek moralists before Christ. Men do not coin new words for old ideas . . ."[15] Even

[14]"We turn to the apostolic letters to Rome, to Corinth, to Ephesus, to Colossae, to the Hebrews, and it is everywhere the same. These disciples of the Crucified, accused, as we know they were . . . of all that was vicious, we here detect, behind the scenes, welcoming the most absolute possible law of virtue and living it out." H. C. G. Moule, *Grace and Virtue*, p. 85.

[15]W. R. Inge, "Religion," in *The Legacy of Greece*, Sir R. W. Livingstone, ed. (Oxford: The Clarendon Press, 1921), p. 42.

the term "virtue," so indispensable to philosophical morality, is not a characteristically biblical word. It is hardly an intrusion into revealed ethics, since the idea is not foreign. Dewar remarks that Paul uses "the normal Greek term for virtue . . . only once (Phil. iv.8) . . . in a passage which is a kind of *a fortiori*. . . . He frequently refers to 'the good' . . . but in a manner very different from a Greek moralist and, with one exception, neither of these expressions occurs in the Corinthian letters."[16] The Bible is properly designated a handbook of virtue. Look where he will, the student of Scripture will invariably find a concern for the highest things, for the side of life which matters most. The word "virtue" is used in the sense of human moral excellence in perhaps only two New Testament passages, 2 Peter 1:5 and Philippians 4:8.[17] Peter exhorts Christians to "add to your faith virtue," Paul implores them familiarly, "if there be any virtue . . . think on these things," or as Handley Moule has suggested, "think these things out."[18] One reason for dissatisfaction with the term "virtue" was that it suggested abstract nebulous ideas of some unattainable good. It was capstone of the life-view of Greek philosophy. Christianity had filled out the form of virtue with a vast amount of detailed content that could actually be realized through the influence of the Spirit. There was nothing nebulous or hazy about the kind of good life the early Christians lived. In the later ante-Nicene era, Christian moralists began to use the vocabulary of Greek and Roman ethical study. This was natural, since the secular philosophers had coined the standard vocabulary of the world to which Christianity addressed itself. But the Christian writers used the old word with new content. Often the end result was injustice to the controlling biblical ideas. But the essential idea of the Greek *arete* and the Latin *virtus* — manly courage devoted to the true and the good, brave loyalty to the moral — was an ideal that was not actually realized until Pentecost. Added help was needed from God for man to live as he knew he should.[19]

If we inquire what virtues Jesus specifically commended, and what vices he especially condemned, the answer is not hard to find. Jesus made the difference between the good life and the life of sin transparently clear. Yet one cannot discuss virtue and Jesus in the same way in which

[16]Lindsay Dewar, *An Outline of New Testament Ethics,* p. 142.

[17]In 2 Peter 1:3, as in 1 Peter 2:9, it may refer to the Divine virtue or perfection. In Mark 5:30, Luke 6:19 and 8:46, it is used for power (not necessarily moral). In the Old Testament, when the Hebrew is somewhat less explicit, suggesting perhaps worthiness rather than virtue, the adjective "virtuous" occurs in the translation of Ruth 3:11, Proverbs 12:4, 31:10, and the adverb "virtuously" in Proverbs 31:29.

[18]Moule, *op. cit.,* p. 30.

[19]Here again a virile Christianity carries alongside its revealed theology a bold pragmatic confirmation. Those who, victimized by the pragmatic and experimental temper of the times, dismissed as speculative curiosities all doctrines which could not be submitted to practical tests, misunderstood the nature of religion and morality alike. But a genuine Christian ethics has least of all moral systems to fear from the test of consequences in its rightful perspective.

he might discuss virtue and Moses, or Isaiah, or Paul, or John. It is not that we have reliable information about virtue only from Jesus. Nor is it that the prophets and apostles only taught morals and failed to live morally. The actual facts are otherwise. Nor is the main difference that Jesus gives us more information about the life of virtue and its implications than do the prophets, although he does teach additional truths about ethics without which Christian morality would be truncated. Jesus and virtue stand apart from all others because Jesus alone is the incarnation of virtue. He is the actual embodiment of ethical perfection. This is a central affirmation of Christian thought, and one already given separate consideration. Here it is enough to note that he alone stands out among all men in history as the only truly virtuous man. His unique sinless life conditions the content of the life of virtue for all other men.

"Purity of heart is the primal Christian virtue." So writes Hartmann,[20] and in this assertion he succinctly expresses the controlling feature of Jesus' approach to morality. But more than this, Hartmann recognizes the striking contrast of this view with that of classic antiquity: "Not only did ancient ethics not know the value of purity in this sense, but by the greatest representatives of philosophy it was consciously set aside. . . . If there be an ethos in an attitude of mind which is anterior to all conflict and in contrast to all energy, then the peculiar value of such an attitude is overlooked in the ancient ethics."[21] The basic value is found in an interior state of the soul, not in ethical performance which is wrested from inner moral conflict, nor in behavior alone under any circumstances. "Blessed are the pure in heart, for they shall see God" (Mt. 5:8).

Such a setting for the moral life brings man face to face at once with universal sinfulness. He needs atonement and a new heart. The virtuous life is impossible apart from the redemption that is in Christ Jesus. The point is not that the Old Testament lacked emphasis on the genuine ethical life as inner and spiritual, nor did it fail to relate the law to the Divine provision of atonement whereby man can find acceptance with God, for both elements are distinctive of biblical ethics in both Old and New Testaments. But Jesus showed the implications of "purity of heart" with a radical inwardness so incisively that his hearers cringed as they realized they stood in the very presence of the Absolute. Jesus unequivocally linked their eternal destinies to himself as the moral judge of man.[22]

The Beatitudes, which summarize the way of blessedness, find the soul's enduring satisfaction in the life of meekness. This is quite contrary to the spirit of Greek philosophy that found it in self-assertion. Hunger for righteousness stands over against the Gentile devotion to a

[20]Nicolai Hartmann, *Ethics,* II, 212.

[21]*Ibid.,* p. 213. Cf. Aristotle, *Nicomachean Ethics,* 1100a, 1ff.

[22]"And every man that hath this hope in him purifieth himself, even as he is pure" (1 Jn. 3:3).

speculative "golden mean" or a pursuit of enough good deeds to outweigh the bad. Unrestricted mercy rather than suppression on the ground of racial or nationalistic distinction; inner singleness of moral intention, or purity of heart, free from all compromise or duplicity of ethical motivation; peaceableness; these are the heart of Christian virtue. The identity of these with the Pauline fruit of the Spirit is obvious. The elements of meekness, kindness and peace are in both, and the prevailing New Testament assumption seen in both is that love is the font of all the virtues. Love is expressed in the Sermon as a hunger for righteousness.

Out of this conception of "purity of heart" rises the ethical vocabulary peculiar to Christianity. The eye that is single; the body full of light (Mt. 6:22, Lk. 11:34); singleness of heart (Acts 2:46, Eph. 6:5, Col. 3:22); the eye or hand that does not offend (Mt. 5:29f., 18:8f., Mk. 9:43ff.); the conscience void of offense (Acts 24:16). These are terms that indicate the whole man devoted exclusively to the will of God in the face of temptation and external pressure. The single-minded are free from judgment that hangs over those who compromise perverse principles and reprehensible motives.[23] This somewhat strange word — "singleness" — leads naturally to the notion of the truth as that which is to be done, not simply to be comprehended. Moral action therefore rises out of the pure heart and its uncompromised devotion to the good. The heart, the eye, the mind, the body, are not to be half-heartedly given to God while still anchored in the world. They are to be instruments of Divine righteousness. The pure heart is not led astray by inordinate desires, nor allured by temptation. What is pure is uncompounded, free from admixture with sin and falsehood. It shares the straightforwardness and guilelessness of unspoiled childhood, a frankness and openness that has nothing to hide; it is unashamed in openness of mind and heart, and requires no mask because nothing is concealed.[24]

In this connection Dewar finds the unwillingness to cause scandal a quality of Christian ethics without parallel in non-Christian views.[25] The words *skandalidzo* and *skandalon* are frequently found on Jesus' lips, indicating his concern with the moral significance of giving offense and causing others to stumble. The word *skandalon* in the New Testament has only an ethical significance: it designates an "offense" that tempts and entices to sin. The word *skandalidzo,* which is not found in Greek writers although it occurs in the Septuagint and Apocrypha, is common in the New Testament. The believer is not to be an occasion of sin, either in his own life or in the lives of others, but is to be separated

[23]Note the extension of this figure to "singleness of heart" (Acts 2:46; cf. Eph. 6:5, Col. 3:22), and the contrastive notion of the "double-minded man" (Jas. 1:8). Purity of heart and single-mindedness are tacitly equated in Jas. 4:8: "Cleanse your hands, ye sinners; and purify your hearts, ye double-minded."

[24]Cf. the Pauline emphasis on simplicity in conduct, or freedom from deceit (2 Cor. 1:12, 11:3; Rom. 12:8), and on purity (Phil. 4:8, 1 Tim. 3:9, 5:22, 2 Tim. 1:3).

[25]Dewar, *op sit.,* pp. 62ff.

from what seduces to unbelief and immorality. He does not provoke false views about the Christian life nor unbelief in Christ. He refuses to be a temptation to the rejection of the Redeemer or to apostasy from the faith. It is man's abnormal moral condition which causes him to be a stumbling block and so give rise to the woes of humanity (Mt. 18:7). Redemptive ethics, in counteracting this condition, seeks to remove whatever imperils moral judgment and behavior.[26] Purity of heart has implications manward as well as Godward, and refuses to cause others to sin or to draw them toward evil. "Whoso offends one of these" is a phrase appearing on Jesus' lips in introduction to some of his sternest warnings (Mt. 18:6, Mk. 9:42, Lk. 17:2), and the theme of unjustifiable offense is caught up again by Paul (Rom. 14:21, 1 Cor. 8:13) and John (1 Jn. 2:10).

Dewar is doubtless right in singling out, alongside of the avoidance of provocative conduct, faith and forgiveness as qualities specially commended by Christ, and in attaching to them an element of uniqueness which Jesus brings to them.[27]

Faith is seldom mentioned as a noun in the Old Testament (Dt. 32:20, Heb. 4:2), although the verb "to trust" is common. But faith as a repose of mind is written into the experience of the Christian community by Jesus' frequent use of the substantive form. Jesus used the word as a state of mind and heart, not merely an act of volition. He brought God nearer to man, and gave faith a firmer grasp, a steadfast reliance and adherence.[28] He sketched the contrast between "no faith" (Mt. 17:17, Mk. 9:19, Lk. 9:41, Jn. 20:27), "little faith" (Mt. 6:30, 8:26, 14:31, 16:8, Lk. 12:28), and "great faith" (Mt. 8:10, Lk. 7:9). To "have faith" or an abiding confidence in God becomes the normal presupposition of a life pleasing to God (Mt. 17:20, 21:21, 23:23, Lk. 17:6, 18:8). The apostles asked for increased faith (Lk. 17:5). " 'They that believed' became a standing name for the followers of Christ (Acts 2:44, Rom. 10:4, 1 Cor. 14:22, Mk. 16:17)."[29] Jesus profoundly impresses his followers that the attitude of faith is virtuous, not merely in the exercise of the charismatic gifts, but as a specific requirement of the moral life. The attitude of unbelief is sin. Indeed, the link between purity of heart and faith is not difficult to discover: the pure heart is impossible for the natural man; it is only in and through faith in the redemptive God that man can rest in the benefits

[26]In this connection it may be well to append a note on ethical compromises which Jesus especially condemns. Dewar lists fornication, covetousness, hypocrisy, and foolishness — each of which holds prominence in Jesus' teaching. In each case, the emphasis falls on the inner disposition as fundamental to the outer manifestation; fornication rises from lust, covetousness from anxiety, hypocrisy from mental dishonesty, and foolishness from pride or the lack of humility.

[27]Dewar, *op. cit.*, pp. 62ff.

[28]The point of contact with singleness of mind is later reflected by James. The man who prays in faith is contrasted with the mind of a doubter (1:6); the inward nature of the doubter is doublemindedness, or a wavering of soul between its direction toward the claim of God and the claim of the world.

[29]G. G. Findley, "Faith," in *H.D.B.*, 256b.

of the atonement and seek to live pleasing to God with a conscience void of guilt.

Another side to the virtue of faith is the virtue of faithfulness. Faithfulness is the trait of fidelity, constancy, firmness, reliability. It speaks of good faith, honesty, and uprightness in men. They who believed were to be steady and firm in their belief and constant in their trust. Only when faithfulness has become an abiding virtue does the attitude of faithlessness appear in its full character as sin. The words "O faithless generation" fall from our Lord's lips (Mt. 17:17), and anticipate the Pauline inclusion of faithfulness as a fruit of the Spirit (Gal. 5:22).

Faith leads appropriately to a consideration of forgiveness as a fundamental virtue stressed by Jesus. Dewar notes that the New Testament words for "forgive" (*aphierni*) and "forgiveness" (*aphesis*) did not bear in classical Greek the sense which they acquire in the gospels. They had only the sense of payment of a material debt. Thus they appear as words which have now acquired wholly new meanings with the Cross as their background. The Christian life is non-vindictive, declining all vengeance. It is positively a forgiving spirit. "That a man should always be willing to forgive" has been called Jesus' "most striking innovation in morality."[30] The forgiveness of others was, of course, not absent from the moral life of the Old Testament, but the gracious Divine erasure of man's many and unending transgressions gives central prominence to this virtue in the New Testament. The Christian thwarts the spirit of his Master if he refuses to forgive seventy times seven times (Mt. 18:22, Lk. 17:3f.). From Jesus' giving of himself for sinners the church learned what forgiveness really means as a virtue (Eph. 4:32). Divine forgiveness is granted conditionally: "Forgive us, as we forgive our debtors" (Mt. 6:12). Jesus declared that whoever refuses to forgive others neither worships God nor prays effectively (Mt. 5:24, Mk. 11:25).

No treatment of the virtues our Lord taught is adequate which does not assign first place to love. Love is the fountain of the pure heart and the forgiving spirit. Love is not simply an attitude which Jesus taught; it is the essence of his very being. He stressed it as the supreme virtue that includes all else in itself. All the commandments are fulfilled by love of God and neighbor (Mt. 22:37f.). Lack of love for God and man is the root of evil (Lk. 11:42, Jn. 5:42, Mt. 5:46). Jesus is the very incarnation of love. Christian expositors have shown that Jesus' conduct supremely fulfilled the requirements of the great Pauline chapter on love (cf. 1 Cor. 13).[31] Yet all discussions of love must sooner or later center about the Cross; the self-giving of Christ for others is love's incomparable manifestation. "Greater love hath no man than this, that a

[30]Marshall, *op. cit.*, p. 90.

[31]fC. Dewar: "If for *agape* we substitute 'Christ' and change the tenses, we find . . . a wonderful description of our Lord's manner of life" (*op. cit.*, p. 127).

man lay down his life for his friends" (Jn. 15:13). "But God commendeth his love toward us, in that while we were yet sinners, Christ died for us" (Rom. 5:8). The dramatic coinage by the New Testament of a new key word for love, *agape,* rises as the climactic manifestation of Divine love. The world of antiquity knew only *eros* or *philos* love, which reached out to its object for the ultimate benefit of the lover. It did not know *agape.*[32] Jesus Christ introduced a unique love, the absolute giving of one's self unto death for the sake of others. He needed nothing from them to fill some essential lack in himself; he was not antecedently obligated to them; indeed, they had done despite to him and were alienated from him. Such love was *agape,* unknown in the world of non-redemptive ethics, but the center of biblical revelation and history in the atonement of Jesus Christ.

Alongside purity of heart, faith, forgiveness and love, room must be made for the virtue of humility. The ancients did not regard humility as a virtue. It may even be said, with Lightfoot (*Commentary on Colossians* 2:18), that the heathen moralists pictured it as a vice, and spoke of it with contempt. Epictetus disparaged it, as must any moral philosophy that regards man in his inmost being as essentially Divine; so did Nietzsche, as must any ethical view that regards man as essentially animal, and hence can hope to lift him above the other brutes only by the deceptive maneuver of unjustifiable pride. To non-Christian ethics, humility appears to be self-degradation and servility. This is because of an antecedent arrogance of spirit, a refusal to acknowledge the proper boundaries of human dignity, a reluctance to confess one's proper status in relation to the Living God. We shall consider humility at length later on.

As one makes the transition to virtues in the apostolic literature, he realizes at once the pervading idea of love as Jesus had developed it.[33] It is not mere coincidence that love appears first in the list of spiritual qualities set forth by Paul. Its primacy is seen in Jesus' teachings and its priority is affirmed elsewhere by Paul (1 Cor. 13, Gal. 5:14). Whether one turns to the triad of virtues, "faith, hope, and love," in the first Corinthian letter, or to the more extended list of virtues in Galatians, Philippians, and Colossians, the priority of love is apparent. It is exalted above ecstasy, preaching power, spiritual insight, and knowledge. It carries us to the center of Pauline ethics no less than to the heart of the ethics of Jesus. The term *agape* hardly occurs in the Septuagint, but it is found sixty-two times in the Pauline epistles. It is

[32]"For it should not be forgotten that agape is a word born within the bosom of revealed religion: . . . there is no trace of it in any heathen writer whatever . . ." (Richard C. Trench, *Synonyms of the New Testament,* p. 41).

[33]Lucian wrote that the Christians "become incredibly alert when anything . . . affects their common interests" and Tertullian sharply registers the contrast of pagan and Christian in immortal phrases: "They say 'look how they love one another!' (they themselves being given to mutual hatred). 'Look how they are prepared to die for one another!' (they themselves being readier to kill each other)" (*Apolog.* xxxix).

the first fruit of the Spirit (Gal. 5:22f.), the "bond of perfection" without which the other ethical virtues fall apart (Col. 3:14). It alone makes possible the fulfillment of the law. Romans 12:9-21 exhibits love in action, providing an exhibition of how love works out in practice. *Agape* is without hypocrisy; it censors the desire for personal superiority over fellow Christians; it promotes industry in man's service of God; it supplies hopeful joy, and powers of endurance, and perseverance in prayer in the face of difficulty; it loosens the pursestrings in almsgiving and hospitality; it promotes mutual sympathy in the joys and sorrows of life; and it promotes harmony in social relations.

First Corinthians 13 is Paul's psalm of *agape,* a reply of biblical ethics to Plato's eulogy of *eros* (*Symposium,* 197) and to every philosophical treatment of love as a virtue. Whoever reads it discerningly will feel compelled to say with Janet and Seailles: "Love is to Christians what wisdom was to the ancients, the principle . . . of all the virtues."[34] It is a personification of love. Since Jesus Christ is supreme love in the flesh, and any portrait of the essential characteristics of love must disclose his features, Jesus Christ and love are interchangeable in the passage. The incarnation and the atonement are love's loftiest illustrations. The *Kenosis*-passage in Philippians (2:5-11) tells where love led the Son of God. Dewar remarks, "Self-renouncing love was not a characteristic of the Jewish picture of the Messiah" but "whenever . . . Paul refers to our Lord's example, it is always to self-effacing *agape* in some form."[35] Love is "poured out" into the hearts of believers through the Spirit (Rom. 5:5), and so has its source in God himself. The Holy Spirit, Christ's other-self, communicates it as a gift to the faithful. It is not, contrary to Marshall, simply "the consideration and care for man . . . based on a lively recognition of human value and of the sacredness of human personality, and which are characterized by the active desire to confer benefits."[36] *Agape* is defined primarily by God's love for unworthy man, and not primarily from any deference to man because of his natural dignity and desert. Love is longsuffering in the face of provocation, remains gracious (1 Cor. 13:4), does not transgress moral seemliness, nor become enraged, nor compute the evil done to her (13:5), nor delight in the moral failure of others, but finds its joy in the right (13:6), bears up under all burdens, believes the good things, faces the future with triumphant confidence, endures all challenges (13:7).[37]

Love is prized above the highest charismatic gifts; those miraculous endowments associated with the apostolic ministry are transient in

[34]Paul Janet and Gabriel Seailles, *A History of the Problems of Philosophy,* Ada Monahan, trans., Henry Jones, ed. (London: Macmillan, 1902), II, 48.

[35]Dewar, *op. cit.,* p. 134.

[36]Marshall, *op. cit.,* p. 291.

[37]For Paul "this affection could be no mere inward rapture. It must go out to others as the love of Christ had gone out to him" (H. A. A. Kennedy, *The Theology of the Epistles,* p. 143). It has been said of love, in contrast with duty, that it "can never do enough."

themselves, and become worthless when love is absent (1 Cor. 13:1ff.).[38] Not only the highest gift of prophecy which grasps the mysteries of heaven by revelation, but also omnipotent faith which bridges mountains, is without value if it lacks love; it then has no ethical significance. Even acts of self-sacrifice which do not proceed from love have no eternal significance. The gifts of the Spirit are temporary; love never falls into decay; it is imperishable (13:8ff.). Prophecy, tongues, and deep knowledge of revelation serve the church only until the Lord's return. Then even perfect knowledge becomes the immediate possession of all and the transitory gifts of chosen individuals are eclipsed. But what goes on into eternity is faith, hope, and love (13:13). The future eschatological age marks the end of all temporary phenomena, but belief and hope and love are vindicated as eternal. While faith, hope, and love are all of lasting import, love holds the highest place and value. It conditions the moral worth of the other virtues (13:13). All the sublime things of life, even those at the pinnacle, are worthless if love is lacking as their cardinal motif. Love endures as the very life of heaven and, in fact, is the Divine life itself (1 Jn. 4:8, 16).[39]

Love is brought to its peak of meaning in the Johannine writings. Perhaps because he was the disciple whom Jesus loved, John wrote of the love of God as did none of the other disciples. Love to John seemed the motivating force of all things in the universe. Love was the "ought" (1 Jn. 5:3, 2 Jn. 6). What one word could best describe God? John easily chose the word: Love. God is love! (1 Jn. 4:8). We are able to

[38]"Now, for the first time," remarks Harnack of the early Christian movement, "that testimony rose among men, which cannot even be surpassed, the testimony that God is love. The first great statement of the new religion, into which the fourth evangelist condensed its central principle, was based entirely and exclusively on love: 'We love, because He first loved us' . . ." and in conjunction with this arises the conviction that "ministering love is the practical expression of love to God" (*The Expansion of Christianity in the First Three Centuries,* I, 183). "The new language on the lips of Christians was the language of love. But it was more than a language, it was a thing of power and action. The Christians really considered themselves brothers and sisters, and their actions corresponded to this belief" (pp. 183f.). It was through this motivation of love that the Gospel in Harnack's phrase "became a social message" (p. 184). Because Christianity inculcated a vast ministry of brotherliness in the ancient world, Harnack is compelled to devote a long chapter to "The Gospel of Love and Charity" in which he calls special attention to these ten distinctive features of Christian life and practice: (1) almsgiving both individually and corporately; (2) support of teachers and officials; (3) support of widows and orphans; (4) support of the sick, infirm, disabled, and poor; (5) care for prisoners and for people languishing in the mines; (6) care of the poor requiring burial and of the dead in general; (7) care for slaves; (8) care for people visited by great calamities; (9) the provision of work; and (10) care for brethren on a journey (hospitality) and for churches in poverty or peril.

[39]"What is it which connects the temporal and the eternal," asks Kierkegaard, "what except love, which just for this reason is before everything, and abides when everything else is past? . . . Love is the bond of the eternal" (*Works of Love,* p. 6). Who loves in truth "will involuntarily and unwittingly expose every hypocrite who comes near him, or else he will make him ashamed; but the lover will perhaps not even be conscious of this" (*ibid.,* p. 13).

love because he first loved us. Love for another is the whole sum of Christian ethics. Luthardt has expressed the thought well. "We learn what it is to love by the love wherewith God has loved us. 'We love Him because He first loved us.' This one saying of St. John expresses the whole mystery of Christian morality. God first loved us is the summary of Christian doctrine. We love Him is the summary of Christian morality."[40] Put this into immediate action and Christ's disciples would make an impact upon the world second only to that of Christ himself.

To the studies of Anders Nygren especially the present generation of biblical scholarship owes a debt for the renewed contrast of *agape* and *eros*.[41] The contemporary studies of love as a Divine perfection often err, especially by so expositing this attribute that inadequate attention is given to justice and righteousness in the nature of God. And they frequently fail to find in human *eros* even some broken refractions of the shattered image of God. But the *agape* school does have the merit of emphasizing how vast an advance over *eros* is involved in the biblical conception of love. The pagan idea of love we distinguish even today as erotic love, although this modern designation unfortunately implies a one-sidedly sensual connotation. The classic philosophers did not hesitate to apply *eros* to the loftiest affective sentiments, even the love of the gods. But the characteristic of *eros*-love is that it reaches out to an object for the sake of what that object can bring to the subject. It springs, therefore, from a deficiency in the subject which requires remedy. But *agape*-love is dramatically dissimilar. *Agape* is bestowed on the object for the sake of the object, and not for a benefit which the object can bring to the lover. It reaches even to an object that can bring no benefit, indeed when the object is a stranger, worse yet an enemy, legitimately under wrath, and when the subject is under no antecedent obligation to bring a blessing into the life of the object. Such is the *agape* of God toward doomed sinners. And whoever withholds love from another, merely because he senses no antecedent obligation, since the other is a stranger, or even an enemy, cuts himself off in principle from the *agape* which God has extended to us in Christ. *Agape* carries its own obligation in the experience of the redeemed sinner; to restrain it is to destroy it.

Only those who fail to see that *agape* — self-giving love — defines the content of Christian love at every level can fall into such an error as that of Nicolai Hartmann. He regards neighbor-love as impersonal, and so contrasts it with personal love for an individual.[42] This is really the retention of an *eros*-concept of love in the philosophic spirit. Neighbor-love becomes a superficial sympathy which exists among a class of people, while at the same time personal-love becomes something uncritically less than its biblical sense. It is true that Hartmann finds in personal

[40]Luthardt, *The Moral Truths of Christianity*, p. 26.
[41]Anders Nygren, *Agape and Eros* (London: S.P.C.K., 1953).
[42]Hartmann, *op. cit.*, p. 368.

love "a pure Being-for-thee on my part, irrespective of any Being-for-me on thy part,"[43] and asserts that "the proverbial bliss which a man experiences only in personal love is not that of being loved, but of loving."[44] One can detect here the importation of an altruistic factor in the exposition of love to which speculative ethics has been a stranger. He will not be disappointed if he expects to find elements in Hartmann's statement which compromise its force. For his act of love keeps always in view a price it pays for the subject's own gain and the value of selfhood, especially the ultimate meaning which it bestows upon human existence.[45] Here the essential idea of *agape* is surrendered. The "self-giving" love of the object is ventured as a means of the "self-realization" of the subject. This is an impossible concept for any who look to the nature of God as supplying the content of personal love. And only now that it is clear in the last analysis that the philosophical is allowed to triumph over the theological is it apparent why Hartmann can declare that "the mistake of Christianity is the belief that the fulfilment of the moral life depends upon brotherly love alone."[46]

The joining together of love with faith and hope is not confined to the classic chapter on *agape*. These virtues are conjoined in Romans, Galatians, Colossians, and First Thessalonians. The word hope, which we must yet discuss, is nowhere found on Jesus' lips; everywhere he is self-assured that he comes to fulfill all that pertains to redemptive promise. The reality that hope looks for is present in his person. The treatment of hope belongs to the epistles. But faith, as we have seen, is central among the virtues Jesus specially commends, and it likewise appears in the Pauline writings as next to love in importance. It is love's constant companion in the spiritual life. The ode to *agape* and the fruit of the Spirit present them in this way, suggesting interdependence. While the term *pistis* occurs on not more than thirty occasions in the Septuagint, it is used at least eighty-seven times in the Pauline letters. Faith does not, in the Pauline treatment, carry the Platonic notion of belief in the absence of proof. Rather, it is an adequately based confidence in the existence and activity of God which is sustained by the indwelling Spirit. It presupposes God's self-revelation and the believer's loyal adherence to the revelation. Faith is an "active principle of trust" whereby one is laid hold on by Christ. The Old Testament concept of faith had the overtone of firmness, steadfastness, reliability in taking hold of God. Faith is an existence *in* the Living God. This idea is expanded by the New Testament wording "believe *in*" as an equivalent of faith. The Revised Version rendering "faithfulness" in the fruit of the Spirit emphasizes the quality of fidelity or reliability to which the spiritual man is introduced and which he reflects. Unreliability casts an aspersion upon spirituality; it is an evidence of faithlessness.

[43]*Ibid.*, p. 373.
[44]*Ibid.*, p. 377.
[45]*Ibid.*, p. 381.
[46]*Ibid.*, p. 463.

"Faith, hope and charity" remained bound together in the early ages of Christian thought. The middle ages superficially regarded hope as the third "theological virtue." Their close association does not rest only upon the classic *agape* chapter but, as we have already observed, occurs elsewhere in the Pauline letters. Yet hope always is in a subordinate position to the others. It is not on that account to be hastily dismissed as of little importance. It shares with love and faith and the other distinctive Christian virtues in dramatic contrast to pagan and secular conceptions.

The absence of hope in the Roman world before the impact of Christianity has long been noted. T. R. Glover remarks that "apart from the Jews there was no nation in the Mediterranean world which consciously hoped."[47] "Students of antiquity have dwelt frequently on the note of despondency, even of despair. . . . Against this background of diffused and dominant pessimism the profession of Christianity presented an arresting spectacle of jubilant hope, untiring activity, habitual cheerfulness and confidence. . . . The secret of the difference lay in the Christian belief that by His Resurrection Christ had validated human effort, and guaranteed the permanence of human achievement."[48] "The ancient world had arrived," Harnack comments, "by all the routes of its complicated development, at the bitterest criticism of and disgust at its own existence."[49] Moreover, the pagan notion of hope mirrored only ambiguous expectation. It was a hesitant anticipation of a future that might as readily be evil as good. Pagan hope lacks both a sure foundation and sure fruits. The historian Thucydides sketched its outlines in drab colors as an empty concept that deceives man. It is not a desirable virtue in early pagan literature, and where hopefulness begins to emerge as a duty it lacks a secure basis and an assurance of final vindication. In the New Testament, however, it uniformly has the sense of a good expectation.

Through the impact of redemptive morality, the word hope loses its ambivalence and acquires positive content. Christianity deleted the bad sense from the Greek word.

The Christian movement was buoyed by a hope that reached through life and the centuries to come to the approaching climax of history. *Finem respice*: "Look to the end"! — that was the great motive-power of Christian morality.

"Perhaps the chief differentiation of Paul from the men and women of today is the high place he assigns to hope. If we were making a list for ourselves, it would hardly occur to any of us to include this quality in it. For us, as for Watts, Hope is a blinded figure holding a shattered lyre and listening for the music of the one remaining string." So writes R. Newton Flew, who is careful to indicate that, from the standpoint of

[47]*Virgil* (5th ed., London: E. Arnold, 1923), p. 331.
[48]H. H. Henson, *Christian Morality,* 183.
[49]A. Harnack, *History of Dogma* (London: Williams & Norgate, 1896-99), III, 127.

the New Testament, "those without hope are the heathen" (cf. 1 Thess. 4:13).[50]

Curiously, both anticipations of the future, the prospect of felicity and the prospect of doom, which Christianity enforces in the consciences of men, carry their tribute to the fact that the religion of revelation stripped away ambiguity about the finale of history.

In pre-Christian times the term *elpis* hardly belonged to the vocabulary of morality. Hope for Paul is a moral idea. The word seldom occurs in a non-theological and non-Christian sense (Rom. 4:18, 1 Cor. 9:10; cf. 2 Cor. 8:5, Phil. 2:23, 1 Tim. 3:14). "For him the future means perfect conformity to the image of Christ; participation in that 'glory' which constitutes the Divine essence."[51] The future fulfills the present in its moral aspirations in Christ: "We by the Spirit eagerly expect the righteousness we hope for" (Gal. 5:5).

For the Christian, the Cross has already wrested the victory from the darkness of the future. The worst that can happen to the believer has already taken place — judgment upon his sins. Moreover, Christianity filled the term with a radiant confidence. The fact that Christ, the moral judge of the universe, has already borne this judgment enables the believer to identify himself with Christ's ultimate triumph in righteousness.

Hope is faith directed toward that glorious future. It is no mere natural expectation, nor is it the extension of natural desire bracketed by the natural course of events.

It is a supernatural virtue with eschatological overtones. It will be crowned at last by the outworking of God's revealed purposes. The Old Testament uses the term with a growing eschatological sense; the believer expects the consummation of his salvation in the future. The word hope and its cognates are not recorded to have been spoken by Jesus, probably because hope and actuality merged in him. "Hope, to Jesus, was certainty."[52]

The object of hope expressed by the various New Testament writers leaves no doubt of its eschatological orientation: the hope of salvation (1 Thess. 5:8); of righteousness (Gal. 5:5); of eternal life (Tit. 1:2, 3:7); of rejoicing (Rom. 12:12); as being something better than the 'former commandment' (Heb. 7:18-19); of the greater glory of the new dispensation (2 Cor. 3:12); of glory (Col. 1:27); of sharing the glory of God (Rom. 5:2); of the grace coming at the revelation of Christ (1 Pet. 1:13); of Christ himself (1 Thess. 1:3, 1 Tim. 1:1, Tit. 2:13). All are summed up in confident expectation of a perfected fellowship and union with the Saviour.

The Christian hope is grounded on Christ's resurrection (1 Pet. 1:3), so that the word gains a fuller sense in the epistles because of the new

[50]R. Newton Flew, *The Idea of Perfection in Christian Theology* (Oxford: University Press, 1934), p. 66.
[51]Kennedy, *op. cit.*, pp. 78f.
[52]P. Shorey, "Hope (Greek and Roman)," in *H.E.R.E.*, 780f.

age that the resurrection inaugurated. The resurrection, as Alan Richardson has remarked, "is, as it were, an eschatological symbol in history of our ultimate salvation and therefore the ground of our hope."[53] The Apostle Paul, who especially expounds the Christian hope in its larger New Testament dimensions, pictures himself as a divinely-appointed minister of the Gospel hope (Col. 1:23). While the vast majority of the approximately fifty occurrences in the New Testament are subjective, dealing with an attitude of mind, some of the references are clearly objective, referring to a future reality (Rom. 8:24, Gal. 5:5, Col. 1:5, Tit. 2:13, Heb. 6:18, 7:19). The subjective attitude of hope blends into the objective reality. This is not illusion; it has an adequate grounding. Hope is inseparable from the cherished expectation of the second advent and final triumph of Christ. "The NT conception of hope has nothing at all to do with any this-wordly prospects; it is as far removed as possible from any notion of an earthly Utopia or any secular optimism. It is through and through eschatological, always bearing reference to the return of the Lord Jesus at the end of the age."[54] Otto Piper expresses a similar verdict. "The biblical hope is teleological and its implementation is expected from a very definite, God-chosen goal, and by the fact that God governs the approach toward that goal. In secular hope, on the other hand, the time process is viewed as being subject to hazard. Thus, while pleasant things may be hoped for from the future, there is no final goal toward which the process moves. Furthermore, hope differs from mere expectation of future events by the fact that the events to which the individual looks forward will be beneficial to him. In the case of the Christian hope, that result is the consequence of divine promise."[55]

The New Testament discloses no foundations for an authentic hope outside the victory of the cross and resurrection and the ultimate eschatological triumph to which these point. George Adam Smith points out that the dual nature of the Christian hope, as personal and social, has its reflection in the moral life of the believer: "Character . . . may be represented as the proper effect of so rich a hope, our grateful and natural response to such a gift, or character may be represented as being the only means of bringing such a hope to pass."[56] It is a strong bridge across the otherwise impossible, a bridge enforced by conscience.

Utter hopelessness in the life of the believer is an impossibility, and flagging hope is sin. Hope is no less constitutive of Christian experience than love and faith. Where it is absent, there has been no genuine appropriation of the Gospel. Those who are devoid of true hope are

[53]Alan Richardson, "Hope," in *A Theological Word Book* (New York: Macmillan, 1951), 109a.

[54]*Ibid.*

[55]Otto Piper, "Christian Hope and History," in *Evangelical Quarterly*, April-July, 1954, p. 82.

[56]George Adam Smith, *The Forgiveness of Sins* (New York: Hodder & Stoughton, 1904), Ch. VII: "The Moral Meaning of Hope," p. 122.

"without God in the world" (Eph. 2:12) and death confronts them only with despair (1 Thess. 4:13).

Next to the love chapter the fruit-of-the-Spirit passage is doubtless the best known of Paul's passages on the Christian virtues. Yet it is only one of several such accounts. Three lists of virtues call for the attention of the student of ethics (Gal. 5:22f., Phil. 4:8f., and Col. 3:12ff.). The Galatian and Colossian statements have, as may be expected, much in common in the supernatural orientation of the moral life and in the particular qualities that are found in them. The Philippian passage, however, is markedly different from the others. Its statement of the Christian mode of action contains no overlapping with the other lists in terminology. Dewar holds that the series of virtues — "whatsoever things are true (*alēthē*), whatsoever things are honest (*semna*), whatsoever things are just (*dikaia*), whatsoever things are pure (*agna*), whatsoever things are lovely (*prosphile*), whatsoever things are of good report (*euphema*); if there be any virtue, and if there be any praise, think on these things. Those things, which ye have both learned, and received, and heard, and seen in me, do . . ." — does not deal with distinctively Christian qualities, but that Paul here meets the Philippians on their own level. The Apostle, he suggests, is dealing with "natural rather than supernatural virtues" which are "not really . . . part of the Christian ideal."[57] But Christian ethics involves a new moral condition. And the retention of "virtues" of the old unchanged nature could only involve a contradiction of the new nature put on by the believer. There is no reason to think that Paul is setting forth something other than Christian morality here. The wellspring of the believer's thought-life and practice is here in view. The true values were to hold the center. Everything real, venerable, upright, unstained, dear, high-toned — this was to be the object of contemplation, action and praise.

The real difference between this passage and the other lists is that the Philippians passage does not specify the particular virtues that distinguish the Christian life. It indicates rather the underlying moral aptitude in disposition and action through which the Spirit articulates the special qualities.

The work of the Spirit is set forth in Galatians 5:22ff. and Colossians 3:12ff., where the internal ethical unity of the life of faith works out into particular virtues. H. A. W. Meyer suggests in connection with the Galatians passage that "the selection of these virtues, and the order in which they are placed, are such as necessarily to unfold and to present to the readers the specific character of the life of Christian fellowship (which had been disturbed and sadly torn among the Galatians)."[58] Yet every reason can be cited for regarding these virtues as expressive at the same time of the qualities that accord with the

[57]Dewar, *op. cit.*, p. 144.
[58]H. A. W. Meyer, *Commentary on Galatians*, 5:22.

nature of the new man. They express the activity of the Spirit in and through regenerate life generally. The-fruit-of-the-Spirit passage (Galatians) lists nine virtues: (1) love, (2) joy, (3) peace, (4) longsuffering (RSV, patience), (5) gentleness (RSV, kindness), (6) goodness, (7) faith (RSV, faithfulness), (8) meekness (RSV, gentleness), (9) temperance (RSV, self-control). The Colossian passage lists eight qualities: (1) bowels of mercies (RSV, compassion), (2) kindness, (3) humbleness of mind (RSV, lowliness), (4) meekness, (5) longsuffering (RSV, patience), (6) forbearing one another, (7) forgiving one another, and (8) charity (RSV, love).[59]

It is, of course, no surprise that love is assigned the determinative position by both lists. The consciousness of Divine love engenders love for God and man, and supplies the principle and presupposition of all virtue. It is mentioned first in Galatians, while in Colossians it is added last as knitting all the virtues into Christian perfection: "above all these . . . charity, which is the bond of perfectness" (3:14). In the absence of love, the individual virtues fall into discord.

The presence of faith in the Galatian list should likewise occasion no surprise in view of Jesus' emphasis on faith. Its absence from the Colossian list, like the omission of hope from both lists, need imply no more than that it is presupposed.

Those virtues mentioned in both passages are love, longsuffering, meekness and kindness.[60] An added correspondence exists between meekness in its sense of mildness or humility and humbleness or modesty of mind. If this partial similarity is ignored, the virtues that appear only in the Galatians list are joy, peace, goodness, faith, and temperance; those in the Colossians list only bowels of mercy, humbleness of mind, upholding one another, and forgiving one another. The scope which is accorded all these virtues elsewhere in the New Testament suggests that Paul does not aim at an exhaustive list in either epistle; rather, he suggests some of that rich moral variety into which the unity of the ethical life centered in love is spontaneously and properly diversified. To seek to force upon every regenerate life the same proportionate and systematic expression would be to straightjacket the spontaneous creative activity of the Spirit and to ignore the facts of Christian growth. At the same time, it is necessary to regard these virtues as more than mere suggestions of what the Christian life disallows by contrast. The life of Christian virtue is superlatively a dynamically positive affair, and these virtues must enter

[59]The passage in Ephesians 4:32 contains three of these virtues — "be ye kind one to another, tenderhearted, forgiving one another, even as God for Christ's sake hath forgiven you" — sharing kindness with both lists, and compassion and forgiveness with the Colossian list.

[60]The RSV translation of *chrestotes* by kindness in the Galatians passage makes more obvious the correspondence with the *chrestoteta* in the Colossians list, but the rendering of *prautes* by gentleness unnecessarily obscures the direct contact with meekness (*prauteta*) in the second list.

in some measure into every good life. To the extent they are cultivated, the ideal moral life is approximated.

Of various virtues mentioned in the Pauline lists, peace and joy occur with outstanding frequency in his letters. The former appears thirty-three times, and the latter nineteen times. Each of the apostle's letters begins with a greeting of peace, so determinative was this concept for the Christian life. But it is not in the frequency of New Testament usage as much as in the novelty of its use of these virtues that the dramatic importance of the Pauline lists is to be found.[61] The term kindness is used regularly in the Septuagint for God's goodness; in the New Testament it is similarly used five times, while here it significantly appears as a characteristic of the believer's life in the Spirit. The term compassion is found frequently in the Septuagint, usually of God's compassion, a sense which it bears in two of its three New Testament occurrences, but here it significantly emerges as a virtue in the life of the believer. The graphic import of *agape* has already been noted; this term, which is hardly found at all in the Septuagint, is the crown of the virtues and appears sixty-two times in Paul's writings. The Greek term for forgiveness is not found at all in the Septuagint in that sense; it appears five times in the New Testament representing as fully as *agape* the Spirit's enlargement of the accepted secular vocabulary of the day to accommodate the realities of redemptive ethics. Likewise, the fact that the term for forbearance is not found at all in the Septuagint as a moral virtue, that the term for longsuffering is very rare, and that for meekness almost as rare, suggests that the enlargement of the life of virtue required at the same time the shaping of a new vocabulary directed to the distinctive realities of the Christian life.

What is so obviously true of certain of the virtues, that they are qualities peculiar to Christian experience, is true also of those virtues which bear a verbal resemblance to secular qualities but which are filled with unique color and tone. This is as true of the virtues of joy, peace, longsuffering, kindness, goodness, meekness, temperance, compassion, and forbearance as it is of love, faith, hope, and forgiveness.

Joy as a virtue has, as Dewar remarks, "no parallel in any other ethical system."[62] Dean Inge tells us that " 'Joy' as a moral quality is a Christian invention, as a study of the usage of *Xapa* in Greek will show. Even in Augustine's time the temper of Christians . . . was one of the things which attracted him to the Church."[63] It is not, of course, that the Christian has a cheerfulness which banishes all sorrow, for the hard experiences of life are presuppositions of his growth in patience. Rather, he knows the consolation of God in life's seemingly bitter provi-

[61]The observations made on this point are derived from Dewar's fine study of the larger use of the terms.

[62]Dewar, *op. cit.*, p. 146.

[63]William R. Inge, *Outspoken Essays* (New York: Longmans, Green, 1920), p. 226.

dences (2 Cor. 4:8f; cf. Mt. 5:4, Jn. 16:20). The ancient Stoic doctrine of resignation meant the privation of all sense of sorrow and joy and the violent eradication of human emotion; Calvin called it an "iron-hearted philosophy." The Christian moves through the whole of life revived by a Divine consolation, not steeled to indifference. Therefore he considers all its providences as God's appointments for blessing, both now and in the future, and as elements in the larger salvation of the redeemed.[64]

The joy that is based merely on human happiness is a fleeting reality, as Zophar remarks to Job: "The joy of the godless is but for a moment" (Job 20:5). While natural joy is almost universal among human beings in some degree — gladness, contentment, satisfaction, mirth, cheerfulness, exultation — as a temporary escape from the pressures of life, yet only the believer can know deep moral joy.[65] It arises from behavior done to the glory of God. Only the believer can experience spiritual joy or rejoicing in view of a vital relationship to the living God (Ps. 43:4, Isa. 41:10) and redemption in Christ (Phil. 3:3, 1 Pet. 1:8) and the promises of which he is heir (Ps. 119:162) and the assurance of future bliss (Rom. 5:2, Mt. 25). Christian joy is an experience unknown to unregenerate people (1 Cor. 2:14). In ideal Christian experience, this joy is constant (Phil. 4:4) and permanent (Jn. 16:22), and so moving as to be unspeakable (1 Pet. 1:8). Joy as a Christian virtue springs from the soul's union with its Redeemer. It is the natural outcome of fellowship with God. The Bible relates it consistently and specifically to the religious experiences of Israel and the church. "In thy presence is fulness of joy; in thy right hand are pleasures for evermore" (Ps. 16:11) writes the Psalmist. The fact of joy is expressed in the Psalms in a number of synonymous terms not easily differentiated: gladness, mirth, to rejoice, to shine, to be bright. But both Old and New Testaments, Everett F. Harrison points out, disclose its dual nature as a bubbling stream and as a deep quiet river. In Old and New Testaments alike, God himself is the object (Ps. 35:9, Isa. 29:19) and the source or ground (Ps. 4:7, 51:12) of the believer's joy. As he neared the Cross, Jesus spoke with his disciples "that my joy might remain in you" (Jn. 15:11). He is as properly called the Man of Joy as the Man of Sorrows. His character and his teaching exemplify that joy despite the grief and tragedy that enter into his life. He guaranteed that the deepest hours of life—the vail of sorrows, the valley of death—can be hours of joy; the most that he said about joy, he said in the hours when

[64]"Because nothing is really amiable to us but what we know to be conducive to our benefit and salvation, our most merciful Father affords us consolation also in this respect, by declaring, that even in afflicting us with the cross, he promotes our salvation. . . . If . . . tribulations are salutary for us, why should we not endure them with grateful and placid hearts?" (Calvin, *Institutes,* III, viii, ii).

[65]Joy is not, Marshall writes, a "mere *joie de vivre* . . . of purely physical origin. . . . Nor again . . . the joy derived from highly privileged circumstances or mere pleasure" but "the unquenchable conviction that all that is meant by goodness is infinitely worth while" (*op. cit.,* pp. 293f.).

he moved toward Calvary. James Orr comments on the added prominence given the element of joy in the New Testament: "It is the appropriate response of the believer to the 'good tidings of great joy' which constitute the gospel."[66] Christian joy arises "in the power of the Holy Spirit" (Rom. 14:17, 15:13), being one of the Spirit's characteristic fruits.

The decline of joy as a spiritual possession[67] today in contrast with primitive Christianity is due to some imperfection in the Christian life. Andrew Fuller has somewhere said: "A vein of sacred enjoyment ran through their lives." They lived amid the realities of Christ's resurrection, in the era of fulfillment — and not of promise merely. From the events after his crucifixion they learned dramatically that God works all things together for good to his followers, so that they could find joy in every circumstance and occasion. They lived in the bloom of Pentecost, and they rejoiced to be counted worthy to suffer persecution. Their labors for Christ were a privilege, not merely a duty. They had adversity, sickness, affliction, but they rejoiced with joy unspeakable and full of glory in the expectation of reunion with Christ and of the boundless prospects of the life to come. The "great voice of much people in heaven saying, 'hallelujah!' " (Rev. 19:1) is a company from whose lips that same spontaneous cry must have been voiced often on earth. They were sharers on this earth of Paul's confidence that the normal response to life situations should be "rejoice in the Lord always" (Phil. 4:4).[68] All the early Christian sources of joy remain for us, but we neglect to draw from the wells. We have a spirit of conformity to the present world, and seek enlarging fortunes which fade away, and are ensnared by the cares of this world and by its fast-withering pleasures. The believer's joy exists in full in anticipation of a final state of bliss — the enjoyment of God forever. Isaiah 12:3, 61:10, 65:18ff., Psalm 126 "see joy as bound up with the fulness of salvation," as "an eschatological reality which is proleptically, and partially, present in human life as an anticipation of the Kingdom of God."[69]

[66]James Orr, "Joy," in *I.S.B.E.*, III, 1755.

[67]Eliseo Vivas points out that "the perfect actualized mode of self-realization of Spirit — as we can see by extrapolating from our own imperfections, is joy," and that this is as important a factor of experience as the anguish on which existentialism concentrates, in order to perpetuate the movement of oscillation between the extremes of nothingness and being. And the absence of the role of joy in German and French atheistic existentialism he traces swiftly to one fact: "That philosophy has lost God." *The Moral Life and the Ethical Life,* p. 340.

[68]This does not mean the Christian must rejoice because of tribulations, sorrow, and trials. Many have the false conception that the Scriptures teach this, regarding 1 Peter 1:6 as a supporting text: "Wherein ye greatly rejoice, though now for a little while, if need be, ye have been put to grief in manifold trials . . ." The correct antecedent for "wherein ye greatly rejoice," however, is "*salvation* ready to be revealed in the last time . . ." (1:5). The true conception, then, is that while we are in trials we are to rejoice in the salvation that God has wrought, and which he shall bring to perfection at the day of redemption.

[69]R. Gregor Smith, "Joy," in *A Theological Word Book,* Alan Richardson, ed., p. 117.

Behind the biblical view of Christian joy is the assurance of a joyful and rejoicing God who delights in his own nature and perfections, who rejoices in his works (Ps. 104:31), in his Son Jesus Christ (Mt. 3:17), and in those who share the benefits of his grace (Ps. 147:11, Zeph. 3:17, Ps. 149:4). The believer's joy is therefore "a gift derived from the joy of God."[70]

While the actual linking of peace as a virtue to Jesus Christ and the realities of redemption occurs but once in so many words — "the peace of Christ" (Col. 3:15) — it is the consistent presupposition of the New Testament that peace as an ethical quality has its reality only on the basis of Christ's work for and in the believer. The Pauline letters throb with the grand reality of peace which the fact of redemption has imported into the spiritual and moral life. "Being therefore justified by faith, we have peace with God through our Lord Jesus Christ" (Rom. 5:1); "He is our peace" (Eph. 2:14). The greeting 'peace' found in most New Testament epistles has rich content by conjunction with God's grace and mercy and love, all manifested in Christ. Peace signifies the removal of estrangement. It is also an inner possession "arbitrating in favour of decisions and actions which produce freedom and love (1 Cor. 7:15, Col. 3:15), is to be pursued in company with fellow Christians (Heb. 12:14, 2 Tim. 2:22), and beggars description because it mounts guard over them and preserves them in their inner being until the Parousia (Phil. 4:7). Life in the church and the calling of peace are coincident (Col. 3:15)."[71]

Peace as a virtue issues from union with God, and is not experienced by the wicked and unregenerate. The Psalmist affirms: "The Lord will bless his people with peace" (Ps. 29:11); "Thou wilt keep him in perfect peace whose mind is stayed on thee," Isaiah writes (26:3). The Scriptures witness that peace as a subjective ethical phenomenon cannot be separated from religious considerations and the questions of conscience and sin.[72] The predominant theme of peace in the Bible is that of peace with God. "The source of peace in all its forms is Jehovah, the God of peace (Judg. 6:24, Isa. 45:7), who overcomes the forces of disharmony in the heavens (Job 25:2), who blesses Israel (Lev. 26:6, Num. 6:26, Ps. 29:11, 85:3-12), the house of David (1 Ki. 2:33), the priesthood (Mal. 2:5), the faithful Israelite (Ps. 4:8), with peace. . . . Peace is central to the preaching of the prophets. . . . They in-

[70]*Ibid.*
[71]C. F. Evans, "Peace," in *A Theological Word Book,* p. 166.
[72]"Peace" is the normal public salutation for a Hebrew and for a Mohammedan, but theirs is not the peace Messiah brings, since both have passed by Christ as the supreme revelation of the Father. The virtue of peace in Christian experience is the lengthened fulfillment of Jesus' promise: "Peace I leave with you; my peace give I unto you" (Jn. 14:27). In the long reach, it is only where this reservoir of peace is known that enduring peace can be brought into human life. Peace of mind, peace of soul, depend upon the peace of Christ. It was he who alone could so confidently designate this strength of his followers: "Blessed are the peacemakers, for they shall be called the children of God" (Mt. 5:9).

terpreted the political and social turmoil as the necessary judgment of God, in the face of which to prophesy security is to pass over sin."[73] Only after judgment is peace offered (Jer. 29:11, Isa. 52:7, 55:12, 57:19; Ezek. 34:25-30, 37:26). "The Suffering Servant brings peace to the nations (Isa. 53:5). A final peace as the gift of God in the coming age is the constituent of Old Testament eschatology, and is envisaged either as the abolition of war and the rule over the nations of Israel's messianic kingdom (Isa. 9:2-7, Zech. 9:9f., Mic. 5:5, Hag. 2:7-9), or as a paradisal existence in which all forms of strife will have been removed (Isa. 11:1ff., 2:2-4, 65:25, Ezek. 34:25-28)."[74] Peace is a gift of the Spirit.[75]

In its classical sense the term *eirene* was primarily of negative significance. It meant the cessation of hostilities and the absence of war. The word has this meaning in some biblical passages. The state of harmony contemplated by the secular use was conceived essentially in terms of a balance of externals, or an adjustment of horizontal relations. But the general New Testament use is far more profound than this secular notion. The Greek term acquires the positive content of the Old Testament term *shalom,* which expresses the ideal state of life both Godward and manward. The Hebrew word looks beyond mere tranquility in the land to tranquility of soul and spiritual soundness. It has in view that peace of soul which is based upon the consciousness of a proper relationship to God. The inward tranquility does not rest on man's feelings or disposition. In this it differs from the *apatheia* of Stoicism, which sought interior calm by the negation of disturbing desires and passions. Biblical peace is based upon the soul's positive relation to God, and rests upon God's work. The man who looks for Divine approval upon his own shabby life, and who does not know redemption by grace, is precluded from knowing peace.

The peace and tranquility that are found in Christ are therefore not a more intense form of what the world calls peace, but they are actually placed in opposition to that of the world: "Not as the world giveth, give I unto you" (Jn. 14:27). The peace that the world has apart from God in Christ is a delusive pseudo-peace which explodes sooner or later into emptiness and vanity, for it does not competently challenge the forces of evil. All peace predicated outside of Christ is foredoomed to disillusionment and judgment. "The peace of unbroken union with the Father in the midst of adversity, which is the supreme gift of Jesus to the disciples and which is to be distinguished from all forms of worldly security (Jn. 14:27), is dependent upon his final victory over the chief

[73]Evans, *op. cit.,* p. 165.

[74]*Ibid.,* p. 165b.

[75]"The overmastering joy of the Man of Sorrows, the calm of Him who said, 'My peace I give unto you, in this world ye will have tribulation but in Me ye have peace,' cannot be understood except through the presence of that Comforter, who is another Christ in the heart." W. T. Davison, *The Indwelling Spirit* (London: Hodder, 1911), p. 112.

enemies, sin and death (Jn. 16:33). Hence it is that after the resurrection the Lord greets his disciples with 'Peace,' shows them the marks of the passion and passes on to them his own mission and victory over sin (Jn. 20:19-23, 26). The life, death, and resurrection of Christ can be called God's gospel of peace for all men (Acts 10:36; cf. Isa. 52:7, Eph. 6:15, 2:17 . . .)."[76] The so-called peace of unregenerate experience provides no durable basis for the removal of human fear and disquiet of soul. It is not that settled quiet of heart in which the stillness of eternity has fashioned the sabbath of God. Biblical peace is inseparable from the grand realities of special revelation and redemption. Christ is the absolute proprietor and dispenser of peace, determining its characteristic qualities. It was on his way to the Cross, when it must have seemed to all sober and righteous judgment that evil had taken the throne and good was outlawed to a cruel finish, that he spoke of his own peace to those disciples whose hearts were troubled and distraught. For his peace looked confidently beyond the crucifixion to the resurrection and the judgment to come; its correlate was the absolute assurance of the ultimate triumph of God's righteousness. The fact that peace takes its place so prominently as a gift of the Spirit in the New Testament marks an advance over the Old Testament. As James Hastings remarks, "In proclaiming peace as the highest good and as an actual present possibility, the gospel of Jesus Christ at once transcends the limits of ancient thoughts and fulfills the vision of the Old Testament. For that which is a dream, a promise, an aspiration in the Old Testament, is a gift and actual possession in the religion of the New Testament."[77]

In the case of longsuffering, also, we find the believer lifted by the Spirit to the level of the Divine life. The spiritual man shares God's "slow to anger." Hence Marshall suggests the translation of *makrothumia* by "long-temperedness," *i.e.*, the endurance of the wrongs of others without passionate and vengeful rage.[78] Lightfoot defines it as "a self-restraint which does not hastily retaliate a wrong," although it would perhaps be more satisfactory to speak of the restraint as that of the Spirit-controlled man. Furthermore, a one-sided emphasis on the passive aspect only makes possible an inadequate equation of longsuffering with patience, whereas they differ. Patience accepts the consequences as final and endures them; longsuffering waits long for their reversal, despite the power to act at once.[79] Cremer asserts that "patience keeps a man from breaking *down* in despair, while long-

[76]*Ibid.*, p. 166a.

[77]James Hastings, "Peace," in *Encyclopaedia of Religion and Ethics* (Edinburgh: T. & T. Clark, 1924-27), IX, 700.

[78]Marshall, *op. cit.*, p. 294.

[79]The religions of negation, in contrast with the religion of redemption, can find value neither in suffering nor in longsuffering. Buddhism proposed an eightfold path to the elimination of suffering, and lost thereby both the discipline of suffering and a meaningful existence via redemption.

suffering keeps one from breaking *out* in word or action."[80] Anger, if consecrated to righteousness, may sometimes be an ethical duty, but it must appear in Christian experience against a background of a God-tempered life and not as a flareup of short temper which lives constantly near the borderline of sudden flight into rage. The spiritual man is not bent toward quarrels, remains unsoured by injustice, exercises forbearance toward those whose conduct is provocative of anger, turns away from wrath with patient magnanimity, bears his injuries patiently, and holds himself aloof from swift passion. The Greek synonym *anoche,* for forbearance, carries this same thought of a delay of punishment. Abbott-Smith defines it as the result and expression of longsuffering, reflecting God's tolerance of sinners.

The fact that the word longsuffering is used fourteen times in the New Testament, and its cognate verb ten times, while it is rarely found in pre-Christian Greek, suggests that the term came into full significance in the early Christian era. To the pagan and unregenerate mind, eager for the self-expression of the natural man, longsuffering in its biblical measure appeared to involve foolish repression. T. C. Edwards clearly points up the difference between the Aristotelian and New Testament conceptions: "It would appear that *megalopsuchia,* which in Aristotle means highmindedness, came to signify in later writers magnificence; and it is, therefore, not improbable that *makrothumia,* which is a later word than *megalopsuchia,* was used in the sense of magnanimity. At the same time it is evident that in the N.T. *makrothumia* has always a tacit reference to difficulties, sorrows, injuries, wrongdoing. For this reason it is said to be an attribute of love in 1 Cor. 13:4. It differs, therefore, in several points from the 'high-mindedness' of Aristotle's Ethics. First, it is not a consciousness of greatness, but a largeness of conception. Second, it is not the loftiness of spirit that great men alone possess, but a moral and godly frame of mind to be exhibited in the life of every Christian. Third, it is not a noble pride that stands aloof, but an interested spectator of life's sufferings, though not an active combatant in the strife."[81] Plutarch carefully distinguishes the longsuffering of men from the longsuffering of God, apparently coining his own term to differentiate what passes for longsuffering in unregenerate experience from the quality of Deity. But the dramatic proclamation of New Testament ethics is that the regenerate man shares through the new life in the Spirit the supernatural virtue of the Godhead. Longsuffering as a Christian virtue is an aspect of sanctification in the life of the believer. What is attributed to God in the dispensation before Pentecost is now in some measure within the reach of Christian experience through the indwelling and infilling of the Spirit.

[80]Cremer, *Biblico-Theological Lexicon of New Testament Greek,* Gal. 5:22. Trans. from German by William Urwick (New York: Scribner, 1880).

[81]T. C. Edwards, *A Commentary on the First Epistle to the Corinthians* (London: Hodder & Stoughton, 1885), p. 343.

The longsuffering of God is often mentioned in conjunction with his mercy (Ex. 34:6, Num. 14:18, Ps. 86:15), as if to show how, as just and holy, he can endure a wayward generation.[82] *Agape* is the secret of longsuffering. The classic Pauline passage asserts that "love suffers long" (1 Cor. 13:4). God's longsuffering of Israel is a main theme of the Old Testament (Ps. 78:39, Isa. 48:9). At the same time, the worldly wicked abuse his longsuffering (Eccl. 8:11, Mt. 24:48f.). In the end, God works doom upon the impenitent wicked, since not even the virtue of longsuffering compromises his righteousness. After his longsuffering, the judgment.

Jesus supplies an example of longsuffering in the face of injustice which amazed even his disciples (Mt. 11:3, 26:52f., Acts 9:4, 1 Tim. 1:16). The Cross is history's superlative illustration. His longsuffering spirit became their inheritance (Jas. 5:6f.). The apostles became partakers both of his sufferings and his longsufferings (1 Pet. 4:12-17). Hastings summarizes the three stages in the progress of the Christian grace of longsuffering: "First, there is the ceasing to render evil for evil (Rom. 12:17 'Render to no man evil for evil,' Eph. 4:2, I Thess. 5:15); this may be merely passive endurance of wrong, and already demands large exercise of longsuffering. Next, there is the active return of good for evil (Matt. 5:39, I Cor. 4:12 'Being reviled we bless'). And finally, there is the close communion with Christ when the longsuffering becomes itself a joy, an assurance of the presence of the Spirit of whom it is a fruit (Gal. 5:22 'the fruit of the Spirit is love, joy, peace, longsuffering')."[83]

Kindness occupies a conspicuous place among the Christian virtues. This is in contrast with the Old Testament, since the Septuagint uses the term *chrestotes* almost exclusively of God. It shares with longsuffering in that its chief objects are to be found among the evil and unthankful. But instead of mere tolerance and the maintenance of a pleasant disposition, it stoops to assist them in their deepest needs, ministering blessing in exchange for cursing. "Christianity let loose a vast, refreshing tide of kindness upon a world in which cruelty abounded," Dewar writes.[84] This basic characteristic, that Christian believers are kind, is among the first qualities upon which observers of the movement have been drawn to comment, for it wins appreciation and sympathy even where the will of others is hostile.

"Paul implies that . . . spirituality is spurious and counterfeit if he

[82]James Denney significantly notes that the prevailing sense which longsuffering bears in the New Testament is "akin, not to endurance but to forbearance; it is a slowness like that of God in avenging wrongs, a restraint of anger . . ." ("Longsuffering," in *H.D.B.*, III, 47). One cannot but wonder whether the RSV preference for "patient endurance" may not perhaps reflect a deeper bias about the character of God, which refuses to regard wrath as a Divine attribute, but subordinates it to his love.

[83]James Hastings, *Expository Times,* Vol. XII, 1901, p. 332.

[84]Dewar, *op. cit.,* p. 147.

fails in kindliness to his fellow-men."[85] And this reading of the Christian life is doubtless accurate, but Marshall identifies Christian kindness too readily with a humaneness that easily moves into mere humanism. There can be no doubt, however, that the greatest impulse to humanitarian movements has come from the reservoirs of Christian kindness. The evangelical revival in England a century ago provides a conspicuous illustration. Humanitarianism may remain as a temporary ideal in a world which has cut the roots of Christian revelation and redemption, but it will not long make its way. It is only as a fruit of the Spirit in regenerate life that the virtue takes its rise and holds its course in a fallen world which is naturally inclined in a contrary direction.

James Seth lists the "subordination of the sterner to the gentler virtues" as one of the laws of moral progress: "Perhaps the most comprehensive statement of the change of standpoint wrought by Christianity is that it substituted for the narrowly and exclusively masculine ideal of the ancient world an ideal which not only included the feminine qualities, but made the specially feminine virtues typical and fundamental — the very essence and presupposition of virtue."[86] Thus the special sphere of operations for Christian virtue was shifted from the battlefield and the market place to the ministry of helping the poor and the sick, the forsaken and the oppressed. Lecky points out that Christianity revealed to the Western mind "the sanctity of weakness and suffering, the supreme majesty of compassion and gentleness."[87]

The virtue of goodness has been called the "practical side of kindness," the extension in conduct of the spirit of the Good Samaritan, ready always to proffer help in the name of Christ. The Greek word *agathosune* occurs only in biblical and later ecclesiastical literature. It was first used in the Septuagint, where it appears approximately sixteen times, and then in the New Testament, where it is found in all four of its occurrences in Paul's letters (2 Thess. 1:11, Gal. 5:22, Rom. 15:14, Eph. 5:9). The absence of the word from classical literature adds to the difficulty of fixing the central force of the term, but at the same time enforces the sense of its biblical uniqueness. It is difficult to draw a precise line of demarcation between the various virtues, and perhaps their inner unity as a single fruit of the Spirit should caution us against excessive partitioning. The term appears, however, to have the specialized sense of benevolence or, better yet, beneficence, as an energetic principle of conduct. It suggests large-heartedness and magnanimous devotion to others.

Paul writes of the believers in Rome as "full of goodness" (15:14), and in the Galatian passage identifies Christian goodness as a fruit of the Spirit. The RSV needlessly departs from the received text in two

[85]Marshall, *op. cit.*, p. 295.
[86]James Seth, *A Study of Ethical Principles* (New York: Scribner, 1905), p. 343.
[87]W. E. H. Lecky, *History of European Morals*, II, 100.

passages (2 Thess. 1:11, where Paul prays regarding the Thessalonian believers that God may "fulfill every desire of goodness . . . with power," and Eph. 5:9, where goodness is said to be "the fruit of the light [Spirit?]" in those who "walk as children of the light"). The consistent impression is that goodness as a Christian virtue originates with the Godhead, and is not to be regarded as a mere cultivation of a native capacity of the unregenerate man. "There is none good, save God only" (Lk. 18:19) is a verdict upon the race in sin. Marshall absorbs the virtue of goodness to Kant's "good will"; but the similarity is only formal, since the autonomous nature of Kantian ethics runs directly counter to a theonomous account of virtue. Man is not a self-sufficient ego who can work out his own good with independent individualism; he is cut off, as sinner, from the springs of goodness, and can be restored to inner harmony and to devotion to true goodness only by regeneration.[88] The goodness of which the Bible speaks is no adjustment of life to an abstract ideal of duty, to an awe-inspiring "I ought." Rather, it flows from a personal abiding in the Spirit. A. B. Bruce points out that in the parable of the sower Jesus furnished "a perfectly definite and adequate characteristic of the class of hearers who attain unto real and abundant fruitfulness" in the assertion that here, side by side, there coexists the fact that "the word is received and retained" and "the noble and good heart."[89]

The virtue of meekness comes to the Christian spirit via the teaching and example of Jesus. The words "Blessed are the meek" stood in the forefront of the Sermon on the Mount (Mt. 5:5), and Jesus' life was a commentary on them. He was sure that the meek will inherit the earth. Someone has suggested that Matthew 5 bears much the same relation to the life of the believer that Philippians 2 does to the life of Jesus Christ. The word *praus,* found there, is used twice in the New Testament of Jesus. Jesus designates himself as "meek and lowly in heart" (Mt. 11:29), and Matthew applies to him the messianic prophecy of the one who comes "meek, and riding upon an ass . . ." (21:5). Its only other occurrence is in 1 Peter 3:4, where "a meek and quiet spirit" is "in the sight of God of great price."

The Greek word for meekness, *praotes,* is rare in the Septuagint. In the Old Testament the meek are pictured as objects of Divine regard, and special blessings are promised them (Ps. 22:26, 25:9, 37:11, 147:6, 149:4, etc.). It is said of Moses that he was "very meek, more than all men on the face of the earth" (Num. 12:3). The idea of poverty and meekness is often closely allied; the one term is used with the basic

[88]Mary W. Calkins' *The Good Man and the Good* (New York: Macmillan, 1918), which discusses the life of virtue without mention of the Holy Spirit as its presupposition and in disregard of the necessity of regeneration, may be taken as representative of the speculative idealistic approach which regards mankind in its present condition as a manifestation of the Absolute.

[89]A. B. Bruce, *The Parabolic Teaching of Christ* (New York: Hodder & Stoughton, n.d.), p. 33.

meaning of poor and humble. But meekness even in the Old Testament suggests a vertical relationship, of a man's attitude toward God. In the Beatitudes it is coupled with poverty of spirit, hunger and thirst for righteousness, and so forth. The New Testament assimilates it to the work of the Spirit in the life of the believer. The word meekness occurs eleven times in the New Testament (1 Cor. 4:21, where Paul contrasts it with the use of "the rod," and 2 Cor. 10:1, Gal. 5:23, 6:1, Eph. 4:2, Col. 3:12, 2 Tim. 2:25, Tit. 3:2, James 1:21, 3:13, and 1 Pet. 3:15). The translations sometimes render it as humility, gentleness, or modesty.

In classic Greek it meant a mild or gracious person. Christianity supplements and enriches this concept. William Barclay pictured its classic use as having "a caress in it." The term meek was used for a beast that had been tamed. Yet such tameness and want of spirit and mere stillness of a retiring disposition are far from its biblical signification. Aristotle regarded meekness as the mean between excessive anger and excessive angerlessness. Meekness then is virtually robbed of all of its standing as a positive virtue. It rather becomes a trait of character which appears only when two *faults* are properly balanced. It is defined only in negative terms, and has no higher significance than the retention of personal equanimity and composure, and the maintenance of peaceful surroundings.[90]

The common concept of meekness today suggests Kasper Milquetoast — a semi-fearful, apologetic spirit, timid, effeminate, pusillanimous and spineless. Thus one of the grandest of Christian virtues becomes ridiculed and debased by its attachment to a Milquetoast morality as a sign of weakness or cowardice. Meekness becomes a deficiency rather than a virtue.

But the Scriptures regard meekness as a virtue, a positive trait of character worthy of the highest commendation. They give it a distinctive content. What is Christian meekness? Assuredly it involves a break with the violence, the arrogance, and the self-assertion of the natural man. It is gentleness and submissiveness. But the suggestion that it is composure under provocation because of the consciousness of personal sin, or that it is a refusal to pretend to be more than one actually is, breaks down when applied to Jesus. It is represented by the New Testament as a condition of soul. The meek man leaves the vindication of his cause to God, and has freed himself from the natural desire to defend his "rights" on the basis of the claims which the ego hurriedly asserts. He refuses to reply immediately to wrongs by retributive action, but leaves vengeance to God. *The Shepherd of Hermas* proposes

[90]The pagan Greek writers were somewhat disagreed as to what trait of character was the contradictory of meekness. To Aristotle it was anger; to Plutarch, severity or relentlessness; and to Plato, fierceness or cruelty. None of these terms approaches the Christian view. In Christian ethics the opposite of meekness is self-assertiveness. It is, on the horizontal plane, that spirit which demands that the ego be defended immediately on every occasion of its abuse. Richard C. Trench, *Synonyms of the New Testament,* p. 151.

to distinguish false and true prophets by meekness as one of the tests: "He who has the Divine Spirit proceeding from above is meek, and peaceable, and refrains from all iniquity and the vain desire of this world" (Bk. II, Commandment XI). To the natural man, whose tendency is pride, such submission may suggest weakness. But Christian sanctification begets virtues that are contrary to the natural inclination. What the world often despises as "feminine virtues" belong to the very epitome of moral strength. Yet they are guarded from cowardice. God does not purpose by them to destroy self-esteem and dignity, but to lift them above abuse. Regeneration makes these virtues the characteristics of the strong, not of the weak. The heroic masculine virtues of the natural man are shown to be the latent source of many of the works of the flesh, while the life which flows from the Spirit produces godliness. Lecky writes that "Christianity for the first time gave the servile virtues the foremost place in the moral type. Humility, obedience, gentleness, patience, resignation, are all cardinal or rudimentary virtues in the Christian character. They were all neglected or underrated by the Pagans." Christianity brought a new rank and standing in the world at large to those qualities which formerly had been, in G. F. Barbour's words, "grudgingly admitted into the accepted catalogue of virtues."[91]

The question of the relationship between humility and meekness here comes to view. Trench suggests that meekness is the vertical relationship from which humility flows. "The Scriptural *praotes* is not in a man's outward behavior only; nor yet in his relations to his fellow-men: as little in his mere natural disposition. Rather is it an inwrought grace of the soul; and the exercises of it are first and chiefly towards God. It is that temper of spirit in which we accept his dealings with us as good, and therefore without disputing or resisting; and it is closely linked with the *topeinophosune* and follows directly upon it (Eph. 4:2, Col. 3:12; cf. Zeph. 3:12); because it is only the humble heart which is also the meek; and which, as such, does not fight against God, and more or less struggle and contend with Him . . . then, or meekness, if more than mere gentleness of manner if indeed the Christian grace of meekness of spirit, must rest on deeper foundations than its own, on those namely which *topeinophosune,* not as more precious than it, but as presupposing it, and as being unable to exist without it."[92] Christ places the two ideas side by side: "Come unto me, all ye that labour and are heavy laden, and I will give you rest. Take my yoke upon you, and learn of me; for I am *meek* and *lowly* in heart: and ye shall find rest unto your souls" (Mt. 11:28f.). "The Gospel of Christ did not rehabilitate *praotes* so entirely as it had done *tapeinophrosune* . . . because the word did not need rehabilitation to the same extent. *Praotes* did not require to be transformed from a bad sense to a good,

[91]G. F. Barbour, *A Philosophical Study of Christian Ethics* (Edinburgh: Blackwood, 1911), p. 13.
[92]Trench, *op. cit.,* pp. 152f.

but only to be lifted up from a lower level of good to a higher."[93] Whereas in classical literature the word signifies a virtue, it is raised to the level of a grace in the New Testament. Wherever the term meekness gathered overtones of humility, the classic spirit was steeled against it. As Yooll remarks: "In no pagan ethics, whether of the cultured Greek or Roman, or of less civilized peoples, has humility been accounted a virtue. It was usually associated with weakness and cowardice. But in Christian ethics it stands in the forefront. It is the clothing of the graces, the basis of sound moral progress, and the condition of true service of others."[94]

As a grace, lowliness of mind (humility) is a Christian creation, and hence pre-eminently and almost exclusively a Christian virtue. Nothing less is involved than a fundamental inversion of the Greek ideas of greatness and service. The virtue was not without an Old Testament basis; Abraham and Moses were humble (Gen. 18:27, Nu. 12:3), and it was inculcated as a chief duty by the prophets (Mic. 6:8). But it gains a new ethical height through the example and character of Jesus, who was "lowly in heart" (Mt. 11:29). The dramatic account of Jesus washing his disciples' feet (Jn. 13:3-15) summarized what was true of his whole ministry. "His whole career in this world was a protracted humiliation or succession of humiliations between humiliation of His incarnation and the humiliation of His crucifixion."[95] We see how far afield Nicolai Hartmann is when he says it is "the consciousness of falling infinitely short of the mark,"[96] a lack of "feeling for the infinite distance between oneself and the ethical ideal."[97] It is consciousness of being neither more nor less than one's actual self in relationship to Deity, and being willing to take a subordinate place in order to better the welfare of others. It is not incompatible with a proper self-regard, yet involves the concealment of an essential dignity by an utter abandon of self in sacrificial service of inferiors. So Jesus, while essentially Divine, humbled himself in the incarnation, assuming the nature of a creature, and suffering death. The Apostle Paul appeals to this example of the Saviour debasing himself to exhort Christians to meekness and lowliness (Phil. 2:4ff.). Jesus made humility a necessary qualification for entrance into the kingdom: "Except ye be converted, and become as little children, ye shall not enter into the kingdom of heaven. Whosoever therefore shall humble himself . . . , the same is greatest in the kingdom of heaven" (Mt. 18:3f.). "For whosoever exalteth himself shall be abased; and he that humbleth himself shall be exalted" (Lk. 14:11, 18:14). Jesus himself furnished the most remarkable illustration of his teaching.

[93]*Ibid.*, p. 151.
[94]Yooll, *op. cit.*, p. 182.
[95]Alexander Gross, "Humiliation of Christ," in *Dictionary of Christ and the Gospels*, James Hastings, ed. (Edinburgh: T. & T. Clark, 1906), I, 756a. The conception of humility which therefore governs Christian ethics is grounded in Christ's revelation of the Divine nature.
[96]Hartmann, *Ethics*, II, 299.
[97]*Ibid.*, p. 298.

The Lord of glory humbled himself so dramatically that Christian theology speaks of the incarnation as his humiliation.

Since pride is pictured often as the root sin, the temptation is always at hand among finite creatures to think over-highly of themselves. The whole pagan enterprise — government, religion, literature, social organization, and even its concepts of life and duty — was predicated upon self-assertion. This suggests perhaps that humility is also one of the most difficult of virtues for the believer. The crucified natural man is its presupposition. Humility which is acquired only by "sudden spurts" is far removed from humility as a Christian virtue. Augustine said humility is first, second, and third in Christianity — an habitual frame of mind. The true Christian looks down his nose at nobody, for he always lifts up his soul to God.

In Trench's words, "Christ came to dethrone the heathen virtue *megalopsyuchia* and set up the despised Christian grace *tapeinophrosune* in its room, stripping that of the honour it had unjustly assumed, delivering this from the dishonour which as unjustly had clung to it hitherto."[98] The word *tapeinophrosune* is found neither in the Septuagint nor in profane authors, except Josephus and Epictetus and there in the bad sense, of something slavish and despicable. It is used in the good sense only after the influence of the Gospel. It is used seven times in the New Testament, mostly in Paul's epistles (Eph. 4:2, Phil. 2:3, Col. 2:18, 3:12). The humiliation of the Son of God in his incarnation, in the circumstances of his earthly life, in the outlines of his public ministry, and finally in enduring that cursed death upon the Cross — these central facts of history provoked the Pauline plea: "Have this mind in you which was also in Christ Jesus, who . . . emptied himself . . ." (Phil. 2:5ff.).

The virtue of temperance (*egkrateia*), understood in the right way, has been a distinguishing feature of the virtuous Christian life from earliest times. Harnack places it alongside of *agape,* summing up early Christian virtue by the two words, self-control and brotherly love. Because of the modern connotation of the word temperance in a restricted association with the use of alcoholic beverages or with sexual attitudes, the translation "self-control" is in wide favor today. It preserves the sense of control over unruly impulses and passions. The secular mind conceived of self-control mainly in terms of the containment of the sensual nature through an activity of the autonomous will. This view of temperance corresponds more nearly with the sense it bears as one of the four Platonic cardinal virtues, or the harmony by which all other virtues are properly balanced. Hence it is often improperly confused with the more specialized biblical sense.

The temperate life is indeed one of spiritual mastery over impulse, desire, and action. But the idea is not that of discreet self-expression through a censorship of instincts and impulses which the natural man

[98]Trench, *op. cit.,* p. 148.

imposes on himself.[99] The flaw of secular ethics is that it regards true self-control as a capacity which the natural man has apart from regeneration and the empowerment of the Spirit; whereas this self needs to be crucified rather than controlled.[100] The Bible has in view rather an inner control of regenerate experience by the Holy Spirit. Thus the necessity for outer controls upon conduct is superseded. Christ becomes the inward rule of life where self-control is true to the biblical manner of life. Self-direction gives way to the Spirit-led life. What self-control means is clearly stated by Paul: "I through the law am dead to the law, that I might live unto God. I am crucified with Christ: nevertheless I live, yet not I, but Christ liveth in me: and the life which I now live in the flesh I live by the faith of the Son of God" (Gal. 2:19f.). This is the discipline which preserves life from both staleness and impropriety.

Before concluding this survey of representative Christian virtues, it will be well to devote some attention to contentment, a quality which is too often given the sense attached to it by the Stoic and Spinozistic ethics. The idea of contentment is intrinsic to New Testament ethics: "I have learned," the Apostle writes, "in whatsoever state I am, therewith to be content" (Phil. 4:11). Does Paul thereby intend nothing but what Epictetus affirms, that the perils of life and death are not to be met with groaning, but with apathy? The phrase *accipio conditionem* — "I accept the conditions" — from Seneca's 26th epistle, fits Pauline ethics and the ethics of the Stoics and of Spinoza, but it means something quite different in its biblical dimensions from the speculative and rationalistic mood of apathy and resignation. The pantheistic moralities regard the whole of reality as a deterministic movement which cares as little about one individual as another. Hence it is futile for one to lament his circumstances. But the ethics of redemptive theism regards the whole of reality as subordinated to the righteous purposes of God whose love for the individual is unveiled by the Cross, and who is pledged to work all the circumstances of life together for the good of those who repose a saving trust in him.

Prayer becomes therefore an element in Christian ethics through which God molds the future and secures the believer's confidence. The ground of Christian contentment is the believer's confidence that faith in Christ is the victory that overcomes the world. The virtue of patience thus becomes significant. Longsuffering is an attribute of God as well

[99]Harold H. Titus writes of virtues as "those qualities or habits of human character which men admire and value," and assumes that these are what "make for the survival and welfare of the group." *Ethics for Today,* p. 200. From the New Testament standpoint, this is highly objectionable. True values, despite the fact that unregenerate humanity ignores them, are the fruit of the Holy Spirit in regenerate experience.

[100]Archibald Alexander overlooks this important distinction: "The pagan virtues are not excluded from the New Testament. They have an acknowledged place in Christian morality. Fortitude and temperance, not to speak of wisdom and justice, are recognized as essential qualities of the Christian character." *Christianity and Ethics,* p. 190.

as of believers, but patience is his gift to man. He is the "God who gives patience" (Rom. 15:5). He has need of none, for things cannot resist him. But among his people, "tribulation worketh patience" (Rom. 5:3) or steadfastness. Impatience in the Christian life is a byproduct of discontent with the will of God and of a restlessness for the regulation of life by the desires and ambitions of the natural man, or of an unexpressed preference to commit one's life to chance rather than to the particular providence which God ordains.[101]

What Henry Swete has said of the fruit-of-the-Spirit passage may be taken as true of the New Testament conception of the virtues in their entirety. "The list begins with those which indicate the attitude of the inner self to God, and from these proceeds to remodel personal and social life."[102] What begins with God must dramatically recreate the natural man. The Christian life is that of a man born of the Spirit, walking in the Spirit, led of the Spirit, filled by the Spirit. That is why godly virtue is a phenomenon that only Christianity can produce. More than this, Christian character is stamped with the die of the nature of the thrice-Holy God. Christians alone are godlike, for God is making them like himself in virtue, holiness, and character.

[101]"No man has rightly renounced himself, but he who has wholly resigned himself to the Lord, so as to leave all the parts of his life to be governed by his will. He whose mind is thus composed, whatever may befall him, will neither think himself miserable, nor invidiously complain against God on account of his lot. . . . The rule of piety is, that God . . . is the arbiter and governor of all events, both prosperous and adverse, and that he does not proceed with inconsiderate impetuosity, but dispenses to us blessings and calamities with the most systematic justice" (Calvin, *Institutes,* III, vii, x).

[102]Swete, *op. cit.,* p. 348.

22

CONSCIENCE AS A CHRISTIAN PHENOMENON

CONSCIENCE, in contemporary life, is a foundling. Its paternity is questioned, its existence annoying, its demands for attention and responsibility burdensome. The dilemma of modern civilization could indeed stem from the failure of influential thinkers to support the Christian view of conscience. Modern thought, in turn, quite easily relegates the foundling to complete abandonment.

The modern mind is prone to conceive all the events of life, moral and physical alike, simply as incidents in the temporal flux. The origin, nature, history, and goal of conscience are restated to accord with this bias. Consequently, the groundwork of an effective morality is stripped away. The naturalistic examination of conscience proceeds to shatter the validity of morality, and imports into conscience a changing and unstable content.

The dogma of all-embracing movement or progress works against a final Divine moral judgment of man and his deeds based on fixed standards. When all ethical reference is depicted as merely finite and relative, the notion of decisive condemnation must be swept away. If moral convictions emerge only gradually, and even then are subject to revision, the notion of a fixed innate factor which pronounces upon the rightness or wrongness of one's actions is indefensible. The appraisal of conscience today depicts its rudimentary nature as standing in need of constant correction and education, not on the ground that conscience has been deflected from its original dignity, but on the hypothesis that ethical distinctions arise only by way of evolution, and that no moral judgments are final and complete. Conscience is degraded into simply a feeling of pleasure or pain, a volitional impulse, or a mere faculty of subjective judgment.

If the notion of Divine revelation goes, so does every significant notion of conscience. What is left is the judgment of motives and deeds simply from a standpoint within particular culture patterns, never from a standpoint addressed to all cultures, and superior to the passing movements of events.

In a true sense, the conflict between theism and atheism reduces to two competitive views of conscience and its significance. Does conscience possess in some sense a sacred and abiding authority or not? Alongside the Christian emphasis on the gravity of sin stands its assurance of the validity of conscience, involving confidence in an objective moral standard. Surrender this confidence, and conscience is stripped of its dynamic as a link between man and the transcendent moral world. Hence, as Dorner rightly remarks, "Conscience is one of the most important topics in the whole of ethics, and even in the whole of theology, especially evangelical theology."[1]

In a recent monograph, C. A. Pierce asserts that modern representations have deteriorated the New Testament view of conscience into idolatrous effigies, even in some Christian pulpits. Conscience often is no longer represented as of Divine origin, but simply as the Divine in man.[2] Conscience retains its high New Testament authority, but gains illicit subjective shades of meaning. Thus it becomes a "diabolical . . . abomination . . . at the last offering 'authoritative' justification for the abandonment of the basic minimum Christian religious observance."[3] The Church widens this rebellion against an authoritative morality when the pulpit champions conscience without interpreting its nature and limitations, and its precise New Testament connotation. "Not only does she permit her children to suppose that conscience is a sufficient guide in all things, but by doing so without clearly defining conscience, she subscribes, in effect, to the popular 'wresting from its proper sense' of the word, and countenances the interpretation of the word that men are only too ready to put upon it."[4] "Liberty of conscience" deteriorates into private interpretation, which the pulpit sanctions as inviolable. To dignify mere human preference or disposition by the term 'conscience' is to falsify the New Testament conception at an idolatrous level. The churches, although called into existence to proclaim a specially-revealed absolute, thus cater to the defense of temporalities, and to the private vindication of conduct. Commissioned to proclaim that 'Christ is Lord,' they shepherd his professed followers toward moral relativism.

Modern schools of ethics divided swiftly into utilitarian and intuitionalist views of conscience. The recent expositions reflect the two competitive interpretations of conscience found in the history of thought, the associational and intuitional. The former holds that cultural attitudes determine the definition of right and wrong. In accord with this approach, the evolutionary view regards conscience as a reflex of the instinct to self-preservation, which sanctions those dispositions and acts making for survival. One weakness of this theory is that it cannot account for great moral reforms in history led by those who challenged the dominant social pattern of their times in the name of conscience, often at the risk of death. Their appeal has been mainly to fixed, eternal claims, worthy of a devotion superior to the reigning moral pattern.

[1]I. A. Dorner, *System of Christian Ethics,* trans. C. M. Mead, R. T. Cunningham (Edinburgh: T. & T. Clark, 1869), p. 226.

[2]C. A. Pierce, *Conscience in the New Testament* (Chicago: Allenson, 1955), p. 122.

[3]*Ibid.,* p. 123.

[4]*Ibid.,* p. 125.

The intuitional view has a basis in biblical ethics. It finds in conscience a mirror of eternal and absolute moral distinctions.

Bishop Joseph Butler stood above the modern tempest over conscience, with a clear emphasis on its ultimate worth. He refused to dismiss conscience as comprehending only an element of feeling. In his *Fifteen Sermons,* expositing his system of ethics to his parishioners, he gave conscience rational significance. In British philosophy he stands out as a proponent of the Christian view. But, instead of representing conscience only as an inner faculty which prods men to do right, he defended the excessive position that conscience still reliably instructs man in the whole content of right and never conflicts with reason. Therefore his defense contributed also to the reaction against conscience.

A major problem faced by every high view of conscience is the diverse claims which conscience seems to impose upon men in different cultures. Apart from the Christian conception of the fall, as well as of the unique moral dignity of man, the intuitional view has no adequate and satisfactory explanation of this difficulty. Speculative Theism or Idealism, which revolt against the biblical doctrine of the fall, often attack the attachment of any objective significance to conscience. Contemporary studies more and more despair of tracing the origin of conscience because they lack a secure account of the origin of man. The implication that human nature and its moral constitution are uniform is disputed from an evolutionary standpoint and in view of the tremendous diversity which scientific examination has uncovered in the study of various races and civilizations.

In an earlier chapter the fact of the diverse judgment of conscience was referred to man's dual moral situation. By creation man bears the image of God but that image is now sullied through his revolt in sin. Heathen social custom, and even religion, sometimes enjoins as ethical duties immoral practices which Christianity regards with revulsion. Yet the Bible, while condemning the iniquity of the pagans, nonetheless insists that unregenerate men everywhere are in revolt against the light of conscience and nature.

The Bible accounts for man's complex predicament by the dual reference to his lofty creation and his tragic fall. But it finds the basis and character of conscience in man's peculiar relation to the eternal moral world and in his accountability to the will of God. While man as sinner is deplorably enmeshed in moral relativism, he is responsibly bound nonetheless to ineradicable principles of eternal moral validity.

The Middle Ages obscured the role of conscience in the moral life by referring ethical decision more and more to ecclesiastically compounded rules of a casuistic nature. The Roman Catholic conception that the church authoritatively mediates between God and man weakens the role of individual conscience. The individual is never permitted, in that system, to be directly confronted by the will of God in Scripture. The Jesuits urge that individual conscience be renounced for the authority of the church, on the alleged ground that the individual cannot know what is right.

But the Reformation saw the reawakening of conscience. Luther at Worms declared it "neither safe nor honest to do anything against conscience." He stressed the right of private judgment and individual soul responsibility as two of Protestantism's great principles. Yet neither the Reformers nor evangelical theologians and moralists since have formulated a complete doctrine of conscience. Meanwhile, secular ethics has attached to "freedom of conscience" a connotation which Luther never intended. The study remains one of the neglected fields of Christian ethics.[5]

It is easy to fall into extreme representations of the inner moral sense, through overstatement or understatement. Secular ethical studies in the last century tended to exaggerate the scope of conscience. Presupposing a pantheistic or idealistic philosophy, they stressed the universal validity of its moral deliverances. Metaphysics aside, Kant felt impelled to remark that "two things fill the soul with ever new and growing wonder and reverence, the oftener and the longer reflection continues to occupy itself with them — the starry heavens above and the moral law within." But in this century naturalistic thought has understated its significance, emphasizing the conflicts in moral practice, and neglecting the ethical correlations in the moral history of man which rule out subjectivism.

That conscience even in its defracted state maintains standards of ethical significance is apparent from the fact that man's judgment of others is adduced in Scripture as one criterion by which man himself will be measured in the Divine judgment of the race. "For the measure you give," Jesus said, "will be the measure you get back" (Lk. 6:38). Man's fall into sin and his long history of moral revolt have not deprived conscience entirely of an ultimate significance.

The word "conscience" meets us first as a technical moral term in the literature of the Greeks, and hence relatively late in history. But the reality it depicts is present from the beginning of human history, and survives today among the most primitive peoples. Even where the term is not expressly formulated, something corresponding to the notion of moral judgment is present in the Gentile world, although often in a more obscure sense than among the Hebrews. The natural experience of the race therefore is laden with this moral phenomenon which revealed religion ventures to interpret. Nowhere is human life without a monitor to remind men that the passage of time makes their crimes and sins no less heinous than they were known to be at the moment of transgression, and that an everlasting power is disapprovingly aligned on the side of justice. Every man carries within him another "I," a second

[5]Among modern works on the theme of conscience are W. T. Davison, *The Christian Conscience*; O. Hallesby, *Conscience*; K. E. Kirk, *Conscience and Its Problems*; C. A. Pierce, *Conscience in the New Testament*; Hastings Rashdall, *Conscience and Christ*; Bishop Sanderson, *Lectures on Conscience and Human Law.*

personality, which observes him from outside, as it were, and passes objective judgment upon his motives and conduct, indeed, upon his whole being.

The speculative development of this inner moral voice is set in motion by Socrates' references to the "Daemon," that intuitive monitor of the ethical life with which man has always to contend in this rationally and morally-ordered world. The treatment of conscience is carried forward by Plato's emphasis on innate standards of morality as the surviving recollection of the world of pre-existence, and by Aristotle's exposition of a ruling faculty within man which distinguishes him from the beasts.[6] But the Stoics first introduce the word *suneidesis,* and among them Seneca perhaps most of all develops its moral significance as an abiding consciousness witnessing and judging man's conduct.

While the New Testament borrows the word *suneidesis* from the Greek climate of the times, it does not do so to enforce an idea which it at first learned only from the Gentile world, but one which already belonged to the Hebrew conception of moral experience, although not in technical philosophical formula. The appeal to conscience is implicit in many segments of the Old Testament. Adam hides in shame among the trees when his "heart smites" him, his descendants carry within themselves a power of moral judgment and criticism. While the Old Testament defines the right by connecting it peculiarly with the revealed will of God, it nowhere disputes the fact that man constantly passes moral judgment upon his motives, thoughts and deeds. Reason is "the candle of the Lord" (Prov. 20:27), supplying man with light in matters of good and evil as well as truth and error. The functions of conscience are attributed to the heart, which smites the transgressor (1 Sam. 24:5, 2 Sam. 24:10), a form of expression which the New Testament retains (Mk. 3:5, 1 Jn. 3:19f.). In the Septuagint, the Greek term *suneidesis* appears but once: "Curse not the king in thy conscience" (Eccl. 10:20), which the versions render "in thy thought" or "in thy heart."

The teaching of Jesus does not provide us, any more than the Old Testament, with what may be denominated as a biblical doctrine of conscience.[7] But the New Testament clarifies and enlarges the conception of conscience, perhaps under the necessities imposed by the increasing prominence the philosophers assigned to that term. "Only in the New Testament can we find full light cast upon this word and all that it implies . . . ; only in Christianity was this mysterious 'consciousness,' the apprehension of which had been growing through the generations, fully explained and its needs met."[8]

While the term nowhere appears in the Gospels as such, it is found thirty-one times in the New Testament. Paul is apparently the first New

[6]Aristotle, *Politics,* i, 1, 11.

[7]C. F. D'Arcy, *Christian Ethics and Modern Thought* (New York: Longmans, Green, 1912), p. 94.

[8]W. T. Davison, *The Christian Conscience. A Contribution to Christian Ethics.* The Fernley Lecture (London: Woolmer, 1888), p. 27.

Testament writer to employ it, and he does so more frequently than any of the others, and alone ventures more than a passing reference to the term's significance. The Pauline use of the word, in fact, has left "more impression on the moral history of the world than all that Aristotle and Seneca ever wrote."[9] More than twenty times the Greek word for "conscience" appears in the Pauline letters (Rom. 9:1, 13:5; 1 Cor. 8:7, 10:25, 27, 28; 2 Cor. 1:12, 4:2, 5:11; 1 Tim. 1:5, 19, 3:9, 4:2; 2 Tim. 1:3, Tit. 1:15). Twice it occurs in Acts, five times in Hebrews, three times in the Petrine epistles. Elsewhere the doctrine may be detected even where the word itself is not found.

It has been argued that the virtual absence of the term *suneidesis* in the Septuagint indicates that the idea enters the New Testament without any special coloring from the Old Testament world of life and thought, and gains its sense wholly from the Gentile world. Pierce argues, however, that Paul could not have derived its use from the Stoics, since they regarded emotion as always faulty, while conscience includes for Paul an emotional element. If Paul derived the term neither from the Septuagint nor the Stoics, its popular employment among the pagan masses, albeit in a non-technical sense, likely supplies its source.

But does the popular use yield its entire New Testament sense? In the pagan usage, it is often noted, conscience is almost invariably regarded as a disapproving phenomenon, so much so as to become practically identical with the bad or guilty conscience. In consequence, conscience when regarded as good is depicted as empty, or as inoperative. Conscience is identified as an adverse moral judgment passed upon acts begun in the past, and completed or in process. Its operation is subsequent; its cause, the specific antecedent act or acts; its verdict, normally condemnatory. Pierce's linguistic studies establish this view as "the usage of the Greek-speaking man-in-the-street, constantly and without significant variation, throughout the history of the Greek language, to a point at least long after the period during which the N.T. was being written."[10]

The Pauline writings contain the earliest and most frequent use of the term in the inspired writings. Several blocks of teaching bear on the subject, *e.g.*, in 1 Corinthians 8:7-12, 1 Corinthians 10:25-29, and Romans 2:14f. Each passage is addressed to believers in vigorous centers of Gentile life.

The first distinctive of the Pauline correlation of the knowledge of good and evil with conduct is that conscience is regarded as bearing on duty which waits to be fulfilled, as well as judging critically such behavior as has already taken place.[11] Paul's discussions give to conscience a future look when he argues that it forbids "the weak" to eat idol-meat (1 Cor. 8:7). This is implied also in Romans 2:15, since

[9]*Ibid.*, p. 28.
[10]C. A. Pierce, *op. cit.*, p. 53.
[11]Rudolf Bultmann, *Theology of the New Testament* (New York: Scribner, 1951), I, 217.

the requirements of the law are said to be stamped on the heart of the Gentiles antecedently to conduct. The appeal for obedience to the state "for conscience sake" (Rom. 13:5) presupposes an advance prescription by conscience. Consequently the New Testament use is not confined to the judging conscience which condemns the performance of bad acts.

The negative sense of conscience is indeed conspicuous in the New Testament. Conscience passes condemnation on the wicked, as an internal monitor which evokes a sense of guilt and terror. But even with regard to the judging conscience, a further distinctive appears. For the judging conscience is assigned the capacity to acquit as well as to condemn. This is obvious from Paul's declaration that his own conscience (here the synonym *suneida* is employed) "has nothing against" him (1 Cor. 4:4), and in those passages in which he invokes conscience to attest his truthfulness (Rom. 9:1) and his sincere life (2 Cor. 1:12). Paul does not even hesitate to interchange the verdict of faith and the verdict of conscience in the experience of the believer in the course of spiritual obedience (Rom. 14:2).

But two equally important distinctives of the Pauline view remain to be developed. Conscience is linked, on the one hand, to the ethical will of God to whom man by creation is always responsibly related. Behind conscience, therefore, stands the transcendent authority of God, whose demand and verdict it mediates to man. At the same time, Paul renounces the adequacy of conscience in fallen man and requires its reorientation to the specially revealed will of God. This latter consideration especially brings into sharp focus the vast divide between the Pauline view and the popular Gentile evaluation of conscience as a self-sufficient barometer of the moral life. Emphatically, and indeed even disdainfully, the Apostle rejects this conception of conscience as the final moral authority. It is therefore necessary to abandon every theory that Paul simply borrows the speculative Gentile conception of conscience, or that he merely modifies such a conception in its details. Whatever point of contact with the Gentile view, both in vocabulary and in life, it is to be comprehended through the larger biblical and not merely through the speculative definition of the term.

Doubtless a connection exists between biblical ethics and the speculative notion of an interior moral sense. Alongside the revealed morality given externally and objectively, an emphasis on an inner moral sense is maintained both in the representation of man on the basis of creation, and in the movement toward the law written upon the regenerate heart of the redeemed man (Jer. 31:31ff.). In the lives of all men the natural conscience assures that moral knowledge which makes the transition to biblical ethics a coherent one. Thus the slander of an absolute antagonism between general and revealed ethics is exposed. Between the secret moral convictions of the unredeemed and the claims of supernatural religion, between the natural and the Christian conscience, no essential contradiction exists. Jesus' words yield the implication that the natural, unregenerate man retains an innate knowledge of the good in some elemental sense: "If ye then, being evil, know how to give good gifts. . ." (Mt. 7:11). Elsewhere, to the multitudes, he addresses the question: "Even of yourselves judge ye not what is right?" (Lk. 12:57). The Apostle Paul attributes "conscience" to the pagan world in the same sense in which he employs it of the Hebrew-Christian world (Rom. 2:15). In his preaching to the Gentiles, he assumed that their consciousness carried an anticipation of Divine wrath. The law of God confronts man not simply as an arbitrary external fiat, but finds endorsement in the inner moral nature. Conscience remains in fallen man the organ whereby he recognizes the ethical Voice which has supreme right to command him, and at the same time the organ whereby man is weighed by that moral claim to which he once corresponded fully on the basis of creation. Thus "the Book and the Breast," as D. S. Adam refers to the twofold moral revelation, stand in no absolute antithesis. for conscience still brings the individual mind in touch with the will of God.[12]

The conscience remains, universally, the organ for perceiving the world of moral facts and truths. It lifts man, spontaneously and often involuntarily, to the consciousness of God and right. To deny its validity entirely is to dismiss experience as an abortive enterprise. Conscience is the creative center of history, and when its bearings are rightly fixed, all goes well with the race. It is the center of gravity morally in human life.[13] In this recognition of conscience as a virile moral constituent of man, biblical and secular ethics wholly agree.

Recent dialectical theology, while supernaturalistic in its stance, assigns conscience a significance inferior to biblical ethics. Whereas the idealistic constructions divinize conscience and obscure Christ in his special redemptive revelation, the dialectical views so one-sidedly emphasize the encounter with the transcendent Christ as to obscure a proper statement of conscience as it survives in fallen man. Motivated by an anti-intellectualistic notion of revelation, dialectical writers find in the condemnatory conscience simply a non-cognitive witness to the Divine summons to obedience. Barth denies even this minimal point of contact

[12]O. Hallesby remarks: "We speak of the judgment of our conscience and the expression is an excellent one, for our conscience can really be compared to a judgment seat. . . . It compares our deeds or our words or our thoughts or our whole being with the moral law, with the will of God." *Conscience,* trans. C. J. Carlsen (4th ed., Minneapolis: Augsburg, 1944), p. 21.

[13]Nicolas Berdyaev remarks: "Conscience may be repressed, hidden and perverted, but it is connected with the very essence of man, with the divine image and likeness in him. In a hidden form it exists even in the Hottentot who defined good and evil by saying, 'It is good if I steal somebody else's wife and bad if my wife is stolen.' In our sinful existence conscience is remembrance of God and of the divine life. When conscience is roused in the most sinful and criminal man, it means that he thinks of God and of living in God's way, even though he may not express it in those words. Conscience is the organ of perception of the religious revelation, of goodness, righteousness and truth in its entirety." *The Destiny of Man,* p. 167.

between conscience and revelation. But Brunner and others insist on this truncated view.

The question at stake is not whether the ethics of special revelation requires a coalition with an equally primary and valid source of moral insight on the basis of general revelation. For the biblical doctrine of the fall and of man's sin precludes any such notion that the dictates of conscience expounded by man as fallen supply an authentic part and to some extent a basic foundation of Christian morality. It is one thing to say that the precepts of creation are written still upon man's heart, that conscience is an aspect of man's capacity for hearing God, and another to say that fallen man actualizes right moral judgments and goals. In the letter to the Romans, Paul concludes his discussion both of the inner light of conscience and of the outer revelation in nature on the same note: that the heathen world does not carry out the will of God. On the contrary, even the heathen conscience has already passed self-judgment, which God will complement by his own judgment in the future (Rom. 2:16).

The issue is rather whether the fall of man involves the destruction of the moral *imago* in every sense, both in respect of form and content. Ramsey virtually acknowledges defeat by the empiricists in the argument over the validity of conscience when he asserts: "Christian ethics . . . is not greatly concerned to prove that there is anything in our moral intuitions not derived from social training. It may be that there is nothing in individual conscience, no content of his moral or value judgments, that is not normally placed there by association of ideas drawn from customary morality."[14] Reinhold Niebuhr, although sharing the anti-intellectualistic approach to revelation, avoids a statement of conscience which is wholly relativistic as to content.[15] Hallesby, who is hardly to be classified as a dialectical theologian (although he asserts that the higher psychological experiences cannot be expressed "without involving ourselves in contradictions")[16] asserts that only the form of conscience (its peculiar function which tells man he ought to perform the will of God) is infallible, while the content of conscience in fallen man is fallible. Even the form, he argues, has been impaired by the fall, to the extent of compromising its strength and clarity.[17] He implies therefore that no trustworthy content survives in the *imago,* a position we regard as excessive.

[14]Paul Ramsey, *Basic Christian Ethics,* p. 88.

[15]"There are of course instances in which practices which are almost universally condemned are actually enjoined by the customs of a particular group; and become the content of conscience for the individuals in that group through the prestige and influence of the custom. In such cases, the moral life may be said to approach a state of total depravity. It is significant, however, that no group custom enjoins lying, stealing, or murder indiscriminately, since such a law would lead to complete chaos within the group. There is thus always a limit to the relativity of law in the conscience of man." *The Nature and Destiny of Man* (New York: Scribner, 1948), I, 275.

[16]Hallesby, *op. cit.,* p. 18.

[17]*Ibid.,* p. 30.

On the other hand, the Christian doctrine of sin involves also a certain depreciation of conscience. Although an inner witness to spiritual and moral truth, conscience is no longer revered as the veritable voice of God. Nor is it the authoritative and ultimate court of appeal in the discrimination of right and wrong. A single phrase from the lips of Jesus — "if therefore the light that is in thee be darkness" (Mt. 6:23, Lk. 11:35) is sufficiently drastic to shut the door upon any notion that the soul cannot be perverted from the service of goodness into the service of wickedness. No man's insight into his duty is so firm that the power of sin cannot overwhelm the authority of conscience and paralyze its operation. If the New Testament links the quickening of conscience with regeneration, Hallesby has good reason for titling a chapter "The Degeneration and the Death of Conscience."

The efficiency of conscience depends largely upon those dispositions and habits of character and will formed by the moral agent. Twice the New Testament (Acts 23:1, 1 Pet. 2:19) links the terms conscience and God in such a manner as to suggest that the act of moral judgment involves an inward realization of God standing in immediate relation to the soul. The plain implication is that knowledge of God and his will is promoted by faithfulness of conscience, and is decreased by unfaithfulness to conscience. No doubt its constraints fall into a variety of patterns, including fear of social disapproval, self-satisfaction and sensitivity to the high example and anticipations of others. But its deeper imperatives proceed from the divinely-implanted sense of the nobility and worth of life, and the conviction of ultimate judgment upon the wrong.

The man in moral revolt is often able to silence his conscience, and to push its reproof out of consciousness. But it is impossible to censor the voice of conscience in the realm of the subconscious. This responsiveness of the subconscious to the pangs of conscience is abundantly attested by contemporary psychological research. In this life, the mental torture of conscience sometimes leads to suicide, being so severe that the pangs of death are preferable. Among the worst terrors of hell is that the conscience will exercise its torment unrestrained, with double rebuke to those who have "explained away" this complex physiological "emergence" in man or this "reflex" of the prejudices of his age. Repressed pangs of conscience will multiply into magnitudes of horror and despair, whereas, had they been given free course in this life, they would have restrained their subject from his wicked pursuits.

The writings of Paul, especially the epistle to the Romans, bring us nearest a doctrine of conscience. The *locus classicus* is Romans 2:14f.: "When the Gentiles, which have not the law, do by nature the things of the law, these not having the law, are a law unto themselves, in that they show the work of the law written in their hearts, their conscience bearing witness therewith, and their thoughts one with another accusing or else excusing them. . ." Here one finds the clear recognition of a law written upon the hearts of men everywhere, the heathen included, and of a faculty which discerns that law and obeys or disobeys it in the sphere of conduct. The text teaches that Gentiles, while lacking the special Old Testament revelation of the law, are morally responsible because of an interior revelation of the good. It implies, therefore, that in no stage of human development and history are moral consciousness and accountability lacking, and that this recognition of the moral law, by whose authority man passes judgment upon himself, hails him accountably before God as surely as does the revelation in the Decalogue. Equally important, the passage implies that conscience is no faculty extraneous to the ego, but is somehow identified with the whole personality in its rational, volitional and emotive life.

How are we to explain this Pauline interest in conscience? Is it that the Apostle, schooled in Gentile universities, simply widened Hebrew-Christian theology to accommodate a phenomenon upon which pagan moral science insists? Does the Romans passage contain simply a discreet concession to the pagan world?

The fact is that the Romans passage does not stand alone. Paul's writings frequently contain the term conscience, in reference to the interior faculty of moral discretion which distinguishes good from bad and approves the one or condemns the other. It is not a phenomenon of the Pauline writings alone, but occurs in the larger New Testament. That Jesus presupposed an interior moral sense has already been indicated.

The universality of conscience is a New Testament emphasis which connects with the biblical doctrine of man as a bearer of the image of God. Knowledge of the good exists in human experience as a Divine gift, which relates man responsibly to God's mind and will. The voice of conscience speaks with an absolute authority to human experience because of this connection with the *imago Dei,* which in fallen man is shattered but not destroyed.

It speaks with dramatic right, addressing man with terrible earnestness as his proximate moral authority. It aspires to become the supreme practical guide of life. It calls man to special inventory by the ultimate personal Good to whom he stands in responsible relations, and reminds him that God is his true but forsaken home. No mere sliding evolutionary scale, it speaks the promise and witness of God that this measure of goodness will be finally vindicated and evil punished. It has been called "God's most intimate presence" within the soul of man — not because man carries a deity within his breast, but because it testifies to the broken good, and mirrors the judgment of the Living God in his life. Hence Luthardt aptly asserts that "conscience is the last thing left to man after he has squandered and lost all else that God has given him. It is the last tie by which God still retains a hold upon the man who has erred and strayed from Him, and by which He reminds him of the home he has forsaken."[18]

The moral agent is called upon, therefore, always to follow his conscience, and never to resist it. He acts ethically only when faithful to the light that he has. To follow one's sincere conviction as to the right course of action is the only course of moral growth. The man who acts conscientiously, although wrongly, is to be commended above the man who acts against the reproach of conscience. Only the moralists who have kept generous faith with the high claims of conscience have emerged as ethical pioneers in the world unenlightened by redemptive morality. Augustine distinguished sins of ignorance — acts in which the subject mistakenly thinks himself to be satisfying the greatest ethical claim — from sins of weakness. Such acts at least preserve the sense of duty, rather than outrage it. The Old Testament ceremonial ritual included sacrifice for sins of ignorance, and hence implied that men may sin without their knowledge of it. Our Lord's reference to the soldiers who put him to death — "Father, forgive them, for they know not what they do" (Lk. 23:34) — may reflect the same standpoint. It is reflected in Paul's apology: "I wist not he was the high priest" (Acts 23:5) after his stinging verbal rebuke to Caiaphas in the dispute following the Apostle's dramatic assertion: "I have lived before God in all good conscience until this day" (23:1). Such moral failure, while mistaken about the moral claim, preserves the sense of duty. In and through conscience as an element of the *imago Dei* God subjectively upholds the moral order. That conscience must always be obeyed is therefore a fundamental principle of Christian ethics. The appeal to conscience becomes an appeal to man's highest dignity.

To act from conscience does not necessarily make an act good, but to act against conscience invariably makes it bad. Only in the course of obedience to conscience does the possibility of further enlightenment exist. Disloyalty to conscience is disloyalty to God, and the man of whom it must be said "he has no conscience" is one skilled in such disloyalty. To stifle the voice of conscience means to shut the door to additional light. The man of high character and ethical concern is never anti-conscience in temper. The Reformation has often been described as an awakening of conscience. The turning-point of the biography of Luther is a crisis of conscience, and his subsequent appeal to the conscience of Germany and Christendom is a well-known story. Behind the Reformation stood the utterance at Worms: "My conscience is bound in the Word of God. I am not able to recall, nor do I wish to recall anything, for it is neither safe nor honest to do anything *against conscience*. Here stand I; I cannot do otherwise. God help me! Amen." Calvin may be claimed for the same emphasis: "Whenever

[18]C. E. Luthardt, *Apologetic Lectures on the Moral Truths of Christianity*, p. 53.

we take a step in opposition to conscience, we are on the high road to ruin."[19]

It belongs essentially to the Protestant outlook that biblical truth must be vindicated to the conscience of the hearer. Whenever the high efficiency of conscience is promoted, the flame of truth flares more brightly. The lively sense of the pure and noble in life, and a strong aversion for evil, appear only where the sense of duty is not left without interior supports. Hence the Christian conscience must be brought to the conscientious performance of every duty. The more frequently one acts in accordance with the claims of conscience, rather than in defiance of it, and cherishes the satisfaction of duty performed and despises rather than muffles the sense of guilt arising from disobedience, the easier the repetition of the right becomes. What distinguishes the believer from the unbeliever is his disposition to act on the side of conscience and to conform the general drift of life to its requirements.

Yet Christian ethics acknowledges at once, and insists, that conscience needs not only to be obeyed, but to be enlightened and educated. Man's duty, therefore, is not mere obedience to conscience, but its proper correction and instruction. The Reformers had no sympathy with "freedom of conscience" in the sense of modern philosophy and ethics which loosens the moral sense from answerability to God and his revelation. Kant's word, "an erring conscience is a chimera,"[20] shaped the modern outlook more than that of Jesus, "Ye do err, not knowing the scriptures" (Mt. 22:29).

Pierce acutely observes that in the Corinthian letter, the earliest in which the term "conscience" occurs, Paul attacks the Gentile presuppositions behind the life and outlook of the day, and that "among these *presuppositions* there stands that which can be summed up in the catchword *conscience*."[21] In Paul's earlier ministry reported in the Acts of the Apostles, the word is not found on his tongue, and it is absent in his earlier writings. But the situation in Corinth requires him to lay the ghost of the popular pagan notion of conscience. His very first recorded reference to conscience (1 Cor. 4:4) declares that human judgments — favorable or unfavorable — are irrelevant except as they are judgments of the Lord. The Apostle denies the competency of any human judgment whatever including his own; only the approbation or disapprobation of God matters. Thus he delivers a staggering blow to the thesis that conscience is the adequate investigator of the moral life.[22]

That the conscience speaks with a transcendent voice does not mean, therefore, that it universally yields a consistent and uniform statement

[19]Calvin, *Commentary on I Corinthians,* 8:11.
[20]Kant, *op. cit.*, p. 206.
[21]Pierce, *op. cit.*, p. 64.
[22]This first Pauline utterance on conscience, the first in Christian literature as a whole, supplies therefore a staggering contrast with the modern tendency, within the Christian churches, to make a beacon of conscience alone.

of moral duties. Alongside the emphasis on Gentile conscience Paul asserts that the conscience of the Israelite has the distinguishing light of special revelation, which the Gentiles — "not having the law" — lack (Rom. 2:14ff.). Both have the light of conscience, damaged by the fall, but repaired for the Hebrews by redemptive revelation.

While viewed as in some sense innate, and not accidental to the moral experience of the race, conscience is nonetheless connected with man's history and moral condition as well as with his response to the specially revealed Word of God. The ethical deliverances it yields are not independent of man's experience. Social influence and individual response and preference are among its conditioning factors. The voice of God, writes Lindsay Dewar, never errs and never hesitates, but the conscience of man falters in both respects.[23] Paul asserts no more than that Gentile conscience involves a knowledge of moral claims sufficient to constitute it responsible and guilty equally with the Hebrews. He gives no hint of the speculative notion that subjective moral criteria are trustworthy in man's fallen predicament apart from an external Divine authority. Nowhere does the New Testament represent conscience as a perfect and unerring organ. The Bible discloses the inadequacy of Buddha's definition of virtue as the agreement of the will with the conscience, and of Fichte's notion that conscience can never deceive us. It points up, also, the fallacy of Kant's view, that the inward law remains the ultimate authority in the moral life, alongside which every other is relative and accidental. "Even the Holy One of the Gospels must first be compared with our ideal of moral perfection before we can recognize Him as such," he writes.[24] The fault with Kant's formula is not his assertion that a genuine moral example "can never authorize us to set aside the true original which lies in reason,"[25] but his assumption that the moral law is autonomous and that it is not seriously clouded in human experience through the fall and sin. Kant presupposes not only a subjective standard of moral development far superior to that which universal conscience vindicates. The dictates of conscience are identified with clear, infallible moral principles before which all other moral phenomena bow. Once this approach is taken, the revision of conscience is precluded from the standpoint of the scriptural revelation and of the Divine incarnation in Christ. Hegel doubtless went to the other extreme when he enmeshed conscience one-sidedly in finiteness and development, but his blunt reminder that a man's conscience may be "the conscience of an ass" fixes attention on Kant's overstatement. Butler too shared Kant's optimistic view that conscience is always right.

Scripture leaves no doubt that conscience can be debased. It may be stained by sin (1 Cor. 8:7), seared so as to be insensible to certain

[23]Lindsay Dewar, *Christian Morals*, p. 173.
[24]Kant, *Fundamental Principles of the Metaphysic of Morals*, trans. Thomas Abbott, (3d ed., rev. London: Longmans, Green, 1883), p. 25.
[25]*Ibid.*

claims of the good (1 Tim. 4:2), insensate to the pangs of reproof and remorse, and at last perverted so that it ceases almost entirely to point upward to God and the good. Hence, conscience in the life of man in rebellion against God is capable of a progressive defilement. Mosley contrasts the wild heathen conscience, tormenting the soul by its accusations, with the Pharisaic conscience "pacified, domesticated, brought into harness — a tame conscience, converted into a manageable and applauding companion vulgarized, humiliated, and chained; with a potent sway over mint, anise and cummin, but no power over the heart" and characterizes the latter as "a dethroned conscience, deserted by every vestige of rank and dignity."[26]

Equally true is the fact that conscience is capable of elevation. Such education may be gradual, as when one grows through the moral earnestness of his culture or circle of acquaintances, or sudden, as in conjunction with a dynamic conversion experience. That conscience is capable of instruction is a fact in the forefront of the biblical representation. Already in man's state of integrity, the deliverances of conscience were supplemented by external commandments. But conscience in fallen man must always find its norm in that moral disclosure which is provided on the basis of special redemptive revelation. The fact that the biblical revelation is progressive is a further reminder that the enlightenment of the redeemed conscience is gradual. During the preliminary Old Testament period, conscience was bound to positive morality of a temporal nature. Even the understanding of revealed morality of permanent validity may be deepened and corrected, as Jesus made plain to his contemporaries by his exposition of the inner meaning of the law.

The regenerate conscience, moreover, is marked by a growth of moral sensitivity, as it matures to the implications of revealed ethics. The New Testament does not represent the conscience of the regenerate man as unerring and perfect. Rather, it indicates that the believer grows in moral judgment. For that reason, the regenerate conscience must not be regarded as self-sufficient and as complete. The morality even of the good conscience stands in continual need of instruction, that it may mature to adulthood. Among believers, conscience is not equally mature and clear in its deliverances. Conscience means "to know with," and the believer's union with Christ involves the progressive shaping of the whole of life. The Christian consciousness must not, in any event, be elevated to a parity with Scripture as an equivalent inward means through which the Spirit speaks. For Christ and his word alone lift the claim of conscience absolutely beyond the level of human fallibility.

The sheer strength of subjective ethical impulses, therefore, does not establish their authority. Only of the experience of Jesus of Naza-

[26]Cited by James Stalker, *The Ethic of Jesus According to the Synoptic Gospels* (New York: G. H. Doran, 1909), pp. 126f.

reth dare it be said that his conscience was nothing but the voice of God in the soul. His moral life alone stands above the reproach of conscience. The last vestige of excuse for the bad conscience is stripped away by the life of Christ, in whom the good conscience is clothed by righteousness in thought, motive, word, and deed. If conscience is the lord of man, Christ is the Lord of the conscience. So long as judgment upon sin is a valid category of history and experience, so long as man longs for a conscience detached from any sense of guilt, so long as the distinction between right and wrong remains ultimate and genuine, so long as the question of values and the good throbs through human interests, that long the name of Jesus will endure. In the world of human conscience, the moral experience of Jesus supplies the only ethical miracle in fallen history.

While conscience is an essential presupposition of man's moral life, it is not, in the view of biblical ethics, unrelated to man's larger experience of knowledge, volition, and emotion. We have already touched this point in the discussion of the *imago Dei.* Conscience is acknowledged by virtually all modern schools to be a more complex phenomenon than philosophers often considered it in pre-evolutionary thought. For Christian ethics, with its emphasis on creation, fall and redemption, it is indeed not a simple entity. The remarkable fact is, as Martineau observes,[27] that psychological inquiry concerning the nature and authority of conscience arose not in classical ethics, but in modern ethics which had for its background the biblical emphasis on human nature more than on nature in general.

The glory of Christian ethics is that it has provided humanity with its most highly trained conscience. It has gone beyond the important emphasis that conscience is the organ through which man is aware that he stands under an absolute moral imperative. Christianity has lifted conscience not merely to the loftiest reflections of Divine providence in history, but to the requirements of God's specially revealed Word. The Christian religion, writes Davison, explains the needs of conscience and supplies them.[28] A remarkable fact, to which moralists only now and then call attention, is that the Mohammedan religion and ethics have no equivalent for this term. If Christian ethics makes any fact crystal-clear, it is the indispensable place and function of both conscience and the Word of God in enlightened moral experience. The conscience of fallen man has but a relative trustworthiness, but the Christian conscience gains absolute compass-bearings from its reorientation to Scripture.

Under the preaching, teaching and pervasive influence of the Word, the enlightenment of conscience by the Holy Spirit takes place. As D'Arcy remarks, "the Bible has been the great moral educator of the Christian conscience as well as man's teacher in the things of religion.

[27]Martineau, *Types of Ethical Theory,* I, 63.
[28]Davison, *op. cit.,* p. 10.

And, as it has been with the race in general, so must it be with the individual. The precepts contained in Holy Scripture, the supreme example of goodness which it sets free, give it the unique potency which it possesses to inspire the heart and to instruct the conscience."[29] The one Spirit of Christ, beyond question, does not contradict himself, and speaks by one voice through the external means of Scripture and the internal voice of conscience, but the moral revelation is published unobscured only in the objective revelation of his will.

The fact of Christian growth explains why, even in the redeemed life, a conflict of conscience seems to arise, so that an area of discrepancy appears in the life of believers. Sometimes the principles by which duty is expressed are inadequate. At other times peculiar subjective proclivities disallow to one life as morally injurious what is a matter of indifference or is morally justifiable in another. An arbitrary and impersonal set of casuistic rules on the details of conduct may guard from evil, but it will do little to promote the good. An internal righteousness which transcends legalism in morality cannot but express itself as a morality of the searched conscience. "Where is the line to be drawn," asks D'Arcy, "between the time to be devoted to duty and the time to be spent upon amusement, between prudent thrift and niggardliness, between liberality and prodigality, between courage and foolhardiness, between courtesy and servility, between tact and time-serving?" and the reply is pointed: "The conscience must get its training in an experience moulded by the influence of the Word of God and Christian civilization on the one hand, and by the will directed by the 'Single eye' upon the other."[30] Freedom of conscience is a necessary correlate of the Christian life. No believer has a right to go beyond the clear requirements of Scripture in drawing up a list of infallible don'ts and imposing it absolutely upon others in the name of a sensitive conscience. Only the healthy conscience, trained to react instinctively in response to the New Testament revelation of the will of God, makes for a spontaneous spiritual morality. The schooling of the fallen conscience in the climate of redemption best conforms actions and moral principles to the requirements of revealed morality.

Since conscience is conditioned by environment, habit and education, the regenerate community bears a responsibility reaching into each of these spheres, as it promotes the redemption of conscience. Believers must place a premium upon the cultivation of the good conscience as a Christian virtue, and thereby rebuke the world's flight from conscience and recall it to moral sensitivity and earnestness. But they dare not stop with the proclamation of the necessity that conscience be honored. Christianity must seek the reorientation of the content of conscience to the revealed morality, and to Jesus Christ as the superlative manifestation of the good conscience and as the pattern for ideal conduct.

[29]D'Arcy, *op. cit.*, p. 99.
[30]*Ibid.*, p. 103.

In fallen history, within the fellowship of the Church, Christianity must create a moral climate sensitive to the high ethical claims of the ethics of revelation, and permit the light of such moral achievement to shine in the dark corners of secular cultural enterprises in our time.

The question of the permanence, or ideality, of conscience is one which gains a new importance through the current emphasis that conscience appears as a moral phenomonen only in man's fallen condition. Conscience admittedly is now connected with circumstances not belonging to human nature originally. Man as sinner cannot determine the original nature of conscience as a reflex of a fallen self-consciousness. In his present experience, the moral agent recognizes conscience largely as ranged in opposition to his ego, as an adversary, a light shining only amidst ethical darkness.

But that conscience has no function nor reality except in the state of sin is a risky theory. It gains support in contemporary ethical literature from the dubious notion that the good cannot arise by conformity to command. Hence the constraint of conscience is regarded as an element present only in the context of moral revolt.

But conscience is a correlate of the possibility of sin, not of its actuality only. James Stalker speaks of sequent conscience, which operates subsequently to performance, pronouncing a judicial verdict of guilty or not guilty, and antecedent conscience, which precedes moral decision or action and declares for one course and against another.[31] Dorner rightly resists the view that conscience is the effect of sin.[32] There is more to conscience than its negative and prohibitory side. Alongside the condemnatory voice of the retributive conscience must be ranged the approving and disapproving voice of the good conscience at the brink of decision. The good conscience is, in fact, the ultimate presupposition of the bad conscience. Just as man as man never falls too low to experience conscience, so he is never wholly above it. It was the pre-Christian world which found the chief significance of conscience in its form of accusation and self-condemnation. But in the New Testament the phenomenon of the "good conscience" comes again prominently into view. Just as man's inner consciousness of a false relation to God is called in Scripture an "evil conscience" (Heb. 10:22), so the conscience which witnesses to man in proper relation to God is good (Acts 23:1, 1 Pet. 3:16, 21, 1 Tim. 1:5, 19, Heb. 13:18), pure (1 Tim. 3:9, 2 Tim. 1:3) and void of offense (Acts 24:16). There is real point to Nicolas Berdyaev's remark that "a 'critique of pure conscience' ought to be written." In an ideal creaturely state, conscience is neither superfluous nor outgrown, but pervades the whole life of thought and conduct and dominates the moral outlook in its entirety.

Creation and glorification thus will once again blend in relation to conscience. Through the reconciliation of redemption, conscience the

[31]James Stalker, "*Conscience*," in *I.S.B.E.* pp. 701f.
[32]Dorner, *op. cit.*, p. 195.

foundling, participates in sonship through adoption, finally to be restored to its original position and nature. Conscience will assure man of Divine approval through a conscious perfect and continuous communion with God. The commandments will be infallibly engraved on the heart. The heart which now condemns us not, on the ground of Christ's meritorious interposition, is the harbinger of a conscience restored to its true home in glorification. The quality of peace and pleasure which attaches to the good conscience is a foretaste of moral glories in the life to come. Redemption restores the lost birthright, and pledges the full possession of inheritance.

23

THE MOTIVES AND SANCTIONS OF THE GOOD LIFE

Men act out of a complex variety of motives and sanctions. Sometimes these motives and sanctions are basically immoral, as when an outwardly "good" life is cultivated because it enables the man to perpetrate secret evils. The bank teller who is prominent in church life and has a place of leadership in the Boy Scouts or Community Chest, while at the same time he is embezzling funds in order to gamble at the race tracks, is a well-known example. In the sincere Christian life conflict arises not so much between proper and improper motives and sanctions as it does out of trying to decide which of the acceptable ones have priority.

The distinction between *motive* and *sanction* may seem artificial. The same considerations sometimes appear in both. But there is a real difference. By motive we mean a subjective reason for obedience — one which can be traced to the personal preferences of the moral agent. By sanction we mean an objective consideration, implicit or explicit, which enforces a moral imperative upon the agent from outside him. That which validates the moral judgment and thereby objectively incites to moral action is a sanction; motives are inner impulsions or inducements to action.

Motives for ethical obedience may include fear of punishment or of God, or desire for future or present reward, or love of the good for its own sake, or the proddings of conscience, or love for God, or imitation of Christ, or gratitude for God's mercies.

Sanctions for ethical conduct include such considerations as the nature of God, the Divine promise of reward, the Divine threat of punishment or the coming judgment, the love of God, and gratitude for the provision of redemption.

It is obvious that the biblical sanctions for moral living are unique. Ethical codes based on majority opinion, or upon the wise prescriptions of a philosophical minority, or upon considerations merely of prudence or utility, do not command the will absolutely.[1] The secular traditions

[1]Walter Lippman says, "Ethical codes cannot lay claim to unhesitating obedience when they are based upon the opinions of a majority, or on the notions of wise men, or on estimates of what is socially useful, or on an appeal to patriotism. For they depend then on the force which happens to range itself behind them at a particular time; or on their convenience for a moment. They are felt to be the outcome of human, and therefore quite fallible, decisions. They are no necessary part of the universe. They were not given by God to Moses on Sinai. They are

are at a loss to show a compelling sanction for morality when Divine sanction is obscured. They have a further inherent weakness. They lack a "good" that is transparently valid for all men in all times and at all places. Such motivations as gratitude for the mercies of redemption, the pursuit of the personal example of Christ, obedience to the injunctions of Scripture, and the eschatological orientation of conduct are obviously peculiar to biblical ethics and set it off from secular views.

Christian ethics sets up its own rules and tests to judge the legitimacy of a person's ethical motivation. For the Christian, fear of punishment ought not to be preached as a motive for repentance, since the believer is delivered from judicial penalty. Arminian ethics is sub-biblical in its emphasis at this point. Nor ought the desire for reward to be preached so as to lead men to expect reward as the just result of their own works. Rather, reward is directly linked to justification by faith as a special grace in view of obedience. Roman Catholic ethics, with its erroneous notions of merit, thrives on this misunderstanding of reward. When the imitation of Christ is conceived as a means to works-salvation, as in the ethics of Liberalism, there is another perversion of biblical ethics. Nor ought the good life to be pursued as "good in itself" in the autonomous sense; nor yet is it to be pursued apart from personal affection for and devotion to the content of his will simply because God had commanded it.

The primary motive for Christian obedience is gratitude for the grace of God in Jesus Christ. All other motives are secondary to this.[2] Of all the newly acquired feelings of the new convert to Christ, none is so natural as that of gratitude. Whoever does not venture the Christian life primarily out of grateful recollection misunderstands the price of his redemption. In relation to the other motives, it is the one, in all its implications, which is most distinctive in revealed ethics. It excludes so completely the motive of salvation by works.[3]

Recognizing the eternal tension between flesh and spirit, Adolf Koberle suggests that this dissension between the "old" and the "new" man necessitates two classes of motives. One would be gratitude or thankfulness arising out of our joyful liberty as the sons of God; the other a bitter compulsion forced upon us by a still partially antagonistic

---

not commandments of God speaking through his Infallible Church. . . . The sanction of a divine morality is the certainty of the believer that it originated with God. But if he has once come to think that the rule of conduct has purely human, local, and temporal origin, its sanction is gone." *A Preface to Morals* (New York: Macmillan, 1929), p. 50.

[2]"In Christian life, grateful love to the redeeming God is the deepest ground of virtue, to which all other motives may be referred. But the love produced by gratitude does not exclude, but includes, adoring love, which loves God for his own sake." R. F. Weidner, *A System of Christian Ethics,* p. 79.

[3]In Adam's state of integrity alone did the possibility of justification for works exist. Those who assert that works never afforded a means of justification either disallow the historicity of unfallen Adam on evolutionary assumptions, or hold the equally objectionable view that human nature is by creation inevitably sinful.

will.[4] The negative commands of Paul — "not to be deceived, not to despise, not to harden, not to cast aside, not to turn aside," are evidence that the battle still rages. Gratitude emerges from and involves the whole biblical soteriology. Koberle points out that the difference between evangelical and Roman Catholic morality has been reduced to the formulas "out of thankfulness," and "for the sake of thankfulness." For the Roman Catholic the highest motive of Christian action is twisted into legalism. What does not proceed only from gratitude falls beneath God's judgment. F. Pieper notes that the believers "present their good works to God not as a ransom to pay for their sins, but as a *thankoffering* for the redemption that Christ has effected . . . Only such worship and service of God is God-pleasing and fitting . . . To non-Christians, however, the worship and service of God is the performance of a 'religious duty,' dictated by the fear of God's wrath and aimed at winning God's favor by keeping the Law. But this . . . evokes God's wrath."[5] Luther called thankfulness the Christian's "most excellent virtue and the highest form of serving God . . . a virtue that no one else can display" except a Christian. The basic sanction for holiness is God's redemptive mercy. To those who contend that the motivation to holy living is nullified if salvation is by grace alone, Calvin states that "by no precepts, by no sanctions, is a pious mind so framed to render obedience to God, as by a serious meditation on the Divine goodness towards it."[6]

The words *grace* and *gratitude* are at root one (*charis*). They are two sides of the same Greek word. Because God's *charis* (grace) is poured out on unmeriting men, man's *charis* (gratitude) springs up in thankful devotion to God and in dedication to his service. The writer of Hebrews graphically expresses this thought: "Wherefore, receiving a kingdom which cannot be shaken, let us *have gratitude* whereby we may offer service well-pleasing to God with reverence and awe" (12:28). The word *eucharisteo,* which the New Testament uses of the expression of thanks and from which the word *eucharist* comes, also springs from *charis,* or grace. Thanksgiving in this spiritual sense is contrasted with the works of the flesh (Eph. 5:4; cf. 2 Cor. 4:15, Eph. 5:20, Col. 4:2). The Heidelberg Catechism sums up all Christian ethics under this heading — "Gratitude."

Newman Smyth concurs with other scholars that both love and gratitude were the motives of obedience to God for the Israelite in Old Testament days.[7] Garrard points out that God's covenant with Israel anticipates an obedience to be rendered gladly from the motive of gratitude[8] (cf. Dt. 4:31, 26:17ff., 29:9; Jer 11:2ff., Ezek. 16.8ff.).

[4]Adolf Koberle, *The Quest for Holiness,* trans. John C. Mattes (Minneapolis: Augsburg Publishing House, 1936), pp. 154ff.
[5]F. Pieper, *Christian Dogmatics,* I, 12.
[6]Calvin, *Commentary on Romans,* 12:1.
[7]Newman Smyth, *Christian Ethics,* p. 484.
[8]L. A. Garrard, *Duty and the Will of God,* p. 58, n.l.

The Decalogue is prefaced with a reminder of God's favor to Israel, of his deliverance of them from Egypt, so that the failure of the Israelite to order his life by God's will could only be the response of ingratitude.

The theme of grateful love is woven also throughout the fabric of the New Testament. Thanklessness is indicted by Paul as one of the two great sins of the pagan world — they "glorified him not as God, neither were thankful" (Rom. 1:21). Yet Christian ingratitude is worse. It mirrors a forgetfulness of God and a breach of fidelity by the redeemed man. G. F. Barbour suggests that "the mainspring of virtue in the Christian scheme" is far deeper than the mere expectation of reward, and is to be found "rather in the sense of responsibility and gratitude, and in the moral necessity of using for unselfish ends a benefit and a life unearned by personal merit."[9] As expressed by Sidney Cave, "the grace of God evoking gratitude, the love of Christ with its constraining power, the present, if partial, experience of the Spirit's power — in these St. Paul found the sources of the Christian life[10] . . . The Christian character springs from Christian gratitude."[11]

Man's chief end in life is "to glorify God" and "to enjoy Him forever." That is the inner spirit of gratitude. Man brings upon himself a detestable guilt when such kindness as that which delivered him from sin is flaunted by his disobedience to the author of that kindness, when he neglects God instead of being devoted to God. This guilt is increased when ungrateful man thanklessly indulges in those temporal blessings that flow from God's goodness.

The Christian motive of gratitude bears none of the overtones of the Aristotelian concept of gratitude. Cicero and Seneca reflect the Greek idea and consider it a reflex of a derogatory dependence upon others. The pagan mood described gratitude as presupposing a feeling of inferiority hurtful to self-respect. This low concept of gratitude provoked one swiftly to repay one favor by a greater in order to overcome the disagreeable feeling of indebtedness. To the contrary, Christianity presupposes no self-debasing inferiority, nor does it seek to transcend man's indebtedness to the Creator and Redeemer, but rather gratitude flows from the very recognition of this indebtedness. There is here no thought of the actual repayment for a benefit, nor of ridding the spirit of a distasteful sense of obligation. Gratitude is the wellspring from which arises the response of love to love. The Giver has given himself. The amazed and overwhelmed recipient gives himself in return. There is no balancing of accounts, no commercial or legal reckoning. There is only an unmeasured and ungrudging outflow of devotion that recognizes that ideally gratitude is without a limit. Like Mary of Bethany, who anointed the Lord's feet with "a pound of spikenard,

[9]G. F. Barbour, *A Philosophical Study of Christian Ethics*, p. 251.
[10]Sidney Cave, *The Christian Way*, p. 133.
[11]*Ibid.*, p. 154.

very costly" — there being now no limit to her purse — and "wiped his feet with her hair" (Jn. 12:3) — nor limit to her personal sacrifice — the believer's works are a living commentary on the truth that "he to whom much is forgiven, loveth much" (Lk. 7:47).

It may seem to many a Christian-in-the-pew that debate over the legitimate priority of motives for conduct is pedantic and void of practicality. But this really is far from the case. God uses the motive of gratitude to mature the believer in the fulfillment of his divinely-assigned vocation in personal and social relationships.

A simple illustration makes plain that the same external act may proceed from a great variety of motives. Some are base, some acceptable, one superlative. The vegetable clerk in a supermart always packages exactly five pounds of potatoes for customer convenience. If he is asked why, he may reply: (1) he wishes to establish a reputation for trustworthiness with his employer, so his job will be secure; (2) he believes that honesty is the best policy as a rule of success in business; (3) he has cheated in the past, and wishes now to placate a guilty conscience by rigorous honesty; (4) he intends to cheat his customers in the future, but first wishes to establish a reputation for integrity; (5) he practices honesty as part of a "salvation by works" philosophy; (6) he desires, as a partaker of God's redemption from sin and its consequences, thankfully to glorify God in his deeds, and he knows that he reflects the character of God when he gives what he promises. Indeed, it is like the grace of God to give "over and above," and if the pointer on the scale must fluctuate one side or the other of the pound mark, he will be inclined to measure with a godly generosity. To the customers who buy potatoes, it may make very little difference what motivation the clerk had. They received their money's worth regardless. But to God it makes every difference.[12] An exact five pounds of potatoes given for the motive (6) is worth its eternal weight in gold, whereas six pounds for most of the other motives may tip the scales of final judgment adversely.

Love that responds to God's love is, of course, a fundamental motive for obedience in the regenerate heart. Yet recent theories of Christian ethics have needlessly and harmfully equated this with gratitude. They are closely related, but they are not identical. Love rises out of gratitude; gratitude issues in love. It may seem that this distinction is pedantic and labored. But a fundamental theological consideration is at stake. The recent tendency to substitute responsive love for gratitude as the primary motive of Christian obedience moves the propitiatory work of Christ to the margin. It finds the basis reference point for

[12]Archibald Alexander asserts: "Men are more accountable for their motives than for anything else . . . . Primarily morality consists in the motives, that is, the affections." *Outlines of Moral Science* (New York: Scribner, 1861), p. 140. It would be fallacious, however, to infer that Christian ethics is disinterested in consequences. Rather, as already suggested, it transcends the secular antithesis between ateleological and teleological ethics.

Christian living not in the substitutionary atonement but in Divine forgiveness apart from propitiatory considerations. The Swedish *agape* school scuttles the motive of gratitude as the connecting link between justification and sanctification. By its emphasis on the repentant sinner's dynamic incorporation into Divine love, it merges justification, regeneration, and sanctification as different descriptions of the same ongoing Divine encounter with man.[13] Justification is no longer the imputation of Christ's righteousness, but becomes man's enlistment in Christ's resurrection victory over evil powers. It is contended that *agape,* which has initiated God's fellowship with man as sinner, thus flows dynamically through human relationship to others without the necessity of regarding love as a reflex of some higher consideration. The traditional view, supposedly, provides no automatic motivation for Christian ethics, since acquittal of the guilty does not in human experience result *eo ipso* in the new birth. This complaint must be understood especially in its protest against Lutheranism, which tries to combine its doctrine of regeneration with infant baptism. A sound Christian ethic will insist that justification is always accompanied by a vital subjective experience, and that the latter is the evidence of the former. The redeemed sinner is doubtless never as fully grateful as he has reason to be; but if he is justified, he will not be completely lacking in sanctification. A second objection is also pressed. A very legalistic and unevangelical conception of Christian ethics may follow out of the motive of gratitude but not out of the motive of *agape.* It has already been noted, however, that a bare notion of *agape* may lead the Christian into antinomian and otherwise quite inadequate and even objectional expressions of Christian behavior. On the other hand, it may be admitted that even when gratitude serves as its presupposition, the Christian life may be conceived legally and unspiritually. But this legalistic and unevangelical expression does not flow necessarily from gratitude. But an *agape*-ethic which misses the propitiatory atonement and is in revolt against God's inscripturated will surrenders the real motivation and direction for Christian living. The *agape*-ethic characteristically overlooks the guilt which attaches to man in view of his wicked past. It proposes his present "deliverance" from evil powers in total disregard of the obstacle which man's cumulative disobedience interposes between himself and Divine forgiveness. The evangelical view does not surrender the biblical role of *agape.* Indeed, it rescues it from loose and unevangelical conceptions which contemporary theology attaches to it. Trust in Christ's blood atonement is an essential element in the motivations to obedience. Gratitude directs a response of love to one who has conferred a benefit upon us. Roget's *Thesaurus* subsumes gratitude under "retrospective sympathetic affections," a classification which focuses attention upon the past, upon the objective propitiatory work of Christ. In Christian ethics, thankful good will

[13]Edgar M. Carlson, *The Reinterpretation of Luther,* pp. 213f.

expresses itself in love for God in view of God's grace. Unless that grace is excessively thinned out, it includes the propitiatory and substitutionary atonement as its presupposition.

Gratitude leads to love; the loveless life is deficient in gratitude. Not only the logic of Christian indebtedness, but the power of the new life in Christ, is such that Christian gratitude is connected with love for God, distinctively love for Jesus Christ the Redeemer. It is no mere commercial view only to favors received in the past and expected in the future. All that has been said against the identification of gratitude and love has been intended to guard against the misconception of both, and not to minimize the indispensable role of love as a motive of Christian living. It has been said to stress the truth that responsive love has as its background the propitiatory death of Christ. Both motives are essential to the Christian life; a morality of love without gratitude threatens to conceive the life of virtue one-sidedly as the imitation of Christ, whereas an ethic of gratitude without love would reduce to a mere "bread and butter" self-serving.

The reciprocated love of God is turned horizontally toward men by an intrinsic necessity. The love for God is inseparable from a sharing of that love with mankind. They are necessary corollaries. Whoever withholds a compassionate love from his fellow man, though that person be outside the circle of his intimate or casual friends, even if he be an enemy, cuts himself off in principle from the love which God has shown the doomed sinner in Christ. Thus the love for God, itself reflexive of God's love for man, becomes in turn the great motivation for man's love to man.[14] The biblical ethic of love is the dynamic of the Church's missionary service and of her concern for a doomed world. Against the conception that love is to be reserved only for those who stand within the circle of faith, the whole Christian moral consciousness reacts in protest.

There are additional motives for obedience in the good life: the example of Christ or of the apostles (2 Thess. 3:7ff., 1 Cor. 11:1, Phil. 4:9); the desire for reward; the avoidance of chastening; the pursuit of happiness. These may be comprehended, with gratitude and love, as included in the desire to exhibit fidelity to the will of God revealed in Scripture. But all must be regarded, Donald MacKenzie indicates, as "colored spectral rays of the real inward motive and sanction of Christian duty, which is the redeeming love of Christ to all men, constraining us to personal holiness and public righteousness."[15]

Marshall lists the motives for Christian conduct as: (1) Christian self-respect, (2) the general good, (3) correct form, (4) the worthy

[14]The motive force behind Communism, by contrast, is hate. "We must know how to hate," writes Lunacharsky, Soviet minister of education, "for only at this price can we conquer the universe." Cited by A. H. M. Lurin, *The Science of World Revolution* (New York: Sheed & Ward, 1938), p. 88. The correspondence between Paul's "works of the flesh" and Communist emphases is remarkable: enmity, strife, anger, dissension, and party spirit.

[15]Donald MacKenzie, "Christian Ethics," in Hastings' *E.R.E.*

walk, (5) reason, (6) fear.[16] Most of these contain some measure of truth, yet they must be guarded from error. The virtuous life does not destroy self-respect nor the general good. Properly understood, it promotes them. Its behavior is comely, and its manner of life "worthy of the gospel of Christ" (Phil. 1:27). Nor is it to be castigated as irrational. But it must still be defined more closely. While fear of chastening is admissible as a motive to good works, fear of condemnation is inconsistent with the filial bond. There can be no proclamation of the fear of hell as a motive of Christian obedience. Only in a limited sense is there room for terror before the Lord within the bond of love. Marshall fails to make this distinction because of his disregard for the eschatological wrath of God. He reduces biblical passages which speak of coming judgment (*e.g.,* Rom. 2:5, 1 Cor. 5:5, 10:8, 11:30) to "the recognition that it is undoubtedly a dangerous thing to trifle with the great issues of right and wrong."[17] One would think that the future reward—which Marshall wholly ignores as a motive—would then reduce to the sheer recognition that morality is an earnest business. It is no great surprise that those whose eschatological convictions have dimmed should seek to detach the Christian life, as we shall presently note, from all orientation to reward. The reasonableness of the good life, which Marshall designates as a motive (appealing to Eph. 5:17 and 1 Cor. 14:20), likewise must not conceal its basis in special revelation and redemption. The appeal to reasonableness is typically Greek, and largely in the spirit of Aristotle and the Stoics. This is quite in contrast to the desire to conform one's life to the specially disclosed will of the living and omniscient God. That the form of Christian behavior is correct, or free from moral objections (Acts 13:50, Rom. 13:13, 1 Cor. 7:35, 12:23, 14:40) and above pagan criticism (1 Thess. 4:12) is doubtless correct. Yet it cannot be admitted that pagan standards as such dictate and measure the content of the ideal life. Even the exhortation to the worthy walk thins out in Marshall's discussion to an appeal to the believer to "pull his weight" and "do his share." This moves toward a one-sided emphasis on meritorious works. Regarding the appeal to the general good, it assuredly is true that the law of love should prevail over expedience. It is the real good of all. But its content is theologically, not merely sociologically, determined. The appeal to self-respect must also be guarded to preserve the distinction between the old and the new natures. Doubtless certain practices are beneath the character of every morally sensitive person. Christian experience recognizes best of all that a certain behavior alone befits the true and created dignity of human nature, and that the great redemptive transaction enforces this lofty emphasis. At the same time, the prevailing cultural modes of thought must not dictate the levels of decency. Even among Christians, a wrong "fear of the world" sometimes thwarts the

[16]L. H. Marshall, *The Challenge of New Testament Ethics,* pp. 309ff.
[17]*Ibid.,* p. 316.

spontaneity of the ethical life. "Self-respect" in the circles of pagan morality is surfeited and vitiated by pride, a tendency of the old nature which even the believer must alertly combat. The "decency" of a pagan society is no doubt preserved against swift deterioration by higher views of self-respect conditioned by Christian influences. However, inner motives of action often remain evil and selfish. This is a far cry from a standpoint of self-respect from which Christian ethics proceeds.

The prime weakness of Marshall's treatment of motive is that his approach is basically practical, whereas actually the Christian life must be first motivated by spiritual considerations from which the practical issue spontaneously. In an incidental reference it is asserted that Paul "recognizes that only love is an adequate motive in the ethical and religious life."[18] Even this statement falls short of an adequate statement of redemption, and fails to do justice to other motives which Paul approbates.

Besides the areas of controversy over motive already discussed, *i.e.*, the question of the priority of motives and the deficiency of responsive love as a substitute for gratitude, a further dispute centers about the legitimacy of reward as a genuine spiritual motivation. This question cannot be separated from the larger issue of the literalness of the eschatological sanction for conduct. Because of the important place which the discussion of the nature of the eschatological sanction once again holds in contemporary ethical and theological thought, the subject is considered separately in the following chapter.

It is appropriate here, nonetheless, to discuss the legitimacy and place of reward as a motive for Christian ethics. The attack upon this motive has proceeded with great vigor in recent decades. Reasons for the attack lay in skepticism or agnosticism about the future, the displacement of biblical by secular anticipations, and a revulsion against low and inadequate views of ethics.

Some forms of secular ethics are linked wholly to reward or beneficent consequences as the validation of good acts. David Hume bases all moral judgments purely upon the pain and pleasure resulting to the individual from his actions. Bentham differs from Hume in distinguishing kinds of reward, rather than emphasizing the mere quantity of it, and seeks to vindicate noble character by noble rewards.

In Judaistic legalism, Floyd Filson holds, the predominant idea was to regard one's life mainly as a means of earning a reward. "The thought of recompense, the desire for reward, predominates, and this militates against tranquil fellowship with God. One must constantly look to his record as the main thing and think of God as the recompenser first of all."[19] Thus the Pharisee Saul must certainly have held that God recompenses men, on the basis of conformity to his law.

[18]*Ibid.*, p. 315.
[19]Floyd W. Filson, *The Recompense Principle in Paul* (Leipzig, 1931), p. 7.

The failure properly to resolve the paradox between reward-motivation and other motives approved in the Bible has resulted historically in many serious errors. It raises many problems. An improper emphasis upon present sacrifice in order to obtain a maximum reward in heaven is firstly, a fertile and well-watered ground for the nurture and growth of pride. Here the custom of venerating saints found its root. Secondly, the question arises whether there will be remorse in heaven over rewards that have been lost. Thirdly, the danger arises of introducing a new form of legalistic bondage; brother strives with brother in good works that one may have a higher position in heaven than the other (Lk. 22:24). Fourthly, the withdrawal from useful life often characterizes those who concentrate improperly upon future reward. Medieval monasticism is the best known example of this misuse of reward.

Christian ethics can only profess an appreciative sympathy for cheap views of morality which make the prospect of future reward or the avoidance of punishment the sole or main motive of behavior. Such a view is grossly deficient for two reasons: it regards the good only as instrumentally good, and not as intrinsically good; and it attaches reward to the good life as a due rather than as a matter of grace. Where such perversions exist, the motive of ethical conduct is nullified by the introduction of an all-controlling egoistic element. The doctrine of salvation through God's grace is threatened, since the blessings of the future are the legal results of good works.

The New Testament itself has no interest in a "morality" which avoids wickedness because it involves penalties. Evil is to be avoided because it is evil. No cheap program of destiny-insurance, no enlightened form of self-interest, can pass muster as a fundamentally Christian ethics. Christianity does not have a merely contingent morality. It deals with what is intrinsically and essentially good. For Christianity the good is never merely instrumental, something to be prized only for the sake of that to which it leads. Whoever feels that he cannot be honest unless he is specially rewarded for it, or who fears dishonesty only because of possible retribution thereby calls his integrity into question. "Crime does not pay" is a repugnant ground for uprightness; even if it did "pay" — as now and then, at least for the time being, it does — no ethical vindication of it would thereby exist. Quite properly does E. Westermarck observe that we cannot feel "moral approval or retributive kindness towards a person if we recognize that he does a thing only in the selfish hope of being benefited by it."[20] The notion that the life of piety and virtue is nothing but a discreet investment which "pays off," here or in eternity, or both, is one which misses the meaning and significance of the good life.

[20]E. Westermarck, *Christianity and Morals* (London: Kegan, Paul, Trench, Trubner, 1939), p. 63.

"It is often contended that, with regard to purity of motive, the ethics of Christianity falls below the ethics of philosophy."[21] When Christian ethics is accused of falling below the ethics of philosophy in the area of rewards and punishment, the contrast is usually made with respect to the purity of motives and on the basis of the philosophical concept that virtue must be first of all disinterested. This extreme view involves the idea that "any form of good action which is prompted by the hope or fear of recompense sinks at once from the level of true virtue to that of prudence; and the one type of conduct which fulfills all the conditions of moral goodness, is that in which the spirit of man ventures all upon the intrinsic righteousness of an action, or seeks an end which is felt to be noble in and for itself, laying aside every consideration of future pain or profit."[22] Over against this view, however, there stands another view which is hardly less universal or insistent; namely, that "virtue shall in the end be recognized and rewarded, and that the struggle shall not be fruitless. . ."[23] In the two views just mentioned, we see the "double demand of the moral and religious consciousness"[24] which has posed such a nettlesome problem to the moral philosophers.

In his *Republic,* Plato argues that if justice is to be proven as a virtue which is superior to injustice, then both qualities must be examined as they are in themselves and all extraneous considerations of reward and punishment are to be strictly excluded. However, Plato still believed that virtue ought to be rewarded. His final conclusion was that righteousness would be vindicated, and that regardless what the lot of a just man might be in this life, he would ultimately find his reward. Socrates accepted the challenge to show that in itself justice was worthy of choice, yet in his Tenth Book we read that, "In the case of the just man, we must assume that whether poverty be his lot, or sickness or any other reputed evil, all will work for his final advantage, either in this life, or in the next. For, unquestionably the Gods can never neglect a man who determines to strive earnestly to become just, and by the practice of virtue is as much like God as man is permitted to do."[25] More recent philosophers such as Spinoza, Kant, and Rashdall are unflinching in their branding of Christianity as a selfish philosophy of life.

Immanuel Kant insists with rigorous logic that reverence for the majesty of the moral must be the only motive of duty and that all motives springing from personal desire or hope of happiness must be severely excluded. It is interesting to note, however, that in the second part of his *Critique of Practical Reason,* Kant proceeds with what Alexander calls "a strange inconsistency to make room for the idea, viz., that virtue is not without its reward, and is indeed united in the end

[21]A. Alexander, *Christianity and Ethics,* p. 15.
[22]G. F. Barbour, *op. cit.,* p. 209.
[23]*Ibid.,* p. 210.
[24]*Ibid.*
[25]*Ibid.*

with happiness."[26] Kant holds that felicity and holiness shall be ultimately one, and that at last virtue shall be seen "to be worthy of happiness, and happiness shall be the crown of goodness."[27] Kant is typical of other philosophers who could be cited here. Although these philosophers contend for purity of moral motive and the disinterested loyalty to the good, nevertheless, at the end they bring in the notion of happiness as a concomitant or consequence of virtue. Alexander is correct in saying that happiness itself "cannot fail to be also an active incentive."[28]

The central problem of philosophy, as we have been viewing it so far, has been to reconcile the two universal demands: first, that virtue must be before all things disinterested, and, secondly, that virtue shall in the end be recognized. This is a real problem to the philosophers, and we have seen with what great difficulty they have tried and failed to remove the idea of recompense as a motive for virtuous conduct.

The charge of egoistic hedonism is the primary accusation which is brought against the New Testament appeal to reward as a motive for Christian conduct. It is alleged, as Alexander quotes the complaint, that "Christianity, while inculcating renunciation in this world, does so for the sake of happiness in the next."[29] The great Utilitarian, Sidgwick, says that the ethics of Jesus is not only hedonistic but that it is to be described as egoistic hedonism, that is "a system which prescribes actions as means to the end of the individual's happiness or pleasure."[30] Nathan Soderblom, the late Archbishop of Sweden, describes the ethics of Jesus as appealing to a "ruthless egoism."[31]

Under the influence of this type of thought many preachers today, unlike their predecessors, believe that it is a serious ethical defect in the teaching of Jesus for him to appeal to either the desire for reward or the fear of punishment as a motive for Christian conduct. They say that "the modern man quite rightly refuses to be enticed into virtue by the hope of reward, or dragooned into it by the fear of punishment."[32] Modern sympathies are rather said to be in favor of the philosophy of the Saracen woman told about in Joinville's life of St. Louis. According to the story, a monk saw her walking down a street of Damascus with a pan of fire in one hand and a pitcher of water in the other. When the monk asked her what she intended to do with these things, she replied that she intended to "burn up Paradise and put out the fires of Hell so that men could do good for the love of God alone."[33]

Dewar agrees that self-centeredness and self-concern are "the chief bugbears of the moral life,"[34] and that the offering of reward does

[26]Alexander, *op. cit.*, p. 158.
[27]Quoted by Alexander, *op. cit.*, p. 158.
[28]*Ibid.*, p. 158.
[29]*Ibid.*, p. 157.
[30]Sidgwick, *The Methods of Ethics,* p. 89.
[31]Westermarck, *op. cit.*, p. 68.
[32]Marshall, *op. cit.*, p. 202.
[33]Barbour, *op. cit.*, p. 210.

appeal to this. But then he goes on to point out a fact which many of the philosophers have overlooked, namely, that to deliberately "exclude any thought of reward appeals to self-centeredness even more strongly; for plainly the temptation to pride oneself on one's virtue in following virtue for its own sake is likely to be very strong."[35] Whether we introduce the idea of recompense or exclude the idea of recompense "we cannot escape the tendency to self-concern."[36] Any philosophy which holds that the appeal to rewards is unethical is placed on the horns of a dilemma, for no man will strive for virtue exclusive of all thought of reward unless he believes he can in some sense have the satisfaction of attaining to purity of motive. However, this satisfaction after which he strives is in itself the reward and thus an unethical motive. The claim for the superiority of philosophical ethics over Christian ethics, on the basis that the appeal to reward is unethical, is a very weak one. Philosophical ethics becomes the victim of its own charge. Moral philosophers may hold that recompense is an unethical motive for their system of moral conduct, but with respect to Christian conduct one is constrained to seek from within Christian philosophy for a more adequate answer.

The notion that the admission of reward as a motivation for ethics leads necessarily to the deterioration of the ethical ideal is erroneous. The secular denial of the validity of reward as a proper motivation for conduct must be repudiated. The battle cry "virtue for virtue's sake, duty for duty's sake" may sound at first like the essence of morality, but it transfers ethics from its theonomous to an autonomous sanction. Clark points out that while Christian ethics "demands sacrifices of men . . . it demands no ultimate sacrifice"[37] in which his self-giving is unrewarded. Christian ethics is not destructive of self-interest, but rather promotes an enlightened self-interest which finds its own welfare in the conformity of creaturely life to the Creator's will. The good is also instrumental to a felicitous destiny; that is why it is eschatologically sanctioned. Better than any other ethical approach, Christianity vindicates the good as at once both instrumentally and intrinsically good. "However loudly it may be protested that virtue is to be pursued for its own sake," writes Barker, "it is not possible to justify a world in which the righteous are the victims of life-long suffering and then pass from existence."[38] The ethical problem cannot be firmly faced apart from a morality in which there will be absolute vindication in the life to come.

Even the belief that goodness will be rewarded by happiness does not commit one to hedonistic or egoistic ethics. Rather than erecting selfishness as the primary motive of ethics, it may with equal assurance

[34]L. Dewar, *An Outline of New Testament Ethics,* p. 49.
[35]*Ibid.*
[36]*Ibid.*
[37]Gordon H. Clark, *A Christian View of Men and Things,* p. 188.
[38]C. J. Barker, *The Way of Life,* p. 40.

"express a conviction about the nature of God and of the moral order. It is, after all, an entrance into a happiness which the moral order validates which is in view."[39] There is nothing unethical in the belief that the virtuous life leads to soul satisfaction, prosperity and happiness. Rather, it would be a defective and fallacious idea of the good life to hold that it must be deprived of such consequences, or that where they do follow, life ceases on that account to be virtuous. Marshall remarks, "If we were living in a universe where virtue brought no reward and vice no punishment, we should no longer be able to believe in a living God."[40] There are noble rewards as well as mean ones, and there is nothing unethical in the idea that virtue brings a noble reward. C. S. Lewis rebukes the notion that reward is a shameful motive. "If there lurks in most modern minds the notion that to desire our own good and earnestly to hope for the enjoyment of it is a bad thing, I submit that this notion has crept in from Kant and the Stoics and is no part of the Christian faith. Indeed, if we consider the unblushing promises of reward and the staggering nature of the reward promised in the Gospels, it would seem our Lord finds our desires, not too strong, but too weak. . . We must not be troubled by unbelievers when they say that this promise of reward makes the Christian life a mercenary affair. There are different kinds of reward. . . Those who have attained everlasting life in the vision of God doubtless know very well that it is no mere bribe, but the very consummation of their earthly discipleship; but we who have not yet attained it cannot know this in the same way, and cannot even begin to know it at all except by continuing to obey and finding the first reward of our obedience in our increasing power to desire the ultimate reward. Just in proportion as the desire grows, our fear lest it should be a mercenary desire will die away and finally be recognized as an absurdity. . ."[41]

The Bible frequently uses the concept of reward to express the certainty that God guarantees the ultimate success and happiness of those who obey his law and serve him. Of its place in Hebrew thought, Abraham Shusterman observes: "Although the greatest Jewish thinkers have preferred to consider goodness as sufficiently desirable in itself, regardless of consideration of material reward or of punishment, the doctrine of retribution has a place in every credal formulation. . . It finds constant expression in Jewish homiletics and in the liturgy. . . In one form or another, the idea of reward and punishment on the part of a righteous God has always remained a fundamental doctrine of Judaism."[42]

[39]"The good life, as set forth in His teachings, is not something that one obtains through the pursuit of his own pleasure and happiness. It comes only through service and devotion to what He called the Kingdom of God." Charles H. Patterson, *Moral Standards*, p. 280.

[40]Marshall, *op. cit.*, p. 207.

[41]C. S. Lewis, *The Weight of Glory* (New York: Macmillan, 1949), pp. 1ff.

[42]Abraham Shusterman, "Reward," in *Universal Jewish Encyclopedia* (1943).

In the prophets it is an inviolable rule that the righteous are rewarded and the wicked punished (Isa. 3:10f., Amos 5:14ff., Hos. 4:1ff.). A decision between obedience and disobedience toward God is always a choice between blessing and curse, and between life and death (Dt. 28:1ff., 30:15ff., Lev. 26:3ff., Josh. 23:14ff.).

So true is this of Jewish ethics that some have thought to explain Jesus' teaching regarding reward and punishment as merely a "relapse" into the common Hebrew idea. No one can deny that Jesus' ethical teaching generally gives a prominent place to the thought of reward. K. E. Kirk has collected an imposing list of the passages in which it figures prominently as a consideration.[43] In Matthew is found: "Blessed are you when men revile you and persecute you and utter all kinds of evil against you falsely *on my account.* Rejoice and be glad for great is your reward in heaven" (5:11f.). "He who receives a prophet *because he is a prophet* shall receive a prophet's reward, and he who receives a righteous man *because he is a righteous man* shall receive a righteous man's reward" (10:41). And again, "And whoever gives to one of these little ones *because he is a disciple,* truly I say to you, he shall not lose his reward" (10:42). Jesus offers the goods of his kingdom as the promised reward of his disciples (Mt. 6:33, 19:29, 24:45ff., 25:34ff., Lk. 6:23ff., 12:33ff., 14:12ff.). The rejection of the reward motive as altogether unworthy ignores many incontrovertible statements in the New Testament concerning reward (Mt. 5:12, 46, 6:1, 10:41, Mk. 9:41, Lk. 6:23, 35, 1 Cor. 3:8, 14, 9:17, 1 Tim. 5:18, 2 Pet. 2:13, 2 Jn. 8, Rev. 11:18, 22:12). "In all cases," Amos N. Wilder admits, "the sanction from the example of Jesus is complicated by the thought of reward present in the context."[44]

Walter Lippmann says that "popular religion is suited to the capacities of the unconverted . . . and is preoccupied with the regulation of the unregenerate appetites of mankind."[45] Such a statement as this is very difficult to reconcile with Jesus' teaching regarding rewards. The rewards which Jesus offers neither appeal to the unregenerate man nor are they available to him, for they have been "placed in a region to which only faith can penetrate and which Jesus himself described in terms of the spiritual life alone."[46]

Marshall discovered the Old Testament view to be that "long life, a large family, prosperity, wealth, health, and happiness" accrue to the good life. He finds this "painfully conspicuous" in Psalm 91, and in Job's final acquisition of twice as much as he lost, as a "rather prudential ideal of virtue," in contrast with which "even Pagan ethics at its

[43]Kenneth E. Kirk, *The Vision of God* (New York: Longmans, Green, 1931, abridged, 1934), pp. 140f.

[44]Amos N. Wilder, *Eschatology and Ethics in the Teaching of Jesus,* p. 132.

[45]Walter Lippmann, *op. cit.,* p. 201.

[46]G. F. Barbour, *op. cit.,* p. 235.

best, declared for virtue for virtue's sake independently of any reward."[47]

The motive of reward is as central and dominant in Pauline thought as it is anywhere else in the Bible. "It seems that Paul's conversion experience of the risen Christ led to a reorganization of his ideas to the extent that God's grace became central instead of God's recompensing activity. But this" — so writes Filson — "was merely a shifting of emphasis and not an abandonment of the recompense principle."[48] Punishment is earned on a strict and absolute basis, for Paul wrote that "the *wages* of sin is death." But salvation and eternal life are not earned by the individual. They are a sharing in Divine mercy. "The gift of God is eternal life in Christ Jesus our Lord" (Rom. 6:23).

What is so often overlooked in appraisals of biblical motive of reward is the fact that the advantages accruing to the people of faith are regarded as the inevitable consequence of their relationship to the Living God who fashions special providences of life, and constitutes men and nature so that virtue produces happy consequences. Dewar pointed out that in the Beatitudes rewards are introduced as the natural consequences of the virtues. "The statements are couched in the form of spiritual laws."[49] Even the Utilitarian recognizes that virtue, on the whole, leads to pleasure; and vice, on the whole, leads to pain. There is nothing unethical in pointing to such a plain fact of experience. The Lord undoubtedly often did appeal to this fact of experience, but he never made careful calculation of prospective pleasure or pain the motive for the ethical life!

The Bible clearly teaches that God will recompense every man according to his deeds. Rather than denying the legitimacy of interested motivation, "the doctrine of Christ constantly stresses the idea of recompense."[50] Although *Young's Analytical Concordance to the Bible* only refers to twenty-two New Testament passages in which *mithros* is used, many other passages definitely teach the doctrine of rewards and punishments.[51] The question with which we must concern ourselves at this time is whether or not such teaching reduces the Christian ethic to the level of egoistic hedonism. Niebuhr says that it is with respect to the ethical problems of rewards that the full rigor and non-prudential character of Jesus' ethic is completely revealed: "Obedience to God, in the teachings of Jesus, must be absolute and must not be swayed by any ulterior considerations. . . The service of God is to be performed not only without hope of any concrete or obvious reward, but at the price of sacrifice, abnegation, and loss. . . In all of these emphases the immediate and the concrete advantages which may flow from right conduct are either not considered at all or their consideration is defin-

[47]Marshall, *op. cit.*, pp. 201f.
[48]Filson, *op. cit.*, p. 14.
[49]Dewar, *op. cit.*, p. 50.
[50]Clark, *op. cit.*, p. 188.
[51]Cf. for example Rom. 8:18.

itely excluded. The ethic demands an absolute obedience to the will of God without consideration of those consequences of moral action which must be the concern of any prudential ethic."[52] Clark replies to the notion that a rewarded conduct is necessarily selfish, "No doubt the Church contains hypocrites; no doubt also many, yes, all sincere Christians fail to live consistently by their principles; but it is exceedingly strange to charge Christianity with inculcating selfishness."[53]

George Walker is correct in saying that "to represent the promised recompense as of a hedonistic or even mercenary kind, proceeds from a misapprehension of what it imports, and of the nature of the expectations which it encourages."[54]

The idea that God is obligated to reward the believer for any good works he may do has no support in the New Testament. Jesus repudiated this conception in his parable of the laborers in the vineyard (Mt. 20:8ff.). Good works are not meritorious in the technical sense, as if they lead to the necessity for reward on the basis of commutative justice in view of their own absolute value and dignity. But if the mercenary nature of a system of rewards is eliminated, what meaning is left to the idea of reward? It becomes obvious again that when the good as a human achievement is spoken of as intrinsically good, it is so only in a borrowed sense. Such works are the product of the Spirit, not an achievement of the flesh (1 Cor. 15:10, Phil. 2:13). In their totality, they represent in regenerate experience only a partial obedience, in contrast with the perfect obedience required by the law (Isa. 64:6, Jas. 3:2). God is not a debtor to those who perform good works, but he approves and inspires such works and has attached a promissory reward to them (Lk. 17.9f., Rom. 5:15ff., 6:23, Eph. 2:8ff., 2 Tim. 1:9, Tit. 3:5). Apart from this promise, believers can expect no compensation for good works.[55] They owe themselves to God, and good works are God's due and their duty. Their moral achievements, imperfect and temporal, are appraised as meritorious deeds, wholly disproportionate to the perfect and eternal reward which God in grace attaches to them. The redeemed sinner cannot establish an absolute merit before God.

Jesus never makes the expectation of reward the chief motive of the Christian life. The opposite indeed is true. The man who seeks to gain the reward by his own efforts thus loses it. He clearly warns of hypocrites who do their good deeds openly with the very end in view that they may be recognized and given their due reward (Mt. 6:1ff.). Yet it is overstatement to contend that only duty which is performed without expectation of reward will be rewarded. Only what is done

[52]Reinhold Niebuhr, *An Interpretation of Christian Ethics,* p. 10.
[53]Clark, *op. cit.,* p. 11.
[54]G. Walker, *The Idealism of Christian Ethics,* p. 244.
[55]*The Westminster Confession* affirms (VII, i) that: "the distance between God and the creature is so great that, although reasonable creatures do give obedience unto Him as their Creator, yet they could never have any fruition of Him as their blessedness and reward, but by some voluntary condescension on God's part, which He hath been pleased to express by way of covenant."

from love will be rewarded, but there is no reason to exclude the expectation of reward from what is so done. It is the "contract" idea of piety and virtue that is excluded. "There is no thought of an equivalent for service rendered, as in the case of a laborer in private life, for the reward has not been the sole motive to action. If reward is to be taken in its strictest sense, it is clear that no one can make demand upon God for recompense. The expectation of a reward becomes a matter of faith and the reward itself a matter of grace."[56]

Of all the approaches to the problem of reward, C. S. Lewis' is the most thoughtful. He has carefully worked out the idea that reward consists of a greater capacity to receive the gifts of God. This is undoubtedly the chief aspect of true reward. The spirit of competition and resentment falls away.[57] Its solution lies in the filial bond. Love will be perfect, so that through the filial bond with the Father, the saints love each other perfectly. Each will delight in the other's reward. Although rewards will differ in accordance with our faithfulness while on earth, we will no more think of being jealous of another's greater reward, or proud that we have been given a higher reward than another, than we would think of being jealous of the position of God as Ruler of all.

Rather than making expectation of reward the chief motive for the Christian life, Jesus taught that if a man were to seek to gain a reward by his own effort he would forfeit it (Mt. 6:1ff., 18:1ff., Mk. 8:35). "Both Jesus and Paul taught expressly that the Christian-ethical life does not spring from reward, but from the Grace of God in us and from the love towards God and our neighbors which it awakens."[58] "The promise of reward may be the condition of action, the ground or premise of strength, but reward is never action's goal. Reward is always added to the nature of the act, not a direct result of it such as might become a part of the agent's own prudential calculation."[59] Jesus taught that if a man were calculating, the nature of his act would change and that it would not be the kind of action for which reward is promised. "In the parable of the Last Judgment, which has been aptly called the Parable of Great Surprises, those who are declared worthy of eternal life are amazed, so completely are they unaware of any merit in their behavior — virtue at its highest is unconscious of itself."[60] If a man acts for the sake of a reward, he will not be rewarded because

[56]O. Kirn, "Reward," in *New Schaff-Herzog Encyclopedia of Religious Knowledge,* p. 20.

[57]The promises of Scripture C. S. Lewis reduces roughly to five heads: "Firstly, that we shall be with Christ; secondly, that we shall be like Him; thirdly, with an enormous wealth of imagery, that we shall have 'glory'; fourthly, that we shall, in some sense, be fed or feasted or entertained; and finally, that we shall have some sort of official position in the universe — ruling cities, judging angels, being pillars of God's temple" (*op. cit.,* p. 7).

[58]M. J. Jackson, *The New Schaff-Herzog Encyclopedia,* p. 20.

[59]Ramsey, *Basic Christian Ethics,* p. 134.

[60]Marshall, *op. cit.,* p. 20.

"he has not yet become entirely trusting and obedient, not yet single minded in obedient love."[61]

"In the New Testament the conception of reward is not employed as a motive for conversion, but as an encouragement to perseverance in the Christian life."[62] In the teaching of Jesus a much greater emphasis is laid upon self-denial and self-sacrifice aspects of discipleship than upon its rewards. "Jesus introduced the thought of reward sparingly as an inducement to those who had not yet cast in their lot with Him,"[63] but he often used it as an encouragement for his followers to persevere in the loyalty which they had already shown. As a rule, it was after his followers had been tested that Jesus encouraged them with the hope that their faithfulness would find its recompense.

Finally, there is no affectation about the teaching of Jesus. He is not a vain prattler about virtue, neither does he represent self-denial or self-sacrifice as being virtuous in themselves. "By denying himself, a man gains something for his own soul. By being the servant of all he becomes the greatest of all. By losing his life he finds it."[64] "Action by which nothing is gained is futile."[65] "Virtue has no meaning except in its relation to its ultimate end."[66] A. B. Alexander says that to be indifferent to all the inherent blessings and joys involved in one's life in God would not be "a mark of pure disinterestedness, but the evidence, rather, of a lack of appreciation of what life really means."[67] A. B. Bruce says that such a "hope is not selfishness, but pure self-consistency. It is simply believing in the reality of the kingdom for which you labor and suffer; involving, of course, the reality of each individual Christian's interest therein, your own not excepted. And such faith is necessary to heroism. For who would fight and suffer for a dream? What patriot would risk his life for his country's cause who did not hope for the restoration of her independence? And who but a pedant would say that the purity of his patriotism was sullied, because his hope for the whole nation did not exclude all reference to himself as an individual citizen? Equally necessary is it that a Christian should believe in the kingdom of glory, and equally natural and proper that he should cherish the hope of a personal share in its honors and felicities."[68]

From what has been said it is apparent that the exclusion of final Divine recompense as an element in the contemplation of moral responsibility leads to incomplete and inadequate systems of ethics. This excision of eschatological reward not only strips the good life of one of its proper and most natural motives, but permits the most subtle forms

[61]Ramsey, *loc. cit.*
[62]Jackson, *op. cit.*, p. 20.
[63]Barbour, *op. cit*, p. 245.
[64]Marshall, *op. cit.*, p. 206.
[65]Statement of E. F. Scott, quoted by Marshall, *op. cit.*, p. 206.
[66]A. Alexander, *op. cit.*, p. 163.
[67]*Ibid.*
[68]A. B. Bruce, *The Training of the Twelve* (New York: Harper, 1871), p. 188.

of egoistic ethics to shape the moral aspirations. Where it is proposed to detach ethics from the reward-motif what we may expect is not a strengthening of the data of morality, but rather their decline. For the Christian belief in a final judgment — in the vindication of the righteous and the reprobation of the wicked — rests upon the sturdiest of moral foundations. The orientation of human conduct toward the future is, in fact, one of the peculiarities structural to personality. Endeavor to free men from all interest in reward though they will, modern secular theories of ethics must acknowledge sooner or later that man as a purposive creature always shapes his conduct toward anticipated consequences, either eternal or temporal. The Utilitarian practices virtue as a means to the pleasure of the greatest number; the Kantian because the pursuit of the good for its own sake brings him peculiar satisfactions. Those whose behavior is guided simply by the expectation of positive earthly rewards need look for none other. But he who lives the good life as God intended it to be lived has a right to lean also upon the Divine promises that its rewards are not exhausted in this present world.

The discussion of motives has bordered frequently upon that of sanctions, which is properly its indispensable background. Except where ethics is misconstrued as autonomous, or self-legislated, the inner motives are admitted to depend for their validity upon an objective basis for the ethical life. Man is impotent to formulate by his own creative ingenuity a scheme of ethics that has universal validity. And were he able to do so, he would be impotent to enforce it. Doubtless it is already apparent that what from one point of view constitutes in Christian ethics a sanction for the virtuous life, serves from another as a motivation. Among the sanctions are the nature (Mt. 5:48f., 6:8) and will of God (Mt. 5:19f., 10:31f., 19:6), the example of God, more particularly of Christ (Jn. 13:15) and the authority of Christ from which his example is inseparable (Mt. 10:24f., 37f.), moral injunctions of the biblical revelation; the fact of the sinner's gracious redemption; the eschatological reward of virtue and punishment of sin (Mt. 7:20ff., 19:27, 24:44; Mk. 8:38, 13:35; Lk. 21:36; Rom. 14:12; 1 Cor. 11:27, 15:58, 2 Cor. 4:14, 5:6ff., 5:11; Col. 3:4; 1 Thess. 5:9; Heb. 10:35; Jas. 5:7; 1 Pet. 4:7; 2 Pet. 1:10, 3:14ff., Rev. 2:5, 3:3, 7:15).

The correspondence between these objective sanctions and their correlative subjective motivations (the desire to conform conduct to the character of God, especially Jesus, gratitude for redemptive grace, the love of God, desire for reward, etc.) is obvious. James Stalker reminds us that "Duty always presupposes a table of laws which have to be fulfilled; but it is one of the most difficult tasks of ethics to determine whence such a table is derived. Is it a primitive writing on the conscience, which experience is, indeed, needed to reveal, but which exists in all mankind alike from their birth: is it a positive revelation like that at Mount Sinai, where the voice of the Almighty thundered forth the law and His finger inscribed it on tables of stone, and has it been propagated from the people of Jehovah to the other races of the earth? or is it the slowly accumulated experience of the race, which, having in the course of time tested every alternative of conduct, has thereby made up its mind as to the benefits resulting from certain acts and the disadvantages flowing from others, and has so steadily rewarded the one class and punished the other, that its convictions now pass almost unconsciously from one generation to another, invested with religious awe?"[69] To raise these questions is to suggest answers, some of which look beyond the more limited horizons of ethics to the larger spheres of theology and metaphysics for their full delineation. The nature of God, the nature of creation, the nature of man, the nature of history, all structure the sanctions of the moral life. This has been sketched in the large in the earlier chapters of this study. But one factor calls for special treatment because of a new prominence assigned to it in contemporary ethical thought. It has been brought to prominence from exile in recent decades. This is the nature of the eschatological sanction for ethics.

[69]James Stalker, *The Ethic of Jesus,* pp. 11f.

24

THE ESCHATOLOGICAL SANCTION FOR ETHICS

THE PHILOSOPHICAL ATTEMPT to divorce ethics from eschatology is not surprising. The concept of a hidden apocalyptic climax of the historical movement is Judeo-Christian. "One of the distinctive ideas in Christianity," wrote Harnack, "was the paradox that the Saviour was also the Judge, an idea by which it rose specially superior to other religions."[1] Because of this conviction, Christianity could give impulse to ethics with a clear doctrine of future rewards and punishments. Because of the eschatological factor, the issues of moral obedience or disobedience are directly linked with the soul's destiny in eternity. The rewards of the blessed are gifts of grace, but they are reserved for those whose faith is attested by works.

Speculative ethics characteristically moves outside the Christian framework of history and nature. It thereby surrenders the vital connection between ethics and biblical eschatology. Even within professedly Christian circles, the tendency to separate ethics from eschatology has thrived in recent decades because of the penetration of speculative ideas. Harnack called for the excision of eschatological legend; mere shell or husk, he called it, non-essential to the biblical structure of theology and ethics.

Nonetheless, modern morality in some speculative forms has accommodated a certain "eschatology." Kant thought that the doctrine of an after life was a necessary postulate in order to justify the very conception of moral law, though he sketched the good life as wholly autonomous. Later idealistic moralities regarded the future life as necessary to preserve those moral values which give subjective worth to human existence. In all such constructions the doctrine of the wrath of God disappears,[2] and the interest in last things reduces to a bare doctrine of immortality. The Protestant liberal "social gospel" ethics conceived the ideal future as a humanly-guided evolutionary kingdom. Communistic ethics blended this with confidence in the future triumph of the

[1]A. Harnack, *The Expansion of Christianity,* I, 111, n.l.

[2]True as it is that the incomplete vindication of the good and right in this life, and man's moral incompleteness in his present state, postulate a future world which lacks this ambiguity, the biblical doctrine of the end does not rise out of an extension of the inherent worth of sinful man, but rather out of the certainties of that revelation of the larger world to which man belongs by the Living God as his Creator, Redeemer and Judge. Hence, as Yooll remarks, "immortality throbs through every fibre of its moral and spiritual teaching." *The Ethics of Evangelicalism,* p. 129.

economic proletariat. The Nazis channeled the theory to the service of the notion of the coming rule of the "master Nordic race."

A confident doctrine of "last things" is always a borrowed element in non-revelational ethics — an unconscious debt to Christianity. It is a distortion of biblical doctrine merged with non-Christian and even anti-Christian ethical features.[3] What is retained is the notion of a consummating final goal toward which the whole movement of things is directed. What is surrendered is the doctrine that this climax will be a transcendent act of God centering in the personal return of Jesus Christ as the final judge of the race. The doctrine of immanental proggress, to which the modern philosophy of history paid obeisance, excludes a catastrophic climax to history. The denial of eschatological wrath by neo-orthodox theologians such as Barth continues to impair the eschatological sanction for ethics. A bias against the full significance for ethics of the Christian doctrine of last things thus continues to be a major problem of ethics in the mid-twentieth century.

The teachings of Albert Schweitzer tended to drive a formidable wedge between ethics and eschatology. If Christ and the apostles taught a short-term morality based on the false expectation of a momentary end to world history, then Christian ethics today must abandon the eschatological since it was a temporary belief centered in the mis-anticipation of the Lord's return. The main question which then remains is, how much of the ethical element can be salvaged? Some scholars contend, as so recent a Gifford Lecturer as Herbert Henson would assure us,[4] that eschatology vitally conditioned none of the content or form of the early Christian ethic. But Paul Ramsey surrenders as irrelevant whole areas of Jesus' ethics in view of his alleged erroneous expectation of the apocalyptic kingdom in the generation after his.[5] "The least that needs to be said is that there are crucial teachings of Jesus whose meaning has been so decisively affected by his Kingdom-expectation that they can be torn from their context only at great peril of complete misunderstanding or with exceeding carefulness to preserve their original meaning."[6]

Dispensational theology resisted the dismissal of biblical eschatology and its import for ethics. But in its extreme forms it also evaporates

[3]In pre-Christian Zoroastrianism, the eschatological element admittedly was prominent. But it did not count decisively for ethics, since ethical dualism left the final outcome uncertain and the triumph of right in doubt.

[4]H. H. Henson, *Christian Morality,* pp. 39f.

[5]Paul Ramsey, *Basic Christian Ethics,* p. 27.

[6]*Ibid.,* p. 35. Ramsey's attempt to salvage some of the ethics on the ground that "genesis has nothing to do with validity" (*ibid.,* p. 41) is unconvincing, simply because genesis has more to do with validity than Ramsey thinks. Ramsey himself states that it was "as a consequence of his Kingdom-expectation" that "Jesus was able to proclaim for the human realm an ethic of obedient love" (p. 42). But Jesus claimed the same absoluteness for his eschatology as for his ethic, and the idea that his eschatology can be radically unabsolute and his morality radically absolute, which in this case has its genesis with Ramsey, has no self-evident validity.

the present-day relevance of much of the ethics of Jesus. Eschatology is invoked to postpone the significance of the Sermon and other segments of New Testament moral teaching to a later Kingdom age. Dispensationalism erects a cleavage in biblical ethics in the interest of debatable eschatological theory. Dispensationalism holds that Christ's Kingdom has been postponed until the end of the Church age, and that Kingdom-ethics will become dramatically relevant again only in the future eschatological era. Liberalism destroyed biblical eschatology and secularized Christian ethics; and the interim ethic school abandoned the literal relevance of Jesus' eschatology and ethics alike; and extreme Dispensationalism holds literally to both the eschatology and ethics, but moves both into the future. New Testament theology will not sustain this radical repudiation of any present form of the Kingdom of heaven.[7]

Other studies have affirmed the inseparability of the eschatological and the ethical, while stressing the contemporary relevance of Christian ethics. Jesus proclaimed a Kingdom that is both present and future. The eschatological element leavens the whole of New Testament ethics. "It is impossible to distinguish strands in it," writes Amos N. Wilder of the eschatological sanction in the teaching of the evangelists, "from which it is absent. It is impossible to presume an absence of it in the teaching of Jesus himself and a subsequent overlaying of Jesus' supposed non-eschatological teaching with this sanction. It is impossible to assign it exclusively to Mark or to pretend its absence from the Source. It is omnipresent in whatever elements or strata we would seek to isolate."[8]

This acknowledged inseparability of the eschatological and the ethical in the New Testament has led in turn to two main positions maintained in our times over against the historic Christian way of relating these elements.

One is projected by existential theologians. Maintaining that the Christian life as a whole can only be understood eschatologically, they transform eschatology into psychology of religion. They restate the New Testament distinction between the present age and the age to come in terms of the spiritual predicament of unfaith or faith in the experience of the individual. Thus eschatology, once the concluding study in Christian dogmatics, becomes the very first doctrine. And it is the whole of ethics, since the entire Christian life is depicted as

[7]George Eldon Ladd, *Crucial Questions About the Kingdom of God.*

[8]Amos N. Wilder, *Eschatology and Ethics in the Teaching of Jesus,* p. 101, where he acknowledges with regard to the eschatological sanction that "It is present in the parables as in the non-parabolic teaching. It is present in the elements that are typically narrative . . . as it is present in the discourse material. It is present in the unique Matthean matter as in the sections dependent upon Mark and the Source, and in the peculiar Lukan material . . . If we . . . try to evaporate the concrete eschatological expectation we soon have to give up the attempt. We find that there are other sanctions present but these do not supplant the eschatological sanction."

eschatological or existential in nature.[9] The eschatological is filled with new meaning: it no longer points to specific future events, but to the existential. The contrast between the present sinful order and the future ideal order is replaced by a subjective conflict between the actual and the ideal, by a tension in the moral life, so that the apocalyptic retains the status only of inner disposition.[10] This reduces eschatology to a value-philosophy grounded in phenomenology and existentialism. It deprives it of its biblical meaning of a literal future end-time. The eschatological, in Bultmann's appraisal, is mythological, pre-scientific, and untenable, except as it ministers to the psychological.

In place of the earlier mistake of historicism, which so concentrated on the first coming of Christ that the second coming was ignored, the existential approach so existentializes the eschatological that it loses hold of the historical at both advents. It thus departs from the standpoint of revealed ethics. Ramsey properly emphasizes that the coming of the Kingdom was not characteristically equated by Jesus with the sinner's repentance, for "the Kingdom was coming no matter what were men's attitudes or what they did."[11] The difference between existential eschatology and biblical eschatology at this level is also laid bare by Harvey K. McArthur. "The existential re-interpretations affirm that history is the arena in which man, individually and collectively, decides for or against God. But they do not affirm that history is the arena in which God's purpose is finally manifestly triumphant. . . Our 'human predicament' may require such a restating of the Christian faith. But if so, let us not pretend that we have simply translated first century eschatology into the terminology of the twentieth century. We have made a translation but in the process have, discreetly or indiscreetly, eliminated the final word that appeared in the dominant Biblical tradition."[12]

Another viewpoint provoked by the acknowledged inseparability of New Testament ethics and eschatology is that of Professor Wilder. He regards the eschatological element as indispensable myth that imaginatively anticipates the complete vindication of God's righteousness. This mythical drama serves as the formal sanction for Christian ethics, but in no sense as its essential sanction. That eschatology is myth-construc-

[9]Sir E. C. Hoskyns contends that "the one fundamental moral problem is what we should still possess if the whole of our world were destroyed tomorrow, and we stood naked before God. The eschatological belief crudely and ruthlessly . . . strips us naked of worldly possessions and worldly entanglements, and asks what survives the catastrophe." *Cambridge Sermons* (New York: Macmillan, 1930), p. 37.

[10]"The historical illusions which resulted inevitably from . . . mythical statement of the situation in which the human spirit finds itself do not destroy the truth in the myth; no more than the discovery that the fall of man was not actual history destroys the mythical truth in the story of the fall." Reinhold Niebuhr, *An Interpretation of Christian Ethics,* p. 58.

[11]Paul Ramsey, *op. cit.,* p. 26.

[12]Harvey K. McArthur, "The Transformation of the Christian Hope," in the *Hartford Seminary Foundation Bulletin,* XVI (Jan., 1954), p. 20.

tion has been the thesis of various schools of ethical thought in the past,[13] but Wilder's erection of the myth-drama into a formal sanction for ethics is distinctive.

The reacknowledgment of the permanent relevance of the ethics of the gospels is now forcing a re-examination of the whole eschatological setting in which the biblical ethic appears. It is now widely conceded that eschatology conditions Christian ethics in two respects: first, by relating all Christian behavior to a final judgment of humanity in which Jesus Christ will be the agent of judgment; and second, by relating the ethical life to the present Kingdom with its new conditions and deepened moral requirement. This present Kingdom is an advance upon the Old Testament dispensation and has present eschatological significance, since the powers of the age-to-come have penetrated into this-present-age. Hence man is confronted by the Kingdom of God in Jesus Christ in both its present and future aspects. This confrontation serves as a sanction for repentance and for a life of obedience in view of the rewards or punishments that will surely follow.

The summons to repentance in view of the coming Kingdom is characteristic of the entire New Testament ethic. Jesus' preaching begins on the note which the forerunner, John the Baptist, had sounded: "Repent . . . for the kingdom of heaven is at hand" (Mt. 3:2, 4:17, Mk. 1:15).[14] Under the canopy of the approaching Kingdom the gospels depict a life of forgiveness in which the moral sense is quickened to a desperate seriousness. The impending Kingdom becomes the sanction of the entire ethical summons. The Beatitudes pronounce a moral universe that is rewarded fully and completely in the future. Main portions of the Sermon on the Mount are validated by eschatology. It is far better to be maimed in this life than to be whole and cast into hell (5:29f.). Treasures are to be laid up in heaven with future dividends (6:19f.). Those who refuse forgiveness to others will be denied Divine forgiveness later (6:15, 18:21ff.). In the woes against Bethsaida, Capernaum and Chorazin, Jesus found a proper motivation for repentance in the future judgment (Mt. 11:20ff., 12:41). In commissioning the twelve, Jesus enforced the claim to repentance by an appeal to future judgment (Mt. 10:7, 14f.). The eschatological sanction for

[13]Cf. Niebuhr: "Placing the final fulfillment at the end of time and not in a realm above temporality is to remain true to the genius of prophetic religion and to state mythically what cannot be stated rationally . . . Since myth is forced to state a paradoxical aspect of reality in terms of concepts connoting historical sequence, it always leads to historical illusions" (*op. cit.*, p. 57). The post-Kantian emphasis on the limitations of human reason, which precludes a conceptual synthesis of supernatural truths, is an obvious underlying motif.

[14]The threat of future judgment is in the forefront of the Baptist's call to repentance: "Who warned you to flee from the wrath to come?" (Mt. 3:7). The Messiah's "winnowing fork is in his hand, and he will clear his threshing floor and . . . the chaff he will burn with unquenchable fire" (3:12). Catastrophic urgency overarches his preaching. Judgment is imminent; sinners are warned against the wrath to come, when the axe will be laid to the root of the tree, and are implored to ready themselves by repentance which brings forth godly works.

repentance reappears in his parables. The disciples were to fear only him who would destroy body and soul in hell (10:28). They would receive thrones and rewards (19:28ff.). Men should be ready for his unannounced future return (24:36ff., 25:1ff.), and those who are not will be cast into outer darkness (25:14ff.). Even simple acts of charity have an eschatological reference (25:31ff.). Mark and Luke reflect at length the standpoint of Matthew's gospel, and a passage in John's gospel maintains its continuity: "He who rejects me and does not receive my sayings has a judge; the word that I have spoken will be his judge on the last day" (12:48; cf. 5:27). The danger of judgment, imminent judgment and final judgment, is everywhere in the forefront as a prominent consideration contributing to the urgency of repentance. Jesus' moral imperatives and ethical demands stand often in inseparable connection with emphatic eschatological declarations. While the setting for reward and punishment is clearly assigned in some statements to the final climax of history, in others rewards and punishment are associated with imminent catastrophe. It is impossible to empty these two aspects the one into the other, and thereby rid ethics of an eschatological sanction, since in some passages both elements appear alongside each other. An example may be drawn from Jesus' declaration that the sin against the Holy Ghost will not be forgiven either in this age or in the age to come (Mt. 12:31).

The ethical appeal gained a heightened urgency from the fact that imminent judgment limited the opportunity to get right with God. The reign of God in its coming form means the doom of all unrighteousness and throws sinners into peril. The Old Testament summons to repentance occurs constantly in the atmosphere of eschatological sanction. This emphasis is directed toward covenant-people, and broadened into a universal appeal before the prophetic message completes its course. The New Testament emphasis is continuous with this scheme of an eschatological-conditioned ethic, although for it the universal implications are everywhere present. The sanction is made desperately relevant by catapulting man into a new eschatological situation in which the threat of judgment is suspended above him with imminent implications. This emphasis on coming judgment and its penalties so structures the teaching of Jesus that Wilder concedes that "Jesus made the coming eschatological event at least the formal motive and sanction for his whole ethical summons."[15] John is identified as the Elijah of Malachi 4:4-6, and judgment is now at the very threshold.[16]

Alongside the negative eschatological sanction of judgment appears the positive sanction of reward; the coming Kingdom has its retribution

[15]Wilder, *op. cit.*, p. 74.

[16]The same connection between the appeal for repentance and eschatology is reflected in Acts (3:17ff., 17:30f.) and the epistles (Rom. 1:32, 2:8f., 2:15f., 13:11ff., 14:10; 1 Cor. 4:1ff., 3:13ff., 6:16ff., 15:32, 58; 2 Cor. 4:16ff., 5:6ff.; Eph. 5:3ff., 5:25f.; Phil. 3:13ff.; Col. 3:1ff.; 2 Tim. 4:1ff.; and many other passages). The standpoint is Petrine as well as Pauline (1 Pet. 1:3ff., 4:7ff., 5:1ff.) and also Johannine (1 Jn. 2:17, 3:1ff.).

for the righteous, whom it vindicates, as well as for the unrighteous, whom it dooms. The reign of God encourages moral earnestness with promises of reward and compensation and blessing. Judgment and reward often appear side by side in the teaching of Jesus. Blessings are added in this life to those who seek first the Kingdom of heaven (Mt. 6:1-6, 16-18, 33; 11:28f.; 13:23; 28:20). "We may be sure," writes Wilder, "that this sanction of reward and penalty in the present age had a part in the actual teaching of Jesus himself."[17] Faithful believers enter into the joy of the Lord in the life to come (Mt. 25:31ff.), participating in eschatological salvation and sharing the vision of God.

The negative sanction of eschatological penalty is minimized by some recent writers who seek to pass over it in deference to the positive aspect of reward. So Wilder, for example, insists that the positive sanction is "the more fundamental" and that the teaching of Jesus was "in its central mood and inspiration, gracious."[18] But, while Jesus' message was a positive message of redemption and fundamentally a message of grace, any effort to force the negative doom for the unrepentant into a marginal or peripheral significance depends upon subjective bias. Wilder is compelled to admit that of the two sanctions "the negative one is more prominent" in Jesus' teaching.[19] It is not surprising, therefore, that the conclusion that the positive sanction is to be regarded as more primary is buttressed by an appeal to Jesus' personality rather than to his teaching, an impossible maneuver. "We may infer this spirit of his teaching from the spirit of his person and action, though enough of his utterance in this vein remains to confirm us."[20] But the spirit of the teaching ought to be established from the teaching and, for that matter, the spirit of the person and action is known to us only through the teaching of the gospels, which assign prominence to the sanction of penalty. Moreover, "enough" of Jesus' teaching "to confirm" the superior importance of the positive sanction can be secured only by first depreciating the gospels as the early church gave them to us in the interest of a modern reconstruction. Wilder is obviously anxious to minimize the punitive eschatological emphasis when he seeks to account for it "by the fact of the sinfulness of the times, and that Jesus is addressing an unrepentant nation," and he thinks, moreover, that "the evangelists all no doubt tended to emphasize unduly this aspect . . . because of the final issue of Jesus' career and because of the rejection of the gospel by Israel and the later history of the church."[21] But none of these elements establishes that the negative sanction is "unduly" emphasized, nor that, whatever the situation to which it was spoken, it has no sufficient basis in the teaching of Jesus. Wilder asserts that, in contrast with the Baptist's "comparatively forbidding form of preach-

[17]Wilder, *op. cit.*, p. 111.
[18]*Ibid.*, pp. 82f.
[19]*Ibid.*, p. 83.
[20]*Ibid.*, p. 82.
[21]*Ibid.*

ing," we may be "confident that Jesus himself spoke a message of a more positive mood."[22] Whatever basis he may have for such an assertion, that basis is not to be found in the actual records from which the historical situation is to be recovered. Wilder seeks to buttress his position by the hopeless approach of questioning the objectivity of the records to which he appeals unquestioningly wherever they appear (by abstracting what he wishes from the teaching as a whole) to lend credence to his special thesis. We are told that the biblical teaching was "spoken under diverse impulses and in diverse situations"[23] an observation that is so matter of fact as to be quite colorless unless one intends the arbitrary inference that it is therefore conflicting and irreconcilable, or that we may dismiss that which issues from some impulses and is directed toward some situations. We cannot argue conclusively from the texts, it is said, because the enforcing motives "may in some cases have been adventitiously attached to or detached from the precepts by the evangelist or others."[24] This position would seem to jeopardize any dogmatic view (including whichever Wilder might care to espouse) unless more objective historical records are available. But Wilder resorts to this favorite critical device to do service for his thesis that "the early community *appears* [ital. sup.] to have colored this (punitative) aspect more highly."[25] "We should not be hasty to conclude," he declares, "that the ruling mood of the gospels is one of warning before judgments to come,"[26] a rather startling conclusion in view of Wilder's acknowledg-

[22]*Ibid.* Some recent writers are more candid in the open admission of the philosophical considerations which sway them: "Perhaps in the last resort our doctrine of the hereafter is, and must be, determined by ethical considerations. If a theory implies a conception of God's character out of accord with our moral convictions, no amount of seeming evidence from scriptural passages can make it a living belief" (C. J. Barker, *The Way of Life,* p. 42). Hence, man's moral sentiments become normative and absolute, even in judgment upon God. We ought not to be surprised to read elsewhere in Barker's work that "every man has within him some conception of justice which, in its broad outlines at least, can usually be trusted to be correct" (p. 52). It is probably not inaccurate to say that the great deterrents to a revival of eschatological study in the literal sense are the modern bias against the New Testament teaching that a man's fate is finally settled at the hour of death and that eternal punishment awaits the wicked. Instead of dealing with the ethical implications of these doctrines, modern moralists prefer to stress the ethical "difficulties" they pose. That they pose difficulties to the unregenerate ought to surprise nobody! The superficiality of such arguments, as that the doctrine that man's destiny is settled at death lacks a deep sense of sin, or that the doctrine of the eternal loss of even one sinner is a defeat for the grace of God (cf. Barker, pp. 42ff.), unmasks such rationalizations for what they are.

[23]Wilder, *op. cit.,* p. 88.

[24]*Ibid.,* p. 86.

[25]*Ibid.,* p. 89.

[26]*Ibid.* Note also Barker's appeal: "Christian ethics depends upon a general attitude towards life: upon certain quite comprehensive convictions, and one of these was that evil can always and everywhere be conquered. . . Secondly, long-suffering and patience are amongst the attributes most persistenly assigned to God. . . Lastly . . . it is essential to ask what forgiveness means on God's part in the light of a man's final destiny" (*op. cit.,* pp. 44f.). His "conclusion" is that an irreversible destiny and final punishment of the lost are inconsistent with the character of God. But our convictions about the nature of God were drawn in the first instance from Jesus Christ and the Hebrew prophets and they did not draw this conclusion, but

ment of the universal presence of the eschatological element, and his concession that this sanction not only has "a large place" in Jesus' teachings,[27] but that "the notion of reward and a frank appeal to it is present in Jesus' teaching and is even fundamental to it."[28] The distinction which Wilder seeks to enforce between the positive and negative elements of the eschatological sanction, to the disparagement of the latter, loses all significance even on Wilder's own approach, however, because he dismisses the eschatological sanction in its totality as merely a formal sanction for ethics, and in no sense the essential sanction. In that event the aspect of reward must be denied a literal significance as well as punishment.

But before we consider Wilder's attempt to dismiss the eschatological sanction in purely formal terms, it is necessary to consider a third way in which the eschatological appeal is tied to ethics in the teaching of Jesus and the New Testament.

The appeal for repentance as imperative because it hastens the coming of the Kingdom is an added way in which New Testament ethics gains an eschatological sanction. The Hebrew mind was familiar through the Old Testament prophets with the idea that the Kingdom may be postponed or hastened according to the spiritual response of the people. Jesus reinforced this conviction alongside his confidence that the time of the consummation of God's plan is fixed in the Father's secret counsel (Mark 13:32, Acts 1:7). Although Bultmann, in line with his speculative conception of the Kingdom as suprahistorical and existential, denies that the Kingdom can be "hastened," Wilder has called attention to the suggestion which the gospels convey of "the immense power of importunate faith in effecting the advent of the kingdom."[29]

Instead of frankly drawing the conclusion that eschatology serves as an essential sanction for Christian ethics, scholars like Wilder are embarrassed by a miraculous philosophy of history and any view of revelation which involves the impartation of knowledge about the future. And so they have sought to break the force of the eschatological element, despite their admission of its controlling place in the New Testament. They call it a formal not an essential sanction. In order to distinguish the essential and eschatological sanctions, Wilder seeks to differentiate sanctions that depend on rewards and penalties and those

---

specifically taught its opposite. Hence, what we tend to get in the modern demand for an eschatological view of life in its relevance for ethics frequently takes the course of a spurious Christian eschatology no less than of a diluted Christian ethics. The content of both elements is drawn no longer from the Scriptures but from philosophical considerations. Marcus Dods once remarked that the theory of evolution has provided the modern era with a new conception of Divine patience. So other theories have furnished it with novel conceptions of ethics and eschatology, which are superficially labelled Christian.

[27]Wilder, *op. cit.*, p. 89.
[28]*Ibid.*, p. 88.
[29]*Ibid.*, p. 85.

that do not (*e.g.*, the summons to mercy or generosity grounded in the nature of God). Thus he tries to eliminate the sanction of reward and penalty from certain strands of the New Testament ethic. The regard for the eschatological as the ruling sanction of Christian ethics is, we are told, a mistake caused by neglect of Jesus' invocation of "other and more fundamental sanctions than that of reward"[30] and a failure to see "the merely formal aspect" of the appeal to reward and punishment.[31] This raises numerous difficulties. For one thing, the eschatological sanction cannot be contrasted with the sanction of the nature of God, if the spirit of the New Testament is to be retained, for the eschatological is as much an appeal to the nature of God as any other sanction.[32] Moreover, as Wilder himself is forced to admit, the sanctions from which the appeal to reward and penalty is absent do not necessarily exclude the latter. But, even more important, the theory falsifies the significance of the eschatological in its biblical dimensions in the interest of alien philosophical considerations.

Wilder can tolerate the eschatological only as myth, as imaginative symbolism. It announces poetically the consequences that flow as compensations out of one's relation to the inner make-up of the moral and spiritual world. In its original Old Testament appearance, eschatology allegedly emerges as a demand of the moral nature in view of the failure of the prophetic call to repentance. Thus the eschatological background of the summons of John the Baptist and of Jesus arises from speculative prophetic self-consolation. The lack of success of the prophetic call to repentance "gave birth to the idea of a repentance eventually worked out by God in the last time."[33] This myth-making about the future is represented at various times by Wilder as a necessity of the human imagination. It is an accommodation on the part of Jesus and the disciples to unphilosophically-minded people, and it is inevitable in view of Jesus' supposed ignorance of the full purport of the future. This is a strange explanation indeed. It suggests that perhaps the author does not know quite how to account for so central an emphasis which requires on his part so comprehensive a depletion. As philosophic justification for eschatological myth, Wilder points out that even profound philosophers, doubtless intending Plato and Kant, have operated with an *als ob* or "as if" sanction for ethics. Others have felt compelled to use a reward-motivation, so that the tendency is one deeply rooted in human nature.[34] In view of the ignorance of the future ascribed to Jesus by Wilder, we are told that only by superhistorical or transcendental expressions of a prophetic and eschatological nature could he express the confidence that God would vindicate his purposes,[35]

[30]*Ibid.*, p. 91.
[31]*Ibid.*, p. 89.
[32]"The character of God is revealed in the way He deals with His children's final destiny" (C. J. Barker, *op. cit.*, p. 42).
[33]Wilder, *op. cit.*, p. 77.
[34]*Ibid.*, pp. 91, 134f.
[35]*Ibid.*, p. 182.

that "the conceptions of the parousia and the regeneration are essentially imaginative."[36] But, if the future is inevitably conceived only in terms of eschatological myth, it is difficult to see how Jesus or the disciples could have "accommodated" themselves by such expressions. For instance, Wilder suggests that "in dealing with simple people good pedagogy demanded that Jesus and the disciples lend concreteness to their teaching," so they dramatized the moral demands for unphilosophical minds by pictures drawn from human compensations.[37] The fact is that in the New Testament the eschatological element is present in material addressed to the profoundest as well as to the simplest minds. Jesus alluded to eschatological material in his discourse with Nicodemus. Luke wrote to the learned Theophilus. The New Testament is critical of false eschatology (2 Thessalonians), but not of eschatology as such, nor of an eschatological ethic which is materially as well as formally sanctioned. Moreover, even when the Apostle Paul and the early Christian movement moved outside the world of Hebrew ideas, they "reasoned of righteousness and temperance and of the judgment to come" (Acts 24:25). Even pagan despotism was overarched by the certainty of final Divine judgment.

Specifically, Wilder tells us that "the conception of . . . eschatological culmination so partook of the nature of myth or poetry that it did not other than formally determine the ethic."[38] The pictures of future reward and punishment are not to be given a crass or literal sense, but are symbolic. "As fictions, it follows that . . . they could never serve as a final and determinative sanction. A fiction however vivid and compelling has not the substance to serve this purpose."[39] This use of the eschatological, we are told, is not adventitious; it may not be impeached as a type of motivation, since the appeal to spiritual and moral realities demands their equivalent so that it expresses an "as if" inherent in the conditions of thought.[40] Wilder therefore dismisses the eschatological element as nothing more than a formal sanction, a special form of ethical presentation that dramatizes the conviction of God's holiness. He contends that the eschatological gains its real force out of a relation to the essential sanction, or subjective experience of God's holiness and power.

This representation of the eschatological raises serious and far-reaching difficulties. For one thing, the interpretation of the eschatological in literal and non-symbolic terms is characteristic of the New

[36]*Ibid.*, p. 187. C. J. Barker presses much the same viewpoint: "The wealth of imagery that gathered round apocalyptic enabled the ethical ideal to be presented to the imagination; and imagination is always a more powerful motive force where moral action is required than mere reasoning" (*op. cit.*, p. 36). The prime significance of eschatology remains only the rousing of emotions which affect the tone and purpose of human life.

[37]Wilder, *op. cit.*, p. 89.

[38]*Ibid.*, p. 161.

[39]*Ibid.*, p. 134.

[40]*Ibid.*, p. 137.

Testament. Wilder himself is forced to concede that even in the gospels the eschatological element "already" takes the form of "crass literalism," although a more candid study of the biblical manuscripts would compel the acknowledgment that they give no support whatever for any distinction between a literal eschatology and a fiction eschatology. The New Testament knows no sanction of myth-eschatology for ethics, but, in point of fact, specifically repudiates "cunningly devised fables" (2 Pet. 1:16) and warns against those who would dispense with the realism of the eschatological (2 Pet. 3:1ff.). Furthermore, when Wilder admits that contemplation of the nature of God leads "inevitably" to reflection upon eschatology and moral consequences, he can no longer seriously allow himself to champion an ethics sanctioned by an appeal to the nature of God but not by an appeal to eschatology. The biblical declarations of the consequences of moral behavior in terms of penalty and reward are not to be contrasted with affirmations about the nature of God, but are made precisely because of that nature. But the key difficulty in Wilder's approach is the psychological impossibility of conjuring an eschatology which is in the first place a product of man's ethical convictions into a sanction for those convictions. Wilder's appraisal of the bearing of the eschatological upon the ethical element in the New Testament resolves itself in the final issue into an unsuccessful and arbitrary attempt to justify his prejudice against giving the eschatological element its biblical due. The prime motivations in his approach are apparent from the following: "Our appeal should not be to an anachronistic and literal Second Coming or forensic Judgment . . . impending in our day. Yet we can properly appeal to rewards and penalties, eschatological and otherwise, as a legitimate way of making clear the fateful character of conduct."[41] But Wilder thereby ceases to view the eschatological as Jesus and the New Testament viewed it. Since the eschatological is dismissed as fictional, and since it is omnipresent in the New Testament teaching as an ethical sanction, Wilder seeks to soften his hostility to it by the device of assigning it a merely formal significance. "We do not wish to rule out entirely the place of such sanction in the teaching."[42] In fact, it is even affirmed to be the dominant ethical sanction. But that it is a ruling and essential sanction is denied. As an ethical sanction Jesus' teaching about the future is "by no means of first importance."[43] Indeed, we are told it is derivative, subordinate, supplementary, and not fundamental.[44] And by the time the eschatological sanction is dismissed in these dimensions, Wilder has lost contact with the New Testament portrayal and is operating within a philosophical scheme which the biblical statement of ethics itself excludes. The significance which Wilder seeks to maintain for the eschatological sanction actually becomes an embarrassment to his

[41]*Ibid.*, p. 193.
[42]*Ibid.*, p. 141.
[43]*Ibid.*, p. 140.
[44]*Ibid.*, p. 141.

viewpoint, for it appears as an artificially grafted appendage with no essential relationship to the whole. If the essential sanction for conduct is spiritual immanence, or an immediate apprehension of God's holiness in present experience, any appeal to a sanction exterior to this can only be an intrusion and an objectionable addition. But Wilder's contrast of vital sanctions for ethics does not appear in the New Testament, for the immediate rewards and penalties are directly linked by Jesus with ultimate rewards and penalties. The Beatitudes, for instance, give assurance of blessing in the Kingdom in its twofold aspect, and a present and future reward is assured to the lowly and ministering and to those giving alms and praying and fasting in secret. Wilder himself refers to the double sanction of "present indemnification and eschatology promise"[45] without sensing the profound problem which this poses for his own dismissal of the eschatological in his attempt to ground Christian ethics in its immediate compensations in relationship to God. The discounting of eschatological teaching cannot but involve a changed relation to New Testament morality.

Rather than serving as a merely formal sanction, the eschatological element has an urgent role as an *essential* sanction in New Testament ethics. The main foci with which the New Testament makes its ethical appeal from the standpoint of eschatology are the motifs of reward-punishment and the personal return of Christ (Mt. 24:36ff., 1 Thess. 4:16, 5:6, 1 Jn. 3:3). The latter is definitely a part of the former, yet Christ's return supplies an incentive above that of desire for reward and fear of punishment. It joins with the motif of gratitude for redemption in his name, and attaches to the warm affection for the Saviour which throbs through Christian devotion.

There are many references to the final judgment and future consummation of the Divine purpose in history; so that the eschatological predictions cannot be emptied of future and exhausted by a contemporary sense. Yet in the gospels the eschatological sanction for repentance and the new life is filled with urgency from the fact that the eschatological age is depicted as somehow already under way with the first advent of Christ. The eschatological period, while it looks for ultimate consummation at the end of the age of grace, gets under way with the proclamation of John the Baptist. It finds its center, and even its hidden climax, in the life, death, and resurrection of the historical Jesus. The Day of the Lord begins with the incarnation and atonement of Christ, and reaches its finale with his anticipated return. The Christian lives no longer merely in the age of Old Testament promise, but in the New Testament era of growing fulfillment. This suggests the element of truth in the statement that what the Jewish apocalyptist saw

[45]*Ibid.*, p. 108. "With whatever sanction drawn from present satisfactions, the strictly eschatological sanctions do not fade into unreality in the least. The twofold considerations of blessing are retained: God's Kingdom and his righteousness, beyond; and all these things, added, here . . . Here, mercy, comfort and satisfaction; in the new age, the eschatological salvation and vision of God" (*ibid.*, p. 112).

was "the *advent* of the Kingdom, but not the Kingdom itself."[46] In his personal teaching Jesus gave the Christian community the content of the Kingdom in its present phase, although its full revelation must wait for the transcendent consummation of all things. "The 'Age to Come' had broken through into this present age," writes Sydney Cave, "and its redemptive powers were already in part realized."[47]

In its larger New Testament outlines, the outpouring of the Holy Spirit in the age of grace links together the present era of eschatological participation with the future era of eschatological climax. The Spirit who indwelled Jesus, and raised him from death, mediates resurrection-life to his followers. It is to the New Testament doctrine of the Spirit to which we must look for suggestions of a "realized eschatology" in the sense that the Spirit brings a measure of the power and reality of the age to come into the present experience of the believer. Believers may live transformed lives with the quality of Godlikeness or Christlikeness because they participate in the powers of the age to come. The eschatological and ethical cannot be contrasted for the simple reason that they are inseparable. Those who seek to find a different and deeper moral basis for New Testament ethics alongside the eschatological[48] misunderstand this intimate connection. All Christian ethics is in a preliminary sense eschatological, is a morality of "eschatological earnest." The separation of the eschatological from the ethical was a corruption of true religion. The eschatological is the vindication of the ethical.

The relevance of eschatology was totally dismissed by modern moralists who sought to limit the concern of Christian ethics only to action in this world; "whatever the Kingdom was to be, it came" in Christ, said William Newton Clarke, so that the eschatological hope is "left behind in the course of events" and "cancelled" as an earnest but inaccurate hope. [49] So James Seth, eager to wrest ethics from an eschatological strangle-hold, maintained that "in the main the moral teaching is not influenced in any way by the eschatology,"[50] a profound miscalculation of biblical ethics. This anti-eschatological bias stemmed from an evolutionary philosophy of history and from a misreading of New Testament apocalyptic as presupposing an immediate end of the present world. Alongside this bias could be ranged another philosophical bias grounded in the appeal to the partiality of human knowledge. This appeal fails to acknowledge the validity of revelation. So T. H.

[46]Lewis A. Muirhead, *The Eschatology of Jesus* (London: A. Melrose, 1904), p. 85.

[47]Sydney Cave, *The Christian Way,* 158.

[48]As G. F. Barbour, who finds the acknowledged eschatological element the "least original and distinctive part of Christian thought" in contrast with the "directly ethical and spiritual principles" and thinks Christianity would have "passed away" had it been "at the center an eschatological faith." *A Philosophical Study of Christian Ethics,* pp. 183f.

[49]William Newton Clarke, *The Ideal of Jesus,* p. 70.

[50]James Seth, *Essays in Ethics and Religion* (Edinburgh: Blackwood, 1926), p. 70.

Green stressed man's inability to analyze conceptually the ideal content of the ethical end, and limited man's knowledge of the ideal moral existence to reflection on past moral experience.[51] Here we move outside the spirit of revealed ethics entirely. Yet the post-Hegelian philosophy encouraged a "vague and partial" conception of the social end of the Kingdom, one that dismissed all specific eschatological features as irrelevant for ethics. This "vague" conception was to a temporary incentive that could be outgrown. Yet this view attempted to retain the motivating power of the biblical view: "The Christian hope which anticipates the progress and final advent of the Kingdom as the *Social* End, has acted at all times as a powerful stimulus to Christian practice."[52] The eschatological teaching colors the whole of the New Testament ethic, and this is precisely one of its distinctives alongside the strictly speculative life-views.

This judgment which focuses its interest on this world exclusively and banishes thought of the world to come is no less extreme than the opposite view that the concern of biblical morality is exclusively other-worldly and strips the present life of its ultimate significance and flees from its duties. The Christian life is, as Cave has suggested, "un-worldly"[53] rather than this-worldly or other-worldly, and it gains this quality supremely through its vital relation to the eternal spiritual realm. "Both worldliness and other worldliness," wrote Keyser, "are avoided by the Christian ethical teaching."[54] The Christian view of the worth of this life stands in contrast to the pagan and ascetic view alike. Martensen observes that the present life does not carry its object in itself; yet it is not on that account valueless.[55] The expectation of the future life serves as an effective present power, for the earthly life must be continuously lived with a view to the end. We pass this way only once, and the road on which we travel has its sure goal. The road and the goal are inseparably inter-related. The eschatological perspective thus brings a wholeness to life because it does not divide the now and the hereafter into two water-tight compartments. It maintains them in a living relationship. The constant element in it is the approval or disapproval of God in the outworking of his great purposes.

Those who minimize eschatology and cast it into the background assuredly do not do so in the interest of Christian ethics. This is true of L. H. Marshall's grouping of all evidences of this sanction under the "appeal to fear." He frankly admits this appeal was made by Jesus and Paul alike, only to contend that "the essential point . . . is the recognition that it is undoubtedly a dangerous thing to trifle with the great issues of right and wrong."[56] Doubtless moral trifling is a peril-

[51]T. H. Green, *Prolegomena to Ethics,* A. C. Bradley, ed. (5th ed.; Oxford: Clarendon Press, 1929), p. 341.

[52]George Walker, *The Idealism of Christian Ethics,* pp. 243ff.

[53]Cave, *op. cit.,* p. 159.

[54]Leander S. Keyser, *A Manual of Christian Ethics,* p. 76.

[55]H. Martensen, *Christian Ethics,* p. 371.

[56]L. H. Marshall, *The Challenge of New Testament Ethics,* p. 316.

ous pursuit, but Jesus and the apostles would surely have been astonished at such an emptying of the eschatological.

The same course is taken when Haering finds the significance of eschatology for ethics almost exclusively in its emphasis that "the present world is only an incomplete stage, a transition: inexpressibly important . . . and certainly not the stage of completeness."[57] Ramsey, too, having dismissed literal eschatological belief as the prerogative of the mentally deficient[58] and then saying that Jesus miscalculated the time-factor and "even more essential elements of his apocalyptic outlook,"[59] is ambiguous in handling his "vastly more important" and "astounding claim that the Messiah of God would judge the world according to the attitude men now display toward him and his movement of preparation for the Kingdom." Despite Ramsey's protest elsewhere against those who transform Jesus' ethics "into an 'eternal idea' more appropriate to the historical Greek temper,"[60] he distills this messianic claim into the bare notion that "Jesus Christ is the standard for measuring the reign of God among men."[61] And Newman Smyth, after assuring us that any apocalyptic mode of restoring the Kingdom is unethical,[62] and after giving no attention to the importance of eschatology for ethics in a 500-page study, closes his work with the note that "Christian ethics adds . . . to the motive of life, in the hard struggle of the good with the evil, an inspiring hope of final victory and perfection . . . The Christian faith holds up for human society the ethical hope of a new heavens and a new earth wherein dwelleth righteousness . . . The Christian social ideal, in some sure world-age to come, is to be realized in the completion of the Messianic Kingdom which the Christ shall give up to the Father."[63]

"Even the strict eschatological teaching of Jesus may have a direct ethical bearing in its implied emphasis on the worth of men," writes King.[64] Yet, he counters this by saying, "Even the future Kingdom . . . is in any case conceived by Jesus as finally ethical and spiritual, so that the eschatological cannot be the dominating conception."[65]

Only a short distance removed in spirit is the deliberate oversimplification of the eschatological to some such thesis as "the rule of God." Granted that this is the heart of the Kingdom-idea, capable of taking many forms, eschatology is structured with a specific content and definite program of future events. These specifics are the heart of the

[57]T. von Haering, *The Ethics of the Christian Life,* p. 142.
[58]Ramsey, *op. cit.,* 36, where he gives even less comfort to the whole range of recent speculative philosophy by suggesting that "apocalypticism is a better myth than the idea of progress prevalent since the eighteenth century."
[59]*Ibid.,* p. 44.
[60]*Ibid.,* p. 31.
[61]*Ibid.,* p. 44.
[62]Newman Smyth, *Christian Ethics,* p. 106.
[63]*Ibid.,* pp. 493f.
[64]Henry C. King, *The Ethics of Jesus,* p. 20.
[65]*Ibid.,* p. 62, n.i.

doctrine of "last things." Shailer Mathews is far afield when he suggests concerning our Lord that "eschatology in his teaching is essentially a recognition of immortality."[66]

When contemplating a golden age, the pagan world turned its thoughts wistfully to the distant past. This feature, coupled with a doctrine of repetitive world cycles, gave no solid sanction for the future realization of the ethical ideal. The doctrine of the intrinsic evil of matter and flesh could lead only to ethical despair in history. The ancient mind unsuccessfully sought to offset that outcome by the equally unpromising doctrine of pantheism: the actual is already the ideal. The Christian view of history shattered this hopeless outlook on things. And it unmasked the fallacious views of the future which were implicit in the pagan outlooks, and banished them until the rise of modern rationalism and its revolt against supernaturalistic Theism. In the last analysis our choice is not between an apocalyptic and a non-apocalyptic ethics. Every life view has implicit within it some concept of the end; the choice narrows to one or another species of apocalyptic morality. "After all," Ramsey has remarked, " 'Eat, drink and be merry, *for* tomorrow we die' is an eschatological ethic."[67] Moralists may dismiss a literal eschatology — as indeed Ramsey himself is prone to do — but they will usually do so in the interest of some rather literal competitor, even if its basis is no firmer than speculative imagination. The sobering feature of this fact is that ethics and eschatology are part of a single whole, and cannot be divorced. Reinhold Niebuhr has declared that "it must be admitted that the ethical rigor of the early church was maintained through the hope of the second coming of Christ and the establishment of his kingdom."[68] The truth of this observation is profounder than Niebuhr's coupling of it with the dubious notion that Jesus and Paul were victims of historical illusions. Christian ethics is bound to a specific view of historical consummation, and no attempted substitution of a dialectical spiritual tension in the life of the believer can compensate for dismissing that view. The Christian view of things tells us, as R. F. Weidner points out, that "history has not merely an aim, but also an *end*,"[69] and it is from this end alone that the problems of human life may be properly comprehended. Biblical ethics and final destiny are inseparable; the Old and New Testaments alike couple the plea for holiness with a summons to remember the end of history and Divine judgment.

It is the eschatological sanction for ethics which surrounds this life with finality, for it reveals God's final purpose to judge man according to the works done in the flesh. It also points out that the moral choices of this life determine our eternal destiny. The repudiation of the factual

[66]Shailer Mathews, *The Messianic Hope in the New Testament* (Chicago: University of Chicago, 1905), p. 123.
[67]Ramsey, *op. cit.*, p. 45.
[68]*An Interpretation of Christian Ethics*, p. 58.
[69]*A System of Christian Ethics*, p. 39.

bearing of eschatology on future history, and the reduction of eschatology to changeless principle imaginatively portrayed, actually conceal one of the great distinctives of Christian ethics and impart a mediocre philosophical morality in its stead. When the significance of eschatology is found only in "underlying principle," while the picture content is regarded as capable of being "painted differently according to the changing ideals and aspirations of successive ages,"[70] the biblical philosophy of history with its assurance of Divine redemptive consummation is obscured. It is true enough that "that alone can have absolute value which contributes to the absolute end,"[71] but eschatological belief involves much more than this. What gives eschatology its driving force is the fact that it cannot be reduced to mere principles; it is the complete enforcement of the will of God as the closing chapter of history, and the assurance that specific human decisions and acts are meaningful and valuable in the light of the final consummation of history. The interim-ethic school at least sensed the indispensability of this factual side of eschatology if its significance for ethics was to be retained. But the interim-ethic school also held that the ethical teaching of Jesus was not of permanent validity in view of his mistaken expectation of an immediate end of the world, and it has profoundly misunderstood the nature and importance of the eschatological background. There is a sense in which the final judgment is imminent for each generation, a factor which has often been overlooked in the controversy over the relevance of Jesus' moral teaching. And for this reason every human life stands removed by less than three score years and ten in principle from the final reckoning.

Jesus himself had declared that the time of the end was known only to the Father. The judgment to come is, Edward W. Hirst noted, imminent "in a moral and religious sense," and hence is "always at hand" requiring every man to live daily under its shadow.[72] Just because it is eschatological, the validity of the judgment is assured for the duration of the present world order. C. H. Dodd is wrong in his conclusions that the early church concluded at last that everything promised by the prophets was already realized in the blessings enjoyed in Christ himself, and that this belief was arrived at as a reflex of the admission that it erroneously expected a speedy and dramatic finish to the world order.[73] But he is assuredly right in the emphasis that the eschatologi-

[70]C. J. Barker, *op. cit.*, p. 36.
[71]*Ibid.*, p. 48.
[72]Edward W. Hirst, *Jesus and the Moralists*, p. 34.
[73]It is striking that Aristides begins and ends his account of the practical morality of second century Christianity with an eschatological reference: "The Christians have received the commandments [of the Lord], which they have engraved on their minds and keep in the hope and expectation of the world to come; wherefore, they do not commit adultery or fornication, they do not bear false witness, they do not deny a deposit, nor covet what is not theirs . . . They labor to become righteous as those who expect to receive the fulfilment of Christ's promises in the life eternal." Ernst von Dobschutz, *Christian Life in the Primitive Church* (New York: Putnam, 1904), pp. xxvf.

cal element clarified the early church's conviction of the transiency of this existence and thus provided a tremendous incentive towards ethical purity.[74]. Rather than attaching great significance to the fact that the note of apocalyptic urgency is not conspicuous in some passages of great ethical vigor in the New Testament and even in Jesus' teaching, we may safely regard that note as presupposed. An eschatologically-based ethic is a timelessly valid ethic, maintaining the duties and responsibilities of man from age to age according to eternally-anchored principles and precepts. "The very concept of the Kingdom," observes C. J. Barker, "never allows ethics to lose sight of an ideal for society that is a final ideal."[75] But it is eschatology viewed as literal history, and not merely as poetry, that marks the Christian ethic with finality.

Principal Salmond, in his classic work on immortality, observed that "Christ's own teaching . . . gives the significance of finality to the moral decision of the present life. If there are possibilities of change, forgiveness, relaxation of penalty, or cessation of punishment in the future life, His words at least do not reveal them. He never softens the awful responsibilities of this life, even by the dim adumbration of such possibilities. His recorded sayings nowhere suggest . . . grace . . . in the after-existence. They nowhere speak of a place of repentance unto life in the other world . . . They never traverse the principle that this life is the scene of opportunity ,and this world the theatre of human fates."[76]Thus the decisive connection of eschatology and ethics, whereby the former serves in the role of essential sanction charging the deeds done in the flesh with an ultimate finality, is apparent. The classical moralists who held to a cyclical theory of history could conceive of no pervading purpose and predetermined goal enclosing the sweep of events and the individual's final destiny. But biblical ethics places man within a purposeful movement of history in which his actions are directly related to an eternal spiritual realm. "The infinite gulf between right and wrong would be hidden," wrote Mackintosh, "if we ceased to think of the infinite contrast between heaven and the outer darkness."[77] For this very reason Christian morality deals with the ethical problem at its very core — the need and provision of redemption. Stalker remarked, "While the question of Moral Philosophy is, What must we do? is it not evident that the question of Christian philosophy must be the far deeper one, What must we do to be saved?"[78] Stalker properly has stressed our debt to Jesus in treating the eschatological atmosphere surrounding ethical living. "It is to Him — and one might also say, to Him alone — that the popular conceptions about a Day of Judgment

[74]C. H. Dodd, *Gospel and Law* (New York: Columbia University Press, 1951), p. 30.

[75]Barker, *op. cit.*, p. 36.

[76]S. D. F. Salmond, *The Christian Doctrine of Immortality* (Edinburgh: T. & T. Clark, 5th ed., 1903), p. 392.

[77]Robert Mackintosh, *Christian Ethics.*

[78]James Stalker, *The Ethic of Jesus,* p. 104.

and the retributions of a future existence are due."[79] Whatever its anticipations in the Old Testament, Jesus' teaching is fuller and even more sobering. Is it conceivable that he simply took over these ideas without intending to make himself responsible for them? Beyond doubt there are figurative elements, as his use of parable forewarned us, but the doctrinal implication is plain: his personal and visible return, the coming bodily resurrection, the final separation of righteous and wicked, and felicity or punishment as a final destiny. What Jesus has so ineradicably stamped upon our minds cannot now be uprooted lightly without holding him to account. What is more likely is that the prejudices of speculative moralists need to be thoroughly scrutinized, until the dubious assumptions on which they rest are exposed. They are unhappy about the conceptions of heaven and hell which Jesus constantly taught and described. A. E. Taylor in a famous series of Gifford lectures spoke his warning to those who would rid ethics of these conceptions. "It seems to me that in its substance . . . the Christian doctrine of a final salvation and reprobation springs less from theological hardness of heart than from seriousness of moral conviction. It is the supreme assertion of the conviction that choice is real and that everything is staked on the quality of our choice. If happiness depends on character and character is genuinely made by our choice, we cannot refuse to contemplate the possibility that character, and with it happiness, may be lost beyond the power of recovery by sufficient persistence in choosing evil or sufficient indolence in choosing good."[80] Jesus' doctrine of heaven and hell goes beyond this notion of a possibility of reversal of destiny from which we alone cut ourselves off, to the idea of divinely fixed limits within which our eternal destiny is determined. Taylor's

[79]*Ibid.*, p. 93.

[80]A. E. Taylor, *The Faith of a Moralist,* I, 131. Against the notion of some that the doctrine of hell must be rejected as morally repugnant, Taylor points out that others argue "that there *is* a Hell because, they are convinced, on moral grounds, that there ought to be one, if eternal justice is not to be mocked" (I, 325). Ian Henderson suggests that the real reason some reject hell is doctrinal rather than moral — its inconsistency with Christ's doctrine of Divine fatherhood. *Can Two Walk Together* (London: Nisbet, 1948), p. 7. But Christ's doctrine of Divine fatherhood is patently consistent with that of hell, as the biblical record of his teaching makes plain. It is the modern doctrine, not his, which contrasts them. A. C. Ewing argues superficially against the idea of retributive punishment that "it is directly in conflict . . . with the teaching of Christianity, which preaches instead the duty of forgiving one's enemies," and argues that the chief justification of punishment is in its effects. *Ethics,* p. 168. C. A. Briggs likewise reflects the readiness to rewrite revealed ethics in conformity with speculative ideas which are enforced by selecting biblical elements out of context and thus given a pious overtone. Briggs attacks as ethically harmful the denial of a middle state of progressive sanctification of the believer after death: "The bugbear of a judgment immediately after death and the illusion of a magical transformation in the dying hour should be banished from the world . . . The former makes death a terror to the best of men, the latter makes human life and experience of no effect; and both cut the nerves of Christian activity and striving after sanctification." "The Authority of Holy Scripture," in *Inspiration and Inerrancy,* Briggs, *et. al.* (London: Clarke, 1891), p. 82. But the fact of judgment upon the works of the flesh and the prospect of conformity to Christ's image constitute in reality dynamic ethical motivations.

words serve as a reminder that the objections levelled against Christian eschatology on professedly ethical grounds may spring in actual fact from sub-moral conceptions. The deepest source of morality and eschatology for the Western world is one and the same, Jesus Christ, who legislated and lived a supreme morality, and forewarned man of his own future role in the judgment of man.

Those who find the eschatological sanction only of formal significance for ethics regard the descriptions of the end time as imaginative symbol rooted in human postulation, an expression of spiritual confidence in the ultimate triumph of right and suppression of wrong. But Christian revelation relates eschatology and ethics far more closely. They are joined in terms not of anthropology merely but in terms of theology. For eschatology gives assurance that the moral ideal actually represents the desired goal of world-history, which moral faith must postulate in order to maintain meaningfulness for the ethical quest. And it also affirms a final change in the present world-course and the establishment of a "new heavens and earth, wherein dwelleth righteousness." D. S. Adam has referred to the eschatological postulate of Christian ethics as a differentiating feature, in view of its affirmation that "the goal is not merely an ideal for the imagination, the pursuit of which is an endless Sisyphus-like task, but an ideal which is realized in God, and which will be realized by all good men in the established kingdom of God under Christ as King."[81] Barbour contrasts the New Testament revelation of the coming triumph of the Divine Kingdom to Plato's hesitation whether an ideal condition might ever be worked out under the conditions of human life. Plato's static "Ideas" lacked dynamic energy to transform the world of change and corruption.[82] For the Christian movement, the eternal world is the world of "living hope" (1 Pet. 1:3).

The futurity of the Kingdom in the New Testament complements rather than counters the present reality of the Kingdom. For this reason the eschatological teaching is to be regarded "not as annulling, but rather as reinforcing the moral ideals" of the Christian outlook by filling life with added earnestness and solemnity.[83] The exalted moral destiny promised the people of God in the future life is a firm incentive to holy endeavor. This life is to prepare them for that existence in righteousness where nothing that defiles may enter and only the pure in heart may see God. The "new heavens and the new earth, wherein

[81]David S. Adam, *A Handbook of Christian Ethics,* p. 47.

[82]Barbour, p. 205.

[83]Archibald B. D. Alexander, *Christianity and Ethics,* p. 139. Alexander, however, spiritualizes the eschatological element due to a tendency to reduce Christian ethics to moral ideals: "Not in a visible reign or personal return of the Son of Man does the consummation of the kingdom consist, but in the complete spiritual sovereignty of Christ over the hearts and minds of men" (p. 139). Why the triumph of the spirit of service and sacrifice should preclude a literal eschatology is wholly unclear; certainly the ethical element does not require such a turn. So too, the final judgment reduces for Alexander to the notion that sin brings its own consequences and automatic punishment (p. 140).

dwelleth righteousness" supply to the Christian an elevated moral atmosphere without such sensualism as there is in the Mohammedan picture of heaven. "How debilitating is the Nirvana of Buddhism, the reabsorption of human personality in the All as taught by Hinduism, and the silence of Confucianism respecting the future," writes Keyser, "in comparison with the uplifting prospect of personal immortality held out to the Christian!"[84] The dramatic fact that the New Testament era is already eschatological, that the future Kingdom is already here in an anticipatory form, gives vigorous life to holy conduct.

The Christian ethic, as a redemptive and eschatological ethic, involves at its very center the recognition that man stands "in a permanent personal relationship to a personal God."[85] And immortality is inextricably bound up with ethical overtures. Barbour has remarked how Jesus, by carrying the doctrine of the worth of the individual man and the supreme importance of personal goodness into the eschatological sphere, radically cut through the class distinctions which prevailed in contemporary Judaism. The future judgment meant something quite different from the separation of the Jews from the Gentiles, or of the pious from the irreligious outcasts; the spiritual quality of the individual was the all-important concern.[86] The conviction that the fellowship of believers in Christ is an eternal relationship breathed a warm quality into the greeting "brother" extended to those otherwise "beyond the pale" of social acceptance. Since man is by creation destined for immortality, all his basic moral relationships must be reviewed in the light of that fact. His immortality guarantees the significance of even the most inconspicuous acts of love.

Another feature is the strength of soul which comes from anticipating "the great spiritual passage from the Seen to the Unseen,"[87] and God's provision of experience which extends "our range of thought and interest, to give distance, permanence and reality to purpose, motive, and expectation." Eschatology lifts the believer out of the mere Cyrenaic present, out of the Epicurean concentration on this life, beyond the Utilitarian concern only with the present well-being of all lives, out of the Platonic eternal which negates time, into an eternal which fulfills time and will be the climax of history. Barker observes that "Eschatology, so far from presenting a mere compensation for present evils, or leading men to despise this world and its affairs, gives zest to life by charging everything with an eternal significance. An existence laden with a sense of futility has an altogether different ethical quality from a life lived in the belief that everything is worth while; that, even if the harvest is delayed, it is sure, provided the seed is good."[88]

[84]L. S. Keyser. *A System of Christian Ethics,* p. 223.
[85]R. L. Ottley, *Christian Ideas and Ideals,* p. 7.
[86]Barbour, *op. cit.,* pp. 197f.
[87]John Hamilton Thom, *Laws of Life after the Mind of Christ* (London: Kegan, Paul, Trench, 1883), p. 391.
[88]Barker, *op. cit.,* pp. 54f.

"All the doctrines of Christian eschatology," affirmed Keyser, "are rife with ethical content and reality, and . . . of a morally inspirational character."[89] The intermediate state, between physical death and bodily resurrection, is to be spent "with Christ." The promise of the resurrection guarantees conformity to Christ's glorified body, a body which is fit for eternity. It will not be an instrument of sin, but will be fashioned for the enjoyments of the spiritual world. The doctrine of bodily resurrection restrains fleshly impulses, and is a constant reminder of the permanent binding of soul and body in the Creator's intention for man, since in eternity as in time the soul will be joined to a body suited to its moral existence. The doctrine of final judgment cannot but shape human behavior differently from the conviction that a day of reckoning will never come. The expectation of the ultimate triumph of righteousness must provide a strong incentive for noble living. The ultimate restitution of all things, grounded in the atoning death of Christ reconciling doomed sinners to God, gives assurance of the reality of the great moral and spiritual purposes. The Christian confidently hopes in this future. It is not guesswork for him, for he has already experienced the first-fruits of the hope. And "everyone that hath this hope set on him purifieth himself, even as he is pure" (1 Jn. 3:3). The influence of the biblical doctrine of last things on the spiritual and ethical life of the believer is incalculable. Not even the Christian doctrine of love can be stated accurately except in relation to One who, though unseen, is yet the center of the believer's devotion. The realities of that unseen world supply the believer's courage in the midst of persecution and tribulation, and when he is threatened with extermination, Christ peers through the shadows, keeping watch over his own. "No duty . . . is too humble to be inspired with the grandest conviction as its ruling motive; no faith is too sublime to consecrate any portion of a life-work that is meant for eternity."[90] One's patience with children, one's use of leisure, one's attitude toward enemies, one's aid to the unfortunate, all are seen in a different light under horizons that are eternal.

The ethical implication of the eschatological means, finally, that Christian morality is not a merely prudential pursuit of goodness only for its future rewards, nor a shunning of evil simply on account of its penalties. This is despite the frequent misinterpretation of Paul's words, "if in this life only we have hope in Christ, we are of all men most miserable" (1 Cor. 15:19) and "if the dead are not raised, let us eat and drink, for tomorrow we die" (1 Cor. 15:32). The moral predicament of man calls for a solution which redeems his total personality by the conquest of death itself. For Paul there is no real deliverance from this sinful plight which does not restore him to acceptance in the eternal spiritual and moral order with which he must make his peace. Only the resurrection of Christ, and of the dead in him, offers hope

[89]Keyser, *op. cit., p.* 224.
[90]Yooll, *op. cit., pp.* 138f.

for the sinner in the face of the righteous God who inhabits the eternities. Apart from that, man is hopelessly doomed in his sins. It may be too much to say that Atheism or Naturalism leads to positive immorality, although two factors need to be kept in mind. One is that modern Humanism borrows much from higher philosophical perspectives to which a proper confinement to its own presuppositions would not entitle it; historically, the world has not received its ethical inspiration from those lives which have militantly espoused a "death ends everything" outlook on life. The other factor is that Christianity so relates the good and the holy that it is impossible by definition to erect a positive morality outside a God-related life view. In fact, because of a universal Divine revelation, men must wrestle with the realities of the ethical life framed in Christian dimensions, and they escape this only in their moral revolt. While Atheism may not lead to gross or positive immorality, and may even escape a moral indifferentism and temporarily acquire a superlative altruism when it is grafted to certain activistic philosophical speculations such as an evolutionary theory, it sooner or later cuts the nerve of moral earnestness and is a doorway to despondency and despair. The problem of the moral life breaks up in frustration on the rocks and shoals of the brevity and uncertainty of life. Man must be tied to the eternal moral order. And only an eschatological ethics, that speaks assuredly of the final goal of things, can assert the ultimacy of the moral duties of this life, and discuss with propriety the moral situation in the life to come. Revelation enables the Hebrew-Christian movement to discuss the morality of the present in terms of justification and sanctification, and provides the basis for discussing the future life in the setting of an ethics of glorification. And in depicting the transition of the soul from its present state in a sinful order to its future perfection, it does not fix attention on the soul's separation from flesh and matter. In this it differs radically from Greek philosophy and from Oriental speculation. "Not because it is withdrawn from the body" does the soul become wholly sanctified in its transition from earth to heaven, since the body as such is not the seat of sin, but for the redeemed who have reposed their trust in him, "by an act of God's power and grace, it is purified from all sin, withdrawn from a sinful environment, and transferred to an environment of perfect purity."[91]

[91]Keyser, *op. cit.*, pp. 220f.

25

CHRISTIAN MORALITY AND THE LIFE OF PRAYER

THE VERY BREATH of prayer sustains the Christian life. Righteousness has interior connections not only with conscience and the indwelling Spirit, but with prayer as the carrier of the soul's sincere desire. George Matheson reminds us that spiritual life by prayer is a necessary consideration in biblical morality. He says, "The moral place of prayer is one of the distinctive features of Christian ethics, and could not by any process be eliminated from a scientific view of the subject."[1] Spiritual existence is "between the two poles, having and not having," and in this holy meeting with God moral endeavor finds its secret access to supernatural aid and its assurance of progress.

Like almsgiving and fasting, prayer falls actually among the religious acts rather than the moral.[2] Doubtless this is the reason even Christian discussions of ethics often make little mention of prayer as an element in the ideal life. But religious acts too are exposed to judgment when sound ethical principles do not underlie them. The ethics of prayer and the place of prayer in morality are therefore not irrelevant considerations.

The prayerless life not only halts short of the ideal, but marks an existence in sin. Prayer is a duty,[3] an indispensable element in the morally complete life. Prayer to the Living God manifests the believer's life as turned aside from idols. Whoever only speaks of God, but never or seldom to God, easily leases body and soul to idols. The Christian thus places his whole future in jeopardy by a stunted prayer life. Prayer is not only the individual's acknowledgment of creaturely dependence, but the whole-souled confession that his true hope is in the supernatural world, above finite satisfactions, and that his only worthwhile destiny lies in the will of God rather than private ambition.

Sometimes the observation is made that over against the New Testament "the law said but little about prayer."[4] Actually, this verdict misses the essential connection between prayer and the worship of God

[1]George Matheson, *Landmarks of New Testament Morality* (London: Nisbet, 1887), p. 117.

[2]C. A. Briggs, *The Ethical Teaching of Jesus* (New York: Scribner, 1904), p. 164.

[3]Cf. Jer. 29:7, Mt. 5:44, 6:6, 9:38, 26:41, Lk. 18:1ff., 1 Thess. 5:17, Jas. 1:5, 5:16, 1 Pet. 4:7.

[4]R. Govett, *The Sermon on the Mount Expounded* (London: Thynne, 1934), p. 273.

which the Scriptures everywhere underscore. The kingly rule of God implies the individual participant's communion and fellowship with him in the present world of experience. "If God is Father," writes R. Newton Flew, "He must desire that His children shall have relations with Him."[5] Love for God, moreover, must always find living expression in communion with him.

Yet the New Testament doubtless brings a new centrality to the place of prayer in the moral life. The fixed worship of Jehovah at one appointed place, at the temple in Jerusalem, where the Hebrew dealt with God through the mediation of a priest, involved restraints upon the scope of prayer which disappear with the equal and universal accessibility of God in prayer. The Christian movement gloried in the Risen Christ as the ascended priest through whom men come to God. In his most sustained ethical discourse, Jesus included prayer by way of command, attaching the promise of an answer. And he was careful to teach his disciples to pray, so there need be no hesitancy. He even left them a model prayer. The exhortation to prayer is made frequently by the apostles, too. The Christian virtues, as a Divine gift, were to be sought by prayer. Through man's fulfillment of this requirement, God dispenses the blessings of grace.

Equally dramatic is Jesus' practice of prayer. He engaged not alone in public and united prayer, but left his disciples an unforgettable example of private prayer. Often he retired to the mountains to be alone with God. On limited occasions the Redeemer took the disciples with him. They sensed what Dorner tells us: "His prayer was the middle point of his activity, the holy altar upon which He ever consecrates and offers anew his humanity to God, and this is always in turn penetrated and illumined by the Divine."[6]

Decades later in the gospels the disciples recorded Jesus' resorting to the mountains for prayer — before sunrise, before men awakened from sleep, sometimes engaging in intercession throughout the long night.[7] Those nights of prayer seem to decide the pivotal choices of his ministry. "Christ does not appear to have been constantly insisting on prayer," writes F. B. Meyer, "but He was constantly praying Himself."[8] The Christian community, in its offense of prayerlessness, has never succeeded in easing its conscience in the presence of this pattern of the praying Redeemer. The very incarnate Son of God experienced the need of prayer and, moreover, satisfied that need to the full.

[5]R. Newton Flew, *The Idea of Perfection in Christian Theology*, p. 24.

[6]Dorner, *System of Christian Doctrine*, III, 370.

[7]Vallings reminds us: "It was while He prayed at the Baptism that the Holy Spirit descended; after a night of prayer that the Twelve Apostles were chosen; in prayer that He was transfigured; in the Gethsemane prayer that an angel comforted Him. It was the sight apparently of Jesus in prayer that prompted the prayer to be taught a form of prayer. At times He would give thanks before what He asked for to human eyes came to pass." *Jesus Christ the Divine Man*, p. 225.

[8]F. B. Meyer, *Directory of the Devout Life* (Grand Rapids: Baker Book House, reprint), p. 112.

The unbroken life of prayer becomes therefore one of the Christian's most desirable goals. Somewhere Karl Barth remarks that it is not enough to say the Reformers "believed" in prayer; they *prayed.* Luther has an interesting comment on the exhortation "ask, and it shall be given you" (Mt. 7:7). The Lord Christ, he tells us, "means hereby to teach that prayer next to preaching is the principal work of a Christian."[9] In modern times the vehement prophetic condemnation of prayerlessness needs to be heard anew. "There is none that calleth upon thy name, that stirreth up himself to take hold of thee," writes Isaiah (64:7), and again, "Yet thou hast not called upon me, O Jacob; but thou hast been weary of me, O Israel" (43:22). Prayerlessness is a spurning of that fellowship with God for which man was fashioned, a snobbish preference for solitude and for self-reflection above conversation with the Almighty. Likewise, it involves a shameful neglect of spiritual and moral resources. Whoever prefers a monologue with himself to a dialogue with the Creator-Redeemer actually shapes an idol of himself.

While prayer is indispensable to the moral life, the habit of prayer does not necessarily imply the good life. No act can be good which is performed in complete detachment from the life of prayer, but no thought and behavior is ideal simply because it is prayer-conditioned. Some of the sternest rebukes in the Bible are aimed at the intercession of false gods, and even at the pursuit of answered prayer on inadequate grounds. Prayer to selfish ends is rebuked as irreligious and immoral: "Ye ask and ye receive not, because ye ask amiss, that ye may consume it upon your lusts" (Jas. 4:3). Pagans often regard their prayers as meritorious external works. Jesus distinguished the intercession of believers from that of the Gentiles who trace the efficacy of prayer to their subjective effort, *e.g.,* "much speaking," "vain repetition" (Mt. 6:7), rather than in the nature of God. He also decried the practice of prayer as a public spectacle (Mt. 6:5ff.).

Such prayer has lost its truth and inwardness, and survives as a hollow witness to the deep interior needs of the soul. Unless it expresses man's sincere, interior relation to God, prayer is a mockery. "The ethics of prayer," Keyser reminds us, "consists in the fact that it must be of the heart; must be utterly sincere; dare not be mere lip-service; and especially should never be engaged in merely 'to be seen of men.' "[10] The secret side of Christian life, which private prayer guards, stands interference against a mere "righteousness of ostentation," like that of many of the scribes and Pharisees. Prayer with a view to public approval rather than to that of the Living God is sinful pretension; the celebrity it seeks is the only reward it gets — and in the discerning company of heaven it loses even that.

[9]Martin Luther, *Commentary on the Sermon on the Mount,* trans. Charles A. Hay (Philadelphia: Lutheran Publication Society, 1892), p. 393.
[10]L. S. Keyser, *A System of Christian Ethics,* p. 251.

Stalker points out the apparent inconsistency in Jesus' injunctions — and the contradiction is only apparent — whereby he enjoins openness (the light that shines) and yet secrecy (the closet of prayer). "The public side of virtue," Stalker urges, "must be balanced and kept in its right place by the private side. If a man's prayers in public are more numerous than his private devotions, he is in a bad way; but, if his testimony in public is accompanied with a hidden life of intercourse with God, it is likely to be salutory for all concerned."[11]

Yet prayer addressed even to the Living God can be something less than moral. Medieval monasticism provides a conspicuous example of professed devotion to God which neglects humanity. More universal is the illicit prayer pursuit of legitimate secondaries which become idolatrous primaries.

Sometimes a Divine sanction is improperly attached to such a misuse of prayer. "If ye ask anything" (Jn. 14:13f., 15:16, 16:23f., 26) is misconstrued as a blank check requiring only the petitioner's signature; the equally fundamental emphasis "in my name," which suggests something more complex than a joint account, is obscured. Those to whom Jesus addressed his assurances of the efficacy of prayer were believers, Judas having already deserted. The assurance of answered prayer which Jesus vouchsafed to his disciples had specially in view their fruitfulness and joy (Jn. 15:16, 16:24). Yet there is scant need to restrict the idea of fruit-bearing, as is often the case, exclusively to soul-winning, especially in view of the broader New Testament conception of spiritual and ethical fruit. The restriction "in my name" guarantees, at very least, that no transactions will be honored which contradict the imperatives God addresses to his followers. For God cannot be glorified by any "answer to prayer" which does violence to the moral law. The petitioner who prays for God to strike dead an officious neighbor, or to assist in the theft of property, needs to change his conception of God as well as of prayer. It may be too much to say that God will hear no plea from unsaved lips but the publican's prayer for salvation, "God be merciful to me, a sinner" (Lk. 18:13). He has nowhere attached the definite promise of an answer. And, indubitably, any prayer whose answer would violate the revealed moral law of God is certain not to be answered, whether it be uttered by a pagan or by an uninformed believer. What links prayer always to ethical dynamism is the fact that it exists not to change but rather to expedite the will of God. Prayer involves always an element of risk — the risk of being found out and unmasked in God's presence as double-minded. "Pray for what you want," a wise pastor once encouraged his flock, "but be sure you want what you pray for."

The Cross is planted squarely in the center of all Christian prayer life. James Strahan reminds us that "The substance of all true prayer is 'Not my will, but Thine, be done,' rather than, "Not Thy will, but

[11]James Stalker, *The Ethic of Jesus*, p. 74.

mine, be done."[12] Martensen asserts that "he who offers no sacrifice in his prayer, who does not sacrifice his self-will, does not really pray."[13] Prayer becomes, therefore, the great school of selflessness. The Lord's Prayer, though it be uttered in secret, begins "*our* Father"; it further enforces the community and solidarity of life by the plural phrases "our daily bread," "our debts," "our debtors." Prayer vivifies the social spirit and militates against selfish motivations.

Christian prayer moves characteristically in the first person plural — as the Lord's Prayer already makes clear — making the transition from isolated selfish concerns to the body of Christ and the body of humanity at large, with both of which the believer stands identified. Intercession is, as Adolf Koberle points out, the Holy Spirit's strongest weapon against egoism and self-love. On the plane of intercession it becomes apparent that prayer is "a preparation for the service of our neighbor and for the battle for God's glory," and not a primary concern with "private religious needs."[14] Abstinence from intercession reflects a surface-piety which is still largely self-centered. Intercession is therefore a culminating manifestation of the inner life.

Yet prayer stands guard also against an opposite danger. Among the moral life's best safeguards against autonomy and humanism is the Christian dependence upon prayer as a means of grace. In our times, ethical duties are often reduced to the service of man, as if this exhausted the claim of God. But the notion that there are no duties toward God distinct from our duties toward men reflects too much Kant's standpoint that the sole purpose of religion is to provide a Divine sanction for man's ethical duties, giving the latter the force of supernatural commands. Not even the duty of prayer can be reconciled with such a theory. Kant could make no room for prayer as an instrument for gaining Divine favor or as the service of God; instead, he held that prayer merely alerts our moral sense by infusing it with the idea of God as a moral lawgiver. The biblical doctrine of prayer was thus bent to Kant's speculative agnosticism.

Prayer is no mere Divine "duty," however. Who understands it only in this way doubtless escapes its use only as an occasional emergency device, but runs the risk of legalizing its practice. The Reformation struck out against the medieval legalizing of prayer, with all its unnatural and morbid Romish rules. Prayer is privilege. Its enjoyment is to be guided by the spontaneous outgoing of the heart to its true fount of blessing.

Nevertheless, God has enjoined prayer. Unbiblical speculations therefore underlie the prevalent notion that true prayer cannot be commanded. Obedience to a command — even the command to pray — need not be legalistic. Prayer in the Spirit alone fulfills the Divine require-

[12]James Strahan, *Hebrew Ideals* (Edinburgh: T. & T. Clark, 1906), p. 131.
[13]H. Martensen, *Christian Ethics,* I, 174.
[14]Adolf Koberle, *The Quest for Holiness,* p. 178.

ment. The act of prayer therefore always forces the Christian to a decision between legal and spiritual obedience.

Virtue is a moral wholeness, not an aggregate of detached precepts. The life of prayer shapes the unity of Christian morality. The one will of God here is allowed to scrutinize the hidden recesses of the heart. The specifics of the moral life are bent beneath the integrating Divine claim. The competition and rivalry of human desires, uttered and unexpressed, are brought to advance judgment. In the alternation between the Scriptures and prayer, conscience gains its renewal, comprehending all moral dispositions in one, and relating their manifold expressions to the Living Lord.

What it means to comprehend all claims from the unified standpoint of prayer is ideally set before us in the Lord's Prayer. Its brevity carries us at once to those major needs characteristic of man universally regardless of race, color, or class. In A. M. Hunter's words, the prayer consists of "six short petitions that go arrow-like to the unseen world."[15] It covers the two tables of the Law and, maintaining the viewpoint of biblical ethics, puts "first things first, heavenly things before the earthly." Stalker notes the brief attention to daily bread, or to the material needs of life, and rather, the concentration on the great things of God.[16] Nothing paralyzes effectiveness more than an uneasy feeling about the propriety of prayer, a sense that what one seeks belongs outside the purview of saintly interests.

"From the earliest days," Flew somewhere reminds us, "the teachers of Christianity have taught a doctrine of prayer far removed from the pagan conceptions which still prevail and are popular in Christian countries." What the Cambridge tutor has specially in mind is the stress in heathen prayer upon earthly and material interests, rather than according the centrality of emphasis to moral discipline and the intellectual devotion to the truth. The teaching of Jesus sets us an example of confidence that God is so aware of the material needs of his children that he may be relied upon to supply the necessary conveniences of life without our making them the all-absorbing interest in prayer. Canon Liddon remarks that the ethics of Christian prayer refers all petitions for merely personal good to the earlier concerns of the Lord's Prayer, summed up in the one supplication which covers the universe as a whole: "Thy will be done."[17] Prayer is essentially conversation with God that has for its main thrust the holy purpose of the Creator and Redeemer in his rescued children.

Yet the implication must be avoided that the material needs of life are in every, or even in any case, an illicit topic of prayer. The phrase "give us this day our daily bread," while it forms a small element in the ideal prayer, nonetheless vindicates the legitimacy of such prayer.

[15]A. M. Hunter, *Design for Life* (London: SCM, 1953), p. 66.
[16]Stalker, *op. cit.*, p. 280.
[17]Canon H. P. Liddon, *Some Elements of Religion,* Lent Lectures, 1870 (6th ed.; London: Longmans, 1898), p. 197.

In times of special need, the believer properly casts all his economic cares, along with all others, upon God. When those cares do not exist, prayer takes preferably the form of thanksgiving for God's provision. Above the yearning for multiplied holdings it reflects a concern for faithful stewardship. But there are also times when financial gain becomes properly an important prayer consideration. Especially is this true when the burden of such prayer springs not out of desire for individual gain, but from a desire to relieve the needs or to extend the frontiers of a spiritual work which God has called into being. George Mueller sustained an orphanage by daily prayer, and God sent the funds.

The intimate study of prayers uttered by Bible characters has rich compensation not only in their testimony to the approachableness of God, but in their publication of the wide range of interests which are a proper burden of ethical prayer.[18] Matheson well reminds us, however, that "the highest effect of . . . petition would, in the eye of Christianity, be its moral effect. Should it lift . . . man from a mere bed of physical sickness to resume an old life of sin, its success, in the view of Christ's religion, would indeed be small. But should it infect the man with its own spirit, should it touch him with somewhat of its own fire, should it wake within him some regret for a misspent past, and some resolve for a desired future, then, whether, physically speaking he should live or die, the verdict of Christianity still would be that the prayer of the righteous man availed much."[19]

Especially the Christian's use or disuse of prayer discloses how profoundly he grasps the essential difference between the revealed Hebrew-Christian world-life view and speculative pantheistic versions. The notion that "prayer changes you, not the objective course of things" is a half-truth which belongs to a fatalistic and deterministic scheme of reality, not to the biblical view. The Stoic scope for teleology and providence was a secondary, and actually inconsistent, admission into their metaphysics. Nowhere is this so clear as in the Stoic disparagement of prayer. The Stoics praised self-observation and self-examination, but were unfamiliar with prayer and thanksgiving. Pagan philosophers often make a point of the fact that unworthy persons receive nothing although they pray, but they do not carefully guard against an implicit thesis that worthy persons gain all there is whether they pray or not. In the biblical view, prayer is one of the means by which God has ordained the ends comprehended in his eternal plan. Thus the vitality of prayer is maintained by biblical Theism without sacrificing the certainty of the ultimate triumph of righteousness and the reality of particular providence. Prayer is therefore an element of Divine creation by which God determines the future in its connection with the destinies of every individual.

[18]Volumes such as Helen C. Hughes and Mary Hodgkin's *Prayers from the Bible* (London: Frederick Muller, 1941) and Elinor Mapes Pierce's *The Prayers of the Bible* (Philadelphia: Judson Press, 1944) are helpful compilations.

[19]Matheson, *op. cit.*, p. 135.

Modern thought has tended to lay increasing stress upon the subjective benefits of prayer. Prayer and peace of mind become its center of reference. And there can be scant doubt that the man of prayer becomes through prayer a different man, with his environment and relations transformed. Prayer turns funeral dirges into songs of praises. It harmonizes the distraught self and conserves the music of life. This psychological mood has been insensitive, however, to the fact that beneficent self-suggestion is inseparable from assurance that an objective Divine resource flows into the life of the finite intercessor. The "last word" in philosophy or in science has often choked prayer into irrelevance by the biased declaration that human desires and words cannot affect the Divine government of the universe. Schleiermacher's conception of a God pantheistically-bound to his own universe allowed to prayer only the roles of thanksgiving or resignation, and proved uncongenial to any confidence that transcendent spiritual forces are released by intercession. Ritschl regarded prayer as a subjective expression of faith in Divine providence, and reduced it to the form of thanksgiving alone. If that be its only value, the religious life declines inevitably into secret unbelief, for prayer becomes an inefficient and insincere use of time. Neglect of prayer is therefore the first result of revolt against the biblical confidence in "answered prayer" and of doubt concerning its objective value. Meager belief in prayer leads inevitably to its even more meager practice.

The modern view operates actually with a conception of the moral order alien to the theistic world-life view unfolded in Hebrew-Christian revelation. Divine purpose is not, in biblical Theism, a blind and inflexible fate. Rather, it includes prayer as one of the conditions of the outworking of God's special providences in the world. The biblical doctrine of prayer has for its corollary the biblical doctrine that God is personal, infinite and sovereign, wise and good. Especially in the tradition of ethical monotheism prayer gains a prospect for power which the polytheistic religions cannot sustain.

While Jesus taught men to subordinate petition to thankfulness, he regarded petitionary prayer among the greatest world-moving forces. Frank Laubach is not untrue to the New Testament in the title of his book *Prayer The Mightiest Force in the World.*

The question of the knowledge of the will of God in particulars, and of Divine guidance, here presses into the picture. Supernatural guidance must be linked to Scripture and to prayer, where the believer stands in the immediate presence of the Spirit of God. The Christian movement voices a proper impatience with those in its ranks who complain that they cannot find the will of God for their lives, while they neglect the Scriptures and prayer. The blunt fact is that every Christian knows more of the will of God than he fulfills. When believers do what they know to be God's will, they may be confident that more of his plan will be readily knowable. This is the assurance of the Scripture itself: "If any man will to do his will, he shall know the teaching" (Jn. 7:17).

The guidance of God centers primarily in the moral and spiritual. Christian living, even devoutly ventured in prayer, is no short cut for achieving such desires of the natural man as riches, fame, health. Some of the greatest saints have lived in near poverty, most others have been ignored by *Who's Who,* and not a few have faced strange and excruciating death. More could be said of prophets and apostles. Sound Christian colleges and seminaries endure financial hardship; they make poor as well as good investments; their ablest faculty men are sometimes bypassed and spurned by religious groups. If prayer and meditation supplied infallible guidance to wealth, fame, and earthly pleasure, the quiet time would not lack for secular addicts.

This is not to deny that God sometimes prospers his followers with exceptional fortune, reputation, and health. Christian commitment does not imply an assured earthly impoverishment, mediocrity, or suffering. Abraham was one of the richest of the patriarchs, Moses and Paul belong in every complete bibliographical dictionary, and the longevity of Joseph and Noah is the envy of modern octogenarians. But God shapes the special providences of life primarily for spiritual and moral ends, and not according to the material and earthly preferences of human beings. Sometimes God gives superlative wisdom or wealth, but the presence or absence of either is no infallible index to moral supremacy. Were every life decision referable to immediate Divine guidance, so man could adjust automatically by a spiritual geiger-counter, what would become of Christian judgment and growth and trust? Christianity prizes faith in God as a virtue; it does not aim to circumvent trust. And it refers man's earthly cares to the general providence of God — "consider the lilies of the field, how they grow" (Mt. 6:28) — and beyond this, to his special interest in man — "Behold the fowls of the air . . . Are ye not much better than they?" (Mt. 6:26). Prayer is a channel for the increase of faith, not an avenue to secret information which dissolves the need of trust.

The sustained practice of prayer, not simply as a habit but in the pursuit of God's will, delivers intercession from the role of an emergency technique for times of crisis. The life of prayer is quite different from the resort to prayers. "Devout men, as their life unfolds, increasingly turn to prayer — not prayers in the plural, but prayer in the singular." So F. B. Meyer reminds us.[20] Doubtless crises occur even in the life of faithful prayer, when saintly believers inarticulately voice their yearnings and needs. But the Spirit, the searcher of hearts, who knows also the deep things of God, takes up their burden of intercession. The writings of some early church fathers contemplate the whole Christian life as but a single prayer in which action is blended with devotion. Yet such a regard for the whole of life as prayer must avoid the modern

[20]F. B. Meyer, *op. cit.*, p. 110.

misunderstanding which rises from bias against personal communion between the soul and God, and reduces prayer to an attitude of mind only. For prayer is, above all else, a person-to-person relationship, and not simply a station-to-station affair.

The complex environment of mid-twentieth century life competes constantly with the maintenance of an effective prayer life. The result is a generation of church-goers whose illiteracy in prayer exceeds even its unfamiliarity with Scripture and with the great doctrines of revealed religion. The conditions and techniques of Western life sustain the illusion of man's self-sufficiency, except in rare and critical times. The climate of life lacks the winds of prayer. The irony of this turn of affairs is the fact that complex human existence in our complicated era calls urgently for more, rather than less, power in prayer. The years are fuller than ever of far-reaching decisions, opportunities, responsibilities for the multitudes, and emptier than ever before of ultimate meaning. If the enterprise of morality is to avoid further descent into the chaotic shadows of nihilism, prayer is no mere option, but an essential.

Prayer alerts man to his high eternal destiny. It quickens the relation between his moral nature and the Divine Lawgiver. Conscience is pricked and renewed in prayer. Wuttke called it "the very life-blood of morality."[21] It gives subjective evidence of Christian fidelity. The Scriptures frequently link prayer with an alert spiritual watchfulness against the dangers of temptation. Apart from prayer, all our virtues are placed in peril, for prayer sustains them in weakness and guards us from pride in their presence. But where regenerate hearts pray, a new ethos is being shaped in human life, for the glory of heaven bends low over the community of true piety.

The fundamental rule for the Christian, in his inevitable contest with an enveloping society of secular and pagan spirits, was not left in doubt by Jesus. It is, to quote a passage from J. Oswald Dykes, "to live by prayer: to fall back on divine help: to keep open that secret avenue of access to the unseen father . . ." Were no supernatural resources available to the moral agent, he would not dare venture to reciprocate the world's evil with the spirit of *agape*. And because prayer is a means of grace, he dare not neglect this exchange of good for evil. Luther's words are memorable: "Oh, if . . . a universal heartfelt cry should ascend to God from the entire nation, what unmeasurable strength and help would result from such prayer! What could happen that would be more terrifying to all evil spirits? What greater work could be done on earth?. . . For the Christian Church on earth has no greater power nor strength than such common prayer against all that may assail her."[22] Eternity alone will disclose the effect of prayer in the turning-

[21]Adolf Wuttke, *Christian Ethics,* trans. John P. Lacroix (New York: Nelson & Phillips, 1876), II, 221.
[22]Luther, *Works* (Erlangen, ed.), XVI, 171.

points of human history and in the great decisions that have shaped the affairs of the successive centuries. Say what one will about Christian action, its main roots are to be found in the soil of efficacious prayer. For prayer remains the hinterland of Christian moral advance. It is the one language of heaven translated into the multi-lingual speech of earth, the redeemed race's spiritual counterpart to the secular world's Babel, and the multiplied tongues of Pentecost turned upward again toward the glory.

BIBLIOGRAPHY

I. THE SERMON ON THE MOUNT

Carpenter, William Boyd, *The Great Charter of Christ, Being Studies in the Sermon on the Mount.* London: Isbister and Company Limited, 1895.

Chambers, Oswald, *Studies in the Sermon on the Mount.* London: Simpkin Marshall, Ltd., 1941.

Chappell, Clovis G., *The Sermon on the Mount.* New York: Abingdon-Cokesbury Press, 1930.

Dykes, J. Oswald, *The Beatitudes of the Kingdom.* London: James Nisbet and Co., 1872.

——— *The Manifesto of the King. An Exposition of the Sermon on the Mount.* London: James Nisbet and Co., 1887 (New Edition).

Devine, Minos, *The Religion of the Beatitudes.* London: Macmillan and Co., Limited, 1918.

Findlay, J. Alexander, *The Realism of Jesus. A Paraphrase and Exposition of the Sermon on the Mount.* London: Hodder and Stoughton Limited, n. d.

Fisher, R. H., *The Beatitudes.* Edinburgh: T.&T. Clark, 1927 (Reprinted).

Fox, Emmett, *The Sermon on the Mount.* New York: Grosset, 1938.

Gore, Charles, *The Sermon on the Mount. A Practical Exposition.* London: John Murray, 1907 (Reprinted).

Govett, R., *The Sermon on the Mount Expounded.* London: Thynne & Co., Ltd., 1934.

Hamilton, E. L., *The Laws and Principles of the Kingdom of Heaven.* London: Marshall, Morgan & Scott, 1927.

Hayes, Doremus A., *The Heights of Christian Living.* New York: The Abingdon Press, 1929.

Hogg, C. F., and J. B. Watson, *On the Sermon on the Mount.* London: Pickering & Inglis Ltd., 1947 (3rd impression).

Hunter, A. M., *Design for Life.* London: SCM Press, 1953.

Jones, E. Stanley, *The Sermon on the Mount. A Working Philosophy of Life.* New York: The Abingdon Press, 1931.

Martin Luther's *Commentary on the Sermon on the Mount.* (Translated by Charles A. Hay). Philadelphia: Lutheran Publication Society, 1892.

Pink, Arthur W., *An Exposition of the Sermon on the Mount.* Grand Rapids: Baker Book House, 1951.

Stafford, Geoffrey Wardle, *The Sermon on the Mount. The Charter of Christianity.* New York: The Abingdon Press, 1927.

Tholuck, A., *Commentary on the Sermon on the Mount* (Translated by R. Lundin Brown from the 4th revised and enlarged edition). Edinburgh: T.&T. Clark, 1869.

Thompson, Ernest Trice, *The Sermon on the Mount and Its Meaning for Today.* Richmond, Va.: John Knox Press, 1953, (Revised).

Trench, Richard Chenevix, *Exposition of the Sermon on the Mount Drawn from the Writings of St. Augustine.* London: Macmillan and Co., 1881 (4th edition, revised).

Vaughan, C. J. *Characteristics of Christ's Teaching. Drawn from the Sermon on the Mount.* London: Strahan & Co., 1874 (6th edition).

White, Mrs. E. G., *Thoughts from the Mount of Blessing.* Mountain View, Calif.: Pacific Press Publishing Association, 1928 (reprint).

Windisch, Hans, *The Meaning of the Sermon on the Mount.* A Contribution to the Historical Understanding of the Gospels and to the Problem of Their True Exegesis (translated by S. MacLean Gilmour). Philadelphia: The Westminster Press, 1951.

Wright, T. H., *The Sermon on the Mount for Today.* Edinburgh: T.&T. Clark, 1927.

II. THE ETHICS OF JESUS

Branscomb, B. H., *Jesus and the Law of Moses.* New York: R. R. Smith, 1930.

Briggs, Charles Augustus, *The Ethical Teaching of Jesus.* New York: Charles Scribner's Sons, 1904.

Clarke, William Newton, *The Ideal of Jesus.* New York: Charles Scribner's Sons, 1915.

Dykes, J. Oswald *The Relations of the Kingdom.* London: James Nisbet & Co., 1874.

King, Henry C., *The Ethics of Jesus* (Noble Lectures, 1909). New York: The Macmillan Company, 1910.

Scott, A. Boyd, *Christ: The Wisdom of Man.* London: Hodder and Stoughton, 1928.

Scott, E. F., *The Ethical Teaching of Jesus.* New York: The Macmillan Company, 1924, 1951.

Stalker, James, *The Ethic of Jesus According to the Synoptic Gospels.* New York: George H. Doran Company, 1909.

Wilder, Amos N., *Eschatology and Ethics in the Teaching of Jesus.* New York: Harper and Brothers, 1950 (Revised Edition).

III. THE ETHICS OF PAUL

Greenhough, J. G., *The Mind of Christ in St. Paul* New York: Hodder & Stoughton, n. d.

Speer, Robert E., *Seeking the Mind of Christ.* New York: Fleming H. Revell Company, 1926.

Thom, John Hamilton, *Laws of Life After the Mind of Christ.* London: Kegan, Paul, Trench & Co., 1883.

IV. GENERAL WORKS

Adam, David Stow, *A Handbook of Christian Ethics.* Edinburgh: T. & T. Clark, 1952.

Alexander, Archibald B. D., *Christianity and Ethics.* London: Duckworth & Co., 1914.

Allen, E. L., *The Structure of Life.* London: Nisbet & Co., Ltd., 1945.

Barbour, G. F., *A Philosophical Study of Christian Ethics.* Edinburgh: William Blackwood and Sons, 1911.

Barker, C. J., *The Way of Life. A Study in Christian Ethics.* London: Lutter worth Press, 1946.

Baxter, Richard, *Christian Directory.*

Bayne, Peter, *The Christian Life, Social and Individual.* Boston: Gould and Lincoln, 1856.

Beach, Waldo (Ed.), *Christian Ethics.* New York: *The Ronald Press* Co., 1955.

Berdyaev, Nicolas, *The Destiny of Man* (translated from the Russian by Natalie Duddington). London: Geoffrey Bles,, 1937. 3rd ed., 1948.

Blaiklock, E. M., *The Christian in Pagan Society.* London: Tyndale Press, 1951.

Bromiley, G. W., *Reasonable Service.* London: The Inter-Varsity Fellowship, 1948.

Browne, Sir Thomas, *Christian Morals.* Cambridge: University Press, 1927.

Bruce, W. S., *The Formation of Christian Character.* A Contribution to Christian Ethics. Edinburgh: T. & T. Clarke, 1908.

Brunner, Emil, *The Divine Imperative.* A Study in Christian Ethics (translated from the German by Olive Wyon). Philadelphia: The Westminster Press, 1947.

Cave, Sydney, *The Christian Way*. A Study of New Testament Ethics in Relation to Present Problems. New York: Philosophical Library, Inc., 1949.

Clark, Henry W., *The Christian Method of Ethics.* Edinburgh: Oliphant, Anderson & Ferrier, 1908.

Coggan, F. D., *The New Testament Basis of Moral Theology.* London: Tyndale Press, 1948.

D'Arcy, Charles F., *Christian Ethics and Modern Thought.* London: Longmans, Green and Co., 1937.

D'Arcy, M. C., *Christian Morals.* London: Longmans, Green and Co., 1937.

Davis, Henry, S. J., *Moral and Pastoral Theology,* 4 vols. London: Sheed and Ward, (5th ed. rev.), 1946.

Davison, William L., *Christian Ethics.* London: A. & C. Black, 1899.

Dewar, Lindsay E., and Cyril E. Hudson, *Christian Morals.* London: London University Press, 1948.

Dewar, Lindsay E., *An Outline of New Testament Ethics.* Philadelphia: The Westminster Press, 1949.

Dickie, Edgar P., *The Obedience of a Christian Man.* London: Student Christian Movement Press, Ltd., 1944.

Dodd, C. H., *Gospel and Law.* The Relation of Faith and Ethics in Early Christianity (Bampton Lectures in America, No. 3). New York: Columbia University Press, 1951.

Dorner, I. A., *System of Christian Ethics* (tr. from the German by C. M. Mead and R. T. Cunningham). Edinburgh: T. & T. Clark, 1887.

Fairbairn, Patrick, *The Revelation of Law in Scripture* (Cunningham Lectures). Edinburgh: T. & T. Clark, 1869.

Garrard, L. A., *Duty and the Will of God.* Oxford: Basil Blackwell, 1938.

Garvie, Alfred E., *The Christian Ideal for Human Society.* London: Hodder and Stoughton Limited, 1930.

———, *Christian Moral Conduct.* London: The Unicorn Press, 1938.

Gore, Charles, *Christian Moral Principles.* London: A. R. Mowbray & Co., Ltd., 1921.

———, *The Philosophy of the Good Life* (Gifford Lectures, 1929-30). London: John Murray, 1930.

Green, Peter, *The Problem of Right Conduct. A Text-book of Christian Ethics.* London: Longmans, Green and Co., 1931.

Gregory, D. S., *Christian Ethics; or, The True Moral Manhood and Life of Duty.* Philadelphia: Eldredge, 1875.

Grubb, Norman, *The Law of Faith.* London: Lutterworth Press, 1947.

Haas, John A. W., *Freedom and Christian Conduct. An Ethic.* New York: The Macmillan Company, 1923.

Haering, Theodore von, *The Ethics of the Christian Life* (tr. from the German by James S. Hill). London: Williams & Norgate, 1909.

Hammond, T. C., *Perfect Freedom. An Introduction to Christian Ethics.* London: Inter-Varsity Fellowship, n. d.

Harless, G. Chr. Adolph von, *System of Christiann Ethics* (translated from 6th enlarged German edition by A. W. Morrison and revised by William Findlay). Edinburgh: T. & T. Clark, 1887.

Hastie, John Stewart, *Triumphant Goodness.* London: H. R. Allenson, Ltd., n. d.

Henson, Herbert Hensley, *Christian Morality, Natural, Developing, Final* (Gifford Lectures, 1935-36). Oxford: Clarendon Press, 1936.

Hildebrand, D. von, *Christian Ethics.* New York: McKay, 1953.

Hirst, Edward W., *Jesus and the Moralists: A Comparative Study of the Christian Ethic* (Fernley-Hartley Lecture, 1935). London: The Epworth Press, 1935.

Hodgson, Leonard, *Christian Faith and Practice.* New York: Charles Scribner's Sons, 1951.

Hovey, Alvah, *Manual of Systematic Theology, and Christian Ethics.* Philadelphia: American Baptist Publication Society, 1877.

———, *Studies in Ethics and Religion;* or, *Discourses, Essays, and Reviews.* Boston: Silver, Burdett, & Co., 1892.

Hughes, P., *The Faith in Practice; Catholic Doctrine and Life.* New York: Longmans, Green and Co., 1938.

Illingworth, J. R., *Christian Character.* London: Macmillan & Co., Limited, 1905.

Jessop, T. E., *Law and Love. A Study of the Christian Ethic.* London: Student Christian Movement Press, 1940.

Keyser, Leander, S., *A Manual of Christian Ethics.* Burlington, Ia.: The Lutheran Literary Board, 1926.

———, *A System of Christian Ethics.* Philadelphia: The Lutheran Publication Society, 1913.

Kilpatrick, Thomas B., *Christian Character. A Study in New Testament Morality.* Edinburgh: T. & T. Clark, 1899.

Kimpel, Ben, *Moral Principles in the Bible.* New York: Philosophical Library, 1956.

Kirk, Kenneth E., *Ignorance, Faith and Conformity. Studies in Moral Theology.* London: Longmans, Green and Co., 1933.

———, (Ed.), *Personal Ethics.* Oxford: Clarendon Press, 1937.

Knight, William, *The Christian Ethic.* London: John Murray, 1893.

Knudson, Albert C., *The Principles of Christian Ethics.* New York: Abingdon-Cokesbury Press, 1943.

Lewis, C. S.. *Christian Behaviour.* London: The Centenary Press, 1943.

Lewis, H. D., *Morals and Revelation.* London: George Allen, 1951.

Lindsay, A. D., and others, *Christianity and the Present Moral Unrest.* London: George Allen & Unwin Ltd., 1926.

Luthardt, Chr. Ernst, *Apologetic Lectures on the Moral Truths of Christianity* (translated from the German by Sophia Taylor), 4th ed. Edinburgh: T. & T. Clark, 1872.

———, *History of Christian Ethics* (translated from the German by W. Hastie), Edinburgh: T. & T. Clark. 1889.

MacLennan, W. G. D., *Christian Obedience* (Kerr Lecture, 1945). London: Thomas Nelson and Sons Ltd., 1948.

Marshall, L. H., *The Challenge of New Testament Ethics.* London: Macmillan and Co., Ltd., 1946.

Martensen, H., *Christian, Ethics.* First Division: *Individual Ethics* (tr. from the German by William Affleck). Edinburgh: T. & T. Clark, 1884.

Matheson, George, *Landmarks of New Testament Morality.* London: James Nisbet & Co., 1887.

Moberly, Sir Walter, *Responsibility.* London: Oxford University Press, 1951.

Monroe, Warner, *An Introduction to Christian Ethics.* Anderson, Ind.: The Warner Press, 1947.

Mortimer, R. C., *Christian Ethics.* London: Cheltenham Press, Ltd., 1950.

———, *The Elements of Moral Theology.* London: Adam and Charles Black, 1947.

Murray, John, *Principles of Conduct* (Payton Lectures) Grand Rapids: Wm. B. Eerdmans Publishing Company, 1956.

Murray, John, *The Daily Life of the Christian.* London SCM Press, 1955.

Murray, John Clark, *A Handbook of Christian Ethics.* Edinburgh: T. & T. Clark, 1908.

Newbigin, J. E. Lesslie, *Christian Freedom in the Modern World.* London: Student Christian Movement Press, 1937.

Niebuhr, Reinhold, *An Interpretation of Christian Ethics.* New York: Harper and Brothers, 1935.

Oldham, J. H., *Life is Commitment.* New York: Harper and Brothers, 1952.

Osborn, A. E., *Christian Ethics.* Oxford: University Press, 1940.

Ottley, R. L., *Christian Ideas and Ideals.* An Outline of Christian Ethical Theory. New York: Longmans, Green, and Co., 1911.

Paget, Francis, *Studies in the Christian Character.* New York: Longmans, Green, and Co., 1902.

Paulus, C. F., *The Christian Life. A Popular Treatise on Christian Ethics* (tr. from the German by F. W. Schneider). Cincinnati: Cranston and Stowe, 1892.

Pike, James A., *Doing the Truth.* New York: Doubleday, 1955.

Quick, O. C., *Christianity and Justice.* London: The Sheldon Press, 1940.

Ramsey, Paul, *Basic Christian Ethics.* New York: Charles Scribner's Sons, 1950.

Robinson, Norman H. G., *Faith and Duty.* London: Victor Gollancz Ltd., 1950.

Row, C. A., *Moral Teaching of the New Testament.* London: Christian Knowledge Society, 1872.

Scott, C. A. Anderson, *New Testament Ethics. An Introduction* (Hulsean Lectures, 1929). Cambridge: University Press (2nd ed., 1934).

Scott, Ernest F., *Man and Society in the New Testament.* New York: Charles Scribner's Sons, 1946.

Scullard, H. H., *The Ethics of the Gospel and the Ethics of Nature.* London: Student Christian Movement, 1927.

Smith, Gerald Birney, *Principles of Christian Living* (2nd ed.) Chicago: University Press, 1942.

Smyth, Newman, *Christian Ethics.* New York: Charles Scribner's Sons, 1903.

Springer, J. Arthur, *Practical Christian Living. An Introduction to Christian Ethics.* Chicago: Moody Press, 1951.

Spurrier, William A., *Guide to the Good Life.* New York: Charles Scribner's Sons, 1955.

———, *Power for Action. An Introduction to Christian Ethics.* New York: Charles Scribner's Sons, 1948.

Storr, V. F., and other members of the Church of England, *The Inner Life. Essays in Liberal Evangelicalism.* London: Hodder and Stoughton, Ltd.,n. d.

Strong, E. L., *Lectures on the Christian Character.* New York: Longmans, Green, and Co., 1923.

Strong, Thomas B., *Christian Ethics* (Bampton Lectures, 1895). New York: Longmans Green, and Co., 1896.

Temple, William, *Christianity in Thought and Practice.* London: Student Christian Movement Press, 1936.

Thomas, George F., *Christian Ethics and Moral Philosophy.* New York: Charles Scribner's Sons, 1955.

Valentine, Cyril H., *Moral Freedom and the Christian Faith.* London: Society for Promoting Christian Knowledge, 1932.

Van Til, Cornelius, *Christian Theistic Ethics* (unpublished syllabus). Philadelphia: Westminster Theological Seminary, 1952.

Wace, Henry, *Christianity and Morality.* London: Basil Montagu Pickering, 1876.

Walker, George, *The Idealism of Christian Ethics* (Baird Lecture, 1928). Edinburgh: T. & T. Clark Co., 1929.

Wand, J. W. C., *God and Goodness.* London: Eyre & Spottiswoode, 1947.

Wardlaw, Ralph, *Christian Ethics; or Moral Philosophy on the Principles of Divine Revelation.* London: Jackson and Walford, 1852.

Warfield, Benjamin B., *Perfectionism,* 2 vols. New York: Oxford University Press, 1931.

Weidner, Revere Franklin, *A System of Christian Ethics.* Based on Martensen and Harless. Philadelphia: G. W. Frederick, 1897.
Wenger, John C., *Separated Unto God.* A Plea for Christian Simplicity of Life and for a Scriptural Nonconformity to the World. Scottdale, Pa.: Mennonite Publishing House, 1952.
Wesley, John, (ed.), *The Christian's Pattern; or, An Abstract of the Imitation of Christ,* by Thomas a Kempis. New York: Abingdon Press, 1954.
Westermarck, E., *Christianity and Morals.* London: Kegan, Paul, Trench, Trubner & Co., Ltd., 1939.
Wuttke, Adolf, *Christian Ethics* (tr. from the German by John P. Lacroix). Vol. I — *History of Ethics.* New York: Nelson & Phillips, 1876. 2nd ed.
Yooll, Henry, *The Ethics of Evangelicalism* (Hartley Lecture, 1906). London: Charles H. Kelley, 1906.

V. FOREIGN WORKS (Untranslated)

Beck, Joh. Tobias, *Vorlesungen über christliche Ethik.* 1882.
Bohlin, Torsten, *Das Grundproblem der Ethik: über Ethik und Glauben.* Uppsala: Almquist & Wiksells, 1923.
Cullberg, John, *Das Problem der Ethik in der Dialektischen Theologie: I. Karl Barth.* Uppsala: A. B. Lundequistska, 1938.
Cullmann, Ph. Theodor, *Die Christliche Ethik.* 1871.
Elert, Werner, *Das christliche Ethos. Grundlinien der lutherischen Ethik.* Tübingen: Furche Verlag, 1949.
Frank, Fr. Reinhold H., *System der christlichen Sittlichkeit,* 1884.
Grimm, Edward, *Die Ethik Jesu* (2 Aufgabe). Leipzig: M. Heinsins Nachfolger, 1917.
Haering, B., *Das Heilige und das Gute. Religion und Sittlichkeit in ihrem gegenseiten Bezug.* 1950.
Herrmann, W., *Ethik* (5 Aufgabe). Tübingen: J. C. B. Mohr, 1913.
Hofmann, J. Ch. Konrad, *Vorlesungen über die theologische Ethik.* 1871.
Koehler, Martin, *Die Wissenschaft der Christlichen Lehre.* 1887.
Kolfhaus, W., *Vom Christlichen Leben Nach Johannes Calvin.* Ansbach: Erziehungsvereins Neukirchen Kreis Moers, 1949.
Kuebel, R., *Christliche Ethik.* 1896.
Lange, J. Peter, *Grundriss der christlichen Ethik.* 1878.
Oettingen, Alexander von, *Die Christliche Sittenlehre.* 1873.
Rothe, Richard, *Theologische Ethic.* 1845, 1868.
Scharling, C., *Die christliche Sittenlehre nach ev.—lutherischer Auffassung,* 1882.
Schleiermacher, Friedrich, *Die Christliche Sitte.* 1843.
Schülke, H., *Einfuhrung in die christliche Ethik.* Muenchen: Reinhardt, 1952.
Schultze, Hermann, *Grundriss der evangelischen Ethik.* 1891.
Seeberg, Reinhold, *Christliche Ethik. Stuttgart: W. Kohlhammer,* 1936.
Soe, N. H., *Christliche Ethik. Ein Lehrbuch.* München: Chr. Kaiser Verlag, 1949.
Steinbuchel, T., *Religion und Moral im Luchte personaler christlicher Existenz.* Frankfurt A. M.: Carolsdruckerei, 1951.
Thielicke, Helmut, *Theologische Ethik.* Tübingen: J. C. B. Mohr, 1952.
Vilmar, August F. L., *Theologische Moral.* 1871.
Wünsch, George, *Evangelische Wirtschaftsethik.* Tübingen: J. C. B. Mohr, 1927.

VI. HISTORICAL

Blackie, John Stuart, *Four Phases of Morals: Socrates, Aristotle, Christianity, Utilitarianism.* Edinburgh: Edmonston and Douglas, 1874 (2nd ed.).
Clogg, F. B., *The Christian Character in the Early Church.* London: Epworth Press.

Gardner, Percy, *Evolution in Christian Ethics.* London: Williams and Norgate, 1918.

Hall, Thomas Cuming, *History of Ethics within Organized Christianity.* London: T. Fisher Unwin, 1910.

McAdoo H. R., *The Structure of Caroline Moral Theology.* London: Longmans, Green, and Co., 1949.

Scullard, H. H., *Early Christian Ethics in the West.* London: Williams and Norgate, 1907.

VII. CONSCIENCE

Chrisholm, Archibald, *Conscience. Its Nature and Authority.* London: Nisbet & Co., Ltd., 1934.

Davison, W. T., *The Christian Conscience. A Contribution to Christian Ethics* (The Fernley Lecture for 1888). London: T. Woolmer, 1888.

Hallesby, O., *Conscience* (translated from Norwegian by Clarence J. Carlsen). Minneapolis: Augsburg Publishing House, 1933. 11th ed., 1944.

Kirk, Kenneth E., *Conscience and Its Problems: An Introduction to Casuistry.* London: Longmans, Green and Co., Ltd., 1927.

Rashdall, Hastings, *Conscience and Christ.* Six Lectures on Christian Ethics. London: Duckworth & Co., 1916.

Raymond, Irving Woodworth, *The Teaching of the Early Church on the Use of Wine and Strong Drink.* New York: Columbia University Press, 1927.

INDEX OF PERSONS

INDEX OF SUBJECTS

INDEX OF SCRIPTURE

BOOKS IN THE SERIES

THE ACTS OF THE APOSTLES .... Richard B. Rackham
APOSTOLIC AND POST-APOSTOLIC TIMES (Goppelt) .... Robert A. Guelich, tr.
THE APOSTOLIC FATHERS .... J. B. Lightfoot
THE ATONEMENT OF CHRIST .... Francis Turrettin
THE AUTHORITY OF THE OLD TESTAMENT .... John Bright
BACKGROUNDS TO DISPENSATIONALISM .... Clarence B. Bass
BASIC CHRISTIAN DOCTRINES .... Carl F. H. Henry
THE BASIC IDEAS OF CALVINISM .... H. Henry Meeter
THE CALVINISTIC CONCEPT OF CULTURE .... H. Van Til
CHRISTIAN APPROACH TO PHILOSOPHY .... W. C. Young
CHRISTIAN PERSONAL ETHICS .... Carl F. H. Henry
COMMENTARY ON DANIEL (Jerome) .... Gleason L. Archer, Jr., tr.
THE DAYS OF HIS FLESH .... David Smith
DISCIPLING THE NATIONS .... Richard DeRidder
THE DOCTRINE OF GOD .... Herman Bavinck
EDUCATIONAL IDEALS IN THE ANCIENT WORLD .... Wm. Barclay
THE EPISTLE OF JAMES .... Joseph B. Mayor
EUSEBIUS' ECCLESIASTICAL HISTORY
FUNDAMENTALS OF THE FAITH .... Carl F. H. Henry, ed.
GOD-CENTERED EVANGELISM .... R. B. Kuiper
GENERAL PHILOSOPHY .... D. Elton Trueblood
THE GRACE OF LAW .... Ernest F. Kevan
THE HIGHER CRITICISM OF THE PENTATEUCH .... William Henry Green
THE HISTORY OF CHRISTIAN DOCTRINES .... Louis Berkhof
THE HISTORY OF DOCTRINES .... Reinhold Seeberg
THE HISTORY OF THE JEWISH NATION .... Alfred Edersheim
HISTORY OF PREACHING .... E. C. Dargan
LIGHT FROM THE ANCIENT EAST .... Adolf Deissmann
NOTES ON THE MIRACLES OF OUR LORD .... R. C. Trench
NOTES ON THE PARABLES OF OUR LORD .... R. C. Trench
OUR REASONABLE FAITH (Bavinck) .... Henry Zylstra, tr.
PAUL, APOSTLE OF LIBERTY .... R. N. Longnecker
PHILOSOPHY OF RELIGION .... D. Elton Trueblood
PROPHETS AND THE PROMISE .... W. J. Beecher
REASONS FOR FAITH .... John H. Gerstner
THE REFORMATION .... Hans J. Hillebrand, ed.
REFORMED DOGMATICS (Wollebius, Voetius, Turretin) .... J. Beardslee, ed., tr.
REFORMED DOGMATICS .... Heinrich Heppe
REVELATION AND INSPIRATION .... James Orr
REVELATION AND THE BIBLE .... Carl F. H. Henry
ROMAN SOCIETY AND ROMAN LAW IN THE NEW TESTAMENT .... A. N. Sherwin-White
THE ROOT OF FUNDAMENTALISM .... Ernest R. Sandeen
THE SERVANT-MESSIAH .... T. W. Manson
STORY OF RELIGION IN AMERICA .... Wm. W. Sweet
THE TESTS OF LIFE (third edition) .... Robert Law
THEOLOGY OF THE MAJOR SECTS .... John H. Gerstner
VARIETIES OF CHRISTIAN APOLOGETICS .... B. Ramm
THE VOYAGE AND SHIPWRECK OF ST. PAUL (fourth edition) .... James Smith
THE VIRGIN BIRTH .... J. G. Machen
A COMPANION TO THE STUDY OF ST. AUGUSTINE .... Roy W. Battenhouse, ed.
STUDIES IN THE GOSPELS .... R. C. Trench
THE HISTORY OF THE RELIGION OF ISRAEL .... John Howard Raven
THE HISTORY OF CHRISTIAN DOCTRINE (revised edition) .... E. H. Klotsche
THE EPISTLES OF JUDE AND II PETER .... Joseph B. Mayor
THEORIES OF REVELATION .... H. D. McDonald
STUDIES IN THE BOOK OF DANIEL .... Robert Dick Wilson
THE UNITY OF THE BOOK OF GENESIS .... William Henry Green
THE APOCALYPSE OF JOHN .... Isbon T. Beckwith
CHRIST THE MEANING OF HISTORY .... Hendrikus Berkhof